D0509051

BISON BOOKS

Encyclopedia of the

Great Plains Indians

DAVID J. WISHART, EDITOR

University of Nebraska Press · LINCOLN & LONDON

© 2007 by the Board of Regents of the University of Nebraska
All rights reserved
Manufactured in the United States of America

∞

Library of Congress Cataloging-in-Publication Data
Encyclopedia of the Great Plains Indians / David J. Wishart, Editor.
p.   cm.
"This encyclopedia consists of 123 entries and an introductory
essay that have been excerpted from the Encyclopedia of the
Great Plains (University of Nebraska Press, 2004), together with
23 new entries and many new photographs"—T.p. verso.
Includes bibliographical references and index.
ISBN-13: 978-0-8032-9862-0 (pbk.: alk. paper)
ISBN-10: 0-8032-9862-5 (pbk.: alk. paper)
1. Indians of North America—Great Plains—Encyclopedias.
2. Great Plains—Encyclopedias.   I. Wishart, David J., 1946–
II. Encyclopedia of the Great Plains.
E78.G73E53   2007
978.004′97003—dc22
2006020334

Project Staff

EDITOR

David J. Wishart. University of Nebraska–Lincoln

REGIONAL EDITORS

Pamela H. Brink.
  Associated Authors and Editors, Inc. Lubbock, Texas (Southern Plains)
Nancy Tystad Koupal.
  South Dakota Historical Society. Pierre, South Dakota (Northern Plains)
Theodore D. Regehr.
  University of Calgary and University of Saskatchewan (Prairie Provinces)

ASSOCIATE EDITORS

J. Clark Archer. University of Nebraska–Lincoln
Frances W. Kaye. University of Nebraska–Lincoln
Martha H. Kennedy. Library of Congress
John R. Wunder. University of Nebraska–Lincoln

PROJECT MANAGERS

Scarlett Presley   (1995–1999)
Sonja Rossum   (1999–2002)

RESEARCH ASSISTANTS

Beth Ritter   (1995–1999)
Akim D. Reinhardt   (1996–1997)
Pekka Hämäläinen   (1996–1998)
Sonja Rossum   (1997–1999)
April L. Whitten   (1997–1998)
Robert Watrel   (1998)
Mark R. Ellis   (1999–2001)
Charles Vollan   (2000–2002)

ADMINISTRATIVE ASSISTANT

Gretchen Walker

The Great Plains region as used in this encyclopedia

physical environments of the Plains with great sacred significance. This is a consecration of environment and place that is generally missing among other populations of the region. The Indians' traditional religions were place-based, the very names of the months in their native languages chronicling changes in the local environment throughout the year. Unlike most European Americans, who moved in and then quickly moved on, Indians were bound to specific places—homelands—by their religions, and by their histories, which were expressed spatially rather than temporally, each place a reminder of something that had happened in the past. The whole environment was revered, but certain landmarks—Bear Butte, for example, to the Lakotas and Cheyennes, and Pahuk, or "Mound on the Water," to the Pawnees—stand out on the sacred map. This is a different, deeper form of regional consciousness, and it is celebrated throughout the encyclopedia.

The organization of the encyclopedia is straightforward: following the introductory essay, entries are presented in alphabetical order. Authors' names and affiliations are given at the end of each entry, and most entries are also followed by suggestions for further reading. A comprehensive index lists the entries in bold lettering, while other information that is presented within entries appears in normal lettering.

Our hope is that the information and analysis included in this encyclopedia will confirm in Plains Indians' minds their right to be proud of their longevity and accomplishments in the Great Plains, while reminding others of the centrality of Indians to life in the region, both in the past and ongoing.

David J. Wishart
University of Nebraska–Lincoln

Preface

This encyclopedia consists of 123 entries and an introductory essay that have been excerpted from the *Encyclopedia of the Great Plains* (University of Nebraska Press, 2004), together with 23 new entries and many new photographs. Most of the original entries, and the essay, come from the Native American chapter in the *Encyclopedia of the Great Plains*, but others were dispersed throughout the book in chapters such as "Literary Traditions" (for example, James Welch and Linda Hogan), "War" (for example, Red Cloud and the Battle of the Little Bighorn), and "Water" (for example, Winters Doctrine). The new entries, focusing mainly on contemporary Plains Indians, were written by Dr. Charles Vollan of the Department of History at South Dakota State University, for which I am most grateful.

There was never any doubt in our minds that our initial paperback spin-off from the *Encyclopedia of the Great Plains* would feature the Indigenous peoples, whose enduring presence is a primary defining characteristic of the region. This is a presence that will only grow in importance, because the reservations in the United States and the reserves in Canada are islands of population increase in a sea of rural population decline. Moreover, the association of Indians with the Plains region is one of great historical depth, extending back at least eighteen thousand years. That means that until relatively recently (really only the last two centuries), all the human landscapes of the Great Plains were shaped by Indians alone.

During the last two centuries, the Great Plains has been both a tragic and a triumphant setting for its Native peoples. The tragedies—nineteenth-century population collapse and dispossession, for example, or the massacres at Sand Creek (1864), the Washita (1868), and Wounded Knee (1890)—come most readily, and disquietly, to mind. But even in the nineteenth century, against a backdrop of violence, disease, and the two federal governments' relentless assimilation policies, there were Indian triumphs, such as Standing Bear's epic trek in 1879 back from Indian Territory to the Ponca homeland on the Niobrara River (in present-day Nebraska) and his equally epic victory in court, mandating that an Indian is indeed a person.

Still, the nineteenth century was mainly a time of loss for Plains Indians, and in the early years of the twentieth century many observers believed that Indians were headed to extinction. Extinction did not occur; population revived; court cases were won (for example, *United States v. Sioux Nation of Indians* [1980], compensating for the illegal taking of the Black Hills in 1876); many ceremonies persisted, and new ones (the Native American Church, for example) were added; most Indigenous languages survived and are now being taught in schools and colleges; and economic conditions have improved in some places, in part because of gaming. And along the way great athletes like Jim Thorpe, singers like Buffy Sainte-Marie, and artists like Oscar Howe have emerged from Indian cultures to enrich the overall fabric of Plains, and national, life.

Finally, it cannot be emphasized too much that over time Indians have endowed the

Encyclopedia of the Great Plains Indians

Introduction

The Plains Indian has been one of the most important and pervasive icons in American culture. Imagine him, for example, as a young man on horseback. Almost without effort, the image conjures up full-blown narratives of buffalo hunts and mounted warfare. Make the "he" into a young woman and imagine romantic tragedies of forced marriage and unrequited love. Make the Indian a wizened elder and see if you don't think of spiritual wonder and almost superhuman ecological communion.

But don't forget that real people peer up from the depths of such timeless images. And while the images can be easily moved to the Hollywood backlot, those real people are not so easily detached from the Great Plains themselves, for this difficult environment framed ongoing historical transformations in Native political organization, social relations, economy, and culture. Along with the nomadic bison hunting popularized in the movies, Native Americans engaged in raiding, trading, pastoralism, agriculture, diplomacy, politics, religious innovation and syncretism, warfare, migration, wage labor, lawsuits, lobbying, and gaming. Through these adaptive strategies, the Plains peoples worked to protect and enhance their political power and their ability to sustain themselves economically, and to maintain their cultural distinctiveness.

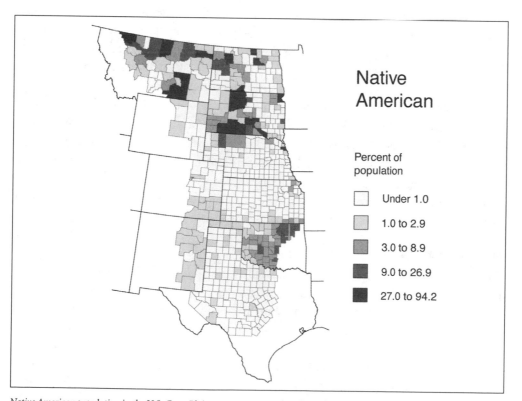

Native American population in the U.S. Great Plains as a percentage of total population, by county in 2000

Rally marchers leave Pine Ridge, South Dakota, on their way to Whiteclay, Nebraska, on June 26, 1999. The demonstration by Native Americans protested the sale of alcohol and unsolved murders in Whiteclay.

Longevity in the Plains

Although some peoples came to the Plains earlier than others, Native Americans have lived there for a long time. Evidence from the Agate Basin site in eastern Wyoming, for example, indicates that humans lived in the Plains at least as early as 8500 BC. Radiocarbon dating of material from the Lewisville site near Dallas, Texas, suggests Indians and their precursors may have been in the Plains for at least thirty-eight thousand years. The oral histories of some tribes refer to long-extinct mammoths and other megafauna. "Star charts" suggest that the Lakota Sioux have associated parts of the Black Hills in South Dakota with astrometrical phenomena since ancient times. Some scholars assert that the Sioux peoples originated in the Great Lakes region and only began moving onto the Plains in the late seventeenth and early eighteenth centuries. Many Lakotas, however, trace the origins of their people to Wind Cave in the Black Hills and suggest that they were simply in the middle of a long, slow migration home after living elsewhere for a time. Clarity on this issue will probably not be forthcoming.

Environmental Adaptations

Their extended tenure in the Plains allowed Native peoples to experience significant alterations in the environment. Between 11,500 and 11,000 BP, precipitation declined, the range of temperatures increased, and free-flowing streams began to turn into small lakes and marshes, eventually becoming part of the expanding grassland. Species adapted to the wetter world—such as mammoths, camels, and horses—died out, opening ecological niches in the Plains grassland. Most of these niches were filled by bison, which were becoming smaller and more mobile, characteristics more effective in the drier climate.

Plains peoples adjusted to these changes as well. Around the time that the larger game disappeared, nomadic hunters shifted from Clovis-style spear points and arrowheads to the smaller Folsom points and heads, which were used until about 8000 BC. Like more recent Native peoples, Folsom hunters and their successors depended heavily upon the bison and relied upon the more sophisticated social organization necessary for group hunting. Such organization allowed for the creation and use of "buffalo jumps," a large funnel of trees, rocks, poles, and people designed to channel stampeding bison over a cliff. Plains hunters used buffalo jumps like the Head-Smashed-In site in southwestern Alberta as early as 5,500 years ago. Along with the bison, Indian hunters' prey included deer, elk, and other smaller game.

Plains residents began experimenting with pottery and more sedentary villages at least as early as two thousand years ago. Ancestors of the Mandans and Hidatsas eventually settled in fortified villages along the Missouri River, where they raised corn, beans, and squash. These villages generally ranged in size from ten to ninety lodges and were built from bracing poles and packed earthen cover. Between spring planting and fall harvest, the villagers probably left the river's bottomland to hunt bison.

Some of the crops these villagers grew became part of the extensive trade networks that linked the horticulturalists with Plains hunters and with peoples outside the Plains. The Caddo and Wichita trade networks included some of the Pueblos in present-day New Mexico, Cahokia (a city built by the Illinois people near the confluence of the Mississippi and Missouri rivers), Hiwasee Island on the Tennessee River, Etowah near the Chattahoochee River, and the Platte River Pawnee communities. The Mandans, Hidatsas, and Arikaras traded with peoples from what is today the American Southwest and with more nomadic Plains hunters like the Crows, Assiniboines, Plains Crees, Cheyennes, Arapahos, Kiowas, and Comanches. Both material goods (agricultural products, dried meat, flint, and animal hides) and cultural products (songs and dances) traded hands.

Migrations

While the rise of sedentary villages and agriculture stood out as a key way that Plains peoples adapted to and shaped their environment, migration played an equally important role in the lives of many Indians. It seems that Plains societies were both amalgamating and splitting apart, and that mobility constituted a common response to both social and environmental factors. The groups that came to be known as Apaches, for example, separated from people in the Northern Plains as early as 600 AD. They moved south, sojourning in Nebraska before moving into the Southern Plains between 1450 and 1525. By the late 1600s they and their Kiowa allies had staked out a territory ranging from northwestern Texas to Wyoming and the Black Hills. At the same time, Shoshones moved east from the Great Basin to eastern Montana. Separating from the Hidatsas and Missouri River horticulture, the Crows migrated west to the Montana-Dakota area.

Such migrations accelerated after 1700, as some groups left the Plains and others entered the region. Moving from what is now eastern Montana, a branch of Shoshones that would come to be known as Comanches swept the Apaches south and by 1775 forced them from the Plains entirely. Cheyennes and Arapahos migrated west from the Great Lakes region. Crees and Assiniboines gradually moved into the Canadian Prairies. Iowas, Missourias, Omahas, Osages, Otoes, Poncas, and Quapaws all came to the Plains after living for some time in what is today Arkansas, Missouri, and Iowa.

Horses, Guns, and Diseases

Migrations also brought Europeans to the Plains, beginning in the sixteenth century. The newcomers brought both opportunities and perils for the Plains peoples in the forms of trade and disease. Horses and firearms were the most important European trade items. The Spanish reintroduced horses into the Plains, in part through trading networks that connected Plains peoples with the Pueblos and Apaches. (Horses had existed in the Americas at one time, but they had become extinct.) Indians acted as middlemen and traded horses to more distant Plains peoples. By the late 1600s, for example, Kiowas and Kiowa Apaches traded horses to the Caddos. Comanches often acquired horses by raiding Spanish and Apache settlements and then traded the animals to other tribes. Utes, Cheyennes, and Arapahos moved horses to the north. Because Spanish law forbade the selling or trading of firearms to Natives, the Plains peoples turned to the English and French for guns, and middleman relationships developed with both mobile traders and trade centers in the Arkansas, Missouri, and Red river valleys.

Access to horses and weaponry came at a high cost. European traders brought European epidemic diseases to which Plains Indians had not been exposed and to which they had limited immunity. Even Natives who had never met a European became ill as a result of contact with Native middlemen in the trade who inadvertently exposed them to smallpox, measles, whooping cough, and many other diseases. Regardless of the source, European diseases spread through the Plains and decimated Native populations, especially those concentrated in villages. Epidemics during the late eighteenth and early nineteenth centuries reduced the Arikaras' population by an estimated 80 percent. The Hidatsas, Mandans, Omahas, Poncas, and other relatively sedentary tribes also suffered great losses.

The combination of European diseases and trade items had a complex impact upon the Plains. Access to horses allowed for the more effective killing and transportation of bison. Consequently, many tribes—such as the Lakota Sioux—rejected a sedentary and horticultural lifestyle and devoted less time to trapping beaver and more time to the hunting of bison. Tribes with the greatest access to horses and firearms could expand their territory and power at the expense of those tribes with fewer guns and horses. The Osages' access to both guns and horses, for example, helped to make them the main power in the region between the lower Missouri and lower Red rivers by the mid-1700s. The Comanches' control of the horse trade and their alliance with the Kiowas gave them command over the area between the Arkansas and Red rivers by the end of the eighteenth century. By the mid–nineteenth century, the Sioux, aided by the Arapahos and Cheyennes, dominated the region bounded by the Minnesota and Yellowstone rivers in the north and the Republican River in the south. The relative power of the nomads was actually increased by disease: they suffered losses, of course, but their dispersed lifestyles made them less vulnerable to epidemics than the concentrated village populations.

Europeans

Unlike their horses, guns, and pathogens, Europeans themselves initially had a relatively limited presence in the Plains. The Spanish first penetrated the region between 1540 and 1542 looking for "cities of gold." When they failed to find the riches they expected, they withdrew and only slowly established missions and colonies in New Mexico and Texas during the seventeenth century. Spain did sponsor an expedition to the Plains under Pedro de Villasur in 1720, but it suffered a military defeat at the hands of the Pawnees and Otoes.

The French expanded into the Southern and Central Plains by the early eighteenth century from bases in the Mississippi Valley. They negotiated commercial and military agreements with Plains tribes. Through these agreements, the French traded with Indians for furs, while using Plains peoples as a defense against rival Europeans and Indians. Few in number and often nomadic themselves, the French posed no threat to Indian autonomy.

In the late eighteenth century, British fur traders from Canada pushed into the Prairie Provinces. Unlike the individualistic French traders, the large British companies built numerous trading posts among the Assiniboines, Plains Crees, Blackfoot, and Gros Ventres, drawing them into market relations. Alcohol, the credit system, and intermarriage created strong linkages and dependencies, but the number of the British and the volume of their trade were too small to dramatically alter the Native cultures. Like the other Plains groups, the Indians of the Canadian Prairies managed to keep their subsistence, political, and cultural systems largely intact until the second half of the nineteenth century.

Americans

When the British, French, and Spanish entered the Plains, they tended to seek peaceful relations with Indian people. In truth, Europeans lacked the power to do otherwise. The same cannot be said, however, of the Americans. U.S. expansion into the Plains in the nineteenth century involved the purposeful or incidental destruction and control of those Plains resources upon which Native Americans depended. To be sure, Plains people adopted various responses to the Americans' actions. Nevertheless, by the end of the century, Native peoples had seen their populations decline precipitously, had lost control over much of their land and other economic resources, and faced the prospect of seeing their societies and cultures forcibly annihilated by outsiders.

Fur traders were the first Americans to enter the Northern and Central Plains in significant numbers in the first four decades of the nineteenth century. In the 1840s large numbers of emigrants passed through the Great Plains on their way to Oregon, Utah, and the California goldfields. The construction of railroads across the Plains after the Civil War made accessible a region with limited navigable rivers, and the Homestead Act of 1862 and other laws drew settlers to the Plains by providing land at a relatively small cost.

The influx presented significant problems for the Plains peoples. Many migrants took old Indian routes across the Plains and codified them for other Americans as "trails"—the Overland or Oregon Trail, which traced the Platte River, and the Santa Fe Trail, which ran along part of the Arkansas River. Migration along these trails destroyed the ecosystems of the Platte and Arkansas valleys. The emigrants drove the bison away, churned the grasslands into mile-wide dust swathes, stripped wood from river bottoms, and polluted water sources—often with diseases such as cholera. Native peoples who depended upon the resources of these areas, such as the Sioux and Pawnees in the north and the Comanches and Kiowas in the south, demanded compensation for this damage and sought substitutes for the lost game. The Comanches and Kiowas, for example, took to raiding for cattle and other items. This led to an escalating series of threats, a cycle of raids, and occasional reprisals by whites.

Treaties, Diplomacy, and Dispossession in the United States

Throughout much of the nineteenth century the U.S. government sought to deal with the conflicts between Indians and non-Indian migrants and settlers through treaties that restricted Native peoples to certain areas. In 1825 the federal government created a Permanent Indian Frontier. Encompassing much of modern-day Nebraska, Kansas, and Oklahoma, it was to serve as a home for displaced eastern tribes. Tribes already in the area, such as the Kansas, Wichitas, Osages, and Pawnees, ceded lands to make room for tribes removed from the east, such as the Delawares and Kickapoos. But this was not a Permanent Indian Frontier. In 1854 the Kansas-Nebraska Act opened up vast areas for American settlement. In a flurry of treaty signing in the second half of the 1850s many Indigenous groups ceded their ancestral lands, retaining only small reservations.

On their reservations Plains Indians were placed under great pressure to change. They experimented with new strategies of resistance but enjoyed limited success. Pawnees in Nebraska and Osages in Kansas, for example, found their livelihoods threatened by Sioux raids and by non-Indian migrants who drove off game. The Indians responded by trying to levy tolls of sugar and coffee on emigrants and by occasionally resorting to harassment and cattle raids. American settlers, crowding in around the reservations, called for the Indians' removal. By the mid-1880s the Pawnees and many of the other Native peoples in Kansas and Nebraska had been relocated to Indian Territory (now Oklahoma), the remnant of the Permanent Indian Frontier.

Many Plains peoples engaged in diplomacy with the United States and other tribes as a strategy to deal with the American newcomers. In 1851, at Fort Laramie, federal agents negotiated a treaty with the Arapahos, Arikaras, Assiniboines, Cheyennes, Crows, Hidatsas, Mandans, Lakota Sioux, and others. Two years later the government entered into a treaty with the Comanches, Kiowas, and Kiowa Apaches at Fort Atkinson. In 1855, along the Judith River, representatives of the Bloods, Piegans, Siksikas, and Gros Ventres made their agreements with the United States. These treaties called for peaceful relations, delineated which tribes got which lands, and stipulated that tribes would be given supplies and services to make up for the destruction of game by non-Indians.

Wars

The treaties did not end threats to Indian lifeways and thus failed to forestall violence for long. The Americans' destruction of game intensified competition among the tribes for the remaining bison and other animals. The U.S. military fought several engagements with the Lakota Sioux, Cheyennes, and Arapahos in the mid-1850s. In the two years after the 1858 discovery of gold in Colorado, thousands of gold seekers flocked into Arapaho territory, violating the 1851 treaty. Some Arapahos responded by moving north of the Platte. For the southern bands who remained, relations with the trespassers deteriorated, and on November 29, 1864, white militiamen massacred Black Kettle's and White Antelope's Cheyennes and Arapahos at Sand Creek, Colorado. In response, members of these tribes, along with some Sioux, Comanches, and Kiowas, resorted to war. They launched a series of attacks against posts along the immigrant trails. Relative peace was restored when the Southern Arapahos, some Cheyenne bands, Comanches, and Kiowas agreed in 1865 and 1867 to treaties that would confine them to reservations. In exchange, federal officials guaranteed that the Indians would be protected from attacks by settlers and soldiers and that they would receive goods to offset the destruction of the bison and other game. When the Comanches and Kiowas resumed raiding because the government failed to provide adequate rations, the army destroyed the Indians' winter camps and forced them back to their reservation along the Red River.

In the Central and Northern Plains, bands of Cheyennes, Arapahos, and Lakota Sioux also waged war to protect themselves. The discovery of gold in Montana in 1862 brought large numbers of non-Indians into and through the area. When the federal government built forts to protect the settlers and the route to the goldfields, the Bozeman Trail, Native Americans laid siege to the forts and forced the United States to negotiate a settlement. In the 1868 Treaty of Fort Laramie, federal negotiators agreed to evacuate the forts, to provide a large reservation (the "Great Sioux Reservation") in South and North Dakota, and to guarantee Indian hunting rights.

Nevertheless, the Sioux and their allies ultimately suffered the same fate as the Comanches and Kiowas. When Americans discovered gold in the Black Hills area of the Great Sioux Reservation in 1874, the federal government unsuccessfully attempted to get the Sioux to sell or lease the land. War broke out between the army and the Sioux and Northern Cheyennes in 1876. The Indians, led by Gall and Sitting Bull (both Hunkpapa Sioux), defeated forces under Gen. George Armstrong Custer at the Battle of the Little Bighorn, but the military's winter campaign of 1876–77 forced most of the Sioux and Cheyennes to return to their reservations or to flee to Canada. Among the latter, those led by Sitting Bull returned to the reservation in 1881, while some others settled in Canada permanently. By the time of Sitting Bull's return, all of the Plains peoples had been settled on reservations.

The army's successes over some Plains tribes stemmed in large measure from the assistance of other Plains Indians as scouts and auxiliaries. Pawnees, Arikaras, and Crows helped the American military fight against the Lakotas, while Pawnees, Caddos, and Wichitas allied with the United States against the Comanches. Military service represented a means for some Indians to adapt to changing conditions. By serving as a scout or auxiliary, an Indian could provide himself and his family with material benefits, including extra rations, food, money, and horses captured in battle. Some Plains Natives saw the United States as a lesser threat than tribes like the Sioux. Service in the army also provided an avenue of escape, albeit temporary, from reservation life and an opportunity to gain honor and status through combat. Similar motivations would later prompt Plains Indians to serve in the U.S. Armed Forces in subsequent conflicts, such as World Wars I and II, Korea, and Vietnam.

Treaties, Dispossession, and War in Canada

On the Canadian Prairies, the fur trade remained the principal medium of interaction between the Indians and whites until the late 1860s. A "middle ground" emerged there between the Blackfoot, Gros Ventres, Assiniboines, and Plains Crees on the one side, and fur traders on the other. Interchange of ideas reduced racial prejudices, gifts created fictive kinship ties, intermarriage bonded companies and bands together, and sexual interaction produced a large Métis (persons of mixed Native, French, and British heritage) population. This cultural accommodation came to an end with the decline of the fur trade in the 1860s. In 1870, after years of deteriorating resources and decreasing profits, the Hudson's Bay Company sold Rupert's Land to the Dominion of Canada.

Like their counterparts in the United States, Canadian officials wanted to move Plains Indians and Métis out of the way of non-Indians who settled the Prairie Provinces in greater numbers following the construction of the Canadian Pacific Railway. Hoping to learn from the United States and avoid a series of financially costly wars, Ottawa officials negotiated a series of seven numbered treaties with the Plains peoples between 1871 and 1877. The Natives agreed to the treaties after a movement led by Métis Louis Riel to establish an independent Métis government in 1869 was crushed and because they wanted government aid to offset the loss of the bison. Plains groups with which the government signed treaties included the Red River Anishinaabes (Chippewas), Plains Crees, Plains Anishinaabes, Siksikas (Northern Blackfoot), Bloods, Northern Piegans, Sarcees, and selected Assiniboines. Generally, the treaties stipulated that the Natives would agree to accept reserves and individual allotments of land in exchange for government aid and assistance in agriculture.

Like their counterparts farther south, Canadian Plains peoples found diplomacy did not produce desired results. Construction of the Canadian Pacific Railway destroyed most of the Blackfoot's hunting territory. Canadian officials often failed to provide adequate aid and sometimes withheld promised aid as punishment for those who called for alterations to treaty provisions. Efforts by leaders such as Crowfoot (Siksika Blackfoot) and Big Bear (Cree) to keep the peace between Natives and whites ultimately proved unsuccessful. In 1884 starving Indians robbed government storehouses and killed several local officials. Crees, Assiniboines, and Métis fended off an attack by troops at Cut Knife Hill, but several key Indian leaders were later arrested.

Troops also crushed the North-West Rebellion of Métis. In March 1885 in Saskatchewan a group of Métis, led once again by Louis Riel, took control of the village of Batoche, arrested the Indian agent, and declared the existence of a new government for the area. Hundreds of Crees and Assiniboines under Big Bear and Poundmaker joined Riel. Government troops recaptured Batoche and eventually forced many of the Métis and Indians, including Riel, Poundmaker, and Big Bear, to surrender (although some escaped to Montana). After a series of trials, the Canadian government hanged Riel and eight others.

As a result of the loss of economic resources and military defeats, Plains peoples found themselves confined to reservations in the United States and reserves in Canada. Reservation life represented a radical departure from the Indians' prior existence. Some groups, such as those Cheyennes and Arapahos who had been resettled in Oklahoma, found themselves far from their homelands, where the environment was unfamiliar and adjustment was difficult. Even for those who remained in relatively familiar territory, the mobility integral to their bison-hunting way of life had been lost. Even if Indians were allowed to leave the reservation or reserve to hunt, their main prey, the bison, was virtually extinct by the early 1880s. For the Caddos, Wichitas, and other Plains peoples who depended on agriculture, the reservation lands often proved inadequate for cultivation. Plains peoples, who had once drawn their existence from the soil and the bison, had in many ways become economically dependent upon the United States and Canada.

For all of the problems with the reservations and reserves, however, they represented homes for peoples and contexts for their cultures. In the United States especially, humanitarian "reformers" worked to take away even this single saving grace. These reformers and their advocates in the government argued that Americans had an obligation to "civilize"—assimilate—Indians by breaking down tribal bonds and absorbing them into white society as individuals.

Several factors helped reformers win support for their ideas. In the context of the Plains Wars and expanding white settlement, absorbing Indians into white society seemed to be the only way to prevent their extinction. Evangelical Christians' desire to create a "righteous Empire" in the United States made conversion of the "red heathens" an important goal. Industrialization and increasing immigration of eastern European Catholics and Jews seemed to threaten traditional rural Anglo-Saxon values and fueled a desire to "Americanize" the First Americans. Reformers also felt that assimilation would end the dependence of many Native Americans upon government rations and annuities.

The 1887 General Allotment Act (along with subsequent acts and amendments) ultimately became the vehicle through which reformers sought to eradicate Indian cultures and societies. Sponsored by Massachusetts senator Henry Dawes, the act provided for ending the tribes' communal landownership and allotting reservation land into individually owned plots. Dawes and the reformers argued that the legislation would sever the peoples' bonds with their "backwards" tribal cultures and societies while forcing them to become hardworking farmers. Unallotted reservation land would then be sold as "surplus lands" to non-Indians. This would further facilitate assimilation by reducing the land available for Indians to use for hunting and would allow Indians to learn from their white neighbors.

Allotment did not become such a significant (and damaging) aspect of Indian policy in Canada. The 1869 Indian Act granted band councils the right to assign full title of specific reserve lands to individuals, who subsequently were allowed to sell, rent, or lease their land only to other band members. Hence, non-Indians simply did not have the same opportunities to buy nonallotted "surplus" lands or to eventually gain access to allotted lands.

Canadians did follow the Americans' lead in using education as a means of assimilation. By the mid-1890s both the U.S. and Canadian governments funded a network of Indian day and boarding schools to foster assimilation. These schools provided academic and vocational education while forbidding students from engaging in such Indian cultural activities as speaking Native languages and practicing Native religions.

Officials in Washington and Ottawa suppressed Plains Indian cultural practices in other ways as well. In Canada, the 1876 Indian Act (with subsequent amendments) outlawed traditional tribal and band governments and banned various religious and cultural practices such as the Sun Dance and Thirst Dance. In the United States, federal agents forced Native Americans to attend Christian services, to adopt "citizens'" clothing and hairstyles, to follow only federally approved Indian leaders, and to abstain from such cultural practices as the Sun Dance and polygamy.

Cultural and Economic Adaptations

Native Americans did not passively accept such strictures, and they found many ways to resist. Sometimes such resistance led to violence, as when conflict with some Lakota Sioux over the Ghost Dance religion ended in the Wounded Knee Massacre in December 1890. Emerging in the late 1880s, the Ghost Dance religion anticipated the destruction of the Earth and the creation of a new world occupied by abundant game and deceased relatives. Many Lakotas, including Sitting Bull, embraced the Ghost Dance and began performing the requisite songs and dances. Some believed that certain "Ghost Shirts" would protect them from harm. Fearing that the dances portended an uprising, the Indian agent at Standing Rock Reservation ordered the arrest of Sitting Bull, who had remained a powerful advocate of Lakota resistance. During the arrest an intense fight ensued, and Indian policemen killed the respected leader. Fearing more violence, Miniconjou leader Big Foot and his band fled south to the Pine Ridge Reservation. There, on December 28, 1890, at Wounded Knee Creek, soldiers attempted to disarm the Indians, and gunfire was exchanged. Who pulled the trigger first remains unclear, but the army's superior firepower turned the encounter into a massacre: from 150 to 250 Sioux men, women, and children died, as did 25 soldiers. Still, the Ghost Dance continued to attract adherents from the Plains, including Oklahoma Kiowas and Comanches, Saskatchewan Sioux, and Wyoming Shoshones.

Some Plains Indians accepted at least some white ways and policies. Big Tree, a Kiowa war leader imprisoned for a time for his raiding activities, converted to Christianity and became a farmer on his Oklahoma allotment. Others resisted assimilation while adapting to the new world that was being thrust upon them. Omaha half-siblings Susette and Francis La Flesche attended white educational institutions and used their education to conduct a campaign to win public support for allowing the Poncas to return to their home in Nebraska. Susan La Flesche graduated from medical school (making her one of the few American women and the only Native American woman in the nineteenth century to do so) and used her training to treat her people.

Religion was a primary means of preserving cultural distinctiveness. Many Indians became involved with peyotism in the late nineteenth and early twentieth centuries. Involving the ingestion of the peyote plant, peyotism is a syncretistic belief system that combines aspects of Christian and traditional Indian spirituality. A Caddo expression of peyotism, the Big Moon ceremony (later known as Cross Fire ritual) incorporated Jesus Christ, the Bible, and other Christian elements.

Multitribal gatherings pointed toward new "pan-Indian" identities that coexisted with more discrete tribal identifications. Native peoples in the Plains came to share certain kinds of cultural display. The Grass Dance, originating with the Pawnees, became a regular part of the growing number of intertribal gatherings across the Plains. Native peoples in the United States and Canada got permission to perform the dance on their home reservations by billing it as a "tribute" to the nation on American Independence Day (July 4) or Canadian Dominion Day (July 1).

Economically, Plains Indians' adaptations varied. The Osages and a few other tribes generated income from oil or other mineral resources. A growing number depended upon seasonal and wage labor. Some Indians reconciled wage labor with more traditional economic enterprises. Cheyenne women, for example, continued to produce moccasins for other Indians and non-Indians, just as they had since before Lewis and Clark. By the end of World War I Cheyennes and Arapahos served as seasonal agricultural laborers harvesting Oklahoma wheat. Many Sioux helped harvest potatoes in Nebraska. Plains peoples experimented with cattle ranching, which looked to be on the path to success until agents and other non-Indians pressured Indians to sell off their herds during World War I. The Gros Ventres, Pine Ridge Sioux, Comanches, and other Indian ranchers sold or leased much of their land to whites.

The Indian cattle industry temporarily fared better on the Canadian Prairies. In an effort to diversify Native economies, Ottawa officials encouraged the Prairie groups to become stock raisers by issuing large numbers of cattle to them. The cattle industry was well established on the Prairie reserves by 1900, but a long dry spell in the 1920s, together with extensive leasing of grazing lands to non-Indians, subsequently decreased the importance of ranching.

The Indian New Deal in the Plains

By the end of the 1920s many Americans had concluded that allotment and assimilation had not been successful. Nationally, the sale of surplus lands and allotments from 1887 to 1934 reduced the Indian's land base by two-thirds, from 138 million to 52 million acres. Ironically, a policy designed to foster self-support produced dispossession and dependency instead. Such economic devastation undoubtedly helped account for Indians' low incomes and high rates of infant mortality and disease.

The growing recognition of these failures led to a shift in U.S. Indian policy that once again changed the environment in which Indians operated. The new changes, like the old ones, created both opportunities and problems for Indians. In 1933 John Collier, a New York social worker and longtime critic of federal Indian policy, became the commissioner of Indian affairs. Collier believed that white society had become too individualistic and had much to learn from Native Americans' community-oriented cultures. He came to office determined to reverse the assimilation policy and to restore an Indian economic base. Collier's reforms, contained in the 1934 Indian Reorganization Act (IRA), ended allotment, increased tribally owned land, and authorized tribes to organize constitutional governments empowered to negotiate with their federal, state, and local counterparts. The act also allowed greater access to economic resources through the establishment of a revolving credit fund from which tribes could finance economic development projects and by making Indians eligible for social welfare programs available to other citizens.

Many Plains peoples availed themselves of the IRA's political and economic provisions. The Cheyenne-Arapahos of Oklahoma, Caddos, Pawnees, Poncas, Iowas, Blackfeet, Pine Ridge Sioux, and other Plains groups adopted written constitutions under the Indian New Deal. The Blackfeet developed a new law code that provided for wildlife conservation. With a $2 million loan, the Northern Cheyennes developed a livestock enterprise. Thousands of Indians found temporary employment through New Deal work programs like the Indian Civilian Conservation Corps and the Works Project Administration. Funds from the latter agency paid for Shoshones to tan elk hides, while the Civilian Conservation Corps and other relief programs provided work for 85 percent of Rosebud Reservation males. The Indian New Deal facilitated the return of millions of acres of land to Native American control as well.

Nevertheless, the Indian New Deal had its share of problems. The IRA's provisions for organizing tribal governments were based on Collier's understanding of the Pueblos and on European American models and thus were often different from tribes' conceptions of government. The secretary of the interior had the power to "review" many decisions made by the new tribal governments. The money in the credit fund usually proved inadequate and only went to the best credit risks and not to those who most needed money. The question of whether tribes should organize under the act often proved divisive. On the Rosebud and Pine Ridge reservations, for example, more acculturated residents tended to favor the act for its economic provisions, whereas traditional residents advocated basing relations with the United States on past treaties and thus tended to oppose it.

World War II and Termination

Like the New Deal, World War II had an enormous impact upon Plains Indians. Thousands served in the armed forces of the United States and Canada, and wartime activities promoted economic opportunities. The Sioux, for example, helped build military facilities in the Northern Plains. In other cases, Indians migrated to urban areas to work in war industries, an out-migration from reservations that has continued to some degree ever since. In Canada, many Indians who served in World War II gained citizenship and political rights, giving them more leverage to fight for religious rights and better education, housing, and health programs. Many of these efforts came to fruition with the 1951 Indian Act, which granted the Natives greater freedom to practice religious and cultural ceremonies and the right to raise political funds and consume alcohol outside reserves.

In 1946 Congress passed the Indian Claims Commission Act, which created the Indian Claims Commission. Through the commission Native Americans could win compensation from the federal government for past mistreatment, such as violations of treaties and land seizures. Numerous Plains Indian groups filed claims with the commission. The Pawnees, for example, were awarded $7.3 million by the Indian Claims Commission in 1962 in recognition of past "unconscionably low" payments for their lands.

The Indian Claims Commission, however, was also a mechanism for clearing the backlog of Indian claims as a prelude to severing federal obligation to the tribes. The success that Indians had had serving in World War II, as well as desires to cut federal spending and to promote national unity during the cold war, convinced many that Indians no longer needed special protection and that they should be "rewarded" through integration into the "mainstream." These views produced the "termination" policy between 1953 and the early 1960s. Termination sought to end Indians' eligibility for certain federal services and to abolish the federal trust status of Indian lands. The latter move would subject reservations to state laws and state taxes and other forces that would presumably erode and destroy Native Americans' distinct cultural status. One Plains tribe, the Northern Poncas, was declared terminated. The federal government also funded a voluntary relocation program to encourage Indians to move to urban areas, such as Denver, where they would supposedly have more employment opportunities and would more readily assimilate.

In some ways, relocation to urban areas could be seen as a revival of the old Plains Indian strategy of physical mobility. The results of relocation often proved mixed, however. As much as 40 percent of relocatees eventually returned to their home communities. City life caused or exacerbated such ills as alcoholism, spouse abuse, and poverty. Nevertheless, some relocatees did find employment, and the interaction of people from different tribes helped foster a "pan-Plains" and "pan-Indian" consciousness.

Native Political Adaptations

Whether they migrated to cities or stayed in their home communities, Plains Indians increasingly utilized intertribal organizing and political tactics—direct lobbying and public protests, for example—to protect and advance their interests. Even before World War II ended, Native peoples met in Denver to form the National Congress of American Indians (NCAI). Osages, Gros Ventres, Blackfeet, Oglala Sioux, Cheyenne-Arapahos, and other representatives of the Plains tribes secured important positions in the organization. Helen Peterson (Oglala Sioux) was executive director from 1953 to 1961. Plains Indians also often proved successful in using their positions to lobby Congress to reject or alter several termination bills during the 1950s. Ironically, termination—designed to break down tribal structures—probably strengthened Plains tribes and organizations by providing a coherent threat that united many Indians in opposition.

Native American lobbying and organization ultimately forced a change in federal policy. Instead of termination, federal policy by the early 1960s came to emphasize "self-determination," which involved allowing tribes greater control over their own affairs. Self-determination was facilitated by the 1960s War on Poverty, which gave local organizations access to federal funds and opportunities to administer antipoverty projects. Indians' inclusion in War on Poverty legislation stemmed largely from the 1964 Indian Capital Conference on Poverty held in Washington DC. Plains Indians played prominent roles in the conference, including NCAI executive director Robert Burnette (Rosebud Sioux), congressional representative Benjamin Reifel (Brulé Sioux), honorary conference chairman Walter Wetzel (Blackfoot), and archdeacon Vine V. Deloria Sr. (Standing Rock Sioux).

Many Plains peoples utilized the federal resources that the War on Poverty made available. The Anishinaabe and Cree residents of the Rocky Boy's Reservation in Montana started a crafts cooperative that produced and sold leather goods to customers throughout the country. The Rosebud Sioux used federal assistance to provide prefabricated housing to reservation residents. Indians not only improved their economic situations, but the experience of managing programs and funds strengthened tribal governments and provided a training ground for Indian leaders.

Sometimes, Plains Indians worked for self-determination through more assertive protest. The organization most commonly associated with this approach in the late twentieth century was the American Indian Movement (AIM). Although originally founded in Minneapolis in 1968 as an outgrowth of the pan-tribal Indian communities that developed in urban areas, the group established chapters throughout the Plains states. In South Dakota in 1970, AIM members occupied the Sheep Mountain area—taken from the Pine Ridge Sioux during World War II—and staged another protest at Mount Rushmore. In 1973, the year after the Trail of Broken Treaties caravan to Washington DC and the seizure of the Bureau of Indian Affairs building, Dennis Banks (Anishinaabe), Russell Means (Oglala Sioux, or Lakota), and other AIM members occupied the Pine Ridge Reservation town of Wounded Knee for more than two months. The occupation grew out of a conflict with tribal chairman Richard Wilson, who was seen by AIM as a corrupt puppet of the United States. The occupation was, in some ways, a rejection of both America's Indian policy and of the tribal council form of government itself.

Since the late 1960s Canadian Indian strategies of protest, lobbying, and lawsuits have forced Ottawa policymakers to acknowledge increased self-government for the Native peoples of the Plains and elsewhere. By the end of the 1960s a growing number of functions once handled for bands by the Canadian government—such as housing and education—had been taken over by Indian councils. Native protests forced the government to reject a termination-style policy recommended by a 1969 White Paper. Indian lobbying and protest also convinced Ottawa policymakers to set up an Office of Native Claims to investigate and negotiate settlements with individual Indians and Native groups who claimed to have lost land because of the government's failure to honor its treaty obligations to the tribes. The government, as part of the 1982 Constitution Act, recognized for the first time Native peoples' title to the land based on Aboriginal status and treaties. However, the measure failed to spell out what such rights entailed, and it did not settle the issue of Natives' relationship with the rest of the country. This became clear in 1990 when Elijah Harper, a Cree and the only Native member of the Manitoba Legislative Assembly, helped block the Meech Lake Accord, which classified French-speaking Quebec as a "distinct" society but failed to recognize the distinct status of Natives. What the future holds for the Plains peoples of Canada and their relationship with other Canadians remains unclear, although legal decisions of the late 1990s point to positive changes in views toward Indian land management and the validity of oral history.

The same uncertainty holds true for the United States. In many respects, Plains peoples' adaptive strategies have succeeded in enhancing their opportunities for political power and economic self-sufficiency. Federal legislation such as the Indian Self-Determination and Education Act (1975) and the Self-Governance Project Demonstration Act (1991) have allowed many tribes greater control over their own political affairs. Several Plains Indians—like Northern Cheyenne Ben Nighthorse Campbell, the first Native American to serve in the U.S. Senate—have filled important government positions. Economic development projects, especially the creation of Indian gaming establishments, have increased the incomes of some groups. On the Pine Ridge Reservation, for example, the Prairie Wind Casino was generating several thousand dollars a month in the mid-1990s.

Such political and economic progress has been accompanied by an even greater success among North American Plains peoples in maintaining distinct identities. Spiritual practices like the Sun Dance are experiencing a revival in both the United States and Canada. By the mid-1990s Buffy Sainte-Marie—a Cree from the Piapot Reserve in Saskatchewan—had recorded several albums of Indian and popular music, written several pieces for Indian publications, and authored a children's book incorporating Indian themes. AIM cofounder and musician John Trudell, a Santee Sioux, mixed Northern Plains Indian musical forms with blues and rock and roll. Trudell, Floyd Westerman, Russell Means, and other Plains Indian actors have appeared in several films. The American Indian Religious Freedom Act (1978) and the Native American Graves Protection and Repatriation Act (1990)—enacted as a result of Indian demands—have, respectively, provided a legal basis for the protection of Native American religious practices and for the repatriation of Indian remains and cultural items held by museums.

Furthermore, the 2000 census shows that Native Americans in the U.S. Great Plains are increasing significantly in numbers, while most Plains counties are losing population. The overall Native American population in North Dakota grew 20 percent from 1990 to 2000, in South Dakota 23 percent, and in Montana 18 percent. During the same years forty-seven of North Dakota's fifty-three counties lost population. The resurgence of Native American population is a result of high birth rates but also of a significant return to the reservations, partly because of job opportunities at casinos. The reservations and surrounding counties stand out on the 2000 census map as places having more than 25 percent, and often more than 50 percent, of their population Native American.

In many ways, however, the Plains peoples of the twenty-first century face significant challenges. Large numbers of Natives in Canada and the United States continue to experience poverty, ill health, substandard housing, and poor health care at rates well above the national average. In the mid-1990s unemployment on the Pine Ridge Reservation ranged from 65 to 85 percent, 1,800 families lacked adequate housing, and many people suffered from alcoholism. Cuts in funding for U.S. Indian programs during the 1980s and 1990s have exacerbated such problems and threaten to cancel out recent gains in self-determination and quality of life. States and private concerns have launched concerted attacks on Indian gaming.

Conclusion

Assertions of a "Native renaissance" may be premature. Nevertheless, Plains Native peoples have proven skilled at adapting to hardship and change while making the most of available opportunities. They have traded and raided, farmed and hunted, ranched and worked for wages, negotiated and made war, danced and prayed, lobbied and protested. Such adaptive strategies have allowed Plains Indians to maintain themselves as distinct peoples despite significant obstacles. One could argue that Plains Indian history has been a succession of "Native renaissances," always coming in response to hard times and always changing the nature of Plains cultures. Native peoples are and will continue to be an integral part of life in the Plains for a long time to come.

Philip J. Deloria
University of Michigan
Christopher K. Riggs
University of Colorado at Boulder

Comeau, Pauline, and Aldo Santin. *The First Canadians: A Profile of Canada's Native People Today.* Toronto: University of Toronto Press, 1990. Deloria, Vine, Jr., and Clifford M. Lytle. *The Nations Within: The Past and Future of American Indian Sovereignty.* Lincoln: University of Nebraska Press, 1984. Fixico, Donald L. *Termination and Relocation: Federal Indian Policy, 1945–1960.* Albuquerque: University of New Mexico Press, 1986. Holm, Tom. *Strong Hearts, Wounded Souls: Native American Veterans of Vietnam.* Austin: University of Texas Press, 1996. Hoxie, Frederick E. *Parading through History: The Making of the Crow Nation in America, 1805–1935.* Cambridge: Cambridge University Press, 1995. Josephy, Alvin M., Jr., ed. *America in 1492: The World of the Indian People before the Arrival of Columbus.* New York: Alfred A. Knopf. 1992. McNickle, D'Arcy. *Native American Tribalism: Indian Survivals and Renewals.* London: Oxford University Press, 1973. Philp, Kenneth R. *John Collier's Crusade for Indian Reform, 1920–1954.* Tucson: University of Arizona Press, 1977. Smith, Paul Chaat, and Robert Allen Warrior. *Like a Hurricane: The Indian Movement from Alcatraz to Wounded Knee.* New York: New Press, 1996. Trigger, Bruce, and Wilcomb E. Washburn, eds. *The Cambridge History of the Native Peoples of the Americas.* Cambridge: Cambridge University Press, 1996. Van Kirk, Sylvia. *Many Tender Ties: Women in Fur-Trade Society, 1670–1870.* Norman: University of Oklahoma Press, 1983. Wood, W. Raymond, and Thomas D. Thiessen, eds. *Early Fur Trade on the Northern Plains: Canadian Traders among the Mandan and Hidatsa Indians, 1738–1818.* Norman: University of Oklahoma Press, 1985.

ADOBE WALLS, BATTLE OF

This battle between buffalo hunters and approximately seven hundred Comanche, Kiowa, and Southern Cheyenne warriors resulted in an Indian defeat, one among several during the course of the large-scale military operation known as the Red River War of 1874–75. Inspired by a recent Sun Dance and Comanche medicine man Isatai's promise of easy victory, the warriors sought to inflict a mortal blow against the hated buffalo hunters who were destroying the vast southern herds in the Texas Panhandle. The young Comanche Quanah Parker joined Isatai as nominal leaders of the raid against the twenty-eight men and one woman residing in Adobe Walls, a small complex of trading stores and a saloon in present-day Hutchinson County, Texas.

During the early dawn hours of June 27, 1874, the Indians attacked the residents, quickly killing two hunters who were sleeping in a wagon. The others were alerted immediately because they had remained awake during the night while repairing a broken beam in the saloon. They held off several assaults, losing only two other defenders—one to Indian gunfire and one to the accidental discharge of a rifle. The siege continued for five days. Indian casualties mounted to several dozen, and faith in Isatai's power faded. On the second day of the siege, Billy Dixon fired his fabled shot, hitting a mounted warrior fully eight-tenths of a mile away. Following abandonment of the Adobe Walls settlement six weeks later, the Indians burned it to the ground. Yet the battle had been a bitter setback for them, and it presaged the larger defeat that would soon follow at the hands of the army.

Michael L. Tate
University of Nebraska at Omaha

Dixon, Olive K. *Life of "Billy" Dixon.* Dallas: P. L. Turner, 1927. Gard, Wayne. *The Great Buffalo Hunt.* New York: Alfred A. Knopf, 1959. Haley, James L. *The Buffalo War.* New York: Doubleday, 1976.

AGRICULTURE

Prior to white contact, Native American agriculture in the Great Plains differed little from farming practices east of the Mississippi River. On the Northern Plains the Mandans and Hidatsas cultivated corn, beans, and squash for their essential food needs. Women, who were expert geneticists, cleared the land and planted, cultivated, and harvested the crops, then stored the surplus in jug-shaped pits. They and other village-based Plains Indians, such as the Pawnees, used floodplain terraces for cropland. The tough prairie sod prevented cultivation of the uplands. Family fields were small, generally less than four acres. Nomadic Plains tribes, such as the Crows and Lakotas (Sioux), traded buffalo meat and hides to the farming peoples for vegetables.

During the nineteenth century the acquisition of Native American lands by the federal government, and its distribution to settlers, led to the creation of reservations where missionaries and government agents attempted to teach Native Americans European American agricultural traditions. A similar policy was instituted in Canada on reserves created in the 1870s and 1880s. Agents often violated Indian culture by providing instruction to men, who viewed agriculture as women's work. Agency farmers also promoted wheat over traditional crops and insisted on row cultivation rather than the intercultivation methods that had traditionally been used.

Often reserves and reservations were located in areas where land could not support agriculture beyond the subsistence level. Both governments also failed to provide adequate equipment, seeds, and training to enable the transition to the new system. On the Canadian reserves, for example, farmers who were supposed to instruct Native Canadians were generally from Ontario and knew nothing of the conditions in the Prairie Provinces.

By the 1880s, in the United States, pressure by settlers for reservation lands became acute, and Congress responded with the General Allotment Act (also known as the Dawes Act) in 1887, which provided for the allotment of land to individual tribal members. Under this legislation, each head of household received a plot of land, generally 160 acres, leaving the remainder of the reservations to be sold as surplus lands. Individuals who took allotments would receive title to their land after a trust period of twenty-five years. The Canadian reserves were also allotted. The U.S. and Canadian governments proposed to teach Native peoples to become self-sufficient farmers on their allotments, but they failed to back the policy with the necessary resources. In 1906 Congress passed the Burke Act, which enabled the secretary of the interior to declare an allotted farmer competent to manage his or her own affairs before the end of the trust period. Landowners who were declared competent received title to their lands and often sold it, a process that further hindered the successful development of Native American agriculture.

During the 1930s the federal government attempted to aid Plains Indian farmers by providing cattle to help build tribal herds, and several tribes organized livestock associations to improve breeding and marketing practices. By the end of World War II, however, high crop and livestock prices accelerated white demands to lease or purchase Indian lands because, it was claimed, they were not being cultivated or grazed to capacity.

Hidatsa Indian woman hoeing squash with a bone hoe, 1912

After 1945 only the white farmers who could command the necessary capital and credit, and who had access to new forms of science and technology and large acreages, could earn a profit from commercial agriculture. Native Americans in the Great Plains remained subsistence farmers, if they practiced agriculture at all. In 1970, for example, only 9 percent of Native Americans on the North Dakota reservations of Fort Berthold, Fort Totten, Turtle Mountain, and Standing Rock were farmers or farm managers.

At the beginning of the twenty-first century, on many reserves and reservations in the Great Plains, Native American agriculture has nearly ceased. There are important exceptions, of course, such as the Montana Reserve in Alberta, which has a successful ranch and feed operation. But many tribes have leased their reservation lands to white farmers and ranchers, and millions of acres of allotted lands have been sold and passed from Indian control. The problems of government-imposed inheritance laws, which divided land holdings into tracts too small for profitable cultivation, and inadequate capital, credit, and education, as well as insufficient machinery, seeds, fertilizer, irrigation, and managerial experience, remain unresolved. As a result, most Native Americans in the Great Plains live in rural areas but are not farmers.

R. Douglas Hurt
Iowa State University

Baillargeon, Morgan. "Native Cowboys on the Canadian Plains." *Agricultural History* 69 (1995), 547–62. Hurt, R. Douglas. *Indian Agriculture in America: Prehistory to the Present.* Lawrence: University Press of Kansas, 1987.

ALLOTMENT

Allotment in severalty is the process of dividing collectively occupied lands into individually owned parcels. European Americans applied the concept to Native Americans many times, beginning in the colonial era and culminating in the passage of the 1887 General Allotment (Dawes) Act. It began as a strategy for rewarding cooperative Native leaders with large parcels of land. Later, the government used allotments to appease Indian peoples who opposed being removed from their homelands. When Native Americans were removed from the southeastern United States in the 1830s, treaties granted allotments of land to families who wished to stay, while dictating the terms of removal to the Southern Plains for all others. Many people who took allotments under these treaties lost them to fraud perpetrated by land speculators.

As the reservation policy emerged in the 1850s, the United States began inserting allotment provisions into land cession treaties. The treaties divided reservation lands into individual parcels at the president's discretion, but this use of allotment served no clear policy objective. In the late 1860s the government reinvented allotment in severalty as an assimilation strategy. Reformers believed that individualized landownership (private property) would help transform Native Americans into farmers, thereby integrating them into the American economy. Development-oriented westerners supported the idea, hoping that allotment would free up "surplus" lands for settlement, mining, ranching, and forestry. The uneasy alliance of these two powerful interest groups helped win passage of the General Allotment (Dawes) Act in 1887, after eight years of congressional debate. Similarly, in the Prairie Provinces in the 1870s and 1880s, newly created reserves for First Nations were allotted into individual and family parcels as part of the assimilation program.

During the debate over severalty legislation in the United States, Native Americans voiced their opinions on the topic. Some, like the Omahas, lobbied for their own allotment acts to secure title to their homelands. Others, like the Five Tribes of Indian Territory, petitioned to be excluded from the Dawes Act, arguing that they were already sufficiently "Americanized."

The Dawes Act mandated the division of reservations into individually owned allotments of land, using a base size of 160 acres for adult males and smaller amounts for other tribal members. Typically, though, allotment sizes were determined on a reservation-by-reservation basis, and often all members of the tribe received the same acreage. Unallotted "surplus" land could be purchased by the federal government and sold to non-Indians. The allotments themselves were to remain in trust (protected against sale and untaxed) for twenty-five years, but Congress eroded this protection in the 1890s and early 1900s.

The president determined which reservations would be allotted, and pressure from development interests usually drove his selections. Tribes in the Plains were singled out more frequently than those in other regions because ranchers and farmers wanted access to their lands. Plains tribes were also disproportionately targeted by competency commissions that decided which allottees were "competent" to handle their own business affairs. "Competent" individuals were compelled to take outright title to their allotments, dissolving the trust status and leaving the land vulnerable to sale.

The Indian Reorganization Act of 1934 officially ended the allotment policy. But many tribes continue to deal with the complex geographic, legal, and economic legacy of the legislation, which turned their reservations into patchworks of tribal lands, allotments, and non-Indian lands.

Emily Greenwald
Historical Research Associates, Inc.

Carlson, Leonard A. *Indians, Bureaucrats, and Land: The Dawes Act and the Decline of Indian Farming*. Westport CT: Greenwood Press, 1981. Greenwald, Emily. *Reconfiguring the Reservation: The Nez Perces, Jicarilla Apaches, and the Dawes Act*. Albuquerque: University of New Mexico Press, 2002. McDonnell, Janet A. *The Dispossession of the American Indian, 1887–1934*. Bloomington: Indiana University Press, 1991. Otis, D. S. *The Dawes Act and the Allotment of Indian Lands*. Norman: University of Oklahoma Press, 1973.

AMERICAN INDIAN MOVEMENT

American Indian Movement, Wounded Knee, South Dakota, March 2, 1973

Eddie Benton Banai and Clyde Bellecourt, two Ojibwa prisoners at Minnesota's Stillwater Prison, began organizing fellow Native American inmates in 1963, preaching a doctrine of Indian pride and self-reliance. After receiving parole the following year, Bellecourt took his message to Minneapolis. By 1968 he and Banai had teamed up with two more Ojibwas, George Mitchell and Dennis Banks. They named their group Concerned Indian Americans. Unhappy with that acronym, they settled upon the American Indian Movement (AIM).

AIM monitored police actions to prevent and report brutality, fought discrimination in jobs and housing, and set up survival schools to equip Indian children with life skills for the urban environment and provide them alternative views of Native history unavailable in public schools. Its approach was also pan-Indian; since the Indian ghettos of American cities contained people from different reservations and tribes, AIM did not represent any single one of them. Instead, they focused on local issues that affected all Indians.

At first, the organization solicited government funds and donations from religious groups. But by 1968 frustration from dealing with these organizations led AIM to adopt a stance that was antagonistic toward mainstream America. They also began to extend their efforts beyond Minnesota. In 1970 an AIM chapter was founded in Cleveland by Russell Means, a Lakota who was born on the Pine Ridge Reservation in South Dakota. Major chapters were subsequently added in Milwaukee, Denver, Chicago, and San Francisco. Throughout its existence, AIM's power structure was largely decentralized, with individual chapters retaining substantial authority and frequently concentrating on local issues. In addition, its national leaders, including Banks, Means, Bellecourt, and Santee Dakota John Trudell, generally led by force of personality and with support from their followers and colleagues.

AIM went beyond urban concerns and made inroads on the Pine Ridge Reservation when it organized protests in nearby Gordon, Nebraska, in early 1972. A Lakota from the reservation, Raymond Yellow Thunder, had been abducted, publicly humiliated, and beaten to death in the town by white racists. When they were charged with involuntary manslaughter instead of murder, many Pine Ridge Lakotas were outraged. AIM marched on the town and forced concessions from local authorities and the governor, thus cementing its presence and reputation on the reservation.

Later that year, AIM moved onto the national stage through its involvement in the Trail of Broken Treaties, a large-scale civil rights march in Washington DC the week before the presidential election of 1972. When the marchers arrived, inadequate sleeping accommodations and federal red tape led to an altercation with police at the Bureau of Indian Affairs (BIA) building, which quickly turned into a riot. The marchers occupied the building. During the standoff, AIM took control of the occupation and dealt with the media and federal negotiators. The occupation ended after less than a week when the government paid AIM more than $66,000 to transport people back home.

After the BIA building incident, AIM was condemned by Pine Ridge tribal chairman Dick Wilson, who himself was embroiled in a major political dispute; many people on the reservation accused him of corruption and intimidation. As conditions became increasingly violent, AIM came to the support of Wilson's opponents. After Means announced he would run against Wilson in the next election, Wilson had him temporarily jailed.

Tensions increased when the federal government stationed FBI agents and U.S. marshals on the reservation in the midst of Wilson's impeachment trial. After Wilson was acquitted amid confusing circumstances, his opponents decided to make a stand by seizing Wounded Knee, the site of the 1890 massacre of as many as three hundred Lakotas by the U.S. Seventh Cavalry. AIM readily supported them. They jointly occupied the hamlet of Wounded Knee on February 27, 1973, and were immediately surrounded by marshals, FBI agents, BIA police, and Wilson's private army, known as the "goon squad."

During the ensuing siege, AIM again took control of the situation, dealing with the national media and negotiating with the federal representatives. After seventy-one days, endless negotiations, the shooting death of two AIM supporters, and the paralysis of one marshal, the siege ended on May 8. It signaled the beginning of the end of AIM.

From then on, AIM endured a two-pronged attack from the federal government. First, a long series of trials against AIM's leaders was designed to bankrupt the organization through costly legal fees and keeping its leaders tied up in court. Meanwhile, the FBI used counterintelligence programs, later deemed illegal, to infiltrate and disrupt the organization. Government repression reached its zenith with the conviction of prominent AIM member Leonard Peltier in the 1975 shooting deaths of two FBI agents on the Pine Ridge Reservation. During the trial, the government intimidated witnesses, manufactured evidence, and committed numerous other infractions. Nonetheless, Peltier was sentenced to two consecutive life terms in 1977. Efforts to win his freedom have since gained international attention, and Amnesty International currently recognizes him as one of the most important political prisoners in the world.

Meanwhile, a virtual civil war between AIM and the "goons" plagued Pine Ridge during Wilson's post–Wounded Knee tenure (1973–76), resulting in more than fifty unsolved murders of AIM members and supporters. In 1979 the mother-in-law, wife, and three children of AIM's national chairman, John Trudell, were killed in an arsonist's fire. The cause of the fire, which was started while Trudell was protesting the Peltier verdict, remains unsolved.

Bankruptcy, paranoia, and repression, combined with AIM's decentralized structure and leadership patterns, led to a spiraling decline within the organization. Individual leaders increasingly worked on their own projects, political and otherwise, and by the 1980s AIM was defunct as a national entity. The FBI closed its active files on AIM in July 1979. Today, a scattering of local chapters continues to work on local issues, and individual members of national prominence continue to invoke the movement's name on behalf of their own programs.

Akim D. Reinhardt
Towson University

Churchill, Ward, and Jim Vander Wall. *Agents of Repression: The FBI's Secret War against the Black Panther Party and the American Indian Movement.* Boston: South End Press, 1988. Josephy, Alvin M., Jr., Joane Nagel, and Troy Johnson, eds. *Red Power: The American Indians' Fight for Freedom.* 2nd ed. Lincoln: University of Nebraska Press, 1999. Kipp, Woody. *Viet Cong at Wounded Knee: The Trail of a Blackfeet Activist.* Lincoln: University of Nebraska Press, 2004. Smith, Paul Chaat, and Robert Allen Warrior. *Like a Hurricane: The Indian Movement from Alcatraz to Wounded Knee.* New York: New Press, 1996.

APACHES

Apaches, along with Navajos, are the southernmost extension of Athapaskan-language speakers. Scholars disagree on which Apaches first lived in the Great Plains. Specialists traditionally argued for a sixteenth-century Apache entry into the region, in part because early Spanish accounts described them in the Plains of Texas and eastern New Mexico. Scholars assumed they were recent arrivals. Archeological work in the 1970s, however, affirmed an Apachean presence in the Central Plains in the fifteenth and sixteenth centuries. Moreover, the Apaches' own stories place them in the Plains as early as the ninth century.

On the basis of archeological evidence, Karl Schlesier postulated four waves of Apachean migration into the Plains between 50 and 1550 AD. The first of these is associated with a proto-Athapaskan movement into Saskatchewan and the Northern Great Plains by 50 AD. Their descendants are the Sarcees (Sarsis). A second movement of people, destined to be known as Southern Athapaskans, arrived in Montana around 200 AD. Schlesier believes that this wave split into three parts, one of which remained in place, while the other two parts continued south into Wyoming and the Black Hills, respectively. From there they moved to the Southern Plains, where Spanish explorers encountered their descendants. A third wave entered the Plains between 950 and 1225 AD. These people became the Navajos (Déné) and Chiricahua Apaches (N'de). This migration is described in traditional stories of Chiricahua and Mescalero Apache peoples. Navajo accounts place their arrival in Colorado and northern New Mexico at about 1100.

A fourth and final wave of Apachean migration, from 1450 to 1650, brought the ancestors of the Jicarillas, Lipans, and lastly, the distantly related Kiowa Apaches (also called Plains Apaches). These Apaches subsisted by food gathering, hunting, and horticulture, augmented by trade with settled farming communities. Autonomous Apache bands collected near the Pueblos, where they traded or raided as conditions warranted.

Spanish entrance into the Southern Plains in the sixteenth century brought profound changes to Apache ways of life. Colonization and forced conversion of Pueblo trading partners created increased hostility between the mobile and settled peoples. Acquisition of European horses and metal weapons presented new opportunities to raid for additional goods.

Spanish officials in New Mexico and Texas had difficulty identifying Apache tribes by name and location. Frequent changes in designation were required to correct mistakes. By 1700 Apaches in the Plains were identified as follows: Lipans, occupying central Texas; Faraons, in the Texas Panhandle; Mescaleros, in eastern New Mexico; Jicarillas, north and east of the Mescaleros; Carlanas, located along the present Colorado–New Mexico border; and Cuartelejos, in eastern Colorado and adjacent western Kansas. Palomas occupied central Nebraska along the Platte River. Plains Apaches (later also known as Kiowa Apaches) were in and around the Black Hills of South Dakota.

By the mid–seventeenth century Apaches had acquired enough horses that their raids became a major concern for Spanish authorities in New Mexico. Colonial governors tried various policies to subjugate them. Military expeditions against scattered autonomous bands produced limited results. Spanish alliances with Pueblos and Comanches were more productive. After 1700 the Comanches swept the Apaches off the plains of Texas and eastern New Mexico. Spanish territorial governors at times attempted to concentrate Apaches near Pueblo communities through dispersal of trade goods, including guns and alcohol. Some bands accepted Spanish annuities and settled under Spanish rule. Most did not. Spain failed to bring Apache bands in the Plains under control. Mexico fared no better. Apache raids, along with Comanche inroads, became the bane of existence in newly independent Mexico between 1821 and 1846.

In independent Texas (1836–45), policy was hostile to Indian populations, Apaches included. Texas, however, focused on war against Comanches, being less interested in Lipans and Mescaleros, who were generally far enough west to be beyond reach. The United States' annexation of Texas in 1845, and occupation and acquisition of much of northern Mexico in 1848, brought immense changes to the Apaches. Gen. Stephen Watts Kearny pronounced the United States' policy at Las Vegas, New Mexico, in 1846, which called for disarming and forcible settlement of all nomadic raiders. That policy was pursued for more than thirty years to an eventual successful conclusion.

From 1849 to 1851 a severe cholera epidemic along overland trails struck the Apaches. Most Lipans perished. Survivors, harried by Comanches and Kiowas, eventually took refuge with the Mescaleros, who absorbed them.

The United States negotiated treaties with the Apaches in the 1850s, but most were not ratified. The U.S. Army carried on a series of campaigns against specific Apache bands in the 1850s. By 1861 war with Apaches had become general. The Jicarillas were fortunate to find refuge on the immense Maxwell Land Grant in northern New Mexico. In 1863 the army was authorized to carry out a war of extermination against the Apaches. Kit Carson directed a campaign against the Mescaleros that resulted in their surrender. They and other Apache bands were gradually placed, by force or agreement, on reservations in New Mexico and Arizona. Apache resistance ended by 1887.

Mescaleros, with surviving Lipans, were established on a reservation in south-central New Mexico, where they still remain, numbering 3,511 in 1992. Jicarillas finally were granted a reservation of their own in northern New Mexico in 1887, to the west of the Great Plains. The reservation was increased in size in 1907 and again in 1908. Their population in 1992 was 3,100. Chiricahua Apaches were held as prisoners of war in Florida and Alabama until 1893. They were then moved to Fort Sill, Oklahoma, and placed as prisoners on land donated by Comanches and Kiowas. In 1913 most of their lands were annexed to Fort Sill. About two-thirds moved to Mescalero; the rest stayed at Fort Sill. They are the Fort Sill Apaches, numbering just over 100. The Plains Apaches were placed at Fort Sill with Kiowas and Comanches at the conclusion of hostilities with those peoples in the 1870s. Most descendants of the Plains Apaches remain in that area, where they are officially recognized as the Apache Tribe of Oklahoma. They have about 1,600 enrolled tribal members.

Donald C. Cole
Bethany College

Basso, Keith H., and Morris E. Opler, eds. *Apachean Culture History and Ethnology*. Tucson: University of Arizona Press, 1971. Hyde, George E. *Indians of the High Plains: From the Prehistoric Period to the Coming of Europeans*. Norman: University of Oklahoma Press, 1959. Schlesier, Karl H., ed. *Plains Indians, AD 500–1500: The Archaeological Past of Historic Groups*. Norman: University of Oklahoma Press, 1994.

ARAPAHOS

Arapahos refer to themselves as Hinanaeina (*hinono'eino*), or "the People." Trappers and trad-

ers in the early nineteenth century used the Crow name for Arapahos, Alappaho ("Many Tattoos"), and Arapahos began referring to themselves by that term in their dealings with Americans. Five dialects of Arapaho (an Algonquian language) existed in historical times and correlated with tribal divisions: Hinanaeina (Arapaho); Hitounena (Gros Ventre); and three others, the speakers of which presumably became absorbed by the other divisions.

Arapahos entered the Northern Plains at least by the early eighteenth century, probably from the northeast. The Gros Ventre division remained in the far Northern Plains, while Arapahos moved in a southerly direction. Wealthy in horses, probably since the 1740s, Arapahos ranged from the headwaters of the Missouri to the Platte River, and west as far as the foothills of the Rocky Mountains. By 1806 they allied with Cheyennes, largely to counter the westward movement of the Sioux (Lakota). With the Cheyennes, they drove the Kiowas and Comanches south of the Arkansas River by 1826 and controlled the region between the Platte and Arkansas rivers. In 1835, diminished by smallpox, they numbered an estimated 3,600.

Arapahos relied on bison for food, clothing, and many other necessities. In the 1830s and 1840s they hunted in the Estes Park area of Colorado (especially the region of the Cache la Poudre River) and the adjacent Plains to the east, which they recognized as their exclusive territory. Men hunted and women dried the meat, collected and dried roots and berries, dressed hides, and made tipi covers, clothing, and containers. The quilled, painted, and, by the nineteenth century, beaded designs applied on hide by women represented prayers for the well being of a relative. After 1857 settlers and miners moved into the Parks area of present-day Colorado, driving off the bison, so that the Arapahos had to hunt more regularly on the open plains east of the Rockies.

Most of the year, Arapahos lived in bands that moved together when large camps were formed or disbanded and affiliated with one of the several named subdivisions of the Hinanaeina, but individuals and households could move from one band to another. Kinship was reckoned on the basis of bilateral descent, although other individuals could be absorbed into kindred by means of "adoption." Arapahos married outside their group of kindred and legalized marriage by gift exchange between the bride's and groom's families.

The Arapaho origin story focuses on Pipe Person's creation of the earth from mud below the surface of an expanse of water. Pipe Person, through prayer-thought, created all life, including the first Arapahos. Arapahos henceforth kept a replica of the Flat Pipe as a symbol of their covenant with the life force or power on which Pipe Person drew. Rites centered on the pipe bundle helped ensure the success of Arapahos generally and of individuals specifically. Seven men's and seven women's medicine bags contained objects and implements that symbolized forms of power, and these passed from one custodian to another. Prayer-thoughts could affect events and lives, and the sincerity of a petitioner's prayer-thought was validated by sacrifices of property or of the body by flesh offerings and fasting. In the major tribal ritual, the Offerings Lodge (also known as the Sun Dance), a petitioner vowed to participate (that is, make a sacrifice) in the ceremony in return for supernatural aid. Individuals also acquired supernatural aid by dreaming or fasting for a vision encounter with a supernatural being. During the early nineteenth century, many of the men's vision fasts were on various peaks in Estes Park, Colorado. Women usually received power in a dream or from a husband or parent.

A governing council and an age-graded series of societies, supervised by the elderly custodians of the medicine bundle, comprised the tribal government. Initiation into each society was precipitated by a religious vow; the age mates of the votary went through the ceremony as a group. Wives were considered to progress through the men's societies with their husbands. These men's groups performed political duties, including keeping order in the camp and supervising the communal hunts. The governing council in the nineteenth century consisted of four leaders representing four tribal subdivisions, the medicine bundle custodians, and the leaders of the men's societies. Beginning in the 1840s "chiefs" served as intermediaries between the governing council and federal officials.

The Arapahos prospered from trading bison robes to Americans in the 1830s, but beginning in the 1840s, American expansion westward disturbed the bison herds. The United States initiated treaty councils, first to prevent troubles along the immigrant routes and later to remove Plains peoples from areas where Americans wanted to settle. In 1851 the Arapahos signed a peace treaty that guaranteed that settlers would not trespass on the tribe's lands in Wyoming and Colorado. Settlers and miners violated the treaty, with little opposition from the federal government, which led to trouble with the Arapahos and Cheyennes. In 1864 Colorado militia massacred a Cheyenne and Arapaho camp at Sand Creek, provoking a two-year war and resulting in the separation of Arapaho bands into politically independent northern and southern divisions. In 1867 the Southern Arapahos, led by Little Raven, signed the Treaty of

Medicine Lodge Creek, ending hostilities. In 1868 the Northern Arapahos, having fought for several years to hold onto the bison range in Wyoming and Montana, signed a treaty under Medicine Man's leadership and agreed to settle on a reservation. Intermediary chiefs negotiated with officials during subsequent months, and in 1869 President Ulysses S. Grant created by executive order a reservation for Southern Arapahos and Cheyennes in Indian Territory (later Oklahoma). In 1878 Northern Arapahos obtained permission to settle on the Shoshone reservation in Wyoming.

When they moved to their reservations, the Southern Arapahos numbered about 1,200 and the Northern Arapahos, 1,000. The Southern Arapahos continued to hunt bison until 1878, when game became scarce. During the 1880s Arapahos on both reservations depended for subsistence on the supplies issued by the federal government and disbursed by band leaders, the most important of whom were Black Coal and Sharp Nose in Wyoming and Powderface, Left Hand, and Yellow Bear in Oklahoma. Leaders also organized communal agricultural labor on both reservations and freighting and livestock raising in Oklahoma. The reservation in Oklahoma was divided into individually owned allotments of land in 1892, and unallotted lands were sold to non-Indians. In Wyoming, allotment occurred in 1901, but the unallotted lands were in an area undesirable for farming, and consequently these lands were never sold. In Oklahoma, the federal government facilitated the sale of most of the allotments over the years, while in Wyoming oil was discovered on the tribally owned unallotted lands. Since 1940 all Northern Arapahos have received monthly per capita payments from mineral royalties and bonuses, which have helped to alleviate poverty and have kept land sales to a minimum.

Both the Oklahoma and Wyoming Arapahos had intermediary chiefs until the third decade of the twentieth century. These chiefs worked to defend the treaty rights of their respective tribes. When the federal government encouraged the formation of elective, representative, and constitutional government, Oklahoma Arapahos instituted a "business committee." Wyoming Arapahos rejected the idea of constitutional government but adopted an elective, representational "business council." In both cases, traditional ideals of leadership became incorporated into the new form of tribal government. Federal programs that created jobs, scholarships, housing, and other kinds of development were introduced, beginning in the 1960s, and these strengthened the role of tribal government. In the late 1990s the population of Arapahos in Oklahoma was about 4,000, in Wyoming at that time there were about 4,400 Arapahos—half of whom live within the boundaries or former boundaries of the reservation. Enrollment in the Northern or Southern Arapaho tribes is contingent on having at least 25 percent Arapaho ancestry; most have more than 25 percent.

The Offerings Lodge continued in Oklahoma until 1939, and thereafter Arapahos took it to Wyoming, where the ceremony continues today, as does the Sacred Pipe ritual. The Ghost Dance movement was important in the 1890s and, in revised form, in the early twentieth century in both the Oklahoma and Wyoming communities. Peyote ritual was introduced to the Southern Arapahos by Plains Apaches in the 1890s and then transferred to the Wyoming Arapahos; the Native American Church continues to be important in both communities. Mennonite and Baptist missionaries introduced Christianity in Oklahoma, and Catholic and Episcopal missionaries in Wyoming. Generally, the practice of Native religion and Christianity are not mutually exclusive. Since the 1970s there has been an elaboration of "traditional" religious and social ritual in both the Oklahoma and Wyoming communities.

Loretta Fowler
University of Oklahoma

Anderson, Jeffrey D. *The Four Hills of Life: Northern Arapaho Knowledge and Life Movement*. Lincoln: University of Nebraska Press, 2001. Anderson, Jeffrey D. *One Hundred Years of Old Man Sage: An Arapaho Life*. Lincoln: University of Nebraska Press, 2003. Fowler, Loretta. *The Arapaho*. New York: Chelsea House, 1989. Fowler, Loretta. *Arapahoe Politics, 1851–1978: Symbols in Crises of Authority*. Lincoln: University of Nebraska Press, 1982. Fowler, Loretta: *Tribal Sovereignty and the Historical Imagination: Cheyenne-Arapaho Politics*. Lincoln: University of Nebraska Press, 2002. Kroeber, Alfred L. *The Arapaho*. Bulletin of the American Museum of Natural History, vol. 18. New York, 1902–7.

ARCHAIC PERIOD SITES

For approximately six thousand years, between about two and eight thousand years ago, the Archaic period in the Great Plains was a time of human adjustment to changing ecological conditions. Paleo-Indian bison hunting decreased markedly after about nine thousand years ago, due to a steady deterioration of ecological conditions. Subsequently there were several late Paleo-Indian groups, such as Lusk, Angostura, Frederick, and James Allen, which were beginning to shift toward the use of small animal and plant resources. By about eight thousand years ago, both bison and human populations in the Great Plains had decreased significantly. Some groups may have moved into the foothills and mountains to the west and others into the prairies on the east. The Plains was not abandoned during the Archaic period, but ecological conditions made it a much less desirable place.

Much of what is known about the Plains Archaic period comes from archeological sites on the edges of, and just outside, the Plains. A widespread change in projectile point styles from lanceolate to notched forms is arbitrarily used to mark the beginning of the Plains Archaic period. Some argue that the change was the result of new groups moving into the area, while others believe it was simply a technological modification accepted by the existing residents. The best evidence for these changes is found in areas adjacent to the Plains and in areas of topographic relief within the Plains, such as the Black Hills of western South Dakota and northeast Wyoming and the Pryor Mountains in southern Montana.

In the Northern Plains, the Early Plains Archaic, also known as the Altithermal, is dated from about 8,000 to 5,500 years ago; the Middle Plains Archaic lasted from about 5,500 to 3,000 years ago; and the Late Plains Archaic lasted from about 3,000 years ago until between 2,000 and 1,500 years ago. A slightly different chronology is used in the Central and Southern Plains. The Early Archaic period there is 8,500 to 6,500 years ago; the Middle Archaic is 6,500 to 4,500 years ago; and the Late Archaic is 4,500 to 2,500 years ago.

Evidence from the Early Plains Archaic suggests that the Black Hills may have been a kind of oasis where bison were able to maintain their numbers. The Hawken site in northeast Wyoming, a 6,500–year-old bison kill site, contained animals that were intermediate in size (probably *Bison occidentalis*), smaller than the ones found in earlier Paleo-Indian kills but larger than the modern bison found in kill sites after about 5,500 years ago. The Itasca site, close to the Plains in Minnesota and dating from between 7,000 and 8,000 years ago, contained similar bison. The Cherokee site in Iowa has Late Paleo-Indian and Early Archaic bison evidence. The Rustad and Smilden-Rostburg sites in western North Dakota are Early Archaic sites with bison remains. The lowest level at the Oxbow Dam site in southern Saskatchewan is Early Archaic. The Logan Creek complex in eastern Nebraska and Iowa and the Sutter site in eastern Kansas are also Early Archaic. Early Archaic sites in the Southern Plains include the Gore Pit site in south-central Oklahoma and the Wilson Leonard site on the Edwards Plateau, which has a stratified sequence of Early through Late Archaic levels.

Pronghorn remains are found in Great Plains sites of all ages. The Trappers Point site at a seasonal migration route along the Green River, just beyond the Plains in western Wyoming, contains communal pronghorn kills dating from about five to eight thousand years ago and is a strong indicator of similar pronghorn procurement throughout much of the Plains.

The Medicine House and Split Rock pit house sites along the North Platte River in southern Wyoming contain evidence of the use of grinding stones, plants, and small animals. Rock shelters and open sites in the Big Horn Mountains of northern Wyoming and in the Pryor Mountains of southern Montana also hold Early Archaic evidence.

Improved climatic conditions and a resurgence of bison hunting appeared during the Middle Plains Archaic, around 5,500 years ago on the Northern Plains. The Head-Smashed-In buffalo jump near Lethbridge, Alberta, is one of the more spectacular of these bison procurement features, showing continuous use from the end of the Early Plains Archaic into historic times. Oxbow Dam, Mortlach, and Long Creek are deep, stratified sites in southern Saskatchewan with both Middle and Late Archaic levels.

McKean sites, named after the McKean site in the Wyoming Black Hills, are widespread over the Northern Plains. The Scoggin site, for example, a bone bed inside an artificial bison corral, is located in western Wyoming close to the North Platte River. The Laidlaw site in southern Alberta is Middle Archaic, with drive lines and a pit used to trap pronghorns. Flat stone grinding slabs, manos (handheld grinding stones), and stone-filled fire pits are numerous in the southern part of the McKean occupation area, indicating a trend toward broad-spectrum hunting and gathering.

The Middle Archaic of the Edwards Plateau of Texas is well represented at the Wilson Leonard site by a wide variety of diagnostic traits. Middle Archaic levels are also present at the Magic Mountain site on the Front Range west of Denver, Colorado.

Late Plains Archaic sites are widely distributed throughout the Great Plains. First thought to be late Paleo-Indian because of large lanceolate projectile points, the Late Archaic Nebo Hill complex, widespread along the Kansas-Missouri border, contains a wide variety of artifact material, features, and faunal and plant food resources. The Late Archaic Pelican Lake complex, named from sites in southern Saskatchewan, is found over most of the Northern Plains. Pelican Lake levels are found at Head-Smashed-In buffalo jump in Alberta and in jump and arroyo bison kills in Montana. South of the Montana border, Pelican Lake demonstrates less dietary emphasis on bison and more on smaller animals, including pronghorn and deer. Grinding stones and stone-filled food-preparation pits are also common. Along the Powder River in northern Wyoming and Montana are arroyo bison kill sites known as Yonkee from a site in southern Montana, with dates of about 2,500 years ago. Stone circles (tipi rings) are widespread features from this period, most of which are believed to have held down the edges of hide coverings of conical lodges.

Besant cultural groups, another Late Archaic group named from sites in southern Saskatchewan, may have been the most sophisticated pedestrian bison hunters to appear in the Plains. The Ruby site in eastern Wyoming is a large bison corral alongside a religious structure. Farther west is the Muddy Creek site, a large Besant bison corral located in a depression, with a wooden ramp built to stampede the animals into the enclosure. Large stone circle concentrations represent associated living areas, and a large boulder pile on a high point overlooking the site is a religious structure.

In the Central and Southern Plains, the Late Archaic subsistence strategy was broad-spectrum hunting and gathering. There is a 2,600-year-old bison jump at Bonfire Shelter at the mouth of the Pecos River in Texas. Late Archaic groups on the eastern margins of the Great Plains may have been encouraging the propagation of native plants, but there is no evidence of corn, beans, or squash.

Following the Archaic in the Northern Plains was the Late Prehistoric period, between about 2,000 and 1,500 years ago, which witnessed the appearance of the bow and arrow and intensified bison hunting. Avonlea, one of the earliest hunting groups to use the bow and arrow, was contemporaneous with some late Besant groups. On the eastern edge of the Plains, agricultural villagers with ceramics and Central American cultigens appeared and persisted into historic times.

George C. Frison
University of Wyoming–Laramie

Johnson, Alfred E., ed. *Archaic Prehistory on the Prairie Plains Border*. Lawrence: University of Kansas, 1980. Larson, Mary Lou, and Julie Francis, eds. *Changing Perspectives on the Archaic on the Northwestern Plains and Rocky Mountains*. Vermillion: University of South Dakota Press, 1997. Wood, W. Raymond, ed. *Archaeology on the Great Plains*. Lawrence: University Press of Kansas, 1998.

ARCHITECTURE, CONTEMPORARY

Before the 1960s and after the demise of traditional architecture, little attention was paid to cultural relevance when designing housing and other structures on Indian reservations. Assimilative pressures, financial exigencies, and supposed efficiency led to reservation housing that was built to resemble housing for other groups, however different the cultural contexts. The standardized buildings also ignored differences in natural environments. Reservation cultural centers and urban social service centers, if built at all, were usually vernacular structures with little indication of the culture in question.

In the late 1960s and early 1970s Native Americans and Canadian First Peoples began to consider

Piya Wiconi Building, Oglala Lakota College, Pine Ridge Reservation, South Dakota

ways in which their cultural expressions could help them overcome difficulties in their private and community lives. Language revival, religious renewal, and other recalled traditions were brought into service. Economic development grants made it possible to use the marketing of heritage to generate employment on reservations in need of jobs. Greater public awareness of past social injustices and a new emphasis on group identity rather than the "melting pot" ideology created a favorable background for efforts to make architecture, as the setting for life, more relevant to the traditions of Native American users. Not all Native American groups are creating specifically Native American modern architecture, but many are, and in increasing numbers.

Cultural relevance can be suggested quickly by adding ornament to a standard building, for example. It can be achieved more substantially by reproducing or paraphrasing building types such as earth lodges and brush shelters that predated the arrival of European American settlers. Architects may use traditional building materials and may align their structures with the movements of the stars and other natural forces. Douglas Cardinal, a Canadian Métis, designs curvilinear forms for both Indigenous and immigrant clients that remind observers of the massive contours of bison or eroded rocks. Some clients and architects prefer to use symbolic forms, incorporating numerological patterns or the shapes of animals or medicine wheels, hoping that the values inherent in the symbols can be transferred to the users. Still others incorporate traditional patterns of use into the building plans, adding ceremonial rooms, central gathering areas, and meditation chambers to schools and hospitals. They may take into account customary desires to observe events in groups, standing, instead of in fixed rows of seats. They may also accommodate

Native peoples' reticence when meeting strangers or the need for storage of crafts and hunted food. Some buildings have been designed by communal processes rather than by standard European American professional practices.

Some tribes restrict culturally appropriate efforts to buildings erected for the direct benefit of all tribal members, including schools, clinics, tribal office buildings, cultural and religious structures, and urban social and service centers, while excluding casinos. Other tribes include windows, trees, and other plantings in casinos, suggesting links between Native Americans and nature and implying that a casino, the "new buffalo," benefits the tribe and is therefore respectable.

In the past decade the United States Department of Housing and Urban Development has become more sensitive to the need for inexpensive housing that also supports customary patterns of Native American life. Multigenerational families and issues of courtesy and privacy are now taken into account. The department has sponsored or encouraged construction with natural materials and with centralized and other unconventional plans inspired by preference polls of prospective residents. Not all tribes take advantage of the department's initiatives, and the available funds cannot meet the urgent need for low income reservation housing units and the repair of existing ones.

Museum buildings and tourist facilities are especially likely to embody aspects of Native American culture or tradition, because one major aim is to celebrate the distinctiveness of the historic cultures in question. Construction of tribal museums has been stimulated recently by the Native American Graves Protection and Repatriation Act of 1990, which provides for the return of artifacts and human remains to descendants of their original owners. There is no standard museum plan,

Crow's Heart's ceremonial lodge. An example of a Mandan earth lodge, ca. 1908–10

so the sponsors can build innovative forms or reproduce older ones. Ceremonial buildings, by contrast, must adhere to certain physical patterns lest the ritual action be hindered. Other religious buildings too, such as the Native American Church at Wounded Knee, South Dakota, are usually traditional in form, though not always in materials. Glass walls or steel beams, for instance, may be used to enlarge such buildings, to economize, or to improve safety.

One design problem is that many Plains people traditionally lived in portable and temporary structures that cannot easily be evoked by fixed buildings made of permanent materials. For this reason, Denby Deegan (Arikara-Sioux) and Dennis Sun Rhodes (Arapaho) have substituted symbolic forms such as the medicine wheel at Deegan's Four Winds School at the Fort Totten Reservation in North Dakota or Sun Rhodes's prairie-side façade (under Thomas Hodne's supervision) for the Piya Wiconi Building at Oglala Lakota College on the Pine Ridge Reservation in South Dakota. Peter Kommers used the morning star to generate a design for the Northern Cheyenne Heritage Center in Lame Deer, Montana. A design by Mark Hoistad for the Omaha interpretive center in Macy, Nebraska, includes totems evoking clan warriors and references to the cosmos reflected in a camp circle as well as a conical container for the sacred pole.

Problems connected to culturally appropriate design include locating sensitive architects (there are still few Native Americans in the profession), securing funds, making decisions by consensus, and devising forms that reflect the cultures. Not all tribal members understand the symbolism in proposed designs, but most will respond favorably to buildings that honor age-old customs and revere traditional patterns of life.

Carol Herselle Krinsky
New York University

American Indian Council of Architects and Engineers. *Our Home: A Design Guide for Indian Housing.* Washington DC: National Endowment for the Arts—Design Arts Program, 1994. Krinsky, Carol Herselle. *Contemporary Native American Architecture: Cultural Regeneration and Creativity.* New York: Oxford University Press, 1996. Landecker, Heidi. "Designing for American Indians." *Architecture* 82 (1993): 93–101.

ARCHITECTURE, TRADITIONAL

Native Americans were living two distinct lifestyles in the Great Plains at the time of first contact with European Americans. Tribes along the eastern edges of the Plains were practicing a semisedentary lifestyle, relying on agriculture for part of their subsistence. Tribes farther west were leading a more mobile lifestyle based on hunting and gathering. These two adaptations are reflected in distinctive patterns of architecture.

The agriculturists developed more permanent structures. These included earth lodges in the Central Plains and farther north along the Missouri River. The prototype earth lodge was probably first developed as an adaptation to a more northerly climate by northward-moving ancestral Pawnee and Arikara groups around 1200 AD. This architectural style then spread to neighboring groups, including the Mandans, Hidatsas, Omahas, Poncas, Otoes, and Kansas by the eighteenth century.

The Pawnee/Arikara earth lodge was constructed by first digging a circular pit thirty to fifty feet in diameter and eighteen inches deep. The central framework consisted of four to eight large center posts, which held up the rafters of the domed roof. An outer circular row of posts held the lower end of the rafters. The rafters were covered with willow branches, a layer of grass, and a thick layer of earth. The earth covering and subsurface floor made the structure easy to heat in the winter and allowed it to stay cool in the summer. The circular roof had a central opening at the peak to allow smoke to exit. An entranceway extended to the east for several feet. The earth lodge was home to from thirty to fifty people, depending on the size of the structure. Larger structures were also used for religious ceremonies.

Pawnee earth lodge symbolism was highly developed. The dome of the roof was the sky, and the circular wall of the earth lodge was the horizon. The house was divided symbolically into four quadrants, each with a center post represented by a symbolic color, wood, animal, and weather pattern. The house was divided into the male east half and the female west half. The west half of the lodge was symbolized by the Evening Star and contained the sacred altar with a bison skull and the sacred bundle with its ears of Mother Corn hanging above. The east half was symbolized by the Morning Star, the god of light, fire, and war. Each morning when the Morning Star rose in the eastern sky it shot beams of light through the entranceway across the lodge to light the fire, symbolizing the first union of the Morning Star with the Evening Star in an act of cosmic procreation. The earth lodge also acted as an astronomical observatory for the village priests. Observations of star positions were made through the central smoke hole, and each of the eighteen to twenty outer wall posts and the four center posts was associated with a star.

On the Southern Plains, the Wichitas, Hasinais, and Caddos built conical-shaped grass lodges with double-curve profiles and wooden frames. Two kinds of grasses were used in constructing these dwellings: the external roof was thatched with coarse prairie grasses, while the interior walls were sealed over with softer grasses from riverbanks. The walls rested on dozens of poles that were bent and bound together at the top. This structure in turn leaned against an interior ring of posts and beams. The frame, which could be sixty feet in diameter, was tightened with horizontal sapling stringers. The grass lodge could be transformed into a cool summer dwelling by exposing the lower ribs. Traditionally, the grass lodges had no smoke holes; instead, the smoke seeped through the grass roofs.

The tipi was used from the Prairie Provinces to the Southern Plains. The tipi is an inverted cone, steeper on the windward side, with an off-center smoke hole at the top. Overall, the floor plan is subcircular. Two types of tipi architecture are recognized: a four-pole framework was more common on the Northern Plains among groups like the Sarcees, Blackfoot, and Crows, and a three-pole variety was more common on the Southern and Central Plains among the Kiowas, Apaches, Arapahos, Lakotas, and Cheyennes. The agricultural groups on the eastern Plains also used the three-pole variety when hunting bison.

Covering for the conical-pole framework was originally made of tanned bison hides sewn together. Before the advent of the horse, when dogs pulled the travois made of tipi poles and loaded with the tipi cover and other belongings, six to ten bison hides were used in the average tipi. Later, horses allowed larger tipis to be moved. Canvas began to replace bison hides for covering the tipi in the late nineteenth century. Some tipi covers were painted to represent events of importance in the owner's life, including a defining vision. In most societies the tipis were owned by the men but were constructed, assembled, and disassembled by the women. Tipi poles were generally lodgepole pine on the Central and Northern Plains, with red cedar more common on the Southern Plains.

The Plains Indians utilized several types of temporary or specialized structures, the most famous of which was the Sun Dance lodge. The centerpiece of the Sun Dance lodge was a forked cottonwood trunk, which directed the dancers' focus toward the sky and the deity. From the center pole, sapling rafters radiated to a circular fence forty to fifty feet in diameter. The side fence and sometimes the rafters were covered with leafy branches. The interior design was dominated by a low, circular barrier of brushes that separated the dancers from the altar, fire pit, drummers, and singers in the middle. Like the earth lodges, grass lodges, and tipis, the Sun Dance lodge opened to the east, toward the rising sun.

Steven R. Holen
University of Nebraska State Museum

Nabokov, Peter, and Robert Easton. *Native American Architecture*. New York: Oxford University Press, 1989. Weltfish, Gene. *The Lost Universe*. Lincoln: University of Nebraska Press, 1997.

ARIKARA EXPEDITION

Early 1823 proved deadly along the upper Missouri River after a series of Indian attacks on fur trappers and trading posts caused staggering economic losses, especially to the Missouri Fur Company. In particular, the Arikaras opposed American attempts to move upriver, which would eliminate their middleman role in the fur trade. On June 2 they attacked William Ashley's trapping party, which was camped near their villages, close to the confluence of the Grand and Missouri rivers, killing fourteen men. When the survivors limped into Fort Atkinson (in present-day Nebraska) on June

View of an Arikara village at Fort Clark, North Dakota, showing a domed lodge and elevated platforms, 1872

18, Col. Henry Leavenworth and Indian agent Benjamin O'Fallon decided that American military strength had to be demonstrated. This would be the first major U.S. expedition against the Plains Indians.

Leavenworth left Fort Atkinson on June 22 with 230 men of the Sixth U.S. Infantry and two cannons to punish the Arikaras. Joining him five days later was trader Joshua Pilcher, head of the Missouri Fur Company, with sixty men and a howitzer. Ashley's men added eighty to the force, and about seven hundred Lakotas joined in to fight their enemies, the Arikaras. As the force neared the villages on August 9, the Lakotas rode ahead and engaged the Arikaras, killing ten to fifteen of them. At dawn on August 10, Leavenworth trained his artillery on the stockaded Arikara villages, but they mainly overshot the target. When the Lakotas deserted the fight to raid the Arikaras' cornfields, the troops were forced to face an expected battle alone. Seizing an opportunity to negotiate with Arikara leaders, Leavenworth asked them to return Ashley's property and to promise future good behavior. The Arikaras were allowed to leave their besieged villages on the night of August 14. Ashley seemingly accepted this outcome, but Pilcher was infuriated.

On August 15 Leavenworth and his troops headed downriver, followed by Pilcher with his contingent of trappers. Angry at the dismal show of force against the Arikaras, Pilcher set fire to both of their villages. This action naturally further alienated the Arikaras, who continued to resist American inroads on the upper Missouri. Forced to seek a new route to the trapping grounds, Ash-

ley and his men forged the overland route into the Central Rockies through South Pass. The new trail set the stage for the enormous future pioneer migration along the Platte Valley and into the West in the 1840s.

Jo Lea Wetherilt Behrens
University of Nebraska–Omaha

Meyer, Roy Willard. *The Village Indians of the Upper Missouri: The Mandans, Hidatsas, and Arikaras.* Lincoln: University of Nebraska Press, 1977. Morgan, Dale L. *Jedediah Smith and the Opening of the West.* Lincoln: University of Nebraska Press, 1964.

ARIKARAS

Long before European Americans entered the Great Plains, the Arikaras, who called themselves Sahnish, meaning "People," separated from the Skiri Pawnees and moved northward to the Missouri River valley in present-day South Dakota. From that time on, they were associated more with the nearby Siouan-speaking Mandans and Hidatsas than with their fellow Caddoan-speaking Pawnees to the south.

Like the Mandans and Hidatsas, the Arikaras centered their lives on the river, using its high bluffs for their earth lodge villages and the rich soil of the bottomlands for gardens of corn, beans, squash, sunflowers, and tobacco. In early spring, Arikara women planted and tended the gardens. Then the people left on summer bison hunts. They returned to the village in the fall to harvest the crops. In late fall they undertook another bison hunt before moving to the winter villages in the bottomlands, where there was convenient wood and water. The earth lodges, like those built by other horticultural tribes of the Plains, were dome-shaped structures large enough to house several generations of a family and all their belongings. Arikara women made clay cooking vessels, decorated with stamped or etched designs, and distinctive willow harvest baskets. These square baskets, marked by brown and white geometric patterns woven around bent wood frames, are unique to the Arikaras, Hidatsas, and Mandans. Most other tools and utensils were common to other Plains tribes. The earth lodges, built and owned by the women, were usually occupied by sisters and their families. This kind of system is often associated with matrilineal clans, but there is no evidence for such a system among the Arikaras. It may be that their village organization and voluntary societies or associations replaced the functions of the clans. Some of these societies were military, encouraging their members to participate in raids and warfare, while others acted as police or cared for the poor. Belonging to a society helped a man attain the military successes and religious devotions that were required for village leadership.

Each Arikara village was autonomous, and leadership was diffuse, organized by rank rather than hierarchically. When the fur trader Pierre Antoine Tabeau called a council meeting in 1804, forty-two of the best-known military and religious leaders—called "men of first rank"—attended. The second level consisted of men and women who had been initiated into the honorary society called Piraskani based on their excellence of character. The third group was composed of men who had significant war honors, probably members of important societies. The lowest level included all remaining warriors.

Men who desired leadership positions also had religious duties. Arikara religious beliefs and practices centered around a belief in a principal creator, Nesharu, and a principal helper, Mother Corn. Mother Corn led the Arikaras out of the underworld and taught them what they needed to know to live in this world. Mother Corn instructed them to build the Medicine Lodge where the sacred ceremonies were held and gave each village a sacred bundle to ensure its well-being and continuance. In addition, each man had to seek a spirit guardian, who gave him prayers and objects to put in a personal sacred bundle. Throughout the year, the owners of sacred bundles sponsored ceremonies associated with corn growing and bison hunting. The Medicine Lodge ceremony took from fifteen to twenty days and marked the end of the year with demonstrations of sacred power, feasting, curing, and other sacred events.

Arikara culture changed dramatically in the eighteenth century, as the Lakotas challenged them for bison-hunting territory and smallpox epidem-

ics decimated the tribe. By 1804, when Tabeau lived with the Arikaras, their eighteen villages had been reduced to three fortified settlements. That same year, Lewis and Clark described the Arikaras as "tenants at will" to the Lakotas. The Arikaras occupied these villages off and on until 1823, when they were attacked by Col. Henry Leavenworth as punishment for Arikara attacks on traders. In 1837, reeling from the effects of another devastating smallpox epidemic, most of the tribe moved north to join the Mandans and Hidatsas at Fort Clark. Ever since, Arikara history has been bound with that of the Mandans and Hidatsas, and in 1862 they settled with them at Like-a-Fishhook Village.

In 1871 the Arikaras, Mandans, and Hidatsas ceded their homeland of about twelve million acres, retaining the eight-million-acre Fort Berthold Reservation (in present-day North Dakota). Allotments subsequently reduced the reservation to about one million acres. At the end of the 1880s Like-a-Fishhook Village was abandoned and the Arikaras settled around the community of Nishu, where they became ranchers and farmers. Spread across the reservation, on both sides of the river, the three tribes led relatively separate lives until 1934, when they accepted the Indian Reorganization Act and adopted the name Three Affiliated Tribes of Fort Berthold Reservation. The damming of the Missouri River in 1954 caused most tribal members to be relocated. The Arikaras centered around the town of White Shield, near some of their most important cultural sites. In the 1970s about 700 Arikaras lived on the reservation, and in 1990 the U.S. census reported a total Arikara population of 1,583.

Mary Jane Schneider
University of North Dakota

Meyer, Roy W. *The Village Indians of the Upper Missouri: The Mandans, Hidatsas, and Arikaras.* Lincoln: University of Nebraska Press, 1977. Parks, Douglas R. *Traditional Narratives of the Arikara Indians.* Lincoln: University of Nebraska Press, 1991. Parks, Douglas R. *Myths and Traditions of the Arikara Indians.* Lincoln: University of Nebraska Press, 1996.

ART, TRADITIONAL

Before Europeans introduced glass beads, metal cones, ribbons, and cloth, Plains Indians decorated themselves, their clothes, and their household belongings with paint, stone, bone and shell beads, animal teeth, and other natural materials. They also carved and painted human and animal figures and various symbolic designs on boulders and rock walls. In the Central and Northern Plains, some groups used stones to create outline figures of medicine wheels, humans, and animals. Shells with faces carved in them and sculptures of buffalo demonstrate that carving, although a minor

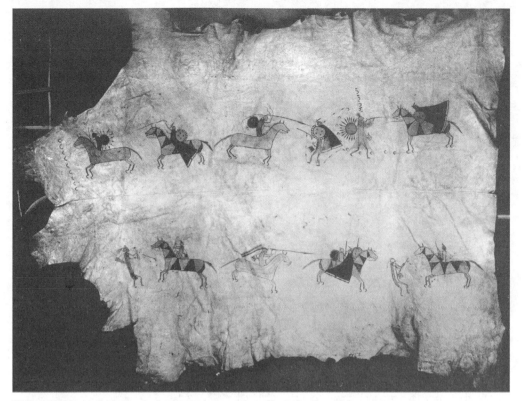

Hidatsa chief's painted robe showing battle episodes in two rows of hunters on horseback, ca. 1900

art form, was done before the introduction of metal tools.

The great diversity in rock-art styles suggests that there were many different tribes or groups inhabiting the Plains. Each region has its own distinct style, and scholars have named and described the works from each area. In the northwestern Plains, works believed to date from between 1000 and 1700 have a recognizable Plains Indian style that connects well to later art forms. Called "Ceremonial" by scholars, the early designs consist of simple outline figures of humans and animals. Some humans are depicted with rectangular bodies, V-shaped necklines, and round heads. Others have large round bodies with arms and legs. The decorations on the bodies suggest that they represent shields, and the designs are referred to as shield-bearing warriors. Animals are shown with elongated, rounded bodies with stick legs and well-defined horns or antlers. Symbolic ribs often appear inside the animal bodies.

Later rock art continued the stick-figure techniques but presents the figures in much more action oriented scenes. This style has been called "Biographical." Hunting and battle scenes seem to tell stories of actual events. Scenes dating from postcontact times show rectangular-bodied, round-headed warriors brandishing guns and rid-

ing horses. Similar scenes appear on the earliest known buffalo robes and men's shirts. A robe collected by Meriwether Lewis and William Clark on their trip up the Missouri River in 1804 shows the same kind of round-headed, rectangular-bodied stick figures as the rock art.

The earliest art, whether rock art or items collected by visitors to the tribes, contains the basic elements of Plains Indian art and shows that the attitudes and aesthetics were very different from European art. Unlike European art, which included large paintings, sculptures, and buildings designed to be regarded as art, Plains Indian art was an integral part of everyday life. Dresses, robes, moccasins, tipis, and rawhide containers were functional whether they were decorated or not, but the decorations enhanced the object and brought pleasure to the people who saw and used them. Both men and women took pride in being well dressed and living among beautiful things.

The designs that were used on clothing and household objects often had spiritual or sacred aspects that connected the creator or the user to tribal beliefs about the world. Plains Indian cosmologies were highly complex, and very simple abstract designs may have had multiple meanings. One common Northern Plains design was a circle composed of elongated triangles painted to look like feathers. The feathered circle represented both the sun and the eagle-feather headdress worn by a successful warrior.

Colors were associated with directions, and directions were associated with sacred beings, whose behavior influenced humans. Using the right color could bring blessings from the spiritual beings. Many different Plains tribes believed that the thunderbird, often shown as a winged, hourglass-shaped figure, caused thunder by shaking its wings. If the bird appeared to a man in a vision or dream, the man could depict the being on a shield, and this would protect him and increase his chances of success in hunting and warfare.

Native American art also differed from European art in its lack of concern with realism. Today, many people still think that an artist should be able to make a tree look just like a tree, but Plains Indians did not think that way. Because the designs often represented mystical or cosmological elements, realism was not a concern. Depicting a thunderbird as an hourglass had the same meaning as showing a bird with widespread wings. Nor was realism necessary to meet the needs of biographical art. A stick figure wearing a distinctive headdress or carrying a unique shield was immediately recognizable. Since realism was not a goal, European ideas of perspective and spatial ordering were not a part of Native American art. When a man painted his war exploits on his robe, he placed the scenes anywhere he thought they looked best, paying little attention to the shape of the robe or how the activities would be seen by others. Because Plains Indian art was so different from what people trained in the European tradition were used to, they considered the Indigenous art childlike or primitive and paid little attention to its meaning.

Another characteristic of Plains Indian art was the fairly strict division between art made and used by men and art made and used by women. Although men and women sometimes cooperated, women usually painted or quilled very balanced, controlled geometric designs on dresses, moccasins, robes, bags, and containers. Men were responsible for the human and animal figures that appeared in the biographical or cosmological art, but women's art had sacred meanings too. Designs placed on women's clothes symbolized prayers for a long life and healthy children. Quillwork was considered a sacred art that a woman had to have the right to do, or disaster would result. Cheyenne and Lakota women gained the right to do quillwork by becoming members of societies in which the art was taught. A woman who excelled in quillwork or other women's arts was publicly honored in the same way as a successful warrior.

The advent of glass beads and other new materials brought changes to the arts, but these were not as immediate or as far-reaching as one might think. Traditional ideas about art were maintained. Women skilled in sewing porcupine quills found that glass beads were not much different and continued to use the old designs. In the Southern Plains, where the porcupine was not found and quillwork had not been developed, the tribes made sparing use of beads and continued to color their clothes with yellow or green paint. In the Central and Northern Plains, however, tribes like the Lakotas and Assiniboines covered large portions of their garments with beaded designs reminiscent of quillwork. In painting, Indian men adopted the European idea of shading to make forms more realistic but did not use perspective or focal points in their work. In the middle to late nineteenth century men began to use paint, colored pencils, and crayons on paper to record scenes of tribal life. Called ledger paintings because many were done on the lined pages taken from account books, these works continued the traditions of earlier times and formed a link to modern Plains Indian painting.

Mary Jane Schneider
University of North Dakota

Berlo, Janet, ed. *Plains Indian Drawings, 1865–1935: Pages from a Visual History.* New York: Harry N. Abrams, 1996. Berlo, Janet, and Ruth B. Phillips. *Native North American Art.* New York: Oxford University Press, 1998. Keyser, James. "A Lexicon for Historic Plains Indian Rock Art: Increasing Interpretive Potential." *Plains Anthropologist* 32 (1987): 43–71.

ASSIMILATION POLICY

Both the United States and Canada developed assimilation policies for their Native peoples. Americans and Canadians both believed that the only way to save the Indians from extinction, and to make room for settlers, was to locate Indians on reservations and convert them into Christian, self-sufficient farmers, complete with a European American sense of individualism and private property ownership. The paradox should be evident: spatial segregation was supposed to lead to cultural integration.

Although assimilation policies were evident in early federal Indian policy and in treaties with Plains Indians in the 1830s, the intensity of the program deepened in the reservation era after the Civil War. The United States applied the policy to the Southern Plains tribes at the 1867 Treaty of Medicine Lodge Creek and to the northern tribes at the 1868 Treaty of Fort Laramie. Tribal leaders were coerced into agreeing to cede to the United States all but a fraction of their land and to locate on reservations. The treaties also committed the Indians to send their children to government schools and provided for the possibility of private property in land. As compensation for the land ceded, Indians were to receive annual payments in cash and goods, as well as the services of physicians, instructors in agriculture, and other government aid. Similar terms, with only details varying, were negotiated with Plains Indians throughout the region from the 1850s through the 1870s.

It was assumed that within decades the Indians would become assimilated. The outcome was far different. There was almost a decade of bloody fighting before all of the western Plains Indians were even located on reservations, and they remained there only because the bison had been nearly exterminated by the late 1870s and early 1880s. Confined to reservations, frequently hungry, and oppressed by officials pressuring them to send their children to school and abandon cherished religious and social customs, Native Americans led a miserable existence. Indian men showed little interest in farming land that would daunt a seasoned white farmer.

Real assimilation had not taken place by the end of the reservation period. The Indian Office then tried to legislate assimilation when it introduced the allotment policy through the General Allotment Act of 1887. Each Indian was to be given a plot of land, generally 160 acres, on which to begin farming. Any remaining reservation land was sold off as "surplus lands." Congress was increasingly reluctant to fund Indian programs, having been told for decades that assimilation was imminent. In an effort to make Indians more employable, the government restructured education programs to prepare the youth for entry-level jobs—the girls as domestic servants and the boys as farm and ranch hands and common laborers. The contexts for this assimilative education were day and boarding schools on reservations as well as off-reservation boarding schools, such as those at Genoa, Nebraska, and Haskell, Kansas.

By the 1920s the failure of assimilation policies was apparent. The United States had destroyed one way of life, and the Indians were struggling to salvage some of their cultures and to survive. The abrogation of the allotment policy in 1934 was recognition that it, and assimilation, had failed.

In Canada developments were similar in many respects. From 1871 to 1885, in a series of seven treaties, the Canadian government acquired Indian lands in the Prairie Provinces and settled the Indians on reserves, where they were put under pressure to assimilate. As was the case in the United States, the Bible and the plow were the principal instruments for assimilation. Reserves were often smaller than their equivalents in the United States, and religious groups were more prominent in Indian education. But again, as in the United States, the rhetoric of the government's assimilation policy was not matched by a genuine commitment in investment: farming instructors were often inept, promised agricultural equipment did not arrive, and Indian self-sufficiency remained a pipe dream.

Consequently, by the 1920s assimilation also seemed to have failed in Canada. Nevertheless, in both countries education and intermarriage were having an effect. Some Indians were merging with the general population, and increasingly, the products of the much-maligned schools were playing more important roles on reservations and reserves. However, the Indians' tenacity in preserving their cultures would be rewarded in the 1970s and 1980s when, in both countries, assimilation gave way to the new policy of self-determination.

William T. Hagan
Norman, Oklahoma

Dickason, Olive Patricia. *Canada's First Nations*. Norman: University of Oklahoma Press, 1992. Hoxie, Frederick E. *A Final Promise*. Lincoln: University of Nebraska Press, 1984. Prucha, Francis Paul. *The Great Father*. Lincoln: University of Nebraska Press, 1984.

ASSINIBOINES

The Assiniboines (the western portion in Alberta are called Stoneys) refer to themselves as Nakota. They are Siouan speakers, linguistically situated in the Dakota-Lakota-Stoney language continuum. They have been distinct dialectically since before the sixteenth century, and 250 years of enmity between Assiniboines and Sioux peoples resulted in many Assiniboines denying that they were ever Sioux. Their closest allies were the Crees and, later, the Ojibwas. The name Assiniboine comes from the Ojibwa *assini-pwa-n*, or "stone enemy."

First noted by Europeans in the *Jesuit Relations* of 1640, Assiniboines were reported in 1658 to be living one hundred miles west of Lake Nipigon and trading in the western Lake Superior regions. Other Assiniboines were encountered on the northern Prairies by Hudson's Bay Company trader and explorer Henry Kelsey in 1690–91 as far west as the Red Deer River in the Rocky Mountain foothills. During the winter of 1754–55, Anthony Henday of Hudson's Bay Company in central Alberta was assisted by "Assiniboine" families who were certainly those farthest west, antecedents of the contemporary Stoneys.

Their geographic concentrations in the seventeenth century included the areas continuously westward from Lake Winnipeg into central Saskatchewan. The Mortlach Aggregate archeological tradition has been identified in this region as representing the prehistoric and protohistoric Assiniboines. The first accounts of Assiniboines from the mid–eighteenth century report portions of groups

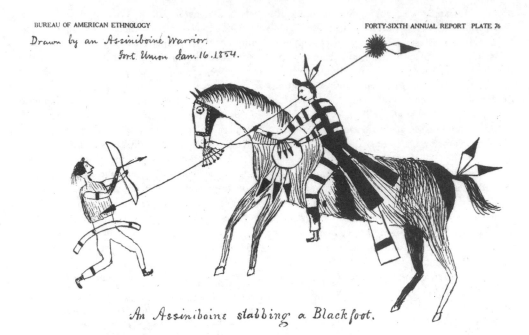

Drawn by an Assiniboine Warrior.
Fort Union Jan. 16. 1854.

An Assiniboine stabbing a Blackfoot.

Drawing by an Assiniboine warrior depicting an Assiniboine stabbing a Blackfoot, 1854

active as middlemen and transporters in the initial postcontact trade networks. La Vérendrye joined an Assiniboine trade expedition to the Mandan villages on the Missouri River in 1738. A portion of the population participated in tribal and intertribal transport expeditions from the interior to Hudson Bay. Other portions of the population were hunters and gatherers, living on processing bison into provisions or, in the case of the Stoney populations, utilizing the variety of resources of the Rocky Mountain foothills. The Stoney territories were reached by competing traders in the 1770s. By 1780 Assiniboines were no longer ranging east of the Forks of the Red River of the North and the Assiniboine River; instead their eastern territories became the confluence of the Souris and Assiniboine rivers and the White Earth River valley to the Missouri.

The Assiniboine subsistence round primarily exploited the parklands between forest and prairie and a series of microclimates found throughout the forests and prairies. The drainages of the Saskatchewan and Assiniboine rivers to the north, the Milk River in the west, and the Missouri to the south framed their homelands. Bison and other large game were primarily hunted, with smaller animals and a wide range of flora rounding out the food resources before annuities and commercial provisions. Bison skin was the major substance for clothing and for making tipi covers for shelter.

Assiniboine social organization involved autonomous bands, each comprising a group of fami-

lies who camped together. Many were related by blood and marriage. Consequently, the band was both the basic political and economic social unit and completely sovereign. Individual affiliation was theoretically flexible, and although kinship bound members to one another, new bands and new headmen could emerge. This caused bands to fragment, as individuals and families realigned themselves to the new social formation. The political order was headed by a group of senior males who comprised the *hungabi*, or "little chiefs," and from among them a *hunga* was chosen to be the executor of this council's will. Senior warriors led the *agi'cita*, or soldiers' society, and they were empowered by the hungabi to fulfill specific tasks that were within their authority.

Assiniboine religion utilizes the longstemmed pipe, which is the fundamental element in all ceremonies: vision quests, sweat lodges, the Sun Dance (which they call the Tibi Tanga, or Big Lodge, also translated as "Medicine Lodge"), hand games (a divinational form of the Pawnee Ghost Dance complex), and feasts, including the Ghost Feast, held within four days of a person's death and during subsequent memorials. Participants in all of these contexts make themselves humble, asking others to pray for them. Individuals pray for their kinsmen and friends and ask that their collective and personal wishes, desires, or vows be fulfilled. A spirit world of helpers is called upon in prayer to prescribe action. Shamans with special powers mediate interpretations and lead ceremonies.

Medicine wheel on top of Medicine Mountain in the Big Horn Mountains near Sheridan, Wyoming, 1917

Contemporary Assiniboine life signals an interest in the revival of religious ceremonies and preservation of their language. This has occurred in part because increased numbers of individuals seek advanced education and follow careers that remove them from their reserve communities. Consequently, these communities have become self-reflective about how effectively to reproduce the language and culture in future generations and how best to coordinate or balance individual development and community development, which is mostly economic and cultural.

Estimates of the historic Assiniboine population give a total of 10,000, prior to their decline by as much as half due to the 1780–81 smallpox pandemic. Subsequent recoveries were offset by other disease episodes that left the Assiniboines with fewer than 5,000 individuals on the eve of reserves and reservations in the 1870s. Numbers continued to dwindle as adjustment was made to a sedentary way of life on reservations in the United States after 1873 and on reserves in Canada after 1874. Shortly after 1900, the population began a steady increase to the present. Contemporary populations of Assiniboine communities in Montana, based on the 1990 census are: Fort Belknap, 2,180 (with Atsinas, Gros Ventres, and others resident and enrolled), and Fort Peck, 5,782 (with Sioux and others resident and enrolled). The resident and enrolled populations on Saskatchewan reserves, based on the 1998 census, are: Carry the Kettle, 1,924; Lean Man/Grizzly Bear's Head/Mosquito, 1,042 (with Crees); White Bear, 1,782, (with Crees); Ocean Man, 321; and Pheasant's Rump, 302. The 1998 populations (on and off reserve) for the Alberta reserves are: Southern Stoney communities at Morley, 3,598 (from among the Bearspaw, Chiniki, and Wesley bands); the same bands at Eden Valley, 479, and at Big Horn, 133; and Northern Stoney communities at Alexis, 1,274, and Paul, 1438.

Important historic leaders include Crazy Bear, who headed the delegation to the 1851 Fort Laramie Treaty Council; Red Stone among the lower Assiniboines in the same period, who led in the transition to reservations in the mid- to late nineteenth century; and Chiefs Jacob Bearspaw, John Chiniki, and Jacob Goodstoney, who were the Stoney signers of Treaty Number 7 in Canada in September of 1877. The earliest documentation of oral history and folklore was by Edwin Thompson Denig in the early 1850s, and the earliest ethnographics were by Robert H. Lowie (1909) and David Rodnick (1938).

David Reed Miller
Saskatchewan Indian Federated College,
University of Regina

Denig, Edwin Thompson. "Indian Tribes of the Upper Missouri." In *Forty-sixth Annual Report of the Bureau of American Ethnology to the Secretary of the Smithsonian Institution, 1928–1929*, 375–628. Washington DC: Government Printing Office, 1930. Lowie, Robert H. "The Assiniboine." *Anthropological Papers of the American Museum of Natural History* 4 (1909). Rodnick, David. *The Fort Belknap Assiniboine of Montana: A Study in Culture Change*. New Haven CT: Yale University Press, 1938.

ASTRONOMY

Like all humans, the Native peoples of the Plains observed the sky, particularly the night sky, and created astronomies. Scholars have used three general methods to describe and understand pre-European astronomies in North America: an examination of myth; archeological data, including astronomical artifacts; and detailed ethnographic and historic studies of specific peoples.

In Blackfoot myth, for example, the Pleiades

were small boys who became stars when their parents would not give them yellow buffalo calf robes. Very young calves have yellow hides in May or June, when the Pleiades are not visible, but become dark around September, when the Pleiades reappear.

Archeology was used by Waldo Wedel to identify astronomies, when he proposed that "council circles" in central Kansas might be solstice registers. These types of data include the well-known medicine wheels, including Wyoming's Big Horn Medicine Wheel. Such sites are also common in the Northern Great Plains and the Prairie Provinces. The most important is the Moose Mountain Medicine Wheel in Saskatchewan, which is aligned to the summer solstice sunrise. Nearby, others mark the rising of the major summer stars: Aldebaran, Rigel, and Sirius.

One of the most important astronomical artifacts is the Skiri Pawnee star chart, drawn on a buffalo scalp and associated with the Big Black Meteoric Star bundle and ceremony. This star is associated with the northeast star pillar position and the color black. It has been proposed that its position is a point north of the celestial pole, a definite black spot in the heavens. The chart seems to be a pictograph of the night sky with key stars and constellations recorded.

Von Del Chamberlain's elegant analysis of the cosmology of the Pawnees is one of the most brilliant ethnographic studies of Native American astronomy. Chamberlain identifies major constellations in Pawnee astronomy, pointing out that they structured the world around the four cardinal, and especially semicardinal, positions. Morning and Evening stars are associated with the east and west, and there are North and South stars and four star pillar positions: the Northeast, Northwest, Southwest, and Southeast. Identifying the particular stars in the heavens with these positions is difficult, but one association is clear: Polaris is the North Star. Chamberlain outlines the problems of identifying the Morning and Evening stars with the planets, but he settles on Mars and Venus, respectively. The sun and moon are also linked: the Sun is Morning Star's younger brother and the Moon is Evening Star's little sister. The semicardinal positions—the star pillars holding up the earth lodge roof and cosmologically the universe—have several interpretations, including that they refer to no celestial bodies. One view sees them linked to planets: Mercury (red) to the Southeast, Saturn (yellow) to the Northwest, and Jupiter (white) to the Southwest. Northeast is a problem, because its color is black and there is no black star. Another view sees them as the stars along the ecliptic, representing Spica (Southwest), Antares (Southeast), Aldebaran

(Northwest), and Regulus (Northeast). A final interpretation has them as the brightest stars: Capella (Northwest), Sirius (Southwest), Vega (Northeast), and Antares (Southeast).

Patricia J. O'Brien
Kansas State University

Chamberlain, Von Del. *When Stars Came down to Earth.* Los Altos CA: Ballena Press, 1982. Wedel, Waldo R. "The Council Circles of Central Kansas: Were They Solstice Registers?" *American Antiquity* 32 (1967): 54–63. Wilson, M. N. "Blackfoot Star Myths—The Pleiades." *The American Antiquarian* 15 (1893): 149–50.

BEECHER ISLAND, BATTLE OF

The Battle of Beecher Island was one of the most publicized engagements fought between Plains Indians and the U.S. Army. On September 17, 1868, on a sandbar in the middle of the Arickaree River in eastern Colorado, a large group of Cheyenne Dog Soldiers, Arapahos, and Lakotas attacked fifty citizen scouts under the command of Maj. George A. Forsyth. The scouts held off repeated charges before the Indians departed.

The scouts survived by eating the meat of their horses for nine days before reinforcements arrived from Fort Wallace, Kansas. Forsyth's command sustained losses of five scouts killed and eighteen wounded. Included among the dead was Lt. Frederick H. Beecher, the nephew of the outspoken New York abolitionist Henry Ward Beecher. Forsyth named the battle in memory of Lieutenant Beecher.

The Indian records obtained years later by George Bent and George B. Grinnell accounted for nine warriors killed and an unknown number wounded. One casualty was the esteemed warrior Roman Nose, a Northern Cheyenne member of the Crooked Lance Society. The Cheyennes referred to the battle as "the fight where Roman Nose was killed." Although the battle held little significance for the Indians, the scouts' successful defensive stand against extreme odds was inevitably compared to the Battle of the Little Bighorn and consequently came to hold epic and symbolic importance for Americans. The sensationalism it generated indirectly led to an infusion of new troops into the Plains, culminating in the Washita campaign.

John H. Monnett
Metropolitan State College of Denver

Monnett, John H. *The Battle of Beecher Island and the Indian War of 1867–1869.* Niwot: University Press of Colorado, 1992.

BERDACHE

In the seventeenth and eighteenth centuries, French explorers, traders, and missionaries in the Mississippi Valley occasionally encountered Native Americans who could be classified neither as men nor women. They called such individuals *berdaches*, a French term for younger partners in male homosexual relationships. In fact, Plains Indian berdaches are best described as occupying an alternative or third gender role, in which traits of men and women are combined with those unique to berdache status. Male berdaches did women's work, cross-dressed or combined male and female clothing, and formed relationships with non-berdache men.

Plains Indian women often engaged in hunting and warfare, but a female role equivalent to that of male berdaches, although common west of the Rockies, has been documented in the Plains only among the Cheyennes (the *hetaneman*). Even so, some Plains Indian women became notable warriors and leaders and behaved much like berdaches. In the early nineteenth century, Running Eagle of the Piegans wore male clothing on war parties, while Woman Chief of the Crows had four wives.

Male berdaches were known among the Arapahos (*hoxuxunó*), Arikaras, Assiniboines (*wi^{n}kta^n*), Blackfoot (*ake:'skassi*), Cheyennes (*he'eman*), Comanches, Plains Crees (*ayekkwe*), Crows (*boté*), Gros Ventres, Hidatsas (*miáti*), Kansas (*mi^{n}quge*), Kiowas, Mandans (*mihdeke*), Plains Ojibwas (*agokwa*), Omahas (*mi^{n}quga*), Osages (*mixu'ga*), Otoes (*mixo'ge*), Pawnees, Poncas (*mi^{n}quga*), Potawatomis (*m'nuktokwae*), Quapaws, Winnebagos (*shiángge*), and the various Siouan-speaking tribes (*winkte*, Lakota; *winkta*, Dakota). The two most common reasons cited for individuals becoming berdaches were childhood preference for work of the other sex and/or certain dreams or visions. The Lakotas credited dreams of Double Woman with influencing men to become *winkte*; others credited the Moon. Such dreams also conveyed valued skills—in particular, proficiency in women's arts, such as quilling, tanning, and beading. Among the Dakotas the saying "fine possessions like a berdache's" was the highest compliment one could pay a household.

Berdaches often had distinct religious roles. A Crow boté selected the central pole used in constructing Sun Dance lodges. Cheyenne he'eman directed the tribe's most important ceremony, the scalp dance. In Hidatsa villages, miáti were an "organized group" of as many as fifteen to twenty-five, treated as a "special class of religious leaders." In several tribes, berdaches were shamans and healers. Other skills attributed to berdaches included the ability to foretell the future and convey luck by bestowing obscene nicknames (Lakota), make love magic (Pawnee), and arrange marriages (Cheyenne). By reputation, many Plains berdaches were sexually active. George Catlin illustrated a Sauk and Fox dance in which a berdache is the central

figure surrounded by "her" male lovers. Dakota warriors sometimes visited berdaches before joining war parties in the belief that such encounters augmented their masculine ferocity. Prominent warriors and chiefs, including the Omaha American Horse and the Lakota Crazy Horse, had berdaches among their wives.

Some observers have explained berdache roles as niches for males unable to fulfill rigorous standards of Plains masculinity. But as Dakotas told anthropologist Ruth Landes, a distinction was made between men afraid to join war parties and berdaches, who "had a dream." In fact, Plains berdaches were active in all aspects of warfare, from providing assistance on war parties to leading war ceremonies and entering battles (and some Dakota berdaches hunted, even as they maintained tipis that women envied). When the Hidatsa chief Four Bears encountered a Lakota winkte, and his arrow failed to penetrate his robe, the winkte exclaimed, "You can't kill me for I am holy. I will strike coups on you with my digging stick." In 1866 a winkte predicted the success of Lakota and Cheyenne forces against the Americans at Fort Phil Kearny. In 1876 the Crow boté Finds Them and Kills Them killed a Lakota warrior in the Battle of the Rosebud.

In the reservation period, American missionaries denounced berdaches, government agents forced them to do men's work, and boarding-school teachers punished children for inappropriate gender behavior. As European American attitudes toward homosexuality were adopted in Indian communities, families often intervened to prevent their own members from becoming (or behaving like) berdaches. Nonetheless, traditional berdaches like Finds Them and Kills Them successfully resisted efforts to change their lifestyles. In the 1980s anthropologist Walter Williams found individuals on Plains reservations still performing traditional functions of the berdache role.

In the 1990s the term "two-spirit" was introduced by Native Americans as an alternative to berdache, and traditional third gender roles became the subject of renewed interest among Natives and non-Natives alike. As Michael Red Earth, a gay-identified Dakota, writes, "Once I realized that this respect and acceptance was a legacy of our traditional Native past, I was empowered to present my whole self to the world and reassume the responsibilities of being a two-spirited person."

Will Roscoe
California Institute of Integral Studies

Gilley, Brian Joseph. *Becoming Two-Spirit: Gay Identity and Social Acceptance in Indian Country*. Lincoln: University of Nebraska Press, 2006. Jacobs, Sue-Ellen, Wesley Thomas, and Sabine Lang, eds. *Two-Spirit People: Native American Gender Identity, Sexuality, and Spirituality*. Urbana: University of Illinois Press, 1997.

Roscoe, Will. *Changing Ones: Third and Fourth Genders in Native North America*. New York: St. Martin's Press, 1998. Williams, Walter L. *The Spirit and the Flesh: Sexual Diversity in American Indian Culture*. Boston: Beacon Press, 1986.

BIG BEAR (CA. 1825–1888)

Big Bear (Mistahimaskwa), 1886

Big Bear (Mistahimaskwa) was a leader of the Plains Crees who carried on a nine-year struggle to gain better treaty terms for his people from the Canadian government. Born about 1825 to Ojibwa parents near Fort Carlton, Saskatchewan, Big Bear was part of a transitional camp that spent its summers on the open Plains but in winter hunted and trapped in the woodlands near Jackfish Lake, Saskatchewan. After the death of his father, about 1865, Big Bear became chief of a band of sixty-five lodges. In addition, he received a number of visions and was a religious leader who opposed the work of Christian missionaries.

In 1876 Big Bear refused to sign Treaty Number 6 with the Canadian government. Instead, he said he would wait five years to see if its promises were honored. As starvation began to beset the Crees, many young dissidents flocked to Big Bear's camp, and he became one of the most important chiefs on the Canadian Plains. During this time, he demanded better terms from the government but was unsuccessful. Finally, he was forced to sign the treaty in 1882 when his own sons rebelled against him.

In the spring of 1885, the Métis launched the North-West Rebellion, and, at the same time, Big Bear's son, Little Bear (Ayimisis), joined with war chief Wandering Spirit (Kapapamahchakwew) to kill nine white residents of Frog Lake. Several others were taken prisoner. Big Bear tried to stop the killing and later protected the prisoners. However, as chief, he was convicted of treason and was sentenced to three years in prison. He became ill while imprisoned and was released after two years. He died within a year of his release.

Hugh A. Dempsey
Glenbow Museum

Dempsey, Hugh A. *Big Bear: The End of Freedom*. Vancouver: Douglas and McIntyre, 1984.

BIG CROW, SUANNE (1974–1992)

SuAnne Big Crow was a Lakota basketball star and an important positive influence on the Pine Ridge Reservation. She was born on March 15, 1974, at Pine Ridge Hospital in Pine Ridge, South Dakota. Big Crow was an All-State player for three years, breaking several state basketball records, including most points in a season and most points in a game (67). She toured Europe as part of the National Indian Team. She led her team, the Lady Thorpes, to the state Class A championship in 1989 and also graduated first in her high school class.

She was a natural leader who hoped to return to Pine Ridge after college to improve the lives of tribal members by battling alcohol and drug abuse and healing inter-tribal divisions. She talked of a place she called Happytime, where children could grow in an atmosphere free of drugs and violence. Her dream was cut short when she died in a car accident in 1991, on her way to a basketball award ceremony.

Big Crow's influence did not die with her. Following her death her mother, Leatrice "Chick" Big Crow, formed SuAnne Big Crow, Inc., and with other family and community members established Happytown, a community center. Not long after, a delegate of the Boys' and Girls' Clubs of America visited and encouraged the group to affiliate with the national organization. Renamed the SuAnne Big Crow Boys' and Girls' Club, it was the first such club on an Indian reservation.

Following her death, SuAnne Big Crow received numerous honors. In 1997 South Dakota's house of representatives honored Big Crow's legacy with a commemoration as "an outstanding member of her community and as an incredible human being." The National Education Association recognized Big Crow's influence on her community by issuing awards in her name to human rights and civil rights pioneers. The South Dakota High School Activities Association presents a "Spirit of Su" award to student athletes who best exemplify her ideals of athletic and academic achievement and community dedication.

In 1999 a visit to Pine Ridge Reservation by President Bill Clinton spurred an effort to build a much larger community center. The organization teamed with the Oglala Lakota community and the departments of Housing and Urban Development, Justice, Interior, and Agriculture to build a thirty-thousand-square-foot facility, with a soccer field, indoor pool, gymnasium, library, and technology center, which opened in 2002. SuAnne Big Crow's dream spread well beyond Pine Ridge. In 2005 there were 117 Boys' and Girls' Clubs serving Indian communities. Eighty thousand children, aged seven to seventeen, attend the clubs each year.

Charles Vollan
South Dakota State University

Frazier, Ian. *On the Rez*. New York: Farrar, Straus, and Giroux, 2000. Rooks, David. "Keeping the Dream: Oglala Lakota Mother Carries On with Her Daughter's Hope." *Indian Country Today* (Oneida NY), August 16, 2000, D1.

BLACK ELK, NICHOLAS (1866–1950)

Nicholas Black Elk and family, ca. 1890–1910

Black Elk was probably the most influential Native American leader of the twentieth century. His influence flows from the enduring beauty and power of his religious teachings, his lifetime of engagement with the problems of his people, and the galvanizing effect of the book *Black Elk Speaks* on the revival of traditional religion and culture.

Black Elk was probably born in 1866, the first year after the Civil War. The end of the war brought western expansion, which led to aggressive efforts to confine and assimilate the Plains tribes. Black Elk's early years were spent living the old nomadic life, and he was present at the Custer fight on the Little Big Horn in 1876. He announced his vocation as a holy man by performing the Horse Dance in 1881, but after the government outlawed the Sun Dance and Native healing practices in 1883, his profession could only be practiced underground. Almost all Black Elk's working life as a holy man was spent in this repressive context, and his religious thought is in part a response to the dominant culture's oppression, missionization, and social engineering. In 1887 Black Elk enlisted with Buffalo Bill Cody and traveled to Europe with his Wild West Show. On his return to the Pine Ridge Reservation in 1889, he became a leader of the Ghost Dance. When the government responded with troops, Black Elk called for armed resistance, and he was present at the Wounded Knee Massacre in 1890.

After Wounded Knee, Black Elk seems to have continued with his medicine practice. In 1904 he accepted Catholicism and became active as a catechist, a position that allowed him to regain a public leadership role. He mastered reservation Catholicism through conversations with the Jesuits, including Eugene Buechel, who cites Black Elk in his Lakota dictionary. In 1931 Black Elk was interviewed by poet John G. Neihardt, which resulted in *Black Elk Speaks* (1932). The book strained Black Elk's relationship with the Jesuits, and he subsequently worked at the Duhamel Sioux Pageant, demonstrating traditional rituals. In 1944 Neihardt interviewed Black Elk for *When the Tree Flowered* (1951). In 1947–48 Black Elk gave an account of Lakota ritual to Joseph Epes Brown that became *The Sacred Pipe* (1953), which provides a Lakota parallel to the seven sacraments and asserts the equal validity of Christianity and traditional religion. Black Elk died at Manderson, South Dakota, on August 17, 1950.

Scholarly work on Black Elk has tended to focus on the authenticity and adequacy of Neihardt's portrait of Black Elk as a traditionalist in *Black Elk Speaks* and on the related issue of the extent of Black Elk's commitment to Catholicism. (The authenticity of *The Sacred Pipe* is a growing topic of discussion.) At one pole of the debate, Michael F. Steltenkamp's *Black Elk: Holy Man of the Oglala* (1993) portrays Black Elk as a progressive Catholic who retains little meaningful commitment to traditional religion. At the other pole, Julian Rice's *Black Elk's Story: Distinguishing Its Lakota Purpose* (1991) portrays Black Elk's involvement in Catholicism as strategic, a response to oppres-

Blackfoot women and a girl standing on a roof in Chicago, Illinois, 1929

sion. Although this debate is illuminating, it is also misleading, because Black Elk retained a lifelong commitment to the central intention of the Ghost Dance, the revitalization of traditional culture through religious ritual. In terms of culture, Black Elk was undoubtedly a nativist, and the symbolism and hope of the Ghost Dance is seldom far from his teaching. On the other hand, his engagement with Catholicism shows that he could assimilate a very different set of religious symbols, something that seems to have been far easier for him than for academic observers obsessed with the colonialist search for authenticity.

Black Elk was not the broken old man who mourns the death of the dream at the end of *Black Elk Speaks*. Nor was he anybody's anthropological informant, a passive source of information on the past. For Black Elk, the dream never died, and he always spoke to the Lakota present. In the simplest terms, he was a leader of his people during a time of troubles, and those troubles should certainly not be forgotten in evaluating his life and work. Black Elk was one of the most gifted spokesmen for the Lakota wisdom tradition, and his farseeing literary collaborations have disseminated his teachings far beyond their original cultural horizon. Lakota

holy men still teach the great lessons of this tradition—respect for sacred power, the relatedness of all beings, and care for the earth—and they still draw on Black Elk's legacy, which continues to confront and challenge European ways of viewing humanity, society, and the cosmos.

Clyde Holler
Morganton, Georgia

Black Elk DeSersa, Esther, and Olivia Black Elk Pourier, *Black Elk Lives: Conversations with the Black Elk Family*. Lincoln: University of Nebraska Press, 2000. Brown, Joseph Epes. *The Sacred Pipe: Black Elk's Account of the Seven Rites of the Oglala Sioux*. Norman: University of Oklahoma Press, 1989. DeMallie, Raymond J., ed. *The Sixth Grandfather: Black Elk's Teachings Given to John G. Neihardt*. Lincoln: University of Nebraska Press, 1984. Holler, Clyde. *Black Elk's Religion: The Sun Dance and Lakota Catholicism*. Syracuse NY: Syracuse University Press, 1995. Holler, Clyde, ed. *The Black Elk Reader*. Syracuse NY: Syracuse University Press, 2000. Neihardt, Hilda. *Black Elk and Flaming Rainbow: Personal Memories of the Lakota Holy Man and John Neihardt*. Lincoln: University of Nebraska Press, 1995. Neihardt, John G. *Black Elk Speaks*. Lincoln: University of Nebraska Press, 2004.

BLACKFOOT

One of the largest Native American groups of the Northern Plains, the Blackfoot Confederacy consists of the Siksikas (Blackfoot proper), Kainahs (Bloods), Northern (Canadian) Piegans, and

Southern Piegans (or Blackfeet, as they came to be known). The Algonquian-speaking Blackfoot may have migrated from the north and northwestern woodlands into the Plains of southern Alberta and northern Montana sometime in the fifteenth century. If so, they adapted to become one of the defining Plains Indian nations, so much so that their own history places their homeland in the Northern Plains.

Early estimates of Blackfoot population varied from fifteen to forty thousand. Blackfoot territory included the area from the North Saskatchewan River south to the Yellowstone River, and from central Saskatchewan west to the Continental Divide. By the middle of the eighteenth century, the Blackfoot had acquired horses from other tribes and guns from British traders. Raiding, gathering, hunting, and trading became the mainstays of their economy, and their power and influence grew. Wider contacts, however, made the Blackfoot vulnerable to smallpox, such as during the 1837 epidemic, and to other diseases which periodically decimated them.

The Blackfoot saw themselves as a part of a vibrant, sacred world, regarding the Sun as one of the most powerful beings. Like other Plains tribes, Blackfoot men and women secured their place in this world through vision quests, through ceremonies of sacred bundles to secure the blessing and protection of powerful bird and animal spirits (the "beaver medicine" being considered among the oldest and most powerful ceremonies), and through reliance on the spiritual guidance of medicine men and women. Although no central authority governed the Blackfoot, the Sun Dance eventually emerged as the principal summer ceremony that brought together dozens of independent, dispersed bands.

In 1806 the Lewis and Clark expedition incurred the enmity of the Blackfoot, resulting in periodic attacks on Americans. The Blackfoot gained a reputation for fierceness due to their opposition to the incursion of American fur trappers into their territory. They remained on friendlier terms with the Hudson's Bay Company, which encouraged the Blackfoot to trade at its posts. After the establishment of Fort McKenzie on the Marias River in 1833, contacts with Americans grew. The Blackfoot exchanged buffalo robes, pemmican, elk and deer hides, and furs for manufactured goods. These contacts occasionally led to trader- or trapper-Native marriages and the appearance of a mixed-blood population.

The transition from independence to reservation life was harrowing for the Blackfoot. In 1855 the Blackfoot, with several other tribes, took part in their first American treaty. The so-called Lame Bull's Treaty set aside for the Blackfoot a portion of a reservation in what became Montana in exchange for annuities and other pledges by the U.S. government. Few promises were fulfilled, and in subsequent years, as whiskey peddlers, miners, cattlemen, and settlers moved into the area, conflicts increased and clamor for the reduction of this reservation grew. Congress failed to ratify two such treaties, and in the 1860s the situation led to a series of raids and clashes called the Blackfoot War. On January 23, 1870, Blackfoot resistance to encroachment on their lands ended with the massacre on the Marias River of 173 men, women, and children by the U.S. Army under Maj. Eugene V. Baker.

In July 1873 an executive order set aside a new reservation for the Blackfeet, Gros Ventres, and River Crows. The 2,750-square-mile reservation was bounded on the west by the Continental Divide, on the north by the U.S.-Canadian border, on the south by the Missouri River, and on the east by Dakota Territory. In 1874, upon the urging of settlers, Congress restored the land between the Sun and Missouri river to public domain.

The remaining bands of the Confederacy signed Treaty Number 7 with the British government in 1877. The Blackfoot and the Kainahs, along with the Sarcees (Sarsis), received as their reserve a four-mile by two-hundred-mile strip of land along the Bow River in southern Alberta. The Kainahs subsequently moved to a new reserve between the St. Mary and Belly rivers, and the Piegans went to a reserve west of Fort Macleod. The land was more suited to hunting than to farming, and the disappearance of the bison from the Northern Plains between 1879 and 1883 brought famine and starvation to the Confederacy. In Canada, an estimated one thousand Blackfoot died, and almost six hundred died of starvation and associated diseases in Montana. As a result, the American Blackfeet were pressured in 1888 and 1896 to trade their only remaining resource, their land, for the prospect of government annuities.

In both countries, efforts to teach self-support through farming and irrigated agriculture initially failed, but by the turn of the century cattle raising began to emerge as a successful enterprise, especially among the growing population of the mixed bloods. In the United States, however, the acts of 1907 and 1919 allotted the reservation, resulting in an erosion of the Blackfeet land base and the crippling of their nascent economy. The Canadian Blackfoot lands were also reduced by the early twentieth century.

The American practice of allotment and assimilation formally ended with the passage of the Indian Reorganization Act in 1934. The Blackfeet chose to organize under this act with a tribal council elected by residents of the various districts of the reservation. Health, education, and economic conditions on the reservation slowly began to improve. During World War II many Blackfeet served in the armed forces and found employment off the reservation. Many consequently chose to relocate to urban centers while maintaining their tribal affiliation. Some entered skilled and professional occupations and pursued higher education.

Since the 1930s the Blackfeet economy has followed the pattern of other tribes with various tribal enterprises—ranching, timber and gas, and light manufacturing industries—which experienced mixed success. The 1.3-million-acre Blackfeet Reservation, adjacent to Glacier National Park (which was once part of it), attracts tourists and visitors. The tribally owned and operated Museum of the Plains Indians houses exhibits and publishes monographs on tribal history and culture. The fully accredited Blackfeet Community College in Browning, Montana, offers standard curriculum as well as courses in the language and traditions of the tribe. Tribal enrollment is about fifteen thousand, with about seven thousand residing on the Montana reservation. The registered population of Canadian Blackfoot is about sixteen thousand, with almost twelve thousand living on the three reserves.

Hana Samek Norton
Albuquerque, New Mexico

Black Kettle (Moketavato), ca. 1860–68

Bullchild, Percy. *The Sun Came Down: The History of the World as My Blackfeet Elders Told It.* Lincoln: University of Nebraska Press, 2005. Eggermont-Molenaar, Mary, ed. *Montana 1911: A Professor and His Wife among the Blackfeet.* Lincoln: University of Nebraska Press, 2005. Ewers, John C. *The Blackfeet: Raiders on the Northwestern Plains.* Norman: University of Oklahoma Press, 1958. Grinnell, George B. *Blackfoot Lodge Tales.* 2nd ed. Lincoln: University of Nebraska Press, 2003. Ground, Mary. *Grass Woman Stories.* Browning MT: Blackfeet Heritage Program, 1978. Kipp, Woody. *Viet Cong at Wounded Knee: The Trail of a Blackfeet Activist.* Lincoln: University of Nebraska Press, 2004. McClintock, Walter. *The Old North Trail: Life, Legends, and Religion of the Blackfeet Indians.* Lincoln: University of Nebraska Press, 1999. Rosier, Paul C. *Rebirth of the Blackfeet Nation, 1912–1954.* Lincoln: University of Nebraska Press, 2001. Samek, Hana. *The Blackfoot Confederacy, 1880–1920.* Albuquerque: University of New Mexico Press, 1987.

BLACK KETTLE (CA. 1800–1868)

Black Kettle (Moketavato) was a leading chief of the Southern Cheyennes through the difficult years of the 1850s and 1860s. Born in the Black Hills before that area was part of the United States, Black Kettle married a woman of the Wotapio band and lived with his wife's people, as was customary. When the chief of that band, Bear with Feathers, died in 1850, Black Kettle was elected chief. In time, Black Kettle married another three women, all sisters to his first wife, and with them Black Kettle had seventeen children.

Black Kettle was a "peace chief," dedicated to strong leadership through nonaggression. After the discovery of gold in Colorado in 1858, the hunting lands of the Southern Cheyennes became increasingly encroached upon by Americans, and resentment developed on both sides. In 1864 Black Kettle and his band, which had avoided hostilities and tried to forge a peace, were camped on Sand Creek, an intermittent tributary of the Arkansas in present-day Kiowa County, Colorado (now called the Big Sandy). On November 28, Col. (and Reverend) John M. Chivington, with six hundred to one thousand men of the Colorado Volunteers, mounted a surprise attack on the village. As Black Kettle hoisted a white flag and an American flag in an attempt to stop the violence, Chivington's men massacred between one and two hundred Indians, mainly women and children.

The Cheyennes retaliated by killing several hundred settlers during the following four years. Black Kettle worked to reestablish peace. His mark, for example, appears second on the Treaty of Medicine Lodge Creek of October 28, 1867, an attempt to establish peace on the Central and Southern Plains. But Black Kettle's efforts all came to nothing on November 27, 1868, when his sleeping village on the Washita River, in present-day Roger

Mills County, Oklahoma, was attacked by troops led by George Armstrong Custer. Black Kettle and more than one hundred of his people were killed.

Bruce E. Johansen
University of Nebraska–Omaha

Hoig, Stan. *The Sand Creek Massacre.* Norman: University of Oklahoma Press, 1961. Moore, John H. *The Cheyenne Nation: A Social and Demographic History.* Lincoln: University of Nebraska Press, 1987.

CADDOS

The Caddo Indians are a tribe whose traditional historic homeland was located along the borders of present-day Louisiana, Texas, Arkansas, and Oklahoma. In the seventeenth and eighteenth centuries, the Caddos occupied a strategic position between Spanish Texas and French Louisiana. In the early nineteenth century, however, Texans forced the tribe out into the Great Plains. After wandering for three decades, they finally settled in western Oklahoma, where most of the Caddos still live today.

The Caddos were the southernmost tribe of the Caddoan language group, whose membership stretched northward to include the Wichitas, Pawnees, and Arikaras. About two thousand years ago the Caddo peoples settled down in small horticultural villages between the Neches and Arkansas rivers. By about 1000 AD, the Caddos had developed complex and socially ranked societies with well-planned civic and ceremonial centers. They conducted elaborate ceremonial practices and mortuary rituals led by a religious and political elite, and engaged in extensive interregional trade.

In 1542 the Caddos were visited by the remnants of Hernando de Soto's Spanish *entrada*, at this point led by Luis de Moscoso. Although the Spaniards spent only a few weeks among the Caddos, they, and later members of other Spanish expeditions, left behind epidemic diseases, which caused the Caddo population to decline catastrophically. By the time Europeans returned to Caddo country in the late seventeenth century, the tribe had abandoned their village sites in the Arkansas Valley. The ten thousand remaining Caddos established permanent farming villages along the Red and Neches rivers. The Red River Caddos consisted of the four tribes of the Kadohadacho Confederacy, as well as the Yatasis and the Natchitoches. To the west, along the upper reaches of the Neches River in East Texas, were the nine tribes that made up the Hasinai Confederacy. Each individual Caddo tribe was led by a hereditary chief, or *caddi*, who presided over a well-defined chain of command that provided the tribe with strong, efficient government.

By 1730 both the French and the Spanish had established themselves in the Caddos' territory. The French maintained trading posts at the Natchitoches, Yatasi, and Kadohadacho villages, while the Spanish set up three Franciscan missions in Hasinai country, as well as establishing the capital of Texas at Los Adaes, only a few miles west of the French post at Natchitoches. Despite the Spanish presence, all of the Caddo tribes obtained French weapons and metal goods, which, together with the adoption of the horse in the seventeenth century, allowed them to better defend themselves against enemies such as the Lipan Apaches to the west and the Osages to the east. By the mid–eighteenth century, however, the Caddos had abandoned most of their traditional crafts and were increasingly dependent upon European metal goods. When Spain obtained Louisiana from France in 1763, it continued to allow French trade goods to flow to the Caddos and their Wichita and Comanche allies in Texas. When the United States acquired the territory in 1803, the Caddos found themselves occupying an undefined border between American Louisiana and Spanish Texas. Seizing the moment, the Kadohadacho caddi, Dehahuit, expertly played the two rivals against one another to gain even further munificence for all of the Caddo tribes for whom he had become spokesman. After 1821, however, the border between Louisiana and Texas was settled, and both the United States and the newly independent Mexico neglected the Caddos. By the 1830s alcohol, disease, and Osage pressure had caused the Caddo numbers to dwindle to about one thousand, and the original fifteen tribes had coalesced into only three: the Hainais, Nadacos, and Kadohadachos. In 1835 U.S. Indian agent Jehiel Brooks forced the Kadohadachos to sign a treaty by which the tribe agreed to move to East Texas to live with the Hainais and Nadacos.

Unfortunately for the Caddos, Texas gained its independence from Mexico the following year and the Anglo-Americans who ruled the republic after 1836 and the state after 1845 were extremely hostile to the Indians of the region. In 1838 Texan settlers drove all three Caddo tribes from their homes in the forests of East Texas out onto the plains of central Texas, where they lived in various settlements for the next sixteen years. In 1854 the Caddos—along with Wichitas, Tonkawas, and Penateka Comanches—settled on two Indian reservations established by the U.S. government on the Brazos River. On the Brazos Reservation, the three Caddo tribes were led by Nadaco caddi Iesh (or José María), an impressive leader who convinced his fellow tribesmen to accept the federal government's "civilization" program and to assist the United States and the Texas Rangers in their struggle with hostile Comanches. Despite this accommodationist stance, in 1859 Texas vigilantes

Calumet, Omaha, Central Plains, ca. 1875. Buffalo Bill Historical Center, Cody, Wyoming, Chandler-Pohrt Collection. Gift of Mr. And Mrs. Richard A. Pohrt. na.502.195.2

forced the Brazos Reservation tribes to move north of the Red River into Indian Territory. The Caddos splintered during the chaos of the Civil War, moving into Kansas and Colorado. The federal government finally brought them together on a reservation in 1872. On the Wichita Reservation, between the Washita and Canadian rivers, the three remaining Caddo groups united into one tribe. Although the Caddos did everything the federal government asked of them in their new homes—farming, stock raising, and submitting to education and Christianity—the Wichita Reservation was dissolved in 1901 and the 534 remaining Caddos went through the allotment process as outlined by the Dawes Act of 1887.

Despite the attempts of the federal government to destroy it, the Caddo tribe remained intact, and a measure of home rule was provided through the terms of the Oklahoma Indian Welfare Act of 1936, which was accepted by the enrolled Caddo voters. The tribe ratified a constitution that remained in effect until 1976, when it was replaced by a completely new document. A measure of compensation for their historical losses came in the 1970s when the U.S. Court of Claims awarded the Caddo tribe $383,475 for abuses in the 1835 treaty and $1,222,800 for inadequate payments for allotments and surplus lands on the Wichita Reservation. Today, the approximately 3,200 Caddos maintain a

tribal complex on thirty-seven acres of tribal-controlled land located at Binger, in Caddo County, Oklahoma.

F. Todd Smith
University of North Texas

Carter, Cecile. *Caddo Indians: Where We Come From*. Norman: University of Oklahoma Press, 1995. Dorsey, George A. *Traditions of the Caddo*. Lincoln: University of Nebraska Press, 1997. La Vere, David. *The Caddo Chiefdoms: Caddo Economics and Politics, 700–1835*. Lincoln: University of Nebraska Press, 1998. Melnar, Lynette R. *Caddo Verb Morphology*. Lincoln: University of Nebraska Press, 2004. Smith, F. Todd. *The Caddo Indians: Tribes at the Convergence of Empires, 1542–1854*. College Station: Texas A&M University Press, 1995. Smith, F. Todd. *The Caddos, the Wichitas, and the United States, 1846–1901*. College Station: Texas A&M University Press, 1996. Smith, F. Todd. *From Dominance to Disappearance: The Indians of Texas and the Near Southwest, 1786–1859*. Lincoln: University of Nebraska Press, 2005.

CALUMET CEREMONY

Native Americans used the calumet ceremony throughout the Plains to trade between different tribes, or between different bands of the same tribe, for food and other needed items. The ceremony evolved in the thirteenth century, possibly among the Wichitas. During the early thirteenth century the climate of the Plains was wetter, supporting more bison and encouraging more tribes to move into the region. Subsequently, as the weather turned drier, many tribes, caught without adequate food supplies following a poor hunt or a local drought, needed to trade with neighbors to survive. In time, the calumet ceremony not only provided food but also often became a primary bond between bands and tribes.

In its fullest form, the calumet was a long and complex ceremony, but even the more common shorter version involved several days of ritual feasting, gift giving, singing, and dancing. The ceremony climaxed with the presentation of the calumet pipe, which made unrelated peoples one "family" through the working of a fictional kinship. Leaders of different bands adopted each other as father or son. Exchanges of gifts then went on for several days, in the later stages accompanied by exchanges between the men and women of each band, who acquired the same fictive father-son relationship to the other band as that established by their leaders. A leader's calumet relationships were considered permanent, and leaders were expected to maintain a number of calumet relationships with other tribes, bands, and villages. The calumet ceremonies also allowed men and women from different bands to meet and court each other, and often trade bonds between bands were supplemented by matrimonial bonds.

Mark A. Eifler
University of Portland

Blakeslee, Donald J. "The Plains Interband Trade System: An Ethnohistoric and Archeological Investigation." PhD diss., University of Wisconsin, Milwaukee, 1975. Fletcher, Alice C. *The Hako: Song, Pipe, and Unity in a Pawnee Calumet Ceremony*. Lincoln: University of Nebraska Press, 1996. Paper, Jordan. *Offering Smoke: The Sacred Pipe and Native American Religion*. Moscow: University of Idaho Press, 1988.

CAMPBELL, MARIA (B. 1940)

Métis author and activist Maria Campbell is best known for her remarkable autobiography, *Halfbreed* (1973), the first document of its kind in Canada. In it Campbell describes her early life in a northern Saskatchewan Métis trapping community in the 1940s (she was born at Park Valley in April 1940), the support of her beloved grandmother Cheechum, and the gradual destruction of her family and community by racism, poverty, and alcohol. Left to care for her seven younger siblings after her mother's death, Campbell quit school and married at fifteen. *Halfbreed* tracks the young Maria's struggle through alcohol, drug addiction, and prostitution and, finally, her healing return to the traditions of her Cree heritage.

Campbell's collaborative theatrical work *Jessica*, based on *Halfbreed*, was first performed in Toronto by Theatre Passe Muraille in 1981. A description of the troubled process of the play's creation was later published with Linda Griffiths under the title *The Book of Jessica: A Theatrical Transformation* (1989).

Campbell's recent writing has been for children and includes informational illustrated works on Plains Indians and Métis heritage. An illustrated collection of narratives, or "told to" stories, from old men of northern Saskatchewan Métis communities, *Stories of the Road Allowance People*, appeared in 1995.

Campbell has helped establish emergency shelters for women and community theater groups, and she has encouraged First Nations writers. She has been writer in residence at several universities and in 1999 was teaching creative writing at the University of Saskatchewan. Campbell lives on the land homesteaded by Gabriel Dumont, commander of the Métis forces in the North-West Rebellion of 1885.

Jeanne Perreault
University of Calgary

Bataille, Gretchen M., and Kathleen Mullen Sands. *American Indian Women: Telling Their Lives*. Lincoln: University of Nebraska Press, 1984. Campbell, Maria. *Halfbreed*. Lincoln: University of Nebraska Press, 1982.

CAPTIVITY NARRATIVES

Captivity narratives are the accounts written by men and women reporting on their experiences as abductees of Native Americans. From the seventeenth century to the end of the nineteenth century such accounts accompanied the westward-moving frontier, and their storylines, established in the first known captivity narrative by Mary Rowlandson in 1682, remained essentially the same: conflict between the settlers and Indians, capture by the Indians, ordeal at the hands of the captors, and a return to European American society.

In general, male captives adjusted easier to their new lives with Native American peoples than did female captives, who, with very few exceptions, feared for their virtue and prayed for a return to civilization. Through the centuries in these captivity narratives, stock phrases are perpetuated—for example, bashing brains out and burning people at the stake. Their descriptions of elements of the captors' cultures tend to be generic and confusing, but the message is clear: Native American cultures are considered inferior to European American civilization, and Native Americans are perceived as emotionless, cruel, and traitorous. The captives' detailed descriptions of torture scenes and the suffering of women and children provided justification for armed conflict on the western frontier and the displacement of Native Americans, whose voices were very rarely heard in the captivity documents.

Women and children brought civilization to the frontier, and in the minds of their contemporaries, their removal from their fledgling communities represented a basic threat to civilization. It was acceptable to convert Native Americans to Christianity and make farmers of them, and thereby to make them part of the mainstream. Women captives, however, found it impossible to exert a civilizing influence on their captors, and their captivity narratives revealed their belief that Native Americans had to disappear in order for civilization to come. Documents and testimonials attached to the narratives were meant to encourage the reader to believe in the historical truth of the narratives and to treat the information contained therein as fact.

Captivities during the settlement of the Plains were much more widely distributed than those during colonial times, and Plains captivity narratives exerted significant influence on their readers. Stories like Fanny Kelly's painted a vivid picture of Native Americans who rejoiced in the killing of women and children. Kelly despairs as she recognizes her small daughter's scalp and then witnesses the hopelessness of a fellow captive forced to "marry" her captor and the degeneration of a captive who, from infancy, had grown up among the Native Americans. Kelly also described "barbaric" customs and physical assaults. These highly emotional descriptions and reports of repeated treachery by the Sioux helped to convince settlers on the Northern Plains that military expeditions were necessary, and that any sympathy with the Native Americans was misguided. Glenda Riley, in her analysis of women's voices on the frontier and especially in the Southern Plains, reveals accounts that reflect Kelly's attitude, as well as accounts of women who came to an understanding of Native American people and their increasingly desperate situation.

The closing of the frontier and the end of Indian wars in the Plains in the late nineteenth century did not diminish the popularity of captivity narratives. They continued to follow the standard form of the genre, but some elements—for example, the heroism of the captives and their deeds—became more exaggerated. At the same time, portrayals of Native Americans became more sympathetic. Instead of condemning Native American cultures wholesale, they allow some noble characters to emerge. An interesting change in the basic plot of captivity narratives has occurred in the last thirty years with the emergence of romance. The captive remains with her Native American captor and exerts a "civilizing" influence over him and his tribe—she achieves what the earlier woman captive could not. There is also hope for some Native American cultures in these romances. These new conventions are evident in such films as *Dances with Wolves* (1990), which, while ethnographically more accurate, as newer audiences demand, romanticizes

traditional Lakota culture and also plays on images of "noble" and "savage" Native Americans (the latter in this case are Pawnees). Captivity narratives remain a formula rather than portrayals of complex and contemporary peoples; they deal with the conflict between Native and European Americans in terms entirely satisfying to the latter audience, while denying complexity and contemporaneity to Native American peoples.

Birgit Hans
University of North Dakota

Kelly, Fanny. *Narrative of My Captivity among the Sioux Indians.* Chicago: Lakeside Press, 1990 [1871]. Riley, Glenda. *Women and Indians on the Frontier, 1825–1915.* Albuquerque: University of New Mexico Press, 1984. Stedman, Raymond William. *Shadows of the Indian: Stereotypes in American Culture.* Norman: University of Oklahoma Press, 1982. Tinnemeyer, Andrea. *Identity Politics of the Captivity Narrative after 1848.* Lincoln: University of Nebraska Press, 2006.

CASINOS

Since the late 1980s, Indian-owned, and sometimes Indian-operated, casinos and gambling halls have expanded rapidly throughout the U.S. Great Plains and, to a lesser extent, the Canadian Prairie Provinces. Their importance to some tribes has been likened to the buffalo because they promise prosperity and economic development. In the United States, Indian-owned gambling operations grew out of the 1987 U.S. Supreme Court decision *California v. Cabazon Band of Mission Indians*, which determined that states could not regulate gambling on Indian reservations. In 1988 the U.S. Congress provided a regulatory framework for Indian-owned gambling establishments by creating the Indian Gaming Regulatory Act (IGRA) and the federal National Indian Gaming Commission (NIGC) to enforce it.

The act created three classes of games, each with different levels of tribal control. Class I games are traditional tribal social games for minimal prizes. These are wholly controlled by the tribes themselves. Class II games include bingo or any variant (such as pull tabs or instant bingo) played in the same location as traditional bingo games. These are allowed as long as the state in which they are run permits such gaming for any purpose, following tribal adoption of regulations acceptable to the NIGC. Class III games have been the greatest source of contention between Indian tribes and their host states. Class III games consist of every other sort of gambling, from slot machines to blackjack and poker (and their electronic equivalents). The IGRA sought to balance state and tribal sovereignty by requiring tribes to make a compact with their host states, subject to approval by the secretary of the interior. This has been the most contentious requirement. Furthermore, tribal gaming ordinance must be accepted by the chair of the NIGC. Thus, Indian casino-style gambling is subject to both state and federal oversight. The issue of Indian gaming is at the forefront of the continuing struggle between tribes, states, and the federal government.

Indian-owned gambling establishments grew impressively but also brought problems, among them questions of sovereignty, non-Indian management of gambling operations, increased social and economic costs for the tribes and their non-Indian neighbors, and allegations of fraud and unequal distribution of benefits. Conflict centered on the right of the states to regulate or even ban casino-style gambling, as well as the issue of revenue sharing. The impact of gaming has been mixed. For some tribes the result has been increased job creation and funds for social programs and infrastructure improvement. Many state-tribe compacts include revenue-sharing provisions, which increased state revenues and attracted support. But while gross gambling revenues rose, so too did the portion paid to the states and to non-Indian managers, often based in Las Vegas, Nevada. Gaming can be very lucrative, but, unfortunately, the tribes most in need of economic development—those far from large metropolitan centers or major travel routes—are the least likely to profit.

Currently, all Great Plains states allow some form of Indian-owned gaming. In 2005 there were approximately fifty such gambling establishments, from bingo to casino style, operating on the U.S. Great Plains, representing forty tribes and sub-bands. South Dakota had the most casino-type operations (nine), while Oklahoma led in numbers of bingo establishments (twenty-nine). Most belong to the Great Plains Indian Gaming Association, founded in 1997, with twenty-eight tribes represented in 2005. Gaming revenues (and construction of new casinos) slowed in the early 2000s, as the industry matured and other avenues for gambling opened.

Indian gaming grew less rapidly in the Canadian Prairie Provinces due to more restrictive laws. A 1985 amendment to the Canadian Criminal Code made the provinces the sole providers and regulators of gaming. While Canadian law generally has favored First Nations sovereignty within their own borders, gaming has been an exception. Attempts to expand First Nations rights met with failure in the 1996 case *Pamajewon v. the Queen*, when the Supreme Court of Canada ruled that neither gaming nor its regulation were integral to the Shawanaga or the Eagle Lake tribes at the time of European contact. While recognizing that wagering games were traditional, the Court ruled that they were not central to the tribes' cultures and that they had never passed laws regulating

gaming or operated commercial-style casinos. According to the Criminal Code, First Nations must win provincial authority for on- or off-reserve gaming. The provincial governments of Manitoba and Saskatchewan allowed their First Nations to build gaming establishments, and in 2001 Alberta adopted a new policy allowing regulated First Nations gaming, but no First Nations–owned gaming establishment had been developed there by 2005.

Charles Vollan
South Dakota State University

National Gambling Impact and Policy Commission. *The National Gambling Impact Study Commission: Final Report.* Washington DC: National Gambling Impact and Policy Commission, 1999. Wilkins, Beth M., and Beth R. Ritter. "Will the House Win: Does Sovereignty Rule in Indian Casinos?" *Great Plains Research* 4 (1994): 305–24. Lane, Ambrose I., Sr. *Return of the Buffalo: The Story Behind America's Indian Gaming Explosion.* Westport CT: Bergin & Garvey, 1995.

CHEYENNES

Between 1820 and 1869 the Cheyenne Nation was the most powerful Indian military force in the Central Great Plains, despite comprising only about 3,500 people. They achieved a dominant military position by allying with the Arapahos and Lakotas, then driving the Shoshones toward the northwest and the Kiowas and Comanches to the south, while keeping the Crows and Pawnees at bay by continual attacks against their villages. Thus, they gained control of the prime bison-hunting areas between the forks of the Platte and on the upper reaches of the Republican and Smoky Hill rivers, and achieved preferred access to trading posts on the Arkansas and South Platte rivers.

The Cheyennes were also successful during this period in their warfare against the U.S. Army, which could not catch them on the open plains, or was often sorry when it did, as at the Fetterman Fight in Wyoming in 1866 and the Battle of Beecher's Island in Colorado in 1868. The military success of the Cheyennes can be attributed mainly to four factors: they could mobilize up to 1,500 warriors, all the active men in the tribe, for a single engagement; their bands were dispersed most of the year so that they could observe anyone entering their territory; their warriors traveled light and took along spare horses for attack, pursuit, and escape; and they maintained ferocious war traditions, which included suicide warfare, dog ropes, medicine lances, and a complex system of war honors that encouraged quick and decisive combat.

The Cheyennes, who speak a language of the Algonquian family and call themselves Tsistsistas, did not see themselves as primarily a militaristic people, however, but as a religious people. Even today their traditional culture is organized around the annual Sun Dances, performed on their Okla-

Cheyenne woman and children with travois, 1889

homa and Montana reservations, and the Arrow Renewal Ceremony, performed in Oklahoma. In addition, most Cheyennes are involved in the Native American Church, or peyote religion, as well as Christian denominations, especially the Catholic Church in Montana and the Mennonite Church on both reservations. The Cheyennes entered written history during the seventeenth century in Minnesota around the shores of Mille Lacs, where they collected wild rice and made occasional trips to the Plains to hunt bison on foot. By 1766, however, some Cheyenne bands had acquired horses and moved their base to the Minnesota River to become mounted bison hunters, while at least one other band occupied an agricultural village on the Sheyenne River in North Dakota, a river that bears the name applied to them by their Dakota neighbors, meaning "red talkers," or people of foreign language. Several decades later the various Cheyenne bands were reunited along the middle Missouri River, where they pursued an economy of mixed agriculture and hunting, based in fortified villages on the riverbanks.

Later still, probably about 1790, the Cheyenne bands moved to the vicinity of the Black Hills, where they acquired more horses, which ultimately enabled them to give up agriculture for a nomadic life of full-time bison hunting. They were urged to do this by their prophet Sweet Medicine, who was given four medicine arrows by sacred persons whom he met in a cave at Bear Butte in South Dakota, known to the Cheyennes as Nowahwas, or Sacred Mountain. Two of the arrows were for killing bison by magical means, and two for killing their enemies.

The Cheyenne political system had two aspects, war and peace, and two kinds of chiefs, war chiefs, or *notxevoe*, and peace chiefs, or *vehoe*. The peace chiefs led the nation's ten or so bands, supervised their trade, and adjudicated disputes. When war threatened, they gave control of the nation to the war chiefs, who planned strategy and tactics and led the attacks. Ideally, there were forty-four peace chiefs in the Chiefs' Council, four of whom were senior, or "Old Man Chiefs," and each of the seven to ten military societies was led by one to four "Big War Chiefs" and four to sixteen "Little War Chiefs."

Most of the daily work in Cheyenne society was done by women, organized along matrilineal lines. A woman usually worked alongside her mother and mother's sisters, her own sisters, her daughters, and her sisters' daughters for her entire life. Women "ruled the camp" and owned the tipis and furnishings, as well as a number of horses. As workers, they organized guilds that honored women who had made tipi covers and liners, clothing, quillwork, and beadwork. Honorable women received the privilege of smoking a pipe after menopause.

Young women were married by ages sixteen to eighteen, the oldest daughter first. Because of warfare, there were more women than men in Cheyenne society, so if possible a second sister was married to her older sister's husband (sororal polygyny). If a man died, his brother was required to marry his widow to maintain ties between the two extended families. If a woman died, an unmarried sister was required to marry the widower, to take care of the children and maintain ties between the families. If there were no unmarried sisters, then a married sister or other woman related in the female line adopted the children. Modern Cheyenne women often "co-mother" their children, playfully calling the practice "Cheyenne health insurance."

The military societies founded in Aboriginal times are still active. They sponsor dinners and powwows to honor their members and families and raise money for the annual ceremonies. Also in existence are local groups of "War Mothers," which were first organized during World War I to honor servicemen and -women and veterans.

Concerning treaties, the U.S. government now admits its failure to live up to the treaties of Fort Laramie (1851) and Fort Wise (1861), and in 1968 paid compensation of approximately $2,000 to each Cheyenne, far less than the actual value of the land taken and annuities not received. In addition, the government has admitted to defrauding Cheyennes of their reservation land through the Jerome Commission, which was certified by the infamous Lone Wolf decision in 1903. The Cheyennes were never compensated for that fraud or for the two hundred noncombatants killed and horses and belongings stolen in 1864 during the Sand Creek Massacre. The descendants of those attacked were promised indemnities under the Treaty of the Little Arkansas in 1865, which had not yet been paid as of 2001, although the Cheyenne Sand Creek Descendants Association continues to make legal efforts to collect the funds.

On their reservations, beginning in the 1870s, the Cheyennes were subjected to an unending series of programs, ostensibly intended to better their condition. Missionary and government schools were set up, and some have continued to modern times. After the passage of the Indian Reorganization Act in 1934 and the Oklahoma Indian Welfare Act in 1936, Cheyennes were able to organize an official government on each reservation and to practice their religion and speak their language freely.

In recent years, the Cheyennes have taken steps to achieve economic self-sufficiency. They have inaugurated bingo halls in Oklahoma and tourist facilities in Oklahoma and Montana. They are presently negotiating with private corporations to bring manufacturing jobs to the reservation areas. Their present population consists of approximately seven thousand Northern Cheyennes enrolled on their reservation in southeastern Montana and another seven thousand Southern

Cheyennes enrolled on their reservation in west-central Oklahoma.

John H. Moore
University of Florida

Berthrong, Donald J. *The Southern Cheyennes*. Norman: University of Oklahoma Press, 1963. Boye, Alan. *Holding Stone Hands: On the Trail of the Cheyenne Exodus*. Lincoln: University of Nebraska Press, 1999. Fowler, Loretta. *Tribal Sovereignty and the Historical Imagination: Cheyenne-Arapaho Politics*. Lincoln: University of Nebraska Press, 2002. Grinnell, George B. *The Cheyenne Indians*. New York: Cooper Square, 1962. Grinnell, George B. *By Cheyenne Campfires*. Lincoln: University of Nebraska Press, 1971. Hardorff, Rivhard G. *Cheyenne Memories of the Custer Fight: A Source Book*. Lincoln: University of Nebraska Press, 1998. Moore, John H. *The Cheyenne Nation*. Lincoln: University of Nebraska Press, 1987. Moore, John H. *The Cheyenne*. Blackwell, 1999. Stands in Timber, John, and Margo Liberty. *Cheyenne Memories*. 2nd ed. New Haven CT: Yale University Press, 1998.

COMANCHES

Studio portrait of Betty Kerchee, a Comanche woman, ca. 1890–1910

The Comanches were the first Native people to adopt the classic horse-mounted lifestyle of the Plains. The ethnonym Comanche probably derives from the Ute word *komantsia*—"anyone who wants to fight me all the time." Their name for themselves is Nemene, or "Our People."

Shoshone speakers, including proto-Comanches, probably moved to the Northern Plains in the sixteenth century. In the late seventeenth century the proto-Comanches began a southward movement, and by the early eighteenth century, if not before, they were in contact with the Spaniards of

New Mexico. The earliest mention of Comanches in Texas came in the 1740s. By the 1840s Comanches were regularly crossing the Rio Grande into Mexico on horse raids.

The Comanche economy can be characterized in three modes: a domestic economy of hunting and gathering, a commercial economy of trade and raid, and a political-diplomatic economy. In the domestic economy, Comanches used both individual stalking of bison and group methods. Group hunts usually occurred in late summer and fall when the animals were fat, robes were good, and there were few flies. Group hunts began with scouts locating a herd. After the scouts reported the herd's location to the chiefs, the hunters were admonished to stay together. The actual hunt was under the direction of the chief or a noted warrior. However, once the chase began, each hunter acted separately. Hunters identified their kills by arrow marks. Other men could claim a portion of the meat by counting coup on it, but the hide remained the property of the killer.

There were three general trade contexts: formal and informal trade fairs and bartering in European settlements; trading posts; and exchange with *viageros*, or "travelers," later called *comancheros*. Comanches traded horses and the products of the hunt with neighboring peoples for agricultural products and, in postcontact times, European industrial products.

Political relations with other peoples probably always included gift exchanges. Political relations with European Americans developed into an economy with significant ramifications. Items in this economy included elite goods such as silver-headed canes, flags, and uniforms. They also included items that could be redistributed downward through the social structure such as foodstuffs, cloth, and metal goods.

Details of Aboriginal clothing are scanty, but it seems that summer dress was minimal. Men wore perhaps only a shirt, a breechcloth, possibly leggings, and moccasins. By the reservation period, photographs and museum collections show mid-thigh-length shirts decorated with twist fringe at the shoulder and elbow. Some side-seam leggings are represented in museum collections, although late-nineteenth-century photographs also show front-seam style, attached by thongs to the belt at the waist and tied with garters below the knee. From knee to ankle, leggings were decorated with long twist fringe. Moccasins were of the two-piece, hard-sole variety. A long triangular vamp was decorated with fringes and tin cone tinklers. The earliest examples of women's apparel are two-part dresses, consisting of a skirt suspended by straps from the shoulders and a separate poncholike blouse; some mid-nineteenth-century photographs show a separate wrap fastened with broaches. In hot weather, or when nursing or in mourning, the blouse could be removed. The later style was a single-piece dress. By the mid– to late nineteenth century, both men and women wore a cloth about the waist outside both leggings and skirt.

Comanche tipis were distinct, with a four-pole base, but with the rest of the poles set as in a three-pole tipi. The cut of the skins forming the cover was also apparently unique.

Comanche relations with the supernatural were considered to be an individual's concern, but despite a range of variation in belief and practice, there were broad features common to Comanche religion. Religious practice centered on *puha*, personal power obtained from the supernatural. Power was available to both men and women, both of whom could become *puhacut*, or a "possessor of power."

In prereservation times, there were four levels of sociopolitical organization: simple family, extended family, local band, and division. The simple family consisted of a man, his wife or wives, and various dependents—children, parents, or parents-in-law. The basic social unit was the bilaterally extended family, or *nemenakane*, "people who live together in a house(hold)." Local bands were composed of one or more extended families, as well as attached simple families and individuals, and were called *rancherias* by the Spaniards. The highest level of Comanche political organization was the division, the tribally organized group of local bands linked by ties of kinship and men's societies. The names and numbers of these groups have changed greatly over the course of Comanche history.

The Comanches were assigned a reservation in southwestern Oklahoma following the Treaty of Medicine Lodge Creek in 1867, but not all the bands were on the reservation until 1876. The reservation was allotted after the General Allotment Act of 1887. Most Comanches now live in the vicinity of Lawton, Oklahoma. They are active, although often partial, participants in the mainstream economy. Fort Sill in Lawton, Tinker Air Force Base in Oklahoma City, and Altus Air Force Base in Altus, as well as several other federal installations, provide employment. As a tribe the Comanches have few independent resources. In 1984 a bingo operation was opened, although it has been the focus of much controversy, and its contribution to the Comanche economy is uncertain.

Although more than half of the 1901–6 Comanche allotments are still in Indian hands, few Comanches actively work them. Rather, allotments are held as undivided joint property by multiple heirs of the original allottee and are leased to non-

Indian farmers or stockmen. A number of oil wells have been drilled on allotments, and several Comanches have become quite wealthy through such revenues.

There are no reliable Aboriginal population estimates; similarly, details of epidemic diseases are scanty and contradictory. In 1870 it was estimated that there were 3,742 Comanches, including possibly 1,000 off-reservation. In 1875, 1,556 Comanches were reported on the reservation south of the Washita River. In 1900 there were 1,499 Comanches, but a year later measles took 98 lives. The low point of 1,399 was reached in 1904, and it was not until the 1930s that the population again surpassed 2,000. In 1990 the tribal population was approximately 9,000.

Thomas W. Kavanaugh
Indiana University

Charney, Jean Ornsbee. *A Grammar of Comanche*. Lincoln: University of Nebraska Press, 1994. Harris, LaDonna. *LaDonna Harris: A Comanche Life*. Lincoln: University of Nebraska Press, 2000. Kavanagh, Thomas W. *Comanche Political History: An Ethnohistorical Perspective, 1706–1875*. Lincoln: University of Nebraska Press, 1996. Mihesuah, Henry. *First to Fight*. Lincoln: University of Nebraska Press, 2002.

COUNTING COUP

Counting coup, or striking an enemy, was the highest honor earned by warriors participating in the intertribal wars of the Great Plains. Native peoples recognized precise systems of graduated war honors, and usually the greatest exploit was counting coup. Key to a man's success in Plains combat was demonstrating his own courage by proving superiority over his opponent and, in a competitive sense, over his own comrades. Killing was part of war, but showing courage in the process was more important for individual status. This was best accomplished by risking one's life in charging the enemy on foot or horseback to get close enough to touch or strike him with the hand, a weapon, or a "coupstick."

Humiliating the enemy also played a part in this fighting, as illustrated by an account from the Jesuit missionary Father Pierre-Jean De Smet. In De Smet's 1848 visit to the Oglala Lakotas, the Oglala leader Red Fish related to the priest how his men had just suffered a disgraceful defeat at the hands of the Crows. The Crows killed ten Oglalas, then chased the others for a distance. The Crows then were content merely to repeatedly count coup on their enemies with clubs and sticks, thus demonstrating to the Oglalas that they were not worth the ammunition needed to kill them.

Counting coup carried over into the battles against American troops. For example, the Northern Cheyenne warrior Wooden Leg related how, as a young man at the Battle of the Little Bighorn, he and his friend Little Bird chased a soldier across the river, counting coup on him with their whips and grabbing his carbine. They did not kill him, said Wooden Leg, because after counting coup it did not seem particularly brave, and besides, it would waste bullets. Counting coup, then, was the epitome of a type of warfare that pitted the skill and daring of one man against another.

Anthony R. McGinnis
Lyons, Colorado

McGinnis, Anthony R. *Counting Coup and Cutting Horses: Intertribal Warfare on the Northern Plains, 1738–1889*. Evergreen CO: Cordillera Press, 1990.

CRAZY HORSE (CA. 1840–1877)

Crazy Horse was born near Bear Butte, South Dakota, around 1840. He was the son of Crazy Horse, a distinguished Oglala Lakota warrior and medicine man, and Rattle Blanket Woman, a Miniconjou Lakota.

The life of Crazy Horse nearly bracketed the years of violent contact between the Lakotas and the United States. A war chief of the Oglalas, Crazy Horse contested American expansion into Lakota lands in the Northern Great Plains. During Red Cloud's War, Crazy Horse demonstrated his military prowess in the Fetterman Fight at Fort Phil Kearny (1866), the Hayfield Fight (1867), and the Wagon Box Fight (1867). The Lakotas' military success persuaded the government to negotiate, and after prolonged discussions Red Cloud and some Lakota chiefs signed the Fort Laramie Treaty of 1868. Crazy Horse and other Lakota leaders, however, refused to acknowledge the treaty.

Crazy Horse's reputation as a war leader earned the admiration of the Lakotas and Northern Cheyennes and of tribal enemies of the Lakotas such as the Crows. His unyielding opposition toward the demands of the U.S. government and toward the reservation regime made him a central figure among the nontreaty Oglala and Miniconjou Lakotas and the Northern Cheyennes, who increasingly looked to him for leadership after 1868. Crazy Horse earned his highest formal honor in 1868 when he was selected as one of the head warriors, or shirt-wearers, of the Oglalas.

Crazy Horse was a shirt-wearer until 1871, when an affair with a married woman (Black Buffalo Woman, Red Cloud's niece) cost him this prestigious position. Crazy Horse kept a sizable following, however, because of his determined opposition to the United States. By the mid-1870s government officials and army officers recognized him as one of the most prominent leaders of the Lakota resistance.

The 1874 discovery of gold in the Black Hills

strengthened the determination of the government to purchase the Black Hills, which angered nearly all Lakota leaders, whether they were signatories of the 1868 Fort Laramie Treaty or not. Negotiations between the government and the Lakotas broke down, and in December 1875 the government ordered Lakota bands living in the unceded areas along the Yellowstone and Powder rivers to report within six weeks to the reservations or face military action.

Not wishing to move their villages during the winter and unsure of the government's intention, Crazy Horse and other Lakota and Northern Cheyenne leaders refused. The government insisted on the move, and in March 1876 army units attacked a Northern Cheyenne village mistakenly identified as that of Crazy Horse. The army's destruction of the Northern Cheyenne village convinced Crazy Horse to prepare for an all-out defensive war against the army.

On June 17, 1876, Crazy Horse and approximately 1,500 warriors defeated a military column led by Brig. Gen. George Crook on Rosebud Creek in southern Montana. On June 25, 1876, Crazy Horse was involved in the destruction of Custer's Seventh Cavalry at the Little Bighorn. Despite these defeats, the army persevered against the Indians in the Powder River–Yellowstone River region through the winter of 1876–77. On May 7, 1877, Crazy Horse and his band surrendered at Fort Robinson, Nebraska.

His contempt for reservation life notwithstanding, Crazy Horse realized there was no viable alternative for the beleaguered Lakotas. Initially, government officials and army officers sought him out, and their attention caused jealousy among Oglala and Sicanju (Brulé) Lakota chiefs, who spread false rumors about Crazy Horse. Junior army officers were persuaded that Crazy Horse was plotting rebellion and they decided to arrest him. On September 5, 1877, during an attempt to imprison Crazy Horse at Fort Robinson, an army sentry bayoneted him. He died a few hours later. He was survived by two wives and no children.

Joseph C. Porter
University of North Carolina–Chapel Hill

Hardorff, Richard G., ed. *The Death of Crazy Horse: A Tragic Episode in Lakota History.* Lincoln: University of Nebraska Press, 2001. Marshall, Joseph M. *The Journey of Crazy Horse: A Lakota History.* Penguin, 2005. Ricker, Eli S. *The Indian Interviews of Eli S. Ricker, 1903–1919.* Lincoln: University of Nebraska Press, 2005. Nebraska State Historical Society Collection, Lincoln, Nebraska. Sandoz, Mari. *Crazy Horse: The Strange Man of the Oglalas.* New York: Alfred A. Knopf, 1942.

CRAZY HORSE MEMORIAL

In the Black Hills, on land taken from the Lakota Sioux, stands a six-hundred-foot mountain. This mountain, blasted away for more than fifty years to expose bare granite, is gradually beginning to represent Crazy Horse, an Oglala Sioux leader and warrior. Korczak Ziolkowski, the self-taught sculptor and artist (born in Boston on September 6, 1908) who started this project has died, but his family is working to keep his dream alive.

Ziolkowski's dream began in the late 1930s, when Henry Standing Bear, an Oglala chief, asked him to create a memorial to Native Americans. Standing Bear wrote, "My fellow chiefs and I would like the white man to know the red man has great heroes too." To honor Standing Bear's wish, Ziolkowski decided to erect a monument—ten times larger than Mount Rushmore—to Crazy Horse, who was born sometime around 1840 and led his people in many fights, resisting white encroachment and refusing to sign treaties. Crazy Horse helped defeat George Armstrong Custer's Seventh Cavalry at the Battle of the Little Bighorn. He was killed at Fort Robinson, Nebraska, in September 1877, reportedly while trying to resist arrest. Crazy Horse remains an important symbol of Native American resistance to European American hegemony.

Ziolkowski dedicated the first blast of the Crazy Horse Memorial in 1948. The monument was just one part of his extensive nonprofit humanitarian project intended to honor Native Americans; Ziolkowski also had intentions to build a museum, university, and medical training center. Only one of his goals ever reached completion, the Indian Museum of North America, which is located below the monument.

The monument can only be what Ziolkowski called a "lineal likeness," since Crazy Horse never allowed anyone to photograph or sketch him. The Crazy Horse Memorial will be the world's largest in-the-round sculpture, measuring 641 feet high and 563 feet long. Four thousand people will be able to stand on his outstretched arm, and below his hand, in three-foot-high letters, a message will read, "My lands are where my dead lie buried."

Although intended to honor Crazy Horse and Native Americans in general, many have questioned the appropriateness of blasting his image out of the sacred Black Hills. According to Virginia Driving Hawk Sneve, Lakotas would rather his image "be cloaked in faceless anonymity to forever symbolize their defeat and the need for inspired leaders once more." However, fifty years after the first blast, Crazy Horse's face was dedicated on June 3, 1998. Some still question whether or not the monument will ever be completed.

Amy Scherer
Reno, Nevada

DeWall, Robb. *Korczak: Storyteller in Stone.* Crazy Horse SD: Korczak's Heritage, 1984. Fielder, Margaret. *Sioux Indian Leaders.*

Seattle: Superior Publishing, 1975. Sneve, Virginia Driving Hawk. *They Led a Nation.* Sioux Falls SD: Brevet Press, 1975.

CROW DOG, LEONARD (B. 1942)

Leonard Crow Dog is a Brulé Sioux holy person and former spiritual leader of the American Indian Movement (AIM). His great-grandfather, Crow Dog, killed the Brulé leader Spotted Tail in 1881. Leonard Crow Dog was born on the Rosebud Reservation on August 18, 1942. He did not attend an American school and only learned English as an adult. His family had been Catholic, but Crow Dog left to follow the Native American Church. He trained to be a *pejuta wichasha*, a spiritual man, from childhood, and ultimately became both a Yuwipi leader and a Road Man for the Native American Church.

He had brushes with the law, and he served more than a year at a reform school in Littleton, Colorado, when he was fourteen. He took on a variety of mostly agricultural jobs in South Dakota and Nebraska and spent a short time in jail at age sixteen for escaping and resisting arrest on an intoxication charge. He had three children with his first wife, Francine, but they divorced while he was still young.

In 1970 Dennis Banks, a founding member of AIM, asked Crow Dog to become the spiritual leader of the organization. He agreed, becoming the first holy person to endorse the group. He was involved in most of the major AIM actions and protests. The Trail of Broken Treaties caravan began at the Crow Dog family's Sun Dance and led to the occupation of the Bureau of Indian Affairs building in Washington DC in November 1972. His family's land, Crow Dog's Paradise, became an AIM center.

He participated in the violent disputes that raged across Pine Ridge Reservation in the early 1970s, pitting traditional Lakotas against tribal president Dick Wilson and his supporters. The federal government supported Wilson and worked to destroy AIM. Following Wilson's contested acquittal for corruption charges, several hundred AIM members, including Leonard Crow Dog, occupied the town of Wounded Knee, site of the 1890 massacre, where they held off federal agents and Dick Wilson's heavily armed GOONs, a paramilitary group, from February 27 to May 8, 1973. Crow Dog acted as spiritual leader as well as "chief engineer," wiring the compound with explosives and healing people wounded by gunfire. His great-grandfather had been a Ghost Dancer, and during the siege Crow Dog brought back the Ghost Dance. He was arrested at the end of the siege and convicted of prohibiting federal officers from performing their duty and for robbery (temporarily disarming fed-

eral postal inspectors) in 1975. He was sentenced to a total of eleven years, but this was suspended and he was put on five years' probation.

Following Wounded Knee II, Crow Dog married Mary Ellen Moore, who had given birth to a child in the Wounded Knee compound. They had four more children together before divorcing. Crow Dog's political activities again caught the attention of legal authorities. After the failed 1975 raid on the Jumping Bull compound on Pine Ridge Reservation, in which two federal agents were killed, Leonard Peltier, the chief suspect, came to Crow Dog's Sun Dance. The FBI arrested Crow Dog, and he was sentenced to five years in jail on November 30, 1975. In January 1976 he was sentenced to five more years for assaulting a man who had accosted his wife in their family home. His earlier probation was revoked, and he faced twenty-one years in jail. With help from author Richard Erdoes, funding from the National Council of Churches, legal aid from attorney William Kunstler, and much celebrity support, he was released in 1976.

In recent years Crow Dog has become disenchanted with AIM and its leaders, claiming that founders Verne and Clyde Bellecourt had forgotten the organization's original purpose. In 1994 he agreed to direct a Sun Dance, open to Indians and non-Indians, in Hallam, Nebraska. He remains an active leader on Pine Ridge Reservation.

Charles Vollan
South Dakota State University

Crow Dog, Leonard, and Richard Erdoes. *Crow Dog: Four Generations of Sioux Medicine Men.* New York: HarperCollins, 1995. Matthiessen, Peter. *In the Spirit of Crazy Horse.* New York: Viking Penguin, 1992.

CROW FAIR

Crow Fair, called the Tipi Capital of the World, is an annual event held the third weekend in August on the Crow Reservation in Montana. It is one of the largest Native American events in North America and is run by a committee of the Crow tribe. Crow Fair combines a celebration of Crow culture, reunion of family groups, powwow, rodeo, horse racing, and commercial vendors. Native Americans of various tribes and many non-Indian people, including visitors from around the world, gather to celebrate and enjoy themselves. There may be one thousand tipis, along with wall tents, pickup campers, trailers, and mobile homes. Each family has its own camp area, and people visit and eat under arbor shades and awnings.

These camps surround an open circular dance arbor with bleachers. Immediately around the dance arbor are commercial booths that serve food as well as sell Native crafts, arts, supplies, and children's carnival toys. Social and popular dances are held for young people in the Round Hall. An all-Indian rodeo and horse races are held at the racetrack arena adjacent to the fairgrounds. Crow Fair runs four days for the tribe and general public. A fifth day is devoted to Crow tribal members and their immediate friends and includes dances, giveaways, feasting, and the Parade Dance around camp with a salute to the mountains.

Each morning there is a parade, and spectators line the edges of the road, sitting on folding chairs, in cars, or in the beds of pickup trucks, many holding umbrellas for shade. The procession is led by a color guard of Native American veterans. The main parade includes people on horseback, on foot, and riding on cars and floats. Most are dressed in powwow finery, wearing traditional Plains regalia, including fancy beaded vests, eagle-feather bonnets, shawls, and elk tooth dresses, mixed with cowboy dress. Many horses are outfitted with traditional Crow saddles, beaded or painted saddlebags, Pendleton blankets, beaded rifle bags, and cradleboards. Vehicles and floats also are covered with traditional finery; along the sides, draped banners declare titles of tribal or family affiliation. The floats have displays such as a small tipi and arbor with elders and children or a drum group with dancers. The paraders smile, wave to the people lining the roadside, and throw candy to the children. The current Crow Fair princess leads "visiting royalty" who have won princess titles at other reservations and powwows. Awards are given for the best dress outfits, decorated horses, and floats.

Drum groups, dancers, and spectators assemble at the central dance arbor for the afternoon and evening powwow. The grand entry is led by an Indian veteran color guard, followed by distinguished individuals, honored guests and elders, and then male traditional dancers, male fancy dancers, women traditional dancers, girl's shawl or fancy dancers, jingle dress, grass dancers, and tiny tots. The powwow includes announcements, jokes, dance competitions in various categories and age groups, and intertribal and social dances. Honor songs and dances, giveaways, and adoption and naming ceremonies occur. After the powwow, there are sometimes forty-nine dances and tipi doorway singing. The all-Indian rodeo and horse races are held at the nearby racetrack arena. The rodeo includes saddle bronc and bareback riding, bull riding, bulldogging, calf roping, team roping, and barrel racing. Quarter horse and Thoroughbred racing are featured. There is much betting on the outcomes of the races.

Crow Fair started in 1904, when the Bureau of Indian Affairs agent and Crow leaders agreed that a country fair format would help induce the Crows to become self-supporting farmers while at the same time allow the people to showcase aspects of Crow culture. Crow women exhibited traditional Native foods, clothing, and handicrafts. People brought ponies, calves, pigs, turkeys, and chickens for exhibit as well as potatoes, pumpkins, squash, grain, jellies, pies, bread, butter, and cakes. Schoolchildren exhibited basketry, embroidery, and various crafts and played band music. A committee of chiefs and elders scheduled entertainment events and arranged a parade, foot and horse racing, relay races, rodeo (including bucking broncos), and dancing to the beat of singers around drums. Storytelling of war deeds by veterans, victory dances, sham battles and reenactments, and the distribution of gifts to tribal members and visitors became popular. Prizes were given for the best-pitched and -decorated tipis, tipi-pitching races, farm exhibits, horse work teams and wagons, buggies, and races.

Federal Indian policy at that time generally forbade traditional singing, dancing, and ceremonies, but the combination of agricultural assimilation and traditional culture coincided with public interest in tourism. Visitors included non-Indians as well as members of many other tribes. The fair became a successful national model for Indian events. After World War II the agricultural aspects of Crow Fair were dropped, and the combined Crow and modern pan-Indian event has grown to become one of the most popular cultural celebrations in the world.

C. Adrian Heidenreich
Montana State University–Billings

Baasaxpilua: Northern Plains Celebration. Video. Denver Museum of Natural History, 1982. Loeb, Barbara. "Crow Fair." Native Peoples 3 (1990): 16–24. Wisherd, Edwin L. "The Friendly Crows in Festive Panoply." National Geographic 52 (1927): 315–22.

CROWFOOT (CA. 1830–1890)

Crowfoot (Isapo-Muxika, or "Crow Indian's Big Foot") was head chief of the Blackfoot (Siksika) tribe. A great orator and warrior, Crowfoot contributed in a significant way to the peaceful settlement of the Canadian West.

Crowfoot was born around 1830 on the Belly River, near present-day Lethbridge, Alberta. He first went to war at about the age of thirteen and showed great bravery in striking an enemy tipi with his whip and rescuing his wounded brother. He was in nineteen engagements with enemy tribes and was wounded six times. His greatest feat of bravery occurred in 1866 when, in full view of his camp, he killed a grizzly bear with a spear. Shortly thereafter he became leader of the Big Pipes band, and by 1870 he was one of three head chiefs of the tribe.

Crowfoot maintained good relations with the Hudson's Bay Company, appreciating that, unlike

Chief Crowfoot (Isapo-Muxika), 1885

"Children of the Large-Beaked Bird." While likely referring to the raven, this term was misinterpreted by early trappers who began to address the Apsaalooke as the Crows. The Crows attribute their origins, as well as the creation of the world, to the trickster Old Man Coyote. The narrative begins with Old Man Coyote traveling alone in a cold and wet world. As four ducks flew over, Old Man Coyote asked his younger brothers to dive beneath the waters and bring up some earth so he could make the land. The first duck dove but was unsuccessful, as were the second and third ducks. Finally, Old Man Coyote asked the fourth duck, Hell Diver, to bring up some earth. The duck dove deep and, after being down a long time, surfaced with a small piece of mud. With this earth Old Man Coyote traveled from east to west and made the land, mountains, and rivers, animals and plants, and gave them life. But the world was still a lonely place. So Old Man Coyote molded from the earth an image he liked and blew a small breath into it. The first man was made. Old Man Coyote was not satisfied. He tried again, and the first woman was created. Old Man Coyote was no longer alone. He taught the people how to live and pray, giving them their language, clan system, and ceremonies.

The historic migration of the Crows from the Lake Winnipeg region of Canada into the Bighorn and Yellowstone river basins of Montana and Wyoming (probably before 1600) predated the arrival of the horse. Horses were acquired by 1750, and the Crows' economic life was transformed from one of sedentary farming to one of bison hunting. The horse became an integral symbol of Crow identity and status. Male leadership roles became predicated on achieving a series of war deeds, such as touching an enemy in combat or leading a successful horse raid against an enemy. Among their enemies were the Blackfeet, Cheyennes, and Lakotas. The Sun Dance became a prominent ceremonial expression, helping unite the tribe and providing a means to obtain spiritual power to avenge the death of a relative.

Despite the changes initiated by the adoption of the horse, the Crows retained elements of their former society. The Tobacco Ceremony, the yearly planting and harvesting of the sacred tobacco seeds, reflected their once-agrarian orientation. The Crows also maintained their matrilineal clan structure, and even today's clan system is based on the thirteen original clans. The Crow language is part of the Siouan family, thus giving them a linguistic affiliation with many other tribes of the region. Today, up to one-third of the population continues to speak the native language.

The central organizing principle around which much of Aboriginal and contemporary Crow soci-

American traders, they did not flood the land with alcohol. Crowfoot also befriended the Catholic missionary Albert Lacombe in 1865 and later rescued him when he was in a camp that was attacked by a Cree war party. Crowfoot allowed Lacombe to preach to his people, though Crowfoot himself paid little attention to Christianity.

In 1874, when the North-West Mounted Police extended their control over western Canada, Crowfoot established friendly relations with its commander, James F. Macleod. In 1877 he willingly signed the Blackfoot treaty (Treaty Number 7) with the Canadian government, ceding much of southern Alberta. However, after the Blackfoot were obliged to live, mired in famine, on their reserve east of Calgary, Crowfoot became disillusioned with the government. Nevertheless, he continued to mediate between his people and government officials. By the last decade of his life, most of his children had died of tuberculosis and he was almost constantly in mourning. Crowfoot died on April 25, 1890, in a tipi in the Bow Valley. He is now considered to be one of Canada's national heroes.

Hugh A. Dempsey
Glenbow Museum

Dempsey, Hugh A. *Crowfoot, Chief of the Blackfeet.* Norman: University of Oklahoma Press, 1972.

CROWS

The Crow people traditionally call themselves Apsaalooke or Absaroka, commonly translated as

Absaroke (Crow) boys playing with a lariat, ca. 1900–1925. Buffalo Bill Historical Center, Cody, Wyoming, Dr. William and Anna Petzoldt Collection. Gift of Genevieve Petzoldt Fitzgerald, Rev. W. A. Petzoldt, D.D., photographer. P.95.92

ety revolves is best understood in the Crow term for clan, *ashammaleaxia*, literally meaning "driftwood lodges." As an individual piece of driftwood has difficulty surviving the powerful eddies and boulders of the Yellowstone or Bighorn rivers, so too does an individual Crow have difficulty surviving the river of life, full of potential adversaries—formerly Lakotas and Blackfeet but now unemployment, substance abuse, and discrimination. But in tightly lodging itself with other pieces of driftwood along the riverbank, the driftwood is protected. So too is an individual Crow protected and nurtured when lodged securely in an extensive web of kinship ties. These are ties made up of both social and spiritual kinsmen and maintained through an extensive pattern of gift exchanges.

The values of ashammaleaxia are clearly evident in oral traditions, kinship relationships, and religious ceremonialism. The story of Burnt Face is an example. A young boy is badly scarred and subsequently ostracized. Burnt Face fasts for several days in the Big Horn Mountains. While on the mountain, he assembles the Big Horn Medicine Wheel as a gift to the Sun. Having given of himself, Burnt Face is adopted by the Little People, who remove his scar. He returns to his people and sub-

sequently becomes a great healer, having extended his kinship ties to the Little People.

Of all kinship relations, that of *aassahke*, or "clan uncle and aunt," is pivotal. A clan uncle or aunt is any male or female member of one's father's mother's clan. Such individuals are to be respected, and gifts of food and blankets are provided to them during giveaways. In return, aassahke bestow on a child an "Indian name," sing "praise songs" for accomplishments, and offer protective prayer.

The principles of ashammaleaxia are expressed in a sweat bath, a Catholic mass, a medicine bundle opening, a vision quest, a peyote meeting, and a Sun Dance. In each instance, individual prayer, the "gift" of sacrificing food and water, or the medicine power of a guardian spirit may be directed at a kinsmen in need. The last "buffalo days" Sun Dance was held in 1875, but with the assistance of the Shoshones, the Crows were again performing the Sun Dance by the 1940s. Today the Shoshone-Crow Sun Dance has become fully integrated into Crow family and religious life. As many as 120 men and women participate in a Sun Dance, several of which are held on the reservation during June and July. Along with the sponsor, each dancer has made a vow to the Creator or his or her own spirit guardian to go without food and water and "dry up" to help another. Typically, dances last three days. During the Sun Dance, individual participants offer prayer for family members, collective morning prayers are given for the welfare of all peoples, the sick are "doctored" by medicine men, and individual dancers may be given a vision.

The ravages of smallpox in the 1830s, the destruction of the bison, the confinement to a reservation in 1868, and its subsequent reduction by treaties and allotment in the late nineteenth and early twentieth centuries all contributed to a decrease in the population to a low of 1,625 by the early 1930s. With improved health care and economic opportunities, the enrolled Crow population had risen to 10,000 by 1998. The Crow Indian Reservation of some two million acres, of which nearly one-third is owned by non-Indians, is located in south-central Montana.

Electing not to adopt most of the specific provisions of the Indian Reorganization Act of 1934, the Crows wrote their own constitution in 1948. It established a general council government made up of every adult member of the tribe. The council elects four officers: a chairman, vice chairman, secretary, and vice secretary. It also establishes various governing committees that oversee such activities as land purchases, industrial development, housing, education, and tribal enrollment.

The resilience of the Crow people is partly the result of persistent great leadership, including that of Plenty Coups, Pretty Eagle, Medicine Crow, Robert Yellowtail, Angela Russell (a state senator), Bill Yellowtail (a state senator and regional director of the Environmental Protection Agency), and Janine Pease Pretty-on-Top (president of Little Big Horn College and a 1994 MacArthur Fellow).

Rodney Frey
University of Idaho

Frey, Rodney. *The World of the Crow Indians: As Driftwood Lodges.* Norman: University of Oklahoma Press, 1987. Hoxie, Frederick. *Parading through History: The Making of the Crow Nation in America, 1805–1933.* New York: Cambridge University Press, 1995. Linderman, Frank B. *Plenty-coups: Chief of the Crows.* 2nd ed. Lincoln: University of Nebraska Press, 2002. Linderman, Frank B. *Pretty-shield: Medicine Woman of the Crows.* 2nd ed. Lincoln: University of Nebraska Press, 2003. Lowie, Robert. *The Crow Indians.* 1935. Rev. ed. New York: Holt, Rinehart and Winston, 1956. Old Coyote, Henry, and Barney Old Coyote Jr. *The Way of the Warrior: Stories of the Crow People.* Lincoln: University of Nebraska Press, 2003. Snell, Alma Hogan. *Grandmother's Grandchild: My Crow Indian Life.* Lincoln: University of Nebraska Press, 2000.

CURTIS, CHARLES BRENT (1860–1936)

Charles Brent Curtis, who served as vice president of the United States from 1929 to 1933, was the first Native American to hold the office. He was born in what is now North Topeka, Kansas, on January 25, 1860. His mother was part Kaw, although he also claimed Indian ancestry through his grandfather's marriage to an Osage woman. In 1878 he was dropped from the Kaw annuity rolls because he neither lived on the reservation nor returned for annuity distribution, but he did legally remain a Kaw. He married Anna E. Baird in 1884. They had one son and two daughters.

An active Republican, Curtis was county attorney in Sherman County, Kansas, represented Kansas in the U.S. House of Representatives from 1892 to 1907, and served in the U.S. Senate from 1907 to 1913. After losing the election in 1912, he returned to the Senate in 1915 and rapidly rose in rank, acting as party whip and replacing Henry Cabot Lodge as majority leader in 1924. He was the first verifiable Native American elected to the Senate.

He held himself up as an example of assimilation. His opponents derisively nicknamed him "the Injun." While serving on the House Committee on Indian Affairs he earned a reputation as a friend of businesses hoping to profit from Indian land and mineral sales. In the House of Representatives he supported the General Allotment Act of 1887. In 1898 he authored the Curtis Act, which brought allotment to the Five Civilized Tribes of Oklahoma. The Curtis Act essentially served as an organic act for Oklahoma, providing for the survey and incorporation of towns, abolishing tribal courts and making all residents subject to federal law, and effectively dissolving the existing tribal governments. In 1889 he won reinstatement to the Kaw tribal rolls, and in 1902 he authored the Kaw Allotment Act, which formally terminated the Kaw government and granted 160-acre allotments to 249 persons, among them Charles Curtis and his children.

In the Senate he earned a reputation as a stalwart Republican, supporting the gold standard, high tariffs, the prohibition of alcohol, and immigration reform. He led the floor fight for the passage of the Nineteenth Amendment, granting women the right to vote. Although supported by railroad interests in Kansas, Curtis retained the support of farmers by consistently voting for the McNary-Haugan Act, which would have established the federal government as the nation's agricultural broker. He ultimately did vote to sustain President Calvin Coolidge's second veto of the bill, leading to its failure.

By this time he had grown less comfortable with post-allotment government relations with the tribes and even with the idea of assimilation itself. He grew to believe that the federal government could help Indians best by removing itself from their affairs.

Hoping to run for president himself, Curtis

bitterly fought Herbert Hoover's nomination, but Hoover won the candidacy on the first ballot. The party ran the farm-state Curtis to balance the ticket. He and Hoover remained estranged. Curtis proved less able as a vice president than as a senator. His term in office was undistinguished, ending with Hoover's defeat by Roosevelt in 1932. He died of a heart attack in Washington DC on February 8, 1936, and was buried in Topeka, Kansas.

Charles Vollan
South Dakota State University

Unrau, William E. *Mixed-Bloods and Tribal Dissolution: Charles Curtis and the Quest for Indian Identity.* Lawrence: University Press of Kansas, 1989.

DANCES WITH WOLVES

Kevin Costner's Academy Award–winning *Dances with Wolves* (1990) is a powerful cinematic reminder of the grandeur of the prairie that once spanned the heart of the North American continent. Although best known for its revisionist treatment of Indians (Lakota Sioux) in the last years of and just after the Civil War, *Dances with Wolves* offers many scenes that help convey the color, breadth, and vastness of the Great Plains. *Dances* was shot on location for five months in South Dakota, and the centerpiece of the film is an extended buffalo hunt during which Costner's character, Lt. John J. Dunbar, kills a wounded buffalo that threatens a young Sioux and is then informally initiated into the tribe. For the hunt, Costner took his actors and crew to a sixty-two-thousand-acre ranch northwest of Pierre, South Dakota. Holding 3,500 head of bison, the ranch offers visiting hunters the chance to shoot bison at $1,500 a head.

Exploiting wide-screen cinematography and an epic format more common to the 1950s and 1960s, *Dances* is a finely crafted film. The acting is outstanding in a genre not known for patient explorations of character; the cinematography of a reimagined Great Plains, cavalry blues, Sioux buckskin and face paint, and horses, wolf, and buffalo blend a wide-screen lushness with the austerity of a nature documentary; the editing is expert; and the gliding camera complements the restrained performances of all the actors. Many scenes and moments use little or no dialogue, encouraging attention to imagery, sound effects, and a now-alien aural environment. Early in the film, Dunbar silently brushes his hand across the waist-high grasses of the prairie. Later in the film, we see Kicking Bird (Grahame Greene) repeat the gesture. The parallelism provides a powerful evocation of the sublime force of the great prairie on people of the period. While classic Westerns had most often been set in valleys over which the Rockies towered or amidst the other-worldly landscapes

of Monument Valley, *Dances with Wolves* carefully and quietly evoked the grandeur of a more subtle geography, where muted earth tones and the big sky dominate.

In November 1993 ABC broadcast a longer version of *Dances* that incorporated footage left out of the original American theatrical release. Much of the material, nearly an hour long, expanded on themes established in the first film. More environmental destruction is seen. A white hunting camp on sacred Sioux grounds is strewn with animal carcasses and empty whisky bottles. The prior inhabitants of Fort Sedgewick are shown, isolated on the Plains and surrounded by Indians, the remainder of the command reduced to savage living in cliff-side dugouts—a dark contrast to Dunbar's successful transition to nature and Indian ways. A recent treatment of the "vanishing American" narrative, *Dances* ends, unsurprisingly, far above the Plains, with Dunbar and his bride, Stands with Fists, ascending a remote, snow-covered mountain, their tribe hunted by the army, the prairie no longer a refuge from accelerating encroachment.

Robert Baird
University of Illinois

Bird, Elizabeth S. *Dressing in Feathers: The Construction of the Indian in American Popular Culture.* Boulder CO: Westview Press, 1996. Blake, Michael. *Dances with Wolves.* New York: Ballantine, 1988. Rollins, Peter C., and John E. O'Connor, eds. *Hollywood's Indian: The Portrayal of the Native American in Film.* Lexington: University Press of Kentucky, 1998.

DAWES ACT

Formally titled the General Allotment Act of 1887, the Dawes Act (also commonly referred to as the Dawes Severalty Act) authorized the president of the United States to subdivide tribal reservations into private parcels of land that would then be "allotted" to individual members of each tribe. Designed to detribalize Indians and assimilate them into mainstream white society by transforming them into self-supporting farmers and ranchers, the Dawes Act became one of the most far-reaching and, for Native Americans, disastrous pieces of Indian legislation ever passed by Congress. By the time the allotment process was stopped in 1934, the amount of Indian-held land in the United States had dropped from 138 million acres to 48 million acres, and, of the remaining Indian-owned land, almost half was arid or semiarid desert.

Under the act, heads of families received quarter-section parcels of 160 acres, while other individuals were granted smaller tracts of up to 80 acres. Allotments deemed to be suitable only for grazing were doubled in size. Once the president directed that a particular reservation be broken up pursuant to the act, tribal members were given four years to select their specific allotment. If no such selection was made, the government made the selection for the individual. Each allotted tribal member received a patent, or trust deed, which provided that the United States would hold title to the land in trust for the benefit of the nominal Indian "owner" for a period of twenty-five years. Proponents of the legislation envisioned that during the trust period Indian allottees would adapt to the farming lifestyle and become increasingly self-reliant through the ownership and control of private property. Perhaps most significantly, the act further provided that tribal lands that were unallocated and therefore deemed "surplus" could be offered for sale to non-Indians, with the revenues to be held in trust by the government for the benefit of the tribes.

The Dawes Act affected reservations throughout the Great Plains, except in Indian Territory, which was not subject to allotment until the establishment of the Dawes Commission in 1893 and the passage of the Curtis Act in 1898. For example, the Devils Lake Sioux Reservation in North Dakota was allotted in 1904 over the objections of many of its residents. The allotments amounted to about 136,000 acres, leaving 92,000 surplus acres to be sold to non-Indians. It was through the allotment process that Plains reservations became "checkerboarded" in complex patterns of white-owned private property and Indian trust lands.

Most modern commentators concede that the proponents of the Dawes Act, including its primary legislative sponsor and namesake, Senator Henry L. Dawes of Massachusetts, were motivated by a sincere interest in the well-being and future prosperity of Native Americans. "Reformers" inside and outside the government viewed tribalism and traditional Indian cultural practices as impediments to the long-term survival and "advancement" of Native Americans—obstacles that could only be overcome by breaking up the reservations and forcing Indians to adopt a more "civilized" lifestyle. Other analysts insist that allotment was never intended to be anything more than a disingenuous legal cover for whites who coveted Indian lands. Whatever the appropriate interpretation of the motivations behind the Dawes Act, the allotment era that the act ushered in is today universally viewed as one of the darkest chapters in the annals of federal-Indian relations. Individual landownership was and is contrary to most traditional Native American beliefs and practices. Moreover, many Indians had no desire to become sedentary farmers and were woefully unprepared and ill equipped to succeed in that occupation even if they had wanted to. The value of the parcels of thousands of allottees was quickly dissipated or lost entirely through tax foreclosures, distressed sales, or unfavorable lease arrangements. Millions of surplus acres were sold or leased away by the government as well, and the ultimate effect of the allotment program was to separate Native Americans from millions of acres of their lands without accomplishing any of the "reforms" intended by the act's proponents.

Mark R. Scherer
University of Nebraska at Omaha

Prucha, Francis Paul. *The Great Father: The United States Government and the American Indians.* Lincoln: University of Nebraska Press, 1986. Washburn, Wilcomb. *The Assault on Indian Tribalism: The General Allotment Law (Dawes Act) of 1887.* Philadelphia: J. B. Lippincott, 1975. Wunder, John R. *Retained by the People: A History of American Indians and the Bill of Rights.* New York: Oxford University Press, 1994.

DELORIA, ELLA CARA (1889–1971)

Ella Cara Deloria, the Yankton Sioux linguist, ethnographer, and author, was born on January 31, 1889, to Mary Sully Bordeaux, the daughter of a Sioux woman and Gen. Alfred Sully, and Philip Deloria, an Episcopal minister from the prominent Deloria family. She spoke Dakota before she spoke English. She had two half-sisters from her father's previous marriages and two younger siblings—a brother, Vine Victor, later a prominent minister, and Susan Mabel, an artist.

Deloria attended the school at her father's mission on the Standing Rock Reservation and then at the All Saint's School in Sioux Falls, South Dakota. She attended three colleges—Oberlin (on scholarship); the University of Chicago; and the Teachers College at Columbia University, where she met the pioneering anthropologist Franz Boas, with whom she had a close professional relationship for the remainder of his life. He hired Deloria as a translator. She graduated with a bachelor of science degree in 1915 and returned to South Dakota. There she began teaching at the All Saint's School in 1915.

Deloria taught at All Saint's School until 1919, then toured the West as the YMCA health education secretary for Indian schools and reservations before taking a position teaching dance and physical education at the Haskell Indian School in Lawrence, Kansas. She resumed translation work for Boas in 1928, aided by her ability to speak all three Sioux dialects. She began to write scholarly works, beginning with "The Sun Dance of the Oglala Sioux," published by the *Journal of American Folklore* in 1929, and *Dakota Texts*, a collection of Sioux stories published in 1932.

Deloria studied the Navajos in 1938–39 for the Bureau of Indian Affairs, and later the Lumbee tribe of North Carolina. Throughout, she collaborated with Boas, publishing *Dakota Grammar* in 1941. When Boas died in 1942, she continued to work with his intellectual heir, Ruth Fulton Benedict, who suggested that Deloria focus on kinship networks and the role of women. Deloria translated a vast quantity of Sioux writings, many of which she had taken down in interviews herself. She won the Indian Achievement Award from the Indian Council Fire in Chicago, then the highest award an Indian could receive. She spent years working on a manuscript describing Dakota family life but never finished it. She published a shorter, popular version in 1944, titled *Speaking of Indians*, which examined historic and contemporary Sioux society and criticized both federal and church policies.

Deloria worked on a historical novel, *Waterlily*, about a young Dakota woman in the early contact era, basing it on twenty years of personal research and translation. She completed the manuscript in 1944, but at Benedict's urging shortened it by half. Deloria tried to interest publishers in the novel, but they uniformly turned her down.

She returned to St. Elizabeth's Mission Home in Wakpala, South Dakota, and taught there for three years. The University of South Dakota hired her as the assistant director of the W. H. Over Museum in 1961. Meanwhile, she worked on a Santee Sioux dictionary.

Deloria died at Wagner, South Dakota, on February 12, 1971, following a series of strokes. In 1988 the University of Nebraska Press published the edited version of her novel, *Waterlily*, to resounding critical success. Following its publication her often neglected work has received much greater interest, and her image as a mere disciple of Franz Boas has largely been replaced with an appreciation of her own true worth.

Charles Vollan
South Dakota State University

Finn, Janet L. "Walls and Bridges: Cultural Mediation and the Legacy of Ella Deloria." *Frontiers* 21 (2000): 158–82. Picotte, Agnes. "Biographical Sketch of the Author." In *Waterlily*, by Ella Cara Deloria, 229–32. Lincoln: University of Nebraska Press, 1988. Gardner, Susan. "Speaking of Ella Deloria: Conversations with Joyzelle Gingway Godfrey, 1998–2000, Lower Brule Community College, South Dakota." *American Indian Quarterly* 24 (2000): 456–75.

DELORIA, VINE, SR. (1901–1990)

Vine Deloria Sr. was the third in a family line of important Yankton Sioux Christian leaders. His paternal grandfather, Saswe, also known as François, had been a subchief and a holy person who adopted Christianity in the 1860s. His father, Philip Deloria, became a priest in the Episcopal Church in 1892 and operated the Standing Rock Mission until 1925. Vine Deloria Sr., born on October 6, 1901, near Wakpala, South Dakota, excelled athletically and academically. His early education came

Vine Deloria Sr., ca. 1980

at the St. Elizabeth's mission on Standing Rock Reservation, but following his mother's death in 1916, he attended the Kearney Military Academy, an Episcopal boarding school in Kearney, Nebraska. He graduated from St. Stephen's College (Episcopal), which later became Bard College. He served as an athletic coach at the Fort Sill Oklahoma Indian boarding school.

His father, Philip, close to retirement, encouraged the reluctant young man to enter the ministry, and Deloria enrolled at the Episcopal General Theological Seminary in New York City. Following his ordination as a deacon he was assigned to the Pine Ridge Mission. There he encountered both the prejudices of his church (he was paid half what a Caucasian classmate received for the same work) and Bishop Blair Roberts, a man with whom he fought for more than twenty years. Deloria's vision of Christianity had a decidedly synchronistic flavor, and his superiors did not always approve.

In 1932 he married Barbara Eastburn of New York and returned to Pine Ridge. They had three children. He led many mixed congregations over the next fourteen years. He moved well between Caucasian and Indian communities but found that the changes in Indian life brought about by the Indian New Deal, World War II, and federal "termination" policy had reduced both the power and appeal of Christianity to Indian peoples. Meanwhile the Episcopal Church reduced funding, closing many missions and chapels.

In 1949 the pressure from his many duties and his difficulties with his church and bishop caused him to suffer a breakdown, and he resigned from his position. From 1951 to 1954 he served in Iowa, in part to free himself from Bishop Roberts. He returned to the Indian missions in 1954 and made a national tour of reservations, but his plan to revitalize the Indian church ran counter to national policy, and he ceased to be an important voice in the church. Despite church acceptance of the termination policy, Deloria spent 1956 and 1957 in Washington DC lobbying against the legislation, even as he served as secretary for Indian work in the Episcopal Church. His superiors forced him out in 1957. He moved again to Iowa to preach but returned to South Dakota in 1961, serving as the archdeacon of South Dakota until his retirement in 1967. He also served as the vice chair of the Episcopal National Advisory Committee on Indian Work. Following retirement he taught courses at Huron College, then relocated to Arizona in 1986, increasingly disillusioned with his own church's program to attract and maintain believers. He died in Tucson, Arizona, on February 26, 1990. His sister, Ella Cara Deloria, was a noted linguist and author. His son, Vine Deloria Jr., was one of the nation's foremost Indian scholars, authors, and educators.

Charles Vollan
South Dakota State University

Deloria, Philip J. "Vine V. Deloria Sr." In *The New Warriors: Native American Leaders Since 1900*, edited by R. David Edmunds, 75–95. Lincoln: University of Nebraska Press, 2001. Deloria, Vine, Jr. *Singing for a Spirit: A Portrait of the Dakota Sioux*. Santa Fe: Clear Light Publishers, 1999.

Dull Knife (Wo'he Hiv)

DULL KNIFE (CA. 1810–1883)

Dull Knife was born in the rugged mountain country of Montana's Rosebud Valley at the beginning of the nineteenth century and died there near century's end. In between, the trajectory of his life encompassed the full sweep of Indian experience in the nineteenth-century Northern Great Plains: warrior, chief, signatory to the Fort Laramie Treaty, statesman, reservation citizen, Cheyenne Outbreak leader, hunted quarry, starving survivor, tribal elder.

To his people, the Northern Cheyennes, he was called Wo'he Hiv', or Morning Star. As a boy, it is said that he showed uncommon bravery and leadership. As a young man, he joined in raids against the Crows, Arikaras, Snakes, and Shoshones, earning a reputation for fierceness and courage. On December 21, 1866, he and Lakota war chief Crazy Horse led a decoy party that helped wipe out Capt. William J. Fetterman and all eighty-one of his men. But not long afterward he began to believe war against the whites was hopeless. A gifted orator and skilled negotiator, he visited the forts, talked to the soldiers, and attended peace parleys, looking for a way out for his people.

In 1868 he was among the chiefs who signed the Treaty of Fort Laramie, agreeing he would never again "sharpen his knife" against the whites. Dull Knife, as he became known, kept his word. Col. George A. Woodward, commander of Fort Fetterman, recalled an 1871 visit to the fort: "Of the three head-men of the Cheyennes, Dull Knife was, I think, greatly the superior. . . . His manner of speech was earnest and dignified, and his whole bearing was that of a leader with the cares of state."

In June 1876, while others left for the Little Bighorn, Dull Knife stayed in his camp a few miles southwest of the battle. Exactly five months after the Custer fight, a surprise predawn army attack wiped out much of his village. On April 21, 1877, after a winter sharing meager supplies in Crazy Horse's camp, Dull Knife and 553 of his people surrendered at Fort Robinson, Nebraska.

Five weeks later, Dull Knife and his Northern Cheyennes were forcibly marched to a reservation in Indian Territory. After a year enduring starvation, disease, death, and acute homesickness, Dull Knife and Little Wolf, another chief and the tribe's most capable warrior, decided to lead about three hundred of their people north on a one-thousand-mile freedom fight back to their Montana homeland. They left on September 9, 1878. Six weeks and more than five hundred miles later—exhausted, hungry, cold, an estimated two thousand troops in pursuit—they had made it deep into the Sandhills of northwest Nebraska, where the chiefs made a decision: Little Wolf and the stronger ones would continue to Montana; Dull Knife and the weaker ones would look for Red Cloud's nearby camp.

On October 23, the cavalry caught up with the weaker group, marching Dull Knife and 148 prisoners on a twenty-eight-mile trek to Fort Robinson. The post commander, Capt. Henry Wessells, told Dull Knife and four subchiefs on January 3, 1879, that a decision had been made: the Northern Cheyennes must return immediately to their Indian Territory reservation. "I am here on my own ground," Dull Knife replied, "and I will never go back. You may kill me here, but you cannot make me go back." On January 5, Wessells ordered all food and heating fuel withheld from the defiant Northern Cheyennes. Two days later, he cut off the water supply. Still, Dull Knife and his people refused to leave their barracks.

Shortly before 10 p.m. on the evening of January 9, with the temperature below zero and half a foot of snow on the ground, the Northern Cheyennes broke out of the barracks, fleeing for the protective bluffs across the White River. Skirmishes between the Northern Cheyennes and cavalry troops continued for two weeks. When the shooting ended on January 23, thirty-nine Northern Cheyenne men and twenty-five women and children had been killed. Dull Knife was not among them. He and several family members eventually made it to the safety of Pine Ridge Agency about sixty miles away, surviving the last few nights by eating the soles of their moccasins.

Later that year Dull Knife, then about seventy, was allowed to return to Montana. In November he rejoined Little Wolf, who—after a journey of seven months and more than one thousand miles—had made it safely back. Dull Knife died of natural causes in his Rosebud Valley homeland in 1883. About a year later, on March 26, 1884, the U.S. government officially set aside a tract of Montana land as the permanent home of the Northern Cheyennes.

Joe Starita
University of Nebraska–Lincoln

Starita, Joe. *The Dull Knifes of Pine Ridge: A Lakota Odyssey.* New York: Putnam, 1995.

EARTH LODGES

The earth lodge was the dominant dwelling of Central and Northern Great Plains village Indians. Earth lodges were circular, dome-shaped dwellings with heavy timber superstructures mantled by thick layers of earth. The type emerged in the 1500s and persisted into the reservation era. Tribes most frequently associated with earth lodge architecture include the Mandans, Hidatsas, Arikaras, Pawnees, Otoes, Kansas, Omahas, and Poncas, although several other groups also adopted the style.

The origins of the earth lodge are not entirely clear, although it was certainly a Northern Plains innovation. Between 1000 and 1400 AD, horticultural villagers in the Central Plains built square houses. During the same time, Northern Plains villagers constructed rectangular structures. Although these types of houses are frequently called earth lodges, they were not; rather, they were vertical walled with thin coverings of wattle and daub or thatch. A few oval to circular structures appeared in northern Nebraska and central South Dakota in the 1400s, but their floor plans do not reflect the fully developed earth lodge style. The earliest true earth lodges were built in central North Dakota and northern South Dakota Missouri River villages in the early 1500s by the ancestors of the Mandans and Arikaras. The earth lodges were thicker and more insulated than the earlier square or rectangular dwellings and were a response to the cooling temperatures of the Neoboreal ("Little Ice Age") climatic regime.

The Mandans, Hidatsas, and Arikaras all constructed earth lodges in the sixteenth century. This architectural style rapidly diffused from the upper Missouri as additional sedentary tribes migrated onto the Plains from the south and east and adopted the form. To the south the Pawnees were firmly established in central Nebraska by 1600 and living in earth lodge villages. Archaeological and ethnohistorical evidence establishes that the Otoes, Omahas, and Poncas were living in earth lodge villages on the eastern margins of the Central Plains by 1700. The Cheyennes briefly adopted earth lodge architecture in the mid–eighteenth century during their occupancy of eastern North Dakota. Some circular floorplan structures encountered by archeologists working at seventeenth- and eighteenth-century villages of Central Plains tribes such as the Wichitas and Kansas are most likely not earth lodges but grass- or thatch-covered houses. Mississippian sites in the southeastern United States occasionally yield earth lodge–type ceremonial structures. The most fully documented are at Ocmulgee National Monument, Georgia. The relationship, if any, between these and the Plains dwellings is unclear.

Earth lodge construction began with the excavation of a shallow circular area typically less than one foot in depth with a diameter varying between twenty and sixty feet. Heavy vertical timbers served

Interior of Hairy Coat's lodge, an Arikara earth lodge, Fort Berthold, North Dakota, 1910

as central roof supports. The Northern Plains earth lodges almost always had four center posts. The Pawnees, Omahas, Otoes, and other Central Plains tribes used four, six, eight, ten, and even twelve center posts. Center posts were forked at the top and connected by horizontal beams. A secondary row of posts was set around the perimeter of the floor pit several feet inside the wall. These were shorter than the center posts but also connected at the top by a series of horizontal cross-stringers. A series of closely spaced sloping posts spanned the area from the top of the stringers to the ground outside the house pit. Rafters extended in spoke-like fashion from the top of the wall stringers to the horizontal beams connecting the center posts. The rafters did not extend across the full radius of the house in order to allow room for construction of a fireplace smoke hole. Thatching and then layers of thick sod and grass covered the sturdy superstructure. A sloping or vertical-walled short entry passage extended from one side of the lodge, typically the south or east.

Interior features included a central fire basin, one or more deep food storage chambers, and altars. Storage chambers were bell-shaped, narrow at the lodge floor and expanding to three to five feet at their bases, and were five to eight feet deep. Such pits were later used for trash disposal. The Hidatsas called the space between the outer vertical posts and the exterior leaners an *atuti*. This area was used for placement of beds and storage of firewood, tools, weapons, and other personal items. Beds were either on the ground or on elevated platforms. Sleeping quarters were generally on the ledge between the outside of the house pit and the edge of the leaners. The central portion of the earth lodge was used for food preparation and social activities. The back wall opposite the entry passage often featured an altar or sacred area. One or more extended families occupied the earth lodge, which could house up to sixty people. Villages consisted of at least a dozen earth lodges and in many cases of more than a hundred. It was not uncommon for villages to be home to several thousand people. Earth lodges were often closely spaced, and during times of conflict an earth or timber fortification wall surrounded the community.

The earth lodge formed the central focus of many aspects of Plains horticultural village life. For some tribes, at least, the structures held important symbolic religious, astronomical, and social significance. In Pawnee cosmology the earth lodge was symbolically considered the heavens. Mandan and Hidatsa lodges also had sacred symbolism attached to them, and special earth lodges were reserved for ceremonial activities such as the Mandan Okipa (a four-day ceremony of renewal).

John R. Bozell
Nebraska State Historical Society

Ahler, Stanley A., Thomas D. Thiessen, and Michael K. Trimble. *People of the Willows: The Prehistory and Early History of the Hidatsa Indians.* Grand Forks: University of North Dakota Press, 1991. Nabokov, Peter, and Robert Easton. *Native American Architecture.* New York: Oxford University Press, 1989. Wilson, Gilbert L. "The Hidatsa Earthlodge." *Anthropological Papers of the American Museum of Natural History* 33 (1934).

EASTMAN, CHARLES (1858–1939)

Dr. Charles Alexander Eastman (Ohiyesa) devoted his entire life to helping Native Americans. He believed that Indians could retain their beliefs, but they also needed to selectively adopt non-Indian ways in order to function in the dominant culture. This was the message he often presented in his lecturers and his eleven books and numerous articles. Elaine Goodale Eastman, his non-Indian wife, assisted him in his publications.

Eastman was born near Redwood Falls, Minnesota, on February 19, 1858, and raised in the traditional manner of a Santee Sioux hunter and

Dr. Charles A. Eastman (Ohiyesa), ca. 1920

warrior. His life drastically changed at age fifteen, when his recently Christianized father convinced Eastman to join him at Flandreau, Dakota Territory, and enroll in Flandreau Mission School. For the next seventeen years Eastman attended a number of schools, including Santee Normal Training School and Dartmouth College, ultimately receiving his medical degree from Boston University School of Medicine in 1890.

His first of several government appointments was as Indian physician at Pine Ridge Agency, South Dakota (1890–93), where he witnessed the massacre at Wounded Knee. Other government positions were outing agent at Carlisle Indian Industrial School, Pennsylvania (1899), Indian physician at Crow Creek Agency, South Dakota (1900–1903), head of the project to revise the Sioux allotment rolls (1903–9), and Indian inspector (1923–25). At times, he clashed with his white superiors regarding policies. His nongovernment work included a brief medical practice in St. Paul, Minnesota (1893), serving as Indian secretary of the International Committee of the YMCA (1894–98), and representing Santee Sioux claims in Washington DC. For several years, the Eastman family ran a summer camp near Munsonville, New Hampshire.

As an active Indian reformer, Eastman helped found and later served as president of the Society of American Indians. He condemned reservation conditions, supported Indian citizenship, and called for the abolition of the Bureau of Indian Affairs. In his final years, Eastman continued to present lectures and worked with the YMCA and Boy Scouts of America and on several research projects. In 1933 he was awarded the first Indian Council Fire Medal for his lifelong work in addressing Indian and white relations. Eastman died in Detroit, Michigan, on January 8, 1939.

Raymond Wilson
Fort Hays State University

Eastman, Charles Alexander (Ohiyesa). *From the Deep Woods to Civilization: Chapters in the Autobiography of an Indian.* Lincoln: University of Nebraska Press, 1977. Eastman, Charles Alexander (Ohiyesa). *Indian Boyhood.* New York: Dover Publications, 1971. Eastman, Charles Alexander (Ohiyesa). *Indian Heroes and Great Chieftains.* Lincoln: University of Nebraska Press, 1991. Eastman, Charles Alexander (Ohiyesa). *Old Indian Days.* Lincoln: University of Nebraska Press, 1991. Eastman, Charles Alexander (Ohiyesa). *The Soul of an Indian: An Interpretation.* Lincoln: University of Nebraska Press, 1980. Wilson, Raymond. *Ohiyesa: Charles Eastman, Santee Sioux.* Urbana: University of Illinois Press, 1983.

ECHO-HAWK, WALTER, JR. (B. 1948)

Pawnee attorney, author, and painter Walter Echo-Hawk was born on June 23, 1948, in the Indian hospital near Pawnee, Oklahoma. He is from the Kitkahahaki band of the Pawnees. He earned a bachelor of science degree in political science from Oklahoma State University in 1970. Motivated by the Indian rights movement of the 1960s and 1970s, he enrolled in the Indian law program at the University of New Mexico and followed his cousin, attorney John Echo-Hawk, to the newly established Native American Rights Fund (NARF), where he clerked. In 1973 after his graduation and passage of the Colorado bar exam he joined NARF as an attorney.

One of the most active and successful Native American lawyers in America, Echo-Hawk has pursued cases throughout the nation but has concentrated on the Pawnees and their battles with the states of Nebraska, Kansas, and Oklahoma. With a focus on religious freedom, prisoner rights, hunting and fishing rights, and burial rights, he used the courts, legislatures, and popular public opinion to confirm Indian sovereignty in crucial areas. His first case for NARF, *Indian Inmates of the Nebraska Penal and Correctional Complex v. Vitek*, won the prisoners the right of access to state-paid spiritual leaders, as well as the right to assemble for educational courses. Other cases addressed the right to wear long hair, to use peyote in Native American Church ceremonies, and to keep sacred objects, such as cedar and sage, in their cells. He and NARF also worked to address more general issues, such as prison overcrowding and censorship of mail.

Echo-Hawk participated in the struggle over peyote use in Oregon and appeared before the U.S. Supreme Court when that court ruled that states could criminalize peyote use, regardless of its re-ligious application. Echo-Hawk and NARF led the effort that culminated in the 1994 passage of the American Indian Religious Freedom Act, which nationally legalized the sacred use of peyote.

His interest in the protection of Native American religious practices extended to the issue of grave protection. For hundreds of years private individuals, museums, universities, and various government entities routinely dug up Native American graves. In doing so they amassed vast collections of human remains and sacred objects. Their resistance to returning them to Indian claimants led Echo-Hawk and NARF to work first at the state level and then at the federal level to win protection of Native American grave sites. The first victory came when Echo-Hawk served as representative of the Pawnee and Winnebago tribes, lobbying the Nebraska State legislature to enact a graves repatriation act and suing the Nebraska State Historical Society for access to its records. Several other states adopted repatriation laws before the U.S. Congress passed the Native American Graves Protection and Repatriation Act in 1990. Echo-Hawk considers graves protection and repatriation his most important work. He also worked to protect sacred artifacts by lobbying for the National Museum of the American Indian Act.

Echo-Hawk has served as a judge on the Pawnee Supreme Court. He has also authored several essays, studies, and a book, *Battlefields and Burial Grounds: The Indian Struggle to Protect Ancestral Graves in the U.S.* (1994). He is married and has three children.

Charles Vollan
South Dakota State University

Echo-Hawk, Roger, and Walter Echo-Hawk. *Battlefields and Burial Grounds: The Indian Struggle to Protect Ancestral Graves in the U.S.* Minneapolis: Lerner, 1994. Quade, Vicki. "Who Owns the Past? Interview with Walter Echo-Hawk." *Human Rights* 63 (winter 1989–90): 24–29, 53–55. Wunder, John. "Walter Echo-Hawk." In *The New Warriors: Native American Leaders Since 1900*, edited by R. David Edmunds, 299–321. Lincoln: University of Nebraska Press, 2001.

ECUERACAPA (D. 1793)

Ecueracapa (Leather Cape) was the name the Spaniards of late-eighteenth-century New Mexico gave to the principal chief of the Kotsoteka Comanches. His Comanche name was apparently Koontyta'nikypa'a, or "Crane on a Stake," but he was also called Cota de Malla (or Maya), "Coat of Mail." This latter citation has led to continuing confusion between the New Mexican Ecueracapa and at least two Texas Comanches also called Cota de Malla.

Ecueracapa first came to the attention of the New Mexican Spaniards in late 1785 when, after peace had been concluded with the Texas

Comanches, Governor Juan Bautista de Anza managed to open communication with the western Comanches. They sent word that Ecueracapa, the "captain most distinguished as much by his skill and valor in war as by his adroitness and intelligence in political matters," was empowered to enter into negotiations, which were conducted in early 1786. In June 1786 a formal agreement was signed at Pecos Pueblo marking the beginning of a Comanche–New Mexican peace that endured until 1821.

In the following years, Ecueracapa appears a number of times in the historical record. In May 1787 he forestalled retaliation against some Jupe Comanche youths who had stolen Spanish horses, and in early 1790 he was involved in an ill-planned joint Spanish-Comanche expedition against the Pawnees. In 1793 Ecueracapa was "grievously wounded" on a campaign against the Pawnees. He probably died sometime that fall.

Thomas W. Kavanaugh
Indiana University

Kavanagh, Thomas W. *Comanche Political History: An Ethnohistorical Perspective, 1706–1875.* Lincoln: University of Nebraska Press, 1996.

ERDRICH, LOUISE (B. 1954)

Louise Erdrich

Since 1984, when she published the collection of poems *Jacklight*, Louise Erdrich has stood out as one of the more captivating and original voices not only in Native American literary circles but also in contemporary American literature generally. Erdrich's popular and critical success stems from her ability to craft evocative narratives that draw heavily on oral storytelling traditions and other aspects of Native American culture.

Born in Little Falls, Minnesota, in 1954, and raised in Wahpeton, North Dakota, Erdrich is a member of the Turtle Mountain band of the Anishinaabe (Chippewas), but she also has German-immigrant roots. She has drawn on these two traditions in her fiction while examining the challenges of coming to terms with mixed ancestry and celebrating the vitality of Chippewa history, culture, tradition, and community in the face of European American intrusion. Drawing on storytelling traditions of the Chippewas, Erdrich repeatedly constructs fictions that employ multiple narrators, including a dog in *The Antelope Wife* (1998), and span several generations, producing what one writer has called a "layered" point of view. But if her narrative style appears nonlinear and disjointed to the reader, what readily emerges is Erdrich's strong sense of place. These stylistic and thematic features have prompted critics and reviewers to compare Erdrich's North Dakota landscape to Nobel Prize–winning author William Faulkner's Yoknapatawpha County, especially as they emerge in her well-known tetralogy (*Love Medicine*, 1984; *The Beet Queen*, 1986; *Tracks*, 1988; *The Bingo Palace*, 1995; and *The Antelope Wife*, 1998), which focuses on three Chippewa families and others on and around the reservation. Erdrich does not shy away from difficult issues such as alcoholism and broken families that confront Native communities; however, by infusing her tales with humor, folklore, and spirituality, Erdrich treats her subjects with both compassion and sensitivity.

Philip R. Coleman-Hull
Bethany College

Bruchac, Joseph. *Survival This Way: Interviews with American Indian Poets.* Tucson: University of Arizona Press, 1987. Smith, Jeanne Rosier. *Writing Tricksters: Mythic Gambols in American Ethnic Literature.* Berkeley: University of California Press, 1997.

EX PARTE CROW DOG

In 1883 the U.S. Supreme Court rendered a decision in *Ex Parte Crow Dog* that reaffirmed a basic promise of federal law as it dealt with the Native American nations: that these nations are political sovereigns and have a right to be ruled by their own law in their own land. Within three years the same Court would break that promise, just as the political branches of the government had broken treaties. Nevertheless, *Ex Parte Crow Dog* remains a foundational case for the tradition of legal pluralism that is today manifested in the laws and institutions of Native American sovereigns.

On the afternoon of August 5, 1881, Kangi Sunka (Crow Dog) shot and killed Sinte Gleska (Spotted Tail) on a road in the Rosebud Indian Agency on the Great Sioux Reservation in Dakota Territory. Both men were respected among the Brulé Lakota. At the time of his death Spotted Tail was attempting to maintain a homeland for his people as both a traditional chief and a leader recognized by the Bureau of Indian Affairs (BIA). Crow Dog had ridden with Crazy Horse yet also served several terms as a BIA-appointed chief of Brulé police. The complex forces of culture and politics that pitted these two men as enemies remain a mystery. The facts of their encounter are still disputed: was it assassination or self-defense?

After the death of Spotted Tail the tribal council met and, following Brulé law, sent peacemakers to both families to restore harmony and order. The families agreed to a payment of $600 and gifts of eight horses and one blanket, which were quickly delivered to Spotted Tail's people. Nevertheless, in contravention of prior policy that had honored Native American self-government, Henry Lelar, the acting agent at Rosebud, ordered the arrest of Crow Dog. He was quickly arrested and imprisoned at Fort Niobrara, Nebraska.

Crow Dog's trial in federal court, Dakota Territory, was tainted by strong anti-Indian prejudice. The lead prosecution witness, Agent John Cook, was in Chicago when the killing occurred, but he testified to Crow Dog's political animosity. Crow Dog, ably represented by attorney A. J. Plowman, was allowed to present his claim of self-defense, but Pretty Camp, his wife and an eyewitness, was not allowed to testify. Moreover, there is unsettling evidence of perjury. But all of this factual controversy is beside the point. The claim of federal jurisdiction, the legal power to make and apply law for Indian-to-Indian matters within Indian Country, is the crux of the matter, and the conviction and death sentence given Crow Dog brought the issue to the Supreme Court.

By writ of habeas corpus Crow Dog urged the Supreme Court to deny federal jurisdiction in the matter. At the same time, the BIA and the prosecution, which had orchestrated the arrest and trial as part of a plan conceived as early as 1874 to extend federal law into Indian Country, argued that treaties and statutes provided federal jurisdiction. The federal government made the following argument: section 5339 of the *Revised Statutes* provides for the death penalty for any murder within the jurisdiction of the United States; title 28 extends the general law of the United States to Indian Country, but it has an exception for crimes committed by one Indian against another Indian; that exception was repealed by the treaty of Fort Laramie (1868), which provided that "bad men among the Indians" shall be delivered to the United States; and the act of 1877 (Congress had prohibited further treaty

making with Native Americans in 1871) provides that Congress shall "secure to [the Sioux Nations] an orderly government; [and] they shall be subject to the laws of the United States."

The Supreme Court rejected the government's argument, stating that such an understanding would reverse an unbroken policy of respect for Native American sovereignty. First, if "bad men" were not delivered, the treaty called for deductions from annuities due the Lakotas; thus it could not mean "bad men" who acted against other Sioux. Second, the statutory promise of "orderly government" meant a pledge of self-government for the Sioux. Finally, to be "subject to the laws of the United States" meant subject to the power of Congress to make federal Indian law for distribution of sovereignty between Native Americans and the United States, not subject as individuals to the generality of federal law. Crow Dog was granted his release.

Crow Dog returned to the Rosebud Agency. He remained a leader among the Brulé, taking Ghost Dancers into the Badlands in 1890 and refusing an allotment until 1910. The BIA repeatedly sought his removal from the Rosebud Agency. He died there in 1912.

Yet *Ex Parte Crow Dog* was tainted by racism. Its concluding language referred to Native Americans living a "savage life" and having a "savage nature," and it described Native American law as the "red man's revenge." This played into the hands of the Interior Department and the BIA, which had since the late 1870s urged Congress to pass a statute extending federal law to Indian-on-Indian crimes within Indian Country. Two years after *Ex Parte Crow Dog*, Congress passed the Major Crimes Act of 1885. The act cut deeply into the promises of self-government and sovereignty by creating federal jurisdiction over seven enumerated crimes when committed by one Indian against another Indian. (Today the statute covers fourteen crimes.)

A year later, in *United States v. Kagama* (1886), the Supreme Court upheld the legality of the act. The Court found a "duty of protection" arising from the "weakness and helplessness" of the Native Americans that granted Congress power despite the lack of any constitutional authority. Civilization was brought to Indian Country in the form of punishment, retribution, violence, and isolation of wrongdoers. The plenary power of Congress over Native American affairs was affirmed, and the people witnessed again the fragile nature of legal promises.

John Rockwell Snowden
University of Nebraska–Lincoln

Harring, Sidney L. *Crow Dog's Case.* Cambridge: Cambridge University Press, 1994.

Marguerite LaFlesche Diddock, a field matron for the Office of Indian Affairs from 1896 to 1900

Field matrons worked for the U.S. Bureau of Indian Affairs (BIA) between 1890 and 1938 in a campaign designed to introduce Native American women to Victorian, middle-class culture. Like the destruction of the collective land base by allotment, the disruption of families by the removal of children to Indian schools, and the steady diminution of sovereignty by federal encroachments, the domestic education of Native American women became, in the hands of the field matrons, yet another tool to destroy tribalism. Convinced that it was possible to "kill the Indian and save the woman [*sic*]," the BIA looked to the field matrons to promote assimilation in reservation communities across the American West.

By the last decades of the nineteenth century, Canadian and American policymakers and reform advocates active in Indian affairs agreed that wholesale "civilization" was the only way to ensure the survival of those remaining Native populations located in the western provinces and states. Only in the United States, though, did a woman-specific assimilation strategy develop. To teach Indian women "to respect and love and seek the ways of White women," the BIA worked with members of Congress, reformers, and missionary activists to create the field matron program.

Sent into the field in 1890, the field matrons eventually worked in nearly every tribal community in the Great Plains, as well as across the West. Those women first employed by the BIA in the late nineteenth century exemplified the era's "certified civilizers." Caucasian, middle-class, and single, they were imbued with Christian missionary spirit. As field matrons they spread among the Indians the American gospel of cleanliness, godliness, corsets, femininity, homebound domesticity, and woman's proper sphere. In the early twentieth century, however, the composition of the group changed. The American women becoming field matrons after 1900 coupled their reformist ambition to "do good" with their personal desire to "do well" financially as BIA employees. From the end of World War I until 1938, women motivated by economic gain rather than rescue dominated the field matron corps.

While the BIA heartily encouraged Native women to become advocates for assimilation in their homes and communities, it only reluctantly included them as full partners in the field matron program. The same ethnocentrism that skewed American and Canadian perspectives on Indian traditionalism resulted in restrictions on the employment of "civilized" tribal women. The BIA rarely accepted Native adoptions of the "American way" as trustworthy because, at base, it was deeply suspicious of the very process of cultural change it hoped to promote. The agency restricted tribal women to the position of assistant field matron and only appointed them between 1895 and 1905. Most of these women served in tribal communities located in the Great Plains.

The decision to phase out the field matron program in the 1930s reflected both the waning significance of Victorian domesticity and the desperate need in reservation communities for medical expertise. Appalling public health conditions plagued Native Americans in both the United States and Canada during the late nineteenth and early twentieth centuries. In the United States, tuberculosis and trachoma ran rampant; infant and child morbidity and mortality robbed tribal communities of their future generations; and destitution revealed itself in malnutrition and hopelessness. Field matrons struggled to adapt their positions by teaching seminars on epidemic diseases and prenatal care instead of homemaking. Their efforts saved lives but also led the BIA to conclude that trained nurses were more valuable than assimilation advocates. After 1938 field nurses replaced field matrons as "civilization" took a backseat to Indian public health education and care in the United States.

Lisa E. Emmerich
California State University–Chico

Bannan, Helen M. "'True Womanhood on the Reservation': Field Matrons in the United States Indian Service." *SIROW* Working Paper no. 19. Tucson: University of Arizona, 1984. Emmerich, Lisa E. "'Right in the Midst of My Own People': Native American

Women and the Field Matron Program." *American Indian Quarterly* 15 (1990): 201–16. Emmerich, Lisa E. "'To Respect and Love and Seek the Ways of White Women': Field Matrons, the Office of Indian Affairs, and Civilization Policy, 1890–1938," PhD diss., University of Maryland, 1987.

FISHER, TE ATA (1895–1995)

Te Ata Fisher was a storyteller, dancer, and singer who spread Native American legends and stories throughout the world. Her father was part Choctaw and Chickasaw. Her mother might have been part Osage. The family did not follow traditional Choctaw or Chickasaw culture or religion, but her father taught her traditional stories that motivated Te Ata throughout her career.

She was born Mary Frances Thompson on December 3, 1895, in Emet, Indian Territory, within the Chickasaw Nation. As a young child her aunt gave her the name Te Ata, which she said meant "Bearer of the Dawn," although the words do not appear to be Chickasaw. She liked the name and used it for the rest of her life. She enrolled in the Oklahoma College for Women in 1915, the school's first Native American student. There she met her mentor, Frances Dinsmore Davis, who encouraged her to focus on her theatrical ability and suggested she base her senior performance on Indian folklore. Te Ata determined to correct stereotypical views of Native Americans as violent and unsuited to modern life. She stressed authenticity but altered the material to fit the tastes of her non-Indian audiences.

Rather than focus on her Choctaw and Chickasaw heritage, of which she knew relatively little, she presented stories from several tribes, such as the Pawnees and the Kiowas, using both anthropological sources and Indian-inspired music and poetry written by non-Indians, such as Longfellow's "Hiawatha." She adopted the traditional dress of numerous tribes because they appeared more authentic than the Calico dresses her Choctaw and Chickasaw forebears had worn for generations.

In 1919 she met members of the University of Nebraska music department faculty and joined a Chautauqua troop they organized to tour the nation. She took graduate courses in performance at the Carnegie Institute of Technology in Pittsburgh. In 1921 she moved to New York City, acting on Broadway and pursuing modeling roles before rejecting both to focus on individual stage performances in the late 1920s. She cultivated friendships with influential people, including Eleanor Roosevelt and Ann Morgan and Mrs. Morgan Hamilton, sisters of financier J. P. Morgan.

As a folklorist Te Ata concentrated on children, believing that they were the best hope for changing the stereotypical view of Native Americans. With support from influential and wealthy friends she toured Europe. She also met her future husband, Clyde Fisher, already married and seventeen years her senior. They married in 1933.

Te Ata achieved rapid success. Her friendship with Eleanor Roosevelt resulted in a 1933 performance at the White House. In 1937 she performed at Roosevelt's Hyde Park estate for England's royal family.

Te Ata and Fisher, both committed to their careers, spent much of their sixteen-year marriage apart. Clyde died in 1949. She remained an active performer until the 1970s. She returned to live in Oklahoma in 1968. Her home state had already honored her by including her in the Oklahoma Hall of Fame in 1957. She was the subject of a 1975 documentary, *God's Drum* (expanded in 1995), and appeared on the *Today Show* in 1976. In 1987 the Oklahoma Arts Council chose her as the state's first "Oklahoma Treasure." In 1989 she collaborated with Lynn Moroney to produce the children's book *Baby Rattlesnake*. She was inducted into the Chickasaw Nation Hall of Fame in 1991. She died in Oklahoma City on October 26, 1995, nearly one hundred years old.

Charles Vollan
South Dakota State University

Fisher, Te Ata, and Lynn Moroney. *Baby Rattlesnake*. San Francisco: Children's Book Press, 1989. Green, Richard. *Te Ata: Chickasaw Storyteller, American Treasure*. Norman: University of Oklahoma Press, 2002. Olivia, Judy Lee. "Te Ata—Chickasaw Indian Performer: From Broadway to Back Home." *Theatre History Studies* 15 (1995): 3–26.

FORT LARAMIE TREATY OF 1868

The Fort Laramie Treaty of 1868 was one of the last major treaties between the United States and the tribes of the Northern Great Plains and a late example of the "concentration" policy, which sought to end Indian resistance and gain territory by forcing Indian nations to live on small, well-defined reservations, where they were to be rapidly indoctrinated in American social and economic ways.

Following a series of massacres of Indians and defeats by American troops, Congress established the U.S. Indian Peace Commission. In theory the Peace Commission was charged with establishing treaties that removed reasons for Indian anger (and causes of war), while peacefully reducing their territory and forcing them to accept American-style civilization. It was an impossible task, for the treaties and land loss were major reasons for tribal discontent. After a failed attempt to negotiate on the Northern Plains, the commission met at Medicine Lodge in Kansas, producing major treaties with the Kiowas, Arapahos, Cheyennes, and Comanches in the summer of 1867.

Moving north, the commission signed treaties with the Northern Arapahos, Northern Cheyennes, the Crows, and representatives from most of the Sioux bands by early May 1868, but the Oglala Sioux proved less willing to sign. Opposition came from two major groups aligned under Red Cloud and Sitting Bull. The commission asked Father Pierre-Jean De Smet to meet on the Powder River with the faction led by Sitting Bull that had refused to sign. De Smet convinced a number of Sitting Bull's followers to come in (although not Sitting Bull himself), and they signed on July 2. Red Cloud refused to sign until the United States abandoned Forts Phil Kearny, Fetterman, and C. F. Smith, which protected the Bozeman Trail to the Montana gold fields. The Sioux believed the road and trail violated the earlier 1851 Treaty of Fort Laramie. Red Cloud, considered hostile but indispensable by the Americans, signed in November after being given assurances that the forts would be dismantled. All evidence shows that he considered this to be the main purpose of the treaty. The tribe celebrated it as a great victory over the United States, but the approaching Union Pacific Railroad had made the trail unnecessary.

While the Western Sioux viewed the treaty as being over the issue of forts, it contained provisions that forever eroded Sioux sovereignty and drastically altered their lifestyle. By signing the treaty, the Sioux further reduced their territory beyond the boundaries established in the 1851 treaty. The treaty had seventeen articles, listing Sioux and American responsibilities. It called for an end to war. It established a procedure to punish Americans who committed crimes against Indians and Indians who did the same against Americans. It created the Great Sioux Reservation in what is now South Dakota west of the Missouri River but also recognized an ill-defined region as unceded territory to the north of the North Platte River and east of the summit of the Big Horn Mountains. It acknowledged Sioux hunting rights, as long as the game should justify it, from the Republican River north.

The tribes acceded to deep cultural changes. They agreed to compulsory education for children. In an effort to transform the signing nations into sedentary farmers, the United States pledged to provide food rations for four years and annuity goods for thirty years. The annuities came in the form of American-style goods—ready-made clothing, hats, and shoes, or the material necessary to make them. Those who wished to farm could receive up to 320 acres, but as little as 80 acres, and on non-mineral-bearing lands only. Those who received land were entitled to receive seeds and agricultural implements for up to four years, as well as a cow each and a broken-in pair of oxen. The United States agreed to establish an agency along the Missouri River that would be provided with a physician, engineer, carpenter, blacksmith, miller, and farmer, as well as teachers.

The United States agreed to abandon its forts along the Bozeman Trail and pledged that "no persons except those herein designated and authorized to do so, and except such officers, agents, and employees of the Government as may be authorized to enter upon Indian reservations in discharge of duties enjoined by law, shall ever be permitted to pass over, settle upon, or reside in the territory." The signing tribes abandoned all permanent claims outside the reservation and unceded territory and accepted the construction of railroads, wagon and mail roads, "or other works of utility or necessity" by the United States. They agreed not to attack Americans.

The boundaries established by the treaty resulted in disagreement and litigation. Ignoring the treaty it signed with the Ponca tribe in 1865, the United States gave the Poncas' territory to the Sioux, their old enemies. The treaty also established the Crow Reservation but did not establish clear ownership of rivers in its future host state of Montana. In the twentieth century, the Crows unsuccessfully sued Montana over use of the Big Horn River and the ability of the tribe to manage and regulate its use (*Montana v. United States*, 1981).

The most famous litigation resulting from the treaty came with the Sioux tribe over the loss of the Black Hills. In 1874, in order to scout the area and establish a fort there to contain the nontreaty Sioux, Gen. George Armstrong Custer led a one-thousand-person expedition to the Black Hills, which the Sioux argued was illegal under the 1851 and 1868 treaties. Custer's reports of abundant gold prompted an invasion by American miners. American civil and military leaders chose to end promised military protection of Sioux territory, and thousands of Americans poured into the Black Hills. The commissioner of Indian affairs ordered all Sioux to return to the agencies by January 31, 1876, or be considered hostile. The message was delivered in winter, when travel was nearly impossible. The U.S. military commenced operations against the tribe in the spring, resulting most notably in the defeat of Custer at the Battle of the Little Bighorn.

The U.S. government had attempted to negotiate the sale of the Black Hills but failed. With Custer's death the nation's mood changed, and the Congress voted to cease all food aid to the starving Sioux until they agreed to give up the Black Hills. The commission convinced 10 percent of the Sioux to agree, far below the 75 percent required to make sales under the 1868 treaty. In 1915 the Sioux began legally battling for the Black Hills. After an unsatisfactory decision by the Indian Claims Commission in 1975, the U.S. Supreme Court reviewed the case, *United States v. Sioux Nation of Indians* (1980), and awarded the tribe the 1877 value of the Black Hills of South Dakota and Wyoming, plus interest. To date, the seven tribal councils of the Sioux have refused to accept the appreciating award and are demanding the return of the Black Hills.

The Fort Laramie Treaty of 1868 proved to be the end of Sioux autonomy. By 1877 almost all Sioux had moved to the reservations, where Indian agents and politicians strived to Americanize the tribe. They had lost their right to hunt outside the reservation. Americanization plans did not progress well, but by this time the tribe had largely ceased to be seen by Americans as problematic or deserving of attention.

Charles Vollan
South Dakota State University

Prucha, Francis Paul. *American Indian Treaties: The History of a Political Anomaly.* Berkeley: University of California Press, 1994. "Treaty with the Sioux—Brule, Oglala, Miniconjou, Yanktonai, Hunkpapa, Blackfeet, Cuthead, Two Kettle, Sans Arcs, and Santee—and Arapaho, 1868." In *Indian Affairs: Laws and Treaties*, compiled by Charles J. Kappler, 2:998–1007. Washington DC: Government Printing Office, 1904. Wilkins, David. *American Indian Sovereignty and the U.S. Supreme Court.* Austin: University of Texas Press, 1997.

GENDER ROLES

Traditionally, Plains Indian gender roles were well defined, and men's and women's responsibilities were equally crucial to the functioning, even the survival, of their societies. Consequently, both men and women were respected for doing their jobs well, although this is not how early European American observers saw it.

Such observers, coming from societies that held that women—gentlewomen, that is—should be cloistered and protected, were aghast at the workload that Plains Indian women carried. They witnessed them, from varying societies and at various times of the year, clearing fields, planting, hoeing, and harvesting; digging cache pits and storing food; erecting and dismantling lodges and tipis; collecting wild plants and firewood; cooking, hauling water, and washing dishes; transporting possessions, generally on foot, on bison hunts; making household items, including pottery and clothing; and child rearing. This workload increased during the first half of the nineteenth century as the fur trade raised the demands for dressed skins and robes. Meanwhile, the European American observers, often only transitory travelers, saw Indian men sitting around the village or encampment, smoking, gambling, perhaps mending a weapon or car-

ing for a horse. The men seemed to have all the power; the women seemed to do all the work.

Visitors who lived with Plains Indians for more extended periods of time, including early anthropologists like Alice Fletcher, saw a much more complex division of labor and distribution of authority. There is no doubt that Plains Indian women worked hard, but they were held in high esteem for the elemental role they played in supporting village life. Among the farming Indians of the eastern Plains at least, women provided most of the food in most years; even in the bison-hunting societies of the western Plains they provided significant amounts of food through collection of wild plants and berries, and they processed the meat obtained on the hunt.

While it is true that the women generally played a subordinate role in ceremonial life and lacked formal political power (you will look in vain for a Plains Indian woman's signature on a treaty with the United States), they had types of political power that contemporary American women lacked. In the agricultural societies—the Pawnees and Omahas of Nebraska, for example—they owned the lodge, tipi, and its contents; they owned the fields, seeds, and implements of production; and they had the right to trade their surplus crops. On the bison hunts they often made the decision on where to camp, and in the lodge the senior wife (for sororal polygamy was the norm) was the main decision maker. Women also had the right to divorce, and since they owned the lodge, an unkind husband could find himself homeless, with only his horse and weapons to his name. Women were also held in high esteem for their craft work; they played an important role in healing (especially in problems associated with childbirth); and they took care of religious items, a responsibility of the highest order.

Men's roles were equally misunderstood by early European American travelers. Men were responsible for hunting, defensive and aggressive warfare, manufacturing of weapons, and nearly all societywide political and religious operations. Observers who saw Indian men in their villages saw them "off work," although often they did help the women in the fields or in the construction of a lodge. Men's work took them away from the village, and it was dangerous. They hunted on increasingly contested bison ranges and journeyed hundreds of miles to enemy encampments to steal horses and to win honors. The reciprocity of the gender roles is made clear by the hard facts of Indian demography: in most, if not all, Plains Indian societies in the mid–nineteenth century there were far more women than men. Women often died at an early age, worn down by a life of hard work and frequent childbearing, but men died in greater numbers and at earlier ages, victims of their dangerous occupations. Only in the late nineteenth century, when wars among the tribes and with the United States were curtailed, did the gender ratios equalize. By that time men and women alike were equally likely to die from diseases caused by poverty, such as tuberculosis.

The gender roles devised over generations by traditional Plains Indian societies persisted for so long because they worked to keep the family and the band or tribe intact. In the last decades of the nineteenth century, the Canadian and U.S. governments launched a concerted attack on the traditional roles of Indian men and women: Indian men were to become farmers or blacksmiths, and Indian women were to become housewives, in keeping with European American concepts of "civilized" divisions of labor. Indian extended families were to be fragmented into nuclear families, each occupying an individual allotment. These imposed changes were resisted, but Indian men's traditional roles were fast disappearing, and as the weight of supporting families fell increasingly on the women, so did relative power. This shift has continued to this day. On Plains reservations and reserves in the early twenty-first century, women are more likely than men to have completed high school and to hold jobs outside the home. They are often the chief providers for the household, while Indian men frequently take over the child care, cooking, and cleaning. Such changes bring with them benefits, such as increased authority for women and closer father-child relationships for men, but they also bring the stresses of added responsibilities and altered self-images.

David J. Wishart
University of Nebraska–Lincoln

Albers, Patricia, and Beatrice Medicine. *The Hidden Half: Studies of Plains Indian Women*. Washington DC: University Press of America, 1983. Billson, Janet Mancini. "Standing Tradition on Its Head: Role Reversal among Blood Indian Couples." *Great Plains Quarterly* 11 (1991): 3–22.

GENÍZAROS

Genízaro was a term used in eighteenth- and nineteenth-century New Mexico for "detribalized Indians," a variety of individuals of mixed Native American, but not Pueblo, parentage who had adopted at least some Hispanic styles of living. They were most common in areas of New Mexico adjacent to the Southern Plains. Genízaros, many of whom were descendants of Native Americans who made their home in the Great Plains, are a little-studied group. They appear to have been a transitional group that appeared and then disappeared as part of the opening, and later closing, of a particular

set of frontier relations in New Mexico. Even the origin of the term *genízaro* is controversial.

The more commonly claimed origin is from the term for captive Christians who were forcibly converted to Islam and served as troops in the Turkish army, called *yeni-cheri*, anglicized as "janissary." Because of the close phonetic equivalence and because of similar roles played by genízaros in New Mexico, this is assumed to be the genesis of the term. Steven Horvath argues persuasively for a different origin. To the root *geno-*, meaning "lineage" or "race," are added suffixes *-izo* and *-aro*, yielding the Spanish word. It referred to people who were the children of parents from two nations, for example France and Spain, or in New Mexico, Comanches and Pawnees. Writing in 1872, Fray Juan Augustín Morfí explained, "This name is given to the children of the captives of different nations who have married in the province." The term became generic for Native Americans who had been born among nomadic groups but who lived in New Mexico.

There were two sources of genízaros. First, they might have been taken captive in the many fights with surrounding nomadic groups. Second, they might have been traded (or "rescued") from friendly Indian groups who had taken them captive in their raids on enemies. Typically, they were children or women and were used as servants and laborers. To skirt the legal ban on slavery, they were officially designated as under the protection of a Spanish household, whose head was to train them in Christianity and Spanish culture generally. In practice they were often slaves. They were desirable because of labor shortages, especially in frontier areas. Consequently, their initial commonality was that they had been born Native Americans but lived in Hispanic society and occupied the lowest of the social strata. Because they often grew up in captivity, they knew little of their natal culture and hence were often described as "detribalized Indians."

Some genízaros eventually earned their freedom and worked as day laborers; a few became landowners or craftsmen. Two avenues to improved status were open to them. They could settle new areas where the Spanish government sought to expand control. Also, men could serve in militia units to fight hostile nomadic Indians. Because of their origins their loyalty was suspect, but they were deemed particularly adept at dealing with or fighting nomadic Indians because of their putative fierceness and because some had at least rudimentary knowledge of one or more languages of nomadic Indians. (This same quality allowed them to participate in locally lucrative but illegal trade with Plains Indians.) Their military role is one basis for the common assumption that *genízaro* was a Spanish term for janissary.

Ghost Dance before Wounded Knee, 1890

Genízaros who stood out in battles eventually could own land or enter occupations other than day laborer or soldier. Land grants to genízaro settlers typically were along frontiers where fighting was heaviest. Through time others of ambiguous ancestry might join such communities. Thus, *genízaro* came to refer to anyone of ambiguous ancestry or lower status. Eventually, more successful genízaros passed into the general Hispanic population. By the late nineteenth century the term gradually fell into disuse. The term is seldom used today except by historians and genealogists studying New Mexico history.

Determining the number or proportion of genízaros is difficult. First, it was a status individuals sought to hide. Second, it changed through time for individuals and for families. Finally, as both social relations and the terms for various groups evolved, just who should be counted as genízaro changed. Estimates range from less than 10 percent of the settled population to as high as one-third—enough to be an important social component of Hispanic society in colonial New Mexico, especially in its interactions with Native Americans who lived in the Great Plains.

For some individuals genízaro might be a multigenerational transitional status in a passage from Indian to Spaniard. Collectively, they were a buffer group created by the combination of a need for labor and a supply of captives from nomadic Indians. When the flow of captives slowed, and finally ceased, the group was no longer refreshed by new members and gradually disappeared.

Thomas D. Hall
DePauw and Colgate Universities

Gutíerrez, Ramón A. *When Jesus Came, the Corn Mothers Went Away: Marriage, Sexuality, and Power in New Mexico, 1500–1846.* Stanford CA: Stanford University Press, 1991. Horvath, Steven. "The Social and Political Organization of the *Genízaros* of Plaza de Nuestra Señora de los Dolores de Belén, New Mexico, 1740–1812." PhD diss., Brown University, 1979. Magnaghi, Russell M. "Plains Indians in New Mexico, the Genízaro Experience." *Great Plains Quarterly* 10 (1990): 86–95.

GHOST DANCE

The Ghost Dance, a messianic Native American religious movement, originated in Nevada around 1870, faded, reemerged in its best-known form in the winter of 1888–89, then spread rapidly through much of the Great Plains, where hundreds of adherents died in the 1890 Wounded Knee Massacre.

In 1869 or 1870, Tävibo, a Northern Paiute and first Ghost Dance prophet, preached that white people would disappear from the earth and dead Indians would return to enjoy a utopian life. He also claimed to communicate with the dead and taught followers to perform a ceremonial circular dance that contributed to the movement earning the Ghost Dance label. The movement spread through

Nevada and to parts of California and Oregon but subsided after the prophecies failed to materialize. Another Paiute prophet, Wovoka, revived the movement in 1889. Rumored to be Tävibo's son, and certainly influenced by his teachings, Wovoka experienced a vision of the Supreme Being in 1889, after which he preached peaceful coexistence and a strong work ethic and taught ceremonial songs and dances to resurrect dead Indians. According to the vision, if Indians followed these practices, they would be reunited with the dead and whites would disappear. Indians who had already subscribed to the first Ghost Dance tended to reject Wovoka's version, but the second Ghost Dance found acceptance among Plains tribes as far east as the Dakotas, Nebraska, Kansas, Oklahoma, and Texas.

The Ghost Dance affected no group more than the Lakota Sioux bands who adopted it. Several Lakota bands sent emissaries to interview Wovoka about his teachings. They reported in early 1890 Wovoka's message that performing Ghost Dance ceremonies and songs would bring back dead Indians, return plentiful buffalo herds, and induce a natural disaster that would sweep away whites, thus restoring the Indian way of life that had existed prior to European contact. The Ghost Dance provided a hopeful message to all Indians, but it proved particularly enticing to Lakotas suffering poor conditions on reservations and to Lakota leaders such as Sitting Bull (Tantanka Iyotanka), who had resisted U.S. Indian policy. Lakota participants added vestments known as ghost shirts to the ceremonies and songs brought by the emissaries. They believed these white muslin shirts, decorated with a variety of symbols, protected them from danger, including bullets. The Lakotas' white neighbors and reservation officials viewed the movement as a threat to U.S. Indian policy and believed the Ghost Dance ceremonies and ghost shirts indicated that the Lakotas intended to start a war. Reservation officials called on the U.S. government to stop the dancing. The government dispatched the U.S. Army and called for the arrest of key leaders such as Sitting Bull and Big Foot (Si Tanka). Indian police killed Sitting Bull while arresting him. Two weeks later, on December 29, 1890, members of the Seventh Cavalry killed Big Foot and at least 145 of his followers (casualty estimates range to higher than 300) in the Wounded Knee Massacre, thus eliminating key leaders most opposed to the United States and its Indian policy. Many historians have pointed to Wounded Knee as the closing episode in the West's Indian wars.

The Ghost Dance died out among the Lakotas after Wounded Knee, but it survived elsewhere in the Plains. A Dakota Sioux community in Canada, for instance, practiced the Ghost Dance into the 1960s. During the 1970s, Leonard Crow Dog, an Oglala Lakota holy man affiliated with the American Indian Movement, revived the Ghost Dance as part of the Red Power movement. To many, the Ghost Dance represented resistance to U.S. Indian policy and American culture and was a rallying point for preserving traditional Indian culture.

Todd M. Kerstetter
Texas Christian University

Hittman, Michael. *Wovoka and the Ghost Dance.* Lincoln: University of Nebraska Press, 1997. Kehoe, Alice Beck. *The Ghost Dance: Ethnohistory and Revitalization.* New York: Holt, Rinehart and Winston, 1989. Mooney, James. "The Ghost-Dance Religion and the Sioux Outbreak of 1890." *Fourteenth Annual Report of the Bureau of American Ethnology, 1892–93,* pt. 2. Washington DC: Government Printing Office, 1896.

GILCREASE, THOMAS (1890–1962)

Thomas Gilcrease was known as a collector of Americana at a time when few others were interested in the art, documents, and artifacts of the Western Hemisphere. Eventually, his collection expanded to include nearly 10,000 works of art, a library of 100,000 items, and more than 250,000 artifacts. In 1949 he opened a public museum on his estate in Tulsa, Oklahoma, to showcase his collection.

Gilcrease was born in Robilene, Louisiana, on February 8, 1890. His early life in the Creek Nation of Indian Territory was marked by little formal education and much hard work. While still in his teens, his life changed dramatically when the allotted land he had received as a result of his Creek tribal membership became part of a major oil field in Oklahoma. Gilcrease proved to be a skillful businessman, expanding his original holdings and founding the Gilcrease Oil Company in 1922. During the 1920s and 1930s extensive travel in Europe and visits to European museums inspired him to initiate his own collection. Pride in his Native American heritage and interest in the history of the American West provided a focus for his collecting activities.

By the late 1930s Gilcrease was spending most of his time developing the collection. In the early 1950s, faced with increasing debts relating to acquisitions for his museum, Gilcrease offered to sell the entire collection in order to keep it intact. In 1954 Tulsans supported a bond issue for the payment of Gilcrease's debts and the acquisition of the collection. Gilcrease allocated oil revenues to the city of Tulsa until the income equaled the amount of the bond, a goal that was achieved in the early 1980s. Thomas Gilcrease died on May 6, 1962, in Tulsa.

Sarah Erwin
Gilcrease Museum

GOVERNMENTS, CONTEMPORARY

One of the most interesting questions that can be asked about contemporary tribal government is, what is its source of authority and power? Unlike the federal government or any state governments, tribal governments in the United States do not have their foundations in the U.S. Constitution. Indigenous North American peoples had sociopolitical organizations that preceded the federal constitutions of both Canada and the United States and were not part of the people or political units that created these federal systems. Treaties in both nation-states provide one source for the ongoing relationships between these nation-states and the Indigenous governments, but these are not the only sources. Executive orders, national legislation, and court cases set further parameters on the interactions of Indigenous peoples with dominant states in North America; however, these are not the sources of tribal authority.

Current research from several directions in the United States and Canada concludes that the most successful tribal development occurs where traditional structures match the contemporary ones. This notion is intuitively satisfying, but it contradicts the historical policy behind the major pieces of legislation affecting the structure of tribal government in the twentieth century. The Indian Reorganization Act of 1934 (IRA) created a centralized corporate model for tribal governments, assuming that traditional systems were inadequate to the demands of modern society. Similarly, the Indian Act in Canada (1876) created band councils. Decision making and development under these model governments has been uneven at best.

One successful fusion of traditional and contemporary governments is the Cheyennes'. Their prophet Sweet Medicine gave the Cheyennes their code of sacred laws, including organization of the council of forty-four chiefs for the ten bands of Cheyennes. The council consulted with warrior societies before making its political decisions. While contemporary Northern Cheyenne government is organized under the IRA, traditional values maintain a strong influence. Tribal government is represented at the annual ceremonies, and ceremonial leaders receive tribal grants and, in some cases, a salary. This has the added benefit of continuity in the formal network between the Northern Cheyennes of Montana and the Southern Cheyennes of Oklahoma. Additionally, while the IRA model centralizes decision making, the Northern Cheyennes use a referendum to allow the community a voice on major decisions.

In a different configuration, the basic political unit for the nomadic Lakotas (Sioux) was groups of families, or *tiyospayes*, each governed by a *wica-*

sitancan, or chief. Through the leaders of fraternal societies the local unit became part of the band, then part of the larger Lakota Nation. A signal value for the Lakotas was autonomy, and the critical level of allegiance was local, to the tiyospaye. Their political structure was designed to maximize and encourage this autonomy. In 1889 the United States forced the Sioux Nation to accept six separate reservations: Cheyenne River, Crow Creek, Lower Brulé, Pine Ridge, Rosebud, and Standing Rock. Those contemporary Lakota governments, later organized under the IRA, emphasize tribal councils, centralized authorities with few mechanisms to include the community or traditional leadership in the decision-making process. Government decisions at the Rosebud and Pine Ridge reservations have been undermined by local and kinship-based allegiances, as would be expected when the formal governing systems are seen as illegitimate by many in the community.

The influence of tribal values in tribal political approaches at the beginning of the twenty-first century is illustrated in a contemporary interpretation of Treaty Number 7 as considered from the position of the Blackfoot Confederacy of southern Alberta. In the treaty the Blackfeet, Bloods, and other signatories promise to "maintain peace and good order." The clause broadly requires order between and among Indigenous people and with other Crown subjects at the time of the treaty (1877) and in the future. Such an agreement, it is argued, requires or implies the authority and power to implement the treaty terms by the Native nations. One avenue is to participate with the federal and provincial governments through guaranteed representation or comanagement.

Despite the amount of influence or interference from the United States and Canada and their efforts to transform, and even terminate, tribal polities, tribal governments persist. Even Indigenous nations that were forced to relocate several times, or those whose governments were repeatedly dissolved by external forces and whose populations were scattered, seem to find the most success when they draw their source of legitimate authority and power today from historic or traditional structures.

Roberta Haines
University of California, Los Angeles

Champagne, Duane. *American Indian Societies: Strategies and Condition of Political and Cultural Survival*. Cultural Survival Report 32. Cambridge MA: Cultural Survival, 1989. Cornell, Stephen, and Joseph P. Kalt. *What Can Tribes Do? Strategies and Institutions in American Indian Economic Development*. Los Angeles: American Indian Studies Center, 1992. Ladner, Kiera L. "Treaty Seven and Guaranteed Representation: How Treaty Rights Can Evolve into Parliamentary Seats." *Great Plains Quarterly* 17 (1997): 85–101.

GRANT, CUTHBERT (1793–1854)

Cuthbert Grant is best known as the captain of the Plains Métis who clashed with the Selkirk settlers at the Seven Oaks Massacre (near present-day Winnipeg, Manitoba) on June 19, 1816. The Métis victory nearly destroyed the fledgling Red River Colony, which later became the province of Manitoba, and enshrined Grant as the founder of the Métis nation. This sense of Métis nationhood would play a role in the Red River Resistance of 1869–70 and the North-West Rebellion of 1885.

Cuthbert Grant was born in 1793 at Fort de la Rivière Tremblante (Saskatchewan) to Cuthbert Grant Sr., a North West Company (NWC) trader, and a Métis woman of French Cree ancestry. He was sent to Montreal to be educated. In 1810 he joined the NWC, returning to the Northwest in 1812 at a time when the Hudson's Bay Company (HBC) and the NWC were engaged in a fierce competition for fur-trade supremacy in British North America. The NWC tried to use the Métis in their struggles against the HBC by instilling in them the idea that they were a nation with rights to the territory. The NWC also appointed Grant as "Captain-General of all the Half-Breeds" with the intention that he and his Métis kinsmen would destroy the Red River Colony, which was backed by the HBC. The Métis, for their part, needed little encouragement after the colony's governor prohibited the export of pemmican from the district and forbade the hunting of buffalo near the settlement.

The Seven Oaks Massacre began when the colony's governor attempted to stop Grant and his men from carting pemmican out of the country. In this battle Governor Robert Semple and twenty-one of his men were killed but only one of the Métis. This violence, which contributed to the eventual merger of the two fur-trading companies in 1821, vastly increased Grant's prestige among the Métis. For this reason the new HBC tried to use Grant as a means of controlling the Métis and winning them over to the settlement. In 1824 they offered Grant a large land grant at White Horse Plains (part of the Red River Colony) with the hope that he would settle the Métis there and prevent them from trading with the Americans. In 1828 the company also appointed Grant as "Warden of the Plains," paid him a large salary, and allowed him to trade in furs if he would prevent his kinsmen from doing the same.

Grant remained a respected leader and chief of the Métis buffalo hunt until the 1840s, when a younger generation of Métis openly defied his authority to trade furs illegally to the Americans on the upper Missouri. No longer effective, Grant was let go by the HBC, and the rest of his life was fairly uneventful. He died on July 15, 1854, after falling from his horse.

Gerhard J. Ens
University of Alberta

Dick, Lyle. "The Seven Oaks Incident and the Construction of a Historical Tradition, 1816 to 1970." *Journal of the Canadian Historical Association/Revue de la Société Historique du Canada* n.s. 2 (1991): 91–114. MacLeod, Margaret, and W. L. Morton. *Cuthbert Grant of Grantown: Warden of the Plains of Red River.* Toronto: McClelland and Stewart, 1974.

GROS VENTRES

The Gros Ventres are an Algonquian-speaking people from the area of the Great Plains between the Missouri River, Montana, and the Saskatchewan River in the Canadian Prairies. Their own name is A'aninin or A'ani, meaning "White Clay People," derived from their belief that they were made from white clay found on the river bottoms.

The Gros Ventres are among the least-known tribes of the Northern Plains, partly the consequence of mistaken identity. The name Gros Ventre ("Big Belly" in French) is a misnomer that originated from a mistranslation of the gesture for the A'aninin in the Plains sign language. The Crees referred to the Gros Ventres as the Water Falls People, Falls Indians, or Rapid Indians because the tribe occupied territory inclusive of the southern branch of the Saskatchewan River, where rapids are frequent. The sign for them was the passing of the hands over the body like water falling. This was mistranslated as a sign representing a large stomach, and hence they became known as the Big Bellies, or Gros Ventres. Adding to the confusion, the Gros Ventres are also known as the Atsinas in some ethnological sources, a Blackfoot word meaning "Belly People." To distinguish them from the Hidatsas, also known as the Gros Ventres, sometimes they were called the Gros Ventre of the Prairies.

Earliest mention of the Gros Ventres places them in the region of the Saskatchewan River in the eighteenth century, far removed from their kindred, the Arapahos. When and where these two tribes split is not known. Trappers and traders of the Hudson's Bay Company and the North West Company located the Gros Ventres on the South Saskatchewan River between 1775 and 1790. As the Gros Ventres ventured farther west and south, they quickly adopted the lifestyle of the Northern Plains. They became mobile and followed the buffalo herds for their primary source of food and clothing. They lived in easily moved tipis and excelled at the elaborate and beautiful beadwork and quillwork of that region.

As in other Plains tribes, the Gros Ventres' spiritual practices were rich and complex. Their principal tribal ceremony was the Sun Dance, or "Sacrifice

Dance." Their major religious possessions were sacred pipes. The Gros Ventres once possessed ten such pipes but now have only two; the Flat Pipe and the Chief Medicine Pipe, or Feathered Pipe, are revered as a direct link to the supernatural. Each spring, the two medicine pipes are used to secure blessings from the One Above.

During the early part of the nineteenth century, the Gros Ventres were driven farther south to the Missouri River country by the Crees and Assiniboines. In the 1820s one band of the Gros Ventres joined the Arapahos in the Cimarron Valley, in the present-day Oklahoma Panhandle. The Gros Ventres band remained there for five years before traveling back north in 1833.

The reunited Gros Ventres took up a precarious position on the Northern Plains, settling in an area between the Blackfoot to the west, the Assiniboines to the east, and the Crows toward the south. Smallpox epidemics had struck the tribe in 1781, 1801, and 1829, significantly reducing their numbers. The great smallpox epidemic of 1837–38 devastated the Blackfoot and the Assiniboines but left the Gros Ventres and the Crows comparatively undisturbed. The Crows proved an enduring enemy, and warfare continued between the two tribes even into the reservation period.

Unlike many other Northern Plains tribes, the Gros Ventres generally remained on good terms with non-Indians. They patronized the American traders at Fort McKenzie and were considered among the more receptive tribes in the region. Jesuit missionaries, including Father Pierre-Jean De Smet and Father Nicolas Point, made sporadic visits to the Gros Ventres and found them generally amicable but resistant to Christianization. Isaac Stephens, governor of Washington Territory, held council with the Gros Ventres, as part of the Blackfoot Nation, in 1855, out of which came a treaty formalizing relations between the tribe and the United States and pressing for intertribal peace on the Northern Plains.

Gold was discovered in what is now Montana in 1862, bringing more and more non-Indians through the hunting territories that supported the Blackfeet, Assiniboines, Crows, and Gros Ventres. The completion of the Union Pacific Railroad in 1869, and the Northern Pacific Railroad in 1883, brought increasing numbers of settlers and made the region less remote. The impact of such rapid settlement greatly reduced the game herds, particularly the bison, already dwindling in numbers. The last of the buffalo herds had disappeared from the Northern Plains by the time the Gros Ventres were confined to the Fort Belknap Reservation in north-central Montana in 1888. At that time, their population stood at 964, and their tribal numbers fell to a low of 576 in 1900.

In 1935 the tribe reorganized its government, the Fort Belknap Indian Community Council, under the terms of the Wheeler-Howard Act (Indian Reorganization Act). In the twentieth century the tribe petitioned the U.S. government for compensation for questionable land transfers in the nineteenth century and battled with mining corporations in an effort to maintain its land base and protect the environment. Despite sharing the Fort Belknap Reservation with the Assiniboines, the Gros Ventres have worked to maintain a distinct culture. There are now few fluent Gros Ventre speakers; however a vigorous program to teach the language begins in primary school and culminates in classes at a local community college. Their economy is agriculturally based, but the federal and tribal governments remain the primary employers, and unemployment remains high. In 2000 the Gros Ventres numbered some three thousand members, the majority living on the 652,593-acre Fort Belknap Reservation.

Walter C. Fleming
Montana State University–Bozeman

Bryan, William L., Jr. *Montana's Indians: Yesterday and Today.* Helena MT: American and World Geographic Publishing, 1996. Flannery, Regina. *The Gros Ventre of Montana: Part I, Social Life.* Washington DC: Catholic University of America Press, 1953. Horse Capture, George, ed. *The Seven Visions of Bull Lodge.* Lincoln: University of Nebraska Press, 1992.

HALF-BREED TRACT

The Half-Breed Tract, also known as the Nemaha Half-Breed Reservation or Reserve, was established on July 15, 1830, with the signing of the Treaty of Prairie du Chien in Michigan Territory. The Half-Breed Tract was established to provide a homeland for tribal members of mixed ancestry, at the request of the signatory Native American nations, the Otoe-Missourias, Omahas, and Iowas, and on behalf of the Santees and Yanktons. Article 10 of the treaty ceded approximately 138,000 acres of Otoe-Missouria land that extended from the Missouri River westward between the Great (Big) Nemaha and Little Nemaha rivers to form a triangular tract located in what is now southeastern Nebraska. This was the first treaty in which Congress authorized the allotment of land in severalty to Native Americans.

On September 10, 1860, following thirty years of controversy regarding the western boundary of the tract, Lewis Neal became the first of 389 individuals to receive a patent of land allotted in severalty. Because there were too many eligible mixed-blood claimants, each allottee received only 320 acres instead of 640 acres originally suggested in the Treaty of Prairie du Chien. By the 1870s most of the land allotted in the Half-Breed Tract had been taken over by white settlers, who sometimes used alcohol to entice mixed-bloods to sell, or who married mixed-bloods and so gained entitlement to allotments. The first test of Native American land severalty in the United States ended in complete failure in terms of the original intention of the Treaty of Prairie du Chien signatories.

William T. Waters
University of Nebraska–Kearney

Chapman, Berlin B. *The Otoes and Missourias: A Study of Indian Removal and the Legal Aftermath*. Oklahoma City: Time Journal Publishing, 1965. Johansen, Gregory J. "To Make Some Provision for Their Half-Breeds, The Nemaha Half-Breed Reserve, 1830–66." *Nebraska History* 67 (1986): 8–29.

HARPER, ELIJAH (B. 1949)

Elijah Harper, 1979

As the Manitoba legislature's only Aboriginal member, Elijah Harper played a major role in defeating the Meech Lake Accord. A Cree Indian, Elijah was born in his parents' log cabin on March 3, 1949, at Red Sucker Lake near the Manitoba and Ontario border. One of thirteen children, he spent much time with his paternal grandparents, living in their home but seeing his parents every day. When he was five years old, he became ill and spent six months under the auspices of the Indian Affairs medical staff without any contact with his parents. He left home to pursue an education, marrying during his second year as a university student in

Winnipeg. After being active in Native organizations and issues, he and his family returned home, where he was elected chief of Red Sucker Lake in 1978. Three years later he was elected as a New Democrat member for the vast Rupert's Land riding, with about 70 percent of the vote. From his remote reservation he forced Aboriginal issues into the constitutional debate.

Attempting to accommodate Quebec and preserve Canada, the Meech Lake Accord proclaimed that Canada had two distinct founding nations. Harper agreed that Quebec's society was distinct but regarded the exclusion of Native peoples from Canada's founding nations as offensive, as did most Native organizations. Prime Minister Brian Mulroney and the provincial premiers signed the Meech Lake Accord on June 9, 1990. After the signing ceremony the legislatures of Manitoba, Newfoundland, and New Brunswick faced a two-week deadline to approve. Harper delayed the vote on the accord forty-eight hours, and a procedural mistake also delayed the accord's introduction to the Manitoba legislature. When debate extension required unanimous consent, Harper again objected, preventing a vote before the deadline expired. His quiet refusal, with an eagle feather in hand, embodied Native resentment over recent and past mistreatment. Harper became a national symbol for Native issues. He is also a controversial figure, however, and at times he has appeared to be prone to political self-destruction, such as when he refused to take a Breathalyzer test following a minor traffic accident.

John M. Pederson
Mayville State University

Cohen, Andrew. *A Deal Undone: The Making and Breaking of the Meech Lake Accord*. Vancouver: Douglas and McIntyre, 1990. Comeau, Pauline. *Elijah: No Ordinary Hero*. Vancouver: Douglas and McIntyre, 1993. Hager, Barbara. *Honour Songs*. Vancouver: Raincoast Books, 1996.

HARRIS, LADONNA (B. 1930)

LaDonna Harris, a Comanche woman born in 1930 in Walters, Oklahoma, is a well-known political activist. Once shy and retiring, but nonetheless aware of the inequities of being an Indian in America, LaDonna blossomed during her marriage to Fred R. Harris, who was later a U.S. senator from Oklahoma and candidate for president. She put her personality and many talents to work as the founder of Oklahomans for Indian Opportunity (OIO), a Native American charitable and educational nonprofit organization. OIO expanded into civil rights activities in the 1960s and was the forerunner of Americans for Indian Opportunity, with its flagship Ambassadors program, a nationwide project headed by Harris. The Ambassadors project takes

LaDonna Harris

some of the nation's brightest and most promising young Indian professionals through an intensive one-year program aimed at rekindling and reinforcing the use of the tribal values in a modern context.

Harris's work takes her all over the country, including Washington DC, where she is well known in Congress as a fighter for, and defender of, Indian rights and programs. She is in demand as a speaker, both locally and nationally, and frequently leaves her home in Bernalillo, New Mexico, to travel in support of Indian issues. Publicly acknowledged by various Indian and non-Indian organizations as a successful activist, LaDonna remains at heart a Comanche woman and returns frequently to her Oklahoma roots, often accompanied by one or more of her three adult children and one grandchild, to draw strength and vitality from her heritage.

H. Henrietta Stockel
Cochise College

Harris, LaDonna. *LaDonna Harris: A Comanche Life*. Lincoln: University of Nebraska Press, 2000.

HEALTH

The history of the health of Great Plains tribes can be characterized as a series of epidemiological transitions highlighted by several distinct eras. Before European American colonization, Plains peoples suffered from low-virulence infections and socially induced mortalities. Paleopathologi-

cal evidence reveals numerous afflictions: malnutrition, anemia, tuberculosis, treponematosis, and other degenerative, chronic, and congenital conditions. Together with periodic trauma, such as accidents and warfare, these afflictions determined morbidity and mortality patterns.

European American contact brought elevated levels of morbidity and mortality. Most tribes experienced deteriorating health conditions and sustained population declines. The crucial factor was the introduction of Eastern Hemisphere infectious diseases such as cholera, influenza, measles, and smallpox. Even before 1730 Plains populations were exposed to epidemics. Then, between 1730 and 1877, approximately fifty epidemics swept across the Northern Plains; Southern Plains societies suffered similar catastrophes. Smallpox was particularly devastating: the 1837–38 epidemic, for example, killed an estimated 17,200 Indians in the Northern Great Plains, including 8,160 Blackfoot.

Epidemics were accompanied by increased warfare, impairment of subsistence activities and consequent famine, breakdown of social systems, which crippled a tribe's capacity to care for its sick, and deep cultural stress. In response, Great Plains societies employed a number of adaptive strategies, altering their kinship, marital, and adoption practices, and modifying their ideological systems to explain the introduced pathogens. Some tribes accepted select Western medical techniques, such as vaccination, adding them to their traditional repertoire of healing practices.

Rudimentary governmental health services were introduced after 1819 under the auspices of the War Department. Army physicians, missionaries, and even traders administered sporadic medical care. Some U.S. government treaties promised medical care, but of the numbered treaties in Canada, only Treaty Number 6 (1876), with the Crees, referred specifically to medical services. Concerted efforts to provide health care for Plains Indians did not occur until long after their confinement to reservations and reserves.

Although epidemics, including influenza, still sporadically occurred, after about 1880 the main causes of morbidity and mortality were afflictions brought about by the impoverished conditions of life on the reservations and reserves, especially tuberculosis, trachoma, and dysentery. For example, in 1898 the high (54 per 1,000) death rate among the Canadian Sarcee (Sarsi) was largely the result of tuberculosis.

In response, in both the Canadian and U.S. Great Plains a rudimentary system of health care delivery was developed that included hospital-based care, civilian physicians, and field matrons. In particular, tuberculosis, trachoma, and high infant mortality rates were targeted. Prior to 1940, however, health care delivery to Plains reservations and reserves was plagued by inadequate facilities, a lack of medical supplies, personnel problems, as well as by a general resistance to Western medicine.

Western medical practices were rejected both because they were culturally alien and also because they undermined Indigenous healing and associated religious beliefs.

In Canada after World War II the responsibility for Native health services was transferred to Health and Welfare Canada, and then, in the 1970s, to the Department of Indian Affairs and Northern Development. In the United States, since the mid-1960s the goal of the Indian Health Service has been to bring Native American health up to the level of the rest of the nation. Still, the health of Native Americans and First Nations remains well below the national averages.

Indeed, the Native peoples of the Plains have epidemiological and demographic profiles similar to those found in the developing world. They are young, poorly educated, and have low income, and their societies are characterized by high fertility and mortality rates, with prevalent occurrences of chronic diseases and social pathologies. Plains Indians have a life expectancy that is seven years lower than the U.S. and Canadian averages. Infant mortality, though falling, was still 3.5 times higher among First Nations of the Prairies than in Canada as a whole in 1996, and in 2000 the infant mortality rate in the Aberdeen, South Dakota, service area exceeded the national average by more than 50 percent.

With the notable exception of another introduced disease, the human immunodeficiency virus that leads to AIDS, infectious diseases on the reservations and reserves have waned because of improvements in sanitation and, to a degree, rising standards of living. The three leading causes of death are now heart disease, malignant neoplasms (tumors), and accidents. Type 2 diabetes, hypertension, and arthritis are also prevalent, and alcoholism, substance abuse, homicide, and family violence also occur at rates substantially higher than the national averages. To one degree or another, these are all afflictions of poverty and associated dysfunctional lifestyles and behavior.

Although such statistics reveal how large the gap is in health equity between Plains Indigenous and non-Indigenous peoples, improvements are being made on a number of health fronts. Great Plains tribes are assuming greater responsibility in defining their health needs and controlling health resources. They are integrating traditional medical practices with Western medical techniques to address their health concerns in a culturally appropriate manner. It is hoped that the result will be sustained improvements in health.

Gregory R. Campbell
University of Montana

Campbell, Gregory R. "Indian Health Service." In *Native America in the Twentieth Century: An Encyclopedia*, edited by Mary B. Davis, 256–61. New York: Garland, 1994. Vernon, Irene S. *Killing Us Quietly: Native Americans and HIV/AIDS*. Lincoln: University of Nebraska Press, 2001. Waldram, James B., D. Ann Herring, and T. Kue Young. *Aboriginal Health in Canada: Historical, Cultural, and Epidemiological Perspectives*. Toronto: University of Toronto Press, 1995. Young, T. Kue. *The Health of Native Americans: Towards a Biocultural Epidemiology*. New York: Oxford University Press, 1994.

HIDATSAS

Section of Like-a-Fishhook Village, photographed by Stanley J. Morrow, October 1872

The Hidatsas, an Indian people of the Northern Plains, have lived in what is now west-central North Dakota for nearly a millennium. The name Hidatsa, which refers to the willows growing on Missouri River sandbars, was once applied to a single band but later encompassed the entire people. Along with the Mandans and the Arikaras, the Hidatsas were the northernmost Plains people to construct large, permanent earth lodge villages and to practice agriculture intensively. Composed in the early historic era of three closely related bands—the Hidatsa-proper, Awatixa, and Awaxawi—each spoke a distinct dialect of Siouan language and maintained unique identities and traditions of separate origin. Awaxawi and Hidatsa-proper traditions describe the people emerging from an underground world near a large body of water, often identified with Devils Lake in eastern North Dakota, and a migration and later meeting with the Mandans, a people with whom the Hidatsas have been intimately associated to the present day. The Awatixas, in contrast, maintain they have always resided on the Missouri River.

During the late eighteenth and early nineteenth centuries, when European and European American observers began to record their encounters with Northern Plains Indians, the Hidatsas lived in three villages perched on bluffs near the junction of the Knife and Missouri rivers. Archeologists now believe the Hidatsas, specifically the Awatixas, had established themselves in the area as early as 1100 AD. Although Hidatsas traveled widely and maintained extensive ties, especially trade ties, to other peoples throughout the Northern Plains and beyond, their villages and river valley environs remained at the heart of their collective life. Villages, with their large numbers of domed, multifamily earth lodges, were principally the domain of Hidatsa women, as well as the children and elderly in their care. For men, villages were a place of return and departure, as their lives frequently led them abroad for hunting and raiding. Rivers provided water, clay for pottery, places for recreation and play, and avenues for travel. Spring floods nourished the river-bottom gardens cultivated by Hidatsa women that yielded an abundance of corn, squash, beans, and sunflowers for their own consumption and for an extensive trade. Men found ample game, including white-tailed deer, along wooded bottoms, but they also turned to the High Plains beyond to hunt bison and pronghorn antelope with friends and family in semiannual hunts.

Clans and societies incorporated each Hidatsa person and bound them together in mutual obligation while also providing care, identity, and community. Membership in the seven or eight clans active in the historic era was matrilineal and cut across the three Hidatsa groups, integrating these distinct communities. Men's and women's societies provided various social services, and membership changed over the course of an individual's life. Likewise, religious observation and devotion were woven throughout daily life. The Hidatsas recognized their world as variously endowed with spirits to be acknowledged and respected, and prayer was offered frequently in a recognition of, and request for, assistance from the power inherent in all things. Individuals, often male, pursued visions and sought guidance even in childhood, presenting acts of self-sacrifice as evidence of their reverence and purpose. Rewarded with a successful vision, an individual would make a small personal bundle as a representation of powers to be called upon for assistance. Larger bundles, associated

with clans or societies, afforded power and protection but required observation of unique ritual care by a trained owner.

The encounter with European and, later, European American newcomers placed unprecedented challenges before the Hidatsas. Some aspects of change were welcome, including the adoption of horses and the expansion of the long-established Aboriginal trade network to incorporate newcomers. But disease, decline in population, and the necessity of defense from the more numerous Sioux (Lakotas) proved especially daunting. Before the cycle of epidemics, the Hidatsas may have numbered 5,000 to 6,000 people, but at least as early as the 1780s their population began to decline. In 1837 a smallpox epidemic killed half of the Hidatsa people in a matter of months, leaving only 1,200 to 1,400 survivors. These losses, combined with even more devastating losses suffered by the Mandans, led to the establishment of a single, shared village, Like-a-Fishhook, in 1845. There the Mandans and Hidatsas were joined by the Arikaras in 1862. In 1870 the three peoples were placed on the eight-million-acre Fort Berthold Reservation in present-day central North Dakota. By the end of the nineteenth century, the Hidatsa population had declined to some 400 people.

Early in the 1880s, in keeping with the government's assimilation policy, the Hidatsas, Mandans, and Arikaras were encouraged to abandon Like-a-Fishhook Village and to establish family farms on individual allotments. While some Hidatsa families chose to do so, many continued to reside in small towns and communities—Lucky Mound, Shell Creek, and Independence—established close to the Missouri River, where they pursued ranching and other enterprises. The size of the reservation was reduced to less than one million acres by allotments.

The 1930s saw a respite from overt demands for assimilation and a revision of Fort Berthold's tribal government as the Three Affiliated Tribes under the Indian Reorganization Act of 1934. But challenges continued.

With the construction of Garrison Dam during the 1950s, some 156,000 acres of Fort Berthold Reservation, home to 90 percent of the tribal community, were flooded. Tribal leaders had resisted the project but finally yielded to congressional pressure and accepted a $12 million compensation package. Relocation continued even as the water rose, and many Hidatsas moved to the town of Mandaree. An additional $143 million was appropriated by Congress in 1992, but the dislocation and disruption caused by the Garrison Dam are felt to this day.

J. Wendel Cox
Arizona State University

Ahler, Stanley A., Thomas D. Thiessen, and Michael K. Trimble. *People of the Willows: The Prehistory and Early History of the Hidatsa Indians*. Grand Forks: University of North Dakota Press, 1991. Bowers, Alfred W. *Hidatsa Social and Ceremonial Organization*. Lincoln: University of Nebraska Press, 1992. Gilman, Carolyn, and Mary Jane Schneider. *The Way to Independence: Memories of a Hidatsa Indian Family, 1840–1920*. St. Paul: Minnesota Historical Society Press, 1987. Meyer, Roy W. *The Village Indians of the Upper Missouri: The Mandans, Hidatsas, and Arikaras*. Lincoln: University of Nebraska Press, 1977. VanDevelder, Paul. *Coyote Warrior: One Man, Three Tribes, and the Trial that Forged a Nation*. Lincoln: University of Nebraska Press, 2005. Wilson, Gilbert H. *Waheenee: An Indian Girl's Story*. Lincoln: University of Nebraska Press, 1981.

HOGAN, LINDA (B. 1947)

Contemporary Native American poet, novelist, and essayist Linda Hogan explores the relationship of humans to the natural world, both past and present. She was born in Denver, Colorado, on July 16, 1947, to a Chickasaw father and a mother of German descent. Her father's family in Oklahoma were gifted storytellers, and this heritage and love for the landscape inform her belief in the sacredness of the earth and its inhabitants. A teacher and political activist, Hogan has taught literature and creative writing at the Universitiy of Minnesota and the University of Colorado. In 1986 she received an American Book Award for her book of poems *Seeing through the Sun*.

An impassioned political and spiritual leader, Hogan catalogs the voices of the disenfranchised, particularly those who have suffered during the settling of the Great Plains. Her historical novel *Mean Spirit* (1990), a finalist for a Pulitzer Prize in 1991, depicts the devastating impact of the 1920s Oklahoma oil boom on an Osage Indian community, especially its women.

Throughout her work, Hogan argues for a balancing of spiritual, intellectual, and physical realms based upon traditional Native beliefs that link past and present into one coherent vision. Contrasting the loud and often violent dominant culture with the voices of her ancestors, Hogan argues that chaos, violence, and greed have silenced the wisdom of the land, yet she seeks to lessen this alienation. The long "distances" she often evokes are the space of the Plains as well as the landscape of lost time and space.

In Hogan's work, women learn from experience that destruction of parts leads to destruction of the whole. She documents a history of extinction and the imposition of a philosophy without reverence or a sense of the future. Harshly rewriting the myths of Plains settlement, she nonetheless holds out hope for healing and rebirth, seeking new stories and habits that nurture the creative power of

this region. There is hope, she says, in the land, the water, and those who listen.

Mark Vogel
Appalachian State University

Hogan, Linda. *Dwellings: Reflections on the Natural World*. New York: W. W. Norton, 1995. Scholer, Bo. "A Heart Made out of Crickets: An Interview with Linda Hogan." *Journal of Ethnic Studies* 16 (1988): 107–17.

HOLLYWOOD INDIANS

In more than a century of film history, the "Hollywood Indian" has rarely reflected the actual Native Americans of the Great Plains. During the years of silent film production, Native Americans were often played by members of the Sioux Nation. "Extras" were brought in by busload for the films, and producer and director Thomas Ince had a Sioux settlement of "Ince Indians" on the California coast. Even during those years, however, Native American roles of importance were generally played by non-Native actors, and the dress and customs of Native American peoples were depicted in whatever costumes suited the director or set designer's taste and rarely reflected those of the individual tribes. However, the Hollywood Indian from the 1920s through the 1980s was more likely to resemble a Plains Indian than any other, largely because the American audience quickly grew accustomed to the exotic look of Plains headdresses and breastplates. In 1914 Alanson Skinner, assistant curator of the Department of Anthropology at the American Museum of Natural History, wrote the *New York Times* to complain about these inaccuracies in film costuming, describing the movies as "grotesque farces" in which Delawares were dressed as Sioux and eastern Indians were shown dwelling in skin tipis of the type used only in the trans-Mississippi West.

In 1940 a Cherokee actor named Victor Daniels (aka Chief Thunder Cloud) led a group of actors in applying to the Bureau of Indian Affairs for recognition as the "De Mille Indians," a new tribe composed only of Native Americans who worked in the film industry. While humorous, the application was also an attempt to show the artificiality of the stereotypes found in the film images. The Western imagination is largely visual, and American audiences have over the course of film history generally accepted as reality the Hollywood Indian, whether Noble Savage or Bloodthirsty Savage.

The Native American has often been used as the metaphorical foe in Westerns. For instance, when the Colonel William F. Cody (Buffalo Bill) Historical Pictures Company made *The Indian Wars* in 1914, the secretary of state sent troops and equipment for the filming, Gen. Nelson Miles agreed to appear in the film, and the War Department put the Pine Ridge Sioux (Lakota) at Cody's disposal. Such overwhelming support was due, presumably, to the fact that the film was to be used for War Department records and to enlist recruits to fight in World War I. Later, films such as *Northwest Passage* (1939) would be similarly used to engender a patriotic response in World War II, with the Hollywood Indian standing in for the German soldiers once more.

During the 1950s the images were more likely to be those of the Noble Savage, as Hollywood, experiencing the effects of McCarthyism, used the Native American to represent the oppressed Other. *Broken Arrow* (1950) and *Cheyenne Autumn* (1964) showed the Native American as gallant and dignified in the face of oppression by the dominant culture. *Little Big Man* (1970) and *Soldier Blue* (1970) used Native Americans as metaphors for the Vietnamese, with the message that innocent and noble people were being killed in an unjust war.

Perhaps the most obvious Hollywood Indian appeared in Elliot Silverstein's 1970 film *A Man Called Horse*, which was intended and well publicized as a "sympathetic and accurate portrayal" of the Plains Indians, particularly the Lakota Sioux. However, according to Ward Churchill, a Native American scholar, the film depicted Indians whose language was Lakota, whose hairstyles ranged from Assiniboine to Nez Perce to Comanche, whose tipis were Crow, and whose Sun Dance ceremony was Mandan. Other important distortions included sending an old woman out into a blizzard to die because her only means of support, her son, was killed in a raid. This was in direct opposition to the reverence with which the Sioux peoples hold the elderly.

The Hollywood Indian of the 1980s and 1990s is more likely to be an actual Native American than in previous decades, and a few films have been made that depict Native Americans less stereotypically, although many still include stereotypes old and new (the Natural Ecologist is among the new ones). Although most films that include Native Americans still take place in the past with tribes that are vanishing or have vanished (as the scroll at the end of Kevin Costner's 1990 *Dances with Wolves* indicates), the images of Native America are occasionally more human than stereotypical. Also, more films are being made by Native American filmmakers, so perhaps it is the Hollywood Indian tribe that will soon vanish.

Jacquelyn Kilpatrick
Governors State University

Bataille, Gretchen, and Charles L. P. Silet, eds. *The Pretend Indians: Images of Native Americans in the Movies*. Ames: Iowa State University Press, 1980. Churchill, Ward. *Fantasies of the Master Race: Literature, Cinema and the Colonization of American Indians*, edited by M. Annette Jaimes. Monroe ME: Common Courage Press, 1992. Kilpatrick, Jacquelyn. *Celluloid Indians: Native Americans in Film*. Lincoln: University of Nebraska Press, 1999.

HORSE

So much has been written about the coming of the horse to the Western Hemisphere with the Spanish invasion that it is often forgotten that the Americas are the home of the modern, single-hoofed horse, *Equus*. Having evolved from the tiny, one-foot-tall and three-toed *Hyracotherium* some two million years ago, the modern horse migrated from North America to Asia over the Bering Strait land bridge.

When the first humans crossed the strait in the opposite direction after about 20,000 BC, they found the Great Plains teeming with horses, which for several millennia were among the many species of megafauna hunted by the first Plains peoples. Then, some eight to ten thousand years ago, the horse followed the mammoth, camel, and other large American mammals into extinction, apparently as the victim of overhunting and a changing climate.

The ensuing intermission in the history of Plains Indian horse use lasted until the early seventeenth century, when the Spanish reintroduced the animal. Although horses began to infiltrate the Plains soon after the Spanish settled New Mexico in 1598, widespread diffusion began only after the Pueblo Revolt of 1680. The subsequent Spanish abandonment of New Mexico put large numbers of livestock into the hands of Pueblo Indians, who embarked on an active horse trade with Plains nomads. Carried forward by Plains Indian raiders and traders, the horse frontier advanced rapidly, reaching the Missouri River in the 1730s and the Canadian Prairies in the 1770s.

The horse that the Spanish brought to the Americas was the famed barb horse, a mix of Arab and Spanish stock. Bred to survive in the North African deserts, these small but sturdy animals found a fitting ecological niche in the dry, grass-covered Southern Plains. By 1800 Comanches, Kiowas, and other Native groups of the area possessed enormous herds. The region between the Rio Grande and the Arkansas River also supported about two million wild horses, which had propagated from strays left by raiders. However, as the horse frontier expanded northward through the Plains, it lost its momentum. The harsh northern winters reduced horses' reproductive success, and the heavy snowfall made feeding difficult, causing severe winter losses. Combined, these factors prevented most Northern Plains groups from becoming fully mounted. While the Southern Plains Indians had as many as four to six horses per person, only the

Piegans in the Northern Plains had enough animals to put all their people on horseback.

Horses revolutionized the Plains Indian way of life by allowing their owners to hunt, trade, and wage war more effectively, to have bigger tipis and move more possessions, and to transport their old and sick, who might previously have been abandoned. The impact of the horse was most dramatic on the Southern Plains, where a true equestrian culture emerged. Comanches, Kiowas, Arapahos, and Cheyennes, who became specialized horse raiders and herders, maintained large herds of surplus animals for trade with other Native groups and European Americans. Horses also became the foundation of status systems by changing relatively egalitarian societies into nascent class societies based on horse ownership. In fact, so attractive was this new horse culture that many groups—most notably Comanches, Lakotas, and Cheyennes—abandoned their traditional homelands for an equestrian existence in the Plains. In doing so, they became some of the most refined and celebrated equestrian societies in history, matched only by the great horse cultures of Asia. However, the large horse herds also disturbed the region's delicate ecological balance, as they competed for water and grass with native species. By the early 1840s the crucial river valleys had already become overexploited, pushing the massive bison herds into an early decline. It is also possible that horses triggered a decline in women's status because the bison hunt became more the domain of the mounted male hunter rather than of the society at large.

The horse culture established weaker roots in the Northern Plains, where the lack of animals prevented the Indians from making a full equestrian transition. Plains Crees, Assiniboines, and other northern groups relied extensively on inferior dog transportation and pedestrian hunting methods. The shortage of animals also encouraged warfare, as tribes tried to stock their herds by raiding their neighbors. Yet another variation of the full-fledged horse culture emerged among the Pawnees, Wichitas, and other horticulturists of the eastern Plains, for whom the horse was a mixed blessing. Horses encouraged these farmers to diversify their economies by allowing them to increase the role of bison hunting in their subsistence cycles. Mandans, Hidatsas, and Arikaras on the upper Missouri River enhanced their role as the paramount traders in the Plains when they started to channel horses from the Southern to the Northern Plains. But horses also overtaxed local ecosystems, obliging the Pawnees, for example, to stay away from their villages for extended periods of time. Horses also attracted raiders. After 1830 Lakota war parties swept down on Pawnee villages almost every year, seeking horses, corn, and honor, and precipitating the decline of this once-powerful people.

The beginning of the reservation period after 1850 marked the end of the Plains horse cultures, but it did not end the association between Indians and horses. During the difficult early years of reservation life, many previously nomadic groups turned to cattle and horse ranching as an alternative to the forced, alien agrarian lifestyle. Rodeo has offered another important way to maintain the connection with horses. On a more abstract level, most people still link Plains Indians and horses almost automatically, and the Hollywood film industry has sold the visual image of the mounted Plains warrior as the stereotype for all North American Indians. To many Indians the horse continues to symbolize their traditional cultures and lifeways as they existed before the European American takeover. From celebration parades and art to actual herds on reservation fields, horses are still integral to Plains Indian life.

Pekka Hämäläinen
University of California, Santa Barbara

Ewers, John C. *The Horse in the Blackfoot Indian Culture.* Bureau of American Ethnology Bulletin 159. Washington DC: Smithsonian Institution, 1955. Holder, Preston. *The Hoe and Horse on the Plains: A Study of Cultural Development among North American Indians.* Lincoln: University of Nebraska Press, 1970.

HOUSER, ALLAN (1914–1994)

One of the most influential Native American artists of the twentieth century, Allan Houser was of Chiricahua heritage; his grandfather was warchief Mangus Coloradas, and his granduncle was Geronimo. Houser was born in Apache, Oklahoma, on June 30, 1914, and grew up near Fort Sill. His early life was filled with stories of Chiricahua resistance. In the 1930s he attended the Indian School in Santa Fe, working with Dorothy Dunn in the Studio. The flat, two-dimensional painting style developed there was too restrictive for Houser, although he executed various Studio-style murals, including some in the Department of the Interior Building in Washington DC. He studied muralism with Olaf Nordmark, who suggested that he turn to sculpture. Beginning in wood, Houser quickly explored other materials, including bronze, marble, and steel. He taught at the Inter-Mountain Boarding School in Utah between 1951 and 1961 and in Santa Fe at the new Institute of American Indian Arts from 1962 to 1975. The institute was founded on principles that Houser held to be deeply important: that Native American artists should be encouraged to explore their cultural heritage as well as to create art in keeping with their own individual goals and self-expression. At sixty-one, he officially stopped

Oscar Howe in his studio at the University of South Dakota, ca. 1968

teaching to devote his energies to his own art, but he never stopped helping students.

Numerous awards filled his life, including a Guggenheim Fellowship (1948) and the French Palmes d'Académiques (1954) for his exemplary work as both artist and teacher. He was inducted into the Oklahoma Hall of Fame and, in 1992, was the first Native American to receive the National Medal of Arts. His unceasing experimentation and creativity were expressed in subject matter that ranged from representations of Native figures of the past to contemporary abstractions without recognizable imagery. Houser died on August 22, 1994, in Santa Fe.

Joyce M. Szabo
University of New Mexico

Allan Houser (Ha-o-zous): A Life in Art. Exhibition Catalog. Santa Fe: Museum of New Mexico, 1991. Perlman, Barbara H. *Allan Houser (Ha-o-zous).* Boston: David R. Godine, 1987. *The Studio of Allan Houser.* Exhibition Catalog. Santa Fe: Wheelwright Museum of the American Indian, 1996.

HOWE, OSCAR (1915–1983)

Internationally acclaimed Yanktonai Nakota painter Oscar Howe was a major force in the evolution of the Native American fine arts movement. In the 1950s and 1960s Howe led his generation in the transition from the highly prescribed Studio style to greater personal expression and active engagement with mainstream modern art.

Oscar Howe was born on May 13, 1915, at Joe Creek on the Crow Creek Reservation in South Dakota. His Indian name, Nazuha Hoksina, translates as Trader Boy, which proved particularly appropriate given his lifelong commitment to bridging Native American and European American cultures. Howe came from a distinguished Yanktonai family that included hereditary chiefs and noted orators. At age seven Howe was sent to the Pierre Indian School, which was administered by the Bureau of Indian Affairs on a military model that actively promoted assimilation. Serious health problems interrupted Howe's education, but he subsequently graduated from the school in 1933. Howe enrolled in the Santa Fe Indian School in New Mexico in 1935, two years after Dorothy Dunn had established an innovative art program known as the Studio. Here he was one of a select group of young artists to receive the training and encouragement necessary to pursue careers in art. Howe graduated in 1938 as salutatorian of his class.

Returning to South Dakota, Howe taught art at the Pierre Indian School until 1940, when he joined the WPA South Dakota Artist Project, illustrating several books and painting murals in Mitchell and Mobridge. In 1942 he was drafted into the U.S. Army and served for three and a half years with combat forces in Europe. Honorably discharged in 1945, Howe returned to his art and in 1947 won the grand prize at the second annual National Indian Painting Competition at the Philbrook Museum of

Oscar Howe. Calling on Wakan Tanka, 1967. *Casein on paper*

Art in Tulsa, Oklahoma. With the prize of $350, he married Adelheid Hample, whom he had met in Germany; their only child, Inge Dawn, was born in 1949. Howe attended Dakota Wesleyan University in Mitchell on the GI Bill, receiving a bachelor of arts degree in 1952. During this period, the artist began designing the murals for Mitchell's "world-famous" Corn Palace, a commission he executed annually until 1971. Howe once again returned to Pierre, South Dakota, between 1953 and 1957 and taught high school art. He entered the master of fine arts program at the University of Oklahoma, graduating in 1954. In 1957 Howe accepted a position as professor and artist in residence at the University of South Dakota in Vermillion, beginning a distinguished twenty-five-year tenure at that institution.

These were the artist's most productive years, marked by over sixty solo exhibitions, fifteen grand or first-place prizes, and numerous awards. By this time, Howe had rejected the last vestiges of the Studio style for strong colors, pulsating space, dynamic movement, and a high degree of abstraction. *Sioux Seed Player* (1974), a casein painting on paper, is an excellent example of Howe's mature style. Masterfully executed, the painting is intensely pristine and compositionally complex, but its most compelling feature is its dynamism. Utilizing highly colorful flat shapes, Howe created

a fluid, ambivalent, and virtually pulsating spatial illusion that is unique in Native American art.

A signature event in Howe's life, often cited as helping to change the direction of Native American art, occurred in 1958. That year the artist challenged the jurors at the Philbrook's annual National Indian Painting Competition after they assessed one of his more abstract submissions as not Indian enough to qualify for an award. In a justifiably famous letter, Howe advanced the cause of personal expression, with the result that a new experimental category was added to future competitions—a decision that was a powerful incentive to younger artists.

During his life Howe was honored with the Dorothy Field Award from the Denver Art Museum (1952); the Mary Benjamin Award from the Museum of New Mexico, Santa Fe (1960); the Waite Phillips Trophy for Outstanding Contributions to American Indian Art from the Philbrook Museum of Art, Tulsa (1966); the South Dakota Governor's Award for Creative Achievement (1973); and the Golden Bear Award from the University of Oklahoma (1978).

Oscar Howe retired from the faculty of the University of South Dakota in 1980 and was recognized with a major retrospective exhibition that toured nationally between 1981 and 1983. After a prolonged illness, he died on October 7, 1983. Throughout his

Howling Wolf's Fight near Ft. Wallace, *drawing from* Fifty-four Ledger Drawings, *ledger page 42, ca. 1874–75. Ink, pencil, and watercolor on paper*

life, Oscar Howe demonstrated a strong connection with the land of his forebears and passionately advanced the creation of a Northern Plains style of Native American fine arts. Today his aesthetic leadership is widely acknowledged, and his work is celebrated for its revolutionary impact and its assertion of the creative vitality of Native American art in contemporary culture. Howe's achievements are memorialized with major collections of his work in South Dakota at the Oscar Howe Art Center in Mitchell, the South Dakota Memorial Art Center in Brookings, and the Oscar Howe Gallery and Archives at the University Art Galleries in Vermillion, South Dakota.

John A. Day
University of South Dakota

Dockstader, Frederick J., ed. *Oscar Howe: A Retrospective Exhibition.* Tulsa: Thomas Gilcrease Museum Association, 1982. Howe, Oscar. *Oscar Howe, Artist of the Sioux.* Vermillion SD: Oscar Howe, 1974. White, Mark Andrew. "Oscar Howe." *American Indian Art Magazine* 23 (1997): 36–43.

HOWLING WOLF (1849–1927)

Active in the Southern Plains wars, then incarcerated at Fort Marion in St. Augustine, Florida, between 1875 and 1878, Howling Wolf was a Southern Cheyenne warrior and noted artist who was born in 1849. He and his father, Eagle Head, were undoubtedly at the Sand Creek Massacre in 1864, and Howling Wolf subsequently engaged in various battles, successfully counting coup or completing his first culturally recognized brave action on a war

party led by the Bowstring warrior Lame Bull in May 1867. Howling Wolf became a secondary Bowstring leader before being selected, together with seventy-one other Southern Plains warriors and chiefs, for exile to Fort Marion, Florida.

Arguably the single most important Plains artist who worked on paper during the late nineteenth century, Howling Wolf is the only artist known to have created drawings during the prereservation era, on the reservation, and at Fort Marion. Using available paper, often lined accountants' ledgers, Plains men drew images of their battles and horse raids in much the same manner they did on hide robes. Howling Wolf's drawings from the first half of the 1870s not only reflect Plains systems of representation, with emphasis on the identity of protagonists and important actions, but also demonstrate experimental creativity and great skill. At Fort Marion he, like many of the younger prisoners, made drawings for various reasons, including to sell to tourists. His Florida drawings are generally nostalgic views of home or records of the men's new experiences rather than battle images. The few drawings he made following his release in mid-1878 demonstrate additional changes in subject and style that may be attributed to the vastly different life of the reservation and to many of the unique experiences he had in the East. Howling Wolf died in Oklahoma on July 5, 1927.

Joyce M. Szabo
University of New Mexico

Petersen, Karen Daniels. *Howling Wolf: A Cheyenne Warrior's Graphic Interpretation of His People.* Palo Alto CA: American West Publishing, 1968. Szabo, Joyce M. *Howling Wolf and the History of Ledger Art.* Albuquerque: University of New Mexico Press, 1994.

HUNTING

The celebrated horse-mounted bison hunters of the eighteenth and nineteenth centuries in the Great Plains have captured the popular imagination, but their reign represents only a relatively short phase in the long and complex history of Plains Indian hunting. Twelve thousand years ago, the Plains was home to eight-ton mastodons, twelve-feet-tall mammoths, giant bison, and wild horses. A growing number of Clovis people hunted these massive animals by driving them into swamps or box canyons and piercing their thick hides with sharp, fluted darts and spears using atlatls, or leverlike spear throwers. Such ventures were dangerous, but the rewards were worth the risk: a single kill could keep a hunting group of thirty to fifty people furnished with meat and fat for weeks. By around 9000 BC, however, warming climate, changing vegetation cover, and, apparently, overhunting pushed the Pleistocene megafauna into extinction, marking the end of the first great hunting culture of the Plains.

The Plains people adjusted to the disappearance of large mammals by concentrating their efforts on smaller animals such as deer, elk, pronghorn antelopes, grizzlies, and modern species of bison. They perfected a wide range of killing techniques: they camouflaged themselves in animal skins and patiently stalked their prey; ambushed individual animals at water holes; drove entire herds into manmade corrals; or stampeded bison over high bluffs and then slaughtered the crippled animals with spears, darts, and stones. About two thousand years ago Plains Indians also learned the use of the bow and arrow, which allowed them to kill effectively from a safe distance.

By about 1000 AD, however, encouraged by a wetter climate, the Plains people began to focus increasingly on farming, and hunting gradually became a secondary economic activity. By the thirteenth century there were still large numbers of nomadic hunters on the western shortgrass Plains (where Spanish explorers would encounter their descendants in the sixteenth century), but most Plains Indians lived along the eastern river valleys, where they based their economies on farming and sporadic hunting excursions.

This trend was suddenly reversed in the seventeenth and eighteenth centuries when horses became available to the Plains Indians. The horse was the missing tool that made it possible for Indians to begin a systematic exploitation of the enormous resource of protein, fat, and hides that was stored in the bodies of an estimated thirty million bison in the Plains. On horseback, hunters could follow the migrating herds more closely and over a wider range, kill the animals more efficiently, and carry back more meat and hides. Attracted by previously unimagined hunting possibilities, Indians poured into the Plains from all directions, creating one of most renowned hunting cultures in history.

By the early nineteenth century the Plains Indians had mastered an array of equestrian bison-hunting techniques that were carefully adapted to the seasonal and geographical variations of the region. In the winter, hunters drove bison into snow-filled gulches or snowdrifts, and in the summer, into swamps, rivers, or corrals. In the Northern Plains, where horses were in short supply, many groups continued to rely on pedestrian hunting techniques, such as the foot surround. Many Plains groups also burned sections of grasslands to make bison migrations and aggregations more predictable. The most popular method was the mounted chase, in which hunters galloped after bison on carefully trained running horses, thrusting lances or shooting volleys of arrows at the sides of the animals. A short bow remained the bison hunters' preferred weapon, because muskets were difficult to load and handle on horseback, and because powder and ball were scarce and expensive, and thus better reserved for warfare.

In the winter and spring Plains Indians usually hunted in small groups of few individuals, but in the summer and fall, when bison congregated into massive herds, hunting became a collective effort of hundreds of people. A typical mass hunt involved several stages, each consecrated by rituals. The preparation began with a bison-calling ceremony, usually a dance, song, or prayer performed by a medicine man. When the herd was located, a camp police of distinguished warriors took over, making sure nobody would try to start the hunt prematurely and stampede the herd. On the chief's order, the entire camp moved out as an orderly column—first the scouts, then medicine men, priests, and leaders, and finally old men, women, and children. Young men rode on both sides of the column, providing protection and ready to charge when the prey came in sight. The actual hunt might take only about thirty minutes, for bison had more endurance than horses and could pull away in few minutes, but that was enough time for most hunters to bring down several animals. After the chase was over, the families moved in to butcher their animals (each hunter used arrows and lances of his own design for recognition), turning the carcasses swiftly into piles of sliced meat, tallow, and hides. A successful hunt ended with ritual smoking, dancing, and feasting, which helped Indians maintain a proper relationship with animal spirits.

Although all Plains groups continued to hunt deer, elk, bears, porcupines, and other animals for clothing, food, tools, and jewelry, by the late eighteenth century most Plains Indians had developed a singular dependency on the buffalo. The western Plains became the domain of highly specialized hunter-nomads who fed, clothed, sheltered, and decorated themselves from the skin, flesh, fat, and bones of the bison. What they could not get by hunting, they acquired by trading surplus hides, dried meat, pemmican, and other products of the hunt. The eastern horticulturists also intensified their hunting practices and began to make extended semiannual hunting expeditions to the western Plains.

This emphasis on bison hunting persisted even after the advent of the commercial fur trade in the late eighteenth century. Some northern groups began producing deerskins and beaver pelts for trading posts, but most Plains Indians refused to take up trapping and instead provisioned European American trappers with bison meat and pemmican. From the 1830s on, following the collapse of the beaver trade, bison robes became the primary focus of the fur trade, and during the following four decades Plains Indians produced more than two hundred thousand hides and skins and forty to one hundred tons of pemmican a year for European American markets.

Such reliance on a narrow ecological base ultimately proved unsustainable, pushing the bison populations into a steep decline by the mid–nineteenth century. The traditional Plains Indian hunting culture came to an end in the 1870s and 1880s with the near extermination of the bison by commercial white hunters and the often violent removal of Indians into reservations, where Indian agents endeavored to transform them from hunters into farmers. Some Indians refused to give up their chosen lifestyle and continued to leave reservations in a desperate search for the few surviving bison. By the 1890s, however, all Plains Indians had been forced to abandon their dream of living as hunters. Today, a few Plains Indians make a living by hunting, or by mixing hunting with other economic activities, but even these efforts are threatened by the ongoing legal struggles among tribal, state, and federal governments over hunting rights.

Pekka Hämäläinen
University of California, Santa Barbara

Frison, George C. *Prehistoric Hunters of the High Plains.* San Diego: Academic Press, 1991. Isenberg, Andrew C. *The Destruction of the Bison: An Environmental History, 1750–1920.* Cambridge: Cambridge University Press, 2000. Lowie, Robert H. *Indians of the Plains.* New York: McGraw-Hill, 1954.

Incident at Oglala is a 1992 documentary film detailing the June 26, 1975, slayings of FBI special agents Jack Coler and Ronald Williams in the Jumping Bull compound near Oglala, South Dakota, and the subsequent conviction of Leonard Peltier for the crime. Although James Eagle, Dino Butler, Bob Robideau, and Peltier were charged with the shootings, Peltier was the only one convicted. Directed by Michael Apted and produced and narrated by Robert Redford, the film provides substantial background on the period of high tension on the Pine Ridge Reservation immediately following Wounded Knee II. The film clearly suggests the unscrupulous lengths to which the FBI and government prosecutors went in order to get a conviction. Peltier, who had fled to Canada, was extradited based on sworn affidavits that government prosecutors later admitted to be coerced fabrications.

Besides giving a feel for the conditions on Pine Ridge and an account of the incident, the film includes interviews and statements with key players and witnesses, including Peltier; American Indian Movement members Dennis Banks and Russell Means; William Kunstler, who served as attorney for Butler and appellant attorney for Peltier; and Myrtle Poor Bear, who claims she was coerced into changing her affidavit in order to extradite Peltier. Two assistant U.S. attorneys and one U.S. attorney speak for the government, but no FBI agents speak due to Bureau policy.

The Peltier case is ongoing. Peltier has become a celebrated example of someone considered by many to be a political prisoner. The incidents surrounding the story were also loosely used in Apted's theatrical film *Thunderheart* (1992).

Larry J. Zimmerman
University of Iowa

Messerschmidt, Jim. *The Trial of Leonard Peltier.* Boston: South End Press, 1983.

INDIAN AGENTS

In both Canada and the United States, Indian agents were responsible for implementing federal Indian policy. They were the governments' representatives on reservations and reserves and, as such, they wielded great power over Native peoples, even to the extent of usurping their traditional political authority, suppressing religious practices, and transforming social roles.

In the United States, Indian policy was transmitted from a commissioner of Indian Affairs (operating, after 1849, from the Office of Indian Affairs in Washington DC), through regional superintendents, to agents, who were responsible for a single tribe or a group of tribes. The agents, in turn, supervised teachers, blacksmiths, farmers, and other agency employees. In the early nineteenth century in the U.S. Great Plains, agents like John Dougherty, who was in charge of the Upper Missouri Agency from 1827 to 1837, were roving ambassadors who strived to maintain peace and to obtain Indian lands. In the second half of the nineteenth century, agents took up residence on their designated reservations and promoted the government's assimilation policy.

In Canada, a separate Department of Indian Affairs was not established until 1880, following the Indian Act of 1876. Federal policy (the federal government was confirmed in its authority over First Nations in the Constitution Act of 1867) was formulated in Ottawa, in the "Inside Service" of the Department of Indian Affairs. From there it passed through regional superintendencies (there were three such districts—headquartered at Battleford, Qu'Appelle, and Calgary—in the Prairie Provinces in 1897) to agents on the numerous reserves that were established after the treaties of the 1870s.

In the early nineteenth century, in the United States, Plains Indian agents were often traders who moved into the Indian service when the fur trade collapsed. Later, their origins were more diverse, but in both Canada and the United States they tended to come from eastern states and provinces, and they were often unsuited for the job. Political patronage played a major role in appointments.

In the late 1860s Quakers and other religious denominations were put in charge of many of the agencies in the U.S. Great Plains in an effort to introduce some honesty into the service; a similar transition occurred in the Prairie Provinces in the 1870s. Military officers were also appointed as agents on some U.S. Plains reservations in the late 1860s and 1870s.

Some agents did their jobs honorably amid the terrible living conditions that prevailed on the reservations and reserves. They were convinced that the only way the Native peoples could survive was by becoming individualized Christian farmers who made a living on their own pieces of private property. Many others were corrupt, taking advantage of the remoteness of their situations by skimming their charges' annuities or by colluding with settlers to steal Indian lands. Because of dismissals for corruption or ineptitude and resignations caused by the hardships of living in such isolated, desperate situations, agent turnover was high. At the Blackfoot Agency in Montana, for example, ten agents came and went in the thirteen years from 1863 to 1876; to the south at the Crow Agency, eight agents served in the nine years from 1869 to 1878. Such frenetic change did not inspire confidence in federal policy.

In the late nineteenth century and early twentieth century, agents imposed the assimilation policy with increasing force. After 1881 on the Canadian reserves, agents were given the powers of justices of the peace and encouraged to use them to control the Indians' behavior, including restricting them to the reserves by enforcing antivagrancy laws. South of the international boundary, agents threatened to withhold the Indians' annuities if their children were not placed in schools or made to work in the fields. In both countries, agents increasingly took over the political decision making that had previously resided with tribal councils.

In the United States, the post of Indian agent was abolished in 1908 by Commissioner of Indian Affairs Francis Leupp. Thereafter, doctors and teachers, officially called superintendents, took over the agents' duties. Leupp believed that they would be more successful in promoting assimilation. On Canadian reserves, agents remained the federal government's representatives, with comprehensive powers to regulate the Indians' lives, until the 1960s. Thereafter, agents were gradually removed from the reserves. The position no longer exists in the Department of Indian Affairs.

David J. Wishart
University of Nebraska–Lincoln

Abbott, Frederick H. *The Administration of Indian Affairs in Canada*. Washington DC: Board of Indian Commissioners, 1915. Hill, Edward E. *The Office of Indian Affairs, 1824–1880: Historical Sketches*. New York: Clearwater Publishing, 1974. *Report of the Royal Commission on Aboriginal Peoples*. Ottawa: RCAP, 1996.

INDIAN BOARDING SCHOOLS, UNITED STATES

Indian boarding schools, a primary focus of federal Indian policy beginning in the late 1870s, were designed as instruments for the assimilation of Native Americans into American society and were established on and off reservations throughout the United States, especially in the Great Plains. Boarding schools first appeared on reservations in 1877, but, beginning in 1879, policy makers seeking higher potential for assimilation channeled their efforts into building them off the reservations. By 1900 officials had reversed their decision, disturbed by the high costs associated with these schools, and, until 1923, they renewed support for on-reservation boarding and day schools. In 1923 pressure from Indian rights activists led the government to decrease its role in Indian education and, with the passage of the Indian Reorganization Act in 1934, to withdraw even further.

From the early nineteenth century, philanthropists and political leaders promoted assimilation through education as the most humane approach to the "Indian problem." Education was initially

Pawnee Manual Labor School, Pawnee Reservation, Nebraska

left to missionaries and philanthropists, who, with the support of church denominations and the government's "civilization" fund, established schools along with missions among Plains Indians during the 1830s. Mission schools remained an important component of Indian education—and assimilation—policy throughout the century, though they declined in importance after 1873, when direct federal financial support was removed. The federal government did, however, continue to contract with religious denominations to support mission schools, but their era was over.

The federal government moved to fill the gap. In 1870 Congress initiated an annual appropriation of $100,000 for Indian education. By 1893 the annual appropriation had risen to $2.3 million. The bulk of the money went to establishing day schools on or near Indian villages and later on reservations. By 1870, 48 day schools were in operation, and the number had risen to 147 by 1900; the majority were on reservations in the Great Plains.

But reformers were not entirely satisfied with day schools. The reservation environment, to which the child returned daily, undermined the process of assimilation. By the end of the 1870s policy makers were promoting reservation boarding schools as a solution to the shortcomings of the day schools; they viewed these schools—and the resultant separation of Indian children from

their families—as a superior context for changing children's attitudes, values, and habits. Like the day schools, which still received support, the majority of reservation boarding schools were built in the Great Plains.

As the idea of reservation boarding schools took hold, so too did the idea of federally operated schools off reservations. These schools followed the model of Richard Henry Pratt's Carlisle Indian Industrial School, founded in Pennsylvania in 1879, with an initial enrollment recruited from the Plains. The children received instruction in academic subjects (English, arithmetic, and geography) and also worked on manual labor projects. Boys labored in the fields, in construction, and in the blacksmith's shop; girls were taught to cook, clean, and sew. The objectives were to instill a work ethic, individualism, and other tenets of American civilization and to suppress all that was Indian.

Federal off-reservation boarding schools first appeared in the Great Plains in 1884 with the opening of Chilocco in Indian Territory near the Kansas border, Genoa in Nebraska, and Haskell in Lawrence, Kansas. Plans were soon under way to expand further. Pratt had urged officials to build off-reservation schools only in completely white communities, as far away from reservation influence as possible, but policy makers were concerned about the cost of transporting Indian children long distances. To save money they decided to build schools closer to the reservations, and in 1882 congressional authorization to use vacated military buildings reinforced this decision.

By the end of the 1880s seven federal off-reservation boarding schools were in operation nationally, enrolling more than 1,800 Indian children. In the 1890s eighteen more were built, including those at Pierre, Flandreau, Chamberlain, and Rapid City, South Dakota. By the end of the century there were also forty-three reservation boarding schools on the Plains and sixty-seven day schools. The on-reservation boarding schools were mainly located in North and South Dakota and Indian Territory; South Dakota, with its eight reservations and large Indian population, had the bulk of the day schools.

Enthusiasm for federal off-reservation boarding schools quickly faded after the turn of the twentieth century. In 1901 Commissioner of Indian Affairs William Jones expressed alarm that $45 million spent on twenty thousand Indian children had produced little evidence of assimilation. His 1904 annual report emphasized the necessity of utilizing existing reservation boarding and day schools more effectively. Arguing that these schools were no less effective than the off-reservation schools for assimilation, Jones proposed a hierarchy of existing schools that would provide the greatest opportunity for assimilating the best students with the greatest potential for surviving in the white world.

The building phase was over. Thereafter, Indian education policy deemphasized off-reservation schools. Policy makers argued that Indians were incapable of (more accurately, resistant to) the rapid assimilation envisioned by Pratt and noted that most Indians educated in the system of schools returned to the reservation. With this shift in emphasis, the number of boarding schools began to decline, and by 1920 seven of the federal off-reservation schools, including the flagship Carlisle as well as Chamberlain, had closed.

By the 1920s the long-lasting and unsuccessful assimilation policy was in decline. John Collier's American Indian Defense Association, founded in 1923, worked for the next decade to change the focus of federal Indian policy from destruction of Native cultures to respect for individual Indian self-identity. Collier became commissioner of Indian affairs in 1933. In 1934 the passage of the Wheeler-Howard Indian Reorganization Act established a "New Deal" for Native Americans, providing for tribal landownership, self-government, control of Indian education, and the closing of many of the remaining federal off-reservation boarding schools. The Great Plains education map

is now dotted with reservation community day schools, Bureau of Indian Affairs postsecondary schools (for example, Haskell Indian Junior College), and tribally controlled community colleges such as Sinte Gleska on Rosebud Reservation in South Dakota, the first Indian-run college to offer bachelor's degrees. The off-reservation boarding schools at Flandreau and Pierre, however, continue to operate.

Ronald C. Naugle
Nebraska Wesleyan University

Adams, David Wallace. *Education for Extinction: American Indians and the Boarding School Experience, 1875–1928.* Lawrence: University Press of Kansas, 1995. Child, Brenda J. *Boarding School Seasons: American Indian Families, 1900–1940.* Lincoln: University of Nebraska Press, 1998. Ellis, Clyde. *To Change Them Forever: Indian Education at the Rainy Mountain Boarding School, 1893–1920.* Norman: University of Oklahoma Press, 1996. Hoxie, Frederick E. *A Final Promise: The Campaign to Assimilate the Indians, 1880–1920.* Lincoln: University of Nebraska Press, 1984. Lomawaima, K. Tsianina. *They Called It Prairie Light: The Story of Chilocco Indian School.* Lincoln: University of Nebraska Press, 1994. Trafzer, Clifford E., Jean A. Keller, and Lorene Sisquoc, eds. *Boarding School Blues: Revisiting American Indian Educational Experiences.* Lincoln: University of Nebraska Press, 2006. U.S. Department of the Interior. *Annual Report of the Commissioner of Indian Affairs to the Secretary of the Interior.* Washington DC: Government Printing Office, 1877–1932.

INDIAN CLAIMS COMMISSION

In 1946, after decades of periodic debate, the United States established the Indian Claims Commission to give Native Americans their "day in court." The commission operated until 1978. Native American tribes and bands were given five years to register claims with the commission, claims relating to past injustices of federal Indian policy, including lands illegally taken, lands taken for "unconscionably low" compensation, and the government's misuse of Indian monies. Most Native American groups did register claims, and many claims were upheld, but ultimately there was little justice delivered in the process.

The Indian Claims Commission, comprised of three (later four) judges appointed by the president, actually functioned as a court that heard arguments of two adversaries—the Native American claimants and the United States as defendant—and then passed judgment. Awards were monetary only; return of land was expressly excluded. In a typical claim involving land, the Native American claimants had first to prove title to that land, then show that the original compensation paid (generally during the nineteenth century) was significantly below its fair market value at the time of taking. The difference between the fair market value and the original compensation (minus lawyers' fees and other offsets) constituted the award. Once an award was accepted or a case dismissed, then that claim was dead forever. Despite platitudes about "belated justice," the United States primarily intended this to be a wiping clean of the slate of outstanding claims as a prelude to termination—the prevailing policy to eliminate tribes as a separate factor in American society.

Altogether, by the deadline, 176 tribes and bands lodged 370 claims, which were separated into 617 dockets. Plains tribes were well represented. From the Lipan Apaches of southern Texas to the Blackfeet and Gros Ventres of northern Montana and from the Omahas of eastern Nebraska to the Crows of Wyoming, Plains Indians took their grievances to the commission.

In all, eighteen Plains tribes and nations lodged claims. The largest award, $35,060,000 for land primarily in West Texas, went to the Kiowas, Comanches, and Apaches in 1974. Other sizable awards included $15 million (1965) to the Cheyennes and Arapahos for lands in northeastern Colorado and adjacent Wyoming, Nebraska, and Kansas; and $10,242,984 to the Crows (1954) for their traditional homelands in Wyoming and Montana. The smallest award—$2,458—was made to the Poncas of Nebraska in 1965 for an accounting claim. In the most notorious case, involving the Lakotas' (Sioux) 1877 cession of the Black Hills, the Indian Claims Commission's award of $17.5 million (without interest) was appealed and eventually reached the Supreme Court, which ruled in 1980 that, because the taking was unconstitutional, not just inadequate, the Lakotas merited interest on the award from 1877 on. Their award, accumulating to more than $600 million by the late 1990s, sits unclaimed in the U.S. Treasury; the Lakotas want their sacred Black Hills back, not a monetary settlement.

On close analysis, even sizable awards diminished to small payments when they were allocated to individual Native Americans. (Sometimes awards were put into tribal investments, but this was often contentious, because the tribal members who did not reside on reservations would not benefit from reservation development.) The Pawnees of central Nebraska, for example, were awarded $7,316,096 in 1964, largely for lands that had been taken in the nineteenth century for unconscionably low compensation. Of this, the lawyers took $876,897 for fees and expenses, leaving $6,439,199. In March 1964 the tribal council voted to distribute the award (with a small amount of accrued interest) on a per capita basis to the 1,883 enrolled members of the tribe. Each Pawnee received about $3,530—no doubt a boon in (always) hard times, but hardly a redress of past injustices. The Omahas, the Pawnees' traditional neighbors, received even less ($750 for each tribal member) in their 1960 settlement, and each Yankton Sioux accepted $249 in 1960 as a reward for enduring ten years of litigation in their land claims case.

The Indian Claims Commission, therefore, should be viewed more as a continuation of the past than a break from it. As in the nineteenth century, most Plains Indians (and Native Americans elsewhere in the country) felt obliged to accept the United States' definition of what constituted justice. At no stage of the litigation process before the Indian Claims Commission was the value that Plains Indians placed on their lands as homelands taken into account.

David J. Wishart
University of Nebraska–Lincoln

Indian Claims Commission. *Final Report.* 96th Cong., 2nd sess., 1980, H. Doc. 96–383. Lieder, M., and J. Page. *Wild Justice: The People of Geronimo vs. the United States.* New York: Random House, 1997. Sutton, I., ed. *Irredeemable America: The Indians' Estate and Land Claims.* Albuquerque: University of New Mexico Press, 1985.

INDIAN COUNTRY

"Indian Country" refers to a variable geographic place where Native Americans reside on trust lands—reserves and reservations. The term is in use in both Canada and the United States, but it bears specific legal meaning only in the latter, where it defines both tribal holdings and individual land allotments, whether still in trust or held in fee (absolute ownership). There is no comparable meaning in Canada, for Native reserves are administered only for Indian communities, not for individual Indians. In both nations the federal government administers most of these lands and thereby generally preempts provincial or state authority over them. Every state and province in the Great Plains includes Indian Country: trust lands abound in the northern tier of states and in the adjacent three provinces—for example, the Rosebud Reservation in South Dakota, the Crow Indian Reservation in Montana, and the Assiniboine Reserve in Saskatchewan. In the Prairie Provinces there are numerous very small reserves, many occupied by brethren of tribes within U.S. borders (e.g., the Blackfeet and Crees); in Alberta there are also a small number of Métis reserves held in fee simple title. In contrast, reservations on the American side of the border are generally much larger, although in the states of Kansas, Nebraska, and Texas, there are only a few small, scattered reservations. Oklahoma—once Indian Territory, to which were relocated tribes from the South, East, and from other parts of the Plains—does not acknowledge Indian Country, despite the existence of the Osage Reservation and so-called former reservations (for the most part, Indian Territory reservations were cancelled through allotment).

Because of conflict and litigation over jurisdiction, other interpretations of Indian Country would apply extralegal meaning in the United States. Such interpretations involve former Aboriginal territory (where, for example, some tribes may continue to hunt and fish but not without controversy); adjudicated claims areas, or lands shown to have historically belonged to tribes, and all former trust lands whether within or outside reservations. State jurisdiction over certain criminal and civil authority may extend to Indians and their lands, but not authority over land use. (Under the Indian Act of 1876 in Canada, provinces do have some jurisdiction over Indians on reserves, but rarely over land in reserves, and provincial zoning authority may apply only if not contrary to that act and constitutional revisions of 1982.)

At one time Indian Country was extraterritorial by treaty and lay beyond local European American jurisdiction. Such was true of the Great Plains until settlers and others, seeking land farther and farther west in both countries, agitated for the cession of tribal reserves or reservations. At first, treaties reserved considerable acreage, as with the Great Sioux Reservation that once dominated Dakota Territory and buffered tribes from adjacent non-Indian communities. Unfortunately, Congress enabled non-Indian homesteading within reservations by declaring remaining acreage "surplus" subsequent to the allotment of tribal lands to individual Indians. Moreover, countless non-Indians also acquired trust lands through sale or inheritance. This aspect of Indian Country is fundamentally inapplicable to Canada.

Where entire counties within Indian Country in some states have become non-Indian in character, litigation has ensued, leading to the diminishment of external boundaries of many allotted reservations. Plains tribes have not escaped this judicial interpretation. In *Rosebud Sioux Tribe v. Kneip* (1977), the Supreme Court determined that four counties in South Dakota were disestablished by earlier allotment laws; consequently, some two thousand tribal members and seven recognized communities occupying trust acreage on the Rosebud Reservation ended up outside the reservation. South Dakota does not delineate on official state maps those counties once part of reservations that now comprise mostly non-Indian citizenry. Recent court decisions have continued to erode the legal meaning of Indian Country and hence its geographic configuration. Fee lands owned, utilized, and resided on by non-Indians constitute a strong demographic factor disqualifying tribal jurisdiction over land-use planning and related environmental management. This interpretation has led the courts in *Devils Lake Sioux Tribe v. North Dakota* PSC to exclude non-Indian holdings from tribal jurisdiction on the Fort Totten Reservation (North Dakota); a similar decision has diminished tribal authority on the Crow Indian Reservation (Montana). According to *South Dakota v. Bourland*, the alienation of Cheyenne River (South Dakota) Sioux lands by flood control and other acts eliminated tribal jurisdiction over non-Indians on certain lands adjacent to the Missouri River. In 1998 a similar decision—*South Dakota v. Yankton Sioux Tribe*—excluded from tribal jurisdiction all former trust lands lying outside diminished reservation borders.

Imre Sutton
California State University–Fullerton

Getches, David H., Charles F. Wilkinson, and Robert A Williams Jr. *Cases and Materials on Federal Indian Law*. St. Paul: West Publishing, 1993. Johnson, Ralph W. "Fragile Gains: Two Centuries of Canadian and United States Policy toward Indians." *Washington Law Review* 66 (1991): 643–718. Sutton, Imre. "Preface to Indian Country: Geography and Law." *American Indian Culture and Research Journal* 15 (1991): 3–35.

INDIAN COUNTRY TODAY

Indian Country Today is the most widely circulated and arguably the most influential Native newspaper in the world. Tim Giago (Nanwica Kciji, or Defender), Oglala Lakota, established the weekly paper in 1981 as the *Lakota Times*. Giago, born in 1934 on the Pine Ridge Reservation and educated at the Holy Rosary Mission School there, served in the U.S. Navy after high school. He attended San Jose State College in California and earned his bachelor's degree from the University of Nevada–Reno. Giago worked a variety of jobs before becoming an Indian affairs columnist for the *Rapid City Journal* in Rapid City, South Dakota, in 1979; he later became a full-time reporter. In 1981 he established the *Lakota Times* to provide news coverage for Pine Ridge. The paper expanded to cover other reservations in the upper Midwest and by 1986 was distributed to all reservations in South Dakota, North Dakota, Nebraska, and Montana. Unlike most Native American papers, which tend to focus on one tribe or reservation, the *Lakota Times* focused on all tribes and reservations. The paper's offices moved to Rapid City in 1989, and in 1991 the *Lakota Times* claimed a readership of fifty thousand. By 1999 circulation had reached seventy-seven thousand, with pass-along readership estimated to be as high as one hundred thousand.

With support from the Gannett Corporation, publisher of *USA Today*, Giago expanded to national coverage in 1992 and changed the name of the paper to *Indian Country Today*. The paper operated bureaus in Albuquerque, New Mexico, and Spokane, Washington, and used freelance reporters to cover other regions. Giago has used the paper and pieces written for national publications such as *USA Today*, the *New York Times*, and *Newsweek* to defend Lakota and other Native American interests. He may be most widely known for criticizing the use of Native Americans as sports team mascots.

Standing Stone Media, Inc., an operation of the Oneida Indian Nation of New York State, bought *Indian Country Today* in December 1998. Corporate headquarters moved to New York, but editorial headquarters remain in Rapid City. The independent paper's sale to a tribal entity raised concern among some members of the Native American Journalists Association, who feared the Oneidas might restrict the paper's editorial voice. Early indications, however, show that the tribe is not changing the paper's editorial process. The paper maintains a bureau in Washington DC and has reporters in the Southwest, California, Oklahoma, and the Northeast. An expanding pool of correspondents provides national coverage. The paper now claims distribution in all fifty states and seventeen foreign countries, and it operates an online version.

Todd M. Kerstetter
Texas Christian University

Andreassi, Diane. "Tim Giago." In *Notable Native Americans*, edited by Sharon Malinowski, 164–65. Detroit: Gale Research, 1995. Fitzgerald, Mark. "A 'New Model' for Tribal Ownership?" *Editor & Publisher*, October 23, 1999: 22–26. Riley, Sam G. *Biographical Dictionary of American Newspaper Columnists*. Westport CT: Greenwood Press, 1995.

INDIAN COWBOYS

Plains Indians have been cowboys for a long time. Their involvement in the cattle industry of the region began in the late nineteenth century and continues to the present. Indian men and women have also been involved for an extended period of time in the world of rodeo. Their participation in ranching and rodeo is significant both in economic and cultural terms.

After the American Civil War, cattle ranching played an important role in the economic development of the Plains. This development came at considerable cost. Native communities lost millions of acres through treaties, agreements, land allotment, land cessions, and long-term leases. With bison hunting no longer possible, Plains Indian peoples had to find alternative means to sustain themselves. Cattle ranching offered Indian men a chance to ride, an alternative to farming, and an opportunity to demonstrate both competence and generosity. Cattle could be given as presents, used to feed people at a gathering, and employed to teach young people about responsibility and

Branding a calf, Fort Berthold Indian Agency, North Dakota, 1948

reciprocity. Given their needs and given the success their new neighbors were enjoying, it is not surprising that so many Indian individuals and communities turned to cattle ranching. Some, like Quanah Parker, knew spectacular, if too brief, success. Others started ranches that continue to our own day. Many Native cowboys also found work as cowboys on ranches owned by non-Indians.

Progress in the Indian cattle industry during the twentieth century was limited by fluctuating federal policies and market conditions, as well as by the problems of fractionated landownership resulting from the division of allotted land through inheritance and sale. Nonetheless, many Indian ranchers continue in the business, either through tribal or community enterprises or as individuals. They know the same satisfactions and experience the same problems as their non-Indian counterparts. Access to better legal counsel has permitted tribes in many instances to obtain more equitable leases or to promote ranching by tribal members.

Plains Indian rodeo dates back to the turn of the century. At agricultural fairs at the Crow Indian Reservation and elsewhere, rodeos began to be featured as prominent components of annual gatherings. The Crows took great pride in their abilities and accomplishments as bronc riders. At Rosebud and other reservations in the Dakotas, Lakota cowboys also demonstrated their talents in various rodeos. The best Indian cowboys, like Sam Bird in Ground (Crow) and George Defender (Standing Rock Sioux), captured world championship titles early in the twentieth century. Tom Three Persons (Blood) won instant immortality by riding Midnight in the first Calgary Stampede rodeo in 1912.

The Plains Indian rodeo tradition continues. Plains Indian cowgirls and cowboys participate in regional competitions, often instructed and judged by relatives eager to pass along their love for the sport, and they have also enjoyed considerable success in the Indian National Finals Rodeo.

Mounted Dakota Sioux Indian Police, Rosebud Agency, South Dakota, 1896

Names like Gladstone and Guardipee, Bird and Bruised Head are immediately recognizable to all those who cherish the history and heritage of Indian rodeo.

Peter Iverson
Arizona State University

Dempsey, Hugh A. *Tom Three Persons: Legend of an Indian Cowboy.* Saskatoon: Purich Publishing, 1997. Iverson, Peter. *When Indians Became Cowboys: Native Peoples and Cattle Ranching in the American West.* Norman: University of Oklahoma Press, 1994. Iverson, Peter, and Linda Mac-Cannell. *Riders from the West: Portraits of Indian Rodeo.* Seattle: University of Washington Press, 1999.

INDIAN POLICE

Indian police forces first appeared on the Great Plains during the 1830s, when the federal government relocated eastern tribes such as the Cherokees to Indian Territory. Known as the Lighthorse, Cherokee police units performed law enforcement duties similar to their European American counterparts of the period. During the 1860s and 1870s Indian agents throughout the American West began to organize police forces to protect reservations from cattle and horse rustlers, timber thieves, and liquor peddlers. In 1862, for example, the Bureau of Indian Affairs (BIA) agent at the Pawnee Agency in Nebraska created a police force to curb horse thefts. Agents at Red Cloud and Spotted Tail Agencies in northwestern Nebraska created similar forces during the 1870s. These police forces operated autonomously, without federal approval or funding. This changed in 1878, when Congress legitimized Indian police forces by providing funds and operational guidelines. BIA agents quickly organized Native police forces, in part because this increased their influence over reservation affairs and removed the need for military troops. By the end of 1878 police forces operated at twenty-two agencies. Three years later forty-nine of sixty-eight agencies had police forces, and by 1890 the number had risen to fifty-nine.

Indian policemen are often viewed unfavorably by historians. Using examples such as the 1890 killing of Sitting Bull by Standing Rock policemen or the role of BIA police officers at Wounded Knee in 1973, many scholars have portrayed Indian policemen as traitors to their own people. This interpretation fails to acknowledge the origins of police forces. The concept of tribal police forces was not new to Plains Indians. All tribes traditionally had law enforcers. Traditional Lakota law enforcers, known as *akicitas*, enforced tribal laws and customs, policed camp moves, and regulated buffalo hunts. When the first agency police force was organized at Pine Ridge (present-day South Dakota) in 1879, it was the akicitas who filled its ranks, suggesting that the Lakotas may have used this institution to continue their traditional roles.

Indian policemen performed an array of duties. Day-to-day tasks included maintaining law and order in and around the agency, including guarding agency property and storehouses, arresting drunks and gamblers, maintaining the agency jail, and serving as messengers and scouts. Armed and mounted policemen also patrolled reservation boundaries, driving off or arresting stock thieves, liquor peddlers, and timber thieves. More controversial duties sometimes included forcing children to attend agency schools and enforcing bans on polygamy, dancing, and traditional ceremonies. In carrying out their duties Indian policemen were often put in danger. Between 1876 and 1906 at least twenty-four Indian police officers were killed in Indian Territory alone. In the deadliest day for Indian policemen, six members of Standing Rock's Indian police force were killed on December 15, 1890, while attempting to arrest Sitting Bull.

Early Indian police forces were usually poorly equipped. With little federal support, agents were left on their own to arm and clothe their police officers. Agents at Rosebud and Pine Ridge Agencies, for example, armed their forces with borrowed weapons from nearby Fort Robinson. By the mid-1880s, however, the Department of the Interior was providing standardized uniforms, badges, and weaponry.

Dismally low remuneration was another problem. Ranking officers in 1880 earned only $8 a month, while enlisted men received a paltry $5 for a month's labor. Even as late as 1927 many Lakota policemen had to supplement their income by farming. Most forces experienced high turnover rates because policemen could earn more money as military scouts or laborers.

Each Indian police force looked and operated differently from the others. On Lakota reservations police units operated almost like the military. Pine Ridge's police force regularly drilled under the command of ex–military officers and patrolled reservation boundaries in small mounted squads. Cherokee and Choctaw police officers, however, operated more like a European American constabulary, performing law enforcement tasks as sheriffs and deputies. Police forces also varied in size. Units at Pine Ridge and Rosebud agencies included the maximum of fifty policemen, while the smaller Cheyenne River Agency had only nine officers on its original force.

The early 1880s were the heyday for Indian police forces on the Great Plains. During these years Indian police forces performed all law enforcement duties on their reservations and operated largely free of federal control. By the mid-1880s, however, federal laws began to encroach on the autonomy of the criminal justice system on reservations. The Major Crimes Act of 1885 gave the federal government jurisdiction in most felonies, limiting the duties of Indian police officers. The Dawes Act further curtailed the authority of Indian police by

placing allottees under the jurisdiction of the state in which they resided. By 1900 the large Indian police forces of the 1880s had disappeared. Without federal financial support, most reservations could employ only one or two police officers by the 1920s; even the largest Lakota reservation employed only seventeen officers. By the 1950s Bureau of Indian Affairs police forces had supplanted most agency forces. In 2000 Bureau of Indian Affairs police forces operated in every Great Plains state except Texas.

Mark R. Ellis
University of Nebraska at Kearney

Ellis, Mark R. "Reservation Akicitas: The Pine Ridge Indian Police, 1879–1885." *South Dakota History* 29 (1999): 185–210. Hagan, William T. *Indian Police and Judges.* Lincoln: University of Nebraska Press, 1980.

INDIAN REMOVAL

The policy of the U.S. government to move Native Americans from their homelands to other locations was part of the clash of cultures brought about by the colonization of North America. There was no such policy of forcible removals from east to west in Canada; even within the Prairie Provinces, First Nations were given considerable choice in the selection of their reserves. U.S. policy was formalized in the Indian Removal Act of 1830, which gave President Andrew Jackson the authority to make treaties with tribes by which they would exchange land east of the Mississippi River for lands to the west. By that time, however, removals had been taking place for more than two decades.

President Thomas Jefferson initiated the idea of removal with the Louisiana Purchase in 1803. He saw a new western territory where Native Americans could live their traditional lifestyles far removed from often deleterious contact with Americans. The rationale was that moving Native Americans to this Permanent Indian Frontier would open up land in the eastern United States for European American settlers, while protecting them until such time as they were willing and able to assimilate into American society. Jefferson also believed that consolidating Native Americans in the Great Plains would create a barrier that would prevent American settlers from dispersing too widely. In the 1820s and 1830s, Baptist missionary Isaac McCoy even campaigned to create a separate Indian state in the Great Plains, where Native Americans could be taught the precepts of American civilization, but the idea did not receive serious attention in Congress.

As early as 1808 the Sauks and Foxes moved voluntarily from Illinois to Missouri to escape the disruption of their lives by white settlers. From 1817 to 1820 federal agents signed treaties with the

Delawares in Ohio and the Kickapoos and Weas in Illinois by which the tribes agreed to exchange their lands for others in Illinois and Missouri. By 1817 leaders of the Cherokees in Georgia had agreed to a treaty that provided individual allotments for those who agreed to be citizens of the state and remain on their land, or a tract of land west of the Mississippi for those who chose to move. The Choctaws signed a similar treaty in 1820. Removal policy led to divisions within tribes between those who agreed to stay in their homelands and adapt to new ways and those who decided to move west and try to retain their cultural identities. Even before formal legislation for Indian removal, some Choctaw and Cherokee families were moving west of the Mississippi to settle on lands guaranteed to them by treaty.

By the time of Andrew Jackson's election to the presidency in 1828, the prospect of ridding the East of Native Americans appealed greatly to land speculators, and Jackson's strong sense of nationalism led him to reject the idea that tribes could exist as sovereign nations within the confines of American territory. Within ten years of the passage of the Indian Removal Act, vast areas of the Midwest and the southeastern United States had been "cleared" and the Native American residents removed to tracts of land in the present-day states of Kansas and Oklahoma.

North of the Ohio River a great variety of Native American communities were shifted west. These included Peorias, Kaskaskias, Sauks and Foxes, Piankashaws, Weas, Shawnees, Ottawas, Wyandottes, Potawatomis, Delawares, and Kickapoos. Many of these groups suffered multiple removals. The Delawares, for example, were originally from eastern Pennsylvania. They subsequently moved to Ohio, Illinois, Missouri, and, in 1829, to Kansas. The Kickapoos also ended up in eastern Kansas in 1832, after first being moved from southern Ohio and then from southwestern Missouri. By 1841 emigrant Native Americans occupied squared-off tracts along the eastern portions of the Great Plains from present-day Nebraska to Texas. They were settled on land that was purchased from Indigenous Plains tribes, such as the Pawnees and Kaws, and frequently conflicts ensued between the emigrants and the local Native Americans.

Major removal treaties were also negotiated with the southeastern tribes. The Choctaws signed the Treaty of Dancing Rabbit Creek in 1830, in large part because the state of Mississippi extended its laws over the tribe and made illegal the operations of the tribal government. The state of Georgia also sought to regulate the Cherokees. The Creeks, Seminoles, and Chickasaws signed treaties in 1832, and the Cherokees signed the Treaty of New Echota in 1835. As a result of these treaties, approximately sixty thousand members of these tribes made the trek west to the land designated as Indian Territory in the eastern half of what is now Oklahoma. For the Creeks, Seminoles, and Cherokees, these were forced marches under the U.S. Army. It is estimated that approximately one-quarter of the refugees died along the trail from illness, exposure, or starvation.

After 1854 the tide of European American settlement reached the Great Plains, and the Permanent Indian Frontier fragmented into reservations, where Indigenous Plains peoples and emigrant tribes were segregated and placed under great pressure to acculturate. In the following three decades, as their reservations were surrounded by settlers, many of these Indians, including the Pawnees, Poncas, Cheyennes, Arapahos, Comanches, Potawatomis, and Kickapoos, made their final migration to Indian Territory, where many of their descendants remain today.

Clara Sue Kidwell
University of Oklahoma

Abel, Annie H. "The History of Events Resulting in Indian Consolidation West of the Mississippi." In *Annual Report of the American Historical Association for the Year 1906*. Washington DC: Government Printing Office, 1908. Foreman, Grant. *Indian Removal: The Emigration of the Five Civilized Tribes of Indians*. Norman: University of Oklahoma Press, 1953. Green, Michael D. *The Politics of Indian Removal: Creek Government and Society in Crisis*. Lincoln: University of Nebraska Press, 1982. Perdue, Theda, and Michael D. Green. *The Cherokee Removal: A Brief History with Documents*. New York: Bedford, 1995.

INDIAN RESIDENTIAL SCHOOLS, CANADA

The modern phase of Canada's residential schools system for First Nations children emerged in the 1880s in the Prairie Provinces, and several of the institutions would continue to exist in that region after the government of Canada decided to phase out the institutions in 1969. Missionaries and colonial governments had experimented with boarding schools for Native children as early as the French colonial regime of the seventeenth century, and other custodial institutions were initiated by Protestant missionary organizations in eighteenth-century colonial New Brunswick and early-nineteenth-century Upper Canada (Ontario). However, the modern era of residential schooling in Canada began in the Prairies in 1883 as a direct consequence of the treaties that Canada had negotiated with the First Nations between 1871 and 1877. The system began slowly in the Prairies in 1883, spread to British Columbia in the 1890s, and expanded to the far North and the northerly regions of Ontario and Quebec in the twentieth century. At the height of the residential school system in the 1920s, more than half of the eighty institutions were located in the three Prairie Provinces.

Father, and children attending Qu'Appelle (Saskatchewan) industrial school, ca. 1900

the many grievances that both residential school students and their families had with the system. Inadequate government funding, especially from the 1890s to the latter part of the 1950s (the government began to improve financing after 1956), led to overwork of the students and inadequate care in diet, accommodation, clothing, and amenities such as recreational equipment. The root of the funding problem was government reluctance to spend much on the First Nations, principally because Canadian society placed little value on Native peoples, and the fact that the per capita funding mechanism that was used induced missionaries to place a greater emphasis on keeping student places in the schools filled than on providing adequate care.

Since, like American schools, Canadian residential schools operated until the 1950s on the half-day system, the administrators had ample occasion to overwork the students. The half-day system theoretically taught both usable job skills and rudimentary academic learning by having students in the classroom half the day and engaged in work in fields, barns, kitchens, and workrooms the other half. In reality, the half-day system proved a means of extracting student labor to keep the underfunded schools running. Besides excessive work and ethnocentrically focused religion, the schools stimulated opposition by providing inadequate care at the best of times and serious physical, emotional, and sexual abuse at the worst. These ills, in conjunction with the obvious fact that the schools were not succeeding as pedagogical, evangelical, or vocational-training operations, provoked strong and organized First Nations opposition by the 1940s. After much hesitation, largely caused by vigorous Roman Catholic opposition to closure, the government decided in 1969 to phase out the schools. Some schools persisted into the 1980s, and a few continued to operate under First Nations control until the 1990s.

In the twenty-first century Canada's residential schools are a festering legal and political problem for Canadians. By the end of 2000 more than 6,200 individual lawsuits involving some 7,200 individuals had been filed against the government and, in some cases, the missionaries; they allege abuse, both physical and sexual, and cultural loss. The number of suits continues to increase weekly. One law firm in the Prairie Provinces is handling over half the suits.

Indian residential schools were joint operations of the federal government and the major Christian churches. The government authorized the creation of schools, provided partial funding for their operation, specified curricula and standards of care, and, in general, oversaw their operation as a system. The day-to-day running of the institutions was in the hands of the churches, with approximately 60 percent of the schools operated by the Roman Catholic Church (mainly through the Oblates of Mary Immaculate and female religious orders), about 30 percent by the Anglican Church, and the remainder by the Methodists and Presbyterians. (The Methodists and most Presbyterians united with the Congregationalists in 1925 to form the United Church of Canada.) Church missionary bodies concentrated on selecting personnel, particularly principals, subject to the approval of the government. A constant source of tension between missionaries and the government was the level of state funding, which was never adequate to cover most of the costs of the schools. The various churches also tended to regard one another with denominational hostility, resulting in a competition for recruits to populate their schools.

The strong emphasis placed by the missionaries on sectarian attitudes toward denominational rivals and the aggressive proselytization of the students under their care constituted but one of

J. R. Miller
University of Saskatchewan

Miller, J. R. *Shingwauk's Vision: A History of Native Residential Schools.* Toronto: University of Toronto Press, 1996. Milloy, J. S. *A National Crime: The Canadian Government and the Residential School System, 1879 to 1986.* Winnipeg: University of

Cheyenne Indian scouts at Fort Reno, Indian Territory

Manitoba Press, 1999. Titley, E. Brian. "Industrial Schools in Western Canada." In *Schools in the West: Essays on Canadian Educational History*, edited by Nancy M. Sheehan, J. Donald Wilson, and David C. Jones. Calgary: Detselig Enterprises, 1986. 133–54.

INDIAN SCOUTS

From the time of the conquest of Mexico onward, Native American–European American conflicts in North America were seldom clearcut; some Native Americans almost always participated on the side of the European Americans, and in conflicts between colonizers, they were likely to be present on both sides. This pattern held true in the campaigns fought in the Great Plains. Pueblo auxiliaries helped Spanish forces in New Mexico defeat the Comanches in the 1780s. Lakota Sioux auxiliaries cooperated with Col. Henry Leavenworth's expedition against the Arikaras in 1823, and Cheyenne and Crow scouts rode with the regular army in the Ghost Dance troubles of 1890–91, the last "Indian war" in the West, though they were not present at the Wounded Knee Massacre.

The very idea of Native Americans assisting European Americans in their conquest has always seemed incongruous to some, leading to distrust by whites at the time, and later to charges by Native Americans that Indian scouts and auxiliaries were mercenaries consciously betraying their own people. In most cases the scouts themselves would have found such accusations meaningless and irrelevant. They often saw themselves as fighting,

beside the best available allies, against bitter—and frequently stronger—enemies who constituted the greater immediate menace. This was the situation with the Pawnees, Arikaras, Crows, and Shoshones who joined the U.S. Army against their enemy, the Sioux, in the 1860s and 1870s. When some Sioux joined up to fight other Sioux who were resisting the United States, they did so hoping for favorable terms for their own bands and for an eventual reduction of further suffering by the "hostile" bands.

The earliest sustained conflicts between European Americans and Plains Indians began in Texas in the 1830s. There, frontiersmen and Texas Rangers, however bitterly they might fight the Kiowas and Comanches, still enlisted the aid of Tonkawas, Lipans, and Delawares, following a pattern set by frontier rangers and Indian fighters in colonial times. As the U.S. Army became increasingly involved in conflict with the Plains tribes after 1848, they followed the frontiersmen's example. The rising tide of conflict during and after the Civil War led in 1866 to a congressional act authorizing the enlistment of Indians as scouts, on the same terms as regular army soldiers, but for shorter terms. As soldiers they could receive pay, rations, weapons, and noncommissioned rank, and a few received the Medal of Honor for bravery. They served not only as individual trackers and intelligence gatherers but often in large contingents of company or even battalion strength. A few units served for extended periods of time, notably the Pawnee scouts under Maj. Frank North, who took the field in 1864 and 1865, served through the Sioux and Cheyenne campaigns of the late 1860s, and campaigned for the last time in the Sioux War of 1876–77. They were admired and praised by the army commanders they served.

Scouts were valued because of their specialized skills and knowledge acquired over a lifetime: knowledge of how to follow a trail and observe the enemy without being seen, knowledge of the country, and ability to identify vital information from tracks. These skills made it possible for soldiers operating in an alien environment to locate and surprise elusive enemies in their own country and greatly enhanced the ability of the military to carry out their mission.

Thomas W. Dunlay
Lincoln, Nebraska

Dunlay, Thomas W. *Wolves for the Blue Soldiers: Indian Scouts and Auxiliaries with the United States Army, 1860–90.* Lincoln: University of Nebraska Press, 1982.

INDIAN TERRITORY

All of Oklahoma was referred to as Indian Territory until 1890, when Congress partitioned Oklahoma Territory and made Indian Territory the formal name for the Five Civilized Tribes' domain. Indian Territory's relevance to the Great Plains thus spans from the 1820s, when the United States cleared title through treaty cessions by the Quapaws (1818) and Osages (1825) and designated the area as Indian Country, to the Oklahoma land runs, beginning in 1889.

The area had long been permanently or seasonally occupied by Great Plains peoples, notably the Wichitas, Kiowas, and Plains Apaches. Comanche, Cheyenne, Arapaho, and Pawnee bison hunters also knew it well in the 1820s, as did hunters from the east, including bands of Cherokees, who came to the Arkansas and Red River areas decades before their nation was forcibly relocated there. The treaties that forced the Five Tribes to remove from their eastern homelands in the 1830s gave them roughly equivalent areas in Indian Territory, overlapping the eastern margin of the Great Plains.

The Five Tribes' three ribbons of Great Plains land included the Cherokee Outlet in the north, a strip between this and the Canadian River shared by the Creek and Seminole Nations, and a wide expanse between the Canadian and North Fork of the Red River owned by the Choctaws and Chickasaws (Texas began west of the North Fork). The Five Tribes' settlements clung to the safe, humid, accessible, alluvial valleys to the east, which left the Kiowas and Comanches to command their western lands.

Beginning in the 1850s western Indian Territory became a dumping ground for dispossessed Plains Indians. When the Chickasaws and Choctaws separated in 1855, they leased the western third of their domain to the United States to resettle Texas Indians. After the Civil War the Five Tribes were forced to cede their western lands to make room for new reservations. The eastern third of the Cherokee, Creek, and Seminole holdings was parceled among a diverse set of Native American refugees, creating a cluster of small, poverty-stricken reservations. The western lands of the Seminoles, Choctaws, and Chickasaws became reservations for the Cheyennes and Arapahos, Comanches, and Kiowas and Apaches following their brutal suppression by the army in the 1860s and 1870s, which also coincided with the era of the cattle drives through the area.

By the 1880s reservation farming was largely unsuccessful, since the most rational land use for land-rich, capital-poor Indians was to lease land to white cattlemen. For quite different reasons, farmers and humanitarian reformers agreed that the communal land tenure on reservations had to end. In 1887 Congress passed the General Allotment (Dawes) Act, which required tribal members to select 160 acres of land for their own use, although title would be held for a period of years by the government. The acreage that remained was then opened to white settlement. The reservations of western Indian Territory were allotted in the late 1880s and early 1890s. This was immediately followed by land runs and lotteries that brought tens of thousands of white families to the region.

Brad A. Bays
Oklahoma State University

Debo, Angie. *And Still the Waters Run: The Betrayal of the Five Civilized Tribes.* Princeton NJ: Princeton University Press, 1940. Gibson, Arrell Morgan. *Oklahoma: A History of Five Centuries.* Norman: University of Oklahoma Press, 1981. Morris, John W., Charles R. Goins, and Edwin C. McReynolds. *Historical Atlas of Oklahoma.* Norman: University of Oklahoma Press, 1986.

INDIAN TRAILS

Plains Indians traveled long distances to hunt, trade, make war, and visit sacred places. To do so, they used trails such as the Great North Trail that ran south from Canada along the eastern front of the Rocky Mountains into New Mexico. A trail that crossed it on the north bank of the Arkansas River ran east to the vicinity of Kinsley, Kansas, then overland to cross the southern part of Missouri to the mouth of the Ohio River. These and many other trails created a web across the face of the Great Plains.

The trails were designed to meet the needs of pedestrian travelers. The most important of these needs was water. People using pack dogs can only travel about ten miles per day, and the most heavily used trails had water holes spaced no farther apart than ten miles. Stream crossings and steep hills were avoided whenever possible; as a result, many trails ran along the divides between stream valleys. Although they were sinuous, these routes had the additional advantage of allowing the traveler to see long distances while passing by the headwater springs of numerous creeks.

Trails converged at good fords across streams and at the rare groves of trees in the High Plains. In some instances, such as the ford across the Kansas River in the Flint Hills, the geologic stratum underlying the divide along which a trail ran created a rocky ford where the ridge was cut by a river. Groves provided shade, vegetable foods, fuel for shelter, and a variety of game animals to hunt. The "Big Timbers" of the Arkansas River in Colorado, of the Smoky Hill River in western Kansas, and of the Republican River in southwestern Nebraska were some of the favored campgrounds.

Operating in cultures that lacked systems of writing and mapmaking, Plains Indians took advantage of natural landmarks whenever possible. This was especially necessary because massive bison herds could erase in a single day pathways worn by decades of human travel. When natural landmarks were absent, stone or sod cairns were sometimes built. Cairns had varied functions. In some spots they marked the main course of a trail, in others they marked a good spring not visible from the trail itself, while in still other places they indicated the route to be used to regain the trail after a river crossing. Some cairns acted as shrines at which travelers added a stone as a prayer.

Well-designed Indian trails had a pronounced effect on the early European American history of the Great Plains. Native guides led explorers along them, traders built their posts beside them, and battles were fought near them. Emigrant trails such as the Oregon and Santa Fe trails developed from Indian trails, although wagon traffic sometimes necessitated modifications to the routes. The well-spaced water holes and gentle grades of many trails led to the use of some as cattle trails and railroad routes. Thus their effects continue to be felt today.

Donald J. Blakeslee
Wichita State University

Blakeslee, Donald J., and Robert Blasing. "Indian Trails in the Central Plains." *Plains Anthropologist* 33–119 (1988): 17–26. Mead, J. R. "Trails in Southern Kansas." *Transactions of the Kansas State Historical Society* 5 (1896): 88–93.

INDIGENOUS

Indigenous is a family blues-rock band of Nakota descent from Marty, South Dakota, on the Standing Rock Reservation. The parents home-schooled the children, encouraging their musical talents and promoting their career. Their father, Greg Zephyr, was an American Indian Movement activist and a guitarist in the 1960s and 1970s band the Vanishing Americans. He played the children music by B. B. King, Santana, Cream, Jimi Hendrix, and Stevie Ray Vaughn. Later influences include Pearl Jam, the Stone Temple Pilots, the Black Crows, and Audioslave.

Their mother encouraged the children to form a band and gave them the name Indigenous. They practiced for five years before performing. It was a family band from the start, with father, mother, and children playing at local bingo halls and schools. Within a few years the children were performing on their own. They cut their first demo in 1992. The band was composed of guitarist and singer Mato Nanji, whose guitar playing has been favorably compared with Stevie Ray Vaughn and Jimi Hendrix, brother Pte playing bass and backing vocals, and sister Wanbdi on drums and backing vocal. An older sister formerly played keyboards with the band but left to raise a family. A cousin, Horse, played percussion but left to pursue a less hectic lifestyle. In 1997 the band contributed the song "Things We Do" to the *Honor the Earth* CD produced by the Indigo Girls to raise money for Indigenous peoples. In 2000 they joined Santana on the Honor the Earth tour. The band recorded a number of low-selling albums to finance their 1998 debut, *Things We Do*, which brought them critical acclaim and a growing audience. In 1999 they released an EP and a live album and joined the B. B. King Blues Festival tour. In 2000 they released *Circle*. Their next release, *Indigenous*, hit the market in 2003. In 2005 they released the EP *Long Way Home*.

The band tours nationally several months a year. They have appeared on *Late Night with Conan O'Brian*, *Austin City Limits*, and the CBS *Morning Show*, among others. They have played with, or toured with, B. B. King, Bob Dylan, Santana, Dave Matthews, the Indigo Girls, and Bonnie Raitt.

Charles Vollan
South Dakota State University

INTERTRIBAL WARFARE

Intertribal warfare was intense throughout the Great Plains during the 1700s and 1800s, and archeological data indicate that warfare was present prior to this time. Human skeletons from as early as the Woodland Period (250 BC to 900 AD) show occasional marks of violence, but conflict intensified during and after the thirteenth century, by which time farmers were well established in the Plains. After 1250, villages were often destroyed by fire, and human skeletons regularly show marks of violence, scalping, and other mutilations. Warfare was most intense along the Missouri River in the present-day Dakotas, where ancestors of the Mandans, Hidatsas, and Arikaras were at war with each other, and towns inhabited by as many as 1,000 people were often fortified with ditch and palisade defenses. Excavations at the Crow Creek site, an ancestral Arikara town dated to 1325, revealed the bodies of 486 people—men, women, and children, essentially the town's entire population—in a mass grave. These individuals had been scalped and dismembered, and their bones showed clear evidence of severe malnutrition, suggesting that violence resulted from competition for food, probably due to local overpopulation and climatic deterioration. Violence among farmers continued from the 1500s through the late 1800s.

Archeological data on war among the nomadic Plains hunters are few, but some nomads were attacking farmers on the edges of the Plains by at least the 1500s. By the eighteenth century, war was common among the nomads, apparently largely because of conflicts over hunting territories.

Prior to the introduction of European horses and guns, Plains warfare took two forms. When equally matched forces confronted each other, warriors sheltered behind large shields, firing arrows; individual warriors came out from behind these lines to dance and taunt their opponents. This mode of combat was largely for show and casualties were light. However, sometimes, large war parties surprised and utterly destroyed small camps or hamlets. Increasing interaction with Europeans from the eighteenth century on changed these patterns dramatically. Massed shield lines could neither stand against mounted warriors nor protect against firearms; this mode of battle largely disappeared with the introduction of horses and guns, although equally matched mounted war parties sometimes used the old tactics. Early access to horses also allowed some groups, notably the Comanches, to overwhelm and displace neighboring tribes who lacked such access. Documentary and archeological evidence indicate that horses and guns contributed mightily to this more destructive mode of Plains warfare, most intensively along the Missouri River.

Raids for horses by small groups of warriors became a primary form of conflict after about 1750, particularly among the nomadic groups. Horse raiders usually entered enemy camps at night to take horses picketed close to their owners. Such raids were dangerous—raiders were killed when caught in the act—and successful raiders often achieved high status. The relation between war and status in the Plains is similarly evident in the practice of counting coup, in which a living enemy (or sometimes a dead enemy) was touched with the hand or a special stick. This act signified ultimate bravery in most Plains tribes and gave a warrior great prestige.

The prestige attached to stealing horses and to counting coup rather than killing has contributed to the view that Plains warfare was a moderately dangerous kind of game driven by individual quests for status rather than "real" war driven by competition for resources. This is misleading. Individual warriors sought status and sometimes avoided killing enemies in battle, but destructive high-casualty warfare was widespread, with documented battles involving thousands of warriors and hundreds of fatalities. Other massacres like that at Crow Creek are known from the eighteenth and nineteenth centuries, and archeological and documentary evidence show great changes in tribal territories resulting from war before and after white contact.

Destructive war in the Plains intensified after contact because of migrations of eastern tribes (the Cheyennes and Lakotas, for example) into the Plains as settlement moved west, because Europeans and Americans manipulated traditional hostilities, and because tribes competed for access to European and American trade, especially in fur-rich areas of the Northern Plains and Prairie Provinces. Contact-period war ended some long-standing hostilities: for example, the Mandans, Hidatsas, and Arikaras, decimated by disease and raiding, banded together for mutual protection during the 1860s. Other hostilities continued, and expanding European Americans exploited them: for example, Crows and Pawnees scouted in military campaigns against the Cheyennes and Lakotas. Intertribal violence in the Plains subsided with the confinement of the tribes to reservations in the late nineteenth century.

Douglas B. Bamforth
University of Colorado at Boulder

Bamforth, Douglas B. "Indigenous People, Indigenous Violence: Pre-Contact Warfare on the North American Great Plains." *Man* 29 (1994): 95–115. Calloway, Colin G. *Our Hearts Fell to the Ground: Plains Indian Views of How the West Was Lost*. New York: Bedford, 1996.

JONES, HAROLD (1909–2002)

Harold Stephen Jones, a Santee Sioux, was the first Native American to be elected bishop of any major denomination. Born in Mitchell, South Dakota, on December 14, 1909, Jones was raised by his grandparents, the Reverend William Holmes, an early Indian Episcopal priest, and his wife, Rebecca, a Caucasian. This dual heritage fostered his eventual ability to serve successfully in a racially conflicted church and society.

Jones's childhood was spent in Niobrara, Nebraska, and Wakpala, South Dakota, where his grandfather served mission churches. His grandfather died while Jones was in his teens. Then came a struggle with discrimination and poverty as he helped support his grandmother and continued his education. He graduated from Northern State College in 1935 and received a licentiate in theology from Seabury-Western Theological Seminary, Evanston, Illinois, in 1938. He married Blossom Steele, a Lakota, in December of 1938, a week after his ordination as deacon.

Beginning with Messiah Chapel in Wounded Knee, Jones was assigned in rapid succession to four small chapels on the Pine Ridge Reservation. There was never adequate compensation, which led to mounting debts on top of unpaid college loans. Three children were born into the Jones family, with only the daughter, Norma, surviving. Moves to the Cheyenne River Reservation in 1947 and back to Pine Ridge in 1952 brought added responsibilities but no financial relief. That finally came when he was called in 1956 to serve a white congregation in Wahpeton, North Dakota.

In 1968 the national Episcopal Church called him to take over the Navajo mission field in Arizona, where he had to adapt to a different language and culture. While there he was elected suffragan (assistant) bishop of South Dakota and was consecrated in a great multiracial service in Sioux Falls on January 11, 1972. His ministry as bishop was severely limited by a stroke after less than a year of service to both white and Indian congregations, and he had to take an early retirement in 1976. Subsequently, the Right Reverend Harold Jones lived with his daughter in Chandler, Arizona, and died there on November 12, 2002.

Mary E. Cochran
Tacoma, Washington

Anderson, Owannah. *Four Hundred Years: Anglican/Episcopal Mission among American Indians.* Cincinnati: Forward Movement Publications, 1997. Cochran, Mary E. *Dakota Cross-Bearer: The Life and World of a Native American Bishop.* Lincoln: University of Nebraska Press, 2000. Sneve, Virginia Driving Hawk. *That They May Have Life: The Episcopal Church in South Dakota.* New York: Seabury Press, 1977.

JUMANOS

Jumano is the standard ethnonym applied by scholars to a Native American people who, between the sixteenth and eighteenth centuries, were variously identified as Jumano, Humana, Xuman, Sumana, and Chouman. Modern interest began in 1890, when Adolph Bandelier observed that the Jumanos, evidently an important Indian nation during the early days of Spanish exploration north of Mexico, had virtually disappeared from the historical record by 1700. Scholars have since ranged far

and wide in pursuit of the identity and the fate of the Jumanos: Frederick W. Hodge believed them to be Caddoans, ancestors of the Wichitas; Carl Sauer favored a Uto-Aztecan affiliation, linking them to the Tarahumaras and other Mexican Indians; Jack D. Forbes argued that they were early Apacheans. In 1940 France V. Scholes and H. P. Mera proposed that "Jumano" was simply a generic term that Spanish colonists had used to designate all Indians who painted or tattooed their faces with horizontal lines; in view of the diversity of opinion, it is not surprising that this suggestion found wide acceptance. Recently, Nancy P. Hickerson has reopened the discussion, citing inferential evidence that the Jumanos' language (never recorded) was actually Tanoan, closely related to that of their trading partners in the eastern Pueblos of New Mexico.

Bandelier's data provided no clues to Jumano prehistory, nor did he speculate about their linguistic or cultural links with other tribes. During the intervening century, archival and archeological research has revealed a fuller—if still incomplete—picture of their adaptation and possible origins. The Jumanos ranged from south of the Rio Grande to the Southern Plains. Within this territory they were essentially nomadic, although there were permanent enclaves at La Junta de los Rios (near present-day Ojinaga, Chihuahua), in the Tompiro Pueblos of New Mexico, and perhaps elsewhere. Their eastward movements were timed to coincide with seasonal rains and prime bison hunting in the Plains; the return trip brought the Jumano bands back to spend the winter at or near the communities of their trading partners. There, meat, hides, and other trophies of the hunt were traded for agricultural produce. Such a relationship of reciprocity between related farmers and hunter-gatherers has many parallels and often develops as an adaptation to changing ecological conditions.

The historical importance of the Jumanos rests primarily on their role as intertribal and interregional traders. This role undoubtedly developed as a consequence of their pattern of seasonal migration. The Southern Plains was a hunting area shared by many Native American groups—Caddoan, Tonkawan, Coahuiltecan, and others. The Jumanos established a close relationship with the Caddos and their neighbors (the "Tejas" alliance) and became active agents in trade between these tribes and those along the Rio Grande. Their routes followed and linked several river systems, including the Pecos, Canadian, Brazos, and Colorado of Texas.

The Jumanos' trade sphere expanded when they adopted an equestrian way of life, and it changed in character as they began to deal in horses.

Records of French explorer La Salle's visits to the Ceni (Caddos) reveal the impact of the Jumano trade, which provided the Caddo elite with Spanish clothing, swords, religious artifacts, and many horses; on the return trip, hides and peltries were carried for sale in New Spain. At this time the Jumano traders were, in effect, serving as Spanish surrogates in promoting friendly relations between the "Nations of the North" (the Caddoan confederacies) and the Spanish Crown.

Even as their interregional trade reached its height, the Jumanos' territorial base was increasingly under attack. Apaches and Jumanos were in contention, both for hunting grounds and for trade access along the Rio Grande. In 1540 Coronado's expedition witnessed the enmity between Querechos (Apaches) and Teyas (probably Jumanos). By 1600 the Apaches had taken control of the trade at Pecos Pueblo, and they dominated a wide area east of that site. In the Tompiro region, farther south, the Jumano population was augmented by refugees from the war in the Plains. When the Tompiros also came under attack, around 1660, the Jumanos abandoned New Mexico for good; thereafter, La Junta de los Rios was their only foothold on the Rio Grande. The Jumanos' trade continued from La Junta following a route along the lower Pecos and Colorado rivers. This route was broken around 1690, when Apache bands pushed eastward to the upper Colorado and the Brazos. Thereafter, the Jumanos had no intact territorial base, and their activities as traders came to an end. Remnant groups around La Junta evidently joined forces with their conquerors after 1700, when Apache occupancy extended southward along the Rio Grande below El Paso.

Throughout the seventeenth century there were several occasions in which Jumano leaders acted as spokesmen for their own and allied tribes, seeking Spanish assistance in defending their territories and trade routes. In 1682 the Jumano chief Juan Sabeata addressed such an appeal to New Mexican authorities at El Paso and escorted a party of soldiers and Franciscan friars to meet with representatives of more than thirty Indian nations on the upper Colorado of Texas. When this effort failed, a remarkable transregional economic and political alliance came to an end, and the Jumanos effectively vanished from the history of the Southern Plains.

Nancy Parrott Hickerson
Texas Tech University

Hickerson, Nancy P. *The Jumanos: Hunters and Traders of the South Plains*. Austin: University of Texas Press, 1994. Kelley, J. Charles. "Juan Sabeata and Diffusion in Aboriginal Texas." *American Anthropologist* 57 (1955): 981–95. Scholes, France V., and H. P. Mera. "Some Aspects of the Jumano Problem." *Contributions to American Anthropology and History* 6 (1940): 269–99.

The Kaw, or Kanza, Indians refer to themselves collectively as the Kaw Nation. The names Kaw and Kanza appear on the tribe's national seal, but Kaw is the identity used by members. Kaw means "Wind People." The Kaws are part of the Dhegiha branch of the Central Siouan–speaking peoples, a group that includes Quapaws, Osages, Omahas, and Poncas. According to their histories, these tribes once lived together along or near the lower Ohio Valley. They began to migrate westward around 1300 AD, and by the 1700s the Kaws were firmly situated in present northeastern Kansas and northwestern Missouri.

From the late eighteenth century until the late 1820s, the Kaws, numbering about 1,500, lived in a single village near present-day Manhattan, Kansas. Their territory extended throughout most of the Kansas Valley and the lower reaches of its tributaries from about the Delaware River west to the Solomon and Smoky Hill rivers. Within this core, the Kaws exercised nearly total territorial control. Their hunting range extended west to the upper Republican River and south to the saline plains of the present-day Kansas-Oklahoma border.

The Kaws' subsistence operated on an annual cycle of hunting, horticulture, raiding, and trading. Beginning in April, Kaw women planted corn, beans, pumpkins, melons, and squash in small fields around the village. They also gathered nuts, berries, roots, tubers, and wood in the riparian forest adjacent to the Kansas and Blue rivers. Kaw males pastured their horses on nearby upland prairie and hunted (mostly elk and deer) along the Kansas River. After planting ended in early May, the Kaws left for their annual summer bison hunt. Along the way to the bison grounds, they hunted deer and elk, and small war parties frequently left to raid Pawnee villages. The Kaws primarily hunted along the middle Solomon, Smoky Hill, and Arkansas rivers, where vast herds of bison sought water in summer. They returned to their village in mid-August to harvest their crops. In winter, the Kaws left their village again and traveled to the woodlands along the Missouri River in present northeastern Kansas and northwestern Missouri. There they scattered into small parties and hunted beaver, deer, elk, turkey, and other smaller game. The furs from these animals were exchanged for goods from French and American traders who regularly traveled the Missouri River. During this season, Kaw war parties raided Otoe, Iowa, Sauk, Fox, and Missouria villages. The Kaws reconvened at their village in mid-March.

This subsistence pattern also provided the Kaws with their material culture (dress, tools, utensils, weapons, and housing). Kaw dress, for instance, consisted of moccasins and leggings (made from deerskins), a breechcloth and girdle (acquired through trade), and a blanket or bison robe. Male warriors often wore necklaces of animal claws or of shells, beads, and metal ornaments (acquired through trade), and they carried a wire apparatus to keep their arms, chins, eyebrows, and scalp plucked (except for a strip of hair on the top of their heads). Both men and women used vermilion to dye their hair.

Circular earth lodges were the most common form of village housing. A lodge measured from thirty to sixty feet in diameter and housed an average of two families (or about ten persons). Each lodge consisted of an outer ring of wooden posts and four taller central posts that were then covered with a frame of stick or twig bundles, over which they laid grass or reed mats, tree bark, and earth. Inside a lodge they maintained a central fire pit (and a hole in the roof's center for smoke to escape) as well as storage pits for dried corn, beans, and other foods. When the Kaws were on the hunt, they lived in portable skin-covered tipis.

Kaw society was patrilineal, and it was divided into two halves, or moieties, each composed of eight clans, or gentes (consisting of several families each), whose members descended from a common ancestor. Politically, the Kaws were organized around a loose confederation headed by several chiefs. There were five civil chiefs, drawn from each of the five leading gentes. There were also several war chiefs, established warriors who ruled in matters of war. Chiefs were elected by a common council of the people because of their demonstrated wisdom, bravery, and generosity. Office was for life, and succession was hereditary. Despite the chieftainships, usually no solid ruling authority was recognized. Most matters were still decided through common council, and some degree of factionalism was characteristic of Kaw politics.

In 1825 the U.S. government convinced the Kaws to cede their land and placed them on a reservation in present northern Kansas. For the next two decades, the Kaws were hemmed in by thousands of relocated Indians from the eastern United States. The influx of emigrant Indians and the expansion of the fur trade depleted small game in the region, and missionaries and government employees on the reservation introduced disease. The Kaws intensified their bison hunting, raided enemies with increasing frequency, and stole crops and animals from neighboring reservations and white settlements.

The Kaws maintained their population of 1,500 persons until midcentury, after which their numbers plummeted. The U.S. government restricted the Kaws to progressively smaller reservations (in 1846, 1859, and 1873). When officials opened Kansas Territory in 1854, settlers pushed the bison farther west, depleted grass and wood, peddled whiskey, and brought more disease to the tribe. Starvation was chronic, and frequent outbreaks of smallpox, cholera, and other illnesses continued to plague the tribe. When the Kaws were removed to Indian Territory in 1873, they numbered 500. By 1900 barely 200 full-blooded Kaws remained. Tragedy extended beyond death. Since religious knowledge was preserved within each gente, the demise of entire gente populations meant the loss of beliefs and customs. By the early twentieth century, much understanding of Kaw society, religion, and history was lost forever.

Congress dissolved the last Kaw reservation in 1902, and the lands were divided into individual allotments. Four years later the former reservation became part of Kay County, Oklahoma. Today, many Kaw descendants still reside in Kay County. According to the 1997 tribal enrollment, there are 2,269 Kaw Nation members. The last Kaw fullblood, William A. Mehojah Sr., died in Omaha, Nebraska, on April 23, 2000.

Benjamin Y. Dixon
State University of New York College at Oneonta

Unrau, William E. *The Kansa Indians: A History of the Wind People, 1673–1873*. Norman: University of Oklahoma Press, 1971.
Wedel, Waldo R. "The Kansa Indians." *Transactions of the Kansas Academy of Science* 49 (1946): 1–35.

KIOWAS

The Kiowas believe that they originated in the Bitterroot Mountains of present-day Montana. They now call themselves K'oigu, the "Principal People." Earlier names, Kwuda and T'epda, or "Coming-Out People," commemorate the Kiowa creation story, when Saynday, the Kiowa trickster, transformed the subterranean-living Kiowas into ants, then commanded them to populate the earth's surface via a hollow cottonwood log. A pregnant woman became lodged in the log, preventing the majority of the ant-people from emerging; hence the small nineteenth-century population of approximately 1,000 to 1,100 Kiowas.

Besides Saynday, other mythological culture heroes include the Zaidethali, or "Split Boys," who slew numerous monsters before one disappeared forever and the other transformed himself into the eucharistic Thali-dai, or "Boy Medicines," known today as the Ten Medicines. During the height of the horse and buffalo culture (ca. 1750 to 1875), these sacred bundles were possessed by ten keepers whose main duty was to pray for the well-being of the people and to settle civil disputes.

Sometime in the mid–eighteenth century, the Kiowas and culturally affiliated Plains Apaches

AMIE AND CARRIE   KIAWAH.

G. A. Addison,   FT. SILL, O. T.

An exhibit of Kiowa women documenting Native American life, photograph ca. 1895

migrated from the Yellowstone River region southeastward toward the Black Hills and befriended the Crows. Between 1775 and 1805 the Kiowas and Plains Apaches were pushed farther south of the Black Hills by Lakotas and Cheyennes. Migrating south to the horse-rich Southern Plains, they initially came into conflict with the more numerous Comanches. After about 1800, however, the Kiowas, Comanches, and Plains Apaches (later referred to as KCA Indians) made an alliance and followed the migratory bison herds between the Arkansas and Red rivers.

Mid-nineteenth-century Kiowa society consisted of ten to twenty hunting bands, each composed of several extended family groups, or kindreds. Each kindred was led by the oldest of a group of brothers, and each band was led by the most prominent man among the coalesced kindreds—the *topadok'i*, or "main chief." The Kiowas recognized four classes: *ondedau*, or "rich" people; the *ondegup'a*, "second best"; the *kwwn*, "poor"; and the *dapom*, or "worthless." Relatives were separated by sex and generation; for example, all cousins were classified as "brothers" and "sisters."

Until about 1847 the Kiowas and Plains Apaches occupied present-day western Oklahoma, southwestern Kansas, and the Texas Panhandle. Winter

and summer camps were located on branches of the Red, Washita, South Canadian, and North Canadian rivers. From this core region, intertribal war parties raided south into Texas and Mexico and southwest into present-day New Mexico. Pawnees, Navajos, Utes, Mexicans, and Texans were common enemies. In the Treaty of Fort Gibson of May 26, 1837, for example, signed by ten Kiowa leaders, including the famous Dohausan, principal Kiowa chief between 1833 and 1866, the Kiowas agreed not to raid the Santa Fe Trail and to guarantee safe passage of all Americans crossing the Southern Plains.

Between 1848 and 1868 the Kiowas expanded their territory north and west into central Kansas and southeastern Colorado. During this period, winter and summer camps were located along the Great Bend of the Arkansas River in Kansas and at the confluence of Wolf Creek and the North Canadian River in northwestern Oklahoma. This northward migration resulted from the expansion of Texas settlements and the arrival of immigrant tribes in eastern Kansas and the Indian Territory. Conflicts with the Pawnees and immigrant tribes were inevitable, because population pressures, dwindling bison herds, and shrinking territory in the Central and Southern Plains created competition for scarce resources. As raiding into Texas and Mexico for horses and plunder continued unabated, the Kiowas began kidnapping children to replace their own children, who had fallen victims to infectious disease. Many Kiowas today remark about the large amount of "captive blood" in the tribe and maintain that all Kiowas are part Mexican.

On October 21, 1867, the KCA Indians signed the Treaty of Medicine Lodge Creek and agreed to a reservation in present southwestern Oklahoma, bounded on the north and south by the Washita and Red rivers. Although the Kiowas abandoned Kansas and Colorado in the fall of 1868, they continued to raid into Texas, which precipitated military action against them. By the end of the 1874–75 Red River War they had capitulated. Renowned Kiowa leaders and warriors were dead or in custody. The remaining topadok'i were demoted to "beef chiefs," in charge of annuity distributions to the former bands, which were now confined in a single village near Fort Sill. The Southern Plains bison herds were extinct by the late 1870s, leaving the Kiowas completely dependent on the government for their subsistence. Most attempts to transform Kiowas into stock herders and farmers failed, so famine persisted during the 1880s and 1890s. Further changes occurred after the Jerome Agreement of 1892, which brought about the allotment of KCA lands. Since the "opening" of the Kiowa Reservation to homesteaders on August 6, 1901, the Kiowa have lived on individual allotments north of the Wichita Mountains, bounded on the west by the town of Lone Wolf and on the east by Anadarko.

Nineteenth-century Kiowa cosmology was based on the concept of *daudau*, or "power," a spirit force that permeated the universe and all natural entities, such as earth, air, mountains, plants, and animals. Power seekers endured vision quests in the Wichita Mountains and other high elevations; the fortunate few who received power visions became great warriors, or curers who painted power symbols on their shields. Before the reservation period several shield societies were in existence, but they died out after 1875. The Sun Dance, the most important Kiowa ceremony, was performed to regenerate the Kiowas and the bison herds. Held in mid-June only if pledged by *ondedau* men, the four dancing days of the ceremony culminated in the final day when the sacred Taime, or Sun Dance bundle, was hung in the forked pole of the Sun Dance altar to bless all tribal members.

Government intervention brought about the demise of the Sun Dance. Although the aborted 1890 Sun Dance "when the forked poles were left standing" marked the death of the Sun Dance religion, the Kiowas turned to the Ghost Dance, which ended in 1891, but was brought back between 1894 and 1916. Missionaries came to Kiowa country in 1887, and by 1918, when the Native American Church of Oklahoma was chartered, most Kiowas were either Christians or peyotists. Today, there are a handful of Kiowa peyote Roadmen, but most Kiowas are Baptist, Methodist, or Pentecostal. Medicine bundle inheritance broke down in the twentieth century, but the eleven tribal bundles—the Thali-da-i and Taime—are still sought out with prayer requests. Despite vast cultural and religious change in the last century, the Kiowas believe that *daudau* still exists in many guises, and that Dauk'i, or "God," is in everything.

Approximately four thousand Kiowas now live in western Oklahoma, and another six thousand live elsewhere in the United States. Kiowas are very much involved in intertribal powwows and cultural activities that promote their tribal identity. Tribal offices are located in Carnegie, Oklahoma, and at the Bureau of Indian Affairs in Anadarko. Kiowa tribal government, chartered by a constitution, consists of a business committee and a tribal chair. Contemporary Kiowas of note include N. Scott Momaday, 1969 Pulitzer Prize winner for literature, and Everett Rhoades, former assistant surgeon general of the United States.

Benjamin R. Kracht
Northeastern State University

Lassiter, Luke Eric. *The Power of Kiowa Song: A Collaborative Ethnography*. Tucson: University of Arizona Press, 1998. Lassiter, Luke Eric, Clyde Ellis, and Ralph Kotay. *The Jesus Road: Kiowas, Christianity, and Indian Hymns*. Lincoln: University of Nebraska Press, 2002. Mishkin, Bernard. *Rank and Warfare among the Plains Indians*. 1940. Lincoln: University of Nebraska Press, 1992. Mooney, James. *Calendar History of the Kiowa Indians, 1895–96*. Washington DC: Smithsonian Institution Press, 1979. Richardson, Jane. *Law and Status among the Kiowa Indians*. Seattle: University of Washington Press, 1940.

KIOWA SIX

The Kiowa Six, sometimes erroneously called the Kiowa Five, had a profound impact on the development of Native American easel painting. The five most commonly known artists in the group are Jack Hokeah (1900–1969), Monroe Tsatoke (1904–37), Spencer Asah (1906–54), James Auchiah (1906–74), and Stephen Mopope (1900–1974). The sixth member was a woman, Lois Smoky (1907–81).

Painting was an important and honored aspect of traditional Kiowa culture. Men painted calendars, chronological records of important events that affected the group as a whole, and records of an individual's heroic deeds. Women usually confined their artistic expression to beading. These early Kiowa artists all spoke Kiowa and were actively involved in traditional Kiowa culture, despite the forced acculturation of the period.

In order to "civilize" and Christianize the Kiowas and turn them into American capitalists, the Kiowa reservation in western Oklahoma was allotted in 1900. Each tribal member received 160 acres. The remaining 480,000 acres of "excess" land were sold to white settlers in 1906. European American education became mandatory. The six Kiowa artists attended St. Patrick's Mission School near Anadarko, Oklahoma. There they were given English names and taught English and how to do manual service jobs. Upon leaving school these artists returned to their community.

At this time Susie Peters was the Indian Service field matron at Anadarko. She is still remembered there for her concern for and support of many Kiowas. By 1920 she had organized a group of Kiowa artists that included the Kiowa Six. She did not give them lessons in art but encouraged them in their work. She also provided them with paints and drawing paper, which, for the most part, they had not had access to previously. During this period these six artists developed what is commonly referred to as the Kiowa style. As in traditional Kiowa painting, the figures in these paintings were drawn on a plain background. Within the lines color was used as a flat filler. This opaque paint was more solid than traditional vegetable dyes or pencil and ink. Partly because of this technique, Kiowa-style paintings, commonly of individual dancers or ceremonies, emphasize design.

Stephen Mopope's Two Indian Dancers and Drummer, All Wearing Feathers

Susie Peters also attempted to market the works of the Kiowa artists in both Oklahoma and New Mexico, and she brought them to the attention of Oscar Jacobson, director of the art department at the University of Oklahoma. In 1927 Jacobson arranged for Stephen Mopope, Monroe Tsatoke, Spencer Asah, and Jack Hokeah to use facilities and supplies at the University of Oklahoma under the guidance of Edith Mahier. Jacobson, however, insisted that they be given no formal instruction. Later, these four artists were joined by Lois Smoky and James Auchiah.

Jacobson, in contrast to Susie Peters, had the contacts to successfully market the artists and their works. Six months after the arrival of the first group of Kiowa artists at the University of Oklahoma, a traveling sales exhibition was organized. Within a year the artists' works had been sold, and an even larger exhibition was mounted. A mere eighteen months after he came to know the artists Jacobson arranged for thirty-five watercolors to be exhibited at the International Congress in Prague, Czechoslovakia, and for a folio of their work to be published in France.

Starting with an exhibition in New York in 1931, the decade of the 1930s was a period of further recognition by European Americans of the beauty of early Kiowa easel painting. The artists were also commissioned under the Public Works of Art Project to paint a number of murals, a medium ideally suited to the Kiowa style with its flat color areas. Other murals were commissioned for the State Historical Building in Oklahoma City and the Department of the Interior Building in Washington DC. The five Kiowa men were involved in these mural projects. Lois Smoky was not. After marrying and having children, she turned her artistic talent to the traditional Kiowa woman's art of beadwork.

The Kiowa Six were among the first Native American painters to be recognized by the European American community. Their work was the model for what is commonly referred to as the traditional flat style, which was refined and developed by Dorothy Dunn at the Indian School in Santa Fe, New Mexico.

Lydia L. Wyckoff
Philbrook Museum of Art

Wyckoff, Lydia L., ed. *Visions and Voices: Native American Painting.* Albuquerque: University of New Mexico Press, 1996.

LA FLESCHE, SUSAN (1865–1915)

Physician and Indian reformer Susan La Flesche Picotte was born in June 1865, the youngest daughter of Joseph La Flesche, last traditional chief of the Omaha tribe. Joseph's commitment to education is reflected in her education. She attended the local Presbyterian mission school, the Omaha Agency Indian School, the Elizabeth Institute for Young Ladies in Elizabeth, New Jersey, and Hampton Normal and Agricultural Institute in Virginia, where she graduated in May 1886. Supported by the Connecticut Branch of the Women's National Indian Association, she attended the Woman's

Dr. Susan La Flesche Picotte

tive as president of the church missionary society, participated in a new chapter of the Eastern Star, and supported various community projects, lectures, and concerts.

In 1909, when the government arbitrarily extended the trust period for protecting Omaha land an additional ten years, she was chosen unanimously by the tribe to head a delegation to Washington DC. The Omahas were subsequently declared competent to rent or lease their lands and handle their own monies.

A product of the nineteenth-century reform movement and its assimilationist policy, she in turn helped her people prepare for the twentieth century. She died on September 18, 1915, and was buried in the Bancroft cemetery.

Valerie Sherer Mathes
Sonoma, California

Mathes, Valerie Sherer. "Iron Eyes' Daughters: Susette and Susan La Flesche, Nineteenth-Century Indian Reformers." In *By Grit and Grace: Eleven Women Who Shaped the American West*, edited by Glenda Riley and Richard Etulain, 135–52. Golden CO: Fulcrum Press, 1997. Mathes, Valerie Sherer. "Susan La Flesche Picotte, MD: Nineteenth-Century Physician and Reformer." *Great Plains Quarterly* 13 (1993): 172–86. Tong, Benson. *Susan La Flesche Picotte, MD: Omaha Indian Leader and Reformer.* Norman: University of Oklahoma Press, 1999.

Medical College of Pennsylvania, graduating in March 1889 at the head of her class. Following an internship at the Woman's Hospital in Philadelphia, she returned to her reservation to practice medicine.

For the next four years, as government physician at the Omaha Agency Indian School, she dispensed medicine and encouraged tribal members to become Christian. Her religious dedication was rewarded years later, when in 1905 she was appointed medical missionary by the Presbyterian Board of Home Missions. Working out of the Blackbird Hills Presbyterian Church, she read the Bible in the Omaha language and held church services.

Ill health forced her resignation as government physician in 1893. She married Henry Picotte, a Sioux Indian from the Yankton Agency, and upon regaining her strength, resumed her medical practice in Bancroft and later in Walthill, Nebraska, among both Indians and whites. She lobbied for required medical inspection of schools, sanitary ice cream dishes and spoons, and free school drinking fountains; fought against tuberculosis and the common housefly; and campaigned against alcohol following the death of her hard-drinking husband. In addition, she organized the Thurston County Medical Association, served on Walthill's health board, chaired the State Health Committee of the Nebraska Federation of Women's Clubs, and organized a hospital for Walthill in 1913. She also helped organize a new church for Walthill, was ac-

LAME DEER, JOHN FIRE (1903–1976)

A member of the Minneconjou Sioux, John Fire Lame Deer was born in South Dakota in 1903 between the Standing Rock and Rosebud reservations. Following a vision quest, he took the name of his great-grandfather, Lame Deer. He attended the reservation school at Rosebud until he was fourteen, when he was forced to move to a boarding school. He took a number of jobs, working as a rodeo rider and clown, picking vegetables, sheep herding, bootlegging alcohol, and operating a pool hall. He fell victim to alcoholic excess and car theft. For a brief time he worked as a tribal police officer. Lame Deer served in the U.S. Army during World War II. For about six years he belonged to the Native American Church, and he determined to focus on traditional Lakota beliefs.

In 1972 Lame Deer's story was published under the title *Lame Deer: Seeker of Visions*. In it Lame Deer described himself as a holy person. The book detailed his early life of alcohol abuse and womanizing, as well as his spiritual growth. It also described many Sioux religious beliefs and practices. Lame Deer later claimed to have trained several other medicine people. After his death, his daughter, Bernice Fire Milk, argued that he had not been a "medicine man" but rather had been a *heyoka*, a person given the responsibility to act as a sacred clown following a vision. Lame Deer associated with Leonard Crow Dog and, at least briefly, with the American Indian Movement, and he was partly responsible for the reintroduction of the Ghost Dance. He died in 1976.

Charles Vollan
South Dakota State University

Lame Deer, John Fire, and Richard Erdoes. *Lame Deer: Seeker of Visions.* New York: Simon and Schuster, 1972. Rice, Julian. "A Ventriloquy of Anthros: Densmore, Dorsey, Lame Deer, and Erdoes." *American Indian Quarterly* 18 (1994): 169–96.

Classification of Native Languages of the Great Plains

CADDOAN

Arikara
Pawnee
Kitsai
Wichita
Caddo
Jumano (?)

ATHAPASKAN

Sarcee
Kiowa Apache
Jicarilla
Lipan
Jumano (?)

SIOUAN

Mandan
Hidatsa
Crow
Assiniboine
Stoney
Santee-Sisseton
Yankton-Yanktonai
Teton
Iowa
Otoe
Missouria
Winnebago*
Omaha
Ponca
Osage
Kanza (Kaw)
Quapaw*

ALGONQUIAN

Blackfoot
Arapaho
Atsina
Cheyenne
Sutai
Plains Cree
Plains Ojibwa
Kickapoo*
Fox-Sauk*
Peoria*

Miami*
Kaskaskia*
Ottawa*
Potawatomi*
Shawnee*
Delaware*

IROQUOIAN

Cherokee*
Seneca*
Wyandotte*

MUSCOGEAN

Choctaw*
Chickasaw*
Creek*
Seminole*

UTO-AZTECAN

Shoshone
Comanche
Jumano (?)

TANOAN

Kiowa
Jumano (?)

KLAMATH-MODOC

Modoc*

SAHAPTIAN

Nez Perce*

ISOLATES

Tonkawa

*Removed to Great Plains by federal order

LANGUAGES

The Great Plains has long been the home to a multitude of distinct Native voices. The language of each family, band, community, or nation has developed to embrace and describe a dynamic life. Through their oral tradition, communities transmit a rich heritage of spiritual, historical, and practical knowledge to their children. The tools of archeologists, linguists, and historians can be combined with the memories of Native elders to study the rise, decline, and survival of these linguistically diverse communities. One useful linguistic device for organizing the many languages of the Great Plains is the "family." It works by placing languages and dialects into groups that exhibit features suggesting a common linguistic origin at some time in the past. Not all languages can be so easily categorized. For example, the Jumano language family of the Southern Plains has been variously identified as sharing features with the Athapaskan, Caddoan, Uto-Aztecan, and more recently, Tanoan language families.

Prior to the European advent on the Great Plains in the 1500s, two language families, Caddoan and Siouan, were already long represented in the region, and several others could be found along the perimeter. Caddoan speakers are some of the oldest communities of the region to survive into contemporary times. They were distributed from the Southern Plains (Wichitas, Caddos, and Kitsais), through the Central Plains (Pawnees), to the Missouri River in the Dakotas (Arikaras). Siouian speakers were the Mandans and Hidatsas of the middle Missouri River and the Crows of the Montana Plains. Except for the Crows, these Caddoan and Siouan speakers were agriculturalists residing near rivers.

Around the margins of the Great Plains were many communities taking seasonal advantage of bison resources. They represented a variety of language families, including Siouan speakers in the north and eastern periphery, Apachean Athapaskan speakers along the western edge, Uto-Aztecan and Tanoan speakers penetrating from the western mountains and moving southward, Algonquian speakers across the northern regions, and some linguistic isolates such as the Tonkawas in the south. The introduction and spread of the horse after the 1750s, together with increasing pressures from European American interests, encouraged many of these groups to become full-time Plains residents. Some entered into trading arrangements with Plains agriculturalists, Puebloans, or Spanish settlements. Communication between these diverse groups was facilitated by fictive kinship relations established through ceremonial adoptions, intermarriage, sign language, and the multilingual abilities of many Plains residents.

In the 1800s the equestrian nomadic bison hunters came to dominate the Great Plains. Their lifestyle became the stereotyped image of the region, including their use of sign language for intergroup communication. While there is no evidence of a single unified sign system, the dynamics of trade, alliances, and warfare created a need for a rich system of nonverbal communication. The greater mobility and contact with linguistically diverse groups in the Great Plains made sign language a necessity. Short-term alliances, such as the one among the Cheyennes, Sioux, Arapahos, Kiowas, Comanches, Apaches, and others against the Utes, may have served to standardize to some degree the gesture language in use by Plains residents.

After 1830 the federal government sanctioned the forced removal of many eastern, and some western, Native American communities into the Great Plains, which dramatically increased the linguistic diversity of the region, adding new voices from the Siouan, Algonquian, Muscogean, Iroquoian,

Klamath-Modoc, and Sahaptian language families. However, catastrophic epidemics and other pressures from both inside and outside of the Native communities worked against the survival of Indigenous languages. Missionary and federal strategies of assimilation operated to vilify and reduce the use of Native languages and the cultural identities and communities they supported. The ongoing effect of such policies has been the slow strangulation of many Native voices. Languages such as Kitsai, Lipan, Missoura, Quapaw, and Tonkawa have been silenced, while many more have been weakened to a whisper.

Language helps to carry a people's history, culture, worldview, and wisdom. It is our great fortune that a diversity of Native languages has survived in the Great Plains. Geographic isolation and local willpower have assisted some communities in resisting assimilation to an English-only existence. Many more communities are joining a rising tide of Native American language awareness, maintenance, and revival efforts. However, their success is not guaranteed. Revival strategies vary between communities, due to differences in local needs, values, and resources. All are faced with the daunting task of securing a place for their voices when the mainstream language has such an overwhelming presence. Without vibrant Native voices lifting into the air with song, story, and prayer, how can we speak to *our* children about the history of the Great Plains?

Mark J. Awakuni-Swetland
University of Nebraska–Lincoln

Campbell, Lyle, and Marianne Mithun, eds. *The Languages of Native America: Historical and Comparative Assessment.* Austin: University of Texas Press, 1979. Hollow, Robert C., and Douglas R. Parks. "Studies in Plains Linguistics: A Review." In *Anthropology on the Great Plains*, edited by W. Raymond Wood and Margot Liberty, 98–109. Lincoln: University of Nebraska Press, 1980. Schlesier, Karl H., ed. *Plains Indians, AD 500–1500: The Archaeological Past of Historic Groups.* Norman: University of Oklahoma Press, 1994.

LAROCQUE, EMMA (B. 1949)

Emma LaRocque is a Plains Cree Métis who was born in a log cabin on January 2, 1949, in Big Boy, northeastern Alberta. Her family made a living from trapping. In *Defeathering the Indian* (1975), she points out that she did not know that she was poor or culturally deprived until she started school. Her book describes a happy childhood, and though she insisted on being sent to school at an early age, in retrospect she is saddened by the fact that this education stole her away from her parents and her culture. LaRocque worked as a teacher on the Janvier Reservation until 1971, then as a reporter and editor for the Alberta Native Communications Society's newspaper, *Native People*. She has earned

Dr. Emma LaRocque

two master's degrees and is now a professor of Native studies at the University of Manitoba.

LaRocque is both a literary critic and a poet. Her early writing began with cogent discussions of colonization and oppression and how these have affected Métis society. She has since become a powerful political writer in the broader fields of social criticism, human rights issues, women's rights, and family violence. She feels that much of her writing has been constrained by her academic training and deplores the fact that if she draws on information from experts within her culture, it is not accepted by the academy. She also resists what she calls the "ghettoization" of Native literature, whereby it is defined as "Native" when indeed it may address universal issues. LaRocque's poetry does indeed address universal issues, as in "Coffins Fell from the Sky," a lament upon the news that her mother had terminal cancer, but the "angry prairie wind of coldstone Canada" (from the poem "1990") also blows through her poems, lodging them in her Métis Alberta background.

Agnes Grant
Winnipeg, Manitoba

Lutz, Harmut. *Contemporary Challenges: Conversations with Canadian Native Authors.* Saskatoon, Saskatchewan: Fifth House, 1991. Perreault, Jeanne, and Sylvia Vance, eds. *Writing the Circle.* Norman: University of Oklahoma Press, 1993.

LAW

The legal history of the Great Plains may be said to begin with the first appearance of organized communities in the region thousands of years ago and long before the arrival of Europeans. The very persistence of these communities over time makes it obvious that they possessed systems of law sufficiently flexible and sophisticated to answer the needs of societies ranging from sedentary agricultural groups with comparatively large population centers to scattered bands of nomads who depended primarily on hunting and gathering for their survival. To some extent they all possessed, for example, rules governing interpersonal relations and well-developed ideas about property that regulated access to the resources of the land. Archeologists have demonstrated that small groups (e.g., individual families) frequently had exclusive or at least first access to the resources in a defined locale. Larger groups (e.g., tribes) likewise occupied defined territories from which they endeavored to exclude others. Unfortunately, little except generalities can reliably be set forth in outlining the finer points of this sort of early legal history and the rules these societies developed to give them structure and cohesion because of the lack of accessible and reliable evidence available to the historian. Unfortunately, this problem is only somewhat abated as we come to consider more recent times and even approach the arrival of Europeans.

In some respects, of course, Native peoples on the Great Plains began to feel the first effects of European influence before—in some cases long before—the actual arrival of the Europeans themselves. The introduction of the horse, new trade goods (notably, firearms), and diseases to which they had little resistance disrupted traditional ways of living and patterns of trade and drastically altered power relationships. The effects of these changes were visible wherever Europeans established themselves, but, like the ripples from a rock thrown in a pond, they spread far and wide, affecting Indigenous people far away from Europeans themselves. Precisely how the societies of the Great Plains adjusted their existing practices to respond to the new realities—or even if they did in every case—is very difficult to determine in the light of existing evidence. There is a body of oral tradition preserved among the various peoples who populated the Great Plains in the years before the arrival of the Europeans, but for very early periods this is a difficult source for historians to use, and it is not always seen as reliable without corroboration.

Nor, it seems, can we say much with confidence about the period when Europeans first had a physical presence, in the form of missionaries, traders, and explorers, on the Great Plains. These harbingers of change produced the first body of written material dealing with the autochthonous population of the Great Plains, but even with this often fascinating body of work in hand the legal historian is too often frustrated. The internal ordering of Indigenous societies was not something in which many of these early writers were interested, and even when it was mentioned, the observers were not always sufficiently sensitive to or even capable of understanding what they saw. With the arrival of larger European populations, though, we are on firmer ground because of the increased abundance of written records and more useful oral accounts.

The latter in particular have proven a valuable source for reconstructing the laws of a number of Plains tribes during the nineteenth century. Both tribes that had a long history on the Plains such as the Blackfoot and those that moved into the region only in the eighteenth century such as the Lakota (Sioux) had to adjust to new realities. The result was approaches to law that share certain broad characteristics such as an emphasis on consensus and restitution. Among the Kiowas of the Southern Plains, for example, there were few conflicts over property, the main exception being horses. Food was shared and stealing was rare. Internal family conflicts were also rare and likely to be settled by reason rather than by law. Criminal actions were deterred by the fear of supernatural reprisal (*taido*). Serious crimes such as murder might result in social ostracism or, if they threatened the integrity of the tribe, in the imposition of the death penalty, a killing "legalized" by the singing of a song, which nullified any supernatural penalty.

There were, however, considerable differences in legal systems (as in most other aspects of life) among Plains Indians. The Kiowas' legal system and, even more so, the Comanches' were rather informal, certainly when compared to the Cheyennes, to whom Llewellyn and Hoebel attributed a "legal genius." In Cheyenne society, for example, the tribal chiefs had exclusive jurisdiction over punishment of a murderer. Punishment generally meant banishment from the society, though remission was possible after a number of years if the perpetrator was penitent. The Cheyenne legal system, it might be added, had a refined classification system of what constituted murder and what might be excused as a justified killing.

The dynamic and varied Indigenous legal systems held on to much that harked back to traditional times but also demonstrated the ability to respond to new needs. The jurisdiction of the chiefs is a good example of the former, and perhaps the best example of the latter in most tribes, including the Cheyennes, is the increasing power of the warrior societies to make and enforce rules. However, the various tribal systems were eventually to come into conflict with ultimately more

domineering legal traditions brought to the region by Europeans.

Spain was active in the southern and France and England originally along the eastern and northern parts of the Great Plains. At first directly and later through colonial offshoots in the Americas, these three European powers, with very different legal cultures, began to transform the region. In all cases it was at first the policy of the European and later American powers not to extend their laws to the Indigenous population. In fact, it was recognized, either explicitly or implicitly, that it was neither desirable nor possible to expect the full body of their national law to apply even to those of European extraction. In theory, then, Native peoples would continue to be governed by their own laws, and Europeans and Americans would be subject to "appropriate" European law. In the United States, Indian Country was territory that was outside the organized territories and states. Settlers were forbidden there, and traders could operate only under license. A series of Intercourse Acts, including the 1834 act, which applied to the Great Plains, regulated trade and imposed fines on violations of the rules governing interactions with Native Americans.

This separation of legal domains was often very difficult and sometimes impossible to apply. Which European or American laws were in effect and which were not? Which rules should apply in disputes involving both Indigenous peoples and European Americans? What was to be done with the increasing numbers of people with both European American and Native ancestry? The result of this period of confusion was twofold. In the first place, there is clear evidence that in some cases contact with European Americans and their ways of doing things profoundly modified Indigenous rules and ways of proceeding. For example, alcohol, forbidden through the Intercourse Acts, continued to flow into the Plains through the fur trade and severely disrupted Native American lives.

But it was the second development that was ultimately to prove more significant. The law of the more powerful party, the European Americans, came to dominate, holding sway in most of the region and over most matters. Indigenous law was, by this steady process, largely marginalized. (Marginalized does not, however, mean exterminated. Indigenous law not only survives but in some jurisdictions—for example, rules concerning access to Native American sacred sites—has been rejuvenated and is even modifying the dominant European-inspired legal system.)

It is difficult to overstate the impact on Indigenous cultures and indeed on the entire ecology of the Great Plains itself that was occasioned by the arrival of large numbers of European Americans coming not simply to explore or trade but also to settle and to make lives for themselves and their children in these new lands. This process began in earnest during the nineteenth century and filled the region roughly from east to west. Friction was often impossible to avoid as the new arrivals sought to take control over the lands and water they needed in order to survive and as a result dispossessed the Native peoples. This process, accomplished by a series of treaties sanctioned by existing European and international law, occasionally led to violence and even wars, especially in the United States but also during two brief episodes in Canada (the Red River Resistance of 1869–70 and the 1885 Riel Rebellion). But these were only the most visible evidences of a kind of low-grade battle that had been in progress for some time as European American and Indigenous ideas about the ownership of property competed.

Traders had earlier confronted the fact that Native peoples often had ideas about private property quite different from their own. This was dealt with in a variety of ways; the Hudson's Bay Company's and American Fur Company's practice of trading literally through a hole in the wall so that their customers had no direct access to the trade goods and could not simply walk off with what they wanted is a good example. This fundamentally different view of property rights remained a source of friction between European Americans and Native peoples as the process of settlement continued and affected everything from land to movables. One particular focus was the horse, which had spread rapidly throughout the Great Plains region after the first Spanish imports had been introduced in the south. Horses became an integral part of the life of many tribes, and possession of horses conferred great status. The result of this was, eventually, a period of near constant raiding—which European Americans, as usual not overly sensitive to Indigenous life and values, termed simply "horse stealing"—during which the aim was to control as many horses as possible. Any and every horse was fair game in this passionate activity, with the frequent result that horses owned by European Americans were run off by Indians. Unfortunately, what was a serious though in some respects a sporting activity for Native peoples was seen as a very serious crime by European Americans, and only the efforts of the military in the United States and lawmen on both sides of the Canadian-American border prevented more serious problems from developing. They were occasionally thwarted by knowledgeable raiders, who knew they could not be chased across the international boundary, sometimes referred to as the "medicine line."

A second problem, related in the minds of most European Americans but in fact quite distinct, concerned the safety of cattle kept on the open range. Native peoples in the Great Plains depended to some extent on hunting for their subsistence, and in the northern regions, where huge herds of bison wandered the prairies, they were almost entirely dependent on this important source of food and its secondary products. It was difficult to persuade Indian hunters, especially after the destruction of the great bison herds was well advanced, that they should not take the cattle that had replaced them, since hunger and even starvation were often the only alternative to killing cattle.

However, the picture so often presented, at the time and since, of Indians as cattle killers and horse thieves has been greatly overdrawn. They did take both cattle and horses in some numbers, but careful reading of the records of the time makes it clear that European American criminals often found it easy to blame Indians for their own crimes and that many complained of Indian depredations simply because they hoped their respective governments would make good their "losses." In fact, members of the North-West Mounted Police in Canada frequently complained in their annual reports that settlers reported that their animals had been stolen simply so that the police would go out and round up their herds for them in the fall free of charge. In the United States, Indian agents often noted that "depredation claims" by settlers seemed to coincide with the arrival of Native American annuity payments.

From the point of view of many in the dominant society, a solution to these and other problems was finally arrived at in both Canada and the United States when the various tribes were confined to lands set aside for them, called reserves in Canada and reservations in the United States. In the United States these areas have preserved an important legal significance, stemming initially from the judgments of Chief Justice John Marshall in the famous Cherokee cases—*Cherokee Nation v. Georgia* (1831) and *Worcester v. Georgia* (1832)—that established the idea of tribes as "domestic dependent nations" possessing limited sovereignty. This sovereignty was further defined by the U.S. Supreme Court in *Ex Parte Crow Dog* (1883), where it was ruled that the United States had no jurisdiction over crimes committed by one Indian against another. Congress subsequently acted to limit this sovereignty, notably, in the Major Crimes Act of 1885, which determined that the United States did have jurisdiction over Indians for seven major crimes, including murder, but it remains an important part of the legal apparatus of the American Plains.

The "checkerboard" nature of landownership

patterns on Plains reservations, however (a product of the 1887 Dawes Act, which imposed allotments on the Indians and permitted the sale of "surplus" reservation lands to Americans), makes for extremely complicated jurisdiction in Indian Country. On many Plains reservations, non-Indians own most of the land, the lines between tribal and federal jurisdictions are blurred, and individual states also try to assert their legal and political authority. Landmark cases, including *Montana v. United States* (1981), have revolved around this complex geography and the extent of tribal jurisdiction over nonmembers of the tribe living on or, in that case, fishing and hunting on the reservation. Recent Supreme Court decisions have even led to the "diminishment" of reservations, especially in South Dakota.

In Canada, however, the approach has not been to recognize group rights, and the various tribes and bands have not had any formal power to make and enforce law. This seems to be changing, though, as a result of the current strong movement toward First Nations self-government, a movement at least partly informed by the perception that the American approach has its virtues. This movement was born in the Prairie Provinces, where more than half of Canada's Status Indians reside, but opposition to Native self-government is also greatest in that same region.

Kenneth Leyton-Brown
University of Regina

Cutter, Charles R. *The Legal Culture of Northern New Spain, 1700–1810.* Albuquerque: University of New Mexico Press, 1995. Knafla, Louis, ed. *Law and Justice in a New Land: Essays in Western Canadian Legal History.* Toronto: Carswell, 1986. Llewellyn, K. N., and E. Adamson Hoebel. *The Cheyenne Way: Conflict and Case Law in Primitive Jurisprudence.* Norman: University of Oklahoma Press, 1941. McLaren, John, et al, eds. *Law for the Elephant, Law for the Beaver: Essays in the Legal History of the North American West.* Regina: Canadian Plains Research Center, 1992. Reid, John Phillip. *Law for the Elephant: Property and Social Behavior on the Overland Trail.* San Marino CA: Huntington Library, 1997. Richardson, June. *Law and Status among the Kiowa Indians.* Vol. 1 of *Monographs of the American Ethnological Society.* New York: J. J. Augustin, 1941. Wunder, John, ed. *Law and the Great Plains: Essays on the Legal History of the Heartland.* Westport CT: Greenwood Press, 1996.

LITERATURE

Native American literature begins with the oral traditions in the hundreds of Indigenous cultures of North America and finds its fullness in all aspects of written literature as well. Until the last several decades, however, Native American literature has primarily been studied for its ethnographic interest. A fruitful intellectual discussion of the place of Native American literature within global literary study—a discussion that includes Native American intellectuals, artists, and writers themselves—only began during the activist period of the 1960s and 1970s.

The written Native American literary tradition commenced as early as the eighteenth century, when a Mohegan Methodist missionary, Samson Occum, published his *Sermon Preached at the Execution of Moses Paul, an Indian* in 1772. William Apess (Pequot), also a Christian minister, wrote an autobiography that protested non-Indians' treatment of Indians, and he also collected the autobiographies of other Christian Indians in *Experiences of Five Christian Indians of the Pequot Tribe* (1833). Other Native Americans published historical and cultural accounts of their peoples during the nineteenth century: David Cusick (Tuscarora); George Copway, Peter Jones, and William Whipple Warren (Ojibwa); Peter Dooyentate Clarke (Wyandot); Chief Elias Johnson (Tuscarora); and Chief Andrew J. Blackbird (Ottawa). These valuable writings represent a range of genres and reflect cultural issues of the times in which they were written.

Plains Indian oral literature includes literary expressions from cultures as different as Blackfeet (northwestern Montana) are from Kiowa (Southern Plains). By far, autobiographies comprise the bulk of written literary materials. During the late nineteenth and early twentieth centuries, academics—mostly anthropologists and historians—took up the idea that Native testimony or life stories needed to be preserved. Many believed that Native Americans were disappearing and with them their languages and histories; great efforts needed to be made to preserve cultural histories and literatures in writing. While many Native Americans wrote their own autobiographies during this period, many more had their life stories recorded as "as-told-to" autobiographies by anthropologists, ethnographers, and "Indian buffs." Plains Indian life stories, particularly those of warriors and chiefs, were so plentiful that they became a genre unto themselves.

Black Elk Speaks (Lakota) is probably the most famous as-told-to narrative, a text "told through" John G. Neihardt. Because the poet Neihardt was most interested in obtaining Black Elk's story for his poetic work on the American West, he omitted aspects of Black Elk's life that did not fit his own poetic purposes. In his study of *Black Elk Speaks*, entitled *The Sixth Grandfather*, Raymond DeMallie presents the transcripts of the initial interviews with Black Elk, enabling us to study the life of Black Elk and the textual creation of that famous work. Other well-known as-told-to Plains autobiographies include *Pretty-shield: Medicine Woman of the Crows* and *Plenty-coups: Chief of the Crows* (both as told to Frank B. Linderman in 1932 and 1930, respectively) and *Cheyenne Memories* (by John

Stands in Timber and Margot Liberty, 1967). Most notable among the self-generated autobiographies of the early twentieth century are Charles Eastman's (Dakota) *Indian Boyhood* (1902) and *From the Deep Woods to Civilization* (1916) and Gertrude Bonnin's (Lakota) *American Indian Stories* (1921), a mixture of short fiction, autobiography, and nonfiction. Contemporary Lakota as-told-to autobiographies continue, for example, *Lame Deer, Seeker of Visions* (1972) and *Lakota Woman* (1990), both written with Richard Erdoes.

European literary genres such as poetry and fiction, for the most part, began being employed by Native American people in the nineteenth century. John Rollin Ridge (Cherokee) wrote the first Native American novel in English, *The Life and Adventures of Joaquin Murieta* (1854).

The most famous Plains Indian writer is N. Scott Momaday (Kiowa), whose first novel, *House Made of Dawn* (1968), won the Pulitzer Prize for literature in 1969. *The Way to Rainy Mountain*, the autobiography he published a year later, traces his journey from the mountains of Montana to Rainy Mountain in Oklahoma, the path Kiowa people followed as their culture was transformed through acquisition of the Taime, the Sun Dance medicine bundle. Momaday's influence since the 1960s cannot be underestimated; through his writing, he created a new voice and a new place for Native American writers in the American imagination.

The era of awakening, dubbed the Native American Renaissance by literary critic Kenneth Lincoln, witnessed the production of many new Indian texts after Momaday's influential novel and autobiographical memoir, including works by Leslie Marmon Silko (Laguna), Simon Ortiz (Acoma Pueblo), and Ray Young Bear (Mesquaki) as well as poetry by Roberta Hill (Oneida), Duane Niatum (Klallam), Joy Harjo (Creek), and Wendy Rose (Hopi-Miwok), and others. James Welch, a Plains writer of Blackfeet and Gros Ventre heritage, has been and remains prominent among Native American writers, with five novels, one book of poetry, and a nonfictional book on the Indian point of view of the Battle of the Little Bighorn.

The substantial amount of writing by Native Americans now enables the identification of clusters of work based on genre, tribal affiliation, geography, theme, style, gender, and sexual preference. The blossoming of nonfictional essay writing and literary criticism by Natives themselves bodes well for the future study of Native American literature. Most notable among contemporary essayists is Elizabeth Cook-Lynn (Crow-Creek-Dakota); her collection *Why I Can't Read Wallace Stegner* (1996) hits at crucial contemporary Native American struggles, challenges, and grievances in tough-minded and bold terms. Although primarily a poet and fiction writer, Cook-Lynn presents "a tribal voice" (the subtitle of the text) that cannot be ignored. Most importantly, Native American literature owes its existence to continuing and vibrant oral traditions.

Kathryn W. Shanley
University of Montana

Allen, Paula Gunn, ed. *Studies in American Indian Literature: Critical Essays and Course Designs.* New York: Modern Language Association, 1983. Ruoff, A. LaVonne Brown. *American Indian Literatures: An Introduction, Bibliographic Review, and Selected Bibliography.* New York: Modern Language Association, 1999. Weaver, Jace. *That the People Might Live: Native American Literatures and Native American Community.* New York: Oxford University Press, 1997.

LITTLE BIGHORN, BATTLE OF THE

On Sunday, June 25, 1876, Lt. Col. George Armstrong Custer led 210 men of the U.S. Seventh Cavalry to their deaths at the Battle of the Little Bighorn. It was the army's worst defeat of the Plains Indian Wars.

The prelude to "Custer's Last Stand" began at the 1868 Treaty of Fort Laramie, which created the Great Sioux Reservation, including the Black Hills, as a homeland for the bands of the Lakotas and Cheyennes. The government's objective was to settle the Indians down on the reservation, where they could be more easily controlled. In 1874 rumors of gold in the Black Hills were confirmed by a geological team accompanying Custer's expedition, and white miners invaded the sacred land. This abrogation of the treaty rights by Americans encouraged the Lakotas and Cheyennes to resist restriction to the reservation and to continue bison hunting on the ranges of Nebraska, Wyoming, and Montana. In December 1875 the United States gave the tribes a thirty-day deadline to return to their reservations or be subject to military reprisals.

In the spring of 1876 the United States launched a three-pronged campaign against the Cheyennes and Lakotas. The first prong, under Col. John Gibbon, marched east from Fort Ellis (near present-day Bozeman, Montana). The second prong, led by Gen. Alfred Terry (and including Custer) headed west from Fort Abraham Lincoln near present-day Bismarck, North Dakota. The third prong consisted of Gen. George Crook's men moving north from Wyoming into Montana. These three units planned to meet near the end of June in the vicinity of the Little Bighorn. Unknown to Terry and Gibbon, Crook encountered the Indians near Rosebud Creek in southern Montana and was defeated by them about a week before Custer's battle. After this, his force withdrew to Wyoming, breaking one side of the triangle. Meanwhile, Terry was moving west up the Yellowstone River to the

Little Bighorn. The Seventh Cavalry, under Custer, scouted ahead on June 22. On the morning of the 25th, they reached the divide between Rosebud and the Little Bighorn rivers. From a spot known as the Crow's Nest, they observed a large Indian camp. Worried the Indians might escape, Custer decided to attack down the valley of the Little Bighorn. He assumed his approximately six-hundred-member command would face at the most eight hundred warriors. Instead he found a camp of five to eight thousand Indians, with about two thousand of them warriors.

Custer divided the Seventh Cavalry into three elements during the early phases of the battle and then subdivided his immediate command into wings. The Lakota and Cheyenne warriors, although surprised by the army's attack, quickly rallied and put all elements of the Seventh Cavalry's attack on the defensive. The Indians fought in small, loosely affiliated groups. They used their superior numbers, took advantage of available cover, and sniped at the soldiers from long distances. The soldiers deployed in open skirmish order, as they were trained, with the result that they were widely dispersed and became easy targets for the warriors' guns. Encircled by mounted forces led by Crazy Horse and Gall, Custer's entire command perished.

The news of Custer's defeat reached the American public during the celebration of the nation's centennial. The reaction was outrage and military reprisals that confined most of the Lakotas and Cheyennes to the reservation by the spring of 1877. Following the Battle of the Little Bighorn, the Black Hills were confiscated by the United States in direct contradiction of the terms of the 1868 treaty. The site of the battle is now the Little Bighorn Battlefield National Monument (previously, before December 10, 1991, the Custer Battlefield National Monument).

Douglas Scott
National Park Service

Scott, Douglas D., Richard A. Fox, Melissa A. Conner, and Dick Harmon. *Archaeological Perspectives on the Battle of the Little Bighorn.* Norman: University of Oklahoma Press, 1989. Utley, Robert. *Cavalier in Buckskin: George Armstrong Custer and the Western Military Frontier.* Norman: University of Oklahoma Press, 1988.

LITTLE BIG MAN

Little Big Man, a film released in 1970 and directed by Arthur Penn, is based on a novel of the same title (1964) by Thomas Berger. Berger and Calder Willingham wrote the screenplay. The film, shot on location in Montana and Canada, is a revisionist history of the mythic Old West, reflecting the social turmoil of the late 1960s.

The central character, Jack Crabb (Dustin Hoff-

man), nearly 120 years old, relates his life story to a young writer. After their parents are killed by Native Americans on the way west, Jack and his sister are taken into a Cheyenne village. His sister escapes, but Jack is raised Cheyenne, in particular by Old Lodge Skins (Dan George).

The story is braided with characters who move in and out of the narrative as Jack ages. Later "rescued" from captivity, Crabb is caught between the worlds of the Cheyennes and European Americans. He moves through life as a gunfighter, a failed store clerk, a muleskinner, a drunkard, and a military scout, but he always moves back to the Cheyennes in order to center his life. The story is told with hyperbole, as a tall tale would be, but with deft humor and irony.

The entire film is a classic retelling of every Western ever written or made. The segments in the European American world are often the most humorous. Jack's religious education is overseen by a missionary and his lusty wife, who later reappears as a saloon prostitute. He assists a snake oil salesman and is tarred and feathered. His tutelage as a gunfighter is overseen by his "manly" sister, Caroline, and Wild Bill Hickok. His stint as an inept businessman includes his marriage to an ill-tempered immigrant woman, who henpecks him. As a drunkard, he ends up becoming a muleskinner and scout for George Armstrong Custer.

Jack's movement in and out of the Native American world is also humorous, but the Cheyennes are presented as victims. Jack is present at the Sand Creek Massacre, after which he takes a Cheyenne wife, only to see her, her sisters, and his child killed by the Seventh Cavalry on the Washita River. He lives to fight in the Battle of Greasy Grass (Little Big Horn), where a childhood rival rescues him from being killed.

The portrayals of the Old West and Native Americans are exaggerated in every way. The film marks the beginning, however, of showing Native Americans as close to nature, spiritual, and victims of the white man. *Little Big Man* was among the first films that made an effort to be ethnographically accurate in its Native American segments. It may also be the first portrayal of Custer as vainglorious and, by the time of the Washita River massacre and Little Big Horn, a raving lunatic. *Little Big Man* reflects the growing resistance to the Vietnam conflict but also incorporates other themes of the day, including more open sexuality, an exposure of religious hypocrisy, and an awareness of environmental issues.

Larry J. Zimmerman
University of Iowa

Kasdan, Margo, and Susan Tavernetti. "Native Americans in a Revisionist Western: *Little Big Man.*" In *Hollywood's Indians: The*

Portrayal of the Native American in Film, edited by Peter C. Rollins and John E. O'Connor, 121–36. Lexington: University Press of Kentucky, 1998.

LONE WOLF V. HITCHCOCK

Lone Wolf and his wife, ca. 1890–1910

Lone Wolf v. Hitchcock (1903) was a U.S. Supreme Court decision that abrogated Native American treaty rights and underscored congressional supremacy (called plenary power) over Indian affairs. Plaintiffs Lone Wolf and several other Indians had sued the defendant, Interior Secretary Ethan Allen Hitchcock, to block allotment of the Kiowa-Comanche-Apache Reservation in southwestern Oklahoma. Kiowa claims, including the condition of article 12 of the Medicine Lodge Treaty (1867) forbidding cession of Indian land unless approved by three-fourths of the tribe's male members, were sidestepped in the Court's opinion. In 1900 Congress had approved a modified 1892 allotment agreement that did not contain sufficient signatures, even with forgeries, and Lone Wolf and his supporters sought judicial relief. Their case had been rejected in federal court in Washington DC and in the District of Columbia Court of Appeals.

The decision was the culmination of a century-long congressional assault on Indian land and treaty rights. The Court held that congressional guardianship over Indian reservation property could not be limited by an Indian treaty and cited its own decree in *Cherokee Nation v. Georgia* (1831) that Congress possessed complete administrative power over Indian tribal property. Referring to the earlier decision in *United States v. Kagama* (1886),

the justices upheld congressional supremacy over the nation's "Indian wards," called paternalism, ruling that congressional plenary authority over Indian relations was not subject to judicial oversight or review, since such congressional power was political.

The Court's decision had reverberations far from Lone Wolf's own reservation, which was quickly allotted. The unallotted "surplus" was opened to a tide of non-Indian settlers, who rapidly engulfed tribal lands. Although Indian land division had been under way before the opinion, the judicial pronouncement spurred a frenzy of allotment. Indian land loss increased, not least on reservations on the Northern Great Plains. Indian Office abuses of Indian land, resources, and rights increased in the ensuing years. Indian nations sank deeper into the mire of wardship, subject to virtually unlimited federal authority. The plenary doctrine of *Lone Wolf* dominated federal Indian law and Indian policy for more than half a century. The decree set back the efforts of humanitarian reformers, who advocated modifications in Indian policy. At the same time in the nation's history, the United States acquired its first overseas possessions, following the conclusion of the Spanish-American War. U.S. authorities viewed local island independence in the same light as that of continental Native American tribal independence, as the attitudes visible in the *Lone Wolf* litigation were applied narrowly to the new possessions.

Although officially repudiated in the judicial system since 1980 (*United States v. Sioux Nation of Indians*), the doctrine periodically has been resurrected in defense of denying Indian rights, such as in Indian religious freedom rights and those dealing with sacred sites. The Indian trust funds scandal at the end of the 1990s, involving Bureau of Indian Affairs mismanagement of Indian trust money, was also a long-postponed but direct outgrowth of the *Lone Wolf* decision and its attendant bureaucratic mind-set.

C. Blue Clark
Oklahoma City University

Clark, C. Blue. *Lone Wolf v. Hitchcock: Treaty Rights and Indian Law at the End of the Nineteenth Century*. Lincoln: University of Nebraska Press, 1994. Wilkins, David E. *American Indian Sovereignty and the U.S. Supreme Court: The Masking of Justice*. Austin: University of Texas Press, 1998. Wyatt, Kathryn C. "The Supreme Court, *Lyng*, and the *Lone Wolf* Principle." *Chicago-Kent Law Review* 65 (1989): 623–55.

LORENTINO, DOROTHY SUNRISE (B. 1912)

Dorothy Sunrise Lorentino opened the door for public school education to Native Americans and educated a nation. The extraordinary contributions to education of this Lawton, Oklahoma,

Alice Young Bear's house and shed on the road, 1952

native began with a battle. At the age of six she was denied access to the Cache Public Schools because of her heritage as a Comanche Indian. She and her parents made a twenty-mile train ride to Lawton, Oklahoma, where her father sued the school district for refusing to admit Native American children to public schools. Lorentino's father won the lawsuit in 1918. Prior to this ruling, all Native American children were required by law to attend only Bureau of Indian Affairs schools.

Lorentino later graduated from the Indian boarding school at Chilocco and earned a bachelor's degree from Northeastern Oklahoma A&M in Talequah in 1938 and a master's degree from the University of Oregon in 1947. Before retiring in 1972, Lorentino taught special education for thirty-four years on reservations in Arizona and New Mexico and later in the public schools of Salem and Tillamook, Oregon. Following her retirement, she continued teaching by substituting at public schools, and she taught the Comanche tribal language and songs to members of her tribe.

Lorentino earned many awards throughout her career as a teacher. In 1997 she became the first Oklahoman and Native American to be inducted into the National Teachers Hall of Fame. Other honors include the National Indian Education Association's Elder of the Year, the Delta Kappa Gamma Society Lifetime Award, and Outstanding Woman of Comanche County. In 1996 Cache High School initiated the Dorothy Sunrise Loren-

tino Award to be presented annually to the Native American graduating senior who best exemplifies the qualities for which Lorentino stands.

Cora Z. Hedstrom
National Teachers Hall of Fame

MANDANS

The Siouan-speaking people now called Mandans referred to themselves as Numangkaki, or "People of the First Man," a name that reflected their creation by First Man. Despite this common name, the people lived in separate, autonomous villages that were identified by their locations on the Missouri River and its tributaries. The two main divisions were the Nuitadi, "People of the West Side," and Nuptadi, "People of the East Side." Two other divisions, the Awigaxa and Istopa, mentioned by early European and European American visitors, disappeared under the pressure of epidemics and American settlement.

In 1797 British explorer David Thompson found some Mandans still living in villages on the Missouri while others had settled among the Hidatsas on the Knife River. Mandan villages differed from those of the Hidatsas by the arrangement of the earth lodges around an open space with a shrine in its center. Like the Arikaras and Hidatsas, the Mandans combined bison hunting with corn, beans, squash, and sunflower agriculture, and this combination set the seasonal round of spring planting, summer hunting, fall harvesting, and winter hunting. While hunting, the tribe lived in tipis and carried only the most necessary tools and clothing. At the village, however, the earth lodge provided plenty of room for storing items such as pottery and baskets, which the women made for cooking and harvesting, respectively. Related women, usually sisters, would build and occupy a lodge with their families.

Family relationships were organized on the basis of matrilineal clans. All the women in a family and their children were members of the same clan. A man who married a woman who was not of his clan moved into her earth lodge, but his primary loyalty was to his clan. The clan cared for its members, especially orphans and the elderly, disciplined its children, assisted its members in acquiring membership in military, social, and religious societies, and helped to purchase sacred bundles that allowed a man to perform religious ceremonies. These sacred bundles were earthly manifestations of the Mandans' origins. Each bundle contained objects, songs, and instructions for the sponsor of the ceremony. These ceremonies ensured the continued success of gardening and hunting activities that supported the tribe. The most important ceremony was the Okipa, a dramatization of the creation of the Mandan world by Lone Man and the gift of the animals. Despite their recognition of common identity, the villages were independent in their government. Each village selected two men—one known for his military abilities and the other for diplomacy—from the general council of sacred bundle owners to lead the village. The leaders served only as long as people accepted their ideas.

The first non-Indians to visit the Mandans found them to be hospitable to outsiders, and this established a long tradition of friendship between the Mandans and European Americans. In 1837 a devastating smallpox epidemic killed most of the Mandans and a large number of Hidatsas, leaving the fewer than two hundred survivors vulnerable to attacks from hostile tribes. As a defensive measure, the Mandans moved up the Missouri and, with the Hidatsas, established Like-a-Fishhook Village. This became a trade and administrative center for the region, attracting fur traders, government officials, and missionaries. The Arikaras moved to the village in 1862, completing the association that eventually became the Three Affiliated Tribes of the Fort Berthold Indian Reservation.

After forty years, Like-a-Fishhook was overcrowded and the local resources were exhausted. Consequently, in the early 1880s, even before allotment officially began, its inhabitants moved to new, kinship-based communities along the Missouri. The Mandans moved to the west side, where they established the settlements of Charging Eagle, Red Butte, and Beaver Creek. There they lived as farmers and ranchers, sending their children to the community school and attending church events and traditional ceremonies. In 1934 the Mandans, Hidatsas, and Arikaras voted to accept the Indian Reorganization Act and, under its auspices, established a tribal council, adopted a constitution, and took the name Three Affiliated Tribes of Fort Berthold Reservation.

In 1954 Garrison Dam, part of the Pick-Sloan Plan, turned the Missouri River into Lake Sakakawea, causing major disruptions in Mandan life. People had to leave the small, kinship-based, bottomland communities and move into new houses in new towns. The new Mandan community of Twin Buttes was built, but not everyone lived there, and tribal activities became more difficult to coordinate. Relatives no longer lived next door to each other, and the removal of the bridge isolated this corner of the reservation from New Town, the new administrative headquarters.

In the years that have passed since the dam was built, the Mandans have strived to maintain their language by teaching it in the elementary school and have revived the Sun Dance and other ceremonies. Nevertheless, marriage with outsiders and work opportunities elsewhere continue to draw young people away. A tenacious core of Mandan identity survives, however, and their population, which was only 241 in 1874, has rebounded to more than 1,200.

Mary Jane Schneider
University of North Dakota

Bowers, Alfred W. *Mandan Social and Ceremonial Organization.* Chicago: University of Chicago Press, 1950. Meyer, Roy W. *The Village Indians of the Upper Missouri: The Mandans, Hidatsas, and Arikaras.* Lincoln: University of Nebraska Press, 1977. Wood, W. Raymond, and Thomas D. Thiessen. *Early Fur Trade on the Northern Plains.* Norman: University of Oklahoma Press, 1985.

MANKILLER, WILMA (B. 1945)

The first woman to lead the Cherokee Nation of Oklahoma, and the tribe's most influential principal chief since John Ross of the nineteenth century, Wilma Mankiller's dedication to her people and their future defines her life of public service and social activism. Among Cherokees and other Native American peoples, Mankiller remains a staunch advocate of Native civil, spiritual, and sovereignty rights, economic independence, women's rights, and education and health reform, all while successfully fighting her own battles with emotional tragedy and personal illness.

Wilma Pearl Mankiller was born at Tahlequah, Oklahoma, on November 18, 1945, to Irene, of Dutch-Irish heritage, and Charlie, a full-blood Cherokee. Material poverty marked her life on the family's allotment tract, known as Mankiller Flats. This poverty would serve as the impetus for her family's move to San Francisco, California, in 1956 as part of the federal government's relocation policies under the auspices of the Bureau of Indian Affairs (BIA). When the BIA's promises of financial security proved false, the family turned to the San Francisco Indian Center for cultural and emotional support. Mankiller and her father developed a particularly strong relationship with the center, and she credits her interests in politics to watching Charlie work as an advocate for the Indian community of San Francisco.

In 1963 Mankiller married Hector Hugo Olaya de Bardi, whom she had met while a student at San Francisco State College, and by 1966 she was the mother of two daughters, Felicia and Gina. Her growing activism for Indian rights was heightened by the Indian occupation of Alcatraz Island; while her siblings joined the protesters on the island itself, Mankiller spent much of her time in fundraising activities for the movement. In 1974, due to fundamental differences in political and personal philosophies, Mankiller and her husband divorced, and in 1977 she returned to Mankiller Flats with her daughters.

Mankiller's work with the Cherokee Nation, as an economic stimulus coordinator, began shortly after her arrival but was interrupted by a near-fatal car accident in 1979, in which her best friend, Sherry Morris, was killed when her vehicle struck Mankiller's car head-on while passing on a blind curve. Mankiller's recovery was compounded by the emotional trauma of Morris's death and the onset of myasthenia gravis, a type of muscular dystrophy in which the immune system attacks skeletal muscles. With help from Cherokee medicine people, surgery, and drug therapy, Mankiller fully recovered and in 1980 continued her work with the Cherokee Nation.

By 1983, after directing a highly successful community revitalization program, Mankiller had developed a strong reputation as an efficient organizer and dedicated advocate of Cherokee people, particularly the poor of the nation. Ross Swimmer, then principal chief, asked her to be his running mate as deputy chief. Swimmer and Mankiller narrowly won the election. In 1985 Swimmer resigned to head the BIA in Washington DC, and Mankiller became the first woman principal chief of the Cherokee Nation. She was reelected in a runoff in 1987, and in 1991, a year after repeated hospitalizations and a kidney transplant, she won her second election with 82 percent of the vote.

The move toward tribal revitalization marked Mankiller's tenure as principal chief, during which she focused on Cherokee self-reliance, independence, and pride. She championed a variety of economic, political, educational, and cultural projects, including Cherokee language and literacy classes, rural development and housing construction, health care initiatives, and land claims settlement. Due to continued ill health, including a second kidney operation and treatment for lymphatic cancer, Mankiller declined in 1995 to run for a third term, but she has since remained active in Cherokee affairs and international Indigenous and women's rights. She and her husband, Charlie Soap, a bilingual full-blood Cherokee, are often seen at multitribal cultural and political events; at powwows, Charlie is a noted Plains-style dancer.

Some of the honors Mankiller has received include induction into the International Women's Forum Hall of Fame, the National Women's Hall of Fame, and the Oklahoma Women's Hall of Fame. She is the recipient of the National Racial Justice award, *Ms.* magazine's Woman of the Year award, and the Oklahoma Federation of Women's American Indian Woman of the Year award, and she was named in the *Marquis Who's Who* as one of the fifty great Americans. In 1998 Mankiller received the Medal of Freedom, the top civilian honor given by the U.S. government, from President Bill Clinton in honor of her work for the rights of women and Native peoples throughout the world.

Daniel Heath Justice
University of Toronto

Mankiller, Wilma, and Michael Wallis. *Mankiller: A Chief and Her People.* New York: St. Martin's Press, 1993.

MEANS, RUSSELL (B. 1939)

Russell Charles Means has been one of Indian America's most controversial leaders for more than thirty years. He was born on November 10, 1939, on the Pine Ridge Reservation in South Dakota but grew up in Southern California. He turned to alcohol, drugs, and crime as a teenager. He graduated from high school and attended several colleges without graduating. Lacking direction, he drifted through a series of jobs before moving to the Rosebud Reservation in South Dakota, where he worked at the Office of Economic Opportunity, a Johnson-era anti-poverty program.

In 1968 he used the federal relocation program to move to Cleveland, Ohio, where he helped organize the Cleveland American Indian Center. There he met Dennis Banks and Clyde Bellecourt, who had organized the American Indian Movement (AIM) in Minneapolis, Minnesota. He joined AIM in 1969 and established the Cleveland chapter, the second AIM chapter after Minneapolis. Means targeted the Cleveland Indians' mascot, "Chief Wahoo." He began to actively protest across the nation, challenging, for example, "pilgrims" on

Thanksgiving Day 1970 at Plymouth, Massachusetts, and occupying Mount Rushmore in South Dakota. Following the murder of Raymond Yellow Thunder in Gordon, Nebraska, Means and other members of AIM traveled to the town, leading 1,300 people, and pressed authorities to fully investigate the killing. Means left Cleveland in 1972 for Pine Ridge Reservation.

Means helped organize the Trail of Broken Treaties, a mass protest in Washington DC, timed to coincide with the 1972 presidential election. In 1972, reacting to the murder of Wesley Bad Heart Bull, Means and others from AIM tried to force authorities to charge his alleged killer with first degree murder rather than involuntary manslaughter. At the historic Custer, South Dakota, courthouse, Means and eighty others were arrested for rioting and arson.

By this point Pine Ridge Reservation was ready to erupt into a civil war between the supporters of tribal president Dick Wilson and more traditional members of the community. Wilson enjoyed federal support, including heavily armed FBI agents. Each side waged war on the other, with beatings, and eventually killings, becoming common. On February 27, 1973, Means led armed supporters to Wounded Knee, the site of the 1890 massacre, and took over the community. The FBI and federal marshals quickly moved in to surround the site. After Means left the compound to negotiate, he was jailed for the remainder of the incident. The siege ended on May 8, 1973, with federal promises to investigate tribal chairman Dick Wilson's government and consider other AIM demands. A federal judge later dismissed all charges against Means, but the organization's demands went largely unmet.

Means challenged Dick Wilson for the tribal presidency in 1974, losing by less than two hundred votes; he claimed that Wilson had cheated. A federal court later agreed, but by then Wilson had been defeated in a subsequent election. When Means ran for the office he was under federal indictment for his actions at Wounded Knee, but a federal judge later dismissed the charges following irregularities by the prosecution.

In subsequent years, Means was arrested for violations of many sorts, most of which he claimed were trumped up. He faced many trials, usually being acquitted, but he did serve time in jail on a number of occasions. He was acquitted of murder in 1976; it was later revealed that he had hidden a pistol in his boot to kill the judge and prosecutor if he was convicted. In 1978–79 he served slightly more than one year of a four-year term in the South Dakota State Penitentiary for rioting; he received a full pardon in 2002. His arrests and trials brought both positive and negative national attention to him and to AIM.

Means became involved in the struggle to regain the Black Hills, participating in the April 4, 1981, occupation of federal land there. He remained in the Black Hills, on and off, for two years. In 1982 he received half of the $35,000 settlement in a lawsuit he filed against the Cleveland Indians for its use of the mascot "Chief Wahoo." In 1983 he helped found KILI, a Lakota-owned radio station on Pine Ridge Reservation.

Means again ran for the Oglala tribal presidency in 1984, promising an end to federal involvement on the Pine Ridge Reservation, but he was removed from the ballot because of his felony conviction for rioting. That year he was *Hustler* magazine publisher Larry Flint's running mate in the Republican party primary but quit because he disagreed with Flint's style. Means remained politically active, and controversial, by supporting the Nicaraguan Miskito Indians in their struggle against the Sandinistas, one of many actions that alienated him from the already unstable AIM. Means had resigned several times from the organization, but following his alliance with the Miskitos, Clyde Bellecourt declared that he was no longer welcome. Means severed his ties with AIM in 1988 and moved more and more to the right of the political spectrum. He became politically involved with Sun Young Moon's Unification Church, then also broke with them. He moved to the Libertarian party, which argued for free market economics and a sharp reduction in the size and scope of government. He competed unsuccessfully to be the 1988 Libertarian party presidential candidate. In 1991 Colorado AIM asked him to be on its board of directors (the group's Web site listed Means as being on its Elders' Council in 2005).

In 1992 Means became involved in film for the first time, starring as Chingachgook in an adaptation of James Fenimore Cooper's *The Last of the Mohicans*, a book Means had previously condemned. His film and television career prospered, including roles in *Natural Born Killers, Under a Killing Moon, Wagons East* (1994), *Windrunner, Buffalo Girls, Pocahantas* (1995), *The Pathfinder* (1996), *Song of Hiawatha* (1997), *Wind River, Pocahantas II, Black Cat Run* (1998), *Thomas and the Magic Railroad* (2000), *Cowboy Up* (2001), *29 Palms* (2002), *Black Cloud* (2003), and *Into the West* (2005). In 1995 he published his autobiography, *Where White Men Fear to Tread*.

In 2002 Means aspired to run for governor of New Mexico under the Independent Coalition party but never filed legal papers. In 2002 and 2004 he campaigned unsuccessfully to be the Oglala Sioux tribal president. He has called himself a

"Lakota Libertarian Republican," arguing that the power of the federal government should be limited. He remains one of the nation's most controversial social and political activists, attacking and being attacked by both the left and the right and by Native and non-Native peoples alike.

Charles Vollan
South Dakota State University

Matthiessen, Peter. *In the Spirit of Crazy Horse*. New York: Viking Penguin, 1992. Means, Russell, and Marvin J. Wolf. *Where White Men Fear to Tread*. New York: St. Martin's Press, 1995. Sayer, John William. *Ghost Dancing and the Law: The Wounded Knee Trials*. Cambridge: Harvard University Press, 1997.

MEDIA

Native American publications in the Great Plains shared many challenges of small-town publications. They faced shortages of supplies and money, carried small subscription lists, confronted dilemmas related to political sponsorship, and found national advertising illusive. Native papers and many Native-owned broadcast stations continue to receive support from their tribal councils, and, as a result, they often face complex political pressures, including the pressure to satisfy patrons while covering the news.

Their traditional dilemmas began with the earliest Native American newspaper, the *Cherokee Phoenix*, published in both English and Cherokee in the late 1820s in the original Cherokee capital at New Echota, Georgia. Editor Elias Boudinot stood up to the power of both the tribal council and their white, racist neighbors. Boudinot waged a courageous fight against white abuse of Cherokees and reported on dissension within the tribal council over Cherokee removal from Georgia to Indian Territory. The editor got caught in tribal factionalism, however, and was killed in Indian Territory in 1839 for signing the treaty that ceded the Cherokees' original land.

The Reverend Samuel Worcester and printer John F. Wheeler, both of whom served Georgia prison time for their work on the *Phoenix*, helped the Cherokees start the *Cherokee Advocate* in 1844 in the new Cherokee capital of Tahlequah in Indian Territory, with William P. Ross, the chief's nephew, as editor. The *Advocate* continued the *Phoenix*'s policies of free distribution and publication in both Cherokee and English. The newspaper's objectives were to spread important news among the Cherokee people, to advance their general interests, and to defend Indian rights. Clearly, the goals reflected a partisan commitment to the cause of Native peoples, but the newspaper also reflected factionalism among the Cherokees and continued, with missionary sponsorship, to advocate assimilation and defend human rights within that

context. Although Cherokee law prevented editors from printing personal and partisan items, political debate occasionally became intensely personal and sometimes violent. After the Civil War, the *Cherokee Advocate* was published under the same format until it ceased publication in 1906. The federal government ordered the Cherokee type preserved in the Smithsonian Institution and the rest of the equipment sold in 1911.

The second Native American newspaper, the *Shawnee Sun* (*Siwinowe Kesibi*), began in 1835 under the editorship of Johnston Lykins and with the assistance of the Reverend Jotham Meeker, a missionary who took a printing press with him to his duties at the large Baptist mission at Shawnee Mission, Kansas. The press at Shawnee Mission published part of the newspaper in the Shawnee language using the English alphabet. Meeker translated religious messages and songs and published Indian material in the Native language. His press was the first in the area that is now Kansas. The newspaper was published monthly or semimonthly until its suspension in 1839. It resumed publication in 1841 and apparently lasted until 1844.

By the end of the twentieth century, one of the three national Native American newspapers was published in the Great Plains. The editorial headquarters for *Indian Country Today*, formerly the *Lakota Times*, are located in Rapid City, South Dakota. Other examples of Native voices from the Great Plains included the two-thousand-watt tribally owned KILI, voice of the Lakota Nation, in Porcupine Butte, South Dakota, and its sister station, KINI, in Rosebud.

William E. Huntzicker
Bemidji State University

Carter, L. Edward. *The Story of Oklahoma Newspapers*. Muskogee: Oklahoma Heritage Association by Western Heritage Books, 1984. Littlefield, Daniel F., Jr., and James W. Parins. *American Indian and Alaska Native Newspapers and Periodicals, 1826–1924*. Westport CT: Greenwood Press, 1984.

MÉTIS

The term "Métis," from the French meaning "mixed," is used by scholars to designate individuals and groups who identify their antecedents with historical fur trade communities, and it refers to people who possess a distinctive sociocultural heritage and sense of self-identification. These descendants of Native American women and European men forged a new identity that was distinct from Indigenous bands and from the European American world of the trading posts. The Métis of the Great Plains could be found almost anywhere the fur trade predominated, and by the early nineteenth century distinct communities were emerging in the valleys of the North Saskatchewan, Assiniboine, and Red rivers in British North America and the Missouri River and its tributaries in U.S. territory.

These communities varied considerably, depending on the locality in which they arose, the Native American bands they were allied to, the ethnicity and nationality of the fur trade fathers, and the particular roles they played within the fur trade economy. What they had in common was that they were bicultural communities that functioned as intermediaries or brokers between European American fur traders on the one hand and trapping bands on the other. It was in these interstitial spaces that unique Métis identities were forged. Being Métis had many advantages in these fur trade worlds. It was an ethnic positioning that allowed individuals to cross boundaries separating Native American and European American societies. It allowed for flexibility in self-definition, whereby an individual could accentuate those personality and kinship aspects to allow entry into both worlds. Some of these communities used "Métis" to identify themselves, though other terms were used, including "Michif," "Bois Brûlé," "Chicot," "Half-Breed," and "Mixed-Blood," among others.

Although these Métis bands were found across the Northern Plains from the Missouri to the Athabasca River, Métis political identity in the early nineteenth century was focused on the Red River Settlement. Their assertion of political rights arose there first in relation to the fur trade wars between the North West Company and the Hudson's Bay Company following the establishment of the Red River Settlement in 1811. The Plains Métis, closely tied to the various bourgeois of the North West Company by consanguinity and employment, were encouraged to oppose the Hudson's Bay Company's efforts to impose any authority over them. This conflict, which ended in violence and the deaths of twenty-one colonists at the Seven Oaks Massacre in 1816, came to be seen by the Métis as the initiation of a "new nation."

Acting as buffalo-hunting provisioners and trappers in the fur trade of the Great Plains, the Métis considered themselves independent of both fur trade and tribal control. By the 1840s the buffalo-robe trade, complementing the summer provisioning hunt, resulted in the establishment of sizable winter villages wherever buffalo could be found. This move into the territory of the Sioux, Crees, and Blackfoot caused violent confrontations, the most famous of which was the Battle of Grand Coteau, on June 16–19, 1851. Here Métis buffalo hunters from the Red River came under sustained attack from Sioux near the Missouri River. Attacked by a much larger force, the Métis circled their two-wheeled Red River carts to corral

their horses and oxen and to shelter their women and children. The men established a perimeter the distance of a gunshot by scraping gun pits in the prairie sod, and from these rifle pits they inflicted enough casualties that the Sioux eventually broke off the attack.

In order to alleviate such hostilities, attempts were made to broker peace treaties between the Métis and the various tribal groups. In 1858 the Métis, Sioux, and Ojibwas met in a Grand Council north of the Sheyenne River, to the west of Devils Lake (present-day North Dakota), to set tribal boundaries and establish peace among the three groups. The Métis, though closely associated with the Ojibwas of the region, were recognized as a separate political and military force and were given the right to hunt in Sioux territory. Still, conflicts would continue to erupt between the Métis and various tribal groups throughout the 1860s and 1870s.

In the treaties negotiated between the United States and Native American groups west of the Great Lakes, various bands insisted that treaties provide some compensation for their "mixed-blood" brothers not living as Indians or as part of the band. When the Red River Métis heard that the American government was planning to negotiate a treaty with the Pembina and Red Lake Chippewas (Ojibwas), many decided to relocate to the American side of the boundary to take advantage of the benefits of this treaty. During the negotiations the Métis claimed that it was their country and that they had long defended and maintained it against the encroachments of enemies. The treaty that was signed between the United States and the Pembina Chippewas on September 20, 1851, however, did not include the Métis as signatories because the government believed it should not treat with people whom it regarded "as our *quasi* citizens." The government negotiator did stipulate that he would not object to any just or reasonable treaty stipulation the Indians might choose to make for the Métis' benefit.

With the transfer of Rupert's Land to Canada in 1869–70, the Red River Métis, led by Louis Riel, initiated a political movement to guarantee their rights in the new political order. The Manitoba Act of 1870, which brought the Red River Settlement into the Canadian Confederation, granted the Métis both land rights and some semblance of constitutional recognition. The rush of settlers into Manitoba after 1870, and the continuing profitability of the buffalo-robe trade, however, induced many Métis to sell their landholdings and move farther west. In 1884 Riel, now claiming to be a religious prophet, led another movement, the North-West Rebellion, aimed at recapturing the political power the Métis had lost in the Red River Settlement. Centered in the communities of the South Saskatchewan River, this movement eventually resulted in armed rebellion against the Canadian state in 1885. The uprising was crushed, and Riel was hanged for treason on November 16, 1885.

Following the North-West Rebellion of 1885 and the demise of the fur trade in the Plains, the Métis lost much of their political influence and cohesiveness. They dispersed northward and westward, with many also fleeing to Montana and North Dakota to escape expected reprisals. There they joined preexisting Métis communities that had been established during the heyday of the fur trade. Although Métis communities survived into the twentieth century in both the United States and Canada, poverty, demoralization, and prejudice against them led many individuals to suppress their biracial heritage and identity. Since the 1970s, however, social, cultural, and political developments that have legitimized ethnicity have produced a renaissance of Métis identity and political activity throughout the Northern Plains and Prairie Provinces. In 1982 the Métis were recognized as one of Canada's Aboriginal Peoples under section 35(2) of the Constitution Act.

Gerhard J. Ens
University of Alberta

Ens, Gerhard. J. *Homeland to Hinterland: The Changing Worlds of the Red River Metis in the Nineteenth Century.* Toronto: University of Toronto Press, 1996. Foster, John E. "Wintering, the Outsider Male and Ethnogenesis of the Western Plains Métis." *Prairie Forum* 19 (1994): 1–13. Peterson, Jacqueline, and Jennifer S. H. Brown, eds. *The New Peoples: Being and Becoming Metis in North America.* Winnipeg: University of Manitoba Press, 1985.

MILLS, BILLY (B. 1938)

Billy Mills, an Oglala Sioux, achieved one of the Olympic Games' most astonishing upsets by winning the gold medal in the ten thousand meters in Tokyo, Japan, in 1964. William Mervin Mills was born on June 30, 1938, on the Pine Ridge Reservation in South Dakota. He entered Haskell Institute, an Indian school in Lawrence, Kansas, after being orphaned at age twelve. Active in various sports, he discovered a penchant for distance running and, in 1957, obtained an athletic scholarship to the University of Kansas.

Mills won several Big 8 Conference cross-country and indoor and outdoor track titles before graduating from the University of Kansas in 1962. He joined the U.S. Marine Corps and, after a two-year break from competitive running, qualified for the 1964 U.S. Olympic team in the ten thousand meters and the marathon. A relative unknown in the ten thousand meters, Mills outran favorites Ron Clarke of Australia and Mohamed Gammoudi

Billy Mills winning the gold medal in the ten thousand meters in Tokyo, Japan, 1964 Summer Olympic Games

of Tunisia in the final few meters, establishing an Olympic record of 28:24.4. He joined Louis Tewanima, another Native American who had won the silver medal in the ten thousand meters in 1912, as the only Americans to garner medals in the event. Mills also won national Amateur Athletic Union (AAU) titles at three miles indoors and six miles outdoors in 1965. After retiring from running, Mills established insurance and public relations firms in California. From 1971 to 1974 he served as an assistant commissioner of Indian affairs in the Office of Recreation and Physical Fitness. In that role, Mills revived the National Track and Field Hall of Fame and the American Indian Athletic Hall of Fame. In 1980 he founded the Billy Mills Leadership Institute to improve social and economic conditions of Native Americans. The 1984 film *Running Brave* depicted his rise to Olympic success.

Adam R. Hornbuckle
Alexandria, Virginia

Mills, Billy. *Wokini: A Lakota Journey to Happiness and Self Understanding.* New York: Crown, 1994.

MISSIONARIES

Christian missionaries promoted strategies to transform Native American communities in the Great Plains. By the end of the nineteenth century few reservations and reserves claimed no Protestant or Catholic presence. Over time, tribal members selectively accepted certain cultural components while actively preserving Native traditions. Intercultural relations involved individuals acting within dozens of tribal and denominational traditions, not conflicts between monolithic "Indian" or "missionary" perspectives.

Missionary contact with Great Plains tribes increased during the nineteenth century. Organized in 1810, the interdenominational American Board of Commissioners of Foreign Missions (ABCFM) led the way among Protestant missionary organizations. In 1819 Congress established a "civilization fund," appropriating $10,000 annually to support assimilation programs for Native Americans. Missionaries, spiritually motivated by the Second Great Awakening of the 1820s and 1830s and partially supported by federal funds, flocked to Indian Country. When Congress passed the Indian Removal Act (1830) and forcibly relocated many eastern tribes to the Plains, Christian representatives followed close behind to minister to relocated tribes as well as to Indians. In 1838 Baptist missionary Evan Jones and Cherokee minister Jesse Bushyhead led two of the Cherokee removal parties to Indian Territory.

Missionaries exerted little influence over tribal members during early interactions. In fact, Christian ministers often lived on the hospitality of tribal leaders. In 1834 ABCFM-sponsored ministers Samuel Allis and John Dunbar joined the Pawnees during their winter buffalo hunt in the Central Plains. During this five-month journey the missionaries lived beholden to tribal members for linguistic and cultural education, as well as for food and shelter. They developed a better understanding of Pawnee ways during the next few years, but claimed no conversions. Pawnee leaders showed interest in the missionaries but ignored their appeals to abandon their seminomadic lifestyle.

Nineteenth-century missionaries arrived in the Great Plains with little experience in intercultural relations. Religious emissaries were drawn from Roman Catholic, Methodist, Baptist, Presbyterian, Lutheran, Mormon, Episcopal, Quaker, and other denominations. Many had extensive educational backgrounds by nineteenth-century standards. In the Plains they endured harsh weather, epidemics, limited support, and cultural isolation. They proved incapable, however, of recognizing the vitality of Native American societies. Instead, their culturally tainted vision saw tribal members as "lazy," "childlike," and "corrupt" members of "offensive" cultural traditions. Some missionaries disagreed on whether they should first promote Christianity or "civilization" within tribal communities. None questioned the premise of advocating both. Many, including Rev. John West, an Anglican stationed in southern Manitoba during the 1820s, considered principles of Christian mission work as indistinguishable from civilization programs.

Despite ethnocentric biases, religious leaders advocated the potential equality of all Christians. Missionaries provided tribes with support for their bodies and minds while hoping to cultivate Christian souls. Jotham Meeker served the Ottawas in Franklin County, Kansas, for more than twenty years as a physician and Baptist minister. Isabel Crawford taught domestic skills at a remote Kiowa camp in western Oklahoma during the late nineteenth and early twentieth centuries. Catholic sisterhoods, including the Grey Nuns, Sisters of the Presentation, Benedictines, and Franciscans, taught in mission schools and developed health-care facilities.

Missionaries found no single assimilation formula that would work for all Native Americans. The effectiveness of programs varied even within divisions of the same tribe. Distinctive tribal histories and missionaries' personalities produced different outcomes at each mission station. Historic contacts with European Americans, community locations, tribal leadership structures, and other variables influenced tribal acceptance, or rejection, of the Christian agenda. Missionary flexibility, communication skills, and attitudes affected tribal responses. In the 1830s, Jesuits recognized a failed mission to the Potawatomis in Council Bluffs, Iowa, at the same time that they recorded success with Potawatomis at Sugar Creek, Kansas. Similarly, during the 1870s, Quaker representatives had varying success with their efforts among the Pawnees, Otoe-Missourias, and Omahas of Nebraska.

Missionaries did not always practice truly Christian behavior. President Ulysses Grant's "Peace Policy" (1869) restricted reservations to a single Christian denomination, reinforcing denominational competition for tribal support. Self-serving actions often came at the expense of tribal interests. During the 1860s, Baptist leaders colluded with federal agents to defraud Ottawas of thousands of acres of their east-central Kansas land under the guise of creating an Indian university. Despite varied commentary from former students about their boarding-school experiences, countless stories reveal physical and emotional abuse at these institutions.

Why did tribal members seek relationships with missionaries? Some recognized the spiritual power of Christian emissaries. The Blackfoot, for instance, described eminent Jesuit missionary Pierre-Jean De Smet as "the man who talks to the Great Spirit." Others saw missionaries of different denominations as potential allies, capable of supporting them against unpopular federal agents and assimilation programs. After their removal to Kansas in the 1820s, Ohio Shawnees sided with Baptist missionaries, while relatives from Missouri cultivated the support of Methodists. On the Lakotas' Pine Ridge Reservation in the 1880s, American Horse's people generally turned to Episcopalians while Red Cloud's folk allied with Jesuit Catholics. In this way, missionary support reinforced preexistent tribal divisions.

Religious leaders often promoted tribal traditions at the expense of the federal assimilation agenda in order to gain converts. Some missions promoted "English only" rules for students in boarding schools while perpetuating adult use of tribal languages. Many missionaries learned tribal languages to cultivate support for their Christian message. ABCFM missionary Stephen Riggs, impatient for the Santee Sioux to understand English, learned the Dakota language to preach Christianity. He also published a Dakota grammar and dictionary in 1851 and *Dakota Odowan*, a hymnbook, in 1853. By the end of his life in 1883, he had published a translation of the Bible in Dakota. Presbyterian missionaries Samuel Irvin and William Hamilton unintentionally supported Iowa and Sac traditions. Their recorded observations of these tribal cultures from 1837 to 1853 stand today as significant ethnographic sources despite their obvious ethnocentric biases. Methodist Rev. John McDougall in southern Alberta went so far as to argue against the Canadian policy of suppressing the Sun Dance and Thirst Dance on the grounds of religious liberty.

Tribal members also crossed cultural barriers. Over time, many joined Christian denominations, even serving within organizational structures as true "Indian" missionaries. Still, they retained their tribal identities. Kickapoo leader Kennekuk cloaked himself in Methodist garb while promoting a nativist agenda. The Kickapoo prophet used his prominence to delay for fourteen years his people's removal from their Illinois homelands to Kansas. In addition, he promoted religious traditions that incorporated rituals and beliefs that drew his people, as well as his Potawatomi converts, beyond Methodist norms. Despite his persistent Lakota identity, Black Elk served as a Catholic catechist on the Pine Ridge Reservation.

Canadian religious leaders, perhaps even more than their American counterparts, promoted the cultivation of Native missionaries. Dakota tribal members John Thunder and Peter Hunter, of the Birdtail Creek Reserve in southern Manitoba, gained employment from the Foreign Mission Committee of the Presbyterian Church. From 1887 to 1912 they served as ministers to their Dakota people in the Northern Great Plains. Both men used their missionary offices to improve their people's status within Canadian and American societies. In these capacities, Thunder and Hunter preached Christianity in the Dakota language and promoted an agenda aimed at improved conditions for Native peoples. Some Indian missionaries crossed tribal lines to spread the Christian message. Ojibwa-born Shahwanegezhick of Ontario, who took the name Henry Bird Steinhauer, introduced Methodist tradition to the Crees of Alberta.

Over time, Native Americans across the Great Plains incorporated Christian traditions into their tribal identities. Missionaries erred, however, in their estimation that they could replace tribal traditions with Christianity. On the Omaha Reservation in Nebraska, prominent La Flesche family members claimed elements of Presbyterian tradition that did not clash with their tribal identities. Some contemporary Native Americans choose to blend tribal traditions with Christianity by praying to Jesus in a sweat lodge and the Great Spirit in churches. Other Native Americans see no need for religious exclusivity. They distinctly practice tribal, Christian, and Native American Church traditions throughout their lives. Many contemporary tribal members still essentially ignore Christian traditions.

Missionary practices changed in tone during the twentieth century. By the 1920s some Christian denominations grew more tolerant of certain tribal traditions. Following World War II, urban ministries arose to work with tribal members drawn to cities for economic and educational opportunities. The later decades of the century witnessed declining ministerial staff and revived interest in Native American communities, leading to increased missionary alliances. Pine Ridge, South Dakota, and Bismarck, North Dakota, now host ecumenical ministries serving tribal members from different denominational backgrounds. Ironically, many contemporary clergy grow increasingly involved in tribal rituals, to the point of suggesting potential Christian "conversion" to Native American traditions.

Robert W. Galler Jr.
St. Cloud State University

Beaver, R. Pierce. "Protestant Churches and the Indians." In *Handbook of North American Indians*, edited by William C. Sturtevant, 4:430–58. Washington DC: Smithsonian Institution, 1988. Bowden, Henry Warner. *American Indians and Christian Missions: Studies in Cultural Conflict*. Chicago: University of Chicago Press, 1981. Burns, Robert I., S.J. "Roman Catholic Missions in the Northwest." In *Handbook of North American Indians*, edited by William C. Sturtevant, 4:494–500. Washington DC: Smithsonian Institution, 1988. Crawford, Isabel. *Kiowa: A Woman Missionary in Indian Territory*. Lincoln: University of Nebraska Press, 1998. Foley, Thomas W. *Father Francis M. Craft: Missionary to the Sioux*. Lincoln: University of Nebraska Press, 2002.

MNI SOSE INTERTRIBAL WATER RIGHTS COALITION

The Mni Sose Intertribal Water Rights Coalition was organized in 1993 to enable the twenty-eight American Indian Nations in the Missouri River basin to seek legal, administrative, economic, and physical control over their water resources. Since its inception, the coalition has been engaged in a constant effort to educate U.S. agencies and congressional committees about the treaty and trust responsibilities of the federal government. For example, under the Flood Control Act of 1944, which authorized the Pick-Sloan Plan, eight reservations relinquished a total of 350,000 acres, or 23 percent of the total land appropriated, for the construction of the five earthen dams to control flooding along the Missouri River. Although a $1.3 billion economic benefit is derived from these projects each year, the tribes have shared in little of the revenues. However, based upon the efforts of the coalition, the tribes are now in the process of approving contracts for allocations of hydropower from the Pick-Sloan dams, which will ultimately result in lower electrical rates on the reservations.

The coalition is also working with federal and other agencies to develop partnerships with tribes to support tribal water uses, conduct research, and encourage technology transfer to improve water resource development and cultural protection of the environment. With the assistance of the Mni Sose Intertribal Water Rights Coalition, tribes are moving from a passive to an active role in protecting their tribal homelands. They are now acquiring the legislative, administrative, and operational capabilities to govern, manage, and protect their tribal water resources.

> Richard Bad Moccasin
> Mni Sose Intertribal Water Rights Coalition

MOMADAY, N. SCOTT (B. 1934)

House Made of Dawn (1968), N. Scott Momaday's Pulitzer Prize winning novel about a World War II veteran's experiences at Jemez Pueblo and in Los Angeles, was a groundbreaking literary event that attracted widespread attention to contemporary Native American writing as well as to much older written and oral Native American literature. Since the publication of that novel, Momaday has written another, *The Ancient Child* (1989), and has also gained international recognition as a poet (*The Gourd Dancer*, 1976; *In the Presence of the Sun: A Gathering of Shields, 1961–1991*, 1992; *In the Bear's House*, 1999), an autobiographer and engaging interviewee (*The Way to Rainy Mountain*, 1969; *The Names: A Memoir*, 1976; *Ancestral Voice*, 1989; *Conversations with N. Scott Momaday*, 1997), an essayist (*The Man Made of Words: Essays, Stories, and Passages*, 1997), and a respected artist.

Navarre Scott Momaday was born in Lawton, Oklahoma, on February 27, 1934. Although he has lived most of his life away from his birthplace, southwestern Oklahoma and other Great Plains

N. Scott Momaday

landscapes have dominated much of his best fiction and poetry. In *The Ancient Child*, some of his most lyric prose poems capture the majesty and seasonal beauties of Devil's Tower (Bear Lodge) in Wyoming and the Wichita Mountains' high meadows in spring. Several fine poems celebrate striking aspects of the Plains landscape (the "prairie fire" of sunrise in "Plainview 3") and Plains culture (*The Gourd Dancer*, "Rings of Bone," and the "Gathering of Shields" prose poems).

It is in *The Way to Rainy Mountain*, however, that Momaday offers his most sustained and moving testimony to the Great Plains. His father's people, the Kiowas, undertook a migration three hundred years ago that traversed the Great Plains from the headwaters of the Yellowstone River to Rainy Mountain in southwestern Oklahoma and continued in later years with horseback travels through Texas to Mexico.

For Momaday, the Plains area of southwestern Oklahoma is "a landscape that is incomparable," in part because it grounds and witnesses a grand paradox for his father's people, "a time that is gone forever, and the human spirit, which endures." To capture this landscape in twenty-four two-page sections, Momaday created three "angles of vision": storytelling (tribal narratives and family lore), history-fact, and personal experience. Together these viewpoints acknowledge the harshness of the Plains—blizzards, a summer heat as fierce as "an anvil's edge," tornadoes powered by a wild mythical horse—and document the tragedies of his people: eight hundred Kiowa horse carcasses rotting near Fort Sill, thousands of buffalo slaughtered, many Kiowas killed and taken into captivity. But in memory, in the present, and in the sense of sacred play of the three perspectives, the vitality of the Kiowa Plains endures in a mountain that "burns and shines" in the "early sun," in a reverence for the grand wanderings of great horsemen, and in the joy of seeing a newborn buffalo that adds life to the returning buffalo herds. Small wonder that Momaday can look at the remote knoll that is Rainy Mountain and see a place "where Creation was begun."

Kenneth M. Roemer
University of Texas–Arlington

Roemer, Kenneth M., ed. *Approaches to Teaching Momaday's "The Way to Rainy Mountain."* New York: Modern Language Association, 1988. Scarberry-Garcia, Susan. *Landmarks of Healing: A Study of "House Made of Dawn."* Albuquerque: University of New Mexico Press, 1990. Schubnell, Matthias. *N. Scott Momaday: The Cultural and Literary Background.* Norman: University of Oklahoma Press, 1985.

MONTANA V. UNITED STATES

In *Montana v. United States* (1981), the U.S. Supreme Court ruled that the Crow Tribe of Montana did not possess the inherent sovereign power to regulate hunting and fishing by nonmembers of the tribe on lands owned by non-Indians within its reservation boundaries. The decision arose out of a dispute between the Crows and the state of Montana over the question of which entity had jurisdiction to control hunting and fishing within the reservation boundaries and primarily focused on the right to regulate fishing and duck hunting on and around the Big Horn River, which flows through the Crow reservation. The Crows based their claim on their inherent powers of tribal sovereignty and the language of the various treaties that created their reservation and, they argued, gave them ownership of the bed of the Big Horn River. Montana, on the other hand, argued that it took title to the riverbed at the time it became a state and that it had always maintained the authority to regulate hunting and fishing by non-Indians within the reservation.

In an attempt to resolve the conflict, the United States, acting as trustee for the tribe, initiated a lawsuit in 1975 seeking a judicial resolution of both the threshold question of title to the riverbed and the accompanying jurisdictional dispute over hunting and fishing rights. The federal district court ruled in favor of Montana, holding that the state rather than the Crows owned the banks and bed of the Big Horn River. The Ninth Circuit Court of Appeals reversed the district court's decision, holding, with some qualifications, that the treaties establishing the Crow Reservation had vested title to the riverbed in the United States as trustee for the tribe and that the Crows could regulate hunting and fishing within the reservation by nonmembers. In its 1981 decision, the Supreme Court reversed the court of appeals, essentially restoring the district court's judgment in favor of the state of Montana.

Two components of the ruling are key. On the question of title to the riverbed, the Court held that, notwithstanding certain ostensibly contradictory language in the 1851 and 1868 treaties by which the Crow Reservation was formed, title to the riverbed passed to the state of Montana upon its admission into the Union in 1889. With respect to the broader issues of inherent tribal sovereignty, the Court acknowledged that Indian tribes still maintain certain powers of self-government but went on to hold that those powers extend only to the control of "internal relations." Extension of tribal power beyond the realm of internal tribal matters, the Court ruled, would be "inconsistent with the dependent status of the tribes." Finding that control of hunting and fishing by nonmembers on lands no longer owned by the tribe (but still within its reservation) bears "no clear relationship to tribal self-government or internal relations," the Court held that the Crows did not possess the "retained inherent sovereignty" to regulate those activities.

The *Montana* decision and others like it are universally perceived by Native Americans and their supporters as troubling judicial assaults on the remnants of tribal sovereignty, confirming the extremely fragile nature of that sovereignty and reiterating the ultimate power of the federal government to define the precise scope and extent of Indian powers of self-determination.

Mark R. Scherer
University of Nebraska at Omaha

Bloxham, Steven John. "Tribal Sovereignty: An Analysis of *Montana v. United States.*" *American Indian Law Review* 8 (1980): 175–81. Canby, William C., Jr. *American Indian Law in a Nutshell.* 3rd ed. St. Paul MN: West Group, 1998.

MORNING STAR CEREMONY

The Morning Star bundle ceremony among the Skiri Pawnees (who lived in what is now central Nebraska) reasserted devotion to the power of the rising Eastern Star (Mars). It was their only ritual involving human sacrifice and was one of only a few not tied to seasonal cycles. For the ceremony to occur, a male member of the tribe had to announce that he had seen Morning Star in a dream and, upon awakening, perceived it rising in the east. Ritual tradition then called for dispatch of the dreamer (now deemed the "warrior leader") to secure a girl captive by raiding neighboring villages. The power of the ceremony was to provide for success in war and for fertility.

Preparation for the ceremony, which ended in a ritual feast and dance by the entire village, involved several stages and sacred songs. After being dressed by the Morning Star priest in sacred raiment from the Morning Star bundle and anointed with red ointment, the captive stayed with the Wolf man, who brought her daily to the warrior leader for meals eaten with utensils from the Morning Star bundle.

On the appropriate predawn morning, the Wolf man led the captive to the scaffold, constructed of different symbolic species of wood. The killing was carried out with a ceremonial bow and arrow. Immediately a stone knife incision was made near the heart, and specially prepared buffalo meat held to receive drops of the victim's blood before being prepared for feasting. Before the body was removed and placed in the prairie facing east, the entire village, including children, lodged dozens of arrows in the victim's back. The Skiris believed that this ceremony allowed the victim's spirit to ascend to the sky to become a star, while her body returned to the earth.

The last known Morning Star Ceremony sacrifice took place on April 22, 1838, with the killing of Haxti, a fifteen-year-old Lakota girl. The United States subsequently suppressed the ceremony, but it also seems that some Skiris themselves wished to stop the human sacrifice.

Byron Cannon
University of Utah

Dorsey, George A., and James Murie. *Notes on Skidi Pawnee Society.* Chicago: Field Museum of Natural History, 1940. Murie, James. *Ceremonies of the Pawnee.* Lincoln: University of Nebraska Press, 1989.

MUSIC

Music lies at the heart of Indian culture. From birth to death, all occasions, sacred and secular, personal and tribal, in the life of the Plains Indian are inextricably intertwined with musical performances.

Music serves numerous functions in traditional Indian culture, including religious ceremonies, healing ceremonies, work songs, game songs, courtship, storytelling, songs to bring success in hunting, agriculture, and war, and social songs and dances. As traditional culture has been influenced through contact with non-Indian cultures, the purposes and functions of music have been adapted so that music retains its meaningful role in cultural identity.

The music of the Plains is the most familiar Na

Members of the Oglala Sioux tribe from Pine Ridge, South Dakota, demonstrate dance steps on the streets of downtown Denver prior to their appearance at the Cheyenne Frontier Days Rodeo, ca. 1966

tive American music to non-Indian peoples, due in large part to its use in television and motion pictures (including the Academy Award–winning *Dances with Wolves,* which featured performances by the Porcupine Singers, a well-known Lakota musical group). The high, tense vocal style, the descending melodic pattern, the vocables (meaningful syllables without a direct English translation), and the rhythmic drumming of the Plains are immediately identifiable as "Indian music" throughout the world. Because of its familiarity, it is often erroneously used in entertainment venues to represent the musical practices of all Indians, regardless of tribal or cultural identity. A recent renaissance of interest in Native cultures has, in large part, corrected this misconception.

The defining characteristics of Plains style music include a tense, tight, and rather strained vocal style; among Northern Plains tribes a high vocal range, among the tribes of the Southern Plains a medium range; "collapsible" melodic contour-melodies that begin high, drop drastically lower over the course of a song, and frequently end with repetitions of the tonic pitch; ululations produced by rapidly fluttering the tongue against the roof of the mouth; singing mostly in unison; and, normally, one large drum played by several musicians to accompany songs. Lyrics may be sung entirely in a tribal language, entirely in vocables, in English, or in any combination.

Drums, the best-known type of Indian instrument, are made in many sizes and shapes and from diverse materials. Both small hand drums—twelve to eighteen inches in circumference and covered on one or both sides with a rawhide head and played by one person—and larger "powwow" drums—sometimes the size of a marching band bass drum and played simultaneously by several musicians—are commonly used among Plains tribes. In contemporary practice, the word "drum" refers not only as a noun to the instrument itself but also as a verb to the performers who play it and sing. Many tribes consider the drum to represent the heartbeat of Mother Earth and to offer a means of communication with the supernatural. Because of this significance, tribes often establish strict protocols for playing the drum.

Rattles are the most ubiquitous type of instrument and display great inventiveness with natural materials. Modern Plains Indians have incorporated virtually every type of material imaginable into the construction of rattles: gourds, turtle shells, carved wood, deer hooves, animal horns, animal hide, and tree bark. Other percussive instruments include large dance bells attached to the arms or legs of dancers to provide an ambient accompaniment to dancing, rasps, and wooden sticks.

Flutes and whistles are the primary melodic instruments among Plains Indians. Members of Coronado's sixteenth-century expedition into the Southern Plains provided the first documentation of flute music by non-Indian sources, while Lewis and Clark noted the use of flutes among Northern Plains peoples in the early nineteenth century. In pre-twentieth-century traditional practices, the flute was used primarily to perform courting songs, though some tribes used flutes and whistles in healing ceremonies. Flute performance among Plains tribes, however, had virtually disappeared by the early twentieth century. Kiowa musician Doc Tate Nevaquaya is credited with reviving the tradition of flute making and playing in the late 1940s and 1950s. Contemporary musicians, including Kevin Locke (Lakota), Joseph Fire Crow (Cheyenne), Tom Mauchahty Ware (Comanche-Kiowa), and Robert Tree Cody (Dakota-Maricopa), have expanded the role of the Indian flute far beyond its traditional role in courtship and healing to embrace social songs, dances, and popular songs. The sound of the Indian flute is now heard in motion picture scores and jazz and rock bands in addition to more traditional venues.

Native American music continues to thrive and evolve. Contemporary musicians are exploring combinations of traditional and non-Indian music to create new styles and genres that retain a distinctively Native American identity. Non-Indian popular music genres such as rock, country, and jazz have been successfully adapted into the modern Indian repertoire by artists such as Tom Bee (Lakota) performing with XIT, the first commercially successful all-Indian rock band, and Keith Secola (Anishinaabe) and the Wild Band of Indians. Indian musicians such as Buffy Sainte-Marie (Cree) and R. Carlos Nakai (Ute-Navajo) contribute to motion picture and television scores, and the orchestral and choral compositions of Oklahoma-born composer-conductor Louis Ballard (Quapaw-Cherokee) mark the beginnings of Indian symphonic and chamber music. Pianist Paul La Roche (Lakota) combines traditional and New Age elements in his unique works for keyboard.

Powwows and tribal fairs held throughout the Great Plains provide opportunities to experience all musical styles and genres of today's Plains Indians, including generations-old traditional songs and dances as well as contemporary popular music. Modern powwows and tribal fairs are celebrations of Native American culture and include displays of tribal arts and crafts, meals of traditional Native foods, and discussions of social and political issues in addition to the music and dance. They are as much community social events as dance performances. Music and dance include ceremonial performances restricted to initiated members of the tribe; competitive dancing featuring world-class performers of grass dances, fancy dances, jingle dress, and specialty dances; and the after-hours social dances referred to as "forty-nine" dances, the popular music and dance of younger tribal members. Among the larger Plains powwows and tribal fairs held annually are Red Earth Powwow, Oklahoma City, Oklahoma; Gathering of Nations, Albuquerque, New Mexico; Crow Fair, Crow Agency, Montana; and United Tribes Powwow, Bismarck, North Dakota. However, smaller local gatherings offer insights into Indian song and dance in a more intimate setting that allows more interaction among performers and audience members.

J. Bryan Burton
West Chester University of Pennsylvania

Burton, J. Bryan. *Moving within the Circle: Contemporary Native American Music and Dance*. Danbury CT: World Music Press, 1993. Heth, Charlotte, ed. *Native American Dance: Ceremonies and Social Traditions*. Washington DC: Smithsonian Institution Press, 1992. Laubin, Reginald, and Gladys Laubin. *Indian Dances of North America—Their Importance to Indian Life*. Norman: University of Oklahoma Press, 1989.

NATIONAL CONGRESS OF AMERICAN INDIANS

The mission of the National Congress of American Indians (NCAI) is to "inform the public and the federal government on tribal self-government, treaty rights, and a broad range of federal policy issues affecting tribal governments." The NCAI provides legal aid to protect Indian civil rights and serves as a watchdog in protection of treaty rights.

Organized in Denver, Colorado, in 1944 by well-educated Native American leaders such as D'Arcy McNickle (Flathead), Archie Phinney (Nez Perce), and Charles E. Heacock (Sioux), the NCAI battled against the federal government's policies of termination of tribal status and relocation. The NCAI also scored an important victory in helping create the Indian Claims Commission. By the 1960s, with the threat of termination fading, the NCAI focused on issues such as poverty and public health. However, during the 1960s the NCAI lost its position as the sole voice for Native Americans. More radical groups, such as the American Indian Movement and the National Indian Youth Council, diverged from the moderate policies of the NCAI by taking a more militant stand. During the 1980s and 1990s the NCAI continued to work to protect Native American cultural rights and the repatriation of Indian artifacts and remains.

The NCAI has grown from an original membership of 50 tribes in 1944 to more than 250 member tribes in 2001. The NCAI functions as a legislative body, with tribes electing delegates to represent them at a national convention. With its headquarters in Washington DC, the NCAI continues to operate as a lobbying agent on behalf of all Native American peoples. Issues concerning the NCAI in 2001 included environmental protection and natural resources management, enhancement of Indian health, and the protection of Indian cultural resources and religious freedom.

Mark R. Ellis
University of Nebraska at Kearney

Cowger, Thomas W. *The National Congress of American Indians: The Founding Years.* Lincoln: University of Nebraska Press, 1999.

NATIVE AMERICAN CHURCH

Native Americans have long been subjected to various policies of the United States in an attempt to "civilize" them. Conversion to Christianity was among such policies. As with most issues dealing with Native Americans, the picture is not complete without providing some insight into both the traditional and legal backgrounds.

Many denominations of mainstream Christianity made initial forays into Indian Country in the attempt to convert Native Americans to Christianity and as part of federal policy. The success of these efforts is reflected in the Christian creeds professed by various tribes. For example, many Omahas originally adhered to Mormonism. Some Sioux tribes are substantially Catholic or Episco-

palian. It depended upon who arrived first to begin the conversion process.

In the early part of the twentieth century, a unique Native Christian religion founded upon the basic tenets of Christianity began to sweep throughout Indian Country. While conversion to Christianity was a slow and painful process, the tenets of the Native American Church were most readily accepted. The exact origins of the Native American Church and its incorporation of peyote as a sacrament of communion are shrouded in oral history, but Native believers generally agree that it began in the Southwest and worked its way up from Mexico. Among the Plains Indians, the Omahas, Poncas, Winnebagos, and Sioux readily accepted the belief system of the Native American Church.

The tenets of the Native American Church are similar to mainstream Christianity. The leap from traditional belief in a universal creative, mysterious, and holy power (God) who now has a son, Jesus Christ, was initially surprising. However, ready acceptance of God having a son was not that difficult, as all things were believed to be possible through the Creator. Peyote is also considered sacred and holy as a sacrament and the means in which to commune with God and Jesus Christ.

The use of peyote, a cactus plant of the mescal family, within the Native American Church has spawned both case law and federal legislation. The legal controversy over peyote resulted in its legal classification as a controlled drug. Therefore, only card-carrying members of the church are allowed to possess, transport, and use peyote for religious purposes.

The Indian Religious Freedom Act of 1978 was passed to provide legal protection for the Native American Church in its use of peyote. All peyote has to be transported from Texas, where it grows. Of the fifty states, only twenty-eight states have enacted laws similar to, or in conformance with, federal regulation intended to protect its use. However, in the U.S. Supreme Court case of *Employment Division v. Smith* (1990), the Court held that the First Amendment does not provide protection for practitioners of the Native American Church. Two subsequent amendments, in 1994 and 1996, were intended to clarify and provide the much-needed protections.

As for the actual religious ceremony itself, it is an act that requires deep commitment and faith. It is generally held in a tipi or, in inclement weather, a large area indoors. The Native American Church also requires that a pastor, priest, or elder conduct the services. This person is referred to as the Roadman, who from time to time must travel from tribal community to community, similar to early

Christian missionaries who covered wide geographical areas.

The Roadman is assisted by a Fireman, whose task is to care for the holy fireplace by making sure that it burns continuously throughout the night. His own instruments for conducting the church services are the prayer staff, his eagle feather, a beaded and feathered gourd, a small drum, cedar, and the peyote chief, which is always present at the altar. Other peyote is ground finely or made into a mush and passed around in a circle to all participants as a sacrament to commune with God and his Son. The Roadman's wife or other female relative prepares seven sacramental foods and the "second breakfast" that are part of the church services. Her part takes place very early, between 4:30 and 5:00 in the morning. The seven sacramental foods are water, shredded beef, corn mush, rice, strawberries, cookies, and soft, individually wrapped candies. To counterbalance the bitterness of the peyote consumed during the services, the sweet foods were added later. The second breakfast is like any other breakfast. It generally includes boiled eggs, toast, hash brown potatoes, coffee, and juice. This meal is served well after sunrise and just prior to the closing of the church services.

Church services are not regular Sunday occurrences but are held in accordance with special requests by a family for celebrating a birthday, or for a memorial or funeral service. Services begin at sundown on either a Friday or Saturday evening and end at sunrise. Thus, a participant "sits up" all night, giving up a full night's rest as part of a small sacrifice to the Great and Holy Spirit and his Son.

The church services culminate in a feast for the whole community the following day. Because peyote is a stimulant, all of the participating members are wide awake, so they too attend the feast. The need for sleep is generally felt in the late afternoon, particularly after the feast. Gifts are given to the Roadman and all his helpers by the sponsoring family at the feast to show deep appreciation for all his hard work.

Wynema Morris
Walthill, Nebraska

NATIVE AMERICAN RIGHTS FUND

The Native American Rights Fund (NARF), based in Boulder, Colorado, is the oldest and largest nonprofit national Indian rights organization in the country. Since its establishment in 1970, NARF has grown from a three-lawyer staff to a firm of forty full-time staff members, with fourteen attorneys. Most of the attorneys and nearly all support staff personnel are Native American. NARF has represented more than two hundred Indian tribes located in thirty-one states, including many Native people who are indigenous to the Great Plains. The hundreds of cases it has handled have involved every major problem and issue in the field of Native American law. The Native American Rights Fund is governed by a thirteen-member board of directors composed entirely of Native people. This board charts the direction of NARF's activities by setting priorities and policies. Board members are chosen on the basis of their involvement in Native affairs, their knowledge of the legal problems facing Native Americans throughout the country, and, most importantly, their dedication to the well-being and survival of Native Americans.

Today, more than fifty-five Indian tribes are an important and integral part of the economic, political, and cultural life of the Great Plains. Most have treaties with the United States that set forth property, political, and legal rights. Each Great Plains state contains Indian reservations that were established by treaties or other federal action and are governed by tribal governments. From legal and political standpoints, each reservation in the United States is a nation within a nation. The power of tribal governments and the jurisdiction over reservation lands among tribal, state, and federal governments are integral aspects of Great Plains governance and are continually being refined by litigation or legislation. At the same time, the protection of and control over the natural resources located on Indian reservations such as water, oil, and natural gas are vitally important to Indian owners. Tribal people are citizens of their respective Indian tribes, the United States, and their respective states, and they aspire to rights of self-determination, tribal sovereignty, cultural rights, and human rights similar to those sought by other Indigenous peoples throughout the world.

NARF attorneys work to tear down barriers to the fulfillment of these rights in Great Plains courtrooms and legislatures. For example, NARF has worked to restore land and federal recognition to the Alabama-Coushatta Tribe, the Kickapoo Tribe, and the Ysleta del Sur Pueblo in Texas and to restore tribal jurisdiction to the Winnebago Tribe in Nebraska. In Oklahoma, NARF has worked to recognize the reservation status of Pawnee lands, to clarify Osage tribal government status, and to confirm Cheyenne and Arapaho tribal oil and gas taxation authority. In the area of human rights, NARF has represented Native American inmates in jails and prisons in North Dakota, South Dakota, Nebraska, Kansas, and Oklahoma. It provided legal representation to tribes located in Oklahoma and North Dakota to protect tribal burial grounds from desecration and to repatriate human remains that had been removed from tribal graves and carried away to museums, historical societies, and other institutions. NARF has also represented tribes and students in South Dakota, North Dakota, Oklahoma, and eastern Colorado on education issues relating to public, tribal, and Bureau of Indian Affairs schools. NARF has represented traditional religious practitioners in protecting their freedom of worship at sacred sites in eastern Wyoming, in prisons, and during the worship ceremonies of the Native American Church. These issues illustrate the problems that confront Great Plains Indian tribes in the United States today as Native peoples strive to live according to their traditional ways of life and the aspirations of their forefathers.

Ray Ramirez
Walter Echo-Hawk
Native American Rights Fund

NEBRASKA INDIANS

From 1897 to 1917 the Lincoln-based Nebraska Indians baseball team toured nationally, compiling an enviable record of wins. They competed against teams in the Negro Leagues as well as against college and minor league teams. They combined excellent play with Wild West show–style antics.

By the 1880s Native American baseball teams had been formed on the campuses of several Indian schools, including the Carlisle Indian School in Pennsylvania, as well as Great Plains schools such as Genoa Indian Industrial School in Nebraska, Haskell Indian Institute in Kansas, and Flandreau Indian School in South Dakota. Unlike African Americans, Native Americans faced no legal discrimination in baseball and played in both the minor and major leagues. They did, however, regularly face opposing crowds who taunted them with cries of "Go back to the reservation!" and "Dog soup!" Newspaper coverage relied on similar stereotypical images of scalping and counting coup.

While there were a number of traveling, or "barnstorming," Native American baseball teams, the Nebraska Indians were billed by their owner Guy Wilder Green as the "Only Ones on Earth" and the "Greatest Aggregation of Its Kind." From 1897 to 1917 they averaged more than 150 games per year, traveling in and beyond the Great Plains. Green's team was mostly composed of Native Americans from the Great Plains, including a large portion from the Winnebago/Ho-Chunk tribe, but there were also a number of Caucasian players (a common practice on "Indian" teams).

The team traveled by Pullman car, but they slept in tents because it was more affordable and avoided confrontations with racist hotel owners. Most players received pitifully low wages and worked only for a few seasons. They played because they enjoyed the game and the adventure of travel. Only one team player, Winnebago/Ho-Chunk, George Howard Johnson of Walthill, Nebraska, moved to the major leagues, playing for the Cincinnati Reds (1913–14) and then the Kansas City Packers (1915). Many others moved around within the minor leagues.

In 1911 or 1912, Green sold the team to James and Oran "Buck" Beltzer, who had earlier organized the Oxford Indians team in 1908, a Sioux/Caucasian team. Under their leadership the Nebraska Indians hired more Caucasians than they had under Green. The team folded in 1917.

Charles Vollan
South Dakota State University

Clark, Jerry E. *Nebraska Diamonds: A Brief History of Baseball Major Leaguers from the Cornhusker State.* Omaha: Making History, 1991. Powers-Beck, Jeff. *The American Indian Integration of Baseball.* Lincoln: University of Nebraska Press, 2004. Seymour, Harold. *Baseball: The People's Game.* New York: Oxford University Press, 1990.

NORTH-WEST REBELLION

The North-West Rebellion, also known as the second Riel Rebellion or the Saskatchewan Rebellion, took place in Saskatchewan's Qu'Appelle River valley in 1885 and was closely related to the earlier Métis resistance at Red River, Manitoba, in 1869–70.

After the Red River Resistance, Louis Riel fled to the United States to escape arrest. With their leader labeled a traitor, the Métis of Manitoba were now seen by the Canadian government as squatters on potential homestead lands. Stripped of their lands, and seeing few alternatives, the majority of the Métis people moved farther west along the Saskatchewan River system into what is now Saskatchewan and Alberta (then the Northwest Territories).

By 1884 the Northwest was home to several thousand Native and Métis peoples. Joining them were a large number of non-Native settlers, recent arrivals from the Canadian provinces, giving a total population of about ten thousand people. In this period the Northwest Territories were administered by a lieutenant governor appointed in Ottawa and a small council made up of appointed and elected representatives. By 1884 the number of elected representatives on the council numbered only five, and the residents of the region did not have territorial representation in the federal House of Commons or Senate.

In the Prince Albert–Batoche area, the Métis and non-Native settlers alike were discontented. Many of them had moved from the Red River region more than a decade earlier to establish prosperous farms along the South Saskatchewan River. Conflict over land tenure, hunting reserves, government surveys, tariff structures, and frustration from the absence of government representation

Hanging of Louis Riel in effigy, July 1885

led the Métis and whites to organize in 1884. As no clear leader emerged, the Métis sent a delegation to Montana to ask Louis Riel to return to unite the English- and French-speaking Native, white, and Métis residents of the region. Riel, now an American citizen, agreed, and he arrived in Batoche amid much fanfare in May 1884. At the same time, the Plains Crees, under the leadership of chiefs Big Bear and Poundmaker, also began to demand the renegotiation of their treaties.

In a move reminiscent of his Red River days, Riel took up the reins to lead the white and Métis settlers, challenging the legitimacy of the Canadian government in the Northwest and proclaiming the formation of a provisional Métis government at Batoche in March 1885.

On March 26 a detachment of the North-West Mounted Police at Fort Carlton (twenty miles from Batoche) sent one hundred men to Duck Lake to head off a possible attack and to prevent the Métis from seizing arms and ammunition stored there. Gabriel Dumont and a large group of Métis met the Mounted Police at Duck Lake, and in the resulting skirmish the Métis killed twelve Mounties and wounded another eleven.

The Duck Lake victory (often called the Duck Lake Massacre by non-Natives) rallied the Native troops and convinced the Crees to join forces with Riel. Cree chiefs Big Bear and Poundmaker tried to maintain calm within the tribes, but the Duck Lake victory had emboldened many of the young Cree warriors who laid siege to Fort Battleford on the North Saskatchewan River. On April 2, 1885, a group of warriors from Big Bear's band attacked the Hudson's Bay Company post at Frog Lake, killing nine non-Native men. Within a few days, the Canadian government sent forces to Batoche, Battleford, and Frog Lake. The main force under Maj. Gen. Frederick Middleton took Batoche on May 12, where Riel surrendered on May 15. Poundmaker surrendered on May 12 and Big Bear on July 2.

Immediately upon his capture, the Canadians brought Riel to Regina for trial. On July 31, 1885, the all-white jury convicted Riel of treason, ignoring both his American citizenship and questions regarding his sanity. Despite a huge public uproar in the province of Quebec, Louis Riel was hanged on November 16, 1885. He was followed to the gallows eleven days later by eight of the Cree warriors who had been involved in the North-West Rebellion.

The Métis gained little from the rebellion. Many of their leaders fled to Montana or were jailed. Citizens of the Northwest received representation in Parliament, but the Métis were forced to either assimilate or move still farther to the margins. The Crees, forced to settle their treaty claims as best they could, suffered under the tightened control of western Indian agents and were relegated to reserve lands, where their death rates climbed rapidly and their population fell dramatically over the next five decades.

Charlene Porsild
Montana Historical Society

Beal, Bob, and Rod Macleod. *Prairie Fire: The 1885 North-West Rebellion.* Edmonton: Hurtig Publishers, 1984. Flanagan, Thomas. *Louis "David" Riel: "Prophet of the New World."* Toronto: University of Toronto Press, 1996.

OJIBWAS

Within the Great Plains, the Ojibwas reside in Montana, North Dakota, Manitoba, Saskatchewan, and Alberta. The name "Ojibwa" is generally translated as "To Roast Till Puckered Up," an allusion to the puckered moccasins worn in the past. In the Great Plains, however, Ojibwa is more likely to be used as a geographical designation rather than a self-identifying term. In fact, no inclusive terms exist to refer to all the Ojibwa communities in the Great Plains. Generally, the term "Plains Bungi" (or Bungee) refers to the Ojibwas residing in Alberta, Saskatchewan, and western Manitoba. "Saulteaux" is often used to designate Ojibwa living in the area near Lake Winnipeg as well as the region south of the lake and extending to the international border. Within the United States, "Chippewas" is frequently used to identify Ojibwas in North Dakota and Montana. In addition to these terms, "Métis" is employed to refer to descendants of French and Ojibwa, Cree, and/or Chippewa ancestors. The Ojibwas speak dialects of the Algonquian language family.

Ojibwas in the eastern portion of their territory sometimes refer to themselves as Anishinaabes, which means "The People" or "Original Man." According to oral traditions, the Ojibwas once belonged to the three fires of the Anishinaabes. This triad represented a confederacy that included not only the Ojibwas but also the Potawatomis and Ottawas. In North Dakota, some local Ojibwas also refer to themselves by the Algonquian word *nakkawininiwak*, which means "those who speak differently." This refers to linguistic differences between the Ojibwa spoken by the Plains and Woodland Ojibwas.

The Plains Ojibwas are descended from Algonquian-speaking Woodland groups located in Michigan, Wisconsin, Minnesota, and Ontario. During the late eighteenth century the expansion of the fur trade and the Iroquois resulted in the migration of some Ojibwas into the Great Plains. Many of these migrants settled in forested areas surrounded by lakes. As a result, substantial communities developed near Lake Winnipeg, in the Turtle Mountain region of North Dakota, and at the confluence of the Red and Red Lake rivers in Montana.

In these areas the Plains Ojibwas began hunting bison, elk, deer, and small game. Fur trapping, fishing, and horse raiding also became important activities in the region. Like numerous other Plains populations, the Ojibwas in the area used bison-hide tipis, the horse and travois, and hard-soled footwear. Like their Woodland ancestors, the Plains Ojibwas continued to use floral designs in their beadwork and to make fish-skin containers. Other similarities between the Plains and Wood-

land Ojibwas continued in the areas of social organization and belief systems.

The Plains Ojibwas retained the concept of nonresidential totemic clans. A number of these patrilineal clans formed bands. Exogamous marriages occurred at both the clan and band level. After marriage, residency was initially matrilocal, due to the two- to three-year bride service (labor due to the bride's family) required of the groom. After that period, the couple practiced patrilocal residency. Husbands practiced mother-in-law avoidance. Joking relationships existed between the wife and her husband's brothers, as well as between the husband and his wife's sisters.

Unlike the Woodland Ojibwas, only a few Plains Ojibwas practiced the Shaking Tent ceremony. Most Plains Ojibwas instead participated in the Sun Dance. Throughout the Ojibwa region, however, belief in Manitou, Windigo, and Nanibush persisted. Manitou refers to a neutral power that permeates all matter. Only through religious training can a person learn to control this essence. Windigo is a giant humanlike monster that resides in the winter forest, and Nanibush refers to a comic hero that continually breaks taboos. During the twentieth century the Native American Church became an important aspect of religious activities among many Ojibwas in the United States.

Currently, the Ojibwas occupy five reserves in Alberta, six in Saskatchewan, two in Manitoba, two reservations in North Dakota, and three in Montana. Generally, members of other Native populations also occupy these reservations and reserves. For example, the Rocky Boy's Reservation in Montana includes Plains Ojibwas, Plains Crees, and Métis, and intermarriage has blurred the lines between the groups.

In Canada, traditional Ojibwa continues to be spoken in many households, while within the United States some adults and fewer children speak the language. Consequently, a number of communities in Montana and North Dakota are establishing bilingual educational programs.

Martha L. McCollough
University of Nebraska–Lincoln

Albers, Patricia C. "Plains Ojibwa." In *Handbook of North American Indians*, edited by William C. Sturtevant, 13:652–61. Washington DC: Smithsonian Institution, 2001. LaCounte, Alysia E. "Ojibwa: Chippewa in Montana." In *Native America in the Twentieth Century: An Encyclopedia*, edited by Mary B. Davis, 399–401. New York: Garland, 1996. Murray, Stanley N. "The Turtle Mountain Chippewa, 1882–1905." *North Dakota History* 51 (1984): 14–37.

OKIPA

The Okipa was the most powerful religious ceremony of the Mandan people of North Dakota. The four-day ceremony was performed every year during the summer. It retold the history of the creation of the Earth and all living things. The main characters are the Okipa Maker, or Lone Man, who created the Mandans and gave them their rituals; Hoita, or Speckled Eagle, who created the animals; and Oxinhede, the Foolish One, who did not believe in the power of Okipa and was cast out of the village at the end. These three dancers are joined by others impersonating buffalo, bald eagles, holy women, swans, snakes, grizzly bears, night, day, wolves, coyotes, meadowlarks, and antelopes. They are supported by drummers playing sacred turtle drums.

The dancers performed inside the Okipa lodge, which was filled by men fasting, praying, and seeking visions. Sacred bundles, containing objects such as buffalo hair, a stuffed raven, a porcupine headdress, buffalo teeth, and a warbonnet of raven and swan feathers, were also presented. These objects represented key elements in the history of the people. The younger men generally underwent torture to demonstrate their bravery. Long wooden skewers were pushed through cuts in the skin on their backs or chests, and they were hung by ropes from beams. Their bodies were weighted down with buffalo skulls hung from other skewers thrust into their thighs and calves. The torment was extreme, but crying out was a sign of cowardice, and those best able to stand the pain became Mandan leaders. Women were not allowed inside the lodge, although some would sit on the roof, where they would fast.

The purpose of the ceremony was to reaffirm the bond between the people and the natural world and to unify the Mandans through a ritual of suffering and bloodshed. The Okipa had been performed for hundreds of years when the artist George Catlin witnessed the ceremony in 1832. The Okipa was probably last held on Fort Berthold Reservation in 1889 or 1890, after which it was suppressed by the United States.

Leslie V. Tischauser
Prairie State College

Bowers, Alfred. *Mandan Social and Ceremonial Organization.* Chicago: University of Chicago Press, 1950. McHugh, Tom. *The Time of the Buffalo.* Lincoln: University of Nebraska Press, 1972. Meyer, Roy W. *The Village Indians of the Upper Missouri: The Mandan, Hidatsas, and Arikaras.* Lincoln: University of Nebraska Press, 1977.

OMAHAS

The Omahas have lived near the middle Missouri River since the early 1700s. Their Sacred Legend describes an origin in a wooded, game-filled region near a large body of water, perhaps the Great Lakes. The Sacred Legend tells how the people developed many subsistence skills, implements,

Omaha chiefs in 1865

and social organizations with focused thought and keen observation. During the course of a slow migration westward, the people adapted to their changing environment. The language they developed is one of five related dialects in the Dhegiha branch of the Siouan language family that also includes the Poncas, Quapaws, Osages, and Kanzas (Kaws). The descriptive name "Omaha" (from umo^nho^n, "against the current" or "upstream") indicates a parting of company from these related peoples during that migration.

After contact with Arikara and Pawnee peoples, the Omahas adopted earth lodge dwellings, bison skin tipis, and local varieties of maize. They settled into the region west of the Missouri between the Platte and Niobrara rivers. Village sites were situated along running streams where the bottomlands provided tillable soil, fuel, and building materials. $To^nwo^nto^ngatho^n$, or "Big Village on Omaha Creek," was the principal Omaha village from 1775 until 1845, with a population estimated to have been more than two thousand people in 1795. The Omahas created a complex schedule of seasonal movements that enabled them to produce substantial gardens of maize, beans, and other cultigens, while conducting large-scale communal bison hunts on the western plains of present-day Nebraska and Kansas.

It was during the summer bison hunts that

Omaha social organization became graphically visible. When the people paused in their daily travels, all of the tipis were erected in a circle on the prairie. The Omahas are divided into ten patrilineal clans, each of which has one or more subclans. The ten clans camped in designated places around the circle.

The Omahas are further organized in a moiety system, or complementary halves, in which one half of the clans are associated with the earth-female cosmic forces, and the other half with sky-male cosmic forces. Each clan and subclan has a catalog of unique personal names for its members, as well as particular duties, rights, and prohibitions. Marriage is to a person outside the clan and, ideally, outside the moiety. Any tendencies toward factionalism are reduced because all ceremonial and political functions require the presence and assistance of multiple clans.

Seven of the ten clans traditionally provided an individual to sit on the tribal council, which deliberated on community affairs and arbitrated disputes. Their authority was sanctioned by the use of two Sacred Tribal Pipes. The eighth clan, as keepers of the Sacred Tent of War, provided military leadership during times of external assault. The two remaining clans did not have a seat on the council but performed important duties for the maintenance of the community.

The Omahas had several social societies that served to foster martial and civic responsibilities. One of the most important of these was the Hethúshka. Membership was restricted to men who had received public war honors. The distinctive dances, songs, and regalia of this society have become the foundation of the "War Dance" of the contemporary Great Plains powwow. Men performing acts of generosity could become members of a chief's society. There were also several doctoring and secret societies.

The Sacred Legend describes the first meeting with Europeans while the Omaha were in the east. This first amicable encounter was followed by the establishment of relations with the French by 1724, the British by 1790, and American traders soon after. The Omahas have maintained a tradition of peaceful relations with European and American visitors ever since. An example of this peace can be seen in the material assistance Omahas rendered to Mormon emigrants residing at their Winter Quarters on the Missouri River in 1846–48.

Until the late nineteenth century amicable relations with nearby Native groups were not always the rule. The need to travel to the western bison-hunting grounds for provisions placed the Omahas in a vulnerable position on two fronts. A successful summer hunt required the presence of religious objects such as the Sacred Pole and the Sacred Buffalo Hide, their aged caretakers, and the entire tribal group. Such a slow-moving company of men, women, children, dogs, and horses burdened with gear made an easy target for enemies. Meanwhile, those people who were too old or infirm to make the journey remained in the earth lodge villages to tend the gardens. The few able-bodied men who stayed to protect them were at a disadvantage if a superior force attacked.

Contact and interaction with European Americans wrought many changes on Omaha society. Subsistence hunting and agriculture shifted to an international fur trade economy. Traditional skills, arts, and crafts declined in favor of the use of trade goods, including firearms. Political and social status shifted as men better able to negotiate trade or hunt successfully for marketable quantities of pelts and bison robes overshadowed customary leaders whose prestige had been gained through oratorical skills, consensus building, and acts of generosity. Women expended more energy in the preparation of furs and hides for market. Recurring epidemic diseases reduced the population several times, causing the Omahas to lose control of the fur trade in their region while becoming increasingly vulnerable to attack by their enemies. They were forced to finally abandon Toⁿwoⁿtoⁿgathoⁿ in 1845 and retreat to a village site closer to the mouth of the Platte.

Under such pressures the Omahas signed treaties relinquishing control of land. The 1830 Treaty of Prairie du Chien ceded their claims to land in the present state of Iowa. To protect their own future they signed an 1854 treaty establishing a reservation in exchange for the remainder of their Nebraska land. The Omahas moved to their present reservation in 1855–56.

Many Omahas embraced some of the more visible "Americanizing" efforts of the federal government by adopting frame houses, new farming techniques, Christianity, and English-language education for their children. Important institutions such as the Sacred Pole, Sacred Buffalo Hide, the Sacred Tribal Pipes, and the Sacred Tent of War were put to sleep. Some of the secret and social societies went underground. Other Native organizations, such as the Native American Church, emerged.

In 1882 some Omahas joined with various non-Indian interest groups to push for the allotment of land. Much of the allotted lands was later sold, or it was forfeited because the taxes could not be paid. Allotments that once blanketed the entire reservation at the turn of the century were eroded to a strip of Omaha holdings along the Missouri River bluffs by the 1950s.

White Bull (left) *recounting the battle of the Little Bighorn to O. D. Wheeler and interpreter William Rowland* (center), *June 1901*

The Omahas voted to accept the provisions of the Indian Reorganization Act of 1934, creating a constitutional government with a tribal council elected by popular vote. The Omaha Tribal Council has emerged as the provider of services or space for many of the secular and sacred activities of the community. These efforts were given a boost in 1962 with a $2.9 million award from the Indian Claims Commission for Omaha lands taken in 1854. Reservation lands stranded east of the shifting Missouri River in Iowa were reclaimed and are being developed. Proceeds from these enterprises, including the Casino Omaha, have been applied to social and cultural revival efforts.

In 1994 about 2,000 of the 5,227 tribal members lived on the reservation, most in the Macy, Nebraska, area. A large number of Omahas make their homes in the surrounding urban centers of Omaha and Lincoln, Nebraska, and Sioux City, Iowa. An annual August encampment and powwow is held at Macy that serves as a homecoming opportunity for the off-reservation tribal members. Many Omahas continue to negotiate their lives between the pressures of mainstream Western society and the traditional values of Omaha culture. Leaders continue to emerge out of this struggle, men and women who emulate the values in the Sacred Legend of focused thought and keen observation. It is their strength and dignity that encourage the Omaha people to continue traveling upstream as a proud nation.

Mark J. Awakuni-Swetland
University of Nebraska–Lincoln

Dorsey, James Owen. "Omaha Sociology." In *Third Annual Report of the Bureau of American Ethnology (1881–1882)*. Washington DC: Government Printing Office, 1884. Fletcher, Alice C., and Francis La Flesche. "The Omaha Tribe." *Twenty-seventh Annual Report of the Bureau of American Ethnology (1905–1906)*. Washington DC: Government Printing Office, 1911. Ridington, Robin, and Dennis Hastings. *Blessing for a Long Time: The Sacred Pole of the Omaha Tribe*. Lincoln: University of Nebraska Press, 1997. Scherer, Mark R. *Imperfect Victories: The Legal Tenacity of the Omaha Tribe, 1945–1995*. Lincoln: University of Nebraska Press, 1999. Stabler, Hollis D. *No One Ever Asked Me: The World War II Memoirs of an Omaha Indian Soldier*. Lincoln: University of Nebraska Press, 2005. Tate, Michael L. *The Upstream People: An Annotated Research Bibliography of the Omaha Tribe*. Metuchen NJ: Scarecrow Press, 1991. Wishart, David J. *An Unspeakable Sadness: The Dispossession of the Nebraska Indians*. Lincoln: University of Nebraska Press, 1994.

ORAL TRADITIONS

For the Indian peoples of the Plains, narratives, or what are often referred to as oral traditions, convey their most cherished values and contribute to the perpetuation of their worlds. The narratives encompass a variety of categories, two of the most prominent being stories of creation and tales of human heroes. While recognizing the rich variation of narratives that issue from the tribal diversity of the region, it can be generalized that creation stories typically involve powerful mythic beings, often identified by animal names, who transform a dangerous world and prepare it for the coming of the human peoples. In the "earth diver" accounts among the Arapahos, Blackfoot, and Crows, for example, mud is brought forth from the bottom of a primordial sea by a waterbird and, with a small piece of the earth, Coyote, or Old Man, fashions the landscape, creates other animals and plants, helps establish various customs and institutions, and ultimately molds from the earth and gives life to the first human beings. These ancient personages simultaneously embrace the traits and qualities of human, animal, and spiritual beings, and, through their deeds, display tremendous transformative powers.

Paramount among these creation mythic beings is the trickster, known by the Blackfoot as Napi or Old Man, by the Crows as Isaahkawuattee or Old Man Coyote, by the Lakotas as Iktomi or Spider, and by many tribes simply as the Coyote. While acknowledged as a benevolent creator, the trickster can also exhibit a self-serving character. Old Man Coyote might attempt to apply deception and trickery to gain a free meal, the woman of his dreams, or some other object of his desires. Yet Coyote's elaborate schemes to outwit an opponent are just as likely to end in failure, with himself being duped by his own trickery and made to look foolish.

Hero tales express the ideals of courage, brotherhood, generosity, and self-effacing valor. In the "Scar Face" (or "Burnt Face") stories of the Blackfoot or Crows, for example, the protagonist finds himself disfigured, poor, and ostracized, and consequently unable to obtain full adult status and marry. Alone, he sets out on a great journey to face seemingly overwhelming obstacles and challenges. Because of his bravery, generosity, and "heart," Scar Face receives a guardian spirit and its powerful assistance, his physical shortcomings are removed and any antagonists overcome, his family position is restored, he is allowed to marry, and he goes on to live a full and bountiful life. In the Blackfoot story, Scar Face, like other culture heroes, also brings an important ceremonial institution, the Sun Dance, to his people.

Embedded within the oral traditions are essential values and discernible lessons. Key among these values is the understanding that the world and its many inhabitants are spiritually endowed and maintained, that the animal peoples share in a fundamental kinship with the human peoples, and that reciprocity is the means by which one should relate to other kinsmen, whether human or animal. An elk is addressed as a "brother" and will offer its meat to a hunter when properly respected. An eagle can become a "father" as a result of the food and water sacrifices offered during a vision quest, and, from the spiritual medicine bestowed during the vision, the eagle can guide, nurture, and bring health to a person throughout his life. From the narratives one learns the likely consequences of being a self-serving Coyote, and from the hero tales one is encouraged to seek the assistance of a guardian spirit and strive to benefit others.

Because the narratives of the Plains Indian emanate from an oral-based medium, the act of storytelling is an essential component of the story. In the past, a storyteller had to have the right to tell stories, typically having inherited the authority. Both men and women could become accomplished storytellers. For most tribes it was only during the winter season, from the first frost in the fall until the first thunder heard in the spring, that the stories of Coyote should be told. Again, acknowledging variation from storyteller to storyteller, it can be said that among the various styles and techniques exhibited by storytellers were the use of repetition of phrases to signal key actions within the narrative, the singing of associated songs, the dramatic use of intonation and pauses, the accentuation of body movement and hand gesturing, and the requirement that listeners of the story affirm their involvement in the story by periodically saying aloud, $\acute{e}e$ ("yes"), or motioning in some other fashion. Should the storyteller fail to receive such acknowledgments, the telling would immediately cease for the evening.

The act of storytelling is made particularly potent through the use of Native language. For example, when told in the Crow language, the words of the story are understood as having the power to bring forth and manifest that which is being spoken. This pivotal notion is conveyed in the Crow term *dasshússua*, literally meaning "breaking with the mouth." That which comes though the mouth has the power to affect the world. The understanding of the creative power of language, coupled with the various techniques used by storytellers, encourages listeners to become participants within the story, traveling the same trails alongside Coyote or Scar Face.

In addition to disseminating the knowledge and

wisdom brought forth by the heroic and mythic figures celebrated in the narratives, oral traditions have another essential role. The narratives help recreate and revitalize the worlds of the Plains Indians. In the act of telling of the deeds of Coyote and Scar Face, that which is conveyed in word and gesture is brought to life, viewed, and engaged in by the participants in the oral tradition. A landscape is renewed and a people are reinvigorated. Today, the telling of the oral traditions remains an essential act of tribal affirmation, identity, and perpetuation, and is a testament to the continued vitality of Plains Indian life.

Rodney Frey
University of Idaho

Dorsey, George. *Traditions of the Arapaho.* 1903. Lincoln: University of Nebraska Press, 1997. Lowie, Robert. *Myths and Traditions of the Crow Indians.* 1918. Lincoln: University of Nebraska Press, 1993. Wissler, Clark, and D. C. Duvall. *Mythology of the Blackfoot Indians.* 1909. Lincoln: University of Nebraska Press, 1995.

OSAGES

Two Osage women and a boy, ca. 1880

The Osages, Dhegiha Siouan speakers, believed in the beginning that there was chaos in the universe. Amid the chaos, the all-powerful, mysterious, and invisible life force, Wakonda, created order by organizing the universe into air, land, and water, creating the Middle Waters. Wakonda brought three groups together, and they became the Wa-zha-she, the "Children of the Middle Waters," or the Osage Nation.

The location of the Osage creation is cloaked in myth and metaphor, but many believe that they formed as a distinct people in the forests along the Ohio Valley and were pushed onto the prairies by Iroquois attacks. Others argue they were survivors of the Oneota cultural complex of the Plains river valleys. By 1673 the Osages were dwelling along the Osage River (in present-day Missouri), and throughout the eighteenth century they hunted in the Ozark Highlands and out onto the Great Plains. They occupied the region from the Republican River in Kansas south to the Red River of Oklahoma and Texas until the early 1830s. In 1839, to make room for the removed eastern tribes, the Osages were forced onto a reservation in southern Kansas. In 1870, as whites invaded their reservation, they were moved south into Indian Territory.

The Osages were semisedentary people who inhabited wooden longhouses in prairie villages in the spring and fall and spent summers in the Plains and winters in the forest. In the spring, after planting their crops, they left their villages to hunt in the Great Plains. In early July they returned to the villages to harvest their crops and store them for winter. They returned to the Plains in September, where they hunted until winter and then traveled back to the forests. They remained there until spring, when they gathered again to renew their seasonal cycle.

Osage men wore deerskin breechcloths and covered their legs with buckskin leggings. They rarely wore anything on their upper bodies, and only in the winter did they wrap themselves in buffalo robes. Osage women wore red and blue dyed buckskin leggings and buckskin tunics. The Osages became well known for their silk ribbon reverse appliqué, in which they cut silk in elaborate patterns and sewed them in layers onto their blankets and clothing.

The Osages believed that all things of the universe were manifestations of Wakonda. They sought to live in peace and harmony with the universe. Clan elders possessed sacred songs, rituals, and bundles, and they used them to sanctify important events and solicit the support of Wakonda.

The basic political unit of the Osages was the village, and according to Osage oral traditions, in the beginning all of the Osages lived in a single village along a river. The village contained twenty-four clans and was divided into moieties, the earth people and sky people. Each moiety had a hereditary leader, and these two chiefs shared power with clan elders. Together they made up the village council, which led the people. For a variety of political, economic, and social reasons, as the Osages moved west they separated into three major bands, with the two northern bands, the Big and Little Osages, occupying southern Kansas, and the Arkansas Osages, occupying the Verdigris River valley, just north of the Three Forks of the Arkansas.

The Osages were a numerous people. The earliest account of their population dates to 1719, when Claude-Charles DuTisné estimated there were two hundred warriors and two hundred lodges in the single village he visited. In 1817 superintendent of Indian affairs William Clark reported six thousand Osages. Great epidemics struck the Osages in the 1830s; hundreds died, as they were simultaneously stricken with cholera and smallpox. Later, on their reservation, pneumonia and tuberculosis continued to take a toll, and their population fell to four thousand by 1870. By 1906 they numbered only two thousand.

In the early twenty-first century, there are now about ten thousand Osages on the tribal roll, but due to the unique nature of the Osage allotment, there are two distinct forms of membership. Osage lands were allotted individually in 1906, but because they had purchased their 1,470,559 acres from the Cherokees and possessed fee simple title to the land, the government had to negotiate with them before they could make more allotments. While allotting the surface rights individually, the Osages successfully preserved communal ownership to the mineral rights to all of their lands. They retain these today. The mineral rights were divided equally into 2,229 shares for the individuals on the roll on July 1, 1907. These shares—headrights—would never be divided, and subsequently, children born to Osage parents were recognized as members of the tribe but were not given additional shares in the tribe's income. After allotment, their reservation became Osage County, where 30 percent of Osages live today. Another 30 percent live elsewhere in Oklahoma, and the remainder live in other parts of the United States.

Willard Hughes Rollings
University of Nevada–Las Vegas

Mathews, John J. *The Osages: Children of the Middle Waters*. Norman: University of Oklahoma Press, 1961. Rollings, Willard H. *The Osage: An Ethnohistorical Study of Hegemony on the Prairie-Plains*. Columbia: University of Missouri Press, 1992.

OTOE-MISSOURIAS

The Otoe-Missourias were two separate peoples until they amalgamated in the last years of the eighteenth century. Members of the Chiwere group of Siouan speakers, they were driven westward from the Great Lakes region in the seventeenth century by the Sioux, who were also moving westward under pressure emanating from the expanding orbit of European colonization. By 1714 the Otoes were living in a village on the Salt Creek

Ar-ka-ke-ta, or Stay-by-It. Photograph by William H. Jackson, ca. 1870

tributary of the Platte River in what is now eastern Nebraska. They occupied that vicinity for the remainder of the eighteenth century. The Missourias joined them there in 1798 after the Sauks and Foxes had driven them out of their former homeland of present-day northwest Missouri. From that time on the Otoe-Missourias were one nation, though the Missourias remained a distinctive constituent throughout the nineteenth century.

They lived, like the neighboring Pawnees and Omahas, in earth lodge villages and divided their subsistence activities between intensive farming at the villages, biannual bison hunts out on the Plains, and a wide array of food collection. They calibrated their annual cycle closely to the signs and rhythms of the physical environment, and they sanctified their activities with ceremonies that enlisted the support of sacred powers. Their way of life worked because they spread their subsistence base over a broad spectrum of Plains resources, and in 1800 they sustained a population of more than one thousand people.

But the outside world crowded in, and with the fur traders, missionaries, Indian agents, and settlers came disease and resource depletion. By 1804, when Lewis and Clark passed by, the Otoe-Missouria population had been reduced by smallpox to fewer than eight hundred; subsequent epidemics and depletion of game, bringing famine, continued the downward plunge to six hundred by mid-century. Fur traders established a post at Bellevue in the 1820s, just to the east of the Otoe-Missouria village, and alcohol became a disruptive force in their society. Enmities that otherwise might have been settled peacefully erupted into violence. Head chief Big Kaw could not preserve unity, and by the 1840s the Otoe-Missourias had splintered into four separate villages.

Mired in poverty, and with starvation a constant companion, they were forced to sell their only resource, their land, merely to survive. The United States obliged, as it needed land on which to settle refugee Indians from the eastern United States in the 1830s and homes for settlers after 1854. The first sale came in 1830 when, at the Treaty of Prairie du Chien, the Otoe-Missourias surrendered their claims to any lands east of the Missouri and also sold a sliver of land in southeastern Nebraska (the Nemaha Half-Breed Reservation) for the resettlement there of mixed-bloods from various tribes. A cession of about one million acres in southeastern Nebraska followed in 1833. The Otoe-Missourias received 4.1 cents an acre for this prime agricultural land. Like subsequent payments for cessions, the money was used by the United States to provide annuities (blankets, farming equipment, and other items) and to finance its assimilation policy, which aimed to transform communal Indians into self-supporting farmers working on separate 160-acre allotments. Even in 1881, when the Otoe-Missourias abandoned Nebraska for Indian Territory, very few, if any, of their men were farming.

When the Kansas-Nebraska Act of May 30, 1854, opened Nebraska for settlement by European Americans, the Otoe-Missourias sold their remaining homeland for 42.6 cents an acre, retaining only a 162,000-acre reservation straddling the Kansas-Nebraska boundary. This was fertile country, and it soon became clear that, as surrounding population pressure mounted and land values escalated, the Otoe-Missourias would have difficulty retaining it. They lived there, in poverty but still defiantly traditional, for twenty-five years. Their agents were generally corrupt until Quakers took over in 1869. Under great pressure to change, and with the old ways increasingly unfeasible, their society cleaved into two opposing segments: one, called the "stable faction" by the Quakers, paid at least lip service to the assimilation policy; the other, the "wild party," led by traditional chiefs Medicine Horse and Ar-ka-ke-ta, remained steadfastly traditional. When the Otoe-Missourias migrated to Oklahoma Territory following the sale of their reservation in two parts in 1876 and 1881, the division persisted and was not healed until after 1890.

In Indian Territory, the Otoe-Missourias settled on a 129,113-acre reservation in what is now Noble County, Oklahoma. Their population continued to plummet, dropping to 340 in 1894. Thereafter, their numbers gradually rebounded to reach 1,550 by 1990. Their reservation was completely allotted in 1907, but when oil was discovered on their lands in 1912, the trust status of their allotments was abrogated, and fully 90 percent of their land base was lost.

The Otoe-Missourias continued to resist the United States' efforts to reshape them. They refused to set up a constitutional government—which would have abolished their traditional tribal government—until 1984, and they have used their resources to buy back some of their lost lands. In the late 1940s, like most other Plains tribes, they lodged their claims with the Indian Claims Commission, and in 1955 and 1964 they received awards of $1,156,035 and $1,750,000 for lands that had been taken in 1830, 1833, and 1854 for payments "so low as to shock the conscience." These awards, large at first sight, diminished to small sums when allocated to individuals. Still, it is remarkable—in fact a triumph—that this small nation, despite the loss of their homeland and the assault on their way of life, has endured into the twenty-first century. Their annual powwow, held in July, and their continued coherence around kinship groups, ceremonies, and social gatherings ensure the continuance of their tribal identity.

David J. Wishart
University of Nebraska–Lincoln

Chapman, Berlin Basil. *The Otoes and Missourias: A Study of Indian Removal and the Legal Aftermath.* Oklahoma City: Times Journal Publishing, 1965. Edmunds, R. David. *The Otoe-Missouria People.* Phoenix: Indian Tribal Series, 1976. Wishart, David J. *An Unspeakable Sadness: The Dispossession of the Nebraska Indians.* Lincoln: University of Nebraska Press, 1994.

PALEO-INDIANS

Paleo-Indians were the earliest people to inhabit the Americas. Between thirty and eleven thousand years ago, small, highly mobile groups of hunter-gatherers extended their hunting areas throughout Beringia (the landmass that joined Siberia and Alaska) and into the Western Hemisphere. This "bridging landmass" emerged slowly from beneath the Bering Sea as more than nine million cubic miles of glacial ice accumulated over southern Alaska, Canada, Labrador, and Greenland. About twenty to eighteen thousand years ago an immense "ice dome" (the Laurentide glacier) towered more than one mile over present-day Hudson Bay. Two lobes of ice spread southward over the eastern edge of the Dakotas and deeper into the Midwest. The Central and Southern Great Plains remained unglaciated at this time, yet the mountains of glacial ice to the north exerted pronounced influences upon the everyday lives of the Paleo-Indians throughout the region.

Archeologists believe that Paleo-Indians expanded into certain ice-free areas of North America's interior, or along its coastal margins. The timing of the arrival of Paleo-Indians in the Great Plains and in North America, in general, is under renewed investigation. Recent genetic studies based on mitochondrial DNA suggest that a founding population composed of four distinct genetic lineages appeared in the Western Hemisphere between thirty-seven and twenty-three thousand years before present (BP). It appears that all contemporary Native Americans are descendants of

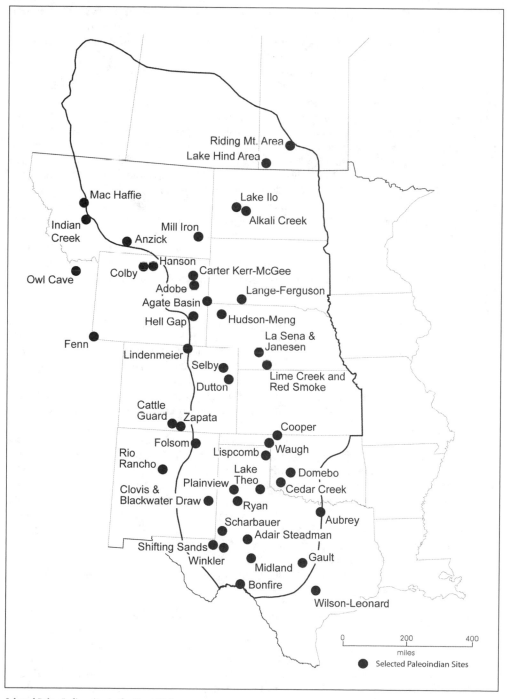

Selected Paleo-Indian sites in the Great Plains

these Paleo-Indian lineages, including the hunter-gatherers who made their appearance in the Great Plains eighteen thousand years ago or earlier.

During the last Ice Age, the Great Plains was inhabited by a diverse array of animals, including the Columbian mammoth, musk oxen, caribou, horse, camel, bison, elk, lion, wolf, arctic ground squirrels, arctic shrews, and lemmings. Around 14,500 BP the Northern Hemisphere began to warm and the glaciers began to shrink. The ice over North America essentially disappeared by 6,500 BP. Mosaic communities of plants and animals were reshuffled and sorted into their characteristic zonal patterns of today. Many large herbivorous and carnivorous mammals were unable to make the necessary shifts in diet, reproduction, and morphology and became extinct between 12,000 and 10,000 BP. Some scientists have attributed the disappearance of many larger mammals to the superior predatory abilities of the Paleo-Indians themselves. There is little reason to believe that Paleo-Indian hunter-gatherers had any significant role in these global animal extinctions; such extinctions had occurred many times before, particularly during abrupt shifts from colder glacial to warmer interglacial periods.

The most abundant physical evidence for Paleo-Indians in the Plains consists of a diverse array of carefully made chipped stone projectile points that were given geographical place-names like Clovis, Goshen, Folsom, Midland, Plainview, Cody, Alberta, Hell Gap, Scottsbluff, and Eden. Hunting weapons were probably constructed from interchangeable parts that were frequently repaired and recycled. Certain chipped stone points (e.g., Clovis, Folsom, and Goshen) were attached to short, fletched "dart" shafts and thrown with the use of a leverlike spear thrower, or atlatl. Paleo-Indian flint knappers developed an extremely efficient eleven-step method for transforming a large flake of high-quality stone into a multipurpose cutting implement and, later, into a Folsom point, two "razor blades," and a "lathe" tool. Larger stone points (e.g., Scottsbluff, Hell Gap, and Alberta) functioned as thrusting spears for dispatching bison that had been driven into natural traps created by parabolic sand dunes, deep gullies, or snowdrifts. Paleo-Indian tool kits also included chipped stone tools required to skin and butcher game, scrape skins and hides, and fashion specialized tools and component parts (e.g., foreshafts, shaft straighteners, and delicate eyed needles) of bone, antler, ivory, and wood.

One of the first documented discoveries of Paleo-Indian stone tools found together with the bones of extinct Ice Age animals in North America was made by H. T. Martin and T. R. Overton in 1895 near Russell Springs, Kansas. A similar find was made by George McJunkin—a cowboy, naturalist, and former black slave—in 1908 near Folsom, New Mexico. But it was not until August 29, 1927, that a fluted spear or "dart" point (Folsom) was found by archeologists among the bones of extinct bison (*Bison antiquus*) at McJunkin's Folsom site. Paleontologists, archeologists, and anthropologists were called to inspect this find in its undisturbed context, and only then did the scientific community agree that humans had lived contemporaneously with these now-extinct animals at the end of the last Ice Age.

These accidental finds sparked the initial systematic studies of the Paleo-Indian presence in the North American Great Plains. In the 1930s Clovis projectile points (dated 11,200–10,900 BP) were found with the remains of extinct Ice Age elephants (mammoths) and also bison near Clovis, New Mexico. Later Paleo-Indian occupations (10,000–8,800 BP), including the Cody complex on the Northern Plains and the Firstview complex on the Southern Plains, featured a number of chipped stone projectile points. With the development of radiocarbon dating in the 1950s, as well as the excavation of "layer cake–like" sites at Blackwater Draw, New Mexico, and Hell Gap, Wyoming, archeologists outlined the time frame for Paleo-Indian life in the Great Plains that is used today.

Paleo-Indians left a scant "trail" throughout the Great Plains. Geographer Vance Holliday has estimated that archeologists have found roughly two Paleo-Indian campsites for each century of their currently documented 2,400–year-long stay in the Great Plains. In the Southern High Plains, this means that there is one Paleo-Indian campsite per 667 square miles (1,733 square kilometers). Yet Paleo-Indian sites are still being discovered, including campsites (e.g., Mill Iron, Montana; Lake Ilo, North Dakota; and Cattle Guard, Colorado), animal kill sites (e.g., Waugh and Cooper sites in Kansas), tool caches (e.g., Anzick, Montana; Fenn, Wyoming; and Ryan, Texas), and tool stone quarries and/or workshops (e.g., Alkali Creek, North Dakota, and Hanson, Wyoming).

Researchers have also intensified their efforts to revise and to reformulate their reconstructions of past environments and Paleo-Indian life. Archeologists had generally assumed that the Great Plains during the late glacial period supported a widespread boreal forest composed predominantly of spruce trees. This spruce forest reconstruction is not supported by a fossil record that is dominated by grazing and browsing mammals. Also, paleoecologists now suggest that much, if not all, of the spruce and pine pollen was not endemic and had actually been deposited over the Plains by westerly winds.

Recent studies suggest that Paleo-Indian hunter-gatherers, specifically Folsom people, lived in small, multifamily groups. These groups or hunting bands may have established from twelve to thirty-six camps per year throughout an area of more than fifty-two thousand square miles (slightly less than the area of North Dakota). Folsom-age projectile points have been found more than three hundred miles (five hundred kilometers) from their geological source. It appears that Paleo-Indians quickly located sources for the highest-quality tool stone in the Plains, including Knife River flint (western North Dakota), Niobrara jasper (Nebraska), and Edwards chert (Texas).

The Great Plains has played, and continues to play, a central role in the study of Paleo-Indian lifeways in the Western Hemisphere. Recent work by Steve Holen (Nebraska State Museum) at mammoth death sites may push the initial human occupation of the Great Plains back to more than eighteen thousand years ago. Such recent research also suggests that the earliest Paleo-Indians may have scavenged food from large mammal carcasses. Archeologists are making use of refined radiocarbon dating methods and more dynamic views of prehistoric technology to reassess the static Paleo-Indian "culture histories" that once dominated their thinking. Archeologists working in the Great Plains have now begun to bring the faint outlines of Paleo-Indian existence into better focus.

Alan J. Osborn
University of Nebraska–Lincoln

Frison, George C. *Prehistoric Hunters of the High Plains.* New York: Academic Press, 1991. Holliday, Vance T. *Paleoindian Geoarchaeology of the Southern High Plains.* Austin: University of Texas Press, 1997. Stanford, Dennis J., and Jane S. Day, eds. *Ice Age Hunters of the Rockies.* Niwot: University Press of Colorado, 1992.

PALO DURO CANYON, BATTLE OF

A battle between Kiowas, Comanches, Cheyennes, and four hundred troopers of Col. Ranald S. Mackenzie's Fourth U.S. Cavalry took place early on the morning of Monday, September 28, 1874, deep in this great canyon of the Red River, one thousand feet below the level plains of the Texas Panhandle. Some Tenth and Eleventh U.S. Infantry assisted Mackenzie's command at a base camp. His command comprised part of a five-pronged campaign against several bands of Native Americans who either had left their reservations in Indian Territory for hideouts in the Staked Plains or who had not yet submitted to reservation life. The Palo Duro Canyon fight was the largest engagement in the Red River War and marked the end of the Southern Plains Indians' military resistance.

Led by Tonkawa scouts, Colonel Mackenzie marched his men most of the night, arriving at the

rim of the canyon at daybreak. They made their way to the floor of the canyon and attacked. Indian women and children retreated up the canyon, while the men engaged the soldiers in combat to allow their families to escape. The Kiowa band was led by Mamanti, the Comanches by O-ha-ma-tai, and the small band of Cheyennes by Iron Shirt. By noon the Indians had escaped, leaving their lodges and horses behind. Mackenzie ordered the lodges searched, then burned. The next day he had his men shoot 1,048 horses to prevent the Indians from recovering them. The Indians straggled into the reservations, having been left with no supplies for the approaching winter. Mackenzie reported that three Indians and one cavalry trooper died.

J'Nell L. Pate
Tarrant County Junior College–Fort Worth

Carter, Robert G. *On the Border with Mackenzie.* Washington DC: Eynon Printing, 1935. Pate, J'Nell L. "Colonel Ranald Slidell Mackenzie's First Four Years with the Fourth Cavalry in Texas, 1871–1874." Master's thesis, Texas Christian University, 1964.

PARKER, QUANAH (CA. 1852–1911)

Quanah Parker

Born between 1845 and 1852 to the white captive Cynthia Ann Parker and the Quahada Comanche war chief Peta Nocona, Quanah Parker grew up within traditional Comanche society, but his later life was marked by a fusion of white and Indian ways. By the time of the 1874–75 Red River War, Quanah had gained such a sufficient following that he helped lead the momentous attack of as many as seven hundred Comanches, Kiowas, and Southern Cheyennes against the two dozen buffalo hunters and merchants at the Adobe Walls trading post in the Texas Panhandle. The failure of this attack, and subsequent army victories on the Staked Plains, forced all the Comanches and Kiowas to their reservation at Fort Sill in western Indian Territory.

Because of his white ancestry and his willingness to accept reservation life, Quanah attracted the attention of various civilians and military officers at Fort Sill. Agent P. B. Hunt established him as a band chief, with authority to preside over the issuance of beef rations and other annuities. This provided Quanah with significant leverage among his own people, even to the detriment of some of the traditional elders. By 1886 he had been appointed one of the three judges of the Court of Indian Offenses, and he used this position to champion an assimilationist course.

Despite his cooperation with white authorities and his determination to have his people "walk the white man's road," Quanah steadfastly honored many Comanche traditions. He retained his long hair, participated in ancient ceremonies, spoke mostly in the Comanche language, and preserved the right of polygamous marriage. The fact that he had eight wives, five of them at one time, angered some important whites, and in 1898 this cost him the coveted position of Indian judge. Significantly, however, he won his battle to serve as a leader of the peyote religion that was expanding rapidly among his people.

Even though Quanah drew most of his authority as "principal chief" from whites, his popularity among Comanches also increased, especially because of his diplomatic skills in negotiating leasing agreements with Texas cattlemen. Although many tribal members initially had opposed the leasing of tribal grazing lands, the collective income soon guaranteed majority support. The greatest challenge to the reservation began in 1892 when the Jerome Commission called for the allotment of tribal lands into individual holdings and the sale of all surplus acreage to white settlers. Quanah made repeated trips to Washington DC to fight this assault on the collective land base and Comanche sovereignty, but, yielding to the inevitable realities, he negotiated the best terms possible and accepted the allotment process in 1900.

Throughout the years of reservation life, Quanah Parker closely aligned his personal interests with those of the broader tribe. He received money and other gifts from Texas cattlemen, lived in the spacious "star house" built by their largess, fenced several thousand acres of tribal land for his own cattle herd and to rent to whites, and rewarded supporters and family members with reservation jobs through supportive agents. Yet no one could doubt that Quanah had gained more benefits for the tribe than any other leader of the era. He died on February 11, 1911. His funeral at Lawton, Oklahoma, was the largest ever held in that region, and was well attended by respectful Indians and whites alike.

Michael L. Tate
University of Nebraska at Omaha

Hagan, William T. *Quanah Parker, Comanche Chief.* Norman: University of Oklahoma Press, 1993. Hagan, William T. *United States-Comanche Relations: The Reservation Years.* New Haven CT: Yale University Press, 1976.

PAWNEES

Unlike many Plains Indians, who moved into the area relatively recently, the Pawnees are longtime residents of the Great Plains. Linguistic and archeological evidence indicates that the Pawnees, specifically the Skiri band, have roots in central Nebraska extending back at least as far as the sixteenth century, and perhaps even further to the Upper Republican peoples who occupied villages along the Republican and Loup rivers from 1100 AD to 1400 AD. This stock was subsequently reinforced by recurrent migrations of other Caddoan-speaking bands from the Southern Great Plains during the seventeenth and eighteenth centuries. The Pawnees' own traditions speak of an origin in the southwestern United States, then a slow migration north, leaving their relatives, the Wichitas, on the Southern Plains. Linguistic analysis suggests that this split occurred in the first few centuries AD. By 1800 the Pawnees were a loose confederation of four bands—the Skiris (Loups), Chauis (Grands), Kitkahahkis (Republicans), and Pitahawiratas (Tappages). Their combined population, according to Lewis and Clark, was 6,850. The Skiris lived in a large village (twenty to forty acres in extent) on a terrace of the Loup River near present-day Palmer, Nebraska; the Chauis occupied two villages on the south side of the Platte River near Bellwood and Linwood; and the Kitkahahkis lived to the south on the Republican River between Red Cloud and Guide Rock. By 1811, under pressure from the Kanzas, the Kitkahahkis moved north to the Loup. The location of the Pitahawirata village, if indeed it was separate from the Chaui sites, is unknown.

Each band was largely independent of the others, with its own chiefs, priests, and ceremonies. The Skiris, especially, maintained an independent

Pawnee Village at Loup Fork, Nebraska, near Genoa. Photograph by William H. Jackson, 1871

stance from the other three bands. The identity of each band was encapsulated in their village bundles, the bison hide packs that contained sacred icons and that represented the peoples' original charter with the gods. Every step in the year's cycle of activities was sanctified by the bundles.

The traditional annual cycle of the Pawnees began in April when the first thunder from the south announced that it was time to clear the fields for cultivation. Corn, beans, squash, and sunflowers were planted by the women along the river floodplains. In late June, when the crops were well established, the Pawnees left for their summer bison hunt. They returned to the villages in late August and harvested and stored their crops. In early November they again abandoned their villages for the bison range, where they remained until March, hunting and camping on the upper reaches of the Republican, Smoky Hill, Solomon, and Platte rivers. The bison hunts not only provided meat and most of the Indians' raw materials but also allowed the Pawnees and their horses (of which there were six thousand in 1806) to spread their subsistence base over an extensive area. This annual cycle was a successful adaptation to the transitional environment of the Great Plains, and in most years the Pawnees produced a food surplus and flourished as the dominant power in the Central Plains.

In the nineteenth century the traditional life-style of the Pawnees was seriously disrupted by war and disease. Their population in 1800 was already only a fraction of the fifteen or twenty thousand people the villages had sustained in previous years. Smallpox struck in 1798, then again in 1830–31, taking at least half the population in one winter. After each epidemic, the Pawnees partly recovered, but after 1831 diseases struck with increased frequency and the population went on a downward spiral that was reversed only after 1906.

Also, after 1831 the Pawnees found themselves caught in a vise, pressed by the Lakotas from the north and by the expanding American frontier to the east. From that time until their departure from Nebraska in 1876, they lived under the shadow of attack. Hunts and harvests were disrupted, food supplies became more precarious, and death rates soared. In the 1840s, mounting traffic along the Oregon Trail led to the depletion of timber and grass, and the bison were driven west beyond the forks of the Platte. By 1854, when Nebraska Territory was opened to settlers, the Pawnees were a beleaguered people.

Traditionally, the territory occupied and claimed by the Pawnees reached from the Niobrara to the Arkansas and Cimarron rivers. The southern part of this territory was sold to the United States in 1833, and subsequent cessions left the Pawnees with only a small reservation, later Nance County,

Nebraska, on the Loup River. There, between 1857 and 1876, their population dropped to fewer than two thousand people, and settlers increasingly hemmed in their lives. In the early 1870s a series of disasters, including a massacre by the Lakotas in southwestern Nebraska in 1873 and the destruction of the crops by drought and grasshoppers, persuaded the Pawnees to relinquish their reservation and take up residency near the Wichitas in Indian Territory.

The migration south and subsequent problems of adjusting to the new homeland resulted in further population decline, the nadir being reached in 1906 when only 650 Pawnees remained. In 1892 the Pawnees accepted individual allotments, and the remainder of their reservation was sold to settlers. The Pawnees were given $30,000 a year for this land. Many of their traditions were forgotten, and ceremonies lapsed. Their culture was resilient, however, and their rich traditions were preserved in the early twentieth century by James Murie, a member of the Skiri band. In 1936 the Pawnees gained tribal government recognition under the Oklahoma Indian Welfare Act. Their identity was further reinforced by lengthy and successful claims-case litigation before the Indian Claims Commission from 1946 to 1962. The Pawnees were eventually awarded $7,316,096 for lands in Nebraska and Oklahoma that had been taken from them for an "unconscionably" low payment in the nineteenth century.

In the late twentieth century the Pawnee population numbered nearly 2,400, most of whom lived around the headquarters of the tribal council in Pawnee, Oklahoma. The tribe owned 726 acres, and another 19,399 acres was allotted to individuals. Unemployment stood at 25 percent. The Pawnees are governed by a council consisting of a president, vice president, and five council members.

David J. Wishart
University of Nebraska–Lincoln

Blaine, Martha Royce. *Pawnee Passage: 1870–1875*. Norman: University of Oklahoma Press, 1990. Blaine, Martha Royce. *Some Things are Not Forgotten: A Pawnee Family Remembers*. Lincoln: University of Nebraska Press, 1997. Dorsey, George A. *The Pawnee Mythology*. Lincoln: University of Nebraska Press, 1997. Weltfish, Gene. *The Lost Universe: Pawnee Life and Culture*. Lincoln: University of Nebraska Press, 1977. Wishart, David J. *An Unspeakable Sadness: The Dispossession of the Nebraska Indians*. Lincoln: University of Nebraska Press, 1994.

PAYIPWAT (CA. 1816–1908)

Payipwat was one of five major chiefs of the Plains Crees (Nehiyawak) after 1860. He was born around 1816, probably in what is now southwestern Manitoba or eastern Saskatchewan, and named Kisikawasan Awasis, or "Flash in the Sky Boy." As a child he and his grandmother were captured and ad-

opted by the Sioux. At age fourteen he was rescued by his own people, and he grew up to be a highly respected spiritual leader among the Young Dogs, a notable Cree-Assiniboine band of the Qu'Appelle Valley region. Because he learned Sioux medicine, his people named him Payipwat (or Piapot), "Hole in the Sioux," sometimes translated as "One Who Knows the Secrets of the Sioux."

An independent and assertive leader, Payipwat agreed to Treaty Number 4 in 1875, after making it clear that it was a "preliminary negotiation." He insisted that the treaty contain a number of additional provisions, and while Treaty 4 was never altered, many of these provisions were written into Treaty Number 6 (1876).

With the disappearance of the bison, Payipwat and other Plains Cree and Assiniboine leaders argued for the establishment of a large Indian territory in the Cypress Hills. However, the plan was thwarted when the federal government coerced their removal to smaller reserves by withholding rations from the starving Indians. The Plains Native coalition for an Indian territory collapsed when the government took advantage of the Métis resistance (1885) to crush it.

Once settled on his reserve near Fort Qu'Appelle, Payipwat continued pressing the federal government to live up to its treaty promises and continued resisting government regulations prohibiting ceremonial practices. Until the end of his life Payipwat resisted Christian conversion and challenged Canadian infringements on Cree sovereignty. A federal order deposing him as chief of his band was issued the day he died, in late April of 1908, on the Piapot Reserve in Saskatchewan.

Winona Wheeler
Saskatchewan Indian Federated College
Saskatoon, Saskatchewan

Tobias, John L. "Payipwat." In *Dictionary of Canadian Biography*, edited by Ramsay Cook, 13:815–18. Toronto: University of Toronto Press, 1994. Watetsch, Able. *Payepot and His People, as Told to Bloodwen Davies*. Regina: Saskatchewan History and Folklore Society, 1959.

PELTIER, LEONARD (B. 1944)

Leonard Peltier is serving two consecutive life sentences at the Leavenworth Federal Penitentiary in Leavenworth, Kansas, for the murder of two FBI agents in 1975. He has received support in his efforts to overturn his sentence from the governments of foreign nations, from U.S. Congresspeople and Senators, from Amnesty International, and from Archbishop Desmond Tutu, Jesse Jackson, the Southern Christian Leadership Conference, the National Congress of American Indians, and a host of other political and entertainment figures.

Peltier was born on September 12, 1944, in Grand

Forks, North Dakota, to parents of mixed Ojibwa, Dakota, and French background. At age fifteen he moved with his mother to Portland, Oregon, under the Relocation Program. Northwestern Indian protests aimed at restoring fishing rights guaranteed in treaties introduced him to political action. He joined the American Indian Movement (AIM) in the late 1960s or early 1970s and participated in some of the more notable AIM activities of the period, including the 1972 occupation of the Bureau of Indian Affairs headquarters in Washington DC.

Peltier moved to Milwaukee, Wisconsin, in 1972 to work as employment manager for a local AIM affiliate. By this point the federal government had targeted Peltier as a leader of the organization. He was confronted by undercover police at a bar, beaten, and charged with attempted murder because he was found to be carrying a (nonworking) pistol. He was later found not guilty.

In 1973 he participated in his first Sun Dance, held by AIM religious leader Leonard Crow Dog. Peltier became a fugitive when he did not show up for his pretrial hearing on the bar incident, and he moved back to the Northwest, again becoming involved in the fishing rights treaty controversy.

Peltier subsequently returned to the Pine Ridge Reservation in South Dakota, which was suffering through a civil war between supporters of tribal chair Dick Wilson (including the heavily armed paramilitary group known as the Guardians of the Oglala Nation, or GOONs) and traditional Lakotas and their AIM allies. Wilson and the GOONs received federal support and arms. Violence flared up across the reservation, and there were dozens of unsolved murders. After receiving a plea for help from traditional elders, Peltier and others established what he called a "spiritual camp" outside the home of elders Harry and Cecilia Jumping Bull near Oglala, South Dakota.

In May 1975 the FBI began building its presence on the reservation, planning a large raid. The raid came on June 26, 1975, when two FBI agents in an unmarked car entered the Jumping Bull compound chasing a red pickup truck, supposedly being driven by Jimmy Eagle, who was wanted for stealing a pair of used cowboy boots. According to Peltier, he awoke to the sound of gunfire. Along with about a dozen others, he returned fire. Immediately the FBI, the GOONs, and tribal police surrounded the compound. Joe Stuntz, a Coeur d'Alene Indian supporter lay dead, as did two FBI agents, Ronald Williams and Jack Coler, both apparently first wounded and then killed by rifle shots to the head.

In November 1975 Peltier, Jimmy Eagle, Bob Robideau, and Darelle Dean Butler were indicted in the deaths of the agents. Peltier had already fled to Canada, believing he could not get a fair trial in the United States. He was arrested in Alberta and extradited back to the United States based on the testimony of Myrtle Poor Bear, who said that she was Peltier's girlfriend and that she had witnessed the murder; she later recanted her testimony, stating that she and her family had been threatened by the FBI. Three other witnesses, young Navajos, also recanted their testimony for the same reason.

Federal authorities dropped charges against Jimmy Eagle (whose alleged boot theft had justified the raid), and Butler and Robideau were acquitted in a Cedar Rapids, Iowa, courtroom—the jury determined that they had fired in self-defense. Peltier's trial was moved to Fargo, North Dakota. The prosecution claimed that Peltier ambushed the agents. It presented little direct evidence of Peltier's involvement other than an AR-15 rifle, damaged in a fire and taken from Robideau. Documents released later under the Freedom of Information Act showed that FBI tests proved that this could not have been the rifle used in the murders. An all-white jury convicted Peltier on April 18, 1977, and he was sentenced to two consecutive life terms in federal prison. He served time at the Marion Federal Penitentiary in Illinois and then at Leavenworth Federal Penitentiary in Kansas, much of it in solitary confinement. In 1978, believing he was going to be killed, he briefly escaped. A fellow escapee was killed. Peltier received an additional seven-year sentence.

Peltier began a long series of appeals. While court after court condemned the abuses of the FBI in the case, including the coercion of witnesses and handling of evidence, Peltier was unsuccessful in his appeals. The U.S. Supreme Court turned down his requests for a new trial in 1978 and 1986. The Court also ruled against Peltier in 2004 when he appealed a 1993 decision by the U.S. Parole Commission, which argued that Peltier could not apply for parole for fifteen years (2008). He has since been granted biannual hearings.

Peltier and the near–civil war on Pine Ridge have been the subjects of several books, a documentary (*Incident at Oglala*, 1992), and a fictionalized feature film (*Thunderheart*, 1993). In 2000 supporters placed pressure on departing president Bill Clinton to grant clemency to Peltier. In December 2000, eight thousand current and former FBI agents signed a petition opposing his release, and five hundred agents protested at the White House itself.

Peltier remains in jail, where he has authored two books, developed his artistic abilities, organized food and clothing drives, and supported charitable organizations throughout the world. He is a foster parent to children in Guatemala and El

Robert Lee Penn's Nightshield

Salvador. He has worked to improve the lives of those on Pine Ridge and Rosebud reservations. In 2004 he was nominated for the Nobel Peace Prize. His sentence will be complete in 2041, when he will be ninety-seven years old.

Charles Vollan
South Dakota State University

Anderson, Scott. "The Martyrdom of Leonard Peltier." *Outside* (July 1995): 44–55, 120–26. Matthiessen, Peter. *In the Spirit of Crazy Horse.* New York: Viking Penguin Books, 1992. Peltier, Leonard. *Prison Writings*, edited by Harvey Arden. New York: St. Martin's Press, 1999.

PENN, ROBERT LEE (1946–1999)

From the late 1960s until his death on February 7, 1999, Robert Lee Penn was one of the most outstanding Northern Plains Indian artists of his generation.

Penn was born in Omaha, Nebraska, on May 3, 1946, to an Omaha father and Brulé Lakota mother. He grew up on the Winnebago Indian Reservation in Nebraska and the Rosebud Reservation in South Dakota, a background that would define his cultural roots and his art. During his years as a student at the University of South Dakota (1967–72), Penn began his formal art studies with the renowned Yanktonai Nakota artist Oscar Howe. After graduation, Penn continued his creative efforts while working as an illustrator, designer, and teacher. Over a period of twenty-five years he exhibited his work regularly in numerous one-man exhibitions and many others.

Penn mastered the technical means of drawing, watercolor, and painting and used them to express his very personal experience of being a traditional Indian in contemporary America. He considered that, as a Native American in contemporary society, his role was that of both artist and interpreter, using his art to convey cultural themes. His work is characterized by sure drawing combined with a strong sense of color and dynamic design, which he used to eloquently express the vital juncture between Plains Indian worlds, past and present.

Evan M. Maurer
Minneapolis Institute of Arts

Maurer, Evan M. *Visions of the People: A Pictorial History of Plains Indian Life.* Minneapolis: Minneapolis Institute of Arts, 1992.

PITARESARU (CA. 1823–1874)

Pitaresaru (Petalesharo) is a Pawnee name meaning "Chief of Men" or "Man Chief." Two or more outstanding chiefs of this name were members of the Chaui band of the Pawnees (there was also a famous Skiri Pawnee chief named Pitaresaru who died in the devastating smallpox epidemic of 1830–31). The elder Pitaresaru of the Chaui band was born in the late eighteenth or early nineteenth century. His name is on the 1833 treaty whereby the Pawnees ceded what is now southern Nebraska to the United States. His son is believed to have been born around 1823 and died as head chief in 1874 in Nebraska, the Pawnee tribal homeland.

The younger Pitaresaru was described as being over six feet tall and of good appearance. He became a chief when he was twenty-nine. He devoted his life to the good of his people, and, as an excellent orator, he attempted to mollify the U.S. government in its often unreasonable demands and treatment. Pitaresaru's name appears first—indicating his primary importance among all four Pawnee bands—on the 1857 treaty in which the Pawnees ceded the balance of their ancestral lands, retaining only a small reservation on the Loup River. Although honoring his own culture, Pitaresaru accepted U.S. government schools so that Pawnee children could learn to read and write the white man's words. He sought to maintain the sovereignty of tribal leaders and forcefully criticized negligent and dishonest agency employees. When his reservation-bound people endured hunger in the 1860s, he successfully pleaded that the tribe be allowed to go on the bison hunt, an activity that countered government policy of spatial restriction and conversion of the Pawnees into farmers.

When pressure came for the removal of the Pawnees from Nebraska to Indian Territory, at first he was resolutely against it, but later he agreed to the removal with a heavy heart. In 1874, before this sad migration was made, Pitaresaru died under mysterious circumstances; he was shot in the leg by parties unknown and subsequently perished from gangrene.

It was later said by a Skiri Pawnee that Pitaresaru ruled all the bands and was a great man. Today, some of his warrior songs are still sung by the Pawnee people in Oklahoma.

Martha Royce Blaine
Oklahoma City, Oklahoma

Blaine, Martha Royce. *Pawnee Passage: 1870–1875*. Norman: University of Oklahoma Press, 1990. Dunbar, John B. "Pitalesharu." *American History Magazine* 5 (1880): 340–42.

PLAINS APACHES

According to our legends, we, the Plains Apaches or Apache Tribe of Oklahoma, have been here since time began. Our earliest oral histories record our existence with the Sarcees (Sarsis) in Canada. These same histories mention that we split from the Sarcees and established ourselves in the Black Hills of South Dakota. At that time, we were known as Kált'inde, "Cedar People." This name was given to us by some other tribe. At that time, the Lakotas granted us the territory south of the Black Hills, while they took the territory to the north. We began to make our way to the south, hunting the bison.

Because of the second name our people were given, our elders believe we must have been very proficient hunters. We again came to be known by our former name, Bek'áhe, or "Whetstone," given to us by another tribe. Our elders believe this came about because we were always honing our knives in order to butcher the many bison our hunters killed. The sign for our people, to this very day, is the sign of honing—moving the outside of the right hand back and forth over the thumb side of the left hand. Today we are known in our own language as Ná'ishą "Stealers or Takers." We were given this name by the Kiowas, with whom we have long been closely associated. It seems that we got this name because of our ability to steal horses in the prereservation period.

We also have had multiple English names. We were first known as the Kiowa Apaches. Our elders believe this name was given to us in order to distinguish us from the Fort Sill Apaches. After the 1867 Treaty of Medicine Lodge Creek, we shared the Kiowa Reservation with the Kiowa and Comanche people. In 1894 the U.S. Army brought a number of Chiricahua Apaches to Fort Sill. At that time, it became necessary to distinguish us from the Fort Sill Apaches. Because we had been closely associated with the Kiowas, we became known as the Kiowa Apaches. The name Plains Apache was given to us by anthropologists and government officials. This name stems from our location and our mobile lifestyle.

We came to this area of the country by wandering with the bison, moving south from the Dakotas. We traveled on the eastern side of the Rocky Mountains, into the Southern Plains. We traveled throughout the Plains, from the northern reaches of the Missouri River to Chihuahua, Mexico. We traded extensively, bartering buffalo hides, salt, and meat for produce and other goods. Through trade, we established peaceful relationships with a number of other tribes, including the Pawnees, Arapahos, and Kiowas. Our people preferred trading to raiding for goods, but we were not passive when hostilities occurred.

Warfare and raiding allowed men to gain power and prestige. To become leaders, men were expected to have outstanding character. The leaders were honest, understanding, levelheaded men who had shown valor in war or had distinguished themselves as providers. Our tribe was governed by chiefs, a council of elders, warriors, and medicine people. When a man appeared to hold the qualities that made a good chief, the warriors would suggest that the council consider him for that position. If the council agreed with the warriors, the man was made a chief. Occasionally, sons or grandsons would inherit their father's or grandfather's positions, but only if the young man had the qualifications. If a chief abused his position or acted irresponsibly, he could be run off or killed.

Women also were important in Ná'ishą society. While women did not hold positions of power, they were in charge of maintaining many of the family possessions. Women were responsible for making and repairing the tipis and all items associated with them. Gathering of plant foods and, occasionally, small game, were women's activities as well. Special skill in tipi sewing, clothing decoration, and food location and preparation was recognized by induction into women's societies, which had their own dances and songs.

Today, we are recognized as the Apache Tribe of Oklahoma. This name was established in 1972 when the Kiowa, Comanche, and Apache tribes officially separated. While each tribe had run its own tribal affairs previously, we all had been supervised by the Bureau of Indian Affairs. Upon establishing our independence in 1972, we became an entity separate from the other two tribes, with our own tribal name and government. Government officers are elected in general elections. There are approximately 1,600 enrolled tribal members. The majority of tribal members live in Caddo and Comanche Counties in Oklahoma. Our tribal offices are located in Anadarko, Oklahoma.

Alfred Chalepah Sr.
Irene Poolaw
Houston Klinekole Sr.
Apache Tribe of Oklahoma
Pamela Innes
Deborah Bernsten
University of Oklahoma

Bittle, William. Fieldnotes. Apache Tribe of Oklahoma Culture Office, Anadarko, Oklahoma. Chalepah, Alfred, Sr., Irene Poolaw, and Houston Klinekole Sr. Oral histories. Apache Tribe of Oklahoma Culture Office, Anadarko, Oklahoma.

PLAINS CREES

Plains Crees traditionally occupied—and still occupy—a large section of the Canadian Plains, extending through much of central Alberta and central and southeastern Saskatchewan. Most of this territory is within the Parkland Belt, a transitional zone between the open grasslands on the south and the boreal forests to the north. Plains Crees speak a dialect of Algonquian.

Archeological remains (Selkirk composite) attributed to the western boreal forest Crees date from at least 1350 AD in northern Saskatchewan. Whether Crees also occupied the Aspen Parklands at this time is not certain, although there are some late archeological materials in this zone that reflect Selkirk influence. Indeed, when Henry Kelsey, the first European known to have visited the Canadian

Cree girl and her brother at Maple Creek, Saskatchewan, 1897

Plains, traveled through the Aspen Parklands of eastern Saskatchewan in 1690, he met Crees there, along with Nakotas (Assiniboines). Certainly, the detailed observations of Hudson's Bay Company employees in the mid-1700s record the presence of at least four named Cree groups—Susahanna, Sturgeon, Pegogamow, and Kiskatchewan—in the Aspen Parklands of Saskatchewan through to central Alberta. The nature of the social and political organization of these groups remains uncertain. It should be noted that the predominant occupants of the Parklands of Saskatchewan and Manitoba at this time were the Nakotas (Assiniboines), who were friends and allies of the Crees. They often located their camps in close proximity, particularly at bison pounds.

Beginning in the late seventeenth century and continuing through most of the eighteenth century, many of these Crees (and Nakotas) played a prominent role in the developing fur trade. In particular, they acted as middlemen traders, and each summer they took canoe loads of furs to York Factory on Hudson Bay. These they traded for European goods, which, upon returning to the borders of the Plains, they exchanged with other Native peoples for furs. Of particular importance was the Blackfoot-Cree alliance, which formed in the 1730s and continued throughout the eighteenth century.

At the heart of this alliance was the provision of guns by the Crees to the Blackfoot in return for furs.

Important changes occurred in the second half of the eighteenth century, including the establishment of a number of fur trade posts on the fringes of the Canadian Prairies, beginning with the French posts in the 1740s and 1750s. By 1780 the Hudson's Bay Company, the North West Company, and some smaller companies operated many posts in the western interior. The Parkland Crees and the Nakotas became much involved in the provisions trade, producing pemmican for the support of the employees of the trading companies. An even more important agent of change was disease, particularly the smallpox epidemics of 1780–81 and 1837–38, which greatly reduced the Cree population. Notably, during 1838 most of the Parkland Crees were vaccinated against smallpox, a reflection of their close relations with the Hudson's Bay Company. Unfortunately, this was not the case with most of the Nakota bands, which were decimated. The Parkland Crees then emerged as the predominant occupants of the Aspen Parklands and adjacent grasslands of central Saskatchewan and Alberta, and very quickly became a new tribal group—the Plains Crees.

Through the mid–nineteenth century, the Plains Crees maintained an economic cycle that positioned them near the grassland/parkland interface during the winter. A common method of taking bison at this season involved building a pound—a circular corral with an opening on one side. Wings extending outward from the opening for a considerable distance were employed to funnel small herds into the pound, where they were dispatched. In the course of the winter, some families traveled into the forest edge to trap fur-bearing animals, an activity that continued through the spring. During the latter season they sometimes built fish weirs on streams in order to intercept spawning runs. Following this they moved out into the Plains for the summer. While the Plains Crees valued horses highly, the number of horses remained low because the northern winters impeded their reproduction and caused a high general mortality. Therefore, dogs remained an important draft animal.

By the second half of the nineteenth century the Plains Crees were divided into eight major bands. Each of these bands had at least one prominent chief who often was the focus of a large camp group; however, all the members of each band gathered together only once a year, during the summer. At this time, in late June or early July, there was a ceremonial gathering at which the Sun (Thirsting) Dance was celebrated. The Plains Crees also observed nine other sacred ceremonies, the most prominent of which was the Smoking Tipi. However, in central Saskatchewan the Goose Dance—a ceremony of certain boreal forest Crees with elements adapted from the Midewiwin (the Grand Medicine Society) of the Ojibwas—was also important.

During the second half of the nineteenth century the bison herds were decimated, their range contracting to the south and southwest. As a result, many Crees were drawn far out onto the grasslands of southwestern Saskatchewan and northern Montana, where they came into conflict with their former allies, the Blackfoot. In the 1870s, with the approaching extirpation of the bison, most of the Plains Cree bands entered into treaty agreements with the Canadian government and took up residence on some twenty-four reserves in Alberta and Saskatchewan, where they survived by farming and ranching.

Over the years, many of the Plains Crees (and Plains Ojibwas) had intermarried with French traders, creating the Métis culture. In 1885, led by chiefs Poundmaker and Big Bear, they joined their relatives in the North-West Rebellion. Defeated after two major battles, Cree leaders were imprisoned, and one group left Canada and eventually settled on the Rocky Boy's Reservation in northern Montana. In the late 1800s the Plains Cree population was about 7,000; by 1998 it had increased remarkably to 62,330 persons, with 37,314 living in Saskatchewan and 25,016 in Alberta. In recent decades there has been considerable out-migration from the reserves to the cities of the Canadian Prairies, and there are now probably more Plains Crees living in urban areas than on the reserves.

David Meyer
University of Saskatchewan

Ahenakew, Freda, and H. Christoph Wolfart, eds. *Kwayask e-ki-pe-kiskinowapahtihicik: Their Example Showed Me the Way.* Told by Emma Minde. Edmonton: University of Alberta Press, 1997. Mandelbaum, David G. *The Plains Cree: An Ethnographic, Historical, and Comparative Study.* Canadian Plains Studies no. 9. Regina: Canadian Plains Research Centre, 1979. Russell, Dale. *Eighteenth-Century Western Cree and Their Neighbours.* Archaeological Survey of Canada Mercury Series Paper no. 143. Hull, Quebec: Canadian Museum of Civilization, 1991.

PLANT LORE

The uses of native plants of the Great Plains for food, medicine, and utilitarian purposes were many and of profound importance to the Native Americans. Plant lore has declined dramatically since European American settlement, and the majority of foods and virtually all medicines today are imported into the region.

The Great Plains has more than three thousand plant species. All Native American tribes of the region used numerous plant species, totaling in the hundreds. Most of the knowledge of their uses for food, medicine, and utilitarian purposes was held in oral histories, and many Native American uses continue today on Plains reservations. Anthropologists and ethnobotanists have recorded much information on the topic. Not surprisingly, most plants utilized were prairie plants, although some trees and shrubs also had important uses.

More native prairie plants (over two hundred) have been documented as being used by Plains Indians for medicine than for any other use. Some, such as yarrow (*Achillea millefolium*) and the purple coneflower (*Echinacea angustifolia*), were widely used for their general medicinal qualities. Others, such as locoweed (*Astragalus*), with its toxic amounts of alkaloids and selenium, were used more successfully to treat both internal and external maladies. Most people knew the many common uses of plants, but there were also highly trained individuals, medicine men and medicine women, who had very specific knowledge about plants and used them in spiritual ceremonies for healing.

In most cases, the belief system was that the spirit healed the individual, and that the plant was a vehicle for this process. The major medicinal plant cures of Plains Indian tribes have plausible scientific explanations for their use and effectiveness. Most of them contain active medicinal constituents. It is extraordinary that many of these uses were discovered. Certainly, much learning occurred through trial and error, but Native Americans also believed that knowledge could be gained through dreams and visions, and plant lore was of course handed down, orally, over generations. In fact, the healing systems of Native Americans are ancient and suggest links to Asia. For example, the Pawnees burned the stems of yarrow and leadplant (*Amorpha canescens*) as short punks placed on rheumatic points to relieve pain, a practice known as "moxabustion," which today is almost completely associated with Asian medicine. Only a very few medicinal plants used by Native Americans were adopted by European American immigrants, primarily because the traditions were vastly different and few European Americans were willing to give credence to Native American learning. One that was adopted was the purple coneflower, which has been imported into Europe and more recently been made available commercially in the United States as an immune system stimulant, used primarily to ward off colds.

Food uses of native plants were vitally important to the Great Plains Indians, and played an essential dietary role. More than 120 native prairie plants were used for food. Many plants were used for seasoning, flavors, tea, or nutritional needs (greens in the spring were used to ward off scurvy). The most important native food plant was the prairie turnip (*Psoralea esculenta*). This starchy, leguminous root was eaten as a staple or added to bison stew. It was also dried and traded or stored. The prairie turnip was so important to the Omahas that they determined the route of their summer buffalo hunt in the High Plains by the locations where the women could find the plant. Since wild food procurement was primarily women's work, little of this knowledge was passed on to European immigrants because interaction between Native American women and women settlers rarely occurred.

Native Americans had many other uses for wild plants, such as cattails and rushes for mats, white sage (*Artemisia ludoviciana*) and eastern redcedar (*Juniperus virginiana*) for ceremonial incense, and trees for lodges and firewood. Of course, Native American women had long cultivated corn, beans, squash, sunflowers, and other crops. With European American settlement, large numbers of new cultivars were introduced for farming and gardening, but the diversity and variety have dramatically decreased over the decades, and farmers now only grow a handful of crops (and indeed only a few genetic varieties of a small number of crops). Only a small number of the native plants originally used by Plains Indians—wild plums (*Prunus americana*), chokecherries (*Prunus virginiana*), wild grapes (*Vitis riparia*), and others—are now used for jams, jellies, and wine by the wider population.

Kelly Kindscher
University of Kansas

Kindscher, Kelly. *Edible Wild Plants of the Prairie: An Ethnobotanical Guide.* Lawrence: University Press of Kansas, 1987. Kindscher, Kelly. *Medicinal Wild Plants of the Prairie: An Ethnobotanical Guide.* Lawrence: University Press of Kansas, 1992. Moerman, Daniel E. *Native American Ethnobotany.* Portland OR: Timber Press, 1998. Snell, Alma Hogan. *A Taste of Heritage: Crow Indian Recipes and Herbal Medicines.* Lincoln: University of Nebraska Press, 2006.

PLENTY COUPS (1848–1932)

Plenty Coups (Alaxchiiaahush, or Aleck chea ahoos) was a Crow warrior, diplomat, and mediator. He was born in 1848 at "the cliff that has no pass" in present-day Billings, Montana. Also known as Bull Who Goes Into (Against) the Wind, he was a Mountain Crow. His parents died when he was about ten years old. Orphaned and in grief, he was encouraged by camp criers to go on vision quests. He was adopted by the Little People and guided by eagles, who became his guardians. In a vision in the Crazy Mountains he saw the buffalo disappear and be replaced by cattle, a windstorm destroy all trees except the one in which the chickadee lived, and himself as an old man sitting by a house.

By his mid-twenties Plenty Coups had accomplished each of four war deeds to achieve the distinction of chieftain, or "good man." He carried a Medicine Pipe and Pipe Holder's bag as a leader of the Fox Warrior Society. One of many Crows who scouted for the U.S. military, he was a leader in the Battle of the Rosebud on June 17, 1876. Years later he stated his reason for aiding the Americans: "We plainly saw that this course was the only one which might save our beautiful country for us." In 1880 he traveled with five other Crow leaders to Washington DC. The main purpose was to negotiate the sale of the western part of the reservation and a Northern Pacific Railroad right-of-way up the Yellowstone Valley. At George Washington's home, he pondered the difficulties of his "small nation." Inspired by the visit, he later willed land in 1928 to be used as a park, recreation ground, and display of his possessions as "a reminder to Indians and white people alike that the two races should live and work together harmoniously." His house, a Montana state park, is a National Historic Landmark.

By 1890 Plenty Coups and Pretty Eagle were recognized as head chiefs of the tribe. Plenty Coups settled in Pryor Valley, on land he had seen in his vision, where he farmed, raised cattle and horses, and established a general merchandise store. He was involved in "pan-Indian" intertribal networks and fought the continual pressure to sell Crow land. In preparation for hearings on yet another bill for opening and settlement of the reservation in 1917, Plenty Coups and other leaders held traditional war ceremonies in a Washington DC hotel room, including burning buffalo chips and offering songs and prayers. He promoted Crow Fair and also led parades at regional fairs. He encouraged Crow support of U.S. efforts during World War I. Chosen to be the representative of all Indians and called "Chief of All Chiefs" for dedication of the Tomb of the Unknown Soldier at Arlington National Cemetery in 1921, he placed his war bonnet and coup stick before the casket; they are on display there today.

Following the example of the chickadee to be observant and learn from others, Plenty Coups lived according to his own Crow values and also accommodated non-Indian culture. He practiced traditional Crow religion, including the vision quest, sweat lodge, and Sacred Tobacco Society. He was baptized into the Catholic Church at St. Xavier on the Crow Indian Reservation. He was married several times, but his two children died young, so he and his wives adopted and raised other children. He considered all the Crows as his "children." He understood that education is important and donated part of his land for a school. His most fa-

mous statement was "Education is your most powerful weapon. With education you are the white man's equal; without education you are his victim." Plenty Coups passed to the "Other Side Camp" on March 4, 1932, at age eighty-four. Funeral services were held according to both Catholic and traditional Crow customs, including proclamation in the Crow language of his deeds. The tribe voted to honor him as their last traditional chief.

C. Adrian Heidenreich
Montana State University–Billings

Hoxie, Frederick E. *Parading through History: The Making of the Crow Nation in America, 1805–1935.* New York: Cambridge University Press, 1995. Linderman, Frank B. *Plenty-coups: Chief of the Crows.* 2nd ed. Lincoln: University of Nebraska Press, 2002.

PONCAS

Since their arrival in the Great Plains, the Ponca Tribe has always been small in numbers. Yet their history and experiences are representative of many of the major themes that have shaped the lives of the Native inhabitants of the region. According to the Poncas' oral history, their original homeland was in the Ohio River valley. For reasons now unknown, the Siouan Dhegiha speakers (Poncas, Omahas, Kanzas, Osages, and Quapaws) undertook a vast migration: as they followed the Ohio, Mississippi, and eventually the Missouri rivers, one cognate tribe after another divided off until only the Poncas and Omahas remained together. The Poncas eventually separated from the Omahas and settled in the Niobrara River valley (in present-day northeastern Nebraska) by the early eighteenth century. As a consequence, the Poncas and Omahas speak mutually intelligible dialects and have similar political and social organization, including hereditary chiefs and patrilineal, exogamous clans.

Settling into their new land, the Poncas jettisoned many of their Woodland adaptations in favor of the archetypal Plains Village Tradition of semipermanent earth lodge villages, maize horticulture, and communal bison hunting. In the nineteenth century, however, as a result of epidemic diseases, the Poncas periodically abandoned horticulture in favor of full-time nomadic bison hunting. Still, they never abandoned their homeland near the confluence of the Niobrara and Missouri rivers, and they continued to return to their sacred sites, villages, and gardens on a regular basis.

The typical seasonal round of the Poncas was organized around the horticultural calendar: planting gardens in the spring and harvesting in the fall, interspersed with communal bison hunts in the summer and winter seasons. Hunting and horticulture were supplemented by gathering wild plants and herbs for food and healing. The Poncas utilized a vast area of the Central Great Plains for trading, hunting, horse raiding, and visiting. In all, they claimed an area extending from the Missouri River on the east to the Black Hills and foothills of the Rocky Mountains to the west, and from the White River in the north to the Platte River in the south.

Given their range, the Poncas had to learn to coexist with their more numerous and powerful neighbors, the Lakotas and the Pawnees. The Poncas forged a tenuous alliance with the Oglala Lakotas, occasionally hunting together and accompanying them on their horse raids against the Pawnees. From the Oglalas the Poncas learned the sacred Sun Dance, but they modified it to fit Ponca horticultural traditions by adding an emphasis on fertility and renewal, consistent with the goals of a horticultural tribe. The Poncas also practiced (and still practice) the sacred pipe religion and expressed a strong belief in their all-powerful creator, Wakonda. The Poncas had a more troubled relationship with the Brulé Lakotas, however, which would eventually contribute to their expulsion from their Niobrara homeland.

The Poncas point with pride to the fact that they never engaged in armed conflict with the U.S. government. In all, they signed four treaties, including a treaty that ceded Aboriginal title to the majority of their land and established a reservation near Niobrara, Nebraska, in 1858. The Poncas tried earnestly to succeed in their transition to reservation-based farming. However, those efforts proved futile when the government ceded away title to the entire Ponca Reservation to the Sioux in the Treaty of Fort Laramie in 1868. Overnight, the Poncas found themselves trespassers on their own reservation. The Brulé Lakotas, under Chief Spotted Tail, were relentless in their harassment of the Poncas and eventually weakened them to the point of desperation. Conditions were so grave by the 1870s that the Poncas considered a plan to abandon their homeland in favor of a new reservation in Indian Territory. After traveling to the proposed site in the winter of 1877, a delegation of Ponca chiefs declined the offer. However, the will of the chiefs was disregarded by the government, and the forced removal of the tribe commenced in the spring of 1877.

This event, known as the Ponca Trail of Tears, was a disaster. Plagued by bad weather and inadequate preparations, the Poncas lost more than one-fifth (158 from 730) of their population within the first two years of removal. Dissatisfaction with their circumstances led to a desperate attempt by Chief Standing Bear to return to the Niobrara homeland to honor the dying wish of his son to be buried with his ancestors. On New Year's Day of 1879, Standing Bear led a small party of Poncas—mostly women and children—back to Nebraska. They were arrested, and a trial ensued in federal district court in Omaha, Nebraska. Judge Elmer Dundy declared that "an Indian is a person under the meaning of the law" and that the United States had no authority to return Standing Bear to Indian Territory.

Standing Bear had won his case, but the victory was a hollow one for the Ponca Tribe. The majority of the Poncas, after spending more than two years settling into their new reservation in Indian Territory, opted to remain there. In 1881 the Ponca Tribe was officially dissolved and legally reconstituted as two separate entities: the Northern Ponca Tribe, residing on a portion of the old Ponca Reservation in northeastern Nebraska, and the Southern Ponca Tribe, with a reservation of 101,000 acres in north-central Oklahoma.

The two Ponca tribes, still linked by family, cultural, and linguistic ties, have faced vastly different fates in the twentieth century. The Ponca Tribe of Oklahoma, organized in 1950, is headquartered in White Eagle, named after the Poncas' charismatic paramount chief at the time of removal. In 1996 the Southern Poncas listed 2,581 enrolled members, of whom more than half resided in Kay County, Oklahoma. The Southern Poncas' land base suffered as a consequence of allotment policy, and they eventually lost the vast majority of their landholdings, including oil-rich lands, to non-Indian interests, particularly the "101 Ranch." The Southern Poncas have been active in the Native American Church, the revitalization of the Heduska, or War Dance Society, and the Plains powwow tradition. The economy of the Ponca Tribe of Oklahoma is based on a successful bingo hall, smoke shops, and various tribal economic development initiatives.

The Northern Ponca Tribe also struggled in the twentieth century with land loss and the out-migration of tribal members. The Northern Ponca Tribe was terminated in 1962, joining more than one hundred tribes that lost their status as a result of federal termination policy. At the time of termination, only 442 Northern Poncas were listed on the tribal roll, and only 847 of their original 27,000 acres remained. Tribal status was legally restored by Congress in 1990 as a result of a prolonged tribal grassroots effort led by the nonprofit Northern Ponca Restoration Committee. The Ponca Tribe of Nebraska is currently headquartered in Niobrara, Nebraska, near their first reservation. The tribe, denied the opportunity to reestablish their reservation by Congress, delivers services to tribal members residing in fifteen designated counties in Nebraska, South Dakota, and Iowa. Enrollment exceeds 2,000. At the turn of the twenty-first century the tribe was engaged in a number of economic developments and cultural revitalization projects, including the reintroduction of bison on tribal trust lands near Niobrara and the establishment of the Ponca Health and Wellness Center in Omaha, Nebraska.

Beth R. Ritter
University of Nebraska at Omaha

Howard, James H. *The Ponca Tribe.* Washington DC: Government Printing Office, 1995. Ritter, Beth R. "The Politics of Retribalization: The Northern Ponca Case." *Great Plains Research* 4 (1994): 237–55. Wishart, David J. *An Unspeakable Sadness: The Dispossession of the Nebraska Indians.* Lincoln: University of Nebraska Press, 1994.

POSEY, ALEXANDER (1873–1908)

Alexander Lawrence Posey, 1908

Alexander Lawrence Posey, a well-known Muskogee Creek poet and journalist, lived in Indian Territory during the turbulent years prior to and one year beyond Oklahoma statehood. He is best remembered for a series of humorous and politically insightful articles printed while he was the owner and editor of the *Eufaula Journal.* "Fus Fixico Letters," some seventy-two in all, became a weekly feature of Posey's newspaper and made use of voices and personae of traditional Creek Indian figures to comment on territorial politicians, elections, members of the Dawes Commission, the issues of coming statehood and an Indian state to be called Sequoyah, as well as the general resistance to "progress" and land allotments led by the Creek historian Chitto Harjo.

Posey was born near present-day Eufaula, Oklahoma, on August 3, 1873, the first child of Nancy and Lewis Henderson Posey. He received his postsecondary education at Bacone Indian University in Muskogee, Oklahoma, where he gained some recognition as a budding poet and as a writer of commencement orations. He was elected as a clerk in the Creek House of Warriors and appointed as superintendent of the Creek Orphan Asylum near Okmulgee. He married Minnie Harris, a schoolteacher from Farmington, Arkansas. In his writings, Posey emphasized the importance of conforming to the new American society and to what he felt were progressive viewpoints.

Although he had achieved a national journalistic reputation, his interests had expanded to include tribal folkways, land development, and even oil and gas speculation. But his life was cut short by a tragic drowning accident on the morning of May 27, 1908. He was survived by his young wife and two children.

Charles Ballard
University of Nebraska–Lincoln

Littlefield, Daniel F., Jr. *Alex Posey: Creek Poet, Journalist, and Humorist.* Lincoln: University of Nebraska Press, 1992. Posey, Alexander. *The Fus Fixico Letters,* edited by Daniel F. Littlefield Jr. and Carol A. Pretty Hunter. Lincoln: University of Nebraska Press, 1993. Posey, Alexander. *Chinnubbie and the Owl: Muscogee (Creek) Stories, Orations, and Oral Traditions,* edited by Matthew Wynn Sivils. Lincoln: University of Nebraska Press, 2005.

POUNDMAKER (CA. 1842–1886)

Poundmaker, whose Indian name was Pītikwahanapiwīyin, was born around 1842. The son of an Assiniboine Indian and a mixed-blood mother of French descent, he was a member of a prominent Plains Cree family from the House band in what today is central Saskatchewan.

Poundmaker was destined to become an influential leader. In 1873 he was adopted by Crowfoot, head chief of the powerful Blackfoot nation of southern Alberta. This happened during a brief truce in the wars between the Crees and the Blackfoot, when Poundmaker visited Crowfoot's camp for the first time. One of Crowfoot's wives, who was grieving the loss of a son in battle, was struck with Poundmaker's resemblance to her dead son and prevailed upon the chief to adopt the Cree as a replacement. For his part, Crowfoot was greatly impressed with Poundmaker's statesmanlike bearing and commitment to peacemaking, and so he readily agreed. The adoption invested Poundmaker with the attributes of a Blackfoot family member; it bestowed new wealth on him in the form of horses gifted by his adoptive family; and it conferred upon him a new Blackfoot name, Makoyi-koh-kin (Wolf Thin Legs). When Poundmaker returned home, he was accorded special standing because of his personal connection to a nation that traditionally had been an enemy of the Crees. Within a few years he was elevated to the rank of a councilor, or minor chief, in the River People band led by Chief Red Pheasant.

Poundmaker proved to be a strong critic of government policy. In 1876, during the negotiation of Treaty Number 6 at Fort Carlton, he took exception to the very notion of confining Indians to reserves. "This is our land!" he protested to the government commissioners. "It isn't a piece of pemmican to be cut off and given in little pieces back to us." He also insisted that the terms offered did not provide adequately for agricultural assistance or for famine relief during hard times. He eventually signed the treaty but remained resistant to taking up reserve life. In 1878, when Red Pheasant agreed to move onto a reserve, Poundmaker formed his own band and made a last-ditch effort to hunt down the few remaining buffalo. A year later he and his starving band accepted a reserve some forty miles west of Battleford, Saskatchewan. Although he made efforts to master farming, he nevertheless remained a determined critic of the government, which routinely ignored both Indian treaty rights and the starvation that stalked the reserves.

Owing to circumstances beyond his control, Poundmaker was implicated in the North-West Rebellion of 1885. Like most Indian leaders, he did not want to join the disaffected Métis who had clashed with government forces at Batoche and elsewhere. While he was known to criticize government policy and the deplorable conditions on reserves, his main aim was to achieve reform through peaceful means, particularly the renegotiation of Treaty 6.

However, soon after the outbreak of hostilities, Poundmaker progressively lost control over his camp, which came to include dissident Métis and a number of Assiniboines who had murdered a farm instructor. At Battleford he was unable to prevent his warriors from looting homes and offices that had been abandoned when the occupants fled for protection to the police barracks nearby. Later, Poundmaker's authority was preempted by his band's warrior society, which, at Cut Knife Hill, Saskatchewan, resisted an assault by government forces led by Lt. Col. William Dillon Otter.

Throughout these events Poundmaker cautioned restraint and took steps to protect prisoners. He is also credited with preventing the warriors from inflicting heavy losses on Otter's troops as they retreated in disarray. Nevertheless, Poundmaker was blamed by a government determined to cripple Indian society by removing its leadership. He was subjected to a humiliating surrender at the hands of Gen. Frederick Dobson Middleton,

placed on trial in 1885 for treason, and sentenced to three years in Stony Mountain Penitentiary, Manitoba. He was granted early release in 1886 but died of tuberculosis four months later, on July 4, while visiting Crowfoot. Initially buried at Blackfoot Crossing, Alberta, his remains were reinterred at Cut Knife Hill in 1967.

F. Laurie Barron
University of Saskatchewan

Jefferson, Robert, *Fifty Years on the Saskatchewan*. Battleford SK: Canadian North-West Historical Society, 1929. Sluman, Norma. *Poundmaker*. Toronto: McGraw-Hill Ryerson, 1967. Stonechild, Blair, and Bill Waiser. *Loyal till Death: Indians and the North-West Rebellion*. Calgary: Fifth House, 1997.

POWWOWS

The word "powwow" is derived from the Narragansett language and refers to a gathering of Native people for the purpose of singing, dancing, celebration, and socialization. It consists of ceremonies, dance competitions, and social dancing. Many are large, annual events and have well-established reputations, such as those held in Calgary, Denver, and Oklahoma City. Powwows are characterized by the use of one or more groups of singers, which are called "drums," and the wearing of elaborate regalia during the dance portions of the event. The style of music and dance that has become standardized in many Great Plains powwows is termed "intertribal" because it is a hybridization of dance and music from several Native American groups. Powwows vary in size from giant affairs attended by people from a wide variety of locations on the North American continent, to small, local gatherings where the population of one community is the primary audience.

The history of the event demonstrates its dynamic nature. During the first part of the twentieth century, there was a great deal of interaction among Native peoples due to relocation on reservations and through increased availability of transportation technology such as the railroad. Native peoples maintained cultural identity by preserving traditional music and dance styles. Participation in World War I, World War II, and the Korean War gave Native American men who might have been members of warrior societies among their own people the opportunity to become active warriors. Traditional dances were held and songs were composed to honor these men. By 1955 there was a great deal of interest in artistic exchange among tribal groups in the Great Plains, who continued to celebrate their warrior societies through song and dance, especially in Oklahoma. These songs and dances were shared with members of neighboring tribes, and an amalgamation of musical and dance

Powwow at Potawatomi Indian Agency, Kansas, ca. 1920

traits resulted that led to the contemporary intertribal powwow.

When these intertribal celebrations began, they did not possess the common elements that can be found today. Although there is still a large amount of variation in format, competition, and participation, many powwows in the Great Plains have an overall form that is predictable and understood by all participants. This form includes a wide variety of events held for specific reasons and, in many cases, in a specific order.

The most impressive event of the contemporary powwow is the Grand Entry, the first part of any dance session. During this time, all dancers who are to compete enter the powwow arena in a specified order. After the Grand Entry, a special ceremony usually takes place that includes the singing of a Flag Song and, sometimes, an Honor Song. After the songs the master of ceremonies may introduce important people at the event, and a prayer is frequently offered. This might be followed by a speech from a dignitary, such as the powwow princess or a visiting politician. During all of this ceremony, the dancers stand quietly in the powwow arena. At its close, the emcee usually calls for an intertribal dance, so that everyone may participate. Several such dances may occur before the competitions begin.

Competition dancing is divided into categories according to the type of songs performed by the drum (the singing group), the type of dance

steps and regalia worn by the contestants, and the contestants' ages. Men's categories usually include traditional and fancy dancers. Women are divided into traditional, fancy, and jingle dress dancers. All categories are further classified by age into adult, junior, and tiny tot divisions. Awards for the competitions are presented for dancing technique, such as stopping on the correct foot with the last beat of the drum and appropriate composure during the entire powwow. Prizes may include cash, trophies, and a wide variety of material objects such as blankets, rifles, food, or household items.

A great diversity of music may be heard at any given powwow. Some of the musical styles include the Omaha dance, social dance, and intertribal. Songs are not improvised but are composed by singers who teach them to other members of the drum. These songs are then dispersed among the population through performance at powwows and through recordings. Songs have appropriate drumbeats that accompany them, including the parade beat, the Omaha beat, the social dance beat, accent or honor beats, and the drum roll. Each of these beats is distinctive, and aficionados will know immediately by the drumbeat which type of song is being performed. The speed of the beat varies according to the type of dance and the style of the drum. Distinctive differences exist between Northern Plains and Southern Plains styles, and these include a faster beat in the north and a slower beat in the south. These differences sometimes make it impossible for a northern-style dancer, for example, to compete while a southern-style drum is playing. For this reason, international drums often perform at powwows in a neutral style so that dancers from both the northern and southern traditions may compete simultaneously.

Competitions are the main focus of the powwow for some participants, but other types of activities occur at various points during the event. Giveaways are common, and intertribal and special dances are interspersed throughout the affair, giving noncompetitive dancers a chance to participate. Raffles are frequently held to raise money in support of the event or to help sponsor the next powwow. After the formal portion of the powwow, young dancers often get together in the late evening for a round of "forty-nine dances." The informal nature of the forty-nines contrasts with the relatively rigid structure of the other powwow dances. This is a time for celebration among the young adults who participate often into the early hours of the morning.

Contemporary powwows play an important role in the social and cultural life of Native Americans. They are a celebration of heritage and tradition that has survived in a unique form apart from the daily lives of the participants. Powwows engender a sense of community and belonging among the people who participate, and those who are on the powwow circuit look forward to making new acquaintances and renewing old friendships as much as to the singing, dancing, and competitions. Music and dance are natural media for dissemination of cultural information because they are so visible, and powwows and recordings of powwow songs disperse important features of Native American culture not only among Native American communities but also among members of other communities.

Kenton Bales
University of Nebraska at Omaha

Ellis, Clyde. *A Dancing People: Powwow Culture on the Southern Plains.* Lawrence: University Press of Kansas, 2003. Ellis, Clyde, Luke Eric Lassiter, and Gary H. Dunham, eds. *Powwow.* Lincoln: University of Nebraska Press, 2005. Horse Capture, George P. *Powwow.* Cody WY: Buffalo Bill Historical Center, 1989. Powers, William K. *War Dance: Plains Indian Musical Performance.* Tucson: University of Arizona Press, 1990.

PUBLIC LAW 280

Public Law 280, passed on August 15, 1953, ended federal law enforcement on tribal lands and brought the tribes of five mandatory states—California, Minnesota, Nebraska, Oregon, and Wisconsin—under state civil and criminal jurisdiction. (Alaska was added later.) In theory this termination-era legislation was applied to these states because their state senators had requested the change and because tribal leaders had apparently accepted state control and federal withdrawal. All other states whose constitutions allowed such action were given the option to accept jurisdiction over their reservations. Congressional testimony reveals two primary justifications for the legislation: a feeling that a condition of lawlessness existed on and near reservations and the belief that tribal peoples should be under the same laws and law enforcement as the majority population.

Although the federal government traditionally administered law on Indian reservations, beginning in 1940 it began to give certain states partial or total jurisdiction. Among these states were Kansas and North Dakota (only on the Devils Lake Sioux Reservation). Following passage of PL 280 other Great Plains states attempted to accept some form of jurisdiction over their reservations. North Dakota accepted civil jurisdiction over its tribes, dependent upon tribal consent. Significantly, no tribe there has consented to state control. South Dakota attempted to apply the law multiple times, including unilaterally extending jurisdiction to its reservations, but, between court battles and electoral decisions, it has not been successful in this endeavor.

Both states and tribal peoples immediately noted problems with the law, problems that would lead to virtually continuous disputes both in and outside of courtrooms for the next four decades as well as jurisdictional uncertainty between tribal, city, state, and federal law enforcement agencies. State arguments against the law were almost universally based on the problem of increased cost to local and state governments. Tribal complaints centered on the fact that the law did not require any form of tribal consent.

Nebraska, the lone mandatory Great Plains PL 280 state, experienced such jurisdictional and law enforcement difficulties. Home to the Omahas and Winnebagos, neither Nebraska nor Thurston County (site of the reservations) hired additional law enforcement officers to replace departing federal officers, despite the fact that allotted lands owned by tribal members were taxed. With diminished law enforcement, crime rose on the reservations. In 1957 the state legislature passed a law known as the Indian Bounty Act, supplying state funds for counties with heavy tribal populations and land bases. This act formed the basis of later tribal complaints that county officials unjustly arrested inordinate numbers of Native Americans in order to receive these funds.

Because of widespread discontent on all sides, Congress included a consent clause to PL 280 in the Civil Rights Act of 1968 and also allowed states to retrocede jurisdiction back to the federal government. It did not give tribal peoples in previous PL 280 states power to demand this retrocession, and the prior consent clause did not have any bearing on the states already affected by PL 280. Under this change, the Omahas and later the Winnebagos successfully won retrocession. They have since created tribal courts and police and have completed cross-deputization and concurrent jurisdiction agreements with county, state, and federal authorities.

Charles Vollan
South Dakota State University

Goldberg, Carol. "Public Law 280: The Limits of State Jurisdiction over Indians." UCLA *Law Review* 22 (1975): 535–94. Hansen, Sandra. "Survey of Civil Jurisdiction in Indian Country." *American Indian Law Review* 16 (1990): 319–75.

PRETTY-ON-TOP, JANINE PEASE (B. 1949)

Janine Pease Pretty on Top is a Crow educator, a former president of Little Big Horn College, and an independent consultant. The *Missoula Missoulan* named her one of the top one hundred influential Montanans of the last century. Pretty-on-Top was born on the Colville Reservation in Washington State in 1949 to a Crow father and an Irish-German mother. She grew up in Washington but spent her summer vacations on the Crow Reservation in Montana. In 1970 she earned degrees in sociology and anthropology from Central Washington University, where she became politically active. In 1971 and 1972 she taught Native American studies, acted as a counselor to minority students, and coached women's basketball at Big Bend Community College in Washington. She briefly taught at the first Native American tribal college, Navajo Community College, in Tsaile, Arizona, before returning to Big Bend Community College. In 1975 she moved to Montana to direct the Crow tribe's Adult and Continuing Education Program. There she collaborated with the Crow Central Education Commission to establish greater tribal control over the education of Crow students. The commission organized GED classes and established a program to enroll Crows in college courses through a local community college. That year she met her first husband, Sam Windy Boy, a Chippewa-Cree educator. They had two children together.

In 1981 Pretty-on-Top became the Indian student advocate at Eastern Montana College (now Montana State University). The next year, the Crow Educational Authority invited her to become executive director of Little Big Horn College, a tribal college established in 1980. The college's physical plant consisted of an old gymnasium donated by the Bureau of Indian Affairs. The student body comprised thirty-two students. Poorly funded and lacking accreditation, the college struggled, charging twenty dollars per credit hour but even then attracting few Crow students. Pretty-on-Top redesigned the curriculum around Crow studies, although the school continued to offer a broad range of courses. After a six-year struggle, the school won accreditation in 1994, and again in 2000.

In 1983 Pretty-on-Top acted as lead plaintiff in the case *Windy Boy v. Big Horn County*, suing the county because its at-large voting system discriminated against Native Americans. That year her marriage dissolved. In 1987 she earned a master of arts degree in education, and in 1994 she earned a doctorate in adult and higher education, both from Montana State University in Bozeman. In 1991 she married John Pretty-on-Top, a leader in the Crow Sun Dance. She served on the American Indian College Fund's board of directors from 1988 to 1995, then again in 1998.

In early 2001 the Crow Tribal Council, following an overwhelming voice vote, removed Pretty-on-Top from the presidency of Little Big Horn Community College, alleging that she violated college procedures. She remained active in the Montana Democratic Party and is a popular public speaker. She now operates her own consulting firm, which raises education money for colleges in Indian Country.

Charles Vollan
South Dakota State University

Shay, Becky. "Ousted: Pretty On Top Removed from Leadership at LBH College." *Billings MT Gazette*, January 14, 2001. Nelson, Douglas, and Jeremy Johnston. "Janine Pease Pretty-on-Top." In *The New Warriors: Native American Leaders Since 1900*, edited by R. David Edmunds, 281–98. Lincoln: University of Nebraska Press, 2001.

PRETTY SHIELD (CA. 1856/1857–1944)

Pretty Shield was a Crow medicine woman, or "Wise-one," born along the Missouri River in what is now southeastern Montana in 1856 or 1857. She was from the Sore-lips band of the Mountain Crows. Her aunt had recently lost her two children and husband in a Lakota attack, so Pretty Shield's parents gave her to her aunt, a member of the River Crows, to raise. She remained in regular contact with her birth parents. She saw her first American at age six. At age thirteen her parents arranged a marriage with a Crow named Goes Ahead. They married when she was sixteen. Goes Ahead later served as a scout for Custer at the Battle of the Little Bighorn, which he survived. Goes Ahead had already married Pretty Shield's older sister, Standing Medicine Rock, and later also married her younger sister, Two Scalps. Pretty Shield and Goes Ahead had five children, two of whom died in infancy. Two more daughters died in early adulthood.

Pretty Shield gained widespread fame after writer Frank B. Linderman interviewed her and wrote the biography *Red Mother*, published in 1932 (reprinted as *Pretty-shield: Medicine Woman of the Crows* in 1972), one of the first attempts to document the life of a Native American woman. She was seventy-four at the time of the interviews and lived near the Little Bighorn battlefield.

Although considered a valuable text, Linderman's work ignored important details, among them that Pretty Shield, at the urging of her husband, was an early Christian convert—the family was listed first in the records of the Congregational Church at Crow agency in 1896. Her granddaughter Alma described Pretty Shield as a Baptist. When Pretty Shield converted she virtually ceased to practice as a medicine woman. But she also retained her belief in Crow spirituality, refusing to attend the Sun Dance, which the Crows learned from the Shoshones in 1940, because it did not conform to Crow tradition.

Pretty Shield died in 1944. Her granddaughter, Alma Hogan Snell, collaborated with anthropologist Becky Matthews to write her own autobiography, *Grandmother's Grandchild* (2000), a work that added many new details to Pretty Shield's story.

Charles Vollan
South Dakota State University

Colasurdo, Christine. "'Tell Me a Woman's Story': The Question of Gender in the Construction of Waheenee, Pretty-shield, and Papago Woman." *American Indian Quarterly* 21 (summer 1998): 385–407. Linderman, Frank B. *Pretty-shield: Medicine Woman of the Crows*. Lincoln: University of Nebraska Press, 1972. Snell, Alma Hogan. *Grandmother's Grandchild: My Crow Indian Life*, edited by Becky Matthews. Lincoln: University of Nebraska Press, 2000.

QUAPAWS

When first encountered by Europeans in the 1670s, some 15,000 to 20,000 Quapaws resided in four permanent villages near the confluence of the Mississippi and Arkansas rivers. They practiced a mixed economy of agriculture and hunting. Socially they were divided into a myriad of patrilineal clans and subclans. Known to their Dhegiha-branch Sioux kinsmen (the Osages, Omahas, Kanzas, and Poncas) as *Ugaxpa*, or "Downstream People," the Quapaws entered into trading and military alliances first with the French and then with the Spanish. The benefits of these relationships hardly compensated for the costs of altered lifeways, weakened social structures, and decimated population (they were reduced to 575 persons by 1800).

In 1803, when the United States acquired Louisiana, American authorities saw the Quapaws as impediments to national expansion. Thirty years later they forced the tribe, led by Chief Heckaton, to remove from its Arkansas homeland to a

150-square-mile reservation in northeastern Oklahoma. The traumatic relocation to Indian Territory divided the tribe into two main groups, one living on the reservation and the other along the Canadian River. Most tribespeople engaged in bison hunting; a few farmed successfully and sent their children to missionary schools.

Tribal fortunes changed markedly with the onset of the American Civil War. Although tribal chiefs War-te-she and Ki-he-cah-te-da signed a treaty with the Confederacy in 1861, within a year the bands had retreated to Kansas with other Indians sympathetic to the Union. There the refugees suffered four years of painful deprivation, resulting in the deaths of one-half of the tribe.

The post–Civil War years brought little relief. In an 1867 treaty with the United States, tribal leaders exchanged reservation land for annuity payments and educational stipends. Led by the last hereditary chief of the Quapaws, Tallchief, a majority of the tribespeople left the reservation to live with their Osage kinsmen. Those who remained leased the domain to non-Indian agriculturists and admitted "homeless" Indians to tribal citizenship. In 1893, fearing forfeiture of the reservation, Quapaw leaders John Medicine and Abner W. Abrams took the unprecedented action of allotting it in 240-acre parcels to 234 enrolled members of the tribe. Federal government approval came after the fact.

In the 1920s and 1930s the discovery of rich lead and zinc deposits on some individual allotments changed the course of Quapaw history. Because wealthy allottees were systematically defrauded, the federal government in 1908 revoked fraudulent leases, obtained higher royalties, and shielded Indian income from local, state, and federal taxes. But this intervention also brought federal control of mining royalties paid to individual allottees. The hated bureaucratic restrictions, however, did not prevent the Quapaws from engaging in uncontrolled spending that left most of them in poverty by 1940. Nor did it prevent a significant number of the wealthy allottees, led by Chief Victor Griffin, from embracing and supporting the Big Moon peyote cult, which had been introduced by John "Moonhead" Wilson in the 1890s.

Because the status quo served the Quapaw leadership well, it rejected the Indian Reorganization Act of 1934 and then refused to organize under the terms of the Oklahoma Indian Welfare Act enacted two years later. The leadership did file a claim under the provisions of the Indian Claims Commission Act of 1946, an action that in 1954 resulted in a favorable judgment of nearly $1 million. In 1961 that money was divided among 1,199 individual Quapaws.

The commission award revitalized the Quapaws

both as a people and as a community. Organized in 1956 as the Business Committee, the tribal government adroitly diverted termination pressures in the 1950s. At the beginning of the twenty-first century it manages varying enterprises ranging from a bingo parlor to a quick-stop gasoline station, a nationally acclaimed powwow, and a gleaming new office building southeast of Quapaw, Oklahoma.

W. David Baird
Pepperdine University

Baird, W. David. *The Quapaw Indians: A History of the Downstream People.* Norman: University of Oklahoma Press, 1980. Baird, W. David. *The Quapaws.* New York: Chelsea House, 1989.

RADIO STATIONS

Radio stations owned and operated by Native Americans and Native Canadians serve much of the Great Plains. The delivery systems are different in the two countries, but the goals are similar: to help preserve and promote Indigenous languages and cultures.

Broadcast media were once negative forces in Indigenous communities because they bombarded the communities with Western languages, cultures, and values. The media of the dominant culture overwhelmed and imperiled fragile traditional cultures. In recent years, however, electronic media owned and operated by Indigenous people have helped to restore the balance.

The first Native American radio station went on the air in 1973. A scattered few additional stations followed during the rest of the decade, but their development was hampered by a lack of funds. A change in federal government policy in the 1980s provided more resources to equip and operate Native stations, and their numbers grew steadily. As of 1999, some forty stations were broadcasting across the United States, and others were being planned.

Fourteen of the Native stations serve the American Great Plains. Each of the stations operates independently. They are licensed variously to tribal councils, community colleges, church groups, and nonprofit corporations. Half of the stations are located in the Dakotas, with three in North Dakota and four in South Dakota. Montana, Wyoming, and Colorado are each home to one station, and there are four in New Mexico. One is being planned for western Minnesota. There are no Native stations in Nebraska, Oklahoma, Texas, or Kansas.

Some stations receive programming from the National Public Radio network, but most do not because of the expense involved in being a member of the network. Most do receive satellite-delivered programming such as *National Native News* (a newscast) and *Native America Calling* (a call-in program) and other services of the American Indian Radio on Satellite Network (AIROS). Many

non-Native stations in the region also broadcast some of these programs. Popular music and public service programs, including coverage of powwows and other cultural events, are also featured on Native stations. Traditional languages are used extensively on some stations, while others do little or no Native-language programming because the languages are seldom used anymore or there are multiple Indigenous languages in a listening area, which limits the use of any single language.

Indigenous stations also serve the Canadian provinces in the Great Plains. Similar to the situation in the United States, Indigenous communities had little control of the media that reached them until the 1980s, when the Canadian government began to fund and support Native-controlled electronic media that would protect and preserve Indigenous languages and cultures. Alberta, Saskatchewan, and Manitoba are each home to sophisticated radio networks that deliver signals to dozens of communities in each province. Corporations in each province provide this service. In Alberta, CFWE-FM radio, owned and operated by the Aboriginal Multi-Media Society, reaches forty-six communities in the province by satellite. In Saskatchewan, the Missinipi Broadcasting Corporation provides the service to more than thirty communities via FM transmitters or cable. In Manitoba, the Aboriginal FM Network of Native Communications Inc. reaches seventy sites. This centralized network system is different from the American model but is an efficient means of reaching the large and sparsely populated regions that are served.

Bruce L. Smith
Southwest Texas State University

Browne, Donald R. *Electronic Media and Indigenous Peoples: A Voice of Our Own?* Ames: Iowa State University Press, 1996. Keith, Michael C. *Signals in the Air: Native Broadcasting in America.* Westport CT: Praeger, 1995. Smith, Bruce L., and M. L. Cornette. "Electronic Smoke Signals: Native American Radio in the United States." *Cultural Survival Quarterly* (spring 1998): 28–31.

RED CLOUD (1821–1909)

Lakota Sioux chief Red Cloud (Makhpyia-Luta), regarded by many historians as the most influential of the Native American leaders living in the Great Plains during the late nineteenth century, was born on Blue Water Creek in May 1821 in what is now Garden County, Nebraska. The creek, a tributary of the North Platte River, was located in a neutral hunting ground disputed by the Lakotas and their hated rivals, the Pawnees. Red Cloud's father, Lone Man, was a Brulé, one of the seven Lakota, or western Sioux, tribes that migrated from the woodlands of Minnesota to the Northern Plains during the sixteenth and seventeenth centuries.

Red Cloud (Makhpyia-Luta)

with whom he had been on good terms, when he closed the Bozeman Trail through Wyoming to prospectors heading north to the Montana gold fields by engineering the decisive Fetterman Fight on December 21, 1866. The aftermath of this battle and two others from the so-called Red Cloud's War was the Treaty of Fort Laramie in 1868. In this treaty the Lakotas were assigned an enormous reservation in Dakota Territory, and their hunting territory in Wyoming's buffalo-rich Powder River country was recognized as unceded. The Lakotas subsequently lost the Black Hills in 1877, partly in retaliation for their victory in the Battle of the Little Bighorn, and had their reservation divided and drastically reduced in size in 1889.

Red Cloud's influence in Lakota affairs, which was dominant for a quarter of a century, was diminished as a result of the Ghost Dance, the chief ceremony of an Indian religious movement Red Cloud eventually opposed, and one that ultimately led to the Wounded Knee Massacre on December 29, 1890. The venerable leader died on the Pine Ridge Reservation in South Dakota in 1909 at the age of eighty-eight. Although Red Cloud has been accused of cruelty in tribal warfare during his younger years and of stubbornness in his negotiations with federal authorities during his older years, his unwavering political and diplomatic leadership on behalf of his people cannot be ignored. Indeed, he demonstrated unusual dedication in his efforts to maintain those provisions in the Treaty of Fort Laramie that he insisted should be honored.

Robert W. Larson
Denver, Colorado

Goodyear, Frank H., III. *Red Cloud: Photographs of a Lakota Chief.* Lincoln: University of Nebraska Press, 2003. Larson, Robert W. *Red Cloud: Warrior-Statesman of the Lakota Sioux.* Norman: University of Oklahoma Press, 1997. Paul, R. Eli, ed. *Autobiography of Red Cloud: War Leader of the Oglalas.* Helena: Montana Historical Society Press, 1997.

His mother, Walks-as-She-Thinks, was an Oglala, another of the seven Lakota tribes. When Lone Man died of alcoholism, a sad result of the early commerce with white traders and trappers, Red Cloud, along with his brother and sister, went to live with his mother's people, who were then under the leadership of an Oglala chief named Smoke.

In 1834, when the Oglalas, led by the domineering Sioux leader Bull Bear, were drawn southward to the North Platte River valley by the commercial possibilities of a trading post, which later became Fort Laramie, Red Cloud, a thirteen-year-old member of Smoke's band, joined this important migration. For more than two decades, Smoke's people frequently encamped near Fort Laramie, allowing Red Cloud to learn more about the ways of the whites than most tribal leaders in the Great Plains. Red Cloud also became a great warrior during these years, killing his first enemy in combat at the age of sixteen. As a result of his participation in battles with enemy tribes, such as the Crows, Pawnees, Utes, and Shoshones, Red Cloud allegedly earned eighty coups, a record never matched by any of his tribal rivals.

Red Cloud became prominent in political affairs when he got involved in a bitter brawl in 1841 that resulted in Bull Bear's death; in his autobiography he took personal credit for firing the fatal shot. He later gained the respect and fear of whites,

RED RIVER RESISTANCE

In 1869 the Métis of Red River, led by Louis Riel, formed a provisional government to stop the Canadian annexation of Rupert's Land. This territory, encompassing most of today's Prairie Provinces, was under Hudson's Bay Company rule and was scheduled to be transferred to Canada in 1869. During the negotiations between the company, the British government, and the Canadian government for the transfer of sovereignty, no one consulted the Métis, who were the vast majority of the twelve thousand residents in the Red River Settlement in the present-day province of Manitoba. Worried about their status in the new Dominion, the Métis took matters into their own hands.

During the summer of 1869, the Métis, comprised

of English-speaking Protestant "mixed-bloods" and French-speaking Catholic Métis, held several public meetings to determine how to respond to the proposed transfer. Two competing factions emerged. One, led by William Dease, argued that the Métis should form a provisional government and negotiate with Canada on the basis of their Aboriginal rights. Louis Riel and the Catholic clergy led a second faction, who argued that the transfer represented the annexation of Red River Settlement by Protestant Ontario and threatened the religious rights of the Catholic Métis. Controlling the largest army, and having the Catholic Church on his side, Riel triumphed in this power struggle. In early November 1869 he seized Upper Fort Garry and effective control of the settlement.

Riel and his Métis supporters suppressed internal dissension in the settlement by imprisoning dozens of Métis opponents and Canadians, and then forged a consensus by calling a number of representative conventions. In January 1870 Red River residents elected a representative provisional government to negotiate the terms of their entry into the Dominion. The resulting Manitoba Act of 1870 created the province of Manitoba, guaranteed the property rights of the Métis, provided for bilingual institutions and denominational schools to protect the interests of the Catholic Church, and granted 1.4 million acres of land to Métis children.

The Manitoba Act and Manitoba's entry into the Dominion was a victory for the Red River Métis that Riel was unable to enjoy. During the Resistance, which lasted from October 1869 until August of 1870, Riel's provisional government had executed an Ontario Orangeman by the name of Thomas Scott. This act made it politically impossible for the Canadian government to grant Riel's government an unconditional amnesty for actions taken during the Resistance. Riel fled to the United States in August 1870 when Canadian troops arrived in Manitoba.

Gerhard J. Ens
University of Alberta

Ens, Gerhard J. "Prologue to the Red River Resistance: Pre-liminal Politics and the Triumph of Riel." *Journal of the Canadian Historical Association* 5 (1994): 111–23. Stanley, George F. G. *Louis Riel*. Toronto: Ryerson Press, 1963.

RELIGION

To generalize about the religious dimension of Plains Indigenous cultures is to ignore the distinctive elements of the numerous individual societies that once flourished in the region. Yet there are sufficient common elements to warrant some summary statements. Location was the paramount factor in determining both cultural and religious style. Those who clustered in villages along the Missouri River and its tributaries in the eastern Plains were oriented more toward agriculture, especially cultivation of corn. What later interpreters would identify as religious rites thus tended to focus on fertility, cementing the close relationship between people and the land. Those to the west, approaching the Rocky Mountains, where a semi-arid climate precluded agriculture, were more dispersed and migratory, and bison hunting was central to their way of life. Among these peoples, vision quests, which brought individuals into contact with supernatural power, thereby increasing their prowess as hunters while connecting them to powerful mythic figures, were basic to the religious beliefs and practices. Sacred sites, such as Bear Butte in present-day South Dakota were, and are, particularly important for such quests.

The case of the Sioux is instructive, although by no means representative of all the peoples of the Plains. Traditionally from what is today part of Wisconsin and Minnesota, the western Sioux by the mid–seventeenth century were pushed by the Ojibwas and drawn by the bison toward the Great Plains. As the Sioux adapted to Plains life, they moved toward dominance because they quickly incorporated the horse (brought first to the Southern Plains by the Spanish) into their culture, and agricultural pursuits gave way to bison hunting. Adaptation in the religious sphere followed, as the concern for fertility was superseded by concern for success in hunting, and vision quests assumed greater importance. One well-known consequence was the emergence of the Sun Dance, an annual rite symbolically recreating and renewing the cosmos in order to assure the well-being of the people. The role of shamans, with their ability to call on supernatural power to effect both healing and success in hunting and other tribal endeavors, grew in importance.

External forces, such as increased migration of non-Native Americans into the Plains, government policies that were frequently inimical to tribal life, and Christian proselytizing, spurred other changes. We should here note three currents that had significant long-term consequences: increased efforts among Christian groups to establish missions among the tribes; the rise to prominence of the Ghost Dance; and the development of peyotism.

Three examples of mission work may be taken as examples. Earliest are the missions among Native Americans started by the Spanish. By the mid–eighteenth century the Spanish had sent around one hundred expeditions into what is now Texas; many included the establishment of missions designed both to convert and, ostensibly, to civilize

Natives by organizing them into something akin to agricultural colonies. The earliest, founded by Franciscans in 1682, lay just outside the Plains near El Paso. Although these missions often served to protect their Native inhabitants from even worse exploitation by the Spanish conquerors, they still disrupted tribal life and represented the imposition of an alien religious style. These missions demonstrate a characteristic that was to mark similar enterprises throughout the Plains, namely the missionary as both friend, who offered security and protection from outside invaders, and foe, whose very presence undermined traditional tribal ways.

To the north, Belgian priest Pierre-Jean De Smet was one of the most influential of the early Catholic missionaries. De Smet's efforts to raise money and call attention to mission needs, beginning in 1838, took him from the Potawatomis in Iowa to the Columbia and Willamette river valleys of the Pacific Northwest. De Smet stands out as well for his genuine appreciation of Native ways, making him repeatedly a valued mediator between tribal peoples and white settlers who encroached on their lands. Twenty years before De Smet began his labors, Joseph-Norbert Provencher assumed leadership of mission work on the Red River of the North, intent on providing spiritual leadership for the French Canadians already there, as well as establishing agricultural colonies and schools for the Indigenous peoples. By the 1830s numerous mission stations were operating, many later sustained through assistance from the French Order of Oblates of Mary Immaculate. Provencher was instrumental in persuading both the Oblates and the Grey Nuns to undertake mission work in western Canada. Also by the 1830s, the Anglican Church Missionary Society, hoping to minister to British Canadians and Native Americans alike, was extending its work from its base along the Red River Valley of the North. Most of these endeavors share another feature that was to mark much mission work, namely the establishment of schools that would provide Native Americans with something like a Western-style education. Even here, however, there was a paternalistic assumption of great import, for many harbored the conviction that education would "civilize" or impress Western ways on the Indigenous inhabitants, rendering them easier to control and more amenable to conversion to Christianity.

This conviction comes into sharp relief in the third example, the work of Stephen Return Riggs, an agent of the American Board of Foreign Missions from 1837 until his death in 1883, who translated both the Bible and secular works into the Dakota language of the Santee Sioux. Riggs was convinced that education would bring a "higher" standard of living to the tribes by preparing them for participation in "Christian civilization." His work, however, also illustrates another long-term impact of the missionary enterprise. In 1862, when armed conflict erupted between the Sioux and American forces, many of Riggs's converts were loath to participate in the fighting. When they, too, suffered reprisals, many of the Sioux believed that white culture had so destroyed the supernatural powers that once shaped tribal life that conversions to Christianity, the religion of the apparently more powerful white culture, increased.

The Ghost Dance, a fusion of millenarian hopes and rituals uniting the living and the dead, began as a revival of Wodziwob's Round Dance of 1870. A Paiute shaman named Wovoka, who lived on the Walker River Reservation in Nevada, had participated in the 1870 movement and had a vision that gave birth to a new revitalization movement that spread quickly to the Plains tribes during the winter of 1888–89. Wovoka's vision endowed him with a message promising the ultimate restoration of tribal integrity at a time when the cohesion of tribal cultures was increasingly challenged by external forces. Wovoka called for the renewal of traditional tribal mores through the practice of trance dances in which supernatural empowerment would come to the faithful. Short Bull and Kicking Bear, Lakota representatives of the Sioux, visited Wovoka and carried the message back to their people. The Ghost Dance also took firm root among the Canadian Sioux, where the movement was known as New Tidings.

In an effort to exert control over the Plains peoples, the American government had banned ritual enactment of the Sun Dance in 1883. The Ghost Dance appeared to be even more of a threat, as it brought renewed solidarity and hope to the tribal cultures. It also increased militant resistance to further external domination, especially among the Sioux who believed that their "ghost shirts" were bulletproof. The massacre at Wounded Knee Creek in 1890 brought these millennial expectations and the hope for revitalized tribal life to a sudden halt for many Sioux, but Wovoka's religion persisted among the Oklahoma tribes, Canadian Native peoples, and the Great Basin peoples well into the twentieth century.

Among the Canadian Crees, the Ghost Dance had a rather different character, reflecting perhaps the generally less violent nature of tribal relations with the Canadian government. In this context, the Ghost Dance served more as a means for the Prairie tribes to form a united front in their dealings with the government. However, the Riel Rebellion of 1885, which was spurred primarily by the Métis but also counted several Cree bands among its participants, essentially thwarted efforts to maintain this united front.

By the dawn of the twentieth century the disintegration of traditional ways among the Plains tribes was evident. Confined to reservations and increasingly dependent on government annuity payments and assistance from Christian missionaries, who rarely appreciated the richness of Native American religiosity, the tribal peoples of the Plains faced what seemed a bleak future. Some sought to return to traditional practices such as the Sun Dance. Others moved toward assimilation into white culture, manifested in part through the adoption or adaptation of practices associated with Christianity. Yet others hoped to revitalize Native American life through promoting a shared "Indian" consciousness. Peyotism, regarded by many as the most important twentieth-century religious development among Native American peoples, fused aspects of all three adjustments.

Long part of tribal religiosity in Mexico where the peyote cactus grows, peyote rites became part of Kiowa and Comanche life around 1870. Peyotism spread rather slowly, usually making its way into tribal life when its advocates, such as Quanah Parker, traveled from tribe to tribe promoting it. Administered under strict ceremonial guidelines, peyote generates visions that often combine Christian symbols with traditional ones, for example, by linking Christ with the Great Spirit. Peyotism also encouraged a return to traditional ethics that would simultaneously renew tribal integrity and allow more peaceful accommodation with white society.

In the United States, the Native American Church, in which peyote rituals are central, was first legally chartered in Oklahoma in 1918. However, as the larger culture developed increasing concern about use of controlled hallucinogenic substances, sporadic efforts were made to quash the practice, culminating first in a U.S. Supreme Court case in 1990 that upheld the right of states to prohibit the practice, and then in federal legislation enacted in the wake of that court decision that protected the practice. Despite the apprehension of the larger culture, peyotism remains one of the most vital means for sustaining a Native American cultural and religious identity. It is estimated that the Native American Church has two hundred thousand members.

Charles H. Lippy
University of Tennessee at Chattanooga

Bowden, Henry Warner. *American Indians and Christian Missions.* Chicago: University of Chicago Press, 1981. Irwin, Lee, ed. *Native American Spirituality: A Critical Reader.* Lincoln: University of Nebraska Press, 2000. Lippy, Charles H., and Peter W. Wil-

liams, eds. *Encyclopedia of the American Religious Experience.* New York: Charles Scribners Sons, 1988.

REPATRIATION

Since the 1970s Native Americans have sought the repatriation of their ancestors' skeletal remains, burial goods, and sacred objects from museums and laboratories. Part of a worldwide Indigenous movement, Native Americans contend that these institutions acquired and retained the remains and objects in violation of the rights of the dead, the tribe, and the sacred. In response, some scholars maintain that the remains provide an important scientific and educational resource and that treatment of the materials has been respectful.

The entire repatriation movement may have started on the fringe of the Great Plains in 1971. An Ihanktonwan (Yankton Sioux) woman, Maria Pearson, protested the differential treatment of Native American remains buried at the edge of a non-Indian, pioneer cemetery near Glenwood, Iowa, that was to be relocated for highway construction. While the non-Indian remains were immediately reburied, the Native remains were taken to the state archeologist's office for study. A court order, Governor Robert Ray's intervention, and substantial media coverage eventually allowed the remains to be reburied.

The case prompted attention by the American Indian Movement (AIM) and the International Indian Treaty Council, which took action against archeologists and their excavations in several locations. Digs in Minnesota and Iowa were disrupted by AIM members. However, other pressing matters, such as the takeover at Alcatraz and Wounded Knee, had turned the attention of AIM elsewhere.

In 1978 the discovery of the massacred remains of nearly five hundred individuals from the prehistoric Crow Creek Village along the Missouri River in South Dakota drew international attention when archeologists and the Army Corps of Engineers–Omaha District agreed to rebury the remains after study. After the remains were reburied in 1981, many archeologists and human osteologists were critical of the agreement, contending that new techniques would have allowed substantially more information to be gleaned from the remains if they had been curated for eventual restudy.

In 1982 the International Indian Treaty Council again turned its attention to repatriation. One of its members, Jan Hammil, determined that organizations, with the Smithsonian Institution as the primary example, should be pressured to return remains for reburial. She also pressured the Society for American Archaeology, the primary organization of professional archeologists in the United States, not to pass a resolution against repatriation.

This struggle continued until passage of major federal repatriation laws in 1989 and 1990.

During this time, several states debated or enacted laws dealing with repatriation. The most controversial case in the Plains involved the Pawnees' efforts to seek the return of skeletons and grave goods curated in the Nebraska State Historical Society (NSHS). In 1988 Lawrence Goodfox Jr. of the Pawnee Tribe of Oklahoma issued several requests to the NSHS for the repatriation of remains and burial offerings long held by the society. NSHS executive director James Hanson refused to respond to the tribe's request, and a long, nationally visible battle ensued. The Pawnees joined forces with other Nebraska tribes and the Native American Rights Fund to seek legislative relief that would force the NSHS to repatriate the remains. In 1989 the coalition eventually saw passage in the Nebraska legislature of the Unmarked Human Burial Sites and Skeletal Remains Protection Act (LB-340). The law required Nebraska public museums to return all tribally identifiable skeletal remains and burial offerings to tribes that requested them for reburial.

Reburial opponents, led by the NSHS, campaigned to derail the legislation. Even after enactment, the NSHS opposed return of remains from the more distant past, in which determining tribal affiliation is often difficult. Eventually, agreements between tribes and the NSHS allowed the return of many more remains than had been originally sought.

While the Pawnees' campaign was going on, the Omahas were working with Harvard University's Peabody Museum to seek the return of Umon'hon'ti, their sacred pole. In 1888, under pressure to abandon their beliefs and accept Christianity, the Omaha tribe had turned Umon'hon'ti and other sacred objects, including the ceremonial war pipes and the sacred shell, over to ethnographer Alice Fletcher for safekeeping. Fletcher transferred them to the Peabody Museum. After an extraordinary effort on the part of the Omahas to reclaim their objects, the Peabody returned the pole in 1989 and has since returned other sacred objects.

In 1989 the World Archaeological Congress met at the University of South Dakota for a forum titled "Archeological Ethics and the Treatment of the Dead." Archeologists and Indigenous people from twenty countries and twenty-seven Native American nations debated the repatriation issue, eventually passing the Vermillion Accord. This accord influenced the passage of several provincial laws in Canada and ethics codes for both the World Archaeological Congress and the Australian Archaeological Association.

In 1989 and 1990, after lengthy negotiations between the Native American Rights Fund, the National Congress of American Indians, the Society for American Archaeology, and other interested parties, the U.S. Congress passed two important federal laws. Targeting the Smithsonian, the National Museum of the American Indian Act (Public Law 101-185) required that the Smithsonian inventory its collection of skeletal remains so that tribes could claim them for repatriation. The Smithsonian has since returned human remains to Plains tribes, including the Pawnees, Cheyennes, and Wahpeton Sioux. In 1990 the Native American Graves Protection and Repatriation Act (Public Law 101-601) extended the earlier law to all federal agencies or institutions with any level of federal involvement. The act requires return of human remains, grave goods, and items of cultural patrimony. It also demands consultation with tribes and requires that a broader range of information, such as oral tradition, be considered when documenting cultural affiliation of remains. After several years of drafting operative regulations, the law has generally worked, although details remain to be worked out. Demonstrations of cultural affiliation have proved contentious for remains from the distant past, and another key issue is the treatment of remains found on private land.

Larry J. Zimmerman
Minnesota Historical Society

Echo-Hawk, Walter, ed. "Repatriation of American Indian Remains." Special issue, *American Indian Culture and Research Journal* 16 (1992). Echo-Hawk, Walter, and Roger Echo-Hawk. *Battlefields and Burial Grounds: The Indian Struggle to Protect Ancestral Graves in the United States.* Minneapolis: Lerner Publications, 1994. Fine-Dare, Kathleen S. *Grave Injustice: The American Indian Repatriation Movement and NAGPRA.* Lincoln: University of Nebraska Press, 2002. Mihesuah, Devon, ed. *Repatriation Reader: Who Owns American Indian Remains?* Lincoln: University of Nebraska Press, 2000. Ridington, Robin, and Dennis Hastings. *Blessing for a Long Time: The Sacred Pole of the Omaha Tribe.* Lincoln: University of Nebraska Press, 1997.

RESERVATIONS

Reservations in the Great Plains are territorial units retained by Native American tribes, either as remnants of their ancestral lands, or as designated areas assigned after removal—from both within and outside the region—following the cession of homelands to the United States. They are places where tribal and federal jurisdictions prevail, to the general exclusion of state jurisdiction, though the legal boundaries here are constantly shifting with new decisions in the courts. Great Plains reservations are generally poor places, mineral resources and revenues from gaming notwithstanding. But they are also treasured homelands where ancestors are buried, sacred sites revered, and cultures preserved; for their Native American residents, they are the surviving geographic connection between past and present.

The first reservations in the Plains, other than the relatively large areas set aside for relocated Indians such as the Delawares in the 1820s and 1830s, were created after the Kansas-Nebraska Act of 1854 opened up the area to European American settlement. Because of this incursion, the idea of a separate, extraterritorial "Indian Country" in the Plains, which had prevailed since 1830, became impractical. Instead, Plains Indians would be restricted to small areas recognized in treaties, laws, or executive orders as belonging to them. The remaining homelands would then be available for resettlement by European Americans. On the reservations, Native Americans would be placed under great pressure to assimilate—to take out individual farms, or allotments, to learn English, and to convert to Christianity. When this occurred, theoretically, the Native Americans would simply merge into the larger society, and any additional reservation lands over and above their allotments would also pass to European Americans. In this sense, then, and despite the recognition in treaties of Indian rights to the lands, reservations were seen by the United States in the mid–nineteenth century as only a temporary expedient until Native Americans assimilated. But Native Americans in the Plains, and elsewhere in the United States, did not disappear through assimilation, or through war and disease. Thus, reservations have remained a significant component of the region's identity.

By 1860 the Indians of eastern Nebraska (e.g., the Pawnees) and eastern Kansas (e.g., the Kaws) had sold their remaining homelands to the United States, retaining only small reservations. In the following decades reservations were created successively west, north, and south (in Indian Territory) from the initial area of European American advance, as tribes, under varying degrees of coercion, were forced to cede their lands. In 1868, for example, at the Treaty of Fort Laramie, the Crows surrendered thirty-eight million acres of their hunting grounds in what is now Montana and Wyoming and agreed to a reservation in south-central Montana. In 1874 and 1888 the Blackfeet relinquished about twenty-seven million acres of land in Montana and took out a reservation where the Plains meets the Rocky Mountains at the forty-ninth parallel. By the latter date, all Plains tribes had been restricted to reservations.

Despite the "recognized" or "reserved" title under which the Plains tribes hold their reservations, their size and the Indians' sovereignty on them have been eroded almost from the beginning. Those early reservations in Kansas and Nebraska were quickly surrounded and coveted by settlers. By 1881

the Kaws, Pawnees, Poncas, and Otoe-Missourias had all been removed to Indian Territory and their reservations thrown open to resettlement. Even when original reservations were retained, as in the cases of the Crows and Blackfeet, the Indians were forced by settlers' demands, and by their own poverty, to sell portions to the United States in return for subsistence. The Crow Indian Reservation, for example, was significantly reduced by cessions in 1882 and 1892, and the size of the Blackfeet Reservation was almost halved in 1895.

Even greater losses from Plains reservations occurred after passage of the General Allotment (Dawes) Act of 1887. At various times thereafter, Indians were allocated individual allotments (generally 160 acres), and the portions of reservations remaining after that allocation were declared "surplus lands" that were opened to European American settlement. In 1904, on the Devils Lake Sioux Reservation in North Dakota, for example, 135,824 acres were allotted to 1,193 Indians, leaving 92,144 acres of surplus lands to be sold to settlers at $1.25 an acre. Subsequently, following a government trust period, many of the allotments were also sold to settlers. As a consequence, non-Indians now own 75 percent of the Devils Lake Sioux Reservation. This is a characteristic pattern on many Plains reservations, which are a "checkerboard" of Indian and non-Indian lands, greatly complicating jurisdiction and compromising tribal sovereignty.

On a map of Indian reservations in the United States, the Northern Great Plains stands out. There are still many Native Americans in Oklahoma, of course, as the successor to Indian Territory, but with the exception of the Osage Reservation, all the reservations were dissolved in the years leading up to statehood. (Many Indian groups in Oklahoma own tribal lands, and some refer to their lands as reservations, but for census purposes they are designated as Tribal Jurisdiction Statistical Areas.) There are no reservations in the Texas Plains, where, after statehood in 1846, the state controlled land disbursement and made no room for the Indigenous inhabitants. There are relatively few (seven) remaining reservations in Kansas and Nebraska, the result of Indian removals in the nineteenth century. But north of the Nebraska–South Dakota border, reservations abound (there are seventeen of them), and most are large. The 1,771,082-acre Pine Ridge Reservation, for example, with its tribally enrolled population of 17,775 in 1995, is one of the largest reservations in the country. It is also one of the poorest places in the country, with 60 percent of families living below the poverty level in 1990. Even on the 2,235,095-acre Crow Indian Reservation in Montana, with its rich resources of coal, oil, and gas, per capita income in 1995 was only $4,243 and unemployment stood at 44 percent.

Despite the promises of the United States, spelled out in treaties and agreements, the status of Plains reservations remains insecure, especially because of state intervention. In an important case in 1981, *Montana v. United States*, the U.S. Supreme Court ruled that the Crow tribe does not have the right to regulate nonmember hunting and fishing on reservation lands that are not owned by, or held in trust for, the tribe. The only exceptions are if the activity threatens tribal integrity or if consensual agreements have been made. Similarly, in federal district court in North Dakota in 1993, the Devils Lake Sioux were held to have the right to contract for electrical services only on lands owned by, or held in trust for, the tribe, which meant only about one-quarter of the area of the reservation. These decisions indicate that the geographic extent of Indian sovereignty is being moved from the exterior boundaries of the reservation to those areas within the reservation held in trust by the tribe or by members of the tribe.

Yet, in other ways, the Indian presence on Plains reservations is resurgent. In a region where rural populations are rapidly thinning, Indian reservations stand out as areas of significant population growth. Birthrates are higher than average, and death rates, though still high, have fallen. Moreover, Indians are returning to reservations to fill jobs created by gaming and other economic development. New revenues mean that reservation lands once alienated can be reclaimed. Far from disappearing, Native Americans and their reservation homelands are reasserting themselves on the landscape of the Great Plains.

David J. Wishart
University of Nebraska–Lincoln

Marino, Cesare. "Reservations." In *Native America in the Twentieth Century: An Encyclopedia*, edited by Mary B. Davis. New York: Garland, 1996. Royce, Charles C. Indian Land Cessions in the United States. *18th Annual Report of the Bureau of American Ethnology, 1896–97*. Washington DC: Government Printing Office, 1899. Velarde Tiller, Veronica E. *American Indian Reservations and Trust Areas*. Albuquerque: Tiller Research, 1996.

RESERVATION TOWNS

The U.S. federal government, railroads, traders, tribal governments, individual Indian proprietors, and missionaries all took part in the planning of towns on Native American reservations in the Great Plains. Prior to allotment, reservation towns were often located on rivers for trading purposes, near missions, or near Bureau of Indian Affairs agencies. As railroads extended through reservations and lands were opened to non-Indians through "surplus" lands acts, new towns were incorporated along railroads and in central places on reservations. Some reservation towns grew haphazardly until incorporation, when gridiron plans were superimposed on the landscape. Others were planned prior to settlement, again commonly laying streets in the four cardinal directions. Regardless of their planning, reservation towns serve as bases for both Indian and non-Indian communities throughout the Great Plains today.

The functions of reservation towns vary from being the seat of tribal governments to being central places for rural Indian and non-Indian populations and bases for economic development. Some towns are largely populated by Indians and house the tribal governments and Bureau of Indian Affairs agencies. For example, Agency Village, Lake Traverse Reservation, South Dakota, was the site of the old Bureau of Indian Affairs agency. After a surplus lands act opened the reservation in 1892, the Bureau of Indian Affairs moved the agency to Sisseton, South Dakota, six miles north of the old agency. Nonetheless, the tribe continued to hold its annual *wacipi* at the old agency site. In the 1960s the tribal government moved its headquarters back to the old agency and named the town Agency Village. This move enabled the tribe to create its own place on the reservation separate from the town of Sisseton, which was populated largely by non-Indians by the 1960s. Today, Agency Village houses one of the tribe's gaming operations, the tribal community college, the wacipi arena, a tribal elementary and secondary school, the offices of the tribal government, and many low-income housing units.

Other reservation towns, especially on the western Great Plains, are populated by both Indians and non-Indians and provide goods and services to vast rural areas. Eagle Butte, South Dakota, houses the tribal government and Bureau of Indian Affairs agency for the Cheyenne River Sioux Tribe. The town provides goods and services to people within the 2.8-million-acre reservation. The landscape of the town reflects the presence of the tribal government, with building after building on the main street displaying the seal of the tribal government. The tribal government owns the telephone authority, the cable company, a hotel, a grocery store, and a small strip mall that service both Indian and non-Indian populations within the reservation.

Reservation towns that are close to major Plains population centers are likely to house casinos today. The economy of Flandreau, South Dakota, a town of 2,400 residents, mostly non-Indians, has become increasingly tribally driven and dependent upon gaming. At the southwestern corner of the town is the Flandreau Santee Sioux's small reservation and large casino. The Royal River Casino has expanded in recent years and now employs some three hundred people. The proximity of Flandreau to Sioux Falls, South Dakota, has enabled the casino to achieve some level of success. Through this success, the tribe has funneled money back into the Flandreau community, thus changing this place through economic development and grants.

Like most Plains small towns, those on reservations have a Main Street, often perpendicular to railroad tracks. The tribal government and Bureau of Indian Affairs offices are located on or near the main street, as are other major tribal services. Low-income housing provided by the tribal housing authority, Housing and Urban Development, or Habitat for Humanity is located in developments on the outskirts of the typical reservation town.

Erin Hogan Fouberg
South Dakota State University

Bays, Brad A. *Townsite Settlement and Dispossession in the Cherokee Nation, 1866–1907*. New York: Garland, 1998. McCormick, Kathleen. "In the Clutch of the Casinos." *Planning* 63 (1997): 4–6. Reps, John W. *Cities of the American West: A History of Frontier Urban Planning*. Princeton NJ: Princeton University Press, 1979.

RESERVES

Indian (First Nations) reserves on the Canadian Prairies were the outcome of a series of treaties negotiated between the new Dominion of Canada and Indian leaders whose peoples had occupied the Prairies for generations. Canada's top priority, when it acquired Rupert's Land from the Hudson's Bay Company in 1870, was to extinguish Indian title to the land and to stabilize the Indian population in anticipation of white agricultural settlement. The Indians' priority was to preserve their way of life in the face of inevitable changes on the Canadian Prairies. Consequently, government officials and Indian leaders held very different views on the purpose of the treaties and reserves.

Treaties numbered 1 through 7 were negotiated between 1871 and 1877 and covered the Prairies of the present-day provinces of Manitoba, Saskatchewan, and Alberta. Treaties 1 and 2 were similar in that each Indian band would receive an inalienable reserve of land using a ratio of 160 acres per family of five and an annuity of $15 per family. Liquor sales were prohibited, and schools would be built by the government on the reserves. Gifts of livestock, farming equipment, and clothing, as well as hunting and fishing rights, were mentioned verbally during negotiations but were not written into the treaties. Subsequently, these two treaties were amended in 1875 to bring them into line with Treaty 3, which set precedents for later treaties. Its terms were: 640 acres per family of five, annuities of $5 per person, a gratuity

of $12, a suit of clothes every three years, salaries for chiefs and band officers, plus gifts of medals and flags. Hunting and fishing rights in unsettled areas were formally acknowledged, and reserves were to be supplied with livestock, farming equipment, and seed. Agricultural instruction would be provided by the government. The only subsequent change was the provision in Treaty 6 of a "medicine chest"—a provision that was then extended to the other treaty areas. Provision was also made for American Sioux (Lakota) refugees from the Battle of the Little Bighorn: they received reserves based on 80 acres per family of five but no annuities, as they had no lands in Canada to cede. The size of all reserves was based on population levels during the 1870s; no provision was made for subsequent population expansion.

Although the government's declared policy was assimilation, in practice it was segregation. The very concept of a reserve is one of segregation. Indians were supposed to select the location of their reserves, but government agents often intervened and clustered the reserves to facilitate bureaucratic administration. In 1882 all the southern reserves except those in southern Alberta were moved north of the Canadian Pacific Railroad to avoid further cross-border raids with American bands. Agents were to terminate the Indians' roaming over the Prairies, to teach them farming, and to settle them on reserves where they would not interfere with white settlement. After the North-West Rebellion of 1885, agents increasingly took control of affairs on the reserves as the power of Indian chiefs was reduced and Indians became wards of the government. In the area of education the government's practice was indeed assimilationist. Schools on the reserves were run by Christian missionaries who sought to "civilize" and Christianize Indian children by stamping out Aboriginal cultural influences. These practices worked against the Indian ideal of preserving as much of their culture as they could on their reserves.

Refusal of the reserve system was scarcely an option for Prairie Province Indians in the 1870s. A smallpox epidemic in the early 1870s, followed by rapid disappearance of the bison, reduced Indian bands to starvation and dependence on government rations for survival. Their plight was desperate by 1880, and despite the pleas of several chiefs such as Big Bear, who argued for Indian unity and renegotiation with the government, many accepted the government's terms. Big Bear even favored clustering of reserves as a step toward creating Indian solidarity and preservation of Indian culture. But even their hunting and fishing rights along the northern margins of the Prairies were ignored, as agents sought to restrict Indian mobility and to seclude them on their reserves. The Indians' distinctive way of life was subjected to the crushing pressures of starvation: sheer survival was possible only on the government's terms. Nevertheless, Indians retained significant elements of their cultures on these small, inalienable reserves of land that had been set aside for them in the early 1880s.

Major changes to the reserve system came after World War II, in which Indians fought bravely in the Canadian armed forces. Veterans refused to accept second-class citizenship, and a revised Indian Act in 1951 gave Indian bands a measure of control for the first time. Although the policy of assimilation continued, Indians were no longer wards of government but were to advance to full rights as citizens. Indians now determined who belonged to Indian bands and who could live on reserves. The Indian Act of 1876 had declared that only "status" Indians could reside permanently on reserves, and the government reserved the right to determine who was a "status Indian." Men who lived off the reserve could lose their status, and the position of women was even more precarious, especially those who married non-Indians. Resolution of these issues now became a matter for Indian bands, although the troublesome problem of women's status was not finally resolved until 1982, when many women were reinstated as band members.

Other changes came more easily. Schools were secularized during the 1960s, and by 1970 Indian bands began to take direct control of education. Bands also took financial control and increasingly policed their reserves—public consumption of alcohol, for example, was permitted in 1970. By the 1980s a pan-Indian movement had been established, which linked Indian reserves on the Prairies with other reserves across Canada, and, as the drive toward Aboriginal self-government was launched, Big Bear's dream of a century earlier became a possibility.

The Canadian government had been determined to treat Indians better than the United States had. Those lofty goals were never achieved, partly through lack of commitment by the government in Ottawa and partly through internal contradictions in policy, but mostly because Indians' wishes were ignored. The result was a marginalization of Canadian Prairie Indians through segregation similar to that of their American cousins for more than a century.

D. Aidan McQuillan
University of Toronto

Canada Royal Commission on Aboriginal Peoples. *For Seven Generations: An Information Legacy of the Royal Commission on Aboriginal Peoples.* Ottawa: Libraxus, 1997. Dickason, Olive P. *Canada's First Nations: A History of Founding Peoples from Earliest Times.* Toronto: McClelland and Stewart, 1992. McQuillan,

D. Aidan. "Creation of Indian Reserves on the Canadian Prairies, 1870–1885." *Geographical Review* 70 (1980): 379–96.

RIGGS, ROLLIE LYNN (1899–1954)

One of Oklahoma's finest playwrights and poets, confidant to Joan Crawford and Bette Davis, and critically acclaimed contemporary of Eugene O'Neill and Tennessee Williams, Rollie Lynn Riggs was an enigma to most who knew him during his short life. He spent his professional career exploring the unique character and spirit of Oklahoma and its precursor, Indian Territory, while shrouding his personal life from public scrutiny. As an acculturated allotment-era Cherokee and a closeted gay man in the first part of the twentieth century, Riggs traveled across the country and the world in search of both artistic acclaim and security. The latter eluded him to the end of his life.

Born in Indian Territory on August 31, 1899, near present-day Claremore, Oklahoma, Riggs was educated briefly at the University of Oklahoma in Norman and lived at various times in Santa Fe, Paris, Chicago, New York, and Hollywood. His poetry and plays focus almost exclusively on the land and people of rural Oklahoma, and he wrote with a dedication to respectfully and accurately representing the speech, philosophies, and cultures of his youth. His poetry follows in much the same fashion but also includes deeply reflective and melancholy elegies and poems of alienation and solitude. His most famous play, *Green Grow the Lilacs* (1929), became the model in 1943 for the Rodgers and Hammerstein musical *Oklahoma!* His only play to focus on Indian issues was also his favorite: *The Cherokee Night* (1930). Riggs died in New York City on June 29, 1954, of cancer.

Daniel Heath Justice
University of Toronto

Braunlich, Phyllis Cole. *Haunted by Home: The Life and Letters of Lynn Riggs.* Norman: University of Oklahoma Press, 1988.

ROCK ART

Rock art in the Great Plains consists of both petroglyphs (markings that have been pecked, scratched, incised, or abraded on natural rock surfaces) and pictographs (painting on nonportable rock surfaces). Petroforms (sometimes called geomorphs, in which large stones or boulders have been used to outline anthropomorphic, zoomorphic, or geometric forms) are found primarily in the northeastern U.S. Plains and southern Saskatchewan. Petroglyphs and/or pictographs have been recorded in all states of the Great Plains. Rock art was noted in the journals of European American explorers, but it was not until the 1930s that petroglyphs and pictographs were thoroughly documented and interpreted for professional publication.

Rock art, southeastern Colorado, Fort Carson Military Reservation

The placement of petroglyphs and pictographs is highly variable in the Great Plains. In the Northern Plains rock art is found in and around major geologic uplifts, especially where rock surfaces are exposed on canyon walls and in rock shelters. On the open Plains rock art is found on sandstone or limestone where streams have cut the underlying bedrock and on boulders on talus slopes and hogbacks. Petroglyphs on isolated boulders also occur along the Missouri River in the Dakotas, in southern Alberta and Saskatchewan, and in central Texas and southern Oklahoma. Rock art in the Central Plains is rarer; however, protohistoric and early historic Native Americans used rock shelters intensively in the Dakota sandstone of the Smoky Hills region of north-central Kansas, where they depicted representational images. Native Americans also made petroglyphs on sandstone bluffs in central Oklahoma. In the Northern Plains some rock art is believed to be associated with bison jumps and kill sites. It is generally acknowledged, however, that in prehistoric social environments the role of rock art as a means of communication varied with its social context. The places where it was produced are usually understood to have had special meanings and functioned, along with myths and stories, to maintain social cohesion.

Despite difficulties in the accurate dating of rock art, it is known that some of the oldest rock art in the Plains is found in the Black Hills of western South Dakota, eastern Wyoming, and the Wyoming Basin. These areas have rock art thought to predate 10,000 BP and also contain sites ranging through the Archaic period (7500–2000 BP). The art is primarily on exposed vertical cliffs and at the base of canyon walls. Zoomorphic figures, usually wapiti (elk) or mountain sheep, are the predominant representations. Some depictions of hunting are found, such as game nets or corrals and the spearing of animals by humans. Some of the most heavily varnished petroglyphs depict apparent hoof prints, vulvas, and grooves. Pictographs

depicting orange to light red finger lines and handprints in central Montana are believed to be more than three thousand years old.

Archaic hunters and gatherers in southern Texas, where the Pecos River, Devils River, and Rio Grande meet, created rock art—considered to be some of the most impressive prehistoric art in the world—in dry rock shelters. Dramatic polychrome pictographs of detailed life-size human-feline composites and anthropomorphic figures with feathers, wings, claws, horns, and weapons are documented. The oldest rock art, the Pecos River style, is nearly four thousand years old. Farther north along the Pecos River at Lewis Canyon are more than 250 pictograph sites and more than 900 petroglyphs. The petroglyphs, many on flat rock surfaces, consist of abstract geometrical designs and representational figures of human hands as well as deer, bison, and bird feet. Depictions of atlatls, a weapon of the Archaic, suggest, in association with other cultural remains, production of the petroglyphs between one and nine thousand years ago. In some of the older glyphs human figures appear to brandish some kind of lance or other weapon. Rock shelters in the Wichita Mountains of Oklahoma contain near life-size anthropomorphic figures and geometric petroglyphs painted with red and yellow ochre.

Pictograph images of animals and anthropomorphs on a massive schist formation at Long Lake along the Manigotagan River in southern Manitoba are thought to have been produced during the middle to late Archaic. In the Milk River valley of southern Alberta a complex of 93 sites and 280 separate rock art panels constitutes one of the largest concentrations of rock art in the Northern Plains. This area, the Writing-on-Stone Provincial Park, includes petroglyphs ranging from up to one thousand years old through the postcontact period (1725–1850 AD). Boulder alignments, many considered solstice-aligned configurations, are found in southern Saskatchewan. Some of the alignments were probably constructed two thousand years ago; others, based on astronomical calculations, may have been constructed in the eighteenth and nineteenth centuries.

Rock art in southeastern Colorado, including many zoomorphic or anthropomorphic representations, has been intensively studied, especially in the rock shelters of the Purgatoire River area. Some rock art in this area is associated with rock structural remains that suggest Native American vision quest activities. Ages of these images range from the middle Archaic (a. 3500 BP) to the late Ceramic stage (a. 250 BP). A cluster of dry caves and rock shelters in the canyon country of Black Mesa in the Oklahoma Panhandle contain petroglyphs and pictographs of bison and anthropomorphs, associated with perishable artifacts such as sandals, basketry, and skin bags, that range in age from the late Archaic through the Woodland (200–1000 AD). The Black Hills of South Dakota include many examples of prehistoric rock art. Stylistic analyses suggest that a chronological sequence of rock art, ranging from the late Paleo-Indian to the early historic period, is reflected in at least seven distinct styles of petroglyph and pictograph imaging. Pecked petroglyphs are also documented, especially in Whoop-Up Canyon in the Black Hills.

The diversity of prehistoric rock art in the Great Plains is indicative of the region's varied modes of social organization and economic systems. Advances in the technology of direct dating will help in assigning rock art to its cultural affiliations, but an understanding of why the markings were made in the places they occur will challenge researchers for years to come and, indeed, may never be known.

Ralph J. Hartley
Midwest Archeological Center

Francis, Julie E., and Lawrence L. Loendorf. *Ancient Visions: Petroglyphs and Pictographs of the Wind River and Bighorn Country, Wyoming and Montana.* Salt Lake City: University of Utah Press, 2002. Kirland, Forrest, and W. W. Newcomb Jr. *The Rock Art of Texas Indians.* Austin: University of Texas Press, 1967. Sundstrom, Linea. *Rock Art of the Southern Black Hills.* New York: Garland, 1990.

ROE CLOUD, HENRY (1884–1950)

Born on the Winnebago Reservation in northeastern Nebraska on December 28, 1884, to parents who still lived mainly by hunting and trapping, Henry Roe Cloud went on to become, in Commissioner of Indian Affairs John Collier's words, the "most important living Indian."

Henry Roe Cloud was originally called Wohnaxilayhungah, or Chief of the Place of Fear. He was given the name Henry Cloud by a reservation school administrator. Later, while an undergraduate at Yale, he was adopted by Dr. and Mrs. Walter C. Roe, and he joined their name to his own. Roe Cloud graduated from Yale in 1910, the first Native American to do so, and he added to his credentials a bachelor of divinity degree from Auburn Theological Seminary in 1913 and a master's in anthropology from Yale the following year.

Though educated in American institutions and convinced that Native Americans should strive to succeed within American society, Roe Cloud was also a Native American activist. As an undergraduate at Yale, he campaigned successfully for the return of Geronimo's Apaches from Fort Sill, Oklahoma, to the Mescalero Reservation in New Mexico.

Also while an undergraduate, he was instrumental in the founding of the Society of American Indians, which advocated higher education for Native Americans. Roe Cloud's persistent hope was that Native Americans could become self-sufficient through education. In 1915 Roe Cloud founded and became president of the Roe Indian Institute in Wichita, Kansas, the first college preparatory school for Native Americans in the United States. The school operated until 1935, though in 1931 Roe Cloud arranged for its takeover by the board of the national missions of the Presbyterian Church as his obligations and ambitions at the national level of federal Indian affairs multiplied. One of those ambitions, to become commissioner of Indian affairs, was never realized, but he played a key role in the preparation of the Meriam Report (1928), which starkly revealed the failings of the federal Indian policy. As a Progressive and New Dealer, he supported Collier's reforms in the 1930s, including the Indian Reorganization Act of 1934.

In 1933 Collier appointed Roe Cloud head of Haskell Institute (Kansas), the largest of the Bureau of Indian Affairs's off-reservation high schools. Cloud's two years at the school were difficult as he fought to integrate Native American traditions into the curriculum and to broaden the existing focus on vocational education. He was appointed supervisor of Indian education in 1936 and superintendent of the Umatilla Reservation in Oregon in 1939, but again he was disappointed when he failed to secure a position on the Indian Claims Commission, and in these later years he felt that he was shunted aside by the bureau. Henry Roe Cloud died in Siletz, Oregon, on February 9, 1950.

David J. Wishart
University of Nebraska–Lincoln

Crum, Steven. "Henry Roe Cloud, a Winnebago Reformer: His Quest for American Indian Higher Education." *Kansas History* 11 (1988): 171–84.

SACAGAWEA (CA. 1780–1812)

The only woman on Lewis and Clark's expedition, Sacagawea was a young Shoshone who had been captured by Hidatsa raiders near the three forks of the Missouri River about 1800. She married trader Toussaint Charbonneau sometime before 1804. A son, Jean Baptiste, called "Pomp" by Clark, was born to them in February of 1805. Together, the family traveled from the Mandan-Hidatsa villages in present-day North Dakota to the Pacific and back.

Sacagawea has been the object of considerable myth and misinformation; her contributions to the expedition have been both exaggerated and minimized. Clark thought more of her contributions than did Lewis, though one must consider here the eighteenth-century tendency to discount contributions of nonwhite peoples. In a letter to Charbonneau after the expedition, Clark wrote, "Your woman diserved a greater reward for her attention and services on that rout than we had in our power to give her." Lewis's view was more dismissive: "If she has enough to eat and a few trinkets I believe she would be perfectly content anywhere."

In fact, Sacagawea's contributions were real: she provided important geographical data to the party at various times, she helped as translator with certain tribes, she rescued important documents during a canoe mishap in May 1805, and, perhaps most important, she gave a friendlier face to the Corps of Discovery. Clark wrote that she "reconsiles all the Indians, as to our friendly intentions, a woman with a party of men is a token of peace."

Sacagawea died of a "putrid fever" in December 1812 near present-day Mobridge, South Dakota, at about age thirty-two. Jean Baptiste and Sacagawea's daughter, Lizette, lived with Clark at St. Louis for a time.

Gerald M. Parsons
University of Nebraska–Lincoln

McMurtry, Larry. "Sacagawea's Nickname." *New York Review of Books* 48 (September 20, 2001): 71–72. Moulton, Gary, ed. *The Journals of the Lewis and Clark Expedition*. 13 vols. Lincoln: University of Nebraska Press, 1983–2001. Ronda, James P. *Lewis and Clark among the Indians*. Bicentennial ed. Lincoln: University of Nebraska Press, 2002.

SACRED GEOGRAPHY

While Great Plains Indian religions differ considerably from one another, they all exhibit a sacred geography. All of nature is regarded as being sacred, yet certain geographical features and areas figure more prominently than others on the sacred map.

Sacred places have multiple levels of meaning to Indigenous cultures. First, sacred places are acts of creation, usually designed by a World Maker. The places are revealed through the society's mythology (sacred truth), thereby becoming the physical manifestations of the mythological system. Second, Great Plains Indians hinge both their religious perceptions and their religious ceremonies on sacred places. The locale where a ritual takes place is as significant as the ritual itself. Third, symbolism is an important component of sacred places. Last, the religious perceptions that Plains Indians have of their physical environment lead to a psychological stability evident in a condition referred to as "existential insideness." Existential insideness is knowing that a particular place is where one belongs, completing the self-identity of an individual. Existential insideness is supported through the spiritual system of the culture when there is an acknowledgment of sacred places.

The mythological traditions of many Plains Indians are located in real places. Thus, place is both mythic and geographical. For example, Pahuk, meaning "Mound on the Water," located in eastern Nebraska on a high bluff above the Platte River, is one of five known Pawnee sacred sites. The Pawnees believe Pahuk is one of the locales where the Sacred Animals (Nahu'rac) held council during mythic times and where a young Pawnee boy learned healing practices from the animal council. The boy took the knowledge to his people, curing his fellow villagers and eventually teaching his skills to other young men of the village. Traditionally, Pawnee doctors would visit Pahuk yearly to renew their healing powers and to give thanks to those mythic beings who bestowed the knowledge on their predecessor.

A place made sacred through mythology is continually consecrated by rituals. The Lakota religion recognizes seven sacred ceremonies. Each of these ceremonies is identified with specific sites where the rituals are performed. The *hanbleceya* (vision quest) ceremony is executed at Bear Butte in western South Dakota near the Black Hills, a place the Lakotas describe as "their most sacred altar." The *hanbleceya* is a prayer for spiritual guidance. The Lakotas recognize Bear Butte as a particularly worthy site for visions because the seeker is generally successful, and visions experienced there can reveal future events that are necessary for the continuation of humanity.

Symbolism plays a primary role in the recognition of sacredness for Great Plains Indian peoples. Natural landforms or human-manufactured structures often symbolize the cosmos: their shapes possess the power of what they symbolize. The "medicine wheel," to many Plains cultures, represents an organization of the cosmos based on a recognition of the four sacred directions. These circular rock formations are found throughout the Plains region and are regularly visited by Indian people on pilgrimages. The best-known example, the Big Horn Medicine Wheel, is sacred to the Cheyennes, Lakotas, Arapahos, and Shoshones.

Existential insideness, the feeling that one belongs to a particular place, characterizes Plains Indians' relationships with their homeland. According to the Lakotas, their religion cannot be practiced without access to the sacred places. When this bond is severed, severe psychological alienation and cultural disintegration can ensue. Many Native American peoples' sense of identity comes from walking on land also walked on by their ancestors, or by being able to identify places that are not only significant to them as individuals but also significant to their ancestors. To lose this identity, through loss of sacred lands, would have devastating consequences for the generations to come.

Kari Forbes-Boyte
Dakota State University

Eliade, Mircea. *The Sacred and the Profane: The Nature of Religion.* New York: Harcourt, Brace, and World, 1957. Vecsey, Christopher. *Handbook of American Indian Religious Freedom.* New York: Crossroad, 1991.

SAINT-MARIE, BUFFY (B. 1941)

Buffy Sainte-Marie is a Cree singer-songwriter, guitarist, mouth-bow player, artist, and educator who was born February 20, 1941, at the Piapot Reserve in Saskatchewan, Canada. Orphaned when a few months old, she was raised by a part Micmac family in Massachusetts and later adopted by a Cree family related to her biological parents. As a college student in the early 1960s, Sainte-Marie became known as a social commentator, initially in New York's Greenwich Village, then internationally in Europe, Canada, Australia, Hong Kong, and Japan. Her songs addressing the plight of Native American people such as "My Country 'Tis of Thy People You're Dying" (1964) generated the most controversy. Several of her songs became widely known in versions by other artists, including "Until It's Time for You to Go" (recorded by Elvis Presley and many others), "Up Where We Belong" (the theme for the film *An Officer and a Gentleman*, which won an Academy Award in 1983 for best song), and the antiwar song "The Universal Soldier" (used as an anthem for the 1960s peace movement).

Sainte-Marie is also noted for her work as a digital artist and as an educator. Her regular performances on the TV show *Sesame Street* (1975–81) taught countless children that Indians still exist. The Cradleboard Teaching Project, founded by Sainte-Marie in 1996, enables mainstream school systems to communicate with Native American communities via computer. Currently residing in Hawaii, Sainte-Marie frequently travels to make recordings, perform concerts, and lecture on a variety of topics, including electronic music, digital art, and Native American women's issues.

Paula Conlon
University of Oklahoma

Miller, Mark. "Buffy Sainte-Marie." In *Encyclopedia of Music in Canada*, edited by Helmut Kallman et al. 2nd ed. Toronto: University of Toronto Press, 1992. Stawarz, Jean. "Songs of Conscience: A Dialogue with Buffy Sainte-Marie." *Runner* (1994): 26–39.

SANAPIA (1895–1984)

Sanapia (Memory Woman), the last known Comanche Eagle Doctor, was born at Fort Sill, Oklahoma, in the spring of 1895. She was one of the most powerful Native women in the Plains during the middle decades of the twentieth century. Her father was a converted Christian, and her mother was a traditional Comanche-Arapaho. Sanapia's mother, maternal uncle, and maternal grandmother were Eagle Doctors, and her grandmother reared the girl in traditional Comanche ways.

From ages seven to thirteen Sanapia was educated at the Cache Creek Mission School in southern Oklahoma. Thereafter, she began training with her mother. She was reluctant at first, but her uncle had cured her of influenza as a child and had made her promise to pursue training as an Eagle Doctor when she was older. He named her Memory Woman to remind her of her pledge. Training included learning herbal medicine, healing skills (including sucking), and eagle power. Tradition, however, stipulated that she could not begin practicing until after menopause.

Sanapia was married three times, the first time, briefly, at the age of seventeen. When her second husband (with whom she had two children) died in the 1930s, Sanapia's grief led her to a period of drinking, gambling, and depression. In 1945 she healed a child at her sister's behest, and subsequently she assumed her role as an Eagle Doctor. She eventually incorporated elements of the Native American Church and Christianity into her traditional teachings.

By the 1960s she was the last surviving Comanche Eagle Doctor with maximum powers. Concerned that she would not be able to pass on her powers before dying, she allowed anthropologist David E. Jones to write an account of her life and her healing powers. They produced a book in 1972, which she hoped would serve as a training manual for the future generations.

Akim D. Reinhardt
Towson University

Jones, David E. *Sanapia, Comanche Medicine Woman.* New York: Holt, Rinehart, and Winston, 1972.

SAND CREEK MASSACRE

Southern Cheyennes and Arapahos will forever remember the Sand Creek Massacre, which occurred on November 29, 1864, when Col. John M. Chivington and his men of the Colorado Third Volunteer Regiment attacked their camp. Cheyennes called this ordained Methodist minister a "holy-speaking white man," yet his statement "Damn any man who is in sympathy with an Indian" expressed his antipathy toward them.

Two opposing forces caused the massacre. On one hand were the men of the volunteer Third Colorado Cavalry, known as the "Bloodless Third" because their one-hundred-day enlistment had nearly expired without action against Native

Americans and led by Colonel Chivington. On the other were the Cheyenne Dog Soldiers, who were opposed to the peaceful goals of Black Kettle and who had been making raids on white settlements—raids that were traced to some warriors of Black Kettle's band. These raids, and blatant land greed thwarted by the failure to acquire mineral-rich Cheyenne and Arapaho lands in treaty conferences in 1851 and 1861, led Governor John Evans to order Chivington's command to attack.

Black Kettle's mostly peaceful band reported to Fort Lyon as "friendlies" and were told by the sympathetic commanding officer, Maj. Edward Wynkoop, that they should camp near Fort Lyon under military protection. Vister, a Cheyenne woman, described their sense of safety as they settled in along Sand Creek on the night before the attack. At dawn they were surprised by the attack, in which Chivington ordered his men to take no prisoners. Vister recalled that a male relative brought her a pony, striking it on its flanks to flee. Instead, she turned to find her younger brother, whom she pulled up behind her as bullets whizzed around them. One bullet struck her in the leg as they raced away from the besieged camp that flew a U.S. flag and a white flag on a lodgepole.

Vister's wound healed, but the trauma ran deep in her spirit. Cheyennes and Arapahos carry the memory of this massacre. In his testimony before a congressional committee, interpreter John Smith described the atrocities: "All manner of depredations were inflicted on their persons; they were scalped, their brains knocked out; the men used their knives, ripped open women, clubbed little children, knocked them in the head with their guns, beat their brains out, mutilated their bodies in every sense of the word."

Upon their return to Denver, Chivington and his men displayed scalps and other body parts from their victims to a cheering crowd in the Denver opera house. Reaction in the East could not have been more opposite—shock and outrage greeted the news, especially when details of the large number of women and children killed, as well as the way in which they died, became public knowledge. The military held an investigation and Congress held two, which transcended their original purpose and became investigations of all U.S. Indian policy. Congress condemned Chivington and his men, but as their enlistments had run out, they were no longer under military jurisdiction.

In response to the massacre, some Cheyennes and their allies the Arapahos and Lakota Sioux initiated raids all over the Northern Plains, particularly along the Platte River. It was the start of roughly ten years of war in the Northern Plains.

On October 14, 1865, U.S. government commissioners negotiated the Treaty of the Little Arkansas River, which read in part, "The United States being desirous to express its condemnation of, and, as far as may be, repudiate the gross and wanton outrages perpetrated against certain bands of Cheyenne and Arrapahoe Indians, on the twenty-ninth day of November, AD 1864, at Sand Creek, in Colorado Territory, while the said Indians were at peace with the United States, and under its flag, whose protection they had by lawful authority been promised and induced to seek, and the Government being desirous to make some suitable reparation for the injuries then done, will grant 320 acres of land by patent," as well as individual payments for property lost to survivors. This promise has not yet been kept.

In 1996 the General Conference of the United Methodist Church adopted a resolution apologizing "for the atrocities committed at Sand Creek, Colorado, by one of their own clergy members." They also offered to "extend to all Cheyennes and Arapahos a hand of reconciliation, and ask forgiveness for the death of over 200 mostly women and children."

Henrietta Mann
Montana State University–Bozeman

Hoig, Stan. *The Sand Creek Massacre.* Norman: University of Oklahoma Press, 1961.

SAN SABÁ MISSION, DESTRUCTION OF

Mission Santa Cruz de San Sabá, founded for the eastern Apaches in April 1757, near present-day Menard, Texas, was sacked and burned on March 16, 1758, by an allied Native American force of about two thousand Comanches, Tejas, Tonkawas, and others. At least eight persons, including two of the three Franciscan missionaries present, were slain during the attack. The nearby presidio, San Luis de las Amarillas, four miles farther up the San Saba River, was powerless to intervene. Although the Spanish Franciscan friars, headed by Fray Alonso Giraldo de Terreros, had failed to congregate the Apaches for religious instruction, the allied northern tribes had been alarmed at the prospect of a Spanish-Apache alliance.

The attack represented the first major conflict between Comanches and European American settlers in Texas. Combined with the failed Spanish punitive military expedition to a Wichita (Taovaya) village on the Red River a year later, it demonstrated that the Spanish faced a new type of enemy with greatly expanded capabilities. French firearms had replaced bows and arrows, and the allied Indians had vastly superior numbers. No longer was a ragged Spanish militia, drawn randomly from untrained civilian settlers, capable of holding the frontier. The Spanish advance from Texas toward the Great Plains was halted.

Robert S. Weddle
Bonham, Texas

Weddle, Robert S. *The San Sabá Mission: Spanish Pivot in Texas.* Austin: University of Texas Press, 1964.

SARCEES

The Sarcees (Sarsis) are an Athapaskan-speaking people living along the eastern foothills of the Rocky Mountains in southwestern Alberta. In 1983 they formally adopted the name Tsuu T'inas, which means "Many People" in their own language.

According to Tsuu T'ina legend, all of the Athapaskan-speaking people once lived together in northwestern Canada and Alaska. One winter, when the people were crossing a frozen lake, a young boy asked his grandmother to get him a stick that was protruding from the ice. When she tried to pick it up, she found the stick to be frozen fast in the ice. As the old lady continued to pull and twist the stick, the water was stirred up and the turbulence angered the Underwater Creature. As he rose, a great fissure split the ice. Terrified, the people ran for shore. Those who headed north became the Dénés of Canada and Alaska. Others moved southward, becoming the Tsuu T'inas, Apaches, and Navajos.

Once in the south, the Tsuu T'inas may have first occupied the upper drainages of the Saskatchewan and Athabasca rivers. By the early nineteenth century they had moved farther south and into a close alliance with the Siksikas (Blackfoot proper). They lived primarily along the central portion of the Bow River and at sites along Wolf Creek (now called Fish Creek), the Weasel Head section of the Elbow River, and at Moose Mountain, which assumed sacred significance.

Through their close association, the Tsuu T'inas adopted much of the material and sacred culture of the Blackfoot. Methods and tools for bison hunting and hide preparation, as well as styles of tipis and clothing, all resemble those of the Blackfoot. Because many sacred objects were left with their northern relatives, the Tsuu T'inas incorporated Blackfoot ceremonies into their own belief system. Today, the people are very private about their beliefs and are reluctant to discuss them publicly.

The Tsuu T'inas lived in kin-based groups, which they referred to as clans. The leader of the clan was acknowledged for his good judgment and ability to bring about a consensus. Individuals were free to move from clan to clan, as they saw fit. The Tsuu T'inas presently recognize five clans, although there may have been more before the epidemics and starvation of the late 1800s.

In 1877 Treaty Number 7 was signed between the government of Canada and the Siksikas, Piegans, Kainahs (Bloods), Stoneys, and Tsuu T'inas. At that time, the population of the Tsuu T'inas was estimated to be only 672 persons, and the government suggested that the Tsuu T'inas be included on a large reserve to be set aside for all of the Blackfoot. Bull Head, an influential Tsuu T'ina leader, recognized the importance of having their own place to preserve their language and culture. He argued successfully for a distinct reserve, and a place was eventually set aside along the Elbow River, near the North-West Mounted Police post at Fort Calgary. By 1881, when the Tsuu T'inas were settled on the reserve, the population had dropped to about 450 persons; it continued to decline over the ensuing years.

In 2001 a population of about 1,100 lived on the reserve. The city of Calgary abuts two of its boundaries, while expanding rural subdivisions encroach on the other edges. An elected council of one chief and eleven council members manage the affairs and revenues from resort and golf course developments, oil and gas exploration, and, until recently, rental for land used as a military base. A large office complex houses several federal government offices, whose rent contributes to the tribal revenue.

The Tsuu T'inas have a cultural research program that is actively collecting oral histories. This information is housed at the Tsuu T'ina Peoples Museum.

Jeanette Starlight
Tsuu T'ina Peoples Museum
Gerald T. Conaty
Glenbow Museum

Jenness, Diamond. *The Sarcee Indians of Alberta.* Bulletin no. 90, Anthropological Series no. 23. Ottawa: National Museums of Canada, 1938.

SATANTA SE-T'ANTE (CA. 1815/1818–1878)

Satanta ("White Bear") was a Kiowa warrior and leader. He was born between 1815 and 1818. Many details of his life remain unknown. He might have been part Arapaho or part Mexican. He married between two and four times and fathered between four and nine children.

Until late in his life he sided with the war-inclined factions of the tribe, and his chief rival was peace leader Kicking Bird. He killed numerous Indians and non-Indians in battle. He was a member of the Kiowa Koiet-senko warrior society, comprised of the Kiowas' ten most daring warriors. He raided into Mexico and into the northern Great Plains. His main enemies were Texans, whom the Kiowas viewed as a separate people from Americans.

He became known to Americans in the 1850s and was a minor rival to the preeminent Kiowa leader Dohansen, who dominated the tribe from the 1830s to the 1860s. Satanta fought in a number of important battles with Americans, including at Adobe Walls, Texas (1866), where he bravely rescued the body of a fellow Kiowa who had been killed by American rifle fire.

In councils and treaty conferences Satanta earned a reputation as a forceful but eloquent speaker. He was a Kiowa representative at the Medicine Lodge treaty negotiations, verbally rejecting American demands that the tribe give up territory and move to a reservation; but he did sign the treaty. When the U.S. Congress failed to provide funds for annuities guaranteed under the treaty, the Kiowas reverted to raiding, and Gen. Phillip Sheridan took Satanta hostage following negotiations in mid-December 1868. Sheridan considered hanging Satanta but instead held him hostage for three months in the hope that the Kiowas would cease hostilities.

Satanta is best known for his role in the Warren Massacre (1871) in Young County, Texas. Kiowa holy person Maman-ti prophesied success for a raid if the Kiowas did not attack the first Americans they saw but instead let them go. The first wagon train that passed the waiting warriors contained Gen. William Tecumseh Sherman, on a tour of Texas in response to settler complaints about Indian raids. The Kiowas attacked. When asked about the raid Satanta not only bragged that he led it but also named other Kiowas as accessories, including Satank, Eagle Heart, and Big Tree. Sherman arrested Satanta, Satank, and Big Tree in a dramatic showdown at Fort Sill, Indian Territory. Sherman turned the three over to Texas authorities. On the way to the trial, troops killed Satank during an escape attempt. A Texas jury found Satanta and Big Tree guilty in July 1871, and the judge sentenced them to die. But Governor Edmund Davis, believing that their deaths would only increase warfare on the Southern Plains, commuted their sentences to life in prison. In an effort to achieve peace, federal negotiators promised the tribe that Satanta and Big Tree would be released by March 1873 (ignoring the fact that they were state prisoners). After complicated negotiations between state, federal, and Kiowa officials, Texas agreed to parole Satanta and Big Tree in October 1873.

Satanta appeared to have rejected war and advocated friendship with Americans. However, during the Red River War in the summer and fall of 1874, he violated his parole by visiting the Wichita Agency, where he was present for a small fight between American troops and Kiowa warriors. He denied involvement but nevertheless surrendered to federal troops in October 1874, saying he was sick of war and wanted to farm. Over the objection of Commissioner of Indian Affairs Edward P. Smith and Secretary of the Interior Columbus C. Delano, Satanta was returned to the penitentiary at Huntsville, Texas. There his health declined rapidly, and the superintendent of the prison recommended his release, but state authorities refused. After hearing that he would likely never be released, Satanta slashed several arteries, but he did not die. A medical attendant left him alone on the second floor of the prison infirmary, and he leapt to his death on October 11, 1878. He was buried outside the prison. In 1963 his grandson James Auchiah brought his remains to Fort Sill, Oklahoma.

Charles Vollan
South Dakota State University

Robinson, Charles M. *Satanta: The Life and Death of a War Chief.* Austin TX: State House Press, 1997. Stanley, Francis. *Satanta and the Kiowas.* Borger TX: Jim Hess Printers, 1968.

SHOSHONES

"Shoshone" comes from the Shoshone word *sosoni'*, which is a plural form of *sonipe*, a type of high-growing grass. Several tribes on the Plains referred to the Shoshones as the Grass House People, and this name probably refers to the conically shaped houses made of native grasses (sosoni') used by the Great Basin Indians. The more common term used by Shoshone people is "Newe," or "People." The name Shoshone was first recorded in 1805 after Meriwether Lewis encountered a group of "Sosonees or snake Indians" among the Crows and noted them in his diary. The Shoshones were also called the Snake People by some Plains Indians. The origin of the term "Snake People" is based on the sign, in Indian sign language, that the Shoshone people used for themselves. The hand motion made during the sign represents a snake to most signers, but among the Shoshones it referred to the salmon, a fish unknown to the Great Plains. Today, many Shoshones have adopted the term "Sosoni'" to refer to other groups of Shoshones besides themselves. The Shoshone language is spoken by approximately five thousand people across Nevada, Idaho, and Wyoming. It belongs to the western branch of the Numic group of Uto-Aztecan languages.

Since the Shoshones are widespread across the West, anthropologists have divided them into three groups based on where they live: the Western Shoshones of Nevada, the Northern Shoshones of Idaho, and the Eastern Shoshones of Wyoming. The different bands of Shoshone speakers share many cultural traits. The Eastern Shoshones are the only band that has adopted a Great Plains way of life.

The early history of the Shoshone people—how their ancestors (the Numa) were able to occupy a large portion of the Great Basin (Nevada and Utah), in addition to the contiguous areas of Idaho and Wyoming—is a debated topic. The origin of the Numa is believed to be the southwestern corner of the Great Basin. By 1500 Shoshones had crossed the Rocky Mountains and begun their expansion toward the northwestern Plains. By 1700 a group of Shoshones had moved into the Southern Plains and eventually developed their own identity as the Comanches. The current location of the Eastern Shoshones in central Wyoming is the result of a period of intense warfare from 1780 to 1825 against the Blackfeet, Crows, and Assiniboines.

The Eastern Shoshones divided themselves into two groups, based on geographical location and primary food resource. Shoshones living in the Green River and Wind River valleys of Wyoming were known as the Buffalo Eaters (Guchundeka') or the Sage Grass People (Boho'inee'). Shoshones living in the Rocky Mountains and Lake Yellowstone areas were known as the Sheep-eaters (Dukundeka') or the Mountain People (Doyahinee').

The subsistence cycle of the Eastern Shoshones in the winter involved the tribe breaking into bands, each loosely associated with a particular mountain or valley. In early spring these bands reunited in the Wind River valley before going to the bison grounds for the spring hunt. After the spring hunt, most Eastern Shoshones spent their early summer in the Wind River valley. Then, in late June and early July, the intertribal rendezvous (or trade fair) was held at Fort Bridger. After the fair the Shoshones broke up into family groups until the fall bison hunt, when the tribe would come together one last time before the winter.

Bison meat played an extremely significant role culturally and economically in the lives of the Eastern Shoshones, accounting for about 50 percent of their diet at the height of the Plains horse culture in the 1700s. Fish caught during the spring and early summer were the second most important resource. Elk, mule deer, beaver, jackrabbit, and mountain sheep were also important sources of protein. Berries were either eaten raw, made into soup, or mixed with dried, powdered meat and fat to produce pemmican. Also, roots were eaten after being baked in earthen ovens.

Shoshone arts and industries exploited wood resources, animal products such as leather, sinew, bone, and minerals such as obsidian, flint, steatite, and slate. Leather working was done mostly by women, except for bowstrings, shields, drums, and rattles, which men produced. Iron, only available through trade, became an important material used in making arrow and spear points as well as knives.

The roles of men and women in Shoshone society were strictly regulated. Women were traditionally in charge of plant gathering, butchering and preparing bison, household chores, crafting items such as tipis and clothing, and child care. Men were in charge of hunting, warfare, and the political and economic decisions for the tribe.

The tribal chief (*daigwahni*) was an older man who had distinguished himself in warfare and possessed supernatural power. The chief controlled collective hunts and the tribe's movements. During times of warfare a special war chief was chosen. There were two Shoshone military societies: the Yellow Brows and the Logs. The Yellow Brows were young warriors who were the advanced forces in battle, whereas the Logs were older men who brought up the rear. These military societies also acted as a police force when the tribe gathered together.

The Shoshone religion is based on belief in supernatural power (*boha*) that is acquired primarily through vision quests and dreams. A shaman (*boha gande*) is a person who uses supernatural power to cure others and also leads special group ceremonies, especially at "Round Dances." The Eastern Shoshones also adopted two pan-Indian religions, the Sun Dance and the Native American Church. The Sun Dance was introduced to the Eastern Shoshones by a Comanche named Yellow Hand around 1800. Originally the Eastern Shoshones had rejected the missionary activities of the peyote religion of the Comanches, but the Native American Church gained influence after it was reintroduced by Arapahos in the early part of the twentieth century.

In 1868 the Shoshones of the Plains ceded their ancestral lands and were placed on a reservation in the lee of the Wind River Range of Wyoming. The Wind River Reservation now extends over 2,268,000 acres and is shared by Eastern Shoshones (who live mainly in the west and northwest) and Arapahos (who live mainly in the east and southeast). The Shoshone population on the reservation was 1,185 in 1988, following years of out-migration in response to dire poverty and high unemployment rates.

Christopher Loether
Idaho State University

Horne, Esther Burnette, and Sally McBeth. *Essie's Story: the Life and Legacy of a Shoshone Teacher.* Lincoln: University of Nebraska Press, 1998. Shimkin, Demetri. "Eastern Shoshone." In *Handbook of North American Indians,* edited by William C. Sturtevant, 11:308–35. Washington DC: Smithsonian Institution, 1986. Trenholm, Virginia Cole, and Maurine Carley. *The Shoshones: Sentinels of the Rockies.* Norman: University of Oklahoma Press, 1964.

SIGN LANGUAGE

The Plains Sign Language (PSL) is the most sophisticated Aboriginal sign language known. PSL is a direct signaling system; its symbols are understood without any reference to a spoken language. At its zenith in the mid–nineteenth century, PSL was the principal lingua franca of the trans-Mississippi West. There were three dominant regional dialects: Southern Plains, Northern Plains, and Plateau (the mountainous region north of the Great Basin). The variation between these was mostly in vocabulary, although sign mechanics also varied.

It is not known where or when PSL originated, but it was likely near the Texas Gulf Coast, where a large number of mutually unintelligible languages were spoken. Given its complexity and wide use, the PSL must be many centuries old. The earliest probable observations of the PSL by Europeans were by Spaniards in the Southern Plains in the first half of the sixteenth century. During the nineteenth century, the PSL was used throughout the Plains, from the Texas Panhandle to the Missouri River and beyond, eventually reaching the Canadian Prairies. But sign use was also prominent outside this area, wherever tribes were influenced by Plains culture.

During the period when the PSL was an ongoing lingua franca, the Kiowas, Comanches, Cheyennes, and Arapahos were known as especially skilled signers. It may be significant that these tribes, who spoke mutually unintelligible languages, were often allies. Adult men are thought to have been the primary users of PSL, although some women knew and used PSL as well. Apart from conversational uses, PSL was also usual in public storytelling. This use survives into the present. Signing was also used for oratory, largely before multilingual audiences.

PSL makes heavy use of the portrayal of meanings by descriptive gesture, thus PSL is heavily pantomimic, but many signs are also merely conventional. PSL is, then, a mixed system varying from gestures whose reading is obvious to gestures whose meaning cannot be inferred and which must be learned. All PSL signs are built from around eighty mutually contrasting basic gestures. Each sign usually includes three or four of these, formed with either one or both hands, which may be used in a stationary position or moved about. Signs are normally produced in a continuous flow of motion, but sentences and longer segments of discourse may be set of by brief pauses. When signing is done at a distance, movements are exaggerated in various ways to make the sign more "readable."

Signing was often accompanied by verbal language. Usually the verbal speech had the same meaning as the signed message. But this does not mean that signed messages were a translation of a spoken analog, following the rules of the spoken language. PSL is an independent language with its own rules. The order of words in a signed sentence is fairly free, and the same thing can usually be said with a number of alternate word orders, though a particular word order is usually preferred. In general, subjects precede verbs, and modifiers follow the element modified.

Unfortunately, PSL is now almost completely obsolete, although some signers can still be found here and there on Plains reservations. But time is short. Soon, only memories will remain as testimony to the former existence of the fascinating and colorful system of communication which we know as the Plains Sign Language.

Allan R. Taylor
University of Colorado at Boulder

Clark, William Philo. *The Indian Sign Language*. Lincoln: University of Nebraska Press, 1982. Taylor, Allan R. "Nonverbal Communication in Aboriginal North America: The Plains Sign Language." In *Aboriginal Sign Languages of the Americas and Australia*, edited by Thomas A. Sebeok and Donna Jean Umiker-Sebeok, 2:223–44. New York: Plenum Press, 1978.

SILVERHORN (1860–1940)

Silverhorn, a Kiowa born in 1860, was the most prolific and influential Plains Indian artist of the late nineteenth and early twentieth centuries. He was also known as Huagoonah. He came from a prominent Kiowa family. He was related to Tohausen ("Little Bluff"), the Kiowa leader from 1833 until 1866 (and an artist himself). Silverhorn's father, Agiati ("Gathering Feathers"), was an artist too, an important band leader, and influential in the Tsentanma warrior society. Silverhorn's son, James Silverhorn, was also a celebrated artist.

The Plains tribes produced the most advanced pictorial art in North America. They did so for spiritual, historical (e.g., "winter counts"), and purely artistic reasons. Silverhorn learned from traditional Kiowa artists and warriors, including those imprisoned at Fort Marian, in St. Augustine, Florida, in the 1870s. He used nineteenth-century styles found in the ledger books, which replaced buffalo skins. As an artist, he acted as a bridge between the generations before and after him, including his nephew Stephen Mopope, one of the "Kiowa Six," who rose to prominence in the 1920s.

Born in the era of the buffalo hunts, Silverhorn experienced the subjugation of his tribe (his family participated in the Kiowa Breakout of 1874) through military conquest, the assimilation process at Fort Sill, Oklahoma, and the adoption of the Ghost Dance and the Native American Church (both of which he participated in). Silverhorn documented what he saw, not by using the same form of traditional Kiowa winter counts, but by developing his own technique and style. Over time Silverhorn grew less specific in his paintings and focused on the distant past rather than on specific events. Other Kiowa artists followed this trend in

Silverhorn (also known as Huagoonah), ca. 1902–20

Hugh L. Scott. More important, Silverhorn drew and painted Kiowa life and physical culture for the Smithsonian anthropologist James Mooney starting in 1901. He also worked with silver and feathers. He mentored younger artists and helped legitimize the sale of traditional art.

In 1901, at age forty-one, Silverhorn married thirteen-year-old Tanguma (Hattie Silverhorn). He had worked unsuccessfully against allotment since the 1890s, but he and Hattie received allotments after the Kiowa reservation in Oklahoma was divided in 1902. He sold half his land in 1910. He and Hattie divorced in 1929. Six of their children survived into adulthood.

Deteriorating eyesight caused by trachoma forced Silverhorn to give up art in the 1910s. He died at his home near Anadarko, Oklahoma, on December 14, 1940, having experienced and documented his people's transformation from independent hunters to sedentary farmers.

Charles Vollan
South Dakota State University

Greene, Candace S. *Silver Horn: Master Illustrator of the Kiowas.* Norman: University of Oklahoma Press, 2001. Donnelly, Robert, Janet Catherine Berlo, and Candace Greene. *Transforming Images: The Art of Silver Horn and His Successors.* Chicago: David and Alfred Smart Museum of Art, University of Chicago, 2000.

SIOUX

The Sioux, and most particularly the Lakota Sioux, are the iconic warrior horsemen of the Northern Plains. They have become perhaps the best known of all Indian nations through paintings and photographs, confrontations with the U.S. military, Wild West shows, and hundreds of Hollywood movies. Sitting Bull, Crazy Horse, Red Cloud, and other Lakota Sioux leaders are among the most famous of all Native Americans, and the Battle of the Little Bighorn in 1876 and the Wounded Knee Massacre in 1890 are among the most widely known events in U.S. history. But the Lakotas are only one division of the Great Sioux Nation.

The Great Sioux Nation, known as Oceti Sakowin, or "Seven Council Fires," is a confederation of closely allied cognate bands. They speak three mutually intelligible dialects of the Siouan language family: Dakota, Nakota, and Lakota. They became known as the Sioux, or a word like it, in the seventeenth century, when their enemies, the Ojibwas, told the French that that was what they were called. The word derives from the Ojibwa term *Na dou esse,* which means "Snakeline Ones" or "Enemies." The French spelled the word "Nadousioux," and the English and Americans shortened it to "Sioux." In recent years, the Sioux, like many other Native peoples, have made a concerted effort to replace their imposed, derogatory name by the names they

the twentieth century. More than one thousand of his images from the 1870s to the 1910s survive and are in museums all over the world.

Silverhorn operated inside and outside of Kiowa culture. He was a medicine man and a Road Man in the Native American Church. He was a calendar keeper. He went to Washington DC as part of a delegation of Kiowas, documenting the trip in sketches. He was a member of the Seventh Cavalry from 1891 to 1894, one of the first Kiowas to serve as a soldier rather than as a scout. While in the army he drew anthropological drawings for Fort Sill's commander, the amateur anthropologist called themselves. Self-identification is commonly based on either band or sub-band names (e.g., Santee, Oglala, or Sicanju), linguistic groups (Lakota, Dakota, or Nakota), or, increasingly, by the name of the reservation of origin (e.g., "Rosebud Sioux" or "Cheyenne River Sioux").

The Great Sioux Nation has seven primary divisions, based on their respective places in the Seven Council Fires. The Isantis (Santees), Dakota speakers, occupy the east and are comprised of four council fires: the Mdewakantunwan, the Sisitunwan, the Wahpetunwan, and the Wahpekute. The Wiciyelas, Nakota speakers, occupy the middle division and are composed of two council fires: the Ihanktunwun (Yanktons) and Ihanktunwanna (Yanktonais). The western council fire is occupied by the Titunwans (Tetons), Lakota speakers, composed of seven sub-bands: Oglala (Scatter One's Own), Sicangu or Brulé (Burnt Thigh), Hunkpapa (Those Who Camp At the Entrance), Mnikowoju or Minneconjou (Those Who Plant By the Stream), Itzipco or Sans Arcs (Without Bows), Oohenunpa (Two Kettles), and Sihasapa (Black Feet).

Europeans first encountered the Sioux in the seventeenth century in the mixed hardwood forests of central Minnesota and northwestern Wisconsin. In the mid–seventeenth century, the Sioux began moving westward and southward, pushed by the Ojibwas, who gradually infiltrated into Minnesota from the Lake Superior area, and pulled by the abundant Plains bison herds and the diffusion of horses from the Southern Plains. While some bands had a few horses by 1707, if not earlier, the Lakotas did not fundamentally become Plains horsemen until 1750–75, by which time they had crossed the Missouri River, displacing the previous residents of the region. By the mid eighteenth century, the Lakotas and Nakotas were closely associated with the Central and Northern Plains. The Dakotas (Santees) remained primarily in Minnesota, where they received reservations in the nineteenth century. The Sioux Uprising of 1862 resulted in the relocation of many Santees to small reservations in South Dakota and Nebraska, although others remained in Minnesota.

As each of the Council Fires adapted to different Plains environments, their lifeways changed and diverged from one another. Yet they maintained their political, economic, and social ties through intermarriage, trade, religious ceremonies, communal hunting, and military alliances.

The Yanktons and Yanktonais, who eventually settled in the eastern Dakotas, became middlemen in a far-flung trade system between the Lakotas, who had pushed westward as far as Wyoming and eastern Montana, and the eastern Santees, who were closely involved in the French fur trade in

Minnesota. While the Lakotas became buffalo-hunting, nomadic horsemen, and the principal grain grown by the Santees shifted from wild rice to corn, some Yanktons and Yanktonais adopted many of the traits of the semisedentary Plains villagers, such as the Mandans and Arikaras, including the building of earth lodges. With the horse for transportation and vast herds of bison, the Lakotas prospered and their numbers grew until, by the nineteenth century, they outnumbered all other bands of the Great Sioux Nation combined. By the mid–nineteenth century, the Lakotas and their allies presented a formidable military and political barrier to European American expansion into the Central and Northern Plains.

The Lakotas eventually controlled a vast hunting territory stretching from the Platte River north to the Heart River and from the Missouri River west to the Bighorn Mountains. Their highly flexible social and political organization was well suited to the demands of maintaining such an empire. The basic unit of Lakota society was the *tiyospaye*, a small group of bilaterally related kin, informally led by a headman. Each of the seven Lakota sub-bands had societies, including *akicitas* (police) and *nacas* (civil leaders). Nacas from each of the sub-bands formed a tribal council (*Naca Ominicia*) with executive committees commonly known as *wicasa* (shirt wearers). When the seven sub-bands congregated each summer for the Sun Dance, the nacas of each of the seven sub-bands constituted a national council. Holy men and medicine people were also consulted on important matters, revealing the centrality of Lakota spiritual and ceremonial life.

The belief systems and rituals of the Lakotas and Nakotas reflect many of the values essential for successful nomadic bison hunting in the Northern Great Plains (e.g., individuality, bravery, sacrifice, vision seeking). The Lakotas are further anchored to the Great Plains by their conviction that they were created by Wakan Tanka (Grandfather, the Great Spirit) and emerged from a cave (Wind Cave) in Paha Sapa, the Black Hills of South Dakota. This place, more than any other, is sacred to the Lakotas. It was in the Great Plains that the Lakotas received their Sacred Pipe and the Seven Sacred Rites, including the Sun Dance, from White Buffalo Calf Woman.

Life within the tiyospaye centered around daily subsistence tasks divided by age and gender. Hunting, raiding, and making tools and weapons were the responsibilities of men, with time left over for trading, counsels, ceremonies, and leisure activities, such as wagering on foot and horse races. Women's responsibilities included gathering wild resources, such as prairie turnips, processing and tanning hides, cooking, sewing, quillwork, and managing the daily needs of the household. Women were responsible for breaking camp, packing belongings on travois, and setting up camp again at the end of the day. Older children and youth frequently had responsibility for gathering firewood and water and tending to horses and dogs. Grandparents and elders were often entrusted with the primary responsibility of caring for small children and infants and assisting with household tasks. In Lakota society, men were allowed to have more than one wife, and men of high status frequently had several wives, ideally sisters or women from the same tiyospaye.

During the first half of the nineteenth century, at the very time the horse-riding nomadic way of life of the Lakotas was flourishing, the grasslands were being invaded by European Americans. The U.S. government initiated an aggressive military policy in the Plains during the 1860s. This policy included building additional military posts and pursuing Indian groups characterized as "hostile," activities that inflamed already tense relations between the federal government and the Lakotas and their allies. The Great Sioux Nation and its allies proved formidable opponents, militarily and politically, and brought the U.S. government to the negotiating table twice at Fort Laramie (1854 and 1868) to sign treaties. The 1868 Treaty of Fort Laramie established the Great Sioux Reservation, spanning more than half of the modern state of South Dakota (west of the Missouri River), and provided annuities and rations for the Sioux. Economic relief was welcomed by the tribe. Bison were an increasingly scarce resource in the Plains by the mid-1870s, and by the mid-1880s they were virtually extinct. The eradication of the bison, mainstay of their economy, had a devastating impact on the Sioux.

By the 1870s intolerable pressures led to a series of "Indian Wars," the most famous of which was the annihilation of Gen. George Armstrong Custer's Seventh Calvary at the Battle of the Little Bighorn in 1876 by Sitting Bull's Lakotas and their Cheyenne allies. Retribution was swift, and even those Lakotas who held out, including the bands of Crazy Horse and Sitting Bull, were eventually settled on the Great Sioux Reservation. In 1889 Congress broke up the Great Sioux Reservation into several smaller reservations in North Dakota and South Dakota. These reservations were loosely based on membership of the sub-bands. Their holdings were further diminished and scattered by allotment in severalty in the 1890s, which forced nuclear families onto small acreages and opened the remaining "surplus" land to non-Indian settlement. Many Lakotas selected their allotments near

other members of their tiyospayes, maintaining a semblance of their old organization. The massacre of Big Foot's band at Wounded Knee Creek in 1890 and the killing of Sitting Bull by Indian policemen the same year marked the end of freedom and the preferred nomadic way of life for many Lakotas.

The 1890s were difficult years for the Sioux. Confined to reservations, where indifferent and self-serving Indian agents controlled them, they were expected to farm arid land. Their children were shipped to boarding schools, such as Carlisle Indian School in Pennsylvania, where they were urged to abandon their Indian ways. The Sun Dance, which had always served as an integrating mechanism for the Lakotas, had been banned along with other Lakota rituals in 1882. Although it was banned, the Lakota Sun Dance was never eradicated; it simply went "underground" to await a more tolerant era. In the 1890s other religions, such as the Ghost Dance and peyotism, helped fill the gap.

The first two decades of the twentieth century were periods of adjustment to reservation life on scattered allotments. Some reservations even began to prosper, to a degree, in the 1920s, only to be devastated during the Dust Bowl and Depression of the 1930s. Still, the catastrophe provided an opportunity to introduce radical reforms. These well-intentioned reforms were introduced by John Collier of the new Roosevelt administration and enacted as the Indian Reorganization Act (IRA) of 1934. The IRA was designed to improve subsistence and employment opportunities on the reservations and to ensure that tribal councils were democratically elected (counter to the traditions of the Lakotas and others). Collier and his staff targeted the Sioux reservations in the Dakotas and pressured them to adopt IRA-style governments and constitutions, which they did. The IRA reforms resulted in short-term moderate relief, as the Lakotas took advantage of some of the economic development programs, but they had negligible long-term benefits, with the exception that allotment policy was ended, which allowed the Lakotas to halt the erosion of their land base.

The second half of the twentieth century was a time of far-reaching change and renewal for many Sioux. Reduction in mortality and high birthrates almost doubled their population, which strained employment on reservations. As part of the termination policy, the Eisenhower administration encouraged Indians to leave their reservations with the 1952 Voluntary Relocation Program. In the 1950s and 1960s regional centers such as Denver, Cheyenne, Bismarck, Minneapolis, Sioux Falls, and Sioux City became home to many Sioux. Poorly educated and discriminated against, many young

Sioux soon returned to their reservations. The turbulence of this period in federal Indian policy, coupled with the civil rights movement, encouraged the birth of the American Indian Movement (AIM). AIM has maintained a close connection to the Great Sioux Nation, with many leaders—Russell Means, Leonard Peltier, and John Trudell—claiming Sioux ancestry.

By the 1970s the once radical position that Indians should be able to follow their own cultural traditions—rather than be forced to assimilate to European American traditions—became more widely accepted. The publication of Dee Brown's immensely popular *Bury My Heart at Wounded Knee* in 1971 and a new confrontation at Wounded Knee in 1973 led by AIM, heightened public consciousness of the plight of the Sioux. Moreover, this era confirmed that the sacred Black Hills were not, nor had they ever been, for sale. In 1980 the U.S. Supreme Court reviewed the fifty-seven-year-old Black Hills land claims case of the Great Sioux Nation and concluded that the taking of the Black Hills by the U.S. government was illegal and that the Great Sioux Nation was entitled to compensation for the taking. That award has now grown to more than $600 million and continues to draw interest in the U.S. Treasury because the Great Sioux Nation has refused the settlement, demanding the return of Paha Sapa, the Black Hills, instead.

Despite the gains reaped from the political and economic programs of the self-determination era, the Sioux reservations in North Dakota and South Dakota remain some of the poorest places in the United States. Many reservations have chosen to open casinos, and some have enjoyed the benefits of large-scale capital infusions into their local economies; others, because of their remoteness from urban population centers, have seen little improvement in their economies, besides improving joblessness rates, as a result of casinos. Today, although transformed through decades of hardship and deprivation, the Great Sioux Nation is in a vigorous, if difficult, renaissance. Many Lakotas continue to speak their language and practice traditions such as the Sun Dance. Tribal community colleges, frequently named after important Lakota leaders, have sprung up on the reservations and are educating tribal members in the skills required to engage the global economy and simultaneously recapture their tribal heritage and traditions.

Guy Gibbon
University of Minnesota

Bettelyoun, Susan Bordeaux, and Josephine Waggoner. *With My Own Eyes: A Lakota Woman Tell's Her People's History*, edited by Emily Levine. Lincoln: University of Nebraska Press, 1998. Buechel, Eugene, and Paul Manhart. *Lakota Dictionary: New Comprehensive Edition*. Lincoln: University of Nebraska Press, 2002. DeMallie, Raymond J., and Douglas R. Parks, eds. *Sioux Indian Religion*. Norman: University of Oklahoma Press, 1987. Feraca, Stephen E. *Wakinyan: Lakota Religion in the Twentieth Century*. Lincoln: University of Nebraska Press, 1998. Hardorff, Richard G., ed. *Lakota Recollections of the Custer Fight*. Lincoln: University of Nebraska Press, 1997. Howard, James H. *The Canadian Sioux*. Lincoln: University of Nebraska Press, 1984. Pickering, Kathleen Ann. *Lakota Culture, World Economy*. Lincoln: University of Nebraska Press, 2000. Price, Catherine. *The Oglala People, 1841–1879: A Political History*. Lincoln: University of Nebraska Press, 1996. Red Shirt, Delphine. *Bead on an Anthill: A Lakota Childhood*. Lincoln: University of Nebraska Press, 1997. Wagoner, Paula L. *"They Treated Us Just Like Indians": The Worlds of Bennett County, South Dakota*. Lincoln: University of Nebraska Press, 2002. Walker, James R. *Lakota Belief and Ritual*. Lincoln: University of Nebraska Press, 1991. Young Bear, Severt, and R. D. Thesiz. *Standing in the Light: A Lakota Way of Seeing*. Lincoln: University of Nebraska Press, 1994.

SIOUX WARS

During the last half of the nineteenth century, Lakota Sioux and their Cheyenne and Arapaho allies defended their homelands and natural resources against incursions by the federal government and European American settlers. Collectively known as the Sioux Wars, major engagements included the Grattan Massacre (1854), Fetterman Fight (1866), Battle of the Rosebud (1876), Battle of the Little Bighorn (1876), and the Wounded Knee Massacre (1890).

The first violent conflict in the Plains involving the Lakota Sioux and the federal government grew out of increased travel along the Oregon Trail. To protect overland travelers, the federal government built Fort Kearny in present-day Nebraska and purchased Fort Laramie in present-day Wyoming. Government agents also negotiated the Fort Laramie Treaty of 1851, which guaranteed the safe passage of emigrants in exchange for annuities and the recognition of tribal territories. Peace held until 1854 when a trivial event—the theft of an emigrant's cow by young Lakotas—led to the Grattan Massacre and subsequent army retaliations. On August 19, 1854, Lt. John Grattan led a detachment of twenty-nine men to recover the stolen cow from the village of Conquering Bear along the North Platte River. Misunderstandings and a belligerent Grattan sparked violence. When the shooting stopped, Grattan and all of his men lay dead; Conquering Bear was the lone Lakota casualty. Army retaliation was certain. The following summer, Col. William S. Harney destroyed a Sioux village at Ash Hollow (present-day Nebraska), killing more than one hundred men, women, and children. Harney then pushed into Lakota territory, briefly occupying Fort Pierre (South Dakota) and finally establishing Fort Randall on the Missouri River. Harney's invasion of the Sioux homeland caused the Sioux to move away from the roads, soldiers, and forts which, in combination with the federal government's preoccupation with the Civil War (1861–65), led to almost ten years of relative peace.

Trouble flared again in 1865–67 when emigrants, in violation of the 1851 Treaty of Fort Laramie, moved along the Bozeman Trail to the Montana goldfields. This pathway cut through the heart of Plains Indian hunting grounds in the Powder River area. Persistent Lakota raids against settlers and soldiers along this route prompted the federal government to build Forts Reno, C. F. Smith, and Phil Kearny to protect emigrant travel. Despite the heavy military presence, Indian attacks continued, and in the second half of 1866 Lakotas led by Red Cloud and Crazy Horse battled federal troops. The most notorious engagement was the Fetterman Fight (December 21, 1866) near Fort Phil Kearny, Wyoming Territory, where eighty men under Capt. William Fetterman were killed. Public cries for decisive action against the Sioux reached a fever pitch, but Congress voted to broker peace with the warring tribes. Red Cloud signed the Fort Laramie Treaty (1868), which guaranteed, among other things, abandonment of the Bozeman Trail forts and creation of a large reservation that included the Black Hills. After agreeing to this treaty, Red Cloud and many Lakota bands moved onto this Great Sioux Reservation, while Sitting Bull, Crazy Horse, and Gall continued to resist encroachment on their lands. They openly rejected the treaty and continued to pursue their traditional life.

Hostilities erupted once again after an 1874 military expedition into the Black Hills confirmed rumors of gold. Gold seekers flooded into Paha Sapa (the Black Hills)—a clear violation of the 1868 Fort Laramie Treaty—forcing leaders such as Crazy Horse and Sitting Bull to defend Sioux territory. To avoid conflict, the federal government in 1875 offered to purchase the land from the Sioux. Overwhelmingly, the Sioux rejected this, and the government provoked a military showdown by issuing an ultimatum requiring all Sioux to report to an agency by January 31, 1876, or be considered hostile. The off-reservation people, now loosely allied under Sitting Bull, were scattered in the Powder River area (southeastern Montana and northwestern Wyoming) in small winter camps, and they largely ignored this arbitrary, impossible demand.

In May 1876 the army launched a three-pronged campaign to force the Lakotas back onto the Great Sioux Reservation: Col. John Gibbon advanced eastward from Fort Ellis (Montana), Gen. George Crook moved north from Fort Laramie, and Gen. Alfred Terry (with George Custer) moved westward from Fort Abraham Lincoln (North Dakota). The military's campaign began to crumble when on June 17, 1876, the Sioux, led by Crazy Horse, routed and turned back Crook's command at the

Battle of the Rosebud. On June 25–26, 1876, in the most famous fight of the offensive, Lt. Col. George Custer's Seventh Cavalry attacked an enormous Indian encampment on the Little Bighorn (Greasy Grass) River. Custer divided his command and attempted to strike the village from both ends but was quickly overwhelmed by superior numbers. Custer and 210 men in his immediate command (263 total) were killed.

After this victory, the Sioux and their allies fragmented into small bands and dispersed. The army initiated a winter campaign and relentlessly hunted down those bands that had not returned to their agencies. In May 1877, Crazy Horse surrendered at Fort Robinson, Nebraska; he was killed four months later, reportedly while trying to escape. Sitting Bull fled to Canada with as many as two thousand followers. In retaliation for defeat at the Little Bighorn, Congress annexed the Black Hills from the Great Sioux Reservation on February 28, 1877.

Essentially, these events marked the end of the Sioux Wars and the start of the reservation era. After Sitting Bull returned to the United States in 1881, all Lakota Sioux bands lived on reservations and any hope of effective resistance was gone. The final conflict between the Sioux and the federal government—the Wounded Knee Massacre—was hardly a military confrontation. Militarily defeated, the Sioux readily adopted the Ghost Dance religion but with a more militaristic twist—some believed they would be impervious to bullets, and most believed that if they danced and prayed with enough fervor the European Americans would vanish. Their newfound focus caused great fear in the Plains, leading to a confrontation with federal troops. On December 29, 1890, while attempting to disarm a fleeing band of Lakotas, the Seventh Cavalry killed more than 250 Lakotas (mostly women and children) on the Pine Ridge Reservation in South Dakota. This massacre marked the end of Sioux resistance and the last chapter in the Plains Indian Wars.

Carole A. Barrett
University of Mary

Olson, James C. *Red Cloud and the Sioux Problem.* Lincoln: University of Nebraska Press, 1965. Utley, Robert M. *The Indian Frontier of the American West, 1846–1890.* Albuquerque: University of New Mexico Press, 1984.

SITTING BULL (CA. 1831–1890)

Sitting Bull (Tantanka Iyotanka) was born in the early 1830s along the Grand River at a place called Many Caches near present-day Bullhead, South Dakota. During the Plains Indian Wars (1865–76) he rose to prominence as a military and political leader among the Lakotas and led resistance against

Sitting Bull (Tantanka Iyotanka), 1885

U.S. military and civilian encroachment through their traditional homelands between the mouth of the Grand and the Yellowstone River basin.

Sitting Bull distinguished himself early as a hunter and warrior and rose to prominence among his own people as a generous man and capable war leader; consequently, he was inducted into a number of prestigious warrior societies. In 1866 he gained attention of the American public for his attacks on soldiers and settlers at Fort Buford (located at the confluence of the Yellowstone and Missouri rivers).

In response to intensifying outside pressures the Hunkpapa and other Lakota bands, principally the Itzipco, Minneconjou, Sihasapa, and a loose alliance of Oglalas under Crazy Horse, attempted to consolidate leadership. In 1866 or 1867 Sitting Bull was recognized as an important political and military leader of these bands. In some accounts he is labeled "supreme chief." Therefore, in 1867 and 1868, when Catholic missionary Pierre-Jean De Smet sought to broker a truce with the Lakotas, he dealt primarily with Sitting Bull. In these negotiations Sitting Bull rejected all overtures and stated his determination to protect his people's homeland and lifeways, a message he repeated often in subsequent years.

For a time tensions abated due to troop withdrawals along the Bozeman Trail as part of the 1868 Treaty of Fort Laramie, which created the Great Sioux Reservation. However, many Lakotas left their agencies to join Sitting Bull when federal officials failed to enforce provisions of the treaty and prospectors poured into the Black Hills after the government-sponsored expedition in 1874, led by George Armstrong Custer, confirmed the existence of gold there. Clashes between the army and "the Sitting Bull people," as they came to be known, were frequent.

In June 1876, during the annual Sun Dance, Sitting Bull had a vision of dead soldiers falling into an Indian camp, and on June 25, 1876, his prophecy came true with the defeat of Custer's command at the Battle of the Little Bighorn. After this fight, the army systematically hunted Native peoples, and by the fall of 1876 Sitting Bull was one of the few leaders still resisting surrender and living outside his agency. In October, Gen. Nelson Miles intercepted Sitting Bull in Montana Territory and demanded his surrender; typically, Sitting Bull stated his determination to continue living in the old way and resist federal demands. By May of 1877 Sitting Bull and about four hundred followers had sought refuge in Saskatchewan, settling between Wood Mountain and Fort Qu'Appelle. Starvation was never far away, and the Dominion of Canada would not provide food or other support, so after lengthy discussion with Canadian and American officials, on July 19, 1881, Sitting Bull and two hundred followers crossed into the United States and handed over horses and weapons at Fort Buford. Despite the U.S. government's assurances he would be repatriated with the Hunkpapas at Standing Rock Agency, Sitting Bull and about one hundred of his people were held in detention at Fort Randall in southeastern Dakota Territory.

In May 1883 Sitting Bull was permitted to join his people at Standing Rock. There he came under the jurisdiction of Indian agent James McLaughlin, and a sustained clash of wills and philosophies ensued. Sitting Bull struggled to maintain a sense of nationhood and to preserve traditional Lakota values, while McLaughlin enforced federal policy. Sitting Bull left the reservation briefly in 1884 and 1885 to tour in two Wild West shows, then returned to Standing Rock to continue his role as outspoken critic of government attempts to divest the Sioux of nine million acres of their land. Nonetheless, the land was lost in 1889, and against this backdrop word of the Ghost Dance spread among the Sioux. Sitting Bull permitted the Ghost Dance in his camp along the Grand River, not far from his birthplace, and Agent McLaughlin quickly seized on this and petitioned the government to order his arrest. On December 12, 1890, arrest orders for Sitting Bull were sent from Washington. By daybreak on December 15, 1890, following an intense fight, Sitting Bull was dead, and eight of his followers and six Indian police lay dead or dying.

Carole A. Barrett
University of Mary

Manzione, Joseph. "*I Am Looking North for My Life*": *Sitting Bull, 1876–1881*. Salt Lake: University of Utah Press, 1991. Utley, Robert M. *The Lance and the Shield: The Life and Times of Sitting Bull*. New York: Henry Holt, 1993. Vestal, Stanley. *Sitting Bull: Champion of the Sioux*. Norman: University of Oklahoma Press, 1932.

SNEVE, VIRGINIA DRIVING HAWK (B. 1933)

Virginia Driving Hawk Sneve is best known as an author, primarily of children's and juvenile literature and nonfiction. She was born on February 21, 1933, on the Rosebud Reservation and is an enrolled member of the Rosebud Sioux. In her 1995 family biography, *Completing the Circle*, she identified herself as being descended from the Santee, Yankton, and Teton Sioux, as well as from French, Scottish, and English ancestors. Her father, James Driving Hawk, was an Episcopal priest. Her paternal great-grandfather, Rev. Charles Frazier, was a Congregationalist missionary. Her grandmothers, particularly her paternal grandmother, Flora Driving Hawk, inspired her to become a storyteller.

Encouraged by a teacher at the Bureau of Indian Affairs (BIA) elementary school she attended, she began to write. In 1950 she graduated from St. Mary's High School for Indian Girls in Springfield, South Dakota. In 1954 she earned a bachelor of science degree from South Dakota State College in Brookings, and in 1969 a master's degree in education at the renamed South Dakota State University.

In addition to writing, Sneve taught English, speech, and drama at public and Indian schools and worked as a guidance counselor at Rapid City High School. She also served as a consultant, producer, and writer for South Dakota Public Television and as an editor at Brevet Press in Sioux Falls, South Dakota. In 1995 she retired from Rapid City High School and also from her position as associate instructor in English at Oglala Lakota College, Rapid City Extension. She is the historiographer of the Episcopal Church of South Dakota and authored *That They May Have Life: The Episcopal Church in South Dakota, 1859–1976* (1977).

She has three children and four grandchildren. Her husband, Vance Sneve, worked for the BIA. She encouraged her children to read but found that children's literature, such as the Little House on the Prairie series, presented only a stereotypical image of American Indians. She decided to write her own books to educate Americans about Indian life, past and present. Many of her works reflect her own experiences, or those of her family and ancestors, including *Jimmy Yellow Hawk* (1972), her first published work. Focusing first on the Sioux, she later wrote nonfiction for juveniles about other tribes, including *The Navajos* (1993) and *The Apaches* (1997).

Sneve published her first work for adults, *Dakota Heritage: A Compilation of Indian Place Names in South Dakota*, in 1973. More recently, in *Completing the Circle*, she described the female half of her family for several generations, placing her female ancestors both within their cultures and within the history of the tribe and tracing the transfer of knowledge and stories from one generation of women to the next. In all, she has written sixteen books. She has received numerous awards, including Writer of the Year from the Western Heritage Hall of Fame (1984), the Native American Prose Award from the University of Nebraska Press (1992), the South Dakota Education Association Human Services Award (1994), and the Human Rights Award from the South Dakota State Counselors Association (1996). She was a National Humanities medalist in 2000.

Charles Vollan
South Dakota State University

Sneve, Virginia Driving Hawk. *Completing the Circle*. Lincoln: University of Nebraska Press, 1995.

SOLDIER BLUE

Soldier Blue (1970), a film directed by Ralph Nelson, is loosely based on *Arrow in the Sun* (1969), a novel by Theodore Victor Olsen (1932–1993), a Wisconsin-born freelance writer of nearly four dozen Western sagas, including the bestsellers *The Stalking Moon* (1965) and *Red Is the River* (1983). As in the film, the novel centers on the fictitious characters of Pvt. Honus Gant, a former schoolteacher from Ohio turned army trooper, and Cresta Marybelle Lee, a young woman from Boston who, while en route to marry an army lieutenant posted on the frontier some years earlier, is captured by a band of Cheyennes and becomes the second wife of the band's leader, Spotted Wolf.

After escaping from the Cheyennes, Lee accompanies an army paymaster's detail that includes Private Gant to Fort Reunion, where her fiancé is stationed. When the paymaster's detail is ambushed and wiped out by Spotted Wolf's band, Gant and Lee, the sole survivors, are forced to try to make it to Fort Reunion on their own. They never do, as their fates become linked to Colonel Iverson's brutal attack on Spotted Wolf's village, which brings the film to a brutal, horrifying, and surreal climax.

Soldier Blue is badly flawed by a glaring anachronism, among other inaccuracies. Action portrayed in the novel supposedly takes place roughly in 1877, more than twelve years after Spotted Wolf had witnessed his entire family being murdered at Sand Creek by Col. John M. Chivington's Colorado Volunteers. Indeed, as we are told in the novel, Spotted

Wolf had been instrumental in George Crook's humiliating defeat at Rosebud Creek, Montana, in 1876, and he had been at Little Big Horn too in that same year. Near the beginning of the film we learn that Private Gant's own father had been killed at the Little Big Horn the previous year, yet by the end of the film it is, inexplicably, November 29, 1864, when we relive the gory and ultraviolent (though poorly re-created) Sand Creek Massacre. Colonel Iverson becomes Lieutenant Calley, and *Soldier Blue* becomes an uneasy parallel to My Lai during which U.S. soldiers wantonly rape, murder, and mutilate hundreds of Native American men, women, and children.

R. B. Rosenburg
Clayton College and State University

SOVEREIGNTY

Sovereignty originally referred to the political attributes of a European king. To be sovereign was to be "above everything." Sovereignty was thought to reside in the physical person of the ruler. The formation of the Swiss Confederation in 1291 and the United Provinces (now the Netherlands) in 1581 introduced a new kind of actor on the political stage: democratic republics that did not have individual dynastic rulers. The seventeenth-century Dutch jurist Hugo de Groot (or Grotius) and eighteenth-century Swiss jurist Emmerich Vattel wrote pioneering legal treatises arguing that sovereignty resides collectively in society itself—that is, in the state and its citizens.

European ideas of sovereignty were culturally applicable to some Aboriginal American contexts. The agricultural city-states of the Mississippi Valley were governed by individual chiefs, as attested by early French descriptions of the city of Natchez. On the whole, however, the chiefs and councils of Indian tribes did not assert absolute lawmaking power over their people.

This was especially true in the Great Plains where, as John Moore has demonstrated for the Cheyennes, group boundaries and leadership remained flexible and could change from season to season. Households not only realigned themselves and chose new leaders within the nation, but they often left the nation altogether, for a season or many years, to travel and hunt with relatives in other nations. While the nation collectively defended a distinct territory with which it identified historically and ceremonially, its constituent families and clans, and its leadership, could be extremely fluid. When the camp crier announced that a respected man planned to break camp at dawn, households individually chose whether to follow him.

Great Plains nations were patches in a boundless, endlessly changing web of kinship relationships, landscapes, and languages. Mobility within this web was sufficient to prevent any persistent concentrations of political power. At the same time, solidarity was sufficient to repel intruders who lacked legitimate claims to local hospitality. Although Great Plains nations could mobilize a formidable military power, as the U.S. Army learned, their leaders generally lacked the institutional means or authority to regulate daily life.

To be sure, most Great Plains nations had "police societies," which could promote good behavior and intervene in disturbances within the camp. In extreme cases, camp police could confiscate malefactors' possessions or even banish them from the community altogether, but only to the extent such actions were supported by collective opinion. When internal disputes could not be resolved by means of negotiation and compromise between families, there was always the option of departure from the camp. A leader misguided enough to try to impose his will on the people would find himself without followers. Plains leaders earned their influence through courage, hard work, and generosity, and they retained it by setting a good example and by respecting the autonomy of others. They were "slow thinkers and silent eaters," as Severt Young Bear puts it so well.

It is accordingly difficult to translate "sovereignty" into Plains Indian languages without changing its meaning. In Lakota, Cree, and Blackfeet societies, for example, "sovereignty" is translated into phrases such as "we do things our own way" or "we are ourselves." This equates sovereignty with freedom rather than power. It has no reference to the existence or legitimacy of states, rulers, or human laws.

Early European explorers nevertheless frequently referred to chiefs as "kings" and showered them with presents in the manner of European court ceremony. What is more important historically and legally is the fact that British, French, Spanish, and Dutch colonists routinely made treaties with Indian nations for trade, military alliances, and the right to build settlements in tribal territories. Warfare and diplomacy with Europeans enhanced the status, wealth, and influence of individual Indian leaders within their own societies. The governance of Indian nations gradually became more centralized and coercive, adopting more and more the political culture of Europeans. Meanwhile, ironically, Europeans began to question whether Indian nations were entitled to be respected as sovereign and independent states—especially after signing treaties that placed them under the protection of European kings.

The first generation of American legal scholars turned to the writings of Grotius and Vattel to explain how a republic could claim to enjoy sovereignty in its diplomacy with European kings. John Marshall, who was secretary of state under President John Adams and then chief justice of the Supreme Court, applied Vattel's legal principles to Indian tribes in the case of *Worcester v. Georgia* (1832). Indian tribes continued to be "distinct, independent political communities, retaining their original natural rights," Marshall concluded, even where they had placed themselves under Europeans' protection by treaty. Although the Worcester decision made it clear that tribal sovereignty was limited only by Indians' consent—in a treaty—Marshall's earlier dictum in *Cherokee Nation v. Georgia* (1831) that Indian tribes are "domestic dependent nations" was resuscitated by late-nineteenth-century judges and has introduced a fundamental ambiguity into the issue of tribal sovereignty. More than a century later, Felix Cohen, a lawyer for the Bureau of Indian Affairs from 1933 to 1948, coined the term "residual sovereignty" to describe the political authority of Indian tribes, and it has continued to be used by lawyers and judges in the United States.

The application of the principle of sovereignty to Native American tribes has changed significantly over time. According to *Worcester*, the sovereignty of an Indian tribe is limited only by the express terms of its treaties with the United States. From 1890 to 1903, however, the U.S. Supreme Court upheld a number of federal laws that interfered with Indian property in violation of treaties, reasoning that Congress has superior sovereignty or "plenary power" over Indians. Finally, in *Oliphant v. Suquamish Indian Tribe* (1978), the Supreme Court ruled that accepting the protection of the United States implicitly stripped Indian tribes of political powers that are "inconsistent with their status" as Indians.

As a result of court decisions, the sovereignty of Native American tribes today is limited by what the tribes surrendered by treaty, what Congress has imposed on tribes by legislation, and what the courts consider to be "inconsistent with their status." Depending on the way particular courts interpret treaties and laws, Indian tribes' residual sovereignty can be very great, or nearly nonexistent.

In Canada, a constitutional monarchy in which the queen is the sovereign and head of state, the courts have not applied the term sovereignty to Indian nations. About half of the territory of Canada was acquired through Indian treaties made in the name of the Crown between 1724 and 1929, however, and most of the rest has been acquired through "modern-day treaties" made since 1975. Since the 1970s, moreover, Canada's Indian nations have in-

sisted that, although they respect the Crown, they possess "unsurrendered sovereignty" of their own. The government of Canada continues to resist this argument, although it has acknowledged as a matter of national policy that Indian nations possess an "inherent right to self-government."

Canada amended its national constitution in 1982 to include, among other changes, a declaration that "the existing aboriginal and treaty rights of the aboriginal peoples of Canada are hereby recognized and affirmed." Indian leaders argue that sovereignty and self-government are Aboriginal rights. This argument has not yet been tested in the Supreme Court of Canada, but it was strongly supported by the Royal Commission on Aboriginal Peoples, a seven-member national policy review body that was established in 1992 and published its final report four years later.

Sovereignty has taken on new meanings for Indian nations in the twentieth century as a result of wider economic and cultural changes and conflicts. The process of centralization of power, which began during the treaty-making period, was enhanced by legislation creating elected tribal lawmaking bodies—in the United States by the Indian Reorganization Act in 1934 and in Canada by amendments to the Indian Act in 1951. Federal funding of tribal government operations, mining of tribal lands, and (in the United States) profits from tribally owned gambling casinos have given many Indian tribal governments large infusions of cash and have turned tribal leaders into corporate managers and employers. Jurisdictional disputes with surrounding state and provincial governments have forced the tribes to assert exclusive territorial lawmaking and law-enforcing powers through the courts. More and more, Native American tribes are exercising sovereignty in the European sense of the word.

At the same time, U.S. and Canadian Indian nations no longer insist on complete independence, but rather a limited sovereignty similar to that of individual states within the American federal system, or individual provinces in Canada's confederation. They tend to accept the inevitability of some degree of congressional (or parliamentary) power over their lives and responsibility for their well-being, while demanding the greatest possible authority over their own territories and citizens. In Canada, this kind of arrangement has sometimes been described as "shared sovereignty," a cooperative political partnership under a freely agreed division of labor.

Although similar political changes have been taking place in Indian communities throughout the United States and Canada, some conflicts over power and resources have been specific to the Great Plains. Plains agriculture has long been based on economies of scale—that is, farming and ranching as much acreage as possible as a single unit. There was considerable pressure on federal officials to open large Indian reservations to leasing or permanent settlement, once the surrounding lands had been fenced. The mechanization of agriculture and soaring grain prices during World War I added to the demand for more acreage. The U.S. and Canadian governments both responded by facilitating the leasing of land within Indian reservations and the diminishment of reservation boundaries.

In the United States, Indian tribes have struggled unsuccessfully to maintain jurisdiction over all of the lands within their original reservation boundaries, including non-Indian settlements. The Supreme Court has taken the view that Congress intended to break up the larger Plains Indian reservations rather than place settlers under the authority of Indian governments. Several Sioux reservations have been considerably reduced (or "disestablished") as a result. The most recent Supreme Court decision, *South Dakota v. Yankton Sioux Tribe* (1998), concluded that Congress intended to dissolve the Yankton Sioux Indian Reservation when it purchased land for settlers from the tribe in 1892. An earlier decision, *Brendale v. Confederated Tribes* (1989), ruled that Indian governments lack authority over predominantly non-Indian settlements inside Indian reservations.

In Canada, leasing and cutoffs are the subjects of hundreds of unresolved land claims in the Prairies. Although the Canadian federal government has accepted responsibility for settling these claims on a case-by-case basis through negotiations, Indians have criticized delays and inadequate compensation. In *Guerin v. the Queen* (1985), Canada's Supreme Court ruled that federal officials have a "fiduciary responsibility" to manage Indian land prudently for Indians' benefit, and that they must pay for any losses attributable to mismanagement. The Royal Commission on Aboriginal Peoples called for the establishment of a tribunal, like the former U.S. Indian Claims Commission, to expedite the processing of land claims.

Meanwhile, water has been replacing land as the main source of friction between Indian tribes and their non-Indian neighbors. Irrigation has surpassed mechanization as the competitive edge in farming the Great Plains, and limited supplies of water must be rationed between long-established non-Indian farms and Indian reservations. In a 1908 decision, *Winters v. United States*, the U.S. Supreme Court reasoned that Congress necessarily intended to include sufficient water for Indian farming when it set land aside as reservations. In-

dian tribes in the Missouri River and Colorado River watersheds have used this legal principle to gain ownership of water and to build their own irrigation systems. Their right to sell unneeded water back to non-Indians is now in dispute.

Irrigation promises to be a growing source of conflict over water allocation in the Saskatchewan River basin, comprising much of southern Alberta and central Saskatchewan. Special Indian water rights have not yet been recognized by Canadian courts, however. To establish an "aboriginal right," according to Canada's Supreme Court in *R. v. Van der Peet* (1997), Indian nations would need to prove that water played a significant role in Aboriginal culture, and that it was neither expressly surrendered through treaty nor explicitly expropriated by Parliament. Since most of the Indians of the Saskatchewan River basin were originally hunters who only began farming and ranching after settling on reserves in the 1880s, it may be difficult for them to convince the courts that they enjoy an Aboriginal right to water.

The growing importance of water in the struggle over Indian sovereignty in the Great Plains highlights the issue of change in Indian nations' political organization and social values. In the arid Plains, water was an object of great reverence and careful stewardship. Important ceremonies, sacred bundles, and pipes were dedicated to water and water dwellers, such as the "beaver bundles" among the Blackfoot and Plains Crees. People exercised collective stewardship of water and shared its use; they did not contemplate altering its flow or allowing anyone to enjoy special privileges. Many Indian governments today associate water rights with large-scale reclamation projects, construction jobs, centrally managed agribusiness, cash flow, and political power.

In the Great Plains context, then, sovereignty has come to be associated more strongly with the power of institutions than with the freedom and responsibility of members of society. To a large extent, this shift in perspective is an understandable and justifiable response to continuing encroachments by Europeans and their governments. Indian nations built statelike institutions and greater power because they needed power to defend themselves. But the power to defend is also potentially the power to oppress people and to disrupt ecosystems. Acquiring sovereignty in the European sense brings new kinds of choices and responsibilities. Many contemporary North American Indians would share the critical viewpoint of Meskwaki (Sauk and Fox) poet Ray Young Bear, who wrote, "By replacing the window of the Cosmic Earth Lodge with aluminum panelling, we encouraged a sudden gust of wind to tear it apart, which made us cringe as the other elements gathered around us in force."

Russel Barsh
University of Lethbridge

Barker, Joanne. *Sovereignty Matters: Locations of Contestation and Possibility in Indigenous Struggles for Self-Determination.* Lincoln: University of Nebraska Press, 2005. Moore, John H. *The Cheyenne Nation: A Social and Demographic History.* Lincoln: University of Nebraska Press, 1987. Young Bear, Ray A. *Remnants of the First Earth.* New York: Grove Press, 1996. Young Bear, Severt, and R. D. Theisz. *Standing in the Light: A Lakota Way of Seeing.* Lincoln: University of Nebraska Press, 1994.

SPANISH-COMANCHE TREATIES

In November 1785 several thousand western Comanches congregated at their favorite wintering spot at the Big Timbers of the Arkansas River to discuss important news: after years of tiring mediation, Juan Bautista de Anza, the governor of New Mexico, wanted to negotiate peace with the Kotsoteka, Yamparika, and Jupe Comanches. Although the eastern Comanche bands had already entered into an accord with the Texan Spanish in October, some western bands remained recalcitrant. The opposition centered on Toro Blanco, who was backed by the bands that supported themselves by raiding New Mexican horse ranches. To resolve the deadlock, the peace faction assassinated Toro Blanco and forced his followers to disperse.

In February 1786 Ecueracapa, a Kotsoteka chief representing the peace proponents, arrived in Santa Fe, where he hammered out the treaty stipulations with Governor Anza. The Spanish promised the Comanches free access to New Mexican markets and trade fairs, distribution of presents to friendly chiefs, and regulation of the fairs so that the shrewd New Mexican traders could not cheat their Native clients. In return, the Comanches agreed to stop raiding, to unite behind one principal chief who would negotiate with the Spanish, and to refrain from trading with foreigners, particularly Americans. There also would be a joint Comanche-Spanish war against the Lipan Apaches, whom both parties wanted to expunge from New Mexico's eastern border. The alliance was sealed in an elaborate ceremony at which Anza distributed lavish gifts, including presenting Ecueracapa with a Spanish flag and a saber. The Comanches returned a New Mexican captive and "buried the war."

This Comanche–New Mexican treaty is one of the major turning points in the history of the Southern Plains. It marked a profound change in Spain's Plains Indian policy by ushering in the abandonment of the traditional military approach in favor of a diplomatic-commercial option. This shift pacified the southwestern Plains for over a generation: from 1786 to 1821 accommodation and trade rather than violence defined Comanche–New Mexican relations. On the other hand, the treaty was a disaster to the Lipans, who were soon forced to retreat to the Sangre de Cristo Mountains by the powerful Comanche-Spanish alliance. The counterpart of the 1786 Comanche–New Mexican treaty, the 1785 Comanche-Texan accord, proved less successful. Comanche-Texas trade did increase after 1785, but the province's officials lacked the necessary funds to maintain a consistent Indian policy. As a result, Comanche raids in Texas continued throughout the Spanish era.

Pekka Hämäläinen
University of California, Santa Barbara

Kavanagh, Thomas W. *The Comanches: A History, 1706–1875.* Lincoln: University of Nebraska Press, 1999.

SPORTS AND RECREATION

Women playing ball, 1916

Traditionally, Native American games were inseparable from their religions. Native American creation stories often involved contests between two opposing Twin Gods armed with clubs or bows and arrows. Games were replays of those creation stories while at the same time providing forums for achievement, recreation, and gambling.

Native American games fall into two broad categories: games of chance and games of dexterity. The former includes dice games and hidden ball games; the latter includes archery, the snow snake, the hoop and pole game, and various ball and running games. Many of these games were played throughout Native North America, but all had their local expressions in the Great Plains.

Dice games, involving dice made from many different materials, were played by every Plains tribe. They were generally played at night after the day's labor was done, and they sometimes went on all night, with considerable stakes involved. More often than not, they were played by women. Blackfeet women in Montana, for example, used four elaborately etched bison rib bones as dice. Sitting opposite each other, the women threw the dice on the ground, adding scores according to which side was up, until a winning score of twelve was attained. Omaha and Cheyenne women used plum stones with patterns burned into one side, and the dice were thrown into a wooden bowl or basket.

The hand game was one of the most widely played games of chance. Because it was done entirely by gesture, it could be played between members of different tribes who did not speak each other's language. In this game, an object made of bone, wood, shell, or hide was moved rapidly from hand to hand by one of the players. The opposing player, carefully tracking the sleight of hand, had to judge which hand held the object. The performance was accompanied by singing, which started out low and built to a crescendo as the swaying player switched the object back and forth until a hand was chosen. This was a man's game and often an occasion of competition between members of different tribes. There is an account of such a game on a Kiowa calendar from 1881–82. A Kiowa leader, Buffalo Bull Coming Out, was challenged by an Apache chief and medicine man. Both claimed the supernatural powers necessary to win. A large crowd waged prized possessions on the outcome, and the victory went to the Kiowa chief.

Games with bows and arrows were ubiquitous in the Great Plains and took many forms. For example, Pawnee boys or men would try to shoot arrows across another arrow that had been placed on the ground. The winner took all the arrows. In one Mandan version, young men, having paid an entry fee of a bison robe or other valued item, would shoot arrows in the air, one after the other. The winner who kept the most arrows in the air at one time took the prizes home.

The snow snake was another game of dexterity that was played wherever frozen conditions prevailed. Played by men and women, young and old, it involved sliding polished rocks, shaped bones, or spears along a track in the ice or snow. The player who slid the implement the farthest or the most accurately to a designated point was the winner.

The hoop and pole game, in a great variety of versions, was played throughout the region. A hoop made of wood, often covered with rawhide and netted in various designs, was rolled down a flattened track. The contestants (two men) tried to throw rods through the hoop or across the hoop as it started to fall. Again, there was gambling on the outcome of the game, but this did not obscure its religious implications. The Skidi Pawnees, for example, played the game to attract the bison, the rods representing bison bulls and the hoop a bison cow.

Lacrosse was played on the Northern Great Plains and in Indian Territory in the second half of the nineteenth century, although it was more common in eastern North America. Shinny, played with a curved wooden bat and a wooden or buckskin ball, was more prevalent on the Plains. Shinny was particularly a woman's game, although it was also played by men and sometimes by men against women. The objective was to knock the ball through the opponent's often-distant goal. Footraces were also common, and, for a man, being a celebrated runner, especially over long distances, was valued only behind being a successful warrior and hunter.

Many of these games died out as European American games and sports were adopted. Of the introduced sports, none was more suited to Native American skills and tradition than rodeo, which continues the horsemanship skills of the Plains Indians. Continuity is also apparent in other developments. The contemporary powwow combines ceremony, gift giving, and the athleticism and grace of dance competition. Gaming, which so rapidly developed on reservations in the 1990s, clearly continues the deeply rooted Native American tradition of gambling. Long distance running remains a Native American specialty, epitomized by Billy Mills, a Lakota from Pine Ridge Reservation who shot from the pack during the final two hundred meters of the ten-thousand-meter final race at the 1964 Tokyo Olympics, breaking the Olympic record in the process. And in any list of the twentieth century's top athletes, Jim Thorpe of the Sauk and Fox Tribe of Oklahoma must surely rank near the top.

Jeff Stuyt
Lubbock, Texas
David J. Wishart
University of Nebraska–Lincoln

Culin, Stewart. *Games of the North American Indians*. Bureau of American Ethnology, 1902–3. Washington DC: Government Printing Office, 1907. King, C. Richard, ed. *Native Athletes in Sport and Society*. Lincoln: University of Nebraska Press, 2005. Oxendine, Joseph B. *American Indian Sports Heritage*. Lincoln: University of Nebraska Press, 1995. Powers-Beck, Jeffrey. *The American Indian Integration of Baseball*. Lincoln: University of Nebraska Press, 2004.

Spotted Tail (Sinte Gleska), his wife, and daughter, ca. 1869–78

Spotted Tail (Sinte Gleska), a major Brulé Sioux leader in the Plains Indian wars, was born to a man named Chunka (Tangled Hair) and a mother named Walks With Pipe, probably along the White River of South Dakota. Known as Jumping Buffalo in his youth, Spotted Tail got his adult name from a striped raccoon pelt that was given to him by a trapper.

In 1855 he was jailed at Fort Leavenworth in retaliation for the defeat of Lt. John Grattan's force the previous year by Brulés, though Spotted Tail had not been involved in the incident. Upon his release in 1856, he balanced Lakota nationalism with conciliation to the United States, as he was convinced of American military superiority. By 1866 he had refrained from hostilities against Americans, unlike his nephew Crazy Horse.

Spotted Tail made several trips to Washington DC on behalf of his people in the 1860s and 1870s. During the most important visit, in 1875, Spotted Tail was among the Sioux chiefs appointed by U.S. officials to negotiate the sale of the Black Hills following George Armstrong Custer's expedition there a year earlier. Spotted Tail, who was one of the few Sioux chiefs who understood the value to Americans of the gold in the hills, demanded that the government's offer of $6 million be declined, but under duress he eventually agreed to its sale.

In the 1870s tension arose between Red Cloud and Spotted Tail after U.S. officials appointed Spotted Tail as chief of the Sioux at the Spotted

Tail and Rosebud Agencies, eventually replacing Red Cloud. Throughout the 1870s Spotted Tail was accused by Red Cloud of pocketing the proceeds from a sale of tribal land. Possibly as part of this dissension, Spotted Tail was shot to death on August 5, 1881, by Crow Dog, a Brulé subchief with whom he had several disputes. Crow Dog's murder case provided the gist of the Supreme Court case *Ex Parte Crow Dog* (1883), in which the defendant was eventually freed when the court ruled that the United States had no jurisdiction over the murder, which had occurred on Indian land.

Bruce E. Johansen
University of Nebraska at Omaha

Hyde, George E. *Spotted Tail's Folk*. Norman: University of Oklahoma Press, 1961. Schusky, Ernest Lester. *The Forgotten Sioux*. Chicago: Nelson-Hall, 1975. Utley, Robert M. *The Lance and the Shield: The Life and Times of Sitting Bull*. New York: Henry Holt, 1993.

STANDING BEAR (CA. 1829–1908)

Standing Bear and his family, ca. 1870s

In the Nebraska Hall of Fame in the State Capitol building is a bust of Standing Bear. He is there among other honored Nebraskans because of the pivotal role he played in resisting U.S. efforts to move his people from their homeland and for his victory in a famous trial, which projected American injustices against Native Americans into the public mind.

Standing Bear was born around 1829 in the traditional Ponca homeland near the confluence of the Niobrara and Missouri rivers. The Poncas sold this homeland to the United States in 1858, retaining a fifty-eight-thousand-acre reservation between Ponca Creek and the Niobrara. In 1865 the reservation boundaries were modified, resulting in a larger reservation that fronted on the Missouri River. On this reservation the Poncas lived a life of deprivation and fear—the United States did little to protect them from attacks from the Brulé Sioux. Furthermore, when the United States created the Great Sioux Reservation in 1868, the Ponca Reservation was included within its boundaries, arguably depriving them of title to their remaining land.

This was the context for the removal of the Poncas to Indian Territory in 1877. Standing Bear was among the chiefs who protested this eviction, and for this he was imprisoned at Yankton in early 1877. But they were forced to move. Standing Bear went with the second, more resistant, group of migrants. On the way, his daughter Prairie Flower died of consumption.

On their new reservation in Indian Territory, the Poncas continued to die in great numbers. The dead included Standing Bear's son. Unknown to their agent, Standing Bear and twenty-nine other Poncas had been storing their rations in preparation for the daunting journey back to the Niobrara. They left on January 1, 1879, and trekked through the Plains winter to reach the reservation of their relatives, the Omahas, in mid-March. Standing Bear carried with him the bones of his son to be buried in the familiar earth along the Niobrara.

Again the federal government intervened. Standing Bear and his followers were arrested by order of Gen. George Crook and taken to Fort Omaha, the intention being to return them to Indian Territory. At this point Thomas Henry Tibbles, an Omaha newspaperman, became interested in their plight and secured two Nebraska lawyers to represent them. The lawyers filed a federal court application for habeas corpus to test the legality of the detention. Judge Elmer Dundy, after permitting Standing Bear to make a moving speech, ruled the detention illegal and the prisoners released. Dundy reasoned that Indians were indeed "persons" under the law and entitled to sever tribal connections and to live where they desired.

Standing Bear subsequently toured the eastern United States with Tibbles, arousing support for the reform of federal Indian policy. In the 1880s he lived with his followers in the bend of the Niobrara, farming successfully. They became known as the Northern Poncas, and their lives increasingly separated from the Southern Poncas who had remained in Indian Territory. Standing Bear died in 1908 and was buried alongside his ancestors.

James Lake Sr.
University of Nebraska College of Law

Lake, James A., Sr. "Standing Bear, Who?" *Nebraska Law Review* 60 (1981): 451–503. Tibbles, Thomas Henry. *The Ponca Chiefs: An Account of the Trial of Standing Bear*, edited by Kay Graber. Lincoln: University of Nebraska Press, 1972. Wishart, David J. *An Unspeakable Sadness: The Dispossession of the Nebraska Indians.* Lincoln: University of Nebraska Press, 1994.

STANDING BEAR, LUTHER (1863/1868–1939)

Studio portrait of Luther Standing Bear, Hollywood, ca. 1920–39

Luther Standing Bear was a Brulé Sioux born either in 1863 (according to Bureau of Indian Affairs records) or 1868 (according to the Sioux winter count). At age eleven he volunteered to go to the Carlisle Indian Industrial School in Pennsylvania, where he was a member of the first class. Originally named Ote Kte, or "Plenty Kill," he adopted his father's name as his surname and chose the name Luther from a list of names on a blackboard. He grew to appreciate his American education, although he found the trade he learned—tinsmithing—to be virtually useless.

While at Carlisle, he and director Richard Henry Pratt grew to respect each other, although Standing Bear questioned Pratt's goal of extinguishing Indian culture. When he left school he returned to the Rosebud Reservation, where he worked as an assistant teacher and tried to influence other Sioux to adopt American ways. He married Nellie De Cory, the daughter of a trader and a Sioux woman.

Although he supported assimilation, Standing Bear often disagreed with the methods used by the agents, many of whom he found to be corrupt, incompetent, or both. At the same time, he distanced himself from his Sioux culture—he was a member of the Episcopal Church and served as a part-time minister. He supported the allotment of the Great Sioux Reservation. In 1891 he moved to the Pine Ridge Reservation, where he acted as assistant postmaster, clerked in his uncle's store, and later led the day school. He operated his own general store and started ranching.

In 1902 he toured England with Buffalo Bill's Wild West Show, acting as an interpreter and performing, once dancing by himself for King Edward VII. In 1905 he was chosen to be the leader of his *tiospaye* (large extended family), and later he claimed to be chief of the Oglala Sioux. He received an allotment for a full section of land in Bennet County, South Dakota, then traveled to Washington DC to meet with the commissioner of Indian affairs, arguing that he deserved the right to control his own property. He eventually did sell his land, then briefly moved to Sioux City, Iowa, working as a shipping clerk, before moving on to Walthill, Nebraska. He traveled to Oklahoma to work at the famous Miller Brothers 101 Ranch but determined the climate did not suit him, and in 1912 he migrated to California, where he spent the majority of the rest of his life.

In California he met Thomas Ince, a film producer who supervised his own band of Sioux, known as the "Ince Indians." Standing Bear worked with many of the most important stars of the era, including Douglas Fairbanks, William S. Hart, and Charles Ray. He sought to convince directors that their movies portrayed Indians unrealistically, in part because they hired so many non-Indians to play the roles. He made twelve films from 1916 to 1939.

Standing Bear worked to advance Indian rights, serving for two years as the president of the American Indian Progressive Association. He advocated Indian citizenship. In 1928 he published the first of his books, *My People the Sioux*, an autobiography. This was followed in 1931 by *My Indian Boyhood*, a children's book intended to develop understanding and sympathy for the Sioux people. In 1933, at the beginning of the Indian New Deal, he published *Land of the Spotted Eagle*, which explored Sioux life and powerfully criticized American Indian policy. In 1934 he published *Stories of the Sioux*, recounting twenty traditional Sioux tales. He is best known today for his writing, which combined a romanticized view of the past with a hopeful, even naïve, view of the benefits of Americanization, along with biting criticism of the methods used to achieve it. Luther Standing Bear died in Huntington, California, on February 19, 1939, while filming *Union Pacific*.

Charles Vollan
South Dakota State University

Ellis, Richard. "I would raise him to be an Indian." In *Indian Lives: Essays on Nineteenth- and Twentieth-Century Native American Leaders*, edited by L. G. Moses and Raymond Wilson, 138–58. Albuquerque: University of New Mexico, 1985. Standing Bear, Luther. *My Indian Boyhood*. Boston: Houghton Mifflin, 1931. Standing Bear, Luther. *My People the Sioux*. Boston: Houghton Mifflin, 1928.

SUMMIT SPRINGS, BATTLE OF

The Battle of Summit Springs, on July 11, 1869, was one of the most decisive engagements fought between the U.S. military and the Southern Plains Indians. In retribution for raids on Kansas settlements in 1868 and 1869, Brig. Gen. C. C. Augur, commander of the Department of the Platte, organized the "Republican River Expedition." His orders to expedition leader Maj. Eugene A. Carr were to clear Indians from the Republican River country with eight companies of the Fifth Cavalry and 150 Pawnee scouts under Maj. Frank North. The command was also to rescue 2 white prisoners, Maria Weichell and Susanna Alderice.

The campaign, which began from Fort McPherson, Nebraska, was directed against the famed Dog Soldier warrior society of the Southern Cheyennes led by Tall Bull. After eluding the soldiers, Tall Bull stopped on the south side of the swollen South Platte River in Logan County, Colorado. On July 11, under the cover of fog, the command advanced on the village of eighty-five lodges. Carr divided his troops into two attack wings and launched the assault about 3:00 p.m. The Pawnee scouts reached the village first, taking the Dog Soldiers by surprise. Guided by Two Crows, women and children took refuge in a nearby ravine. Tall Bull died defending his people, as did the highly regarded Wolf With Plenty of Hair, allegedly the last Dog Soldier to "stake himself out" with a symbolic "dog rope" in warfare. Carr officially reported one trooper wounded, fifty-two Indians killed, and seventeen women and children captured. Susanna Alderice was killed in the attack, and Maria Weichell was severely wounded.

Summit Springs ended conflict with Native Americans in the Colorado Plains. According to George Bent, who later related the history of the Cheyenne people, the Dog Soldiers were never again an important factor.

John H. Monnett
Metropolitan State College of Denver

Grinnell, George B. *Two Great Scouts and Their Pawnee Battalion: The Experiences of Frank J. North and Luther H. North.* Lincoln: University of Nebraska Press, 1973. Monnett, John H. *The Battle of Beecher Island and the Indian War of 1867–1869.* Niwot: University Press of Colorado, 1992.

SUN DANCE

The Sun Dance is a distinctive ceremony that is central to the religious identity of the Indigenous peoples of the Great Plains. It developed among the horse-mounted, bison-hunting nations who populated the Great Plains in the eighteenth and nineteenth centuries. Those nations at the core of its practice in the bison-hunting era that have continued its practice into the contemporary period include the Arapahos, the Cheyennes (Southern and Northern), the Blackfoot (who include the Siksikas or Blackfoot proper, the Bloods or Kainahs, and the Northern and Southern Piegans or Pikunis), and the Sioux (including in particular the westernmost Sioux, who are the seven tribes of the Lakota nation, but also including the Yanktons and Santees, who comprise the six tribes of the Dakota nation). From these four nations, the Sun Dance ceremony spread to the Kiowas and Comanches, who ranged the Southern Plains, and to Northern Plains nations such as the Plains Crees of Saskatchewan and the Sarcees of Alberta, as well as to virtually every other Plains nation in the land between these two extremes, including the Arikaras, Assiniboines, Crows, Gros Ventres, Hidatsas, Mandans, Pawnees, Plains Ojibwas, Poncas, Shoshones, and Utes.

The Canadian and U.S. governments perceived this ceremony as superstitious rather than religious and suppressed it, and full liberty to practice the Sun Dance was regained only after the mid–twentieth century. Some Sun Dances, including the Kiowa, Comanche, and Crow ceremonies, ended in the nineteenth century. Others persisted clandestinely through the time of suppression. The Crows in 1941 formally renewed practice of the ceremony by receiving the Shoshone form as their own.

The name "Sun Dance" derives from the Sioux identification of it as *Wi wanyang wacipi,* translated as "sun gazing dance." Other Plains peoples have names for the ceremony that do not refer to the sun. The Arapaho, Cheyenne, and Blackfoot names for the ceremony all refer to the medicine lodge within which the ritual dancing occurs. The medicine lodge is constructed of pole rafters radiating from a sacred central pole. However, the best-known and most widely practiced contemporary form of the ceremony is that of the Sioux, who do not construct a medicine lodge. Instead, the Sioux make a *hocoka,* or ritual circle, with a sacred cottonwood tree erected in the center and a circular

arbor built around the entire perimeter, except for an open entrance to the east, so that the dancing takes place within a central arena that is completely open to the sky and to "sun gazing." However, both traditions, whether that of the medicine lodge or of the hocoka, involve ritual ways of making local space sacred as a setting for renewal of the people's relationship with the land itself and with all the beings of their life-world, both human and other-than-human.

The ceremony is highly variable because its performance is intimately connected to the authoritative guidance of visions or dreams that establish an individual relationship between one or more of the central participants and one or more spirit persons. In all cases, however, the primary meaning is understood to be the performance of acts of sacrifice in ritual reciprocity with spiritual powers so that the welfare of friends, family, and the whole people is enhanced. The Arapaho, Cheyenne, Blackfoot, and Sioux nations all practice sacrificial acts of piercing the flesh, often described pejoratively as "torture" by outsiders. Others, such as the Ute, Shoshone, and Crow nations, perform sacrificial acts of embodying their spiritual intentions through fasting and intense dancing, but not through piercing.

Some Indigenous interpreters have suggested an analogy between the piercing of sun dancers and the piercing of Jesus on the cross, seeing both as acts of voluntary sacrifice on behalf of other beings and the cosmic welfare. While this interpretation may facilitate understanding for some, interpreters must be wary of imposing any religious category that clashes with the central concern of the Sun Dance: to establish and maintain kinship with all the people's relatives, including other humans, the animal and plant relatives of this earth, and the cosmic relatives of the spirit realm.

Dale Stover
University of Nebraska at Omaha

Densmore, Frances. *Teton Sioux Music and Culture.* Lincoln: University of Nebraska Press, 1992. Dorsey, George Amos. *The Arapaho Sun Dance: The Ceremony of the Offerings Lodge.* Field Columbian Museum Publication no. 75. Chicago: Field Museum of Natural History, 1903. Farr, William E. *The Reservation Blackfeet, 1882–1945: A Photographic History of Cultural Survival.* Seattle: University of Washington Press, 1986.

SWEAT LODGE

The sweat lodge is a contemporary religious ritual of ancient origin used by Native Americans throughout the Great Plains. Eastern Indian groups removed to the Plains by the U.S. government also engage in ceremonial sweating. Groups like the Cherokees and Chickasaws originally utilized permanent, dome-shaped log houses with subterranean floors that were also used for sleeping in winter. This entry will focus on the original Plains groups, among whom the ceremony takes place in a small, circular domed structure constructed of pliable saplings (often willow) with a single entrance facing a specific cardinal direction. The frame of this impermanent structure is tightly covered, formerly with skins but today with blankets, tarps, and sometimes sheet plastic. A pit is dug in the lodge to receive stones that are heated in a fire outside the lodge. This fireplace and frequently a mounded altar constructed of earth excavated from the interior pit are aligned with the entrance of the lodge.

The ceremony consists in entering the lodge, filling the pit with hot stones that are reverenced as ancient and spiritual in nature, pouring water on the hot rocks, praying, singing, speaking from one's heart, closing and opening the door a set number of times, and emerging from the lodge. Important elements in the ceremony that vary in emphasis from group to group are communication with the spiritual realm, moral and/or physical purification, the humbling of oneself, healing of self and/or others through the physical and/or spiritual agency of the sweat, and voluntary suffering to achieve a specific need or to fulfill a pledge for requests already granted.

Variations in the ceremony and structure of the lodge are accounted for by three factors: historic era, cultural group, and specific ritual leader. Nevertheless, there is remarkable consistency in the core ritual and structure across time and among different Plains groups. Variations include the incorporation of a prayer pipe and a variety of symbolic objects such as a buffalo skull placed on the altar outside of the sweat lodge; the erection of a pole on which to tie offerings; the use of switches made of sage, willow, cherry, buffalo tail, or horse hair; song accompaniment with a drum and/or rattle; the sacred use of plants such as sage, cedar, or pine needles; the pouring of herbal infusions on the rocks; drinking water between rounds and sometimes pouring it on oneself; spiritual supplication through crying; spiritual talks, particularly by the leader and sometimes other participants; joking when the door is open; and bathing in a cold stream at the conclusion of the ceremony.

The sweat lodge can be a ceremony in itself but is also used in preparation for other ceremonies such as the Sun Dance, sacred bundle ceremonies, vision quests, and sometimes Native American Church meetings. Among some tribes, men and women sweat together, while in others they are segregated. There are ritual restrictions for women in menses.

The ritual is widely used for marking significant life events, consoling and encouraging, protecting the group from misfortune such as disease, succeeding in battle and hunting, predicting future events, and averting future disaster. Many traditional stories of the revival of the dead through the agency of the sweat lodge attest to the great power of this ceremony.

The ceremony has markedly increased in practice since the beginning of the twentieth century, not only by Indian people on the reservations but more recently in urban areas, correctional facilities, veterans groups, and substance abuse treatment facilities. The spiritual strengthening and social conviviality inherent in the sweat serve to unite family members, Indians from different tribes, and non-Indians, although the proper place and role of outsiders in the sweat lodge and in Indian ritual in general are controversial.

Raymond A. Bucko
Creighton University

Bruchac, Joseph. *The Native American Sweat Lodge: History and Legends.* Freedom CA: Crossing Press, 1993. Bucko, Raymond A., S.J. *The Lakota Ritual of the Sweat Lodge: History and Contemporary Practice.* Lincoln: University of Nebraska Press, 1998. Vecsey, Christopher. "The Genesis of Phillip Deere's Sweat Lodge." In *Imagine Ourselves Richly: Mythic Narratives of North American Indians,* edited by Christopher Vecsey, 206–32. New York: Crossroad, 1988.

TALLCHIEF, MARIA (B. 1925)

Born in Fairfax, Oklahoma, on January 24, 1925, Elizabeth Marie Tall Chief became the first American classical dancer to earn international acclaim as a prima ballerina. Her parents, Alexander Joseph Tall Chief and Ruth Parker, had acquired their wealth from Osage oil money, and from her early years Elizabeth Marie was schooled in music and dance. In 1930 Ruth moved the family to Hollywood, California, specifically to advance the music and dance careers of Elizabeth Marie and her younger sister Marjorie. Elizabeth Marie's talents as a pianist and dancer blossomed, and by her senior year at Beverly Hills High School, she had chosen ballet for her career.

Elizabeth Marie joined the Ballet Russe de Monte Carlo in 1942 and gained soloist status in 1943, the same year she changed her name to Maria Tallchief. Following her 1946 marriage to George Balanchine, the Russian-born choreographer acclaimed as the father of American ballet, Tallchief became the first American featured as a guest artist with the Paris Opera Ballet. She joined Balanchine's Ballet Society in 1947 and contributed to the company's development into the New York City Ballet the following year. Tallchief was featured in twenty-two major works created by Balanchine and is recognized as the prototype for what is known today as the "Balanchine ballerina." During her career with the New York City Ballet, which ended in 1965, she appeared as guest artist with companies such as the American Ballet Theatre during its 1958 Russian tour and the Royal Danish Ballet. In addition to honors bestowed on her by the Osage Nation, the state of Oklahoma, and the dance world, Tallchief was named Indian of the Year in 1963. She received the Capezio Award in 1965, a Kennedy Center Honors in 1996, and a National Arts Award in 1999.

Lili Cockerille Livingston
Tulsa, Oklahoma

Livingston, Lili Cockerille. *American Indian Ballerinas*. Norman: University of Oklahoma Press, 1997. Reynolds, Nancy. *Repertory in Review: 40 Years of the New York City Ballet*. New York: Dial Press, 1977.

THORPE, JIM (1887–1953)

Jim Thorpe, ca. 1910

James Francis Thorpe, widely acknowledged as the greatest American athlete of the twentieth century, was born on May 28, 1887, near Prague, Indian Territory, in what is now the state of Oklahoma. His impoverished parents, Hiram and Charlotte Thorpe, were members of the Sauk and Fox Indian Nation. They gave their son the Native American name Wa-Tho-Huk, or Bright Path. To this day, Thorpe remains the only American athlete to perform at the world-class level in three major sports: track and field, baseball, and football.

Thorpe grew up hunting, fishing, and breaking horses with his twin brother, Charlie. Charlie died of pneumonia at age nine, and Thorpe came to believe he inherited a measure of his brother's physical energy and strength. Thorpe's mother died when he was a teenager, and his father subsequently sent him to the Carlisle Indian Industrial School in Pennsylvania, one of several schools founded by Richard Henry Pratt with the intent to assimilate Native American youths into European American society. After he enrolled at Carlisle, Thorpe returned to the Great Plains only intermittently throughout the remainder of his life.

While playing halfback for Carlisle, Thorpe earned football all-American honors in 1911 and 1912, leading Carlisle to the collegiate national championship in 1912. Although he did not become an official citizen of the United States until 1917, Thorpe was a member of the U.S. track and field team at the Olympic Games of 1912 held in Stockholm, Sweden. His gold medal performances in both the pentathlon and decathlon inspired King Gustav V of Sweden to remark, "You, Sir, are the greatest athlete in the world." Thorpe's gold medals were stripped from him by the Amateur Athletic Association when it was revealed that he had previously played semiprofessional baseball, but these medals were posthumously restored to him in 1982. It has been argued that the worldwide publicity inspired by Thorpe's accomplishments in Stockholm helped to ensure the future viability of the Olympic Games.

After his triumph in Stockholm, Thorpe signed a $5,000 contract to play baseball with the New York Giants. He played major league baseball for seven seasons, with New York, the Boston Braves, and the Cincinnati Reds. In 1915 Thorpe agreed to play football for the Canton Bulldogs. He led Canton to unofficial world championships in 1916, 1917, and 1919. Thorpe went on to play football for an assortment of teams, including the New York Giants and the Chicago Cardinals. In 1920 he become the first president of the American Football Association, which later became the National Football League. After retiring from sports, Thorpe worked as an actor and casting director in Hollywood, lectured around the country on Native American sports and culture, and during World War II served in the U.S. Merchant Marine. He died in his trailer in Lomita, California, on March 28, 1953. He is buried in the eastern Pennsylvania town that bears his name.

Thorpe was elected to the Pro Football Hall of Fame in 1963. In 1999 the Associated Press ranked Thorpe third on its list of the one hundred top athletes of the century, behind only Babe Ruth and Michael Jordan. In the same year, both the U.S. Senate and the U.S. House of Representatives passed resolutions that designated Thorpe "American Athlete of the Century." Prior to the 2000 Super Bowl, ABC Sports honored Thorpe as "Athlete of the Century," and the National Football

Decorated Blackfeet tipis, ca. 1900–1903

League renamed its most valuable player award in his honor.

Russ Cunningham
Poway High School

Schoor, Gene. *The Jim Thorpe Story: America's Greatest Athlete.* New York: Messner, 1951. Wheeler, Robert W. *Jim Thorpe: World's Greatest Athlete.* Norman: University of Oklahoma Press, 1981.

TIPIS

Tipis are the conical skin- or canvas-covered dwellings used by the Plains Indians as permanent or seasonal dwellings. The Sioux word *tipi* literally translates as "used to live in." In the nineteenth century each tipi accommodated, on average, eight to ten adults and children. Minimally, tipis consist of a number of long, thin poles placed vertically to form a conical framework, a hide or canvas cover, and tent pegs, rocks, or sod used to hold the cover to the ground.

The framework of tipis consists of peeled poles trimmed of all knots and branches and thinned at the base. Tipis normally utilize fifteen to twenty-five poles, two to adjust the smoke flaps and the rest for the frame. The poles are tied together at the peak of the cone, but poles extend several feet beyond the point where they cross. Size is limited by available pole size. An eighteen- to twenty-foot-diameter tipi uses sixteen to eighteen poles, each twenty-two to twenty-five feet long. Some tribes, particularly the Crows, preferred longer poles that extended higher above the cover. The poles were usually two to three inches in diameter where they crossed and three to six inches at their butts.

In many parts of the Northern Plains, lodgepole pine was the preferred tree for poles because it tends to grow tall and straight and requires less thinning at the base. Where lodgepole was not available, other conifers such as yellow pine, tamarack, and cedar were used, but these were normally heavier or required more trimming.

The tipi cover was made by piecing together hides or lengths of canvas. Buffalo hides were used until the second half of the nineteenth century, when they were gradually replaced by canvas. The hides were thinned, tanned, and cut to the desired shapes. The entire cover is a semicircle with a smoke flap on each side of the center point. The radius of the semicircle is close to the basal diameter of the finished tipi. A traditional tipi with a diameter of fifteen to sixteen feet required thirteen to sixteen buffalo hides. A modern tipi with a diameter of eighteen feet requires sixty-eight square yards of canvas.

Some tipi covers were painted. The painting was done before the tipi was erected. Designs included geometric shapes, sacred animals important to the designer, legends, and battle scenes. Women usually made, erected, dismantled, and maintained tipis, but men painted the designs, and the overall design was exclusive to the painter. The Kiowas of the Southern Plains and the Blackfeet of the Northern Plains were particularly renowned for their painted tipis.

Plains Indians set up tipis by first lashing three or four poles to form the frame. Most Siouan-speaking groups used a three-pole frame, whereas western Plains tribes such as the Crows and Blackfeet favored the four-pole frame. The remaining poles are placed on the frame, and the cover is stretched over the poles. The cover is laced together in the front of the tipi from the ground to the smoke flaps, leaving an opening for the doorway. The final step is to secure the bottom of the cover to the ground. Today, tipis are tied down with tent pegs. In the past, stones or sod blocks often secured the base of the cover. When the tipi was removed, the rocks were rolled off the cover and left as circular alignments, now called tipi rings. These provide the main archeological evidence of early tipi use.

Tipis are not perfectly circular. The poles on the back are usually slightly closer to the center, creating a steeper surface. This produces a slightly tilted cone, with the steeper back side facing windward and a more gradual slope on the leeward side with the doorway. This arrangement improves stability in strong winds. The difference between the long and short axis is less than 10 percent, and the floor plan is slightly egg shaped.

Tipis are, surprisingly perhaps, quite heavy. The poles for an average tipi weigh around 400 pounds, and a hide cover adds another 100 to 150 pounds. When Plains Indians acquired the horse, they could travel ten to fifteen miles a day using the poles as a travois and putting portions of the cover on each travois. Before the horse, however, dogs were the only pack animals, and it was a strenuous job for a family to move 500 to 600 pounds of tipi poles and cover, plus another 100 pounds or more of bison robes, stored food, and personal possessions five or six miles a day.

Tipis have probably been used since the Middle Archaic period, about 4,000 years ago. Most archeological evidence dates to the period 2,500 to 500 years ago. Tipi use increased steadily over time and was probably one of the major factors that enabled more intensive and specialized use of the open Plains. Virtually all tribes in the Great Plains from Texas to southern Canada used tipis. Eastern Plains groups who lived in earth lodge villages used them seasonally when hunting; western Plains hunting and gathering groups used them as year-round dwellings.

Tipis were ideal, adaptable dwellings for the semi-nomadic Plains Indians. They could be taken down or erected in a few hours and moved to anywhere the group chose to set up camp. They could be adapted to accommodate the number of occupants. In inclement weather they could be modified to include liners and insulation, and, with an internal fire, they offered protection from strong winds and frigid temperatures.

Today, tipis are important symbols of ethnic and tribal identity. They symbolize adherence to traditional ways, evoking lifestyles that persisted for centuries but that have since been effaced. Nevertheless, tipi designs, the knowledge of how

to erect tipis, and the right to paint them remain a prized part of the rich Plains Indian heritage.

Ken Deaver
Sherri Deaver
Billings, Montana

Ewers, J. C. *The Blackfeet: Raiders on the Northwestern Plains.* Norman: University of Oklahoma Press, 1958. Frison, G. C. *Prehistoric Hunters of the High Plains.* New York: Academic Press, 1978. Laubin, Reginald, and Gladys Laubin. *The Indian Tipi: Its History, Construction, and Use.* Norman: University of Oklahoma Press, 1977.

TONKAWAS

The Tonkawas were a combination of a number of independent bands. The name Tonkawa translates as "they all stay together." From at least the eleventh century until their removal to a reservation in Indian Territory in 1884, the Tonkawas occupied the pin oak prairie and grassland that stretched from the Llano River in central Texas to the Canadian River in Oklahoma.

The Tonkawas, who numbered several thousand before contact with Europeans, were led by a selected tribal chief. Maternal clans were the basic societal unit, with children becoming members of the mother's clan and the husband living with his wife's clan. The Tonkawas subsisted by hunting bison and other game and by gathering a wide variety of wild fruits, roots, and nuts. Unlike most other Plains Indians, they also ate fish and shellfish. They practiced agriculture, unsuccessfully, and only when the elimination of the bison drove them to it. Their traditional homes were short tipis made of bison hides. When this resource was no longer available, in the second half of the nineteenth century, they lived in tipi-like structures made of brush and grass, and later in flat huts roofed with brush. The Tonkawa language is thought to be unrelated to any other Native American language.

The Tonkawas initially came in contact with Spanish explorers in the sixteenth century. They came into permanent association with European settlers in 1722, when Juan Rodriguez, the chief of the southern Tonkawas (Ervipiames), demanded and received a mission, San Francisco Xavier de Najera, at San Antonio de Béjar in Texas. Although the Ervipiames and their allies never settled at San Antonio's missions in any numbers, the Tonkawas began to interact with the Spaniards as allies against the Lipan Apaches and Comanches. But Spain saw the advantages of Comanche friendship at the expense of the weaker Tonkawas, and by the 1770s the Tonkawas were left to make a place for themselves on the borderland between the Comanches and the Europeans. Under a chief named El Mocho they aligned themselves with the Lipans and Bidais. While successfully fending off Spanish and Comanche attacks, they moved closer to the forests of East Texas and absorbed the remnants of the Karankawas, a coastal tribe.

By 1821, when Stephen F. Austin's colonists arrived on the Brazos River, the Tonkawas were in need of powerful allies. They offered to serve the American settlers as scouts and fighters. Throughout the years of the Austin Colony, the Texas Revolution, and into the decade of Texas's independence, the Tonkawas served loyally as auxiliaries to the military arm of Anglo Texas in its battles with Iscanis (a sub-tribe of the Wichitas) and Comanches. Their reward, after the United States had annexed Texas, was to be removed to a reservation on the Clear Fork of the Brazos in 1856, a time when Texans were demanding that all Indians be exiled from the soil of the state. In 1859 the Tonkawas were removed to Fort Cobb on the Washita River in Indian Territory, along with the other tribes of the Texas frontier.

Old enmities died hard, however, as did old friendships. Tonkawas continued to help United States and Texas troops fight the Comanches. With the outbreak of the Civil War, the Tonkawas sided with the Texans, while most Indians at Fort Cobb favored the Union. On October 24, 1862, pro-Union Indians attacked the Tonkawas, killing half the tribe and driving the survivors back into Texas, where Confederate authorities provided them with food and clothing and enlisted them as scouts on the frontier.

When the Civil War ended, the relentless push of Americans westward into Comanche country once again provided the Tonkawas with employment. Enlisted by the U.S. Army as scouts, they were settled at Fort Griffin in north-central Texas and employed continually until the Comanche defeat in 1878. Tonkawa scouts distinguished themselves in every major action of the post–Civil War era in Texas. When the Comanches and their allies had been confined to a reservation, the Tonkawas expected to be rewarded for their long service to the United States. Instead Fort Griffin was abandoned in 1881 and the Tonkawas' funds were cut off. For three years the tribe survived mostly on rations, until they were forcibly removed to lands abandoned by Chief Joseph's Nez Perces near the present-day town of Tonkawa, in Kay County, Oklahoma. In 1896 their reservation was allotted, and their land base was further reduced. They now hold 399 acres of land. Their population plummeted to 34 in 1921, then began a slow revival to 43 in 1936 and 186 in 1993.

In recent years Tonkawas have developed an interest in their past and their role in Texas settlement. A powwow in Austin and local gatherings in Oklahoma have served to create a renewed interest in a people who are among the original settlers of what is now Texas and the most loyal of American allies.

Thomas F. Schilz
San Diego Miramar College

Carlisle, Jeffery D. "Tonkawa Indians." In *The New Handbook of Texas*, edited by Ron Tyler, 6:525–26. Austin: Texas State Historical Association, 1996. Smithwick, Noah. *The Evolution of a State, or Recollections of Old Texas Days*. Austin: Gammel Book Company, 1900.

TRADE

Native peoples of the Great Plains engaged in trade between members of the same tribe, between different tribes, and with the European Americans who increasingly encroached upon their lands and lives. Trade within the tribe involved gift-giving, a means of obtaining needed items and social status. Trade between Plains tribes often took the form of an exchange of products of the hunt (bison robes, dried meat, and tallow) for agricultural products, such as corn and squash. European and American items, such as horses and guns and other metal products, were incorporated into the existing Plains trade system after the seventeenth century.

Trade among the Plains Indians has a long history. The archeological record shows an active trade in Knife River flint in the Northern Plains beginning before 2000 BC. Moreover, copper, obsidian, and marine shell artifacts suggest an existence of an early east–west trade route crossing the Northern Plains and connecting to the Great Lakes and the Atlantic Coast in the east and the Rocky Mountains and the Pacific Coast in the west. Farther south, the people living along the lower Missouri, Arkansas, and Red rivers traded in copper and marine shells with the Mississippi Valley people after 2000 BC. There is also evidence of local trade for this period. While the Northern Plains trade system remained relatively stable throughout the following centuries, the Southern and Central Plains trade patterns changed dramatically around 1200 AD, when the ties between the Mississippi valley and the lower Missouri, Arkansas, and Red river societies were cut. Further changes came in the fourteenth and fifteenth centuries, when the Southern Plains societies began to trade in corn, pottery, and bison products with the Pueblos of the Southwest.

At the time of European contact, there were two types of Native American trading sites in the Great Plains. The first was associated with permanent agricultural villages, including those of the Mandans and Hidatsas in present-day North Dakota and the Arikaras in present-day South Dakota. These sites hosted trading parties from the Crows, Shoshones from the west, Assiniboines and Crees from the north, and Plains Apaches, Cheyennes, Arapahos, and Pawnees from the south. Lewis and Clark, who wintered with the Mandans in 1804, noted that traders in the villages obtained items from as far as Mexico and the Pacific Coast. In the Southern Plains, the Wichita villages on the Arkansas and Red rivers served as trading sites for Jumanos, Apaches, Comanches, and Pawnees.

The second type of trading site was a trade fair, or rendezvous, in which bands met to exchange goods away from a permanent village, generally at a point convenient to nomadic bands. The Dakota rendezvous, held on the James River in present-day South Dakota, and the Shoshone rendezvous, held in southwestern Wyoming, were regular trading fairs at the beginning of the nineteenth century. A major trading site—perhaps as important as those at the Mandan, Hidatsa, and Arikara villages—was operated by the Western Comanches in the valley of the upper Arkansas River from the 1740s to around 1830.

An integral part of the trade system was the middlemen who operated between the various trade centers. The Cheyennes served as intermediaries between the upper Missouri villages and the Southern Plains hunter-pastoralists and carried firearms and other European American goods to the south and horses to the north. The Crows trafficked in horses and firearms between the central upper Missouri and the Shoshone rendezvous. The Assiniboines and Plains Crees carried manufactured goods to the upper Missouri from Canadian fur traders and took back horses and corn. In the Southern Plains, the Jumanos and Apaches and later the Apaches and Comanches competed for the lucrative middleman position between the Wichitas and the Pueblos. By linking the trade centers, these middleman groups integrated the Plains tribes into a compact commercial network that covered the whole region.

The trade systems were maintained through a variety of sustaining mechanisms, including the calumet ceremony, redundancy trading, and sign language. The calumet ceremony made unrelated peoples one family through the working of a fictional kinship. Leaders of different bands or tribes adopted each other as father or son, allowing trade to take place even between traditional enemies. In such exchanges, tribes gained access to foodstuffs that would otherwise have been difficult to acquire. However, Native peoples often exchanged corn for corn, or meat for meat. The Pawnees, for example, traded corn for corn with the Arikaras. This redundancy trading was a security mechanism, setting up avenues for exchange in case of local crop failure. Sign language allowed linguistically diverse tribes to negotiate the terms of the trade.

European traders began to engage in this trade from the edges of the Plains. Spanish settlers in Santa Fe exchanged goods of European manufacture, such as beads, mirrors, and blades, for hides, foodstuffs, and services early in the seventeenth century. British traders infiltrated the network from the northeast, and French and Spanish traders pushed up the Missouri River from St. Louis in the late eighteenth century. By the early nineteenth century, American and British fur companies had created networks of fixed trading posts throughout the Missouri and Saskatchewan river drainage basins. At these points European and American manufactured products were exchanged for bison robes, beaver pelts, and other furs and skins. The Plains Indians became the primary producers in an international trade system controlled from New York and London. American and Canadian traders also sought to bypass the traditional middlemen and used alcohol as a means to curry favor. The Indians would not have participated if they had not valued the introduced products (especially guns), but a dependency on outside supplies was created, and when there no longer were furs to trade the Indians could not obtain the goods they had come to rely upon.

The increased market demands resulted in the collapse of the resource base. By 1840 beaver had been eliminated from large parts of the Plains, and the virtual destruction of the bison herds in the 1870s brought an end to the traditional Plains Indian trade. Restricted to reservations in both Canada and the United States, the Indians' trade was often a sale of annuity goods, at inadequate prices, at the local trader's store. Native American conventions of trade continued, and continue within tribes and in contexts like powwows between tribes, but the traditional Plains trade system that had endured for so long fell victim to imposed European American economies.

Mark A. Eifler
University of Portland

Hämäläinen, Pekka. "The Western Comanche Trade Center: Rethinking the Plains Indian Trade System." *Western Historical Quarterly* 29 (1998): 485–513. Jablow, Joseph. *The Cheyenne in Plains Indian Trade Relations, 1795–1840.* Vol. 19 of *Monographs of the American Ethnological Society.* New York: J. J. Augustin, 1950. Swagerty, William R. "Indian Trade in the Trans-Mississippi West to 1870." In *Handbook of North American Indians,* edited by William C. Sturtevant, 4:351–74. Washington DC: Smithsonian Institution, 1988.

TRANSPORTATION

For the Native peoples, the Great Plains was a world of enormous distances. All Indigenous groups of the Plains, whether nomads or semi-nomads, spent much of their time following the wide-ranging bison herds. In addition, the scarcity of streams and scattered distribution of springs, the primary sources of water, forced these peoples to cover enormous distances on a daily basis. Finally, most Plains tribes were engaged in long-distance commerce at trade centers such as the Arikara and Mandan-Hidatsa villages on the upper Missouri River, which, for some tribes, meant covering hundreds of miles.

The primary reason that made the distances so demanding was the lack of efficient transportation facilities in the period before contact with Europeans. Native Americans lacked large beasts of burden such as camels and horses. Their only domesticated animal was the dog, which was used to carry loads and to draw the travois. Native peoples employed the travois to transport household utensils, weapons, tools, tipi covers, firewood, and meat, but a dog could haul only about sixty pounds, which meant that human beings, particularly women, did most of the carrying themselves. Most Plains rivers were dry for too long each year to be useful channels for water transportation. As a result, only a few Plains tribes, including the Assiniboines, Blackfoot, and Crees, used canoes, while others relied only on land transportation. The Assiniboines, Blackfoot, and Crees were particularly skillful in using the canoe. In the early eighteenth century, for example, the Blackfoot canoed to the Hudson Bay to trade with the British. More locally, the tribes along the Missouri River developed bullboats—small, light, bowl-shaped vessels made of bison hides—for transportation of goods.

The event that changed the traditional transportation system was, of course, the introduction of the horse to the Plains by the Spanish. (Actually, the proper term would be *reintroduction*, for horses had lived on the Plains until they became extinct around 8000–6000 BC.) Coronado and other early Spanish conquistadors explored the Southern Plains on horseback in the sixteenth century, but horses did not begin to spread among the Indians until the Spanish established a permanent colony, New Mexico, at the southwestern edge of the Plains at the end of the sixteenth century. Gradually, through trade and theft, horses spread from the New Mexican ranches in all directions, so that by the end of the eighteenth century all Plains tribes were mounted.

In time, the introduction of the horse was to have far-reaching cultural, economic, and political effects among the Plains Indians, but the most immediate consequence was a transportation revolution. The horse was about eight times as efficient as the dog: it could carry on its back or haul on a travois a load four times heavier than the load a dog could manage, and it could travel twice as far in a day. Thus, horse transport allowed Indians to carry more tools and utensils, extra foodstuffs, and larger tipis, and suddenly nomadism did not require giving up all but the bare minimum of possessions. It also made it possible for Indians to hunt bison more effectively, and this enticed horticulturists—the Omahas, for example—to increase the role of hunting in their economies. Interaction between tribes increased as sheer distance became less of an obstacle. In short, like railroads in the late nineteenth century, horses reduced the friction of distance, opened new economic possibilities, and raised the standards of living on the Plains.

The adoption of horses also resulted in the abandonment of canoes, usually within a generation after the Indians received their first horses. Dogs, on the other hand, continued to be used for transportation throughout the prereservation period. This was particularly the case on the Northern Great Plains, where distance from the source of horses and cold winters, which made herding more difficult and labor intensive, reduced the availability and numbers. The Southern Plains Indians, who had the largest herds, continued to use dogs to carry small items such as moccasins and household utensils.

H. Roger Grant
Clemson University

Ewers, John C. *The Horse in Blackfoot Indian Culture*. Bureau of American Ethnology Bulletin 159. Washington DC: Smithsonian Institution, 1955. Haines, Francis. "The Northward Spread of Horses among the Plains Indians." *American Anthropologist* 40 (1938): 429–37.

TRAVOIS

Unique to the Plains, the travois is a wooden load-bearing frame fastened by a leather harness to a dog or horse. The basic dog travois consists of two aspen or cottonwood poles lashed together at one end with buffalo sinew. The other ends rest splayed apart. Crossbars are lashed between the poles near the splayed ends. The finished frame looks like a large letter A with extra crossbars. The apex of the A, wrapped in buffalo skin to prevent friction burns, rests on a dog's shoulders, while the splayed ends drag over the ground.

Used by Plains Indian nations, travois were perfectly suited to their environment. Over native grasslands the dragging travois ends sweep silently and nearly without friction; they appear almost to float through the same prairie that cracks and breaks wheel axles. Outside of grasslands the travois is not much used, for bush and gullies are impassable.

Native women both built the travois and managed the dogs, sometimes using toy travois to train puppies. Bison meat and firewood were typical travois loads. Dogs could tack up and down grassy

Husky and travois, in contemporary scene

hill slopes and ford shallow rivers with a travois. But temperature was a serious constraint on travois work, for on warm days dogs overheated easily.

In historic times Plains Indians constructed much larger versions of the dog travois and hitched them to horses. Horse travois allowed the transport of the increased material wealth accumulated by some Native nations skilled in the mounted bison hunt. Children or ill adults could ride on the horse travois load rack as well. Their rack ride was smooth, but the legs of the saddle rider, typically female, hung uncomfortably over the travois poles.

Norman Henderson
University of East Anglia, England

Ewers, John. *The Horse in Blackfoot Indian Culture.* Bureau of American Ethnology Bulletin 159. Washington DC: Smithsonian Institution, 1955. Henderson, Norman. "Replicating Dog Travois Travel on the Northern Plains." *Plains Anthropologist* 39 (1994): 145–59.

TREATIES

In both the United States and Canada, negotiated treaties were the instrument for obtaining Indian lands and more generally for extending federal control over Native peoples, while at the same time recognizing the sovereignty they retained. In the United States, the Constitution gave the executive branch the authority to negotiate treaties and the Senate the authority to ratify them. Treaty making was abolished in 1871, but similar bilateral agree-

ments between the federal government and the tribes continued thereafter. In Canada, the provision for a treaty process was established with the Royal Proclamation of 1763, whereby the Crown reserved the sole right to purchase Indian lands. That authority was continued through the British North America Act of 1867, which passed on the Crown's authority over First Peoples to the new Dominion of Canada.

In both Canada and the United States, early treaties proclaimed peace and friendship between the government and the Native peoples. The fact is, neither of the colonizing powers had the military power to defeat the Indians, and treaties were a pragmatic alternative. After 1812, however, the population balance swung in favor of the European Americans, and treaties became the means to acquire Indian lands. Especially in the United States, it was a buyer's market. Pressured by settlers and mired in poverty, Indians rarely had any option but to sell. In many cases, consent to treaties was obtained only through fraud and duress. The surrender of the Black Hills by the Lakotas (Sioux) in 1877 and the sale of the Red River Valley of the North by the Red Lake and Pembina bands of the Chippewas are notable examples of such manipulation.

In the American Great Plains, treaty making for the purpose of obtaining Indian lands began with the cession of what is now southern Oklahoma by the Quapaws in 1818. This land, and vast areas

U.S. Army commissioners in council with chiefs, Fort Laramie, Wyoming, 1868

subsequently obtained in the 1820s and 1830s in present-day Oklahoma, Kansas, and southern Nebraska, were bought from Plains Indians to make room for relocated Indians from the eastern United States. The next wave of treaties came in eastern Nebraska and southeastern Dakota Territory in the second half of the 1850s when the Pawnees, Omahas, Poncas, Otoe-Missourias, and Yanktons sold their ancestral lands, retaining only small reservations. European Americans moved in to settle the newly acquired public domain. This process was repeated westward and northward throughout the Great Plains in the following four decades. Indian dispossession, achieved through treaties, was the prerequisite for frontier settlement.

In Canada, the clearing of Indian title to the Prairie Provinces was done more quickly. From 1871 to 1877, in a series of seven numbered treaties, the many bands of Crees, Chippewas, Assiniboines, and Blackfoot relinquished their claims to the land and settled on reserves. The terms of each treaty varied only in detail. Through Treaties 1 and 2, for example, concluded in 1871, the Swampy Crees and Chippewas ceded 52,400 square miles of southern Manitoba and Saskatchewan in return for a reserve, a school, farm implements, a onetime payment of $3 per person, and an annuity of $3 per person.

Similar types of compensation were given south of the forty-ninth parallel. In both coun-

tries, payments for lands—the monies due the Indians—were used to fund the government's "civilization" programs, which aimed to assimilate the Indians as independent, self-sufficient, Christianized farmers. But payments for Indian lands were so low (they averaged ten cents an acre in the Central and Northern Great Plains) and the quality of services and goods so poor, that the end product of treaty making was poverty, not self-sufficiency.

On the one hand, then, treaties can be viewed as a subterfuge, a means of acquiring Indian lands legally and without the more expensive and disruptive warfare. Negotiations took place, the Indians had their say, and the federal governments set the conditions of the divestiture. On the other hand, treaties established reservations and reserves where tribal law and government still prevail despite challenges. Treaties are not merely historical documents; they are contracts between sovereign powers, the foundation of Indian law, and often the legal justification for claims cases.

David J. Wishart
University of Nebraska–Lincoln

Cohen, Felix S. *Handbook of Federal Indian Law.* Buffalo: William S. Hein, 1988. McQuillan, Aidan D. "Creation of Indian Reserves on the Canadian Prairies, 1870–1885." *Geographical Review* 70 (1980): 219–36. St. Germain, Jill. *Indian Treaty-Making Policy in the United States and Canada, 1867–1877.* Lincoln: University of Nebraska Press, 2001. Wilkinson, Charles F. *American Indians, Time, and the Law.* New Haven CT: Yale University Press, 1987.

TRIAL OF STANDING BEAR

On May 12, 1879, in Omaha, Nebraska, in the U.S. Circuit Court for the District of Nebraska, Judge Elmer Dundy ruled that noncitizen Indians—in this case, a group of Poncas led by Chief Standing Bear—were defined as persons in terms of federal law and entitled to review under habeas corpus protections (a constitutionally based appeal used to determine whether a person is restrained or imprisoned without due process). The writ of habeas corpus specifically stated that Standing Bear and his followers had withdrawn from the Ponca tribe. Standing Bear's case not only played a central role in four crucial decades of Ponca-federal relations, but it also directly influenced landmark Indian policy changes of the 1880s.

In an 1858 treaty, the Poncas ceded all their lands except for a small reservation (in present-day northeastern Nebraska) on the lower Niobrara River. Dutifully taking up farming the white man's way, the Poncas endured terrible hardships when their crops regularly failed and Indian agency supplies remained woefully inadequate. Yet their long-standing friendship with the United States failed to prevent their forced removal to Indian Territory in the spring of 1877. The Poncas' conditions worsened due to the Office of Indian Affairs' complete lack of preparation for their arrival—no lands had been reserved and no appropriation secured to provide food, clothing, and housing. As many as two hundred Poncas died from related hardships. In January 1879 Standing Bear and twenty-nine others fled back to their Nebraska homeland. When they reached the Omaha reservation in March, the U.S. Army arrested them and escorted them to Fort Omaha (located four miles north of Omaha, Nebraska).

On March 30 *Omaha Daily Herald* assistant editor Thomas Henry Tibbles interviewed Standing Bear and dispatched a stream of features to newspapers in Chicago, New York, and other eastern cities. Tibbles also inaugurated a legal challenge against Standing Bear's arrest, obtaining the services of two prominent Omaha attorneys, John Lee Webster and A. J. Poppleton. In May, Judge Dundy delivered his extraordinary ruling that habeas corpus safeguards applied to Standing Bear, even though as a Native American he was a noncitizen and in spite of the fact that for all practical purposes he had renounced his Ponca tribal affiliation. Moreover, because federal statutes authorized the army to deliver prisoners only to civil authorities, making the Ponca detainment at Fort Omaha illegal, Dundy ordered Standing Bear and the Poncas released and directed that there would be no appeals to a higher court.

Judge Dundy's bold decision protected Stand-

ing Bear's Poncas from being returned to Indian Territory, but it provided no lands for them. In 1890 they finally secured allotments on their former reservation. Equally important, Standing Bear's struggle for justice significantly influenced the national movement to reform Indian policy. In the fall of 1879 Tibbles featured Standing Bear on a highly successful Indian reform tour that included Chicago, Boston, New York, Philadelphia, and Washington. In Boston, Standing Bear's eloquence so impressed Massachusetts senator Henry L. Dawes that he plunged into the Indian reform movement. He joined the Senate Indian Affairs Committee, and his leadership on Indian issues and prominence on the popular issue of Indian assimilation led directly to passage of the 1887 General Allotment (or Dawes) Act. Standing Bear lived on his family allotment on the Niobrara until his death in 1908.

Dennis J. Smith
Morningside College

Hoxie, Frederick E. *A Final Promise: The Campaign to Assimilate the Indians, 1880–1920.* Lincoln: University of Nebraska Press, 1984. Lake, James A., Sr. "Standing Bear, Who?" *Nebraska Law Review* 60 (1981): 451–503. Tibbles, Thomas Henry. *The Ponca Chiefs: An Account of the Trial of Standing Bear,* edited by Kay Graber. Lincoln: University of Nebraska Press, 1972.

TRIBAL COLLEGES

Thirty-eight tribal colleges across the United States and Canada enroll thirty thousand students from more than two hundred Native American and First Nations tribes. Tribal colleges are unsurpassed in their ability to provide the knowledge and skills Indian students need to become successfully employed, and their job placement rates are high. In addition, 42 percent of graduates from these colleges continue their education in other postsecondary institutions. Indian students who transfer from tribal colleges are four times more likely to complete four-year degree programs than those who enter mainstream institutions as freshmen.

Twenty-five tribal colleges are located in the Great Plains: seven in Montana, five in North Dakota, four in South Dakota, three in Alberta, two in Nebraska, two in New Mexico, one in Kansas, and one in Saskatchewan. Maskwacîs Cultural College in Alberta was the first tribally controlled college in Canada. In July 1988 the Legislative Assembly of Alberta passed the Maskwacîs Cultural College Act, which established the college as a private postsecondary institution with authority to grant certification to students at the certificate and diploma levels. Since then, Maskwacîs Cultural College has grown to offer nine one- and two-year program certificates and eight bachelor's degrees. Founded in 1884 as an Indian boarding school, Haskell Indian Nations University in Lawrence, Kansas, became the first federally chartered Indian college in the United States in 1970. Two tribally controlled colleges in the Great Plains were founded in 1971: Oglala Lakota College in Kyle, South Dakota, and Sinte Gleska University in Rosebud, South Dakota. Most recently, Little Priest Tribal College was chartered in Winnebago, Nebraska, in 1996.

In the United States tribal colleges are situated on land that is considered to be federal trust territory. This means that individual states are not required to provide any funding, making most tribal colleges dependent upon the federal government's treaty obligation and trust responsibility to provide education for Native American tribes. With unemployment on Native American reservations ranging from 30 to 70 percent, the greatest challenge faced by administrators, faculty, staff, and students at tribal colleges is funding. This is reflected in the White House Executive Order on Tribal Colleges and Universities (1998), which lists increasing core funding for operations as the first priority for the thirty federal departments and agencies involved in tribal college education.

The mission statements of the twenty-five tribal colleges in the Great Plains stress three fundamental concepts. First, all of the colleges focus on the importance of students understanding their sense of self-identity. For example, Dull Knife Memorial College in Lame Deer, Montana, states that the college operates "in the belief that all individuals should be treated with dignity and respect." A second common concept emphasized by tribal colleges is the preservation and perpetuation of their Native cultures. Blackfeet Community College in Browning, Montana, for example, which serves students from both Montana and Canada, states that, "most importantly, it is the mission of Blackfeet Community College to serve as a living memorial to the Blackfeet Tribe, in preserving the traditions and culture of a proud and progressive people."

Finally, tribal colleges stress the importance of students being able to understand the differences between Native culture and Western society. For example, Cankdeska Cikana Community College in Crow Agency, Montana (formerly Little Hoop Community College), states that "the mission of Cankdeska Cikana Community College is to provide comprehensive post-secondary education which addresses both traditional and contemporary aspects of learning. The college focuses on educating our students to live successfully by assisting each in reaching a goal that is desirable and attainable for their needs in this multi-cultural world." These examples, or philosophies, may well explain why tribal colleges are so successful in educating Native peoples.

Charles A. Braithwaite
University of Nebraska–Lincoln

American Indian Higher Education Consortium and the Institute for Higher Education Policy. *Tribal Colleges: An Introduction.* Washington DC: Tribal College Research and Database Initiative, 1999.

TRICKSTER

The trickster is the embodiment of lawlessness and paradox. He is a divine buffoon, a hero who breaks taboos, a rebel, a coward, and a creator. Trickster helps establish social rules, and he deliberately flouts them. He is commonly depicted as deceitful and humorous. He is amoral, rather than immoral, and he has a voracious appetite for food and sex. In his traditional and mythic incarnations, he is almost always male. As the supreme boundary-crosser, trickster is always *between* classifications—between what is human and what is animal, between what is cultural and what is natural.

Native American tricksters tend to be associated with animal spirits (such as Coyote, Rabbit, or Raven). Their tales are both sacred myths and simple folk tales. Among the Indigenous peoples of the Great Plains, the trickster's name is Old Man (Crow and Blackfoot), Iktomi (Lakota), and Veeho (Cheyenne). The most common incarnation of the Plains trickster, however, is Coyote.

In his various (and strikingly similar) cultural guises, trickster is the self-indulgent clown who dupes women into having sex with him; he steals food from his industrious neighbors; he cross-dresses and becomes temporarily a woman; he dies and is reborn. As expected, his tomfoolery frequently backfires. He juggles his eyes and loses them in a tree; he accidentally sleeps with his wife; he drowns in his own feces; he uses his enormous penis to attack a chipmunk (who in turn bites his penis off to "human" size). Further, trickster is a cultural hero. In some narratives, he creates the Earth; he creates animals or substantially alters their bodies; he steals tobacco from the gods; and, more recently, he tricks the white man.

Symbolically, the trickster is always located at the periphery of the community (though, importantly, never totally separated from it). From this "outer" vantage point, trickster reveals "inner" communal structures. His very presence determines the limits of social boundaries. Trickster thus serves as a political tool with which to subvert (or endorse) social practices. Indeed, trickster continually offers us the possibility of transcending (or renewing) social codes. As such, trickster is arguably an incarnation of creativity itself. At the very least, trickster allows us to poke fun at the powers that restrain us. He reveals the *structure* of social structures and offers us glimpses of new (and terrifying) world orders. Not surprisingly, many contemporary authors use tricksterlike characters as creative forces that both define and critique dominant cultural practices.

Ultimately, the trickster is disturbing, not because of his difference but because of his lack of difference. As purely a cultural construct, the trickster's body is a cultural body—our body. He is always a part of us, and he exists only to be interpreted. And when we interpret trickster, we interpret ourselves. Even though we often attempt to alienate ourselves from the trickster—by making his body grotesque, indistinguishable—wherever we are, there is trickster, laughing at what we've become.

Anthony Farrington
University of Arkansas–Monticello

Babcock, Barbara. "'A Tolerated Margin of Mess': The Trickster and His Tales Reconsidered." In *Critical Essays on Native American Literature*, edited by Andrew Wiget, 153–84. Boston: G. K. Hall. Ballinger, Franchot. "Living Sideways: Social Themes and Social Relationships in Native American Trickster Tales." *American Indian Quarterly* 13 (1989): 15–30. Radin, Paul. *The Trickster: A Study in American Indian Mythology*. New York: Philosophical Library, 1956.

TROPA DE GENÍZARO

During the eighteenth century, Indian slavery and the slave trade were important components in relations between the New Mexican Spanish and Native Americans of the Great Plains. Captives who had been acculturated and paid their ransom debt were discharged by their Spanish masters and entered Spanish society as *genízaros*. The term is from "janissary," which referred to Christian captives who entered Turkish service.

The genízaros, many of whom came from the ranks of such Plains tribes as Plains Apaches, Jumanos, Comanches, Kiowas, Pawnees, Wichitas, and possibly Crows, lacked legal and social status and land; consequently, they settled at frontier outposts from El Paso to north of Santa Fe, where they received land and protected the colony from surrounding Indian raiders—Apaches, Comanches, Navajos, and Utes. In time they developed civilian (trader, weaver, rancher, farmer) and military occupations. Many traded with Plains Indians during peaceful times. They continued as an unorganized military force known for their bravery and fighting ability, both as militia troops and scouts. Their economic status improved with the horses, livestock, and other goods that they were allowed to keep from successful campaigns.

The genízaro militia was officially recognized and formally organized in 1808 as the Tropa de Genízaro. It was commanded by a corporal from their own ranks and based in Santa Fe. It had an organized supply system, which provided the militia with equipment and expendable supplies. With the end of Spanish rule in 1821, the segregated genízaro troops disappeared as they merged with the regular Mexican militia.

Russell M. Magnaghi
Northern Michigan University

Magnaghi, Russell M. "Plains Indians in New Mexico: The Genízaro Experience." *Great Plains Quarterly* 10 (1990): 86–95.

TRUDELL, JOHN (B. 1946)

A Santee Dakota, John Trudell was born in Omaha, Nebraska, on February 15, 1946, and raised on the Santee Sioux Reservation. Initially, he achieved national notoriety for his political activism on behalf of Native Americans. He was a leader of the Indians of All Tribes' occupation of Alcatraz in 1969, and in that capacity he hosted a radio program in 1970, *Radio Free Alcatraz*, that was broadcast in Berkeley, Los Angeles, and New York City. From 1973 to 1979 he served as the national chairman of the American Indian Movement (AIM). After the fire-bombing death of his wife, mother-in-law, and three daughters at their home on the Duck Valley Reservation in Nevada on February 11, 1979, Trudell began moving away from direct political action and devoted more of his time to artistic and intellectual endeavors.

In 1981 he wrote his first book, *Living in Reality*. In 1985 he formed the Graffiti Band with Jesse Ed Davis, a prolific studio guitarist from Oklahoma City who was of Seminole and Kiowa descent. Together they wedded Trudell's poetry, which ranged from political and social commentary to love poems, with Davis's unique musical style. They released *AKA Graffiti Man* and *Heart Jump Bouquet* before Davis's death in 1988. *AKA* was subsequently rereleased on a major label (Rykodisk) in 1992 and was executively produced by Jackson Browne. It featured the original tapes of Davis and Trudell, which were remastered and fleshed out with additional musicians. Guest appearances were made by Browne and Kris Kristofferson. *AKA* received high critical acclaim (Bob Dylan called it the best album of the year) and was followed by *Johnny Damas and Me* (1995).

Trudell has also acted in several feature films, including *Thunderheart* (1992), *On Deadly Ground* (1994), and *Smoke Signals* (1998). In 1994 he published his second book, *Stickman*.

Akim D. Reinhardt
Towson University

UNITED STATES V. SIOUX NATION OF INDIANS

In *United States v. Sioux Nation of Indians* (1980), the U.S. Supreme Court held that an 1877 act of Congress, by which the United States wrested control of the Black Hills of South Dakota from the Sioux Indian Nation, constituted a "taking" of property under the Fifth Amendment, giving rise to an obligation to fairly compensate the Sioux. The Court affirmed a prior decision of the court of claims, which had awarded the Sioux $17.1 million for the taking of the Black Hills, and further held that the tribe was entitled to interest on that amount from 1877. By the late 1990s, the amount due the Sioux had risen to more than $600 million—a payment that the tribe still refuses to accept, choosing instead to continue to seek the return of the land itself.

The 1980 decision represented the judicial culmination of more than sixty years of litigation and lobbying in the Court of Claims, the Indian Claims Commission, the U.S. Congress, and the Supreme Court, in which the Sioux sought retribution for more than a century's worth of bad faith and fraudulent dealings relating to the Black Hills. The fundamental basis for the continuing claim is the 1868 Fort Laramie Treaty, in which the government pledged that the Great Sioux Reservation, including the Black Hills, would be permanently preserved for the "absolute and undisturbed use and occupation" of the tribe. The treaty further provided that no change to the reservation boundaries would be effective unless approved by at least three-fourths of the adult male population of the Sioux Nation. In 1877 Congress enacted a statute that, in effect, unilaterally abrogated the provisions of the 1868 treaty. The act codified the terms of a new treaty, signed under military duress by only about 10 percent of the adult male Sioux population, under which the Sioux purportedly ceded another seven million acres, including the Black Hills, to the United States.

Some forty years after losing the Black Hills under those dubious circumstances, the Sioux embarked upon a long judicial and legislative quest for their return. In 1920 they brought suit in the Court of Claims, alleging that the government had taken the Black Hills without just compensation in violation of the Fifth Amendment. The Court of Claims ultimately dismissed that claim in 1942, and the Sioux then reasserted their arguments before the Indian Claims Commission, beginning in 1946. The commission held that the 1877 act was in fact a compensable taking for which the Sioux were entitled to $17.5 million, without interest. On appeal, however, the Court of Claims again dismissed the Sioux claim, holding that the tribe's arguments were barred by the Court's 1942 decision. There the

matter stood until 1978, when the Sioux obtained a special act of Congress authorizing a new review of the tribe's Black Hills claim without regard to the earlier decisions of the Court of Claims. This time the Court of Claims held that the government had indeed acted in bad faith in taking the Black Hills and that the Sioux were entitled to $17.1 million in damages, plus interest from 1877. When the Supreme Court affirmed the Court of Claims ruling in 1980, the Sioux's long decades of legal tenacity were seemingly vindicated.

Yet even before the Sioux achieved this monumental Supreme Court victory, controversy arose within the tribe and between some members of the tribe and their attorneys over whether or not a monetary judgment should even be sought, much less accepted. For growing numbers of Sioux, monetary compensation was not acceptable as a resolution of their claims—only the return of the sacred Black Hills themselves would suffice. Those sentiments have controlled subsequent events in this prolonged drama, and the Sioux continue to refuse to accept the payment dictated by the Court's decision.

Mark R. Scherer
University of Nebraska at Omaha

Lazarus, Edward. *Black Hills, White Justice: The Sioux Nation versus the United States, 1775 to the Present*. New York: HarperCollins, 1991. Pemberton, Richard, Jr. "'I Saw That It Was Holy': The Black Hills and the Concept of Sacred Land." *Law and Inequality: A Journal of Theory and Practice* 3 (1985): 287–311.

URBAN COMMUNITIES

Urban Indian communities are mainly the products of the federal relocation program for Native Americans following World War II, which was associated with the "termination" movement. The relocation impetus derived from the harsh winter of 1947–48 on the Navajo Reservation, where freezing conditions resulted in starvation for both the Navajos and their livestock. The government responded by airdropping hay to sheep and horses and by moving many Navajo families to Denver, Salt Lake City, and Los Angeles. Convinced that this drastic action had been a success, the government sponsored a wider relocation through the Bureau of Indian Affairs. From 1952 to 1973 an estimated one hundred thousand Native Americans relocated to urban areas such as Chicago, Los Angeles, Seattle, San Francisco, Dallas, and, in the Great Plains, Wichita, Denver, Oklahoma City, and Tulsa. The relocation program promised Native Americans jobs and housing in the cities, but it actually began a new era of federal efforts to assimilate Native peoples into the mainstream culture of America.

The first Indian relocatees were so-called gatekeepers who helped each other in this urban frontier experience. In the 1950s and 1960s urban Indians lacked sufficient education and needed job skills to compete successfully in the cities. Many did not make this adjustment, and becoming frustrated, they returned to their reservation or resorted to drink. A second generation of Native Americans migrated to the cities in the 1960s and 1970s, often settling near relatives who were already living there. By the 1980s this generation had grown up in the cities and felt closer to Indian friends and relatives there than to those on reservations. They did not know the reservation culture like their parents and grandparents did, although they did visit on a regular basis. They developed an urban Indian culture quite unlike the way of life on the reservation. Urban Indian centers, which had been established in the early 1970s with government funding, became stronger, with more independent funding and community support. They provided counseling and sponsored bowling leagues, softball teams, and other outings for their Indian communities. Such centers—in the Great Plains at Fort Worth, Oklahoma City, Tulsa, Wichita, Lincoln, Denver, Rapid City, and Sioux Falls, for example—brought together Native Americans from different tribes, creating a new overall Indian identity.

Los Angeles became the largest urban Indian community, drawing Native Americans from all over the United States but mainly from the Southwest and Oklahoma. About 113,000 Native Americans lived in the greater Los Angeles metropolitan area by 1997. In the Great Plains in the late 1990s, about 25,000 Native Americans, mostly Navajos and Lakotas, called Denver their home; 22,000 to 25,000 Cherokees, Choctaws, Chickasaws, Creeks, and Seminoles, and various Southern and Northern Plains tribes lived in Dallas–Fort Worth; 48,196 Native Americans, drawn mainly from the Five Civilized Tribes and eastern Oklahoma tribes, resided in Tulsa; and 45,720 of the Five Civilized Tribes and western Oklahoma tribes lived in Oklahoma City. Smaller, but significant, Native American populations also lived in Rapid City (10,000 to 12,000, mainly Lakotas) and Sioux Falls (12,000 to 15,000, also mainly Lakotas) in South Dakota and in Omaha and Lincoln, Nebraska (with 10,000 and 1,150 Poncas, Lakotas, and Omahas, respectively).

Donald L. Fixico
Arizona State University

Danziger, Edmund, Jr. *Survival and Regeneration: Detroit's American Indian Community*. Detroit: Wayne State University Press, 1991. Fixico, Donald L. *The Urban Indian Experience in America*. Albuquerque: University of New Mexico Press, 2000. Weibel-Orlando, Joan. *Indian Country, L.A.: Maintaining Ethnic Community in Complex Society*. Urbana: University of Illinois Press, 1991.

Reserve towns are not as prevalent in the Canadian Prairies as reservation towns are in the U.S. Plains. However, the recent development of urban Indian reserves is unique. In 2000 there were fourteen urban reserves in Saskatchewan, one each in Manitoba and Alberta, with more in the planning stage. The number of urban reserves in the Canadian Prairies will continue to increase.

Following the treaty process (1871–77), many reserve surveys allowed for the development of village sites. Churches and the Hudson's Bay Company, for example, often secured lots on reserves, and over time small villages grew around them. Non-Indian town sites on alienated reserve lands were established as a result of the land rush accompanying the building of the Canadian Pacific Railway.

Many Indian reserves within the railway belt were subject to expropriation for railway right-of-ways or to accommodate growing municipalities. The town of Hobbema (population 9,000), for example, is situated on lands once reserved for the Samson First Nation in the Bear Hills (Maskwacîsihk), Alberta. The reserve was surveyed in 1881 but a few years later fell within the reach of the proposed Edmonton-Calgary line. Reserve lands were expropriated or surrendered to accommodate the line and siding (train station landings and town sites).

Often urban pressures resulted in the loss of entire reserves. Papascase First Nation was surveyed in 1884 well beyond the city limits of Edmonton, but the railway line and the urban explosion soon targeted it for future development. Within a few years most of the band members enfranchised (withdrew from treaty), and their reserve was surrendered. The Mill Woods area, south of Fifty-first Avenue and north of the Tourist Information Centre, sits on the surrendered Papascase reserve. Often First Nations surrendered reserves after relentless pressures from government officials and local settlers; sometimes the legalities of the appropriations were questionable.

In Saskatchewan, very few reserves were established near settler villages and towns largely because federal Indian policies for the Prairies were developed to facilitate clearing the fertile region for railway and settlement and to suppress First Nations' resistance to treaties and their demands for the creation of a large Cree-Assiniboine territory in the southern Prairies. The Plains Cree movement was crushed in 1885, and the disbanded dissenters were removed to small, isolated reserves north of the railway belt.

More recently, urbanization and economic diversification trends have precipitated First Nations' investments in urban properties. Currently, there are two types of urban First Nations landholdings: those subject to municipal jurisdiction like other private holdings, and those that have been converted to Indian reserve status, now referred to as urban reserves.

The process by which lands are converted to reserve status is defined by two instruments: section 9.3.2 of the 1987 Additions to Reserves Policy of the Department of Indian Affairs and Northern Development and article 9 of the 1992 Saskatchewan Treaty Land Entitlement Framework Agreement, a comprehensive land claims agreement between Saskatchewan First Nations, the federal government, and the province of Saskatchewan. Both instruments were precipitated by First Nations' specific and Treaty Land Entitlement claims. Once transformed into Indian reserves, urban reserves are subject to the Indian Act and have the same legal status as rural Indian reserves: they are held in trust by the federal government, fall under First Nations jurisdiction, and are exempt from municipal and provincial taxation and most laws.

While formal agreements between First Nations and municipalities are not required, they are encouraged and are becoming the norm. Comprehensive agreements between First Nations and municipalities address a range of substantive issues: the application and enforcement of provincial and municipal laws and their compatibility with First Nations bylaws; compensation for lost tax revenue; First Nation taxation jurisdiction over Indian and non-Indian residents; service delivery (e.g., sewage, water, garbage disposal) to urban reserves; and dispute-resolution mechanisms.

In January 1997 the Centre for Municipal-Aboriginal Relations (CMAR) was created by the Federation of Canadian Municipalities and the Indian Taxation Advisory Board. CMAR serves as a clearinghouse and resource center and undertakes applied research in the area of municipal-Aboriginal relations.

Winona Wheeler
Saskatchewan Indian Federated College

Barron, F. Laurie, and Joseph Garcia, eds. *Urban Indian Reserves: Forging New Relationships in Saskatchewan*. Saskatoon: Purich Publishing, 1999. Tobias, John L. "The Subjugation of the Plains Cree, 1879–1885." *Canadian Historical Review* 64 (1983): 519–48.

VETERANS

Native Americans have served with the U.S. armed forces as auxiliaries, allies, scouts, volunteers, and conscripts since the Revolutionary War, and Canadian First Peoples fought for Great Britain as early as the mid–eighteenth century. During both world wars, Native Americans and First Peoples served (and died) in numbers exceeding their relative populations and distinguished themselves on battlefields from the Argonne Forest to Iwo Jima. For example, more than four thousand First Peoples enlisted in World War I, including every eligible man in Saskatchewan's File Hill community. Native North Americans' record of service extended to the hills of Korea, the rain forests of Vietnam, and the deserts of Saudi Arabia and Iraq during the Gulf War of 1991 and 2003 invasion of Iraq.

The reasons why Native North Americans enter the armed forces are many and complex. They serve to earn a guaranteed wage or perhaps because they believe that tribal treaty agreements obligate them to volunteer for military duty. For some, military service was a natural step from militarized Indian boarding schools. For Mike Mountain Horse of the Blood band of Alberta, and no doubt many others, fighting in World War I was proof that the warrior tradition had not been suppressed by reservation life.

Whatever their reasons for entering the military, those who returned had to face challenging problems of readjustment to civilian life. Information from the U.S. Department of Veterans Affairs and statistical data from the Bureau of the Census reveal that by 1980 there were more than 159,000 Native Americans eligible to receive veterans' benefits. The majority of these veterans came from the Great Plains. Many of them rarely used their hard-earned benefits because of the distances involved in traveling from reservations to VA hospitals, benefits offices, and veterans' outreach clinics.

Adjustment to civilian life was much more than taking advantage of veterans' benefits, however. Returning veterans had to readjust emotionally, economically, and culturally. The adjustment was eased for some by strong family relationships and by ceremonies designed to cleanse the veteran of his or her war-related trauma or to honor their sacrifices. Economic adjustment was difficult. Many veterans of the wars of the twentieth century returned to Plains communities, whether urban or reservation, that were among the poorest in the nation, with few opportunities for work. Still, these veterans revived warrior societies, took part in time-honored ceremonies related to warfare, and founded all-Indian VFW and American Legion posts.

Nowhere were these revivals, ceremonies, and organizations as important as in the Great Plains. The Kiowas, for example, rejuvenated the Gourd Dance, a warriors' society ceremony, and the Black Leggings, another warrior sodality, following World War II. Several other societies were revived among the Cheyennes, Lakotas, Arapahos, Pawnees, and Osages. These revivals, initiated and kept alive largely by veterans, have become an important part of the post–World War II movement to preserve tribal cultures.

Militarization quite often has an effect of democratizing societies. It was clear, for example, that after World Wars I and II Native North American veterans were prepared to demand their full rights of citizenship. Their service in the military had, in effect, legitimized their quest for better treatment. A great number of veterans of World War II became tribal officials almost immediately following the conflict. One, a Lakota from the Lower Brulé Agency of South Dakota, was elected tribal chairman at the young age of nineteen. In 1945, all the tribal council members of Crow Creek Reservation (also in South Dakota) were veterans. By 1946 more than one-third of all tribes in the United States had veterans serving as tribal council members. Numerous others went on to lead the fight against the federal policy of termination and later to promote self-determination and tribal self-sufficiency.

Tom Holm
University of Arizona

Bernstein, Alison R. *American Indians and World War II*. Norman: University of Oklahoma Press, 1991. Gaffen, Fred. *Forgotten Soldiers*. Penticton BC: Theytus Books, 1985. Holm, Tom. *Strong Hearts, Wounded Souls: Native American Veterans of the Vietnam War*. Austin: University of Texas Press, 1996.

VISION QUEST

For thousands of years, the nations of the Great Plains celebrated their interdependency with nature in ceremonies such as the vision quest. They accounted the environment that sustained them to be sacred. They saw how the buffalo gave itself to the people, how the grass gave itself to buffalo, how the rain gave itself to grass—how the people, like all their earthly relations, gave themselves back to the vast Plains that sustained them. They called the dark earth "Mother" and the great sun "Father," and they revered the Great Creator, not as some abstract principle, but as the palpable design, function, and constant presence of their environment.

Hence, the great sun, the dark earth, and the endless horizon, particularly as viewed from the traditional precincts of Mateo Tepee (Devils Tower), the Black Hills, and the Northern Rockies, became the Great Creator's initiation ground, the passageway for individuals in life transition. Their rites involved spiritual education that was fundamental to their existence. If, indeed, they lived in the home of the Great Creator, then clearly they would consider the significant growth events of their lives to be occasions for ceremony and spiritual edification.

Largely "confirmatory" in function (marking the attainment of changed social status), these rites followed the classic anthropological definition of rites of passage: severance (preparation to leave the former life and go into a sacred time and space, including rites of purification in a sweat lodge); threshold (existence—often three or four days and nights—alone in a sacred world of taboo and self-abnegation, where the individual sacrificed the self to a greater whole and attained "medicine" or visionary power); and incorporation (return to a council of elders and subsequent reintegration within the community as individuals with changed social status).

The objective of the threshold, or mountaintop, experience, was a medicine vision of benefit to the people as a whole. Without food, water, companionship, shelter, or defenses against predators, sometimes in great pain from self-inflicted wounds, the body longed for spiritual answers. The sacred ancestors sent dreams to console and inspire, and the Great Spirit provided "allies" or "helpers." When the initiates returned from this time with the Great Creator and the sacred ancestors, they were considered to have confirmed visionary intent. If the intent were not confirmed, the candidates would often return again—and again—until signs from nature indicated that the quest had been consummated. Thus, the community was blessed by the spiritual growth of its members, and every vision took its place in the legendary annals of the people.

Many forms of what, in the English language, has become known as the vision quest were practiced among the people of the Great Plains. Traditions were passed down from medicine men to their apprentices for many generations. The most widely published traditions were recorded by observant Europeans when medicine chiefs were willing to teach them the old ways. Black Elk's *Sacred Pipe* (as told to Joseph Epes Brown) contains a classic depiction of the seven rites of the Oglala Sioux, including a thorough description of the *hanblecheyapi*, or "crying for a vision." Similar noble rites existed among the Crows, Blackfoot, Cheyennes, Arapahos, Pawnees, Kiowas, Crees, and many other peoples, including the Native nations of the Northwest Coast, Great Basin, Eastern Woodlands, and Southwest.

This same ritual vision quest archetype is known by many other names in cultures throughout the world. Although this tradition has declined in the face of modern life, the rite is still practiced among the Indigenous people of the Great Plains.

Steven Foster
School of Lost Borders
Big Pine, California

Brown, Joseph Epes. *The Sacred Pipe: Black Elk's Account of the Seven Rites of the Oglala Sioux*. Norman: University of Oklahoma Press, 1953. Mails, Thomas E. *The Mystic Warriors of the Plains:*

The Culture, Arts, Crafts, and Religion of the Plains Indians. New York: Mallard Press, 1972. Van Gennep, Arnold. *The Rites of Passage.* Chicago: University of Chicago Press, 1972.

WAR CHIEFS

Since superior performance in warfare constituted a principal measure of leadership potential, many Native American societies of the Great Plains during the preconquest era embraced the concept of a war chief (e.g., *toyopki* to the Kiowas; *blotahunka* among the Oglala Sioux) and constructed a cultural order that reinforced a military tradition. For instance, male warriors belonging to Plains tribes such as the Arapahos, Blackfoot, Cheyennes, Comanches, Crows, Kiowas, and Lakotas elevated their status by winning battle distinctions. As honors accrued, men embellished brave deeds through public recitations and symbolic ornamentation. Assiniboine males acquired eagle feathers for each martial exploit; Blackfoot warriors accumulated white weasel skins; and successful Crow soldiers attached wolf tails to the heels of their moccasins. Such recognition did not require the killing of an enemy or the taking of a scalp. In fact, in many Plains societies the practice of counting coup, or touching an enemy with one's hand or a special stick, outranked killing as a heroic deed. A Blackfoot warrior, for example, always dwelt on the number of horses and guns he captured, not on the quantity of enemies extinguished. One of the principal avenues for achieving exalted warrior status was affiliation with a military society. Sporting names such as the Dog Soldiers, Fox Soldiers, and Kit Foxes, war societies extended membership only to the most promising young men of the band.

Most Indigenous societies of the Great Plains practiced some form of hereditary chieftainship and recognized a head chief. In theory, the head chief presided over a council composed of war chiefs, headmen, warriors, and holy men. In practice, however, charismatic, self-made war-party leaders often exercised the most significant authority, especially in times of crisis. The career of the Oglala Lakota leader Red Cloud is illustrative. Red Cloud became a war chief of an Oglala band in the early 1840s. His power and prestige increased over the next two decades as a result of military successes against the Crows, Pawnees, and Shoshones, as well as his strategic intervention against whites along the Bozeman Trail. By the late 1860s the American government regarded Red Cloud, who still retained only war chief status among the Oglalas, as the principal Lakota chief. American officials sought Red Cloud's influence in negotiating a peaceful resolution to the warfare raging in the Northern Plains at the time.

Conflict among the Plains tribes, regardless of warfare's exalted status, was not a "natural" condition or simply the result of the "aggressive instincts" of male warriors. Instead, wars took place primarily in light of pragmatic considerations—acquiring horses, expanding trade, capturing hunting grounds, or defending compatriots from the incursions of the U.S. military. In addition, the dynamics of Plains Indian warfare changed over time in relation to the shifting cultural landscape. For example, the acquisition of horses from the Spanish Southwest during the seventeenth and eighteenth centuries accelerated the nomadic lifestyle of bison hunters like the Kiowas, Cheyennes, and Lakotas, thereby intensifying the competition for buffalo hunting grounds. In conjunction with the horse, the procurement of guns from French, British, and American traders between the seventeenth and nineteenth centuries contributed to various military imbalances in the Great Plains, to the benefit of groups such as the Blackfoot, Comanches, and Lakotas. During the late eighteenth and early nineteenth centuries, the spread of disease pathogens exacerbated these imbalances. Horticultural peoples like the Arikaras, Mandans, and Hidatsas suffered grievously from smallpox epidemics. On the other hand, migratory hunters like the Lakotas escaped the wholesale ravages of disease, enjoyed unprecedented population growth in the early 1800s, and used their demographic advantage to dominate much of the Central and Northern Plains by the mid–nineteenth century.

By the 1850s, however, the onrush of white competitors into the trans-Missouri West posed new military challenges for Native Americans and forced innovative responses. The mounting threat gave rise to alliances among various Plains groups, formed to protect resources as well as one another from the white invasion. In the Northern Plains, the Lakotas, Arapahos, and Cheyennes joined forces; to the south, the Comanches and Kiowas built alliances with the Cheyennes and Arapahos. Emphasis on military accomplishment within tribes assumed even greater significance in the nineteenth century, when white intrusion made martial readiness a prerequisite to a group's survival. Consequently, the closing frontier era produced some of the most notable war chiefs, including Quanah Parker (Comanche), Satank (Kiowa), and Crazy Horse (Oglala Lakota).

James O. Gump
University of San Diego

Mishkin, Bernard. *Rank and Warfare among the Plains Indians.* Lincoln: University of Nebraska Press, 1992. Secoy, Frank Raymond. *Changing Military Patterns of the Great Plains Indians.* Lincoln: University of Nebraska Press, 1992. Utley, Robert M. *The Indian Frontier of the American West, 1846–1890.* Albuquerque: University of New Mexico Press, 1984.

WASHITA, BATTLE OF THE

The Battle of the Washita occurred on November 17, 1868, in western Indian Territory, about one mile west of present-day Cheyenne, Oklahoma. Before dawn, Lt. Col. George Armstrong Custer peered over a snow-encrusted ridge into the valley of the Washita River. There he saw a large Cheyenne village in a wooded bottom on the south side of the stream. At daybreak, 700 men of the Seventh U.S. Cavalry struck the village of Black Kettle, a Cheyenne peace chief. Completely surprised, the warriors offered only token resistance as women and children fled to the surrounding woodlot and hills. Troopers occupying the village began burning its fifty lodges, killing approximately eight hundred horses and destroying supplies. Throughout the day, soldiers skirmished with a growing number of warriors from camps downstream who converged on the smoldering village. In late afternoon, Custer assembled his troops and withdrew, with 53 captives. Cavalry casualties included 22 men killed and 13 wounded. Also, Indians murdered Clara Blinn, a white captive, and her young son during the attack. Precise Native losses are unknown. Some estimates placed the dead at 9 to 20 men, including Black Kettle, and 18 to 40 women and children, while others suggest that as many as 103 were killed in total.

The Battle of the Washita emerged as the only significant engagement of the winter campaign of 1868–69. Frustrated by elusive Cheyenne and Arapaho warriors who raided the Central Plains frontier the previous summer, Gen. Philip H. Sheridan had organized the expedition to chastise the Indians. He also hoped a show of force would coerce the Cheyennes and Arapahos onto a reservation created for them by the 1867 Treaty of Medicine Lodge Creek. Custer's attack on Black Kettle's village, some of whose warriors participated in the summer raids, accomplished both of Sheridan's objectives. In 1997 the battlefield was designated a National Historic Site by the National Park Service.

William Corbett
Northeastern State University

Hoig, Stan. *The Battle of the Washita: The Sheridan-Custer Indian Campaign of 1867–1869.* Garden City NY: Doubleday, 1976. Utley, Robert M. *Cavalier in Buckskin: George Armstrong Custer and the Western Military Frontier.* Norman: University of Oklahoma Press, 1988.

WELCH, JAMES (1940–2003)

Born in Browning, Montana, where the mountains break into foothills and then prairie, James Welch, a writer of Blackfeet and Gros Ventre heritage, remained rooted in Montana. His writings reflected a lifetime spent primarily in the magnificent and variable geographic terrain of the West. Welch attended schools in Montana, Oregon, and Alaska before graduating in Minneapolis, Minnesota, in 1958. He received a bachelor of arts degree in liberal arts from the University of Montana in 1965, where he also enrolled in the master of fine arts in creative writing program from 1966 to 1968 but did not earn a degree.

Since the publication of his first novel, *Winter in the Blood* (1974), Welch has been widely recognized as a leading figure in Native American literature. His novels have been translated and published in France, Italy, Germany, Holland, Japan, Sweden, and England. Subsequent to the rave reception his first novel received (it was reviewed on the front page of the *New York Times Book Review*), Welch republished his first and only collection of poetry, *Riding the Earthboy 40* (1971; reprint, 1976). In 1979 *The Death of Jim Loney* appeared, a second novel set around the Fort Belknap Reservation in Montana. Both novels' protagonists grapple with their familial histories, the deaths of loved ones, and excessive alcohol use.

With his third novel, *Fools Crow* (1986), Welch moved to depictions of historical events. Set in the Rocky Mountains, home of the Piegan (Pikuni) band of the Blackfeet Confederacy in the 1870s, *Fools Crow* offers a fictional view of Pikuni life around the time of the virtual extinction of the bison and just before Blackfeet people signed a treaty that forever changed their way of life. Based on historical figures such as Pikuni leader Heavy Runner and U.S. Army officer Gen. William Tecumseh Sherman, the novel takes as its central subject the growth into manhood of White Man's Dog into Fools Crow, a chief. Fools Crow must grapple with what living with honor versus shame is and might be in the face of cultural upheaval. That same year Welch coedited *The Real West Marginal Way* (1986), a volume based on Richard Hugo's life and work, together with his wife, Lois Monk Welch, and Ripley Hugo, widow of Richard Hugo.

In his fourth novel, *The Indian Lawyer* (1990), Welch drew on his ten years of experience as vice chairman of the Montana State Board of Pardons (1979–88) to depict another sort of Indian protagonist. Sylvester Yellow Calf, a descendant of Fools Crow, becomes a lawyer and a U.S. Senate hopeful. In *The Indian Lawyer* Welch moves beyond depictions of familial and personal identity struggles to present a man who learns he can make or break himself.

The traumatic events in U.S.-Native relations gripped Welch's imagination more fully after he wrote *Fools Crow* and *The Indian Lawyer.* Along with Paul Stekler, he created a video, *Killing Custer: The Battle of the Little Bighorn and the Fate of the*

Plains Indians (1994), that reflects Native American points of view regarding the Battle of the Little Bighorn. In his last novel, *The Heartsong of Charging Elk* (2000), Welch told the poignant story of a Lakota who is left stranded and sick in Marsailles when the Wild West show that had employed him moved on.

Welch occasionally taught at the University of Washington and Cornell University as a visiting professor, and lived in Missoula, where he wrote full-time. Welch died of a heart attack August 4, 2003, in Missoula.

Kathryn W. Shanley
University of Montana

Beidler, Peter G., ed. "James Welch's *Winter in the Blood*." *American Indian Quarterly* 4 (1978): 93–172. McFarland, Ron. *James Welch*. Lewiston ID: Confluence Press, 1986. Velie, Alan R. "James Welch's Poetry." *American Indian Culture and Research Journal* 3 (1979): 22–23.

WHITE BULL, JOSEPH (1849–1947)

Studio portrait of Chief White Bull (Pte san hunka), ca. 1870–90

One of the leading Sioux warriors of the nineteenth century, White Bull (Pte san hunka) was credited by some historians and Indians with killing George Armstrong Custer at the Battle of the Little Bighorn in 1876. He was the son of Chief Makes Room and the nephew and adopted son of Sitting Bull. He was from the Minneconjou band of the Sioux.

From a young age, White Bull was interested in warfare, becoming a warrior when he was sixteen or seventeen years old. He fought traditional Sioux enemies including the Crows, Utes, Shoshones, Flatheads, and Omahas. He participated in many of the most notable battles between the Sioux and the Americans, including the Fetterman Fight (1866), the Wagon Box Fight (1867), the Battle of the Rosebud (1876), and the Battle of the Little Bighorn (1876), where he fought beside Crazy Horse, counted coup seven times, and killed at least two soldiers.

White Bull married for the first time at age nineteen and ultimately married fifteen or sixteen times. He had several children. Following Gen. Nelson Miles's punitive Milk River Expedition in October 1876, White Bull surrendered and settled at the Cheyenne River Agency. In 1879, with the help of missionaries, he learned to read and write. He used these skills in his role as a keeper of the winter count, which he wrote in Lakota. White Bull converted to Christianity in 1879, becoming a Congregationalist, which he blended with traditional Lakota beliefs. He served as a leader of a young men's church group, as church treasurer, and as a member of the church's board. He was a tribal judge for four years, chairman of the tribal council, and a member of the Indian police for twelve years in total. Upon the retirement of his father, he became a Shirt-wearer, or chief. He worked tirelessly for his people, representing them several times in unsuccessful efforts to maintain the Sioux land base and regain the Black Hills.

In 1926 White Bull led the Sioux delegation at the fifty-year anniversary of the Battle of the Little Bighorn, catching the attention of historian Stanley Vestal. Vestal's biography, *Warpath*, introduced Americans to White Bull in 1934. In 1957, in a new edition of his biography of Sitting Bull, Vestal claimed that White Bull had killed Custer, a claim popularized in a short essay, "The Man Who Killed Custer," published in *American Heritage* magazine in February 1957. Vestal reasoned that he had withheld the claim to protect White Bull. The claim received further support when James Howard translated and edited White Bull's winter count (a version from the early 1930s) as *The Warrior Who Killed Custer* in 1968 (republished as *Lakota Warrior*).

Later historians have been skeptical of the idea that White Bull killed Custer. Raymond DeMallie, in his introduction to *Warpath*, discredited Vestal's story, noting that the claim was not included in Vestal's extensive notes and that White Bull had admitted that he had never seen Custer before the fight and could not identify him. In notes to his biography of Sitting Bull, *The Lance and the*

Shield, historian Robert Utley argued that no serious student of Indian history believed that White Bull had killed Custer. White Bull's place in Sioux history remains firm, regardless of any connection to Custer's death. White Bull died on July 21, 1947, at age ninety-eight.

Charles Vollan
South Dakota State University

Utley, Robert. *The Lance and the Shield*. New York: Henry Holt, 1993. Vestal, Stanley. *Warpath*. Lincoln: University of Nebraska Press, 1984. White Bull, Joseph. *Lakota Warrior*, edited and translated by James H. Howard. Lincoln: University of Nebraska Press, 1996.

WICHITAS

When the Spanish explorer Coronado traveled across the Southern Plains in 1541 in search of the fabled riches of Quivira, he encountered large villages of a distinctive tattooed people along the Great Bend of the Arkansas River, near present-day Arkansas City, Kansas. This was the initial European contact with the Native Americans now recognized as the Wichita and Affiliated Tribes.

Early historic accounts from Coronado's *entrada* and the later Oñate expedition found the Wichitas referring to themselves as the Quicasquiris or Quirasquiris (or Ki'dikir' eis, based on interviews conducted with tribal members in 1949). Close study of Spanish and French explorers' visits with the Wichitas reveals a loosely aligned confederacy of a number of bands. These included the Taovayas, Tawakonis, Iscanis-Wacos, and the Wichitas proper. By the eighteenth century the Kitsais, another tribe related to the Wichita subgroups, had been assimilated by the Wichitas.

Linguistically, the Wichita language belongs to the Caddoan language family that also includes the Pawnee, Kitsai, Caddo, and Arikara languages. Historically, Wichita is most closely related to the Northern Caddoan subfamily languages of Kitsai and Pawnee and is more distantly related to Caddo of Proto-Caddoan derivation.

While many Native groups traditionally recognized as Plains societies (for example, the Cheyennes) have a relatively recent history in the Southern Plains, the Wichitas have been there for 2,000 to 2,500 years. They were among a diffuse group of people, possibly from Louisiana or Mississippi, who began a westward movement some three thousand years ago. This migration gradually extended across the Plains, displacing existing residents. During this expansion, the newcomers began to develop regional distinctions in material culture, means of subsistence, and social, political, and religious organization. Archeologists now link these regional expressions to the historic Caddo, Kitsai, Wichita, Pawnee, and Arikara tribes. Archeological evidence and historic accounts reveal that the Wichitas ranged over much of the Southern Plains, including what is currently north-central Texas, Oklahoma, and south-central Kansas.

Wichita subsistence practices reflected a dual economy based on farming and hunting. During the spring and summer they cultivated sizable plots of corn, beans, and squash and harvested wild plants such as amaranth and sunflower. Bison, deer, and small game were hunted. In the fall and winter the Wichitas conducted large-scale communal bison hunts. Greater reliance on hunting by a traditionally agricultural people was probably connected to the introduction of the horse in the seventeenth century.

The Aboriginal material culture of the Wichitas closely parallels that of other Plains village societies. A variety of natural products, such as animal bones and hides, wood, plant fiber, stone, and clay, were used in the manufacture of domestic goods, clothing, and ornaments. Much of the traditional technology was abandoned by the late nineteenth century in favor of European American goods. The most distinctive aspect of the Wichita material world was their beehive-shaped grass houses. These houses ranged from fifteen to thirty feet in diameter and twelve to twenty feet in height. The dwelling, consisting of fourteen to sixteen cedar posts with a frame of smaller cedar and willow poles, was covered with bundles of coarse grass. Four small poles extended about three feet from the peak of the house, representing the four world quarters or gods. Wichita dwellings were designed to house extended family units of roughly eight to ten people. Villages had from thirty to several hundred such residences. Wichita settlements in the eighteenth century also typically contained a palisade or fortification, although not all the houses of the village would be within this protected area.

Wichita society has been generally viewed as highly egalitarian, with male status acquired through individual achievements in hunting and warfare. However, there are indications that some Wichita subgroups, such as the Tawakonis, had chiefs or rulers with greater authority; inheritance of these positions appears likely to have occurred in some instances. A typical Wichita village would have a principal chief elected by the head warriors, a leader responsible for finding new village locations, shamans or medicine men, warriors, elders, and "no-count men," who were servants to the chief, leader, or priests. Women of the village were responsible for planting and tending the crops as well as most of the labor-intensive tasks, such as building houses, collecting firewood, and hauling water. Men were principally involved in hunting and warfare. As was the case in many Native American farming societies, kinship was matrilinear, or traced through the woman's side, and matrilocal, meaning that the husband moved to the residence of the wife's family after marriage.

The Wichitas recognized a host of sacred figures. These were divided into the gods and goddesses of the earth and sky. Supreme among these was the god known as Kinnikasus (Man Never Known on Earth), who was responsible for the creation of the universe and its parts. Other male gods controlled the heavens (with the exception of the moon goddess), whereas goddesses—the goddess of water, for example—reigned on earth. The Wichitas also believed that all animate and inanimate objects possessed a spirit and that everything could assume more than its apparent natural characteristics. These concepts played a significant role in the development of supernatural powers among the medicine men. The Wichitas have also been credited with establishing the calumet ceremony as a means of initiating truce conditions among Plains societies.

The arrival of Europeans on the Southern Plains dramatically transformed Plains tribes. The presence of the horse and European goods, weapons, and diseases brought about drastic changes in demographics, subsistence economies, and political structures of most tribes, including the Wichitas. The French and Spanish also manipulated the tribes, pitting them against each other in an effort to gain control of the Southern Plains. In the seventeenth and eighteenth centuries, the Wichitas had continuous conflicts with the Apaches and Comanches to the west and the Osages to the east. By the mid–eighteenth century, they had established peace with the Comanches. Conflicts continued with the Apaches and Osages. In the 1750s the Osages forced the Wichitas from the Great Bend of the Arkansas River to the middle reaches of the Red River. The Wichitas maintained good relations with the French but never fully embraced Spanish authority. They won a major victory over the Spanish in 1759 when Col. Diego Ortiz Parilla failed in his attack on a Wichita village on the Red River.

The Wichitas may have had a total population of around 10,000 in the 1700s. Subsequently, introduced diseases and continuing conflicts with whites and other Indians led to significant population decline. By the late eighteenth century their population had dropped to about 4,000, and by the 1890s only 153 Wichitas remained.

In 1872 the Wichitas ceded all claims to their ancestral lands in Texas and Indian Territory to the United States and were left with a 743,000-acre reservation in present-day Caddo County, Oklahoma. However, this agreement was never ratified, and their title to the land remained in doubt. In 1901 the reservation was allotted and greatly reduced by the sale of "surplus lands."

The Wichita and Affiliated Tribes currently reside adjacent to the Anadarko Agency just north of Anadarko, Oklahoma. They hold some 1,260 acres of land in common trust with the Caddo and Delaware tribes. In 1995 there were 1,798 Wichitas, most of whom lived in Oklahoma.

Robert L. Brooks
University of Oklahoma

Dorsey, George A. *The Mythology of the Wichita.* Washington DC: Carnegie Institution, 1904. John, Elizabeth A. H. *Storms Brewed in Other Men's Worlds.* College Station: Texas A&M University Press, 1975. Newcomb, W. W., Jr. *The Indians of Texas.* Austin: University of Texas Press, 1961.

WINTERS DOCTRINE

The judicially crafted Winters Doctrine (1908) provides water for the needs of Native Americans who reside on federally reserved lands. This judicial guarantee, while not absolute, is highly significant given the demands for this critical natural resource in a region where water is often not abundantly available.

Water policy in the Great Plains is shaped by powerful political forces. Economic demands translate into political pressures and ultimately into water law. State water laws are generally designed to allocate water for "beneficial uses," following the doctrine of prior appropriation. Stressing uses, rather than needs, is inconsistent with Native American ideals, whereby water, like other aspects of the environment, is connected to a higher sacred order. Consequently, European American water schemes have often been in conflict with Native American concepts.

In 1908, however, Native Americans prevailed in the landmark case *Winters v. United States.* The case involved the Gros Ventres and Assiniboines of the Fort Belknap Reservation in Montana and their right to use the water of the Milk River. When farmers upstream diverted water from the river the United States brought an injunction against them, reasoning that this left insufficient water for agriculture on the reservation. The farmers appealed. On January 6, 1908, the Supreme Court ruled in favor of the United States and the Native Americans, arguing that the establishment of the Fort Belknap Reservation entitled the Native Americans to perpetual use of the water that it contained. Their rights were "reserved" at the date of establishment (1888), and, contrary to the doctrine of prior appropriation, those rights could not be lost through nonuse.

The Winters Doctrine was a major victory for all Native Americans, serving notice that state laws are secondary to federally reserved water rights and preventing prior appropriation schemes from extinguishing Native American needs. In 1976, in *Cappaert v. United States*, the doctrine was extended to groundwater use on or near federally created reservations. Subsequently, however, an increasingly conservative Supreme Court has ruled against tribes in a number of water rights disputes. While the Winters Doctrine protects Native American water rights, this protection is still vulnerable to changes in the prevailing political climate.

Peter J. Longo
University of Nebraska–Kearney

Burton, Lloyd. *American Indian Water Rights and the Limits of Law.* Lawrence: University Press of Kansas, 1991. Hundley, Norris. "The Winters Decision and Indian Water Rights: A Mystery Reexamined." In *The Plains Indians of the Twentieth Century*, edited by Peter Iverson, 77–106. Norman: University of Oklahoma Press, 1985.

WOMEN OF ALL RED NATIONS

Women of All Red Nations (WARN) was founded in 1978 in San Francisco, California, and to date remains the most prominent activist Native American women's organization. WARN advocates for Native American treaty rights and for social, economic, and environmental justice for Native American peoples. WARN was created at the height of Indian activism in the 1970s, when the virtually all-male national leadership of Indian activist groups became targeted by federal and state law enforcement agencies and courts. After the national American Indian Movement leaders were prosecuted and imprisoned by the federal legal system, women were called to the fore of Native American issues and WARN was born.

From its beginning, WARN has sent spokeswomen to international forums concerning colonialism, land struggles, energy resource protection, and Indigenous rights recognition. WARN was instrumental in stopping the uranium mining that was planned for the sacred Black Hills of South Dakota. The organization built coalitions with non-Indians so that uranium mining would never be conducted in lands sacred to the Lakota, Dakota, and Nakota people.

WARN also conducted a health study of the water on the Pine Ridge Reservation in South Dakota, which found that the groundwater system was highly radioactive. Since then, federal funds have been allocated for the construction of a safe drinking-water system, called Mni Wiconi, or the Water of Life, for the greater reservation area. WARN has worked on numerous issues relating to human health, specifically the epidemic proportions of Type II diabetes in Indian Country, as well as the terrible problems associated with fetal alcohol syndrome and fetal alcohol effect.

Today, WARN continues its advocacy, predominantly through the efforts of women's circles in local communities both on and off reservations. WARN's ongoing community organization and advocacy on issues affecting Native Americans at the grassroots level remain highly focused and effective.

Madonna Thunder Hawk
Eagle Butte, South Dakota

WOMEN WARRIORS

Raiding and warfare were an integral part of the men's role among Plains Indian nations, but it was by no means uncommon for women to engage in these activities as well. Their motivations were the same as those of the men: revenge, defense, and a desire for prestige and wealth. Most frequently, a woman would join or even lead a war party in order to take revenge for relatives slain by some enemy. Women would also take up arms to defend their camp against hostile intruders. In other cases, women, by means of visions, received the command to go to war. Capturing horses and other property on a raid also brought great prestige to both men and women.

The term "woman warrior," while commonplace, is misleading. To be a warrior was a lifetime occupation for Plains Indian men, but most women who went to war did not pursue a warrior's life permanently. Many women went to war only once or twice in their lives. Others were married and accompanied their husbands on war or raiding parties, especially while the couple was still young and childless.

Some women served as sentries and messengers; others fought in battle alongside the men, counted coup, and took scalps. Eventually, they quit warring and raiding, raised children, and did their share of work within the gendered division of labor. In this they differed from the female two-spirits, or *berdaches*, who took up the culturally defined man's role completely and permanently.

In some cases, however, success as a warrior would pave a woman's way to a quasi-masculine role and status. The war deeds of Woman Chief, who lived among the Crow around 1850, were so daring that the men invited her to join their council meetings, where she ranked as the third leading warrior in a group of 160 lodges. She became an accomplished trader and hunter and eventually married four wives, who processed the hides and did the other standard women's chores around her lodge. Another example is Brown Weasel Woman, a Piegan female warrior. A major battle with an enemy tribe brought her—the only female in her tribe's history to be so honored—a man's name, Running Eagle, that was reserved for famous warriors.

Gathering Up the Dead, *Wounded Knee, South Dakota*

The role of the woman warrior was socially accepted wherever it occurred among the Plains nations. The same holds true for other role alternatives in which women could gain prestige by exhibiting behavior culturally defined as masculine. The prestige system of the Plains cultures was clearly male-dominated, centering on warlike activities and personality traits considered masculine. It is true that Plains Indian women could gain great prestige by excelling in women's occupations such as beadwork and agriculture, by assuming certain roles in ceremonies, and by expressing culturally valued ideals of femininity. Yet the masculine prestige system was the measure for both sexes. Even feminine achievements were sometimes expressed in masculine terms. Within that system, however, women could compete for the prestige associated with war and raiding on equal terms with men and did so if they had the inclination.

Sabine Lang
Hamburg, Germany

Hungry Wolf, Beverly. *The Ways of My Grandmothers*. New York: Quill Books, 1982. Lang, Sabine. *Men as Women, Women as Men: Changing Gender in Native American Cultures*. Austin: University of Texas Press, 1998. Medicine, Beatrice. "'Warrior Women': Sex Role Alternatives for Plains Indian Women." In *The Hidden Half: Studies of Plains Indian Women*, edited by Patricia Albers and Beatrice Medicine, 267–80. Washington DC: University Press of America, 1983.

WOUNDED KNEE MASSACRE

On December 29, 1890, on Wounded Knee Creek in southwestern South Dakota, a tangle of events resulted in the deaths of more than 250, and possibly as many as 300, Native Americans. These peo-

ple were guilty of no crime and were not engaged in combat. A substantial number were women and children. Most of the victims were members of the Miniconjou band of the Lakota Sioux who had been intercepted by military forces after they fled their reservation in South Dakota for refuge in the Badlands.

The story begins in October 1890, when Daniel F. Royer arrived at Pine Ridge Agency, home of the Oglala Lakotas, to assume responsibility as agent. His selection as agent could not have been worse: he knew nothing about Native Americans and was irrationally fearful of them, and from the time of his arrival the dispatches he sent back to Washington were peppered with warnings of an outbreak similar to the one in Minnesota in 1862 in which hundreds of settlers were killed by Santee Sioux. Royer's appointment was also ill timed. In 1890 drought replaced the bountiful rainfall of the 1880s, resulting in crop failures and economic depression. On their reservations, Native Americans were forced into dependence on the federal government for food and clothing. When Royer took over as agent, there was widespread anxiety among the Oglalas regarding the adequacy of government provisions.

A year earlier, the Ghost Dance had appeared on the Pine Ridge Reservation. Born from the vision of a Paiute named Wovoka (aka Jack Wilson), the Ghost Dance blended the messianic account of Christianity with traditional Native beliefs. This new religion told of the return of the Messiah to relieve the suffering of Native Americans and promised that if they would live righteous lives and perform the Ghost Dance in the prescribed manner, the European American invaders would vanish, the bison would return, and the living and the dead would be reunited in an Edenic world. But in Royer's paranoid mind the Ghost Dance was a war dance that threatened imminent bloodshed. His dispatches to Washington urged that troops be sent to protect citizens from war.

In mid-November 1890 President Benjamin Harrison responded to the fears of an Indian outbreak by ordering troops into the area. Regular troops were sent from Fort Robinson, Nebraska, and on November 18, 1890, the Second Nebraska Infantry left Fort Omaha in two special trains. On the train was also a cadre of newspaper reporters. From that point on, the crisis at Pine Ridge was a significant news item in newspapers across the country and around the world.

The trains unloaded their travelers at Rushville, Nebraska, on November 20, 1890, and from there the troops and reporters made their way to Pine Ridge Agency, where they all soon discovered that there was no crisis to be found. Soon a regular fare of rumors and lies began to appear in the national press, fed by merchants who wanted to keep the reporters, and their expense accounts, engaged in the economically strained communities south of the Pine Ridge Reservation. These fantastic stories fed a growing national anxiety about impending war. They also appeared on the reservations, where Lakotas who had been educated in the nation's Indian schools read the reports of troop activities and the rumors of outbreak to other members of their community. In this manner, the press became an important factor in stoking the anxiety both on and off the reservation.

By mid-December 1890 the combination of news reports, governmental reports (particularly those of the panic-stricken Royer), and Ghost Dancing had every nerve in the region on edge. The Lakotas polarized into political camps commonly referred to in the press as "hostiles" and "friendlies," a distinction between those who were opposed and those who were reconciled to reservation life. The Ghost Dancers were generally assigned to the "hostiles" camp. On December 15, 1890, the Hunkpapa holy man and Ghost Dance leader Sitting Bull was killed at Standing Rock Agency. Sitting Bull's death was seen by many as the fate that awaited all who failed to accept reservation life. To the south, at Cheyenne River Agency, the Miniconjou Lakotas grew nervous. Their leader, Big Foot, was also engaged in the Ghost Dance, and though not considered a major threat, he was under close observation by the military. In an attempt to quiet the Miniconjous, the military asked a local squatter named John Dunn to persuade them to acquiesce

to the military's wishes that they stay in their own village on the reservation. Dunn's tactics are inexplicable: he is reported to have told the Miniconjous that the military planned to take their men prisoner and deport them to an island in the Atlantic Ocean. He apparently advised them to take sanctuary on Pine Ridge Reservation.

On December 23, the Miniconjous left their village in the dead of night and fled south toward the Badlands. Big Foot soon contracted pneumonia, which slowed the escape. Nonetheless, the tribe managed to avoid the military pursuit for five days. But on December 28, the Seventh Cavalry intercepted the ailing Big Foot and his people and ordered them into confinement on Wounded Knee Creek. On the morning of December 29, Col. James W. Forsyth convened a council with the Miniconjous. He demanded that they surrender all their firearms and told them that they would be relocated to a new camp. The order to a new camp was interpreted by the Miniconjous as exile, probably to Indian Territory, a prospect that they found intolerable.

While these discussions proceeded in the Lakota camp, a number of Indians began singing Ghost Dance songs, with some rising to throw handfuls of dirt in the air. The troops who surrounded them perceived the singing and dirt throwing as signals to attack, and at this tense moment the fuse was lit. A man named Black Coyote (sometimes called Black Fox) refused to surrender his rifle to a soldier. The two began wrestling over the gun, and in the struggle it discharged. Immediately the nervous troops began firing, while the Miniconjous retrieved their weapons and returned fire. The military's rifle fire was complemented with cannon rounds from Hotchkiss guns, whose accuracy and exploding shells were formidable. The outnumbered and outgunned Lakotas fled, and for several hours intermittent gunfire continued, with the military in pursuit. Bodies were found as far away as three miles from the camp. Firing ceased, and by midafternoon the troops had gathered up their dead and wounded, as well as Lakota wounded, and returned to Pine Ridge Agency. The fear of a reprisal attack kept troops and civilians entrenched at the agency until January 3, 1891, when a military-escorted civilian burial party proceeded to the site of the massacre. There they buried 146 Lakotas in a single mass grave. Other dead were accounted for later, bringing the total to more than 250 Lakotas; the Seventh Cavalry lost 25 men.

Photographers accompanied the burial detail and made a total of sixteen photographs. A snowstorm that occurred shortly after the massacre added a cold and grim edge to the scene of carnage. The photographs sold well and, together with news stories, carried the story of the massacre at Wounded Knee worldwide. Soon the event developed a meaning that transcended the reality of the tragic loss of life, and Wounded Knee became, and remains, the symbol of the inhumanity of U.S. government policy toward Native Americans.

John E. Carter
Nebraska State Historical Society

Jensen, Richard E., R. Eli Paul, and John E. Carter. *Eyewitness at Wounded Knee*. Lincoln: University of Nebraska Press, 1991. Mooney, James. *The Ghost-Dance Religion and the Sioux Outbreak of 1890*. Fourteenth Annual Report of the Bureau of Ethnology, Smithsonian Institution. Washington DC: Government Printing Office, 1896. Utley, Robert. *The Last Days of the Sioux Nation*. New Haven CT: Yale University Press, 1963.

YELLOWTAIL, ROBERT (1887/1889–1988)

The dominant political voice on the Crow Reservation in the mid-twentieth century, Robert Summers Yellowtail was born on the banks of the Little Bighorn River near Lodge Grass, Montana, in either 1887 or 1889. His family followed traditional Crow religious practices but also engaged with Christianity—Yellowtail was baptized twice and attended six churches before settling on the Baptist Church.

From 1908 to 1917 the Indian Office pressed the Crows to sell "surplus" land, but Crow leaders resisted. In 1913 Yellowtail traveled to Washington DC as a translator for elders defending Crow lands. With support from Crow leader Plenty Coups, Yellowtail developed as a leader in his own right and quickly made a name as an eloquent speaker. He returned to Washington in 1915, 1916, and 1917, making alliances with non-Indian politicians and lawyers. When Senate leaders asked the Crows to compromise, Yellowtail sided with the young leadership, which favored dividing the entire Crow lands among the tribe, with limits on non-Indian landholdings and outright fee simple land ownership for Indians without a trust period. The Crow Act became law in 1920.

While defending tribal rights, Yellowtail was also a proponent of economic development. He operated the Little Horn Ranch for decades. Although he was a lifelong Republican, he supported the candidacy of Franklin Delano Roosevelt, hoping for law reform and the appointment of his old acquaintance and long-time critic of the Bureau of Indian Affairs John Collier as commissioner of Indian affairs. Once in office, Collier appointed Yellowtail superintendent for the Crow Agency, the first Native American to be superintendent of his own reservation. He supported Collier's program for greater Indian self-determination but only gave lukewarm support to the Indian Reorganization Act, and the Crows decisively rejected it.

Yellowtail worked to achieve two goals: gaining control over tribal lands, including those leased to white ranchers, and tribal economic development. He convinced the National Park Service to transfer a bison herd to the tribe and worked to bring the benefits of the New Deal to the reservation. He also defended traditional Crow culture, opposing the Indian Office's restrictions on traditional dancing and religious ceremonies. In 1941 he helped usher in the return of the Sun Dance.

His effort to accommodate white land owners angered many Crows, who blamed him for being too willing to support large leases in return for loose promises to hire more Crows or support community gatherings. The result was that these leases locked the tribe into long-term contracts that gave white ranchers control over large amounts of Crow land. In 1945 Yellowtail resigned as superintendent to run, unsuccessfully, for the U.S. House of Representatives. He turned his attention to the federally proposed damming of the Little Big Horn River valley, which he opposed because it would take Crow land while offering few benefits to the tribe. He remained active in politics, being elected tribal chairman in 1948 and coauthoring the 1948 Crow constitution. In 1951 the federal government increased pressure on the tribe to agree to the construction of the ironically named Yellowtail Dam. The project bitterly divided the tribe, with Yellowtail leading the anti-dam Mountain Crows against the pro-dam River Crows. The tribal council ultimately backed the River Crow faction, and the dam was completed in 1964.

The dam fight was Yellowtail's last major political battle. He had failed to win the Republican nomination to the U.S. Senate in 1954, and he was increasingly out of the mainstream on his own reservation. He focused on his ranching operation, coming out of retirement only in the 1970s to advocate tribal ownership of coal leases. In 1985 he collaborated on the documentary *Contrary Warriors: A Film of the Crow Tribe*. He died on June 18, 1988, only yards from where he had been born.

Charles Vollan
South Dakota State University

Contrary Warriors. Directed by Pamela Roberts. Los Angeles: Direct Cinema Limited, 1985. Hoxie, Frederick, and Tim Bernardis. "Robert Yellowtail." In *The New Warriors: Native American Leaders Since 1900*, edited by R. David Edmunds, 54–77. Lincoln: University of Nebraska Press, 2001. Poten, Constance J., "Robert Yellowtail, the New Warrior." *Montana: The Magazine of Western History* 39.3 (summer 1989): 36–41.

YUWIPI CEREMONY

The Yuwipi ceremony is practiced by the Sioux for healing physical problems and gaining advice in life matters. The name comes from the Siouan word *yuwi*. Translations vary—the term has been used to refer to both the little sacred stones and tobacco wraps used in the ceremony and to the act of tying the holy person up as part of the sacred process. While the Yuwipi is a Sioux ceremony, similar ceremonies are practiced throughout North and South America. The Sioux call the ceremony a Yuwipi "sing," and each healer has singers as accompaniment. The sing is usually preceded by a sweat lodge ceremony and sometimes is associated with vision quests. Many prominent holy leaders have been Yuwipi healers, including Frank Fools Crow, Lame Deer, and Leonard Crow Dog. Yuwipi healers, depending on their ability, are said to receive help from as many as 405 spirits, which have been called Stone White Men and are embodied in sacred stones. After having a vision, devotees apprentice, sometimes for years, with older healers. The songs, prayers, and materials they use are their own sacred property. They often assist in other ceremonies, such as the Sun Dance.

When a person needs to know something, such as where an item has been lost or what types of medicines will cure an ailment, they approach the healer with a sacred tobacco pipe to ask for help. The room is prepared by taking out all furniture and modern items, such as anything metal. The ceremony is held in darkness, all windows covered and lights extinguished. Sweetgrass is used to purify the room, and tobacco is offered as a sacrament. Men sit on the north side of the room; women sit on the south side (menstruating women are not allowed in the ceremony). The singers sit to the west. No one wears shoes. Two helpers tightly bind the Yuwipi healer, fingers together, hands and arms tied to the body. He is covered completely, formerly with a buffalo hide but currently with a blanket or star quilt.

Participants describe visits from the spirits of deceased friends and relatives, who may offer spiritual, medicinal, or lifestyle advice, answer a question, find or retrieve lost items, or even scold participants for bad behavior or thoughts. Sometimes the spirits are said to be angry, at other times playful. Participants describe hearing noises, seeing lights, and being physically touched. When the singers cease singing, the lights are turned on and the Yuwipi healer is shown to be free of bonds. The healer then interprets the ceremony and the knowledge gained from it. The sing always ends with a meal, usually of dog, which is held to be especially sacred, *wojapi* (chokecherry pudding), and corn *wasna* (kidney fat and corn pounded together).

Charles Vollan
South Dakota State University

Powers, William. *Yuwipi: Vision and Experience in Lakota Ritual.* Lincoln: University of Nebraska Press, 1982. Lewis, Thomas H.

ZITKALA ŠA (1876–1938)

Zitkala Ša, 1898

Zitkala Ša, a Yankton Sioux, was among the first Native American authors to tell her own story without the aid of an editor or translator, and she was a significant figure in pan-Indian politics during the first part of the twentieth century. She was born Gertrude Simmons on February 22, 1876, on the Yankton Reservation in South Dakota. As a little girl, at the enticement of missionaries, she left her mother and homeland to attend boarding school. In compelling narratives published in the *Atlantic Monthly* and *Harper's Magazine* in the early 1900s, Gertrude described her life on the reservation and her experiences in White's Manual Labor Institute boarding school in Indiana and as a teacher at Carlisle Indian School in Pennsylvania. She also published short stories and a collection of traditional Sioux tales, *Old Indian Legends* (1901). Gertrude renamed her literary and public persona Zitkala Ša, or Red Bird.

In 1901 Gertrude returned to the Yankton Reservation, where she met and married Raymond Bonnin. They worked for the Indian Bureau on the Uintah and Ouray Reservation in Utah, where Gertrude collaborated with William Hanson on the *Sun Dance Opera* (1913) and became involved with the Pan-Indian Society of American Indians. After she was elected secretary in 1916, she and Raymond moved to Washington DC, where she worked for the society and edited and wrote for *American Indian Magazine*.

In 1921 she published her earlier writings along with several new, more political pieces in *American Indian Stories*. With Raymond, she continued her activism, lobbying for the American Indian Citizenship Act of 1924, against violence and injustice on reservations, and for land claims and tribal rights. Zitkala Ša died on January 26, 1938, in Washington DC. She was buried in Arlington National Cemetery.

P. Jane Hafen
University of Nevada–Las Vegas

Rappaport, Doreen. *The Flight of Red Bird: The Life of Zitkala-Ša*. New York: Dial Books, 1997. Zitkala-Ša. *Dreams and Thunder: Stories, Poems, and The Sun Dance Opera*, edited by P. Jane Hafen. Lincoln: University of Nebraska Press, 2001. Zitkala-Ša. *American Indian Stories*. 2nd ed. Lincoln: University of Nebraska Press, 2003.

Illustration Credits

Crampton. *Music:* Denver Public Library, Western History Collection, Photo by Melvyn E. Schieltz, Call Number: X-31647.

North West Rebellion: Provincial Archives of Manitoba, Neg. No. N9582, Collections: Events 145.

Omahas: Nebraska State Historical Society. 1394–97. *Oral Traditions:* Photo by L. A. Huffman. Montana Historical Society, Helena. 981–149. *Osages:* ca. 1880, Call Number: 2002.183, National Cowboy & Western Heritage Museum, Oklahoma City, Oklahoma. *Otoe-Missourias:* Nebraska State Historical Society. 1395:4–4.

Paleo-Indians: Map by Alan Osborne. *Parker, Quanah:* NARA-NWDNS, ID 111–SC-87722, Gallery of the Open Frontier at gallery.unl.edu. *Pawnees:* Photo by W. H. Jackson. Nebraska Historical Society. 1396:1–1.

Penn, Robert Lee: The Minneapolis Institute of Arts, The John R. Van Derlip Fund. *Plains Crees:* Glenbow Archives NA-3811–12. *Posey, Alexander:* Archives and Manuscripts Division of the Oklahoma Historical Society, Barde Collection, Photo Number 4213. *Powwows:* NARA-NWDNS, ID 75–PT (PHO)-4, Gallery of the Open Frontier at gallery.unl.edu.

Red Cloud: NARA-NWDNS-11–SC-82537. Photo in the Archival Research Catalog (ARC ID #530816).

Rock Art: Photo courtesy of Ralph Hartley.

Silverhorn: Denver Public Library, Western History Collection, Call Number: X-32436. *Sitting Bull:* NARA-NWDNS,ID 79–PS(SB)(PHO)-2559, Gallery of the Open Frontier at gallery. unl.edu. *Sports and Recreation:* Minnesota Historical Society, Photo by Gilbert Wilson, Call Number: IX-49–[1916]. *Spotted Tail:* Denver Public Library, Western History Collection, Photo by Stanley J. Morrow, Call Number: X-31905. *Standing Bear:* Nebraska State Historical Society. 1397:1–2. *Standing Bear, Luther:* Denver Public Library, Western History Collection, Call Number: X-31857.

Thorpe, Jim: Photo #15A-02–01, Cumberland County Historical Society, Carlisle, Pennsylvania. *Tipis:* Glenbow Archives NA-919–37. *Travois:* Photo by Norman Henderson, published in *Plains Anthropologist* (1994, vol. 39, pp. 145–59, fig. 1). *Treaties:* Photo courtesy of Smithsonian Institution National Anthropological Archives. Neg. 3686.

White Bull: Denver Public Library, Western History Collection, Call Number: X-31640. *Wounded Knee:* Nebraska State Historical Society. RG2845:13–10.

Zitkala-Ša: National Portrait Gallery, Smithsonian Institution, Photo by Joseph T. Keiley, NPG.79.26

Index of Contributors

General Index

Aboriginal FM Network of Native Communications Inc., 165

Aboriginal Multi-Media Society, 165

Abrams, Abner W., 164

activism. See political activism

Adobe Walls, Battle of (1874), **17**; Quanah Parker, 148; Satanta, 181

Agate Basin site, 2

Agency Village (SD), 172

agents, Indian. See Indian agents

Agiati, 183

agriculture, **17–18**; Arikaras, 29; assimilation policy and, 32, 33; Blackfoot, 41; Cheyennes, 48; Crow Fair, 54; Dawes Act and, 58, 59; Fort Laramie Treaty of 1868, 70; gender roles and, 71; Hidatsas, 81; and hunting, 88, 89; Indian agents and, 90; Kaws, 105; Pawnees, 149; plant lore and, 156; Poncas, 157, 158; religion and, 167; sovereignty and, 192; Tonkawas, 203; and trade, 204; traditional architecture and, 27; Wichitas, 219. See also ranching

AKA Graffiti Man (Trudell), 211

akicitas, 96, 185

Alabama-Coushatta Tribe, 134

Alberta: Archaic period sites in, 25; Assiniboines, 33, 35; Blackfoot, 41; casinos in, 47; Crowfoot, 54–55; Head-Smashed-In buffalo jump, 3, 25; Indian Country, 93; LaRocque, Emma, 112–13; missionaries in, 128; Native agriculture in, 18; Ojibwas, 137; Plains Crees, 154–55; radio stations in, 165; reserves in, 173–74; rock art in, 175; Sarcees, 180; tribal colleges in, 209; urban Indian reserves in, 213; water rights in, 193

Alberta complex, 146

Alcatraz Island occupation, 122, 211

alcohol: and Europeans, 5; La Flesche, Susan, and fight against, 110; Lame Deer, John Fire, 110; Otoe-Missourias, 144; reserves and, 173; trade, 205; urban communities and, 213; Women of All Red Nations, 221

Alderice, Susanna, 198

Algonquian languages, 111, 112

Allis, Samuel, 127

allotment, **18–19**; agriculture, 17; American expansion into the Plains, 9; Arapahos, 23; Arikaras, 30; assimilation policy and, 33; Blackfoot, 41; Caddos, 44; cattle ranching and, 95; Coman-

ches, 50; Crows, 57; Curtis, Charles Brent, 57; Dawes Act and, 58–59; Eastman, Charles, 64; Half-Breed Tract, 77–78; Hidatsas, 81; Indian Country, 93, 94; Indian New Deal, 11; Indian police, 97; Indian Territory, 101; Kaws, 106; Kiowas, 107–8; and the law, 116; *Lone Wolf v. Hitchcock*, 119; Omahas, 139; Osages, 143; Otoe-Missourias, 144; Parker, Quanah, 148; Pawnees, 150; Posey, Alexander, 159; Quapaws, 164; reservations and, 171; Sioux, 186; Standing Bear, Luther, 198; Wichitas, 220. See also Dawes (General Allotment) Act (1887)

Altithermal (Early Plains Archaic) period, 24

Ambassadors program, 78–79

American Board of Commissioners of Foreign Missions, 127, 168

American expansion into the Plains, 5–8

American Fur Company, 115

American Horse, 37, 128

American Indian Citizenship Act (1924), 226

American Indian Defense Association, 92

American Indian Magazine, 226

American Indian Movement (AIM), **19–21**; Crow Dog, Leonard, 53; *Incident at Oglala*, 89; Lame Deer, John Fire, 111; Means, Russell, 122–23; National Congress of American Indians, 133; Peltier, Leonard, 151; political adaptation of, 14; repatriation and, 169; Sioux, 187; Trudell, John, 211; Women of All Red Nations, 221

American Indian Progressive Association, 198

American Indian Radio on Satellite Network, 165

American Indian Religious Freedom Act (1994), 15, 65

American Indian Stories (Bonnin), 117, 226

Americanization, 9, 139

Americans for Indian Opportunity, 78

The Ancient Child (Momaday), 129

Anglican Church Missionary Society, 168

Angostura group, 24

animals: hunting, 88–89; oral traditions and, 141; Paleo-Indians, 146; rock art, 175; traditional art, 30–32; trickster, 210. See also buffalo (bison); dogs; horse

Anishinaabes, 137

The Antelope Wife (Erdrich), 66

antivagrancy laws, 90

Anza, Juan Bautista de, 66, 194

Apaches, **21–22**; genízaros, 72–73; Houser, Allan, 84–85; Indian Claims Commission, 93; Indian scouts, 100; Jumanos, 105; language, 111, 112; and

tion, 206; travois, 207; war chiefs, 216; Wichitas, 220; women warriors, 221

Horse Dance, 39

Horvath, Stephen, 72

House Made of Dawn (Momaday), 117, 129

Houser, Allan, **84–85**

housing: contemporary architecture, 26; earth lodges, 62–64; grass lodges, 28, 181, 219; longhouses, 142; reservation towns, 173; tipis, 202–3; traditional architecture, 27–28. *See also* earth lodges; tipis

Howard, James, 218

Howe, Oscar, **85–87**, 152; *Calling on Wakan Tanka*, 86; *Sioux Seed Player*, 86

Howling Wolf, **87–88**

Hudson's Bay Company: Assiniboines, 33; Blackfoot, 41; Crowfoot, 54–55; Grant, Cuthbert, 76; Gros Ventres, 76; and the law, 115; Métis, 125; North-West Rebellion, 136; Plains Crees, 154, 155; Red River resistance, 166; Rupert's Land, 8, 125, 166, 173; urban Indian reserves, 213

Hugo, Richard, 217; *The Real West Marginal Way*, 217

human rights, 134

human sacrifice, 130–31

Hunkpapa, 185

Hunt, P. B., 148

Hunter, Peter, 128

hunting, **88–89**; Archaic period sites, 24; contemporary architecture, 27; Assiniboines, 34; Cheyennes, 48; Comanches, 50; environmental change, 2–3; gender roles, 71; Hidatsas, 81; and the horse, 4, 83, 84; Kaws, 105; Mandans, 120–21; *Montana v. United States*, 129; Paleo-Indians, 146, 147; pronghorn, 24, 25, 81, 88; religion, 167; reservations, 172; reserves, 173; trade, 204; traditional art, 31, *31*; war chiefs, 216; Wichitas, 219. *See also* buffalo (bison)

Ice Age, 146

Iesh, 43

Ince, Thomas, 82, 198

Incident at Oglala (film), **89**, 151

Indian Achievement Award, 60

Indian Act (1876), 10, 75, 90, 94, 174, 192

Indian Act (1951), 12, 174, 192

Indian agents, **89–90**; agriculture, 17; *berdache*, 37; and hunting rights, 89; Indian police, 96; and the law, 115; Otoe-Missourias, 144; Sioux, 186; Sitting Bull, 189; Standing Bear, Luther, 198; Wounded Knee Massacre, 222

Indian boarding schools, United States, **90–92**; American expansion into the Plains, 10; assimilation policy, 33; *berdache*, 37; Genoa Indian Industrial School, 33, 91, 135; Haskell Institute, 33, 59, 91, 92, 126, 135, 176, 210. *See also* Carlisle Indian Industrial School

Indian Bounty Act (1957), 162

Indian Boyhood (Eastman), 117

Indian Capital Conference on Poverty (1964), 13

Indian Civilian Conservation Corps, 12

Indian Claims Commission, **92–93**; National Congress of American Indians, 133; Omahas, 140; Otoe-Missourias, 144; Pawnees, 150; Quapaws, 164–65; Roe Cloud, Henry, 176; termination policy, 12–13; *United States v. Sioux Nation of Indians*, 212

Indian Country, **93–94**; Indian Territory, 101; and the law, 114; reservations, 171

Indian Country Today (newspaper), **94–95**, 124

Indian cowboys, **95–96**

Indian Gaming Regulatory Act (1988), 46

Indian Health Service, 80

Indian Lawyer (Welch), 217

Indian Museum of North America, 52

Indian National Finals Rodeo, 95

Indian New Deal, 11–12, 92

Indian police, **96–97**

Indian Religious Freedom Act (1978), 133

Indian removal, **97–98**; American expansion into the Plains, 6; languages, 112; missionaries, 127; reservations, 171

Indian Removal Act (1830), 97, 98, 127

Indian Reorganization Act (1934): allotment, 19; Arikaras, 30; Blackfoot, 41–42; Cheyennes, 49; contemporary governments, 75; Crows, 57; Gros Ventres, 77; Hidatsas, 81; Indian boarding schools, United States, 90, 92; Indian New Deal, 11–12; Mandans, 121; Omahas, 140; Quapaws, 164; Roe Cloud, Henry, 176; Sioux, 186; sovereignty, 192; Robert Yellowtail, Robert, 224

Indian residential schools, Canada, 10, **98–100**

Indian scouts, **100–101**; American expansion into the Plains, 7–8; and Battle of Palo Duro Canyon, 147; and Battle of Summit Springs, 198; Plenty Coups, 157; Tonkawas, 204

Indian Self-Determination and Education Act (1975), 15

Indian Taxation Advisory Board, 214

Indian Territory, **101**; American expansion into the Plains, 6; Battle of the Washita, 217; Caddos, 44; Indian boarding schools, United States, 91, 92; Indian Country, 93; Indian police, 96, 97; Indian removal, 98; Kaws, 106; Kiowas, 107; Osages, 142; Otoe-Missourias, 144; Pawnees, 150; Pitaresaru, 153; Poncas, 158, 197, 209; Quapaws, 164; reservations, 171; Riggs, Rollie Lynn, 174; Tonkawas, 204. *See also* Oklahoma

Indian trails, **101–2**

Indian wars: American expansion into the Plains, 6–7; Arikara expedition, 28–29; Battle of Adobe Walls, 17; Battle of Beecher Island, 36; Battle of Palo Duro Canyon, 147; Battle of Summit Springs, 198; Battle of the Little Bighorn, 117–18;

Kitsais, 219

Klamath-Modoc languages, 111, 112

Knife River flint, 147, 204

Koiet-senko warrior society, 180

Kommers, Peter, 27

Kunstler, William, 53, 89

labor, division of, 71

Lacombe, Albert, 55

lacrosse, 195

La Flesche, Francis, 10

La Flesche, Susan, 10, **109–10**

Lakota linguistic group, 185

Lakota Sioux: agriculture, 17; Arapahos, 22; Arikara expedition, 29; Arikaras, 30; in Battle of Beecher Island, 36; in Battle of the Little Bighorn, 117–18; *berdache*, 37; Black Elk, 39–40; Cheyennes, 47; and contemporary governments, 75; counting coup, 51; Crazy Horse, 51–52; Crazy Horse Memorial, 52; *Dances with Wolves*, 58; *Ex parte Crow Dog*, 66–67; Fort Laramie Treaty of 1851, 6, 186; Ghost Dance, 10, 74; and the horse, 84; Indian Claims Commission, 93; *Indian Country Today*, 94; Indian cowboys, 95; Indian police, 96, 97; Indian scouts, 100; and intertribal warfare, 103; Kiowas, 107; and the law, 114; literature, 117; longevity in Great Plains, 2; missionaries, 128; and oral traditions, 141; Pawnees, 149, 150; Plains Apaches, 153; Poncas, 158, 197; Red Cloud, 165–66; reserves, 173; sacred geography of, 177; Sioux, 184–87; Sioux Wars, 187–88; Sitting Bull, 188–89; sovereignty, 191; Spotted Tail, 196; Standing Bear, Luther, 197–98; Sun Dance, 199; tipis, 28; traditional art, 32; treaties, 207; urban communities, 213; veterans, 214; war chiefs, 216; Wounded Knee Massacre, 222–24

Lakota Times (newspaper), 94, 124

Lakota Woman (Lame Deer), 117

Lame Bull's Treaty (1855), 41

Lame Deer, John Fire, **110–11**, 117, 225; *Lakota Woman*, 117

land: Fort Laramie Treaty of 1868, 70; Indian agents, 90; Indian Claims Commission, 92–93; Indian Country, 93–94; law, 115–16; *Lone Wolf v. Hitchcock*, 119; Native American Rights Fund, 134; as sacred geography, 177–78; treaties, 207–8; *United States v. Sioux Nation of Indians*, 212. *See also* allotment

Landes, Ruth, 37

landmarks, 102

Land of the Spotted Eagle (Luther Standing Bear), 198

languages, **111–12**; Deloria, Ella Cara, 59–60; "English-only," 112, 128; missionaries, 128; radio stations, 165; sign language, 182–83. *See also* sign language

La Roche, Paul, 132

LaRocque, Emma, **112–13**

Late Plains Archaic period, 24, 25

La Vérendrye, Pierre Gaultier de Varennes de, 34

law, **113–16**; Echo-Hawk Jr., Walter, 65; Native American Rights Fund, 134–35; sovereignty, 191–94; Supreme Court of Canada, 192, 193. *See also* law enforcement; sovereignty; Supreme Court (U.S.)

law enforcement: Indian police, 96–97; Public Law 280, 162–63

Leavenworth, Henry, 29, 30, 100

ledger paintings, 32, 87

Left Hand, 23

Lelar, Henry, 67

Leupp, Francis, 90

Lewis and Clark: Arikaras, 30; Blackfoot, 41; music, 132; Otoe-Missourias, 143; Pawnees, 148; Sacagawea, 176–77; Shoshones, 181; and trade, 205; traditional art, 31

Libertarian party, 123

Liberty, Margot, 117

The Life and Adventures of Joaquin Murieta (Ridge), 117

life expectancy, 80

Lighthorse, 96

Like-a-Fishhook Village, 30, *80*, 81, 121

Lincoln, Kenneth, 117

Linderman, Frank B., 116, 164; *Pretty Shield: Medicine Woman of the Crows*, 116, 164; *Red Mother*, 164

Lipan Apaches, 21, 22, 43, 100, 111, 194, 203

literature, **116–17**; captivity narratives, 45–46; Erdrich, Louise, 66; Hogan, Linda, 82; LaRocque, Emma, 112–13; Momaday, N. Scott, 129–30; Riggs, Rollie Lynn, 174; Zitkala Ša, 225-26; Sneve, Virginia Driving Hawk, 190; Standing Bear, Luther, 198; Welch, James, 217–18;

Little Arkansas, Treaty of the (1865), 49, 179

Little Bear, 38

Little Bighorn, Battle of the (1876), **117–18**; Black Elk, 39; counting coup, 51; Crazy Horse, 52; Dull Knife, 61; Fort Laramie Treaty of 1868, 70; *Little Big Man*, 118; reserves, 173; Sioux, 184, 186; Sioux Wars, 187, 188; Sitting Bull, 189; *Soldier Blue*, 191; Welch, James, 217–18; White Bull, Joseph, 218–19

Little Big Horn College, 163

Little Big Man (film), 83, **118–19**

Little Hoop Community College, 210

Little House on the Prairie series, 190

Little Priest Tribal College, 210

Little Raven, 23

Little Wolf, 61–62

Living in Reality (Trudell), 211

Locke, Kevin, 132

locoweed, 156

Lone Wolf v. Hitchcock (1903), 49, **119**

Water Rights Coalition, 128–29; Omahas, 138, 140; religion, 167; rock art, 175; sign language, 183; trade, 204, 206

Mitchell, George, 19

Mnikowoju, 185

Mni Sose Intertribal Water Rights Coalition, **128–29**

moccasins: Comanches, 50; Ojibwas, 137

moieties: Kaws, 106; Omahas, 139; Osages, 142

Momaday, N. Scott, 108, 117, **129–30**; *The Ancient Child*, 129; *House Made of Dawn*, 117, 129; *The Way to Rainy Mountain*, 117, 129–30

Montana: Arapahos, 23; Archaic period sites, 24, 25; Assiniboines, 35; Battle of the Little Bighorn, 117–18; Blackfoot, 41, 42; Cheyennes, 48, 49; Crow Fair, 53–54; Crows, 55, 57; Dull Knife, 61–62; Fort Laramie Treaty of 1868, 70; gold, 7; Gros Ventres, 77; Indian Claims Commission, 93; Indian Country, 93, 94; *Indian Country Today*, 94; Métis, 126; *Montana v. United States*, 129; Native American population, *1*, 15; Ojibwas, 137; Paleo-Indians, *145*, 146; Plains Crees, 155; Plenty Coups, 156–57; Pretty-on-Top, Janine Pease, 163; radio stations, 165; reservations, 171; Sioux Wars, 188; tribal colleges, 209, 210; Welch, James, 217–18; Yellowtail, Robert, 224

Montana Reserve (Alberta), 18

Montana v. United States (1981), 70, 116, **130**, 172

Mooney, James, 184

Moore, John, 191

Moose Mountain Medicine Wheel, 36

Mopope, Stephen, *108*, 109, 183

Morfí, Juan Agustín, 72

Mormons, 127, 139

Morning Star, 36

Morning Star ceremony, 28, **130–31**

Mortlach Aggregate archeological tradition, 25, 33

Mother Corn, 28, 30

Mountain Horse, Mike, 214

Mount Rushmore, 14, 123

moxabustion, 156

Mulroney, Brian, 78

murder, 114

Murie, James, 150

Muscogean languages, 111, 112

Museum of the Plains Indians, 42

museums: contemporary architecture, 26–27; Gilcrease, Thomas, 74; Indian Museum of North America, 52; Museum of the Plains Indians, 42; repatriation, 169–70

music, **131–32**; Indigenous, 102; powwows, 160–62; Saint-Marie, Buffy, 178; Trudell, John, 211

My Indian Boyhood (Luther Standing Bear), 198

My People the Sioux (Luther Standing Bear), 198

Nakai, R. Carlos, 132

Nakota linguistic group, 185

Nanibush, 137

Nanji, Mato, 102

Nanji, Pte, 102

Nanji, Wanbdi, 102

National Congress of American Indians (NCAI), 13, **132–33**, 170

National Indian Gaming Commission, 46

National Indian Painting Competition, 86

National Indian Youth Council, 133

National Medal of Arts, 85

National Museum of the American Indian Act, 170

National Native News (radio program), 165

Native America Calling (radio program), 165

Native American Church, **133–34**; Cheyennes, 48; contemporary architecture, 27; Crow Dog, Leonard, 53; Echo-Hawk Jr., Walter, 65; Kiowas, 108; Lame Deer, John Fire, 110; missionaries, 128; Native American Rights Fund, 135; Ojibwas, 137; Omahas, 139; peyotism, 169; Poncas, 158; Sanapia, 178; Shoshones, 182; Silverhorn, 183, 184; sweat lodge, 200

Native American Graves Protection and Repatriation Act (1990), 15, 65, 170

Native American Journalists Association, 95

Native American Renaissance, 117

Native American Rights Fund (NARF), 65, **134–35**, 170

Native People (newspaper), 112

natural resources: Native American Rights Fund, 134; oil and gas, 11, 51, 74, 134, 144, 158; Osages, 143; Quapaws, 164; reservations, 171–72; Sioux Wars, 187

Navajos: Apaches, 21; Tropa de Genízaro, 211; urban communities, 212, 213

The Navajos (Sneve), 190

Neal, Lewis, 77

Nebraska: Archaic period sites, 24; earth lodges, 62; Echo-Hawk Jr., Walter, 65; Half-Breed Tract, 77; Indian boarding schools, 33, 91, *91*; Indian Claims Commission, 93; Indian Country, 93; *Indian Country Today*, 94; Indian police, 96; Indian removal, 98; La Flesche, Susan, 110; missionaries, 127; Morning Star ceremony, 130–31; Native American population as percentage of total population, *1*; Native American Rights Fund, 134; Omahas, 138, 139, 140; Otoe-Missourias, 143, 144; Paleo-Indians, *145*, 147; Pawnees, 148–50; Permanent Indian Frontier, 6; Poncas, 157–59; Public Law 280, 162; radio stations, 165; repatriation, 170; reservations, 171; sacred geography of, 177; Sioux, 185; Sioux Wars, 187, 188; Standing Bear, 196–97; treaties, 208; Trial of Standing Bear, 209; tribal colleges, 209, 210; urban communities, 213

Nebraska Indians (baseball team), **135**

Nebraska State Historical Society, 170

redundancy trading, 205

Regina v. Van der Peet (1997), 193

Reifel, Benjamin, 13

religion, **167–69**; Arapahos, 22–23, 24; Arikaras, 30; Assiniboines, 34; *berdache*, 37; Black Elk, 39–40; Blackfoot, 41; Cheyennes, 47–48; Comanches, 50; contemporary architecture, 27; cultural adaptation, 10–11; Echo-Hawk Jr., Walter, 65; gender roles, 71; Ghost Dance, 73–74; Hidatsas, 81; Kiowas, 108; Lame Deer, John Fire, 110–11; Native American Church, 133–34; Native American Rights Fund, 135; Ojibwas, 137; Plains Crees, 155; sacred geography, 177–78; Shoshones, 182; Sioux, 185; Sun Dance, 199; traditional art, 31–32; Wichitas, 220. *See also* ceremonies, religious; Christianity; Ghost Dance; Native American Church; peyotism; sacred geography

relocation policy: Mankiller, Wilma, 121; Sioux, 186; urban communities, 212–13

repatriation, **169–70**; Echo-Hawk Jr., Walter, 65; National Congress of American Indians, 133; Native American Rights Fund, 134–35

Republican River Expedition, 198

reservations, **170–72**; agriculture, 17; allotment, 18–19; American expansion into the Plains, 9; Apaches, 22; Arapahos, 23; Arikaras, 30; assimilation policy, 33; Assiniboines, 35; Blackfoot, 41, 42; Caddos, 43, 44; Cheyennes, 49; Comanches, 50; contemporary architecture, 25; Crazy Horse, 52; Crows, 57; Dull Knife, 61–62; field matrons, 68; Fort Laramie Treaty of 1868, 71; gender roles, 72; Gros Ventres, 77; health, 79–80; Hidatsas, 81; and the horse, 84; Indian agents, 90; Indian boarding schools, United States, 90, 91–92; Indian Country, 93, 94; Indian police, 96–97; Indian removal, 98; Indian Territory, 101; Kaws, 106; Kiowas, 107–8; and the law, 115–16; missionaries, 127; *Montana v. United States*, 129; Native American population, 15; Native American Rights Fund, 134; Ojibwas, 137; Omahas, 139; Osages, 142; Otoe-Missourias, 144; Pawnees, 149–50; Poncas, 158, 197; Public Law 280, 162–63; Quapaws, 164; religion, 169; reservation towns, 172–73; Shoshones, 182; Sioux Wars, 188; sovereignty, 192; termination policy, 13; Tonkawas, 204; and trade, 205; treaties, 208; urban communities, 213; Wichitas, 220

reservation towns, **172–73**

reserves, **173–74**; agriculture, 17; assimilation policy, 33; Assiniboines, 35; Canadian expansion into the Plains, 9; gender roles, 72; health, 79–80; Indian agents, 90; Indian Country, 93, 94; and the law, 115; Ojibwas, 137; Payipwat, 150; Plains Crees, 155; Poundmaker, 160; Sarcees, 180; treaties, 208; urban Indian reserves, 213–14

residual sovereignty, 192

revenue sharing, 47

Rhoades, Everett, 108

Rhodes, Dennis Sun, 27

Rice, Julian, 39

Ridge, John Rollin, 117; *The Life and Adventures of Joaquin Murieta*, 117

Riding the Earthboy 40 (Welch), 217

Riel, Louis: Métis, 125–26; North-West Rebellion, 8, 135, 136; Red River resistance, 8, 166, 167

Riel Rebellion. *See* North-West Rebellion

Riggs, Rollie Lynn, **174**; *The Cherokee Night*, 174; *Green Grow the Lilacs*, 174

Riggs, Stephen Return, 128, 168

Riley, Glenda, 46

Roadman, 133–34

Roberts, Blair, 60, 61

Robideau, Bob, 89, 151

rock art, **174–76**; traditional art, 30–31

Rocky Boy's Reservation (MT), 14, 155

rodeo, 84, 95–96, 195

Rodnick, David, 35

Rodriguez, Juan, 203

Roe Cloud, Henry, **176**

Roe Indian Institute, 176

Roman Nose, 36

Roosevelt, Eleanor, 69

Roosevelt, Franklin Delano, 224

Rose, Wendy, 117

Rosebud, Battle of the (1876): Battle of the Little Bighorn, 117; Crazy Horse, 52; Plenty Coups, 157; Sioux Wars, 187, 188; *Soldier Blue*, 191; White Bull, Joseph, 218

Rosebud Reservation (SD): and contemporary governments, 75; *Ex parte Crow Dog*, 66–67; Indian Country, 93, 94; Indian cowboys, 95; Indian New Deal, 12; Indian police, 97; Lame Deer, John Fire, 110; Means, Russell, 122; Sinte Gleska community college, 92; Sneve, Virginia Driving Hawk, 190; Standing Bear, Luther, 197–98; War on Poverty, 14

Rosebud Sioux Tribe v. Kneip (1977), 94

Ross, John, 121

Ross, William P., 124

Round Dance, 168, 182

Rowlandson, Mary, 45

Royal Commission on Aboriginal People, 192, 193

Royal Proclamation of 1763, 207

Royer, Daniel F., 222, 223

running, 126, 195

Running Brave (film), 126

Running Eagle (Brown Weasel Woman), 37, 221

Rupert's Land, 8, 125, 166–67, 173

Russell, Angela, 57

Sabeata, Juan, 105

Sacagawea, **176–77**

sacred bundles: Arikaras, 30; Blackfoot, 41; Hidatsas, 81; Kiowas, 106; Mandans, 121; Okipa, 138; Osages, 142; sweat lodge, 200

Sioux Seed Player (Howe), 86

Sioux Uprising (1862), 168, 185, 222

Sioux Wars, **187–88**; Battle of the Little Bighorn, 117–18; Fetterman Fight, 47, 51, 61, 166, 187, 188, 218; Indian scouts, 101; White Bull, Joseph, 218; Wounded Knee Massacre, 222–24. *See also* Little Bighorn, Battle of the (1876); Rosebud, Battle of the (1876); Wounded Knee Massacre (1890)

Sitting Bull, **188–90**; Battle of the Little Bighorn, 7; Fort Laramie Treaty of 1868, 70; Ghost Dance, 10, 74; Indian police, 96, 97; Sioux, 184, 186; Sioux Wars, 188; Wounded Knee Massacre, 223

Skinner, Alanson, 82

Skiris, 36, 130–31, 148–49, 152

slavery, 211

smallpox: Arapahos, 22; Arikaras, 30; Assiniboines, 35; Blackfoot, 41; Crows, 57; epidemic of 1780–81, 35, 77, 155; epidemic of 1837–38, 41, 57, 77, 79, 81, 121, 155; Gros Ventres, 77; health, 79; Hidatsas, 81; Kaws, 106; Mandans, 121; Osages, 143; Otoe-Missourias, 143; Pawnees, 149; Plains Crees, 155; war chiefs, 216

Smith, Edward P., 181

Smith, John, 179

Smithsonian Institution, 169, 170

Smoking Tipi ceremony, 155

Smoky, Lois, 109

Snell, Alma Hogan, 164

Sneve, Virginia Driving Hawk, 52, **190**; *The Apaches*, 190; *Completing the Circle*, 190; *Dakota Heritage: A Compilation of Place Names in South Dakota*, 190; *Jimmy Yellow Hawk*, 190; *The Navajos*, 190

snow snake, 195

Soap, Charlie, 122

societies: Arapahos, 23; Arikaras, 30; Assiniboines, 34; Cheyennes, 49; Comanches, 50; Hidatsas, 81; Omahas, 139; Plains Apaches, 154; police societies, 191; Shoshones, 182; Sioux, 185. *See also* warriors' societies

Society for American Archaeology, 169, 170

Society of American Indians, 64, 176

Soldier Blue (film), 83, **190–91**

South Dakota: Archaic period sites, 24; Arikaras, 29; Big Crow, SuAnne, 38; casinos, 47; Crazy Horse, 51–52; *Dances with Wolves*, 58; Deloria, Ella Cara, 59–60; Deloria, Vine Sr., 60–61; earth lodges, 62; Howe, Oscar, 85–87; Indian boarding schools, 92; Indian Country, 93, 94; *Indian Country Today*, 94, 124; Indigenous, 102; infant mortality, 80; intertribal warfare, 103; Jones, Harold, 103–4; Lame Deer, John Fire, 110; longevity of Native Americans in, 2; media, 124; missionaries, 128; Native American population, *1*, 15; Native American Rights Fund, 134, 135; Paleo-Indians, *145*; radio stations, 165; reservations, 171; reservation towns, 172–73; rock art,

175, 176; sacred geography of, 177; Sioux, 185, 186, 187; Sitting Bull, 188–89; Sneve, Virginia Driving Hawk, 190; Standing Bear, Luther, 197–98; tribal colleges, 209, 210; *United States v. Sioux Nation of Indians*, 212; urban communities, 213; Wounded Knee Massacre, 222–24. *See also* Black Hills; Pine Ridge Reservation; Rosebud Reservation; Standing Rock Reservation

South Dakota Artist Project, 85

South Dakota v. Bourland, 94

South Dakota v. Yankton Sioux Tribe (1998), 94, 193

Southern Athapaskans, 21

Southern Piegans, 41

sovereignty, **191–94**; casinos, 47; *Ex parte Crow Dog*, 66–67; Fort Laramie Treaty of 1868, 70; and the law, 115; *Montana v. United States*, 129; Native American Rights Fund, 134; Parker, Quanah, 148; Pitaresaru, 153; treaties, 207, 208

Spaniards: Apaches, 21; Caddos, 43; Comanches, 49–50; destruction of San Sabá Mission, 179–80; Ecueracapa, 65–66; Europeans, 5; *genízaros*, 72; and the horse, 4, 83; Indian scouts, 100; Jumanos, 104, 105; and the law, 114; religion, 167–68; and sign language, 183; Spanish-Comanche treaties, 194; Tonkawas, 203–4; and trade, 205; Tropa de Genízaro, 211; Wichitas, 220

Spanish-Comanche treaties, 66, **194**

sports and recreation, **194–95**; Big Crow, SuAnne, 38–39; Mills, Billy, 126; Nebraska Indians baseball team, 135; rodeo, 84, 95–96, 195; Thorpe, Jim, 201–2

Spotted Tail, 66–67, 158, **196**

Standing Bear, 158, **196–97**, 209

Standing Bear, Henry, 52

Standing Bear, Luther, **197–98**; *Land of the Spotted Eagle*, 198; *My Indian Boyhood*, 198; *My People the Sioux*, 198; *Stories of the Sioux*, 198

Standing Rock Reservation (SD): agriculture, 18; Deloria, Ella Cara, 59; Vine Deloria Sr., 60; Indigenous, 102; Sitting Bull, 10, 189

Standing Stone Media, Inc., 95

Stands in Timber, John, 116–17

Stay-by-It, *143*

Steinhauer, Henry Bird, 128

Stekler, Paul, 217; *Killing Custer: The Battle of the Little Bighorn and the Fate of the Plains Indians*, 217–18

Steltenkamp, Michael F., 39

Stephens, Isaac, 77

Stickman (Trudell), 211

stone projectile points, 146

Stone White Men, 225

Stoneys, 33, 34, 35, 111

Stories of the Sioux (Luther Standing Bear), 198

storytelling, 141, 183

Studio style, 84, 85, 86, 109

Stuntz, Joe, 151

Lodge Creek, Treaty of; Treaty Number 7; *and other treaties by name*

Treaty Land Entitlement Framework Agreement, 214

Treaty Number 1, 173

Treaty Number 2, 173

Treaty Number 3, 173

Treaty Number 4, 150

Treaty Number 6, 38, 79, 150, 160, 173

Treaty Number 7: Assiniboines, 35; Blackfoot, 41; contemporary governments, 75; Crowfoot, 55; Sarcees, 180

Trial of Standing Bear, **209**

tribal colleges, **209–10**

tribal fairs, 132

Tribal Jurisdiction Statistical Areas, 171

trickster, **210–11**; Crows, 55; Kiowas, 106; oral traditions, 141

Tropa de Genízaro, **211**

Trudell, John, **211**; AKA *Graffiti Man*, 211; American Indian Movement, 20; *Living in Reality*, 211; music, 15; Sioux, 187; *Stickman*, 211

Tsatoke, Monroe, 109

tuberculosis, 79, 110, 143

Two Crows, 198

"two-spirit" people, 37. See also *berdache*

Umon'hon'ti, 170

unemployment, 15

Union Pacific Railroad, 77

United States v. Kagama (1886), 67, 119

United States v. Sioux Nation of Indians (1980), **212**; Fort Laramie Treaty of 1868, 71; Indian Claims Commission, 93; *Lone Wolf v. Hitchcock*, 119

United Tribes Powwow, 132

Unmarked Human Burial Sites and Skeletal Remains Protection Act, 170

Upper Republican peoples, 148

urban communities, **212–13**; Blackfoot, 42; results of relocation, 13; Sioux, 186

urban Indian centers, 213

urban Indian reserves, **213–14**

U.S. Indian Peace Commission, 69

Utes, 4, 199, 211

Utley, Robert, 219

Uto-Aztecan languages, 111, 112

Vanishing Americans (band), 102

Vattel, Emmerich, 191–92

Vermillion Accord, 170

Vestal, Stanley, 218; *Warpath*, 218

veterans, **214–15**; Crow Fair, 54; powwows, 160; reserves, 174

Villasur, Pedro de, 5

vision quest, **215–16**; Assiniboines, 34; Blackfoot, 41; Crows, 56; Kiowas, 108; Lame Deer, John

Fire, 110; Plenty Coups, 157; religion, 167; sacred geography, 177; Shoshones, 182; Yuwipi ceremony, 225

Vister, 179

Wagon Box Fight (1867), 51, 218

Wakan Tanka, *86*, 185

Wakonda, 142, 157

Wandering Spirit, 38

war: *berdache*, 37; gender roles, 71; and the horse, 84; intertribal warfare, 102–3; traditional art, 31; Tropa de Genízaro, 211; veterans, 214–15; war chiefs, 216; women warriors, 221–22. *See also* Indian wars; veterans

war chiefs, 182, **216**

War Dance, 139

War Dance Society, 158

War Mothers, 49

War on Poverty, 13–14

Warpath (Vestal), 218

Warren, William Whipple, 116

Warren Massacre (1871), 181

warriors' societies: Assiniboines, 34; Cheyennes, 49; Dog Soldier warrior society, 198, 216; Shoshones, 182; veterans, 214; war chiefs, 216

Washita, Battle of the (1868), **217**; Black Kettle, 42–43; *Little Big Man*, 118

water: Indian trails, 102; Mni Sose Intertribal Water Rights Coalition, 128–29; sovereignty, 193; Winters Doctrine, 220–21; Women of All Red Nations, 221

water holes, 102

Waterlily (Deloria), 60

The Way to Rainy Mountain (Momaday), 117, 129–30

Webster, John Lee, 209

Wedel, Waldo, 36

Weichell, Maria, 198

Welch, James, 117, **217–18**; *The Death of Jim Loney*, 217; *Fools Crow*, 217; *The Heartsong of Charging Elk*, 218; *Indian Lawyer*, 217; *Killing Custer: The Battle of the Little Bighorn and the Fate of the Plains Indians*, 217–18; *The Real West Marginal Way*, 217; *Riding the Earthboy 40*, 217; *Winter in the Blood*, 217

Welch, Lois Munk: *The Real West Marginal Way*, 217

Wessells, Henry, 62

West, John, 127

Westerman, Floyd, 15

Wetzel, Walter, 13

Wheeler, John F., 124

whistles, 132

White Buffalo Calf Woman, 185

White Bull, Joseph, *140*, **218–19**

White House Executive Order on Tribal Colleges and Universities (1998), 210